HISTORICAL DICTIONARIES OF ASIA, OCEANIA, AND THE MIDDLE EAST
Edited by Jon Woronoff

Asia
1. *Vietnam*, by William J. Duiker. 1989. *Out of print. See No. 27.*
2. *Bangladesh*, 2nd ed., by Craig Baxter and Syedur Rahman. 1996. *Out of print. See No. 48.*
3. *Pakistan*, by Shahid Javed Burki. 1991. *Out of print. See No. 33.*
4. *Jordan*, by Peter Gubser. 1991
5. *Afghanistan*, by Ludwig W. Adamec. 1991. *Out of print. See No. 47.*
6. *Laos*, by Martin Stuart-Fox and Mary Kooyman. 1992. *Out of print. See No. 35.*
7. *Singapore*, by K. Mulliner and Lian The-Mulliner. 1991
8. *Israel*, by Bernard Reich. 1992
9. *Indonesia*, by Robert Cribb. 1992. *Out of print. See No. 51.*
10. *Hong Kong and Macau*, by Elfed Vaughan Roberts, Sum Ngai Ling, and Peter Bradshaw. 1992
11. *Korea*, by Andrew C. Nahm. 1993. *Out of print. See No. 52.*
12. *Taiwan*, by John F. Copper. 1993. *Out of print. See No. 34.*
13. *Malaysia*, by Amarjit Kaur. 1993. *Out of print. See No. 36.*
14. *Saudi Arabia*, by J. E. Peterson. 1993. *Out of print. See No. 45.*
15. *Myanmar*, by Jan Becka. 1995
16. *Iran*, by John H. Lorentz. 1995
17. *Yemen*, by Robert D. Burrowes. 1995
18. *Thailand*, by May Kyi Win and Harold Smith. 1995. *Out of print. See No. 55.*
19. *Mongolia*, by Alan J. K. Sanders. 1996. *Out of print. See No. 42.*
20. *India*, by Surjit Mansingh. 1996
21. *Gulf Arab States*, by Malcolm C. Peck. 1996
22. *Syria*, by David Commins. 1996. *Out of print. See No. 50.*
23. *Palestine*, by Nafez Y. Nazzal and Laila A. Nazzal. 1997
24. *Philippines*, by Artemio R. Guillermo and May Kyi Win. 1997. *Out of print. See No. 54.*

Oceania
1. *Australia*, by James C. Docherty. 1992. *Out of print. See No. 32.*
2. *Polynesia*, by Robert D. Craig. 1993. *Out of print. See No. 39.*
3. *Guam and Micronesia*, by William Wuerch and Dirk Ballendorf. 1994
4. *Papua New Guinea*, by Ann Turner. 1994. *Out of print. See No. 37.*
5. *New Zealand*, by Keith Jackson and Alan McRobie. 1996. *Out of print. See No. 56.*

New Combined Series

25. *Brunei Darussalam*, by D. S. Ranjit Singh and Jatswan S. Sidhu. 1997
26. *Sri Lanka*, by S. W. R. de A. Samarasinghe and Vidyamali Samarasinghe. 1998
27. *Vietnam*, 2nd ed., by William J. Duiker. 1998. *Out of print. See No. 57.*
28. *People's Republic of China: 1949–1997*, by Lawrence R. Sullivan, with the assistance of Nancy Hearst. 1998
29. *Afghanistan*, 2nd ed., by Ludwig W. Adamec. 1997. *Out of print. See No. 47.*
30. *Lebanon*, by As'ad AbuKhalil. 1998
31. *Azerbaijan*, by Tadeusz Swietochowski and Brian C. Collins. 1999
32. *Australia*, 2nd ed., by James C. Docherty. 1999
33. *Pakistan*, 2nd ed., by Shahid Javed Burki. 1999
34. *Taiwan (Republic of China)*, 2nd ed., by John F. Copper. 2000
35. *Laos*, 2nd ed., by Martin Stuart-Fox. 2001
36. *Malaysia*, 2nd ed., by Amarjit Kaur. 2001
37. *Papua New Guinea*, 2nd ed., by Ann Turner. 2001
38. *Tajikistan*, by Kamoludin Abdullaev and Shahram Akbarzedeh. 2002
39. *Polynesia*, 2nd ed., by Robert D. Craig. 2002
40. *North Korea*, by Ilpyong J. Kim. 2003
41. *Armenia*, by Rouben Paul Adalian. 2002
42. *Mongolia*, 2nd ed., by Alan J. K. Sanders. 2003
43. *Cambodia*, by Justin Corfield and Laura Summers. 2003
44. *Iraq*, by Edmund A. Ghareeb with the assistance of Beth K. Dougherty. 2004
45. *Saudi Arabia*, 2nd ed., by J. E. Peterson. 2003
46. *Nepal*, by Nanda R. Shrestha and Keshav Bhattarai. 2003
47. *Afghanistan*, 3rd ed., by Ludwig W. Adamec. 2003
48. *Bangladesh*, 3rd ed., by Craig Baxter and Syedur Rahman. 2003
49. *Kyrgyzstan*, by Rafis Abazov. 2004
50. *Syria*, 2nd ed., by David Commins. 2004
51. *Indonesia*, 2nd ed., by Robert Cribb and Audrey Kahin. 2004
52. *Republic of Korea*, 2nd ed., by Andrew C. Nahm and James E. Hoare. 2004
53. *Turkmenistan*, by Rafis Abazov. 2005
54. *Philippines*, 2nd ed., by Artemio Guillermo. 2005
55. *Thailand*, 2nd ed., by Harold E. Smith, Gayla S. Nieminen, and May Kyi Win. 2005.
56. *New Zealand*, 2nd ed., by Keith Jackson and Alan McRobie. 2005.
57. *Vietnam, 3rd ed.,* by Bruce Lockhart and William J. Duiker, 2006.

Historical Dictionary of Vietnam

Third Edition

Bruce M. Lockhart
William J. Duiker

*Historical Dictionaries of Asia, Oceania,
and the Middle East, No. 57*

The Scarecrow Press, Inc.
Lanham, Maryland • Toronto • Oxford
2006

Rowman + Littlefield 06/07

SCARECROW PRESS, INC.

Published in the United States of America
by Scarecrow Press, Inc.
A wholly owned subsidiary of
The Rowman & Littlefield Publishing Group, Inc.
4501 Forbes Boulevard, Suite 200, Lanham, Maryland 20706
www.scarecrowpress.com

PO Box 317
Oxford
OX2 9RU, UK

British Library Cataloguing in Publication Information Available

Library of Congress Cataloging-in-Publication Data

Lockhart, Bruce McFarland, 1960–
    Historical dictionary of Vietnam / Bruce Lockhart, William J. Duiker.
    —3rd ed.
        p.   cm.— (Historical dictionaries of Asia, Oceania, and the Middle
East ; no. 57)
    Rev. ed. of: Historical dictionary of Vietnam / William J. Duiker.
2nd ed. 1998.
    Includes bibliographical references.
    ISBN 0-8108-5053-2 (hardcover : alk. paper)
    1. Vietnam—History—Dictionaries.   I. Duiker, William J., 1932– .
II. Duiker, William J., 1932– . Historical dictionary of Vietnam.
III. Title.   IV. Series.
    DS556.25D85   2006
    959.7'003—dc22   2005020145

∞ ™ The paper used in this publication meets the minimum requirements of
American National Standard for Information Sciences—Permanence of Paper for
Printed Library Materials, ANSI/NISO Z39.48-1992. Manufactured in the United
States of America.

Contents

Editor's Foreword

Vietnam is, if anything, a survivor—sometimes a loser, often a winner, but always a survivor. It has proven this not only over decades or centuries but over millennia. It managed to resist encroachment and domination by the huge Chinese empire (and the People's Republic) several times. It fought off other aggressive neighbors while bearing down on some of the weaker ones, like Laos and Cambodia. It was colonized by the French, but reemerged as a nation, though a divided one. And it was taken over by the Japanese, but not for long. It pitted its seemingly puny military might against the overwhelming technology of the United States . . . and won. Now, the biggest struggle is against itself. The ideologies adopted, sometimes wisely, sometimes not, to regain its independence have not served it well in the present period, so it has to find something else. That is not easy and Vietnam's leaders are rather hesitant, but progress is being made, although no one can say yet what the ultimate result will be. Nonetheless, Vietnam is at last opening up and this is important for its closest neighbors, most of Southeast Asia and also East Asia, and indeed the rest of the world.

With a long and dense history, there is a lot to be packed into a one-volume encyclopedia like this. There are the formative centuries, with a number of kingdoms and countless kings, the colonial period with its innovations and ultimate demise, and most important, the particularly intractable Vietnam War. They are all covered in the dictionary section, which has entries on the political units, the persons running them, the significant institutions and events. Other entries describe the economy, society, and culture. Some inevitably look beyond its frontiers to foreign policy. The whole story is not very tidy or easy to grasp, but this book is facilitated by a chronology and ruler lists. And, as much as possible, the introduction offers a general overview. As for all these historical dictionaries, conceding that not everything can fit in the limited space, a key section is the bibliography with reference to other useful sources of information.

The first and second editions of the *Historical Dictionary of Vietnam* were written by William J. Duiker, who studied East Asian history at Georgetown University and then put his education to practical use with the U.S. Department of State, serving in Saigon among other posts. He has written many articles and several notable books on Vietnam. This third edition is the work of Bruce M. Lockhart. Dr. Lockhart became interested in Vietnam with the arrival of the first refugees in 1975, and then proceeded to study Southeast Asian history. During the early 1990s, he spent several years teaching in Laos and Vietnam. Now he is teaching about both of them, and more broadly, as assistant professor of history at the National University of Singapore. He has also written extensively on Vietnam, including his dissertation, a journal article, book chapters, and a book, *The End of the Vietnamese Monarchy*. He has done an amazingly good job of expanding and updating this work without detracting from it, providing our readers with another generation of information on a country that should again move to the forefront.

Jon Woronoff
Series Editor

Preface

This third edition of the *Historical Dictionary of Vietnam* represents a collaboration between a senior scholar of modern Vietnamese political history and a junior scholar from the "postwar" generation who has lived and worked in Vietnam after its opening in the 1990s and who is particularly interested in how its people perceive and explain their culture and history. The earlier editions' solid core of information on colonial and postcolonial developments has been maintained, but entries and details on premodern history and culture have been considerably revised and new ones added, along with information on political and economic developments since the second edition. Some attention has also been given to the more subtle issues, ironies, and paradoxes that dot the study of the Vietnamese past, and we have attempted to take note of perspectives from recent revisionist scholarship on Vietnam's history.

The bibliography at the end of the volume has been considerably updated with entries for English- and French-language scholarship. Although the bibliography is divided into categories and subcategories for the reader's convenience, the decision to assign a particular entry to a particular heading is admittedly subjective, and the reader is encouraged to peruse the whole bibliographical section.

The authors of a historical dictionary, more than most writers, are dependent on the entire community of scholars and other specialists who have added to the common knowledge of civilization in which we share a mutual interest. William Duiker would particularly like to acknowledge the comments and experience of two of his former colleagues at the Pennsylvania State University—Arthur F. Goldschmidt and Charles S. Prebish—both of whom have written historical dictionaries of their own for Scarecrow Press. Bruce Lockhart is grateful to the History Department and to the Asia Research Institute of the National

University of Singapore (NUS) for a semester's writing leave, which gave him time to work on various projects, including this dictionary. He is also fortunate to have had access to the resources of the libraries at NUS and the Institute of Southeast Asian Studies during the preparation of the new edition. He thanks Claudine Ang and Marius Rummel for their help with the maps. Needless to say, however, the responsibility for any errors of fact or any omissions from this volume are ours.

William J. Duiker   Bruce M. Lockhart
Southern Shores, North Carolina   National University of Singapore

Reader's Notes

One important feature of this third edition is the decision to use Vietnamese diacritical marks throughout the dictionary; the only exceptions are the names *Vietnam, Hanoi,* and *Saigon.* Those who do not speak or read Vietnamese will not see the importance of these marks and may choose to ignore them. Although modern Vietnamese is written in a Romanized script known as *quốc ngữ* or "national language," the alphabetical order of words in a Vietnamese-language dictionary does not entirely follow Western usage. For example, there are two forms of the letter "D." One, written like the English letter, is pronounced as "z" or "y," depending on one's regional accent. The other, written as "Đ" or "đ," is pronounced like a hard "d" in English. In a Vietnamese dictionary, these two letters are listed separately, but in Western-language works, both letters are written the same. This dictionary maintains the written distinction between the two but for purposes of alphabetization, treats them as a single letter. Another issue related to spelling is that Wade-Giles orthography for Chinese words and names has been replaced by Pinyin.

Another problem familiar to Vietnam specialists is the question of names. Like the Chinese, the Vietnamese place their family name first, while given names follow. In Vietnamese usage, however, it is the practice to refer to individuals by the last word appearing in their name. President Ngô Đình Diệm, for example, was commonly known as *President Diệm,* although his family name was Ngô. Hồ Chí Minh, on the other hand, was known as *President Hồ,* probably because the name *Hồ Chí Minh* was a pseudonym that he had adopted from the Chinese. We have attempted to conform with current usage as much as possible. Thus, names are listed in this dictionary according to the family name (the first element), but when individuals are referred to in the text, the personal name (the last element) is frequently used.

Still another issue is that of the geographical divisions of Vietnam. In addition to the separate villages, districts, and provinces into which the state of Vietnam is divided, the Vietnamese often refer to their country in terms of three separate regions: the North (known in Vietnamese as *Bắc Bộ* or *Bắc Kỳ*), the Center (*Trung Bộ* or *Trung Kỳ*), and the South (*Nam Bộ* or *Nam Kỳ*). These divisions correspond roughly with the colonial divisions adopted by the French for the protectorates of Tonkin and Annam and the colony of Cochin China. Although these regions are often not subject to precise definition, they are meaningful to the Vietnamese in a geographical, linguistic, and cultural sense, and we have used *Northern, Central,* and *Southern* in this way. The terms *Tonkin, Annam,* and *Cochin China* are used for the colonial period, while *North Vietnam* and *South Vietnam* refer specifically to the Democratic Republic of Vietnam and the Republic of Vietnam respectively during the period between 1954 and 1975. Notice also that Vietnamese toponyms (Đà Nẵng, Hội An) are preferred over their French equivalents (Tourane, Faifo).

Another change from previous editions is that many organizations (particularly political parties) are now indexed according to their Vietnamese names, though with cross-references for the common English equivalents. If readers consult scholarly works on Vietnam, they will find that many of these organizations are referred to by their original names and that the English translations vary from author to author. There are a few exceptions, such as *Indochinese Communist Party* and *Vietnamese Communist Party.* In these cases, the standard English term has been used.

As a number of entries refer to rulers, it is necessary to say something about Vietnamese imperial titles and reign dates. A Vietnamese monarch bore several different titles during his lifetime and after his death; in addition, upon his ascension to the throne, he adopted a reign title that was used as a basis for dating documents, inscriptions, and events. A ruler who remained on the throne for several years might change his reign title one or more times, and the dating would start over; for example, "The ninth year of Hội Phong" would be followed by "the first year of Long Phù," but with no change in emperor. The Nguyễn dynasty (1802–1945) broke with tradition by using only one reign title for each ruler, and therefore the emperors of this dynasty are known by their respective reign titles (*Gia Long, Minh Mạng,* etc.), and the dictionary has conformed to this practice. The emperors of the three other long-lasting dynasties in Vietnamese history—the Lý (1009–1225), Trần (1225–1400), and Lê (1428–1788)—are ordinarily known by imperial titles ending in *Tông* (sometimes spelled *Tôn*). Entries for rulers from these dynasties are listed under their family name (e.g., Lê Thánh Tông), but frequently within an entry only the specific title (Thánh Tông) is used.

Precise dating of imperial reigns is complicated by the fact that most emperors did not formally take the throne until the beginning of the next lunar year (in late January or early February) following the death of their predecessor. Thus, if a ruler died in July 1300, his successor's reign would be recorded as beginning in January or February 1301. In fact, however, barring factional struggles or other challenges to the new ruler, there was no gap or interregnum following the death of the old one. When indicating reign dates, we have tried as far as possible to make them correspond with historical reality rather than Vietnamese tradition, but readers consulting other sources might find discrepancies of one year for the dating of some reigns.

Acronyms and Abbreviations

AFIMA	Association pour la Formation Intellectuelle et Morale des Annamities
ARVN	Army of the Republic of Vietnam
ASEAN	Association of Southeast Asian Nations
CIA	Central Intelligence Agency
CORDS	Civil Operations and Revolutionary Development Support
COSVN	Central Office of South Vietnam
CPRP	Cambodian People's Revolutionary Party
DMZ	Demilitarized Zone
DRV	Democratic Republic of Vietnam
EFEO	École Française d'Extrême-Orient
FEF	French Expeditionary Forces
FULRO	Front Uni pour la Libération des Races Opprimées
ICC	International Control Commission
ICP	Indochinese Communist Party
KCP	Khmer Communist Party
MAAG	Military Assistance Advisory Group
MACV	Military Assistance Command, Vietnam
MIA	Missing in Action
NCRC	National Council for Reconciliation and Concord
NLF	National Liberation Front
NVA	North Vietnamese Army (People's Army of Vietnam)
PAI	Parti Annamite de l'Indépendance
PAVN	People's Army of Vietnam
PLAF	People's Liberation Armed Forces
PRG	Provisional Revolutionary Government
PRP	People's Revolutionary Party
RVN	Republic of Vietnam
SRV	Socialist Republic of Vietnam
UBC	Unified Buddhist Church
USSR	Union of Soviet Socialist Republics
VCP	Vietnamese Communist Party
VLA	Vietnamese Liberation Army

VNA	Vietnamese National Army
VNQDD	Vietnam Quốc Dân Đảng (Vietnamese Nationalist Party)
VWP	Vietnamese Workers' Party

Geographical Regions of Vietnam

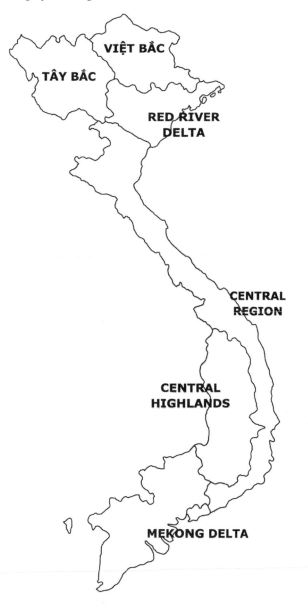

Note: The regional "boundaries" drawn here are rough approximations. The western part of the "Central Region" along the Lao border is upland territory, but is not usually included in the area specifically called the "Central Highlands." The "Mekong Delta" region has been extended eastward here to include the lowland areas extending up to the edge of the Central Highlands.

Đại Việt Around 1500

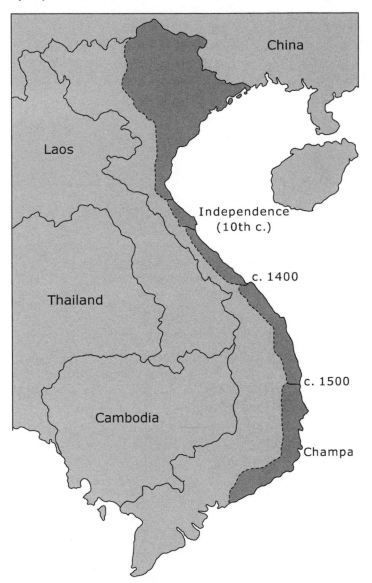

Note: This map represents the expansion of the Vietnamese polity until the time of the civil wars in the 16th century. During the 14th and 15th centuries, Vietnam acquired territory from Champa by both peaceful and violent means, as indicated by the dates "c. 1400" and "c. 1500." However, some historians argue that Vietnamese control over this territory remained loose until after the division of the country into two kingdoms at the beginning of the 17th century.

The Southern Kingdom of Đàng Trong

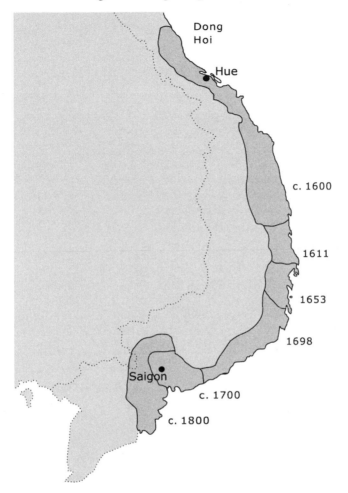

Note: This map shows the expansion of the southern kingdom of Đàng Trong under the Nguyễn Lords during the 17th and 18th centuries. This territorial expansion took place at the expense first of the Cham along the coast and then of the Khmer in the Mekong Delta. The progressive annexation of Cham territory is known with considerable accuracy; the successive stages of acquisition of different parts in the Mekong Delta are much less certain, and what is shown on the map for the latter process is only an approximation. The map draws on information from Po Dharma, "Les frontières du Campā (Dernier état des recherches)" in P. B. Lafont (ed.), *Les frontières du Vietnam: Histoire des frontières de la péninsule indochinoise* (Paris: L'Harmattan, 1989), pp. 128–135, and Mak Phoeun, "La frontière entre le Cambodge et le Viênam du XVIIᵉ siècle à l'instauration du protectorat français présentée à travers les chroniques royales khmères," in the same volume, pp. 136–155.

Vietnam Under French Rule

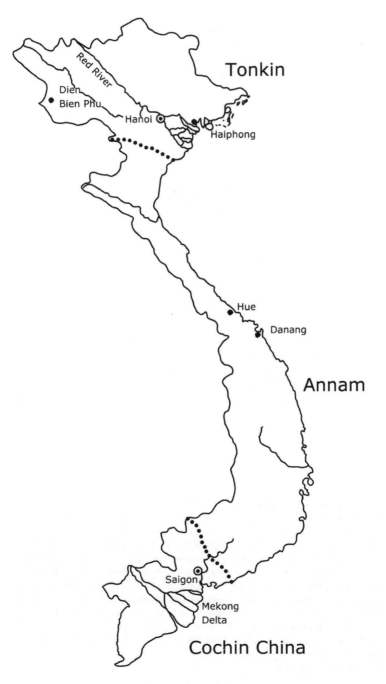

Red River

Tonkin

Dien
Bien Phu

Hanoi

Haiphong

Hue

Danang

Annam

Saigon

Mekong
Delta

Cochin China

Chronology

Prehistory and Chinese Period until 900 C.E.

258 B.C.E. An Dương Vương establishes Kingdom of Âu Lạc after conquest.

207 B.C.E. Foundation of Kingdom of Nam Việt (Nanyue) by Triệu Đà (Zhao Tuo) in southern China.

179 B.C.E. Triệu Đà conquers Âu Lạc.

111 B.C.E. Conquest of Nam Việt by Han dynasty.

39 C.E. Revolt of Trưng Sisters against Chinese rule.

43 Suppression of Trưng Sisters Revolt by Ma Yuan.

192 Foundation of Kingdom of Linyi/Lâm Ấp in present-day central Vietnam.

248 Revolt by followers of Lady Triệu (Bà Triệu).

542–600 Lý Bí Rebellion against Chinese rule, continued by Lý Phật Tử, Triệu Quang Phục.

722 Mai Thúc Loan (Mai Hắc Đế) Rebellion.

Age of Independent Vietnamese Kingdoms, 10th to 19th Centuries

939 Proclamation of Ngô Quyền as king after first battle of Bạch Đằng.

968 Proclamation of Đinh Bộ Lĩnh as emperor.

980 Proclamation of Lê Hoàn (Lê Đại Hành) as emperor.

982 Vietnamese seizure of Indrapura, Cham capital at Đồng Dương.

1009 Foundation of Lý Dynasty by Lý Công Uẩn (Lý Thái Tổ).

1010 Transfer of capital from Hoa Lư to Đại La, renamed Thăng Long (now known as Hanoi).

1070 Construction of the Temple of Literature in Hanoi.

1225 Foundation of Trần dynasty (1225–1400) by Trần Thủ Độ.

1257 First Mongol attack on Vietnam.

1284 Second Mongol attack on Vietnam.

1287 Defeat of Mongols at second battle of Bạch Đằng.

1400 Foundation of Hồ dynasty (1400–1407) by Hồ Quý Ly.

1407 Conquest of kingdom of Đại Ngu (Đại Việt) by Ming dynasty in China.

1418 Launching of Lam Sơn rebellion (led by Lê Lợi) against Chinese rule.

1428 Foundation of Lê dynasty (1428–1788) by Lê Lợi.

1471 Seizure of Cham capital Vijaya by Vietnamese forces.

1527 Usurpation of power by Mạc dynasty (1527–1592).

1592 Restoration of Lê dynasty in Hanoi.

ca. 1600 Effective partition of Vietnamese territory into two autonomous kingdoms, Đàng Ngoài and Đàng Trong.

1627 Civil war between the Trịnh and the Nguyễn (1627–1672). Arrival of Alexandre de Rhodes in Hanoi.

1692 Champa annexed to Vietnam as protectorate.

1698 Gia Định (Saigon) comes under Vietnamese control.

1771 Eruption of Tây Sơn Rebellion.

1786 Tây Sơn armies enter Hanoi.

1787 Treaty of Versailles between Nguyễn Ánh and kingdom of France.

1788 Defeat of the Lê and Trịnh and foundation of Tây Sơn dynasty (1788–1802) by Nguyễn Huệ (Emperor Quang Trung).

1802 Final defeat of the Tây Sơn and foundation of Nguyễn dynasty (1802–1945) by Nguyễn Ánh (Emperor Gia Long).

1833 Lê Văn Khôi Rebellion in southern Vietnam (1833–1835).

1846 Establishment of joint Vietnamese-Siamese protectorate over Cambodia.

French Colonization and Colonial Rule
1858–1954

1858 French and Spanish fleet attack Vietnam in Đà Nẵng harbor.

1859 French conquest of three provinces in Mekong Delta.

1861 Battle of Kỳ Hoà, near present-day Hồ Chí Minh City (Saigon).

1862 Treaty of Saigon, ceding three provinces in Cochin China to France.

1863 Declaration of French protectorate over Cambodia.

1867 Conquest of three remaining provinces in Mekong Delta by the French.

1873 French adventurer Francis Garnier killed near Hanoi by Black Flags.

1874 Philastre Treaty recognizing French sovereignty over all of Cochin China, establishing first stage of protectorate over Vietnamese Empire.

1882 French captain Henri Rivière seizes Hanoi.

1883 Harmand Treaty establishing French protectorate over Vietnamese Empire.

1884 First Treaty of Tientsin between France and Qing Empire. Harmand Treaty is replaced by Patenôtre Treaty, confirming French protectorate over Annam (central Vietnam) and Tonkin (northern Vietnam).

1885 Flight of Emperor Hàm Nghi from imperial court at Huế and launching of Cần Vương Movement.

1887 Indochinese Union established in Vietnam and Cambodia.

1888 Hàm Nghi captured and exiled to Algeria.

1896 Dissolution of Cần Vương Movement with final pacification by French.

1904 Foundation of Modernization Society (Duy Tân Hội) by Phan Bội Châu.

1905 Foundation of Đông Du (Study in the East) Movement.

1906 Foundation of Đông Kinh Nghĩa Thục (Tonkin Free School) in Hanoi.

1912 Foundation of Vietnamese Restoration Society (Việt Nam Quang Phục Hội) by Phan Bội Châu.

1915 Abolition of civil service examinations in Tonkin.

1917 Thái Nguyên Rebellion in Tonkin.

1918 Abolition of civil service examinations in Annam.

1919 Hồ Chí Minh (then known as Nguyễn Ái Quốc) presents petition to Versailles Peace Conference demanding Vietnamese independence.

1924 Hồ Chí Minh arrives in Canton from Moscow.

1925 Formation of Vietnamese Revolutionary Youth League (Thanh Niên) in Canton. Seizure of Phan Bội Chau by French police in Shanghai; deported to Vietnam, he is placed on trial and sent to house arrest in Huế.

1926 Foundation of Cao Đài religion by Ngô Văn Chiêu.

1927 Foundation of Vietnamese Nationalist Party (Việt Nam Quốc Dân Đảng, VNQDĐ) by Nguyễn Thái Học in Hanoi.

1929 May: Congress of Thanh Niên in Hong Kong.

1930 February: Unification of radical factions into a single Vietnamese Communist Party (VCP) in Hong Kong. Outbreak of Yên Bái revolt, led by VNQDĐ. **May:** Beginning of Nghệ-Tĩnh Revolt in Annam. **October:** VCP adopts new name of Indochinese Communist Party (ICP).

1931 April: Seizure of ICP leadership by the French. **June:** Hồ Chí Minh arrested in Hong Kong. **July–August:** Suppression of Nghệ-Tĩnh Soviets.

1932 September: Emperor Bảo Đại returns from schooling in France and assumes limited imperial powers.

1933 December: Hồ Chí Minh is released in Hong Kong and returns to the Soviet Union.

1935 March: The Indochinese Communist Party holds its first national congress at Macao.

1936 Formation of the Popular Front in France.

1938 Hồ Chí Minh leaves the Soviet Union and travels to China.

1939 Foundation of the Hoà Hảo religious movement in Cochin China. **September:** Outbreak of war in Europe. Indochinese Communist Party driven underground.

1940 August: Franco–Japanese Treaty granting Japan military facilities in northern Indochina. **September–October:** Bắc Sơn uprising in northern Tonkin. **November:** Nam Bộ uprising in Cochin China.

1941 May: Eighth Plenum (Pác Bó Plenum) of the Indochinese Communist Party sets up the League for the Independence of Vietnam (popularly known as the Việt Minh).

1942 August: Hồ Chí Minh arrested in southern China. Foundation of Vietnamese Revolutionary League (Đồng Minh Hội) by exiles in southern China.

1943 September: Hồ Chí Minh is released from prison and joins the Đồng Minh Hội.

1944 December: Creation of the first Armed Propaganda Brigades by the Indochinese Communist Party.

1945 9 March: Japanese *coup d'état* abolishes French administration in Indochina and offers emperor Bảo Đại independence under Japanese protection. **April:** Vietnamese puppet government is formed under Prime Minister Trần Trọng Kim. **May:** Armed Propaganda Brigades are merged with National Salvation Army into Vietnamese Liberation Army. Hồ Chí Minh returns from China, sets up ICP headquarters at Tân Trào. **August:** ICP conference is held at Tân Trào and decides on national insurrection. Japan surrenders. National Congress of the Việt Minh appeals for general uprising throughout Vietnam and declares Hồ Chí Minh president of a provisional republic. General uprising in Hanoi. Việt Minh forces seize imperial capital of Huế. Uprising of communist and nationalist forces allied in Committee for the South in Saigon. Emperor Bảo Đại abdicates and accepts position as supreme political adviser to new provisional republic. **September:** Hồ Chí Minh declares Vietnamese independence in Hanoi. Chinese occupation forces arrive in Hanoi as part of Potsdam Agreement. British occupation forces begin to arrive in Saigon. Committee for the South orders general strike in Saigon. British commander announces martial law in Saigon. **October:** French military forces begin to arrive in Cochin China. Việt Minh forces retreat from Saigon and begin guerrilla operations against French administration in Cochin China. **November:** ICP dissolved and replaced by an Association of Marxist Studies. Agreement between Communist and nationalist parties on formation of a coalition government in Hanoi. Hồ Chí Minh is selected as president of the Democratic Republic of Vietnam (DRV).

1946 January: Provisional coalition government takes office in Hanoi. National elections held throughout the North for a National Assembly. **February:** Sino–French Agreement on withdrawal of Chinese troops from northern Vietnam. **March:** Signing of preliminary Hồ-Sainteny Agreement creating "free state" of Vietnam and calling for a referendum in Cochin China. **April–May:** Đàlạt Conference between representatives of France and DRV fails to resolve issues between the two governments. **June:** Formation of Republic of Cochin China by pro-French elements. **July:** Opening of Fontainebleau Conference between representatives of France and the DRV held near Paris. **September:** Hồ Chí Minh signs *modus vivendi* in Paris and returns to Hanoi. **October:** National Assembly of the DRV convenes and reorganizes government without participation of non-Việt Minh nationalist elements. **November:** National Assembly approves adoption of first Constitution of the DRV. French ships bombard native quarter in Hảiphòng. **December:** Việt Minh attacks on French installations in northern Vietnam mark beginning of Franco–Việt Minh conflict. DRV government flees to rural areas to reorganize for guerrilla war.

1947 May: French scholar Paul Mus meets with Hồ Chí Minh, who refuses to accept French terms for an end of the conflict. **December:** First Hạ Long Bay Agreement reached between ex-emperor Bảo Đại and French high commissioner Emile Bollaert in Gulf of Tonkin. Later, Bảo Đại denounces the agreement as providing too little independence for projected new state of Vietnam.

1948 June: Second Hạ Long Bay Agreement between Bảo Đại and French representatives. France recognizes the independence of a provisional central government formed in May but retains control over foreign affairs and defense. Other functions are to be discussed at a future conference. **July:** Bảo Đại denounces Second Hạ Long Bay Agreement as inadequate.

1949 March: Élysée Agreement signed between representatives of France and new Associated State of Vietnam. The new state has many of the attributes of independence, but France retains control of foreign relations and national defense and Vietnam enters the French Union. **June:** Bảo Đại assumes office of Head of State of the new government. **July:** Official establishment of the Associated State of Vietnam.

1950 January: The new People's Republic of China (PRC) grants diplomatic recognition to the DRV, and the USSR officially recognizes its independence. **February:** The United States officially recognizes the independence of the State of Vietnam; Great Britain follows suit. France requests U.S. aid in fighting the Việt Minh insurgency movement. **May:** President Harry S. Truman approves $15 million in military aid to the French in Indochina. U.S. announces intention to set up economic aid mission in the Associated States of Indochina (Vietnam, Laos, and Cambodia). **June:** Outbreak of Korean War. Opening of Pau negotiations to transfer sovereignty to the State of Vietnam. **September–November:** Việt Minh border offensive destroys French outposts along Chinese border.

1951 January–May: Abortive Việt Minh general offensive on fringes of Red River Delta.

1952 November: Việt Minh offensive in the mountains north of Hanoi forces French evacuation of much of the border area.

1953 April: Việt Minh offensive in northern Laos. **May:** Appointment of General Henri Navarre as commander in chief of French forces in Indochina and adoption of the Navarre Plan to win the Franco-Việt Minh War. **November:** French forces occupy military outpost at Điện Biên Phủ to hinder Việt Minh movement into Laos. In interview with Swedish reporter, Hồ Chí Minh offers to negotiate an end to the war.

1954 January–February: Conference among Great Powers held in Berlin agrees to discuss a settlement of the Indochina War at a conference to be convened at Geneva in May. **May:** French outpost of Điện Biên Phủ falls to Việt Minh forces after two-month siege. Opening of discussions on Indochina at Geneva. **July:** Ngô Đình Diệm appointed prime minister of the Associated State of Vietnam. Geneva Conference concludes with military agreement on a cease-fire and a political protocol calling for national elections in 1956. **September:** Creation of Southeast Asia Treaty Organization in Manila. **October:** Return of DRV government to Hanoi. President Eisenhower promises aid to State of Vietnam.

1955 July: Ngô Đình Diệm refuses to hold consultations on elections with representations of the DRV. **October:** Diệm defeats Bảo Đại in a referendum, announces formation of Republic of Vietnam with its capital in Saigon.

1955–1956 Land reform program in the Democratic Republic of Vietnam redistributes land holdings throughout the country. Excesses committed against individuals lead to the firing of several government officials and the demotion of Party General Secretary Trường Chinh.

1957–1958 Discontent rises among various elements of the population in South Vietnam over the policies of President Ngô Đình Diệm.

1958–1960 Adoption by DRV of three-year plan launches collectivization in the North.

1959 January: Central Committee of Vietnamese Workers' Party adopts program to resume revolutionary war in South Vietnam. **31 December:** DRV adopts its second constitution.

1960 September: Third National Congress of the Vietnamese Workers' Party held in Hanoi. The Congress decides to escalate the revolutionary struggle in South Vietnam. Lê Duẩn is elected general secretary of the Party. **11 November:** Abortive coup against Diệm in Saigon. **20 December:** Formation of the National Front for the Liberation of South Vietnam (NLF).

1961 May: President John F. Kennedy promises continued U.S. aid to the Republic of Vietnam. Vice-President Lyndon Johnson visits South Vietnam. **October:** General Maxwell Taylor visits South Vietnam and reports to the president.

1963 May–June: Buddhist demonstrations lead to government repression in South Vietnam. **Summer:** Dissident military officers contact Kennedy administration with plans to overthrow Diệm regime. **1 November:** Diệm and his brother Ngô Đình Nhu are overthrown and killed in Saigon. A Military Revolutionary Council is formed to continue the struggle against the NLF. **December:** Central Committee of the VWP decides to escalate the struggle in the South.

1964 January: General Nguyễn Khánh seizes power in Saigon. **August:** First Tonkin Gulf Incident leads U.S. Congress to pass Tonkin Gulf Resolution. Deterioration of the political situation in South Vietnam as several governments succeed each other in Saigon. Revolutionary forces take advantage of the situation to extend their control over rural areas.

1965 February: Attack by revolutionary forces on U.S. base at Pleiku provides Johnson administration with a pretext to launch bombing campaign on North Vietnam and begin dispatch of U.S. combat troops to South Vietnam. **June:** Young Turks under Nguyễn Cao Kỳ and Nguyễn Văn Thiệu seize control of government in Saigon. **October:** Battle of Ia Drang Valley pits U.S. troops against revolutionary forces in the South in sustained battle for the first time.

1966 February: Honolulu Conference between U.S. and South Vietnamese representatives on war strategy. Saigon regime agrees to seek political stability in the South. **September:** Election of a Constituent Assembly in South Vietnam.

1967 January: U.S. and South Vietnamese forces cooperate in Operation Cedar Falls to destroy revolutionary emplacements in the Iron Triangle. **April:** New Constitution of the Second Republic of Vietnam is approved by the National Assembly. **September:** In national elections held in South Vietnam, Nguyễn Văn Thiệu is elected president of the RVN.

1968 February: Communist-led forces launch Tết Offensive throughout South Vietnam. Heavy fighting in Saigon, in Huế, and along the Demilitarized Zone, where the U.S. firebase is under heavy attack for several weeks. **May:** The United States and the DRV agree to hold peace talks in Paris.

1969 January: Peace talks open in Paris. **June:** Formation of the Provisional Revolutionary Government of the Republic of South Vietnam (PRG) under the guidance of the DRV. **2 September:** Hồ Chí Minh dies on DRV National Day. **23 September:** Hồ is succeeded as president by Tôn Đức Thắng.

1970 29 April: U.S. and South Vietnamese forces invade Cambodia in an effort to eliminate the sanctuaries. Demonstrations against the war mount in the United States.

1971 3 October: Thiệu reelected president of South Vietnam.

1972 March: North Vietnamese forces launch Easter Offensive in South Vietnam. **December:** President Nixon approves "Christmas bombing" of North Vietnam.

1973 27 January: Paris Agreement signed, ending direct U.S. participation in the war.

1974 September: As Paris Agreement breaks down, party leadership in the DRV undertakes policy review and decides to launch a major military offensive in South Vietnam the following year.

1975 January: Communist forces launch general offensive designed to liberate South Vietnam from the Saigon regime. **April:** Thiệu resigns as president of the RVN and is replaced by Trần Văn Hương. The latter gives way to Dương Văn Minh, only days before Communist forces occupy Saigon and accept his surrender. South Vietnam comes under the control of the PRG. **May:** First border clashes take place between Vietnam and Khmer Rouge from Democratic Kampuchea. **June:** Government begins forced relocation of refugees and other urban residents to New Economic Zones. **September:** New government launches a campaign against the "comprador bourgeoisie" in the South. All commercial transactions in the South are suspended for one day, and the former Republic of Vietnam currency is replaced by a new *đồng*, separate from the currency used in the North. Politburo announces that national reunification will take place as soon as possible and that "socialist construction" in the South will begin immediately.

1976 25 April: Elections held throughout Vietnam to create a new National Assembly for the entire country. **May:** SRV and Democratic Kampuchea begin unsuccessful border negotiations. **2 July:** Announcement of the creation of a new Socialist Republic of Vietnam (SRV), uniting North and South into a single country. **December:** Fourth National Congress of the Communist Party held in Hanoi; the name of the Party is changed to *Vietnamese Communist Party (VCP)*. Five-year economic plan is announced. The DRV president (Tôn Đức Thắng) and premier (Phạm Văn Đồng) retain their positions in the SRV. North-South rail link is completed, known as the *Thống Nhất* (Reunification) railroad.

1977 3 January: Government establishes Inspectorate Committee to oppose corruption and other abuses at lower levels of the system. **July:** Vietnam and Laos sign a 25-year Treaty of Friendship and Cooperation. **10 September:** Politburo establishes a committee to coordinate the "socialist transformation" of the South. **October:** Vietnam launches major incursions into Cambodian territory after a series of border incidents and raids by Khmer Rouge forces. **31 December:** Democratic Kampuchea breaks diplomatic relations with the SRV.

1978 23 March: Government announces the nationalization of all private manufacturing and commercial enterprises above the family level throughout the SRV. **April:** Refugees, many of them overseas Chinese, begin to flee Vietnam. China accuses the SRV of mistreating its Chinese residents and cuts off economic aid. **May:** Single currency is put into use for the entire country. **June:** Vietnam's membership in the socialist bloc's Council for Mutual Economic Cooperation is fast-tracked and pushed through by the USSR despite little consultation with other members. **July–September:** Severe flooding damages the economy. **3 November:** The SRV signs a 25-year Treaty of Friendship and Cooperation with the Soviet Union. **25 December:** Vietnamese military forces invade Democratic Kampuchea.

1979 9 January: After the Vietnamese occupation of Phnom Penh, a new pro-Vietnamese government is established under Heng Samrin, entitled the People's Republic of Kampuchea (PRK). **17 February:** Military forces of the PRC cross the border in a brief but bitter attack on Vietnam. **5 March:** China announces impending withdrawal of forces after penetrating only a few miles into Vietnamese territory. **April:** Peace talks between China and Vietnam begin, but the two sides are unable to agree on a settlement. **May:** The party carries out a review of membership qualifications as preparation for a cleansing of its ranks. **September:** Sixth Plenum of the Fourth Party Central Committee takes first steps toward reversal of socialist economic policies. **October:** National census shows the SRV population to be 53 million.

1980 February: Cabinet reshuffle replaces Võ Nguyên Giáp with Văn Tiến Dũng as minister of defense and installs a number of younger men in top positions, including Nguyễn Cơ Thạch in the Foreign Ministry. VCP begins a purification campaign of its membership. **30 March:** SRV President Tôn Đức Thắng dies. **July, September:** Major typhoons cause serious damage to the rice crop. **18 December:** The SRV promulgates a new constitution, the third since the declaration of independence in 1945; the new charter calls for a rapid advance to a fully socialist society. However, the Ninth Plenum of the Central Committee pursues a more pragmatic line away from socialist economic policies.

1981 April: Elections are held for the National Assembly. **June:** Prominent intellectual Nguyễn Khắc Viện circulates a private letter to government leaders criticizing many official policies. **July:** National Assembly elects top government leaders for the Council of Ministers and Council of State (an organ newly created by the 1980 Constitution), headed by Phạm Văn Đồng and Trường Chinh, respectively. The SRV and USSR sign a five-year agreement detailing Soviet economic assistance.

1982 March: Fifth National Congress of the VCP held in Hanoi, several months later than scheduled because of disputes over economic policy. The Congress approves a compromise program calling for a cautious advance to socialism but recognizes that the country is facing serious problems. **April:** Foreign Minister Nguyễn Cơ Thạch begins a "peace offensive" travel program to improve ties with Europe and India. **June:** Formation by rebel groups of a Coalition Government of Democratic Kampuchea to force the withdrawal of Vietnamese occupation forces from Kampuchea. **July:** Government issues a directive against economic crimes, including smuggling, hoarding, and speculation. **November:** China and Vietnam both withdraw some units from their border region, temporarily reducing tensions. **December:** Government launches a campaign to "restore socialist order in the market."

1983 February: Tax regulations are amended to clearly favor the state and cooperative sectors over private economic activities. **June:** Fourth Plenum of the Fifth Central Committee emphasizes the ongoing struggle between the "capitalist" and "socialist" paths. **December:** Government campaign is launched to sell bonds (denominated in both *đồng* and kilograms of rice) to "build up the fatherland."

1984 Prolonged cold weather, drought, insects, and flooding cause extensive damage to rice crops around the country. **July:** At the Sixth Plenum of the Central Committee, General Secretary Lê Duẩn makes a speech outlining his concept of "collective mastery," intended to establish a middle way between centralist and individualist excesses. He acknowledges the need for economic policies to use incentives rather than coercion. **November:** New fighting breaks out along Chinese border.

1985 June: Eighth Plenum of Central Committee announces price, wage, and currency reforms but maintains strict price controls, thus significantly slowing the pace of reform. **September:** Ill-conceived currency changes and salary increases trigger a bout of major inflation that eventually reaches 1,000 percent. **October:** Vice-Premier Võ Văn Kiệt makes a speech severely criticizing the overall state of the economy and calling for more consistent planning and implementation.

1986 March: Party launches a criticism/self-criticism campaign to address problems in policy implementation. **10 July:** Party General Secretary Lê Duẩn dies in Hanoi. He is replaced by Politburo member Trường Chinh. **August:** Politburo meeting lays the official groundwork for *đổi mới* (renovation) reforms. **December:** Sixth National Congress of the VCP is held in Hanoi later that year, launching *đổi mới*. Trường Chinh and other veteran members of the party are retired from the Politburo, and Nguyễn Văn Linh is elected general secretary.

1987 February: Another Party purification campaign is launched targeting bad cadres. **March:** Controls over the flow of goods are lifted and checkpoints along roads are abolished. **April:** Second Plenum of Sixth Central Committee acknowledges widespread economic hardship, legalizes moonlighting activities by civil servants. Elections are held for the National Assembly. **June:** Trường Chinh and Phạm Văn Đồng resign as chief of state and premier, respectively, and are replaced by Võ Chí Công and Phạm Hùng. General Secretary Nguyễn Văn Linh tells the National Assembly at its opening session that it needs to play a more active role in the government. **October:** Linh promises a congress of writers and artists that the Party will loosen its control over intellectuals and their work. **December:** Liberal foreign investment code is passed.

1988 March: Premier Phạm Hùng dies and is replaced by reformist Võ Văn Kiệt. New regulations on the family economy allow households to sign production contracts with the state and cooperatives and grants them land ownership rights. Clashes erupt in the Spratly Islands after Chinese forces fire on Vietnamese freighters. **June:** Kiệt is replaced by the more conservative Đỗ Mười after serious intra-Party debate. **July:** A Politburo resolution says that the private sector needs to be "consolidated" along with the state sector. The first Jakarta Informal Meeting (JIM) is held in Indonesia as part of an Association of Southeast Asian Nations (ASEAN) initiative to promote a resolution of the conflict in Cambodia. **30 September**: Trường Chinh dies. **December:** Border trade is officially resumed with China.

1989 January: The Vietnamese deputy foreign minister visits China, the highest-level official contact with Beijing since the 1979 invasion. **February:** ASEAN organizes a second JIM. Party General Secretary Nguyễn Văn Linh takes the Vietnamese press to task for being overly critical of the government. **April:** Vietnam announces that it will withdraw all of its forces in Cambodia by September. **September:** Vietnam completes the withdrawal of its troops from Cambodia. **28 December:** National Assembly passes a tough new press law.

1990 March: Politburo member Trần Xuân Bạch loses his Party leadership posts after calling for greater freedom of information in order to avoid the fate of East European socialist regimes. **June:** The USSR announces a reduction in its aid to the SRV, at the time averaging $150 million a year. **September:** A secret summit in Chengdu, China between the SRV and PRC premiers and Party general secretaries lays the groundwork for normalization of ties. **13 October:** Lê Đức Thọ dies. **December:** Draft plan for promoting economic growth during the next decade is discussed. Party calls for continued economic reform with political stability.

1991 June: At the Seventh Congress of the VCP, Nguyễn Van Linh retires, and Đỗ Mười is named general secretary of the Party, to be replaced as premier by Võ Văn Kiệt. **23 October:** Paris Agreement ends civil war in Cambodia. **November:** Normalization of relations with the PRC. The first Export Processing Zone is created at Tân Thuận Đông near Hồ Chí Minh City. **December:** Collapse of USSR brings an end to the Soviet–Vietnamese relationship. Mười publicly affirms that socialism remains the "correct course" for Vietnam.

1992 April: Revised constitution is promulgated, reducing role of Marxism–Leninism in Vietnamese society. It eliminates the Council of State structure, and the Council of Ministers is replaced by a Cabinet. Work begins on a North–South power line. **June:** New law is passed that allows for the sale of state-owned enterprises as part of the process of "equitization." The first steps are taken to ease the U.S.-led trade embargo. **July:** Elections are held for the National Assembly, whose size is trimmed from 496 to 395 members (though this reduction will later be reversed). **September:** Lê Đức Anh becomes chief of state (president), and Võ Văn Kiệt is reelected as premier. **October:** Following Vietnamese protests and threats, China withdraws forces from some Spratly Islands, which it has been occupying since February.

1993 January: Fourth Plenum of the Seventh Central Committee focuses on the "human factor," passing resolutions pertaining to social and cultural issues. **July:** The United States ends its veto of a plan to help Vietnam repay its arrears to the International Monetary Fund.

1994 February: Lifting of U.S.-led economic embargo on trade with the SRV. **27 May:** Vietnam's North–South power line begins operation.

June: National Assembly passes labor law to address issues of workers in market economy. **July:** Government launches the first of several campaigns against "social evils."

1995 July: United States and Vietnam agree to establish diplomatic relations, although no ambassadors are exchanged. Vietnam joins ASEAN as a full member. Vietnam and the European Union sign a treaty of cooperation. **October:** National Assembly passes Civil Code as part of effort to develop "rule of law." Government undergoes major Cabinet reshuffle and merging of several ministries; "super-ministry" is established for investment and planning.

1996 April: Đào Duy Tùng, a prominent Party ideologue, drafts a very conservative political report for the upcoming Party Congress, apparently in a bid for power that costs him his position within the Party. **June:** The Eighth Congress of the VCP is held, but with no immediate change in the top leadership positions. Lê Mai, key Vietnamese diplomat and one of the architects of normalization with the United States, dies suddenly. **September:** SRV and United States begin negotiations on a Bilateral Trade Agreement. **October:** National Assembly passes an amended Law on Foreign Investment meant to streamline procedures for investors, though many of the latter feel it is inadequate for the task. Eight provinces are subdivided into 15 provinces and one city as part of shift away from larger, combined administrative units. **November:** President Lê Đức Anh suffers a stroke, which helps pave the way for his retirement, along with Party General Secretary Đỗ Mười and Premier Võ Văn Kiệt.

1997 March: Vietnam asks for and receives ASEAN's support after China sets up an oil-drilling rig in a disputed area of the South China Sea, leading Beijing to remove the rig. **May:** Douglas "Pete" Peterson arrives as the first U.S. ambassador to the SRV. Violent protests break out over land and corruption issues in Thái Bình province. **June:** A plenum of the Party Central Committee chooses Trần Đức Lương as president of the SRV and Phan Văn Khải as premier. **July:** National Assembly elections include "self-nominated" candidates for the first time. **August:** Opening ceremonies are held for Vietnam's first stock exchange, though it will not actually come into operation until 2000. **November:** Unrest occurs in Đồng Nai province over land issues.

Hanoi hosts a Francophone Summit to improve its ties with French-speaking countries. **December:** Lê Khả Phiêu is selected as the new Party general secretary after months of anticipation and debate.

1998 February: The government issues new rules on foreign investment in another attempt to satisfy the expectations of investors. The State Bank allows the value of the *đồng* to slide as part of an gradual but steady devaluation of the currency. During a visit to restive Thái Bình province, Premier Phan Văn Khải acknowledges that the Party has failed to respond to popular complaints about corruption and abuses by cadres. **August:** Government attempts to tackle official corruption with a major decree requiring officials to declare their assets. **October:** Khải makes an official visit to Beijing—the first by a premier since normalization of relations in the early 1990s. **December:** Vietnam hosts its first ASEAN summit.

1999 January: Trần Độ, an army general and prominent dissident, is expelled from the Party for his critical views. **February:** Lê Khả Phiêu visits China and works out a "new mechanism" for Sino-Vietnamese relations. **May:** The Party launches a self-criticism campaign intended to address problems of corruption and wrong attitudes within its ranks. **July:** Hanoi and Washington reach in-principle agreement on the text of a Bilateral Trade Agreement (BTA). **September:** Vietnam suddenly backs off from its agreement to sign the BTA. **30 December:** A land border agreement is signed with China, but the details are kept secret, causing widespread dissatisfaction; they will only be published officially (though very quietly) in Vietnam in August 2002.

2000 January: New Enterprise Law takes effect, intended to promote individual entrepreneurship. **July:** Bilateral Trade Agreement signed with the United States. Vietnam's first stock exchange begins operation in Hồ Chí Minh City. **November:** U.S. President Bill Clinton makes a landmark visit to Vietnam. **December:** China and Vietnam sign a treaty delineating the maritime border, but ratification is delayed until 2004.

2001 January–February: Serious protests break out in the Central Highlands over issues of land and religious repression. **April:** Ninth Party Congress sees Lê Khả Phiêu replaced as general secretary by Nông Đức Mạnh, a member of the Tày ethnic minority. The positions of senior advisors (held by retired leaders Đỗ Mười, Lê Đức Anh, and

Võ Văn Kiệt) are formally abolished. **June:** Mạnh endorses a large hydroelectric project in Sơn La province that will displace up to 100,000 people. **September:** Mạnh personally visits the three Central Highland provinces where unrest took place earlier in the year. **October:** Dissident Catholic priest Father Nguyễn Văn Lý is sentenced to 15 years in prison for having submitted testimony to a U.S. Congressional committee looking into religious persecution in Vietnam. Russia announces that the last of its forces at Cam Ranh Bay will be withdrawn. **10 December:** U.S.–Vietnam Bilateral Trade Agreement officially comes into force.

2002 Prosecution of Năm Cam scandal, Vietnam's biggest corruption case to date, involving many high-level officials. **January:** Government announces decision to rotate high-level state and Party leaders through different posts on a regular basis in attempt to reduce corruption and abuses of power. **March:** Premier Phan Văn Khải publicly comments that private enterprise brings a "glorious victory" to the country. **May:** Government announces formal guidelines for the future direction of "equitization" of State-owned enterprises that seems to encourage wider privatization. National Assembly elections take place, with a drop in non-Party winners from nearly 15 percent to 10 percent. **September:** Vietnam attempts to protect its domestic motorbike industry by reducing quotas on imported parts, seriously irritating Japan. **December:** Seventh Plenum of Ninth Party Central Committee recognizes problem of "erosion of popular confidence" in the Party.

2003 January: Official concern over religious activities leads to new legislation aimed at controlling religion in Vietnam. Government scraps the controversial limits on imported motorbike parts after widespread criticism. **February:** Hanoi and Washington begin negotiations for quotas on textile exports to the United States. **19 March:** Government issues amendments to Foreign Investment Law meant to redress some of the problems that have hampered investors. **July:** Eighth Plenum of Central Committee pays particular attention to issues concerning ethnic minorities as a response to unrest in the highlands. A U.S. warship makes a port call to Vietnam, the first since the war. **October:** Party General Secretary Nông Đức Mạnh holds high-level meeting to tackle problems of corruption and flawed implementation of government directives. **November:** Amended Land Law is passed that is meant to offer more flexibility for land use and transactions. An amended Criminal Code is ratified that promises more "democracy" within the legal system. **December:** Vietnam hosts the SEAGames.

2004 20 January: First hearing in Washington on the dumping petition by U.S. shrimp producers against Vietnamese exporters. **March:** A new income tax law is issued, which raises the minimum taxable income for Vietnamese; the stated goal is to increase tax revenue while taxing fewer people. **April:** New unrest breaks out in Central Highlands. United Airlines announces its plans for daily flights from the United States to Vietnam via Hong Kong, the first service by a U.S. carrier since 1975. The International Monetary Fund terminates its main aid program to Vietnam after the government refused to allow an independent audit of the State Bank's foreign exchange reserves. **June:** Vietnam finally ratifies 2000 maritime border agreement with China. National Assembly ratifies new Ordinance on Beliefs and Religions, which is criticized by foreign observers as potentially repressive. A new law permits the existence of 100 percent foreign-owned banks. **July:** Vietnam accedes to the Berne Convention on copyright protection, the first time it has signed a multilateral agreement on intellectual property. **October:** Substantial oil reserves are discovered in the Tonkin Gulf. Hanoi and the European Union conclude talks paving the way for Vietnam's entry into the World Trade Organization. **November:** U.S. Department of Commerce issues list of tariff rates for Vietnamese shrimp exporters after the conclusion of the dumping case. Most of the companies on the list will have a tariff of less than 5 percent, with a rate of nearly 26 percent for the other few. By comparison, most Chinese shrimp exporters will have tariffs of at least 55 percent, and some as high as 112 percent. The National Assembly passes a Competition Law to regulate commercial competition.

2005 January: Long-time peace-activist monk Thích Nhất Hạnh returns to Vietnam for the first time since 1967. **February:** Catholic priest Father Nguyễn Văn Lý and several other prominent dissidents are amnestied and released from prison. **March:** A second stock exchange (Securities Trading Center) begins operation in Hanoi. **June:** Premier Phan Văn Khải makes a historic visit to the United States.

Introduction

Vietnam became significant for the English-speaking world only around the end of World War II, and for France roughly a century earlier. It is thus all too easy to forget that Vietnam as a geographical and historical entity is in fact one of the oldest in Southeast Asia, and that the ethnic Vietnamese of the 21st century trace their roots to a civilization dating back to the Bronze Age. For an entire generation "Vietnam" evokes memories of wars and protests. More recently, however, a Vietnam that is reunited and finally at peace has become a place of reconciliation and discovery, a popular tourist destination, and—for the commercially minded—a potentially lucrative market.

Vietnam has never existed in isolation from its neighbors. This is partly by choice, as the Vietnamese have maintained long-term diplomatic and trade links with other countries in the region, and partly a fact of geography, because much of Vietnam's territory is easily penetrated by outsiders. These realities have produced a long-term pattern of defensive warfare (against, among others, the Chinese, French, and Americans) combined with territorial expansion (at the expense of the Cham and Cambodians). The latter process in particular is a major historical factor in the geographical, ethnic, and cultural diversity that characterizes present-day Vietnam.

Like most of its neighbors, Vietnam has experienced drastic social and political changes over the last century. French colonization in the mid- to late 1800s eroded much of the traditional imperial system, as well as the traditional structures at the village level, even though colonial rule preserved at least the outer shell of many of these institutions. Although various strains of nationalism emerged during the colonial period, the version that ultimately triumphed was blended with Marxism under the leadership of Hồ Chí Minh and the Communist Party. This "socialist/nationalist revolution" defeated first the French in 1954 and,

1

eventually, the anti-Communist Republic of Vietnam and its American ally as well.

Although for "true believers" within the Party, the successive victories against various enemies proved the correctness of the socialist path for Vietnam, this consensus began to break down within a decade of national reunification in 1976. The Stalinist economic policies of the Democratic Republic of Vietnam proved ineffective in the new Socialist Republic of Vietnam, as attempts to impose them on the southern half of the country met with serious obstacles. The decision taken in the mid-1980s to adopt market-oriented reforms (known collectively as *đổi mới* or renovation) has moved the country further and further away from orthodox socialism. At the same time, however, the Vietnamese leadership has elected to follow the example of the People's Republic of China in making drastic changes in the economy while avoiding any significant political reform that would dilute the power of the Party.

LAND AND PEOPLE

Geography

Vietnam is best understood as a patchwork of geographical regions, each with its own character, resources, and history. Modern Vietnamese have come to think of their country as broadly divided into three parts—North, Center, and South—which refer particularly to the lowland areas that have been the traditional home of the ethnic Vietnamese majority. The heart of the northern region is the Red River Delta, with Hải Phòng as its major port and Hanoi as its political center. This region, along with the large province of Thanh Hoá to its south, is home to many of the myths and legends associated with the Vietnamese race, as well as the various Stone and Bronze Age cultures that archeologists link to their earliest ancestors.

The long central region stretches from Thanh Hoá along the southern edge of the Red River Delta to the northern edge of the Mekong Delta. It is often compared to a long shoulder pole with the two deltas as baskets full of rice dangling at either end because these two regions are the most agriculturally fertile in the country. Although agriculture is important in the central region, the frequently poor quality of the land

and the proximity of the sea have made fishing and maritime trade an important part of its economy. Mountains stretch along the western edge of the central provinces, and trade in the products of these highland areas has also been a long-standing feature of the region; the coast is dented by a series of bays and ports with rivers stretching inland. Much of central Vietnam was once the territory of the Cham people, who were gradually conquered, colonized, and absorbed by the Vietnamese.

Southern Vietnam is almost completely lowland territory, except for some mountainous areas along the region's northwestern border with Cambodia. The Mekong Delta, which is the core of the region, was originally occupied by ethnic Cambodians or Khmer but underwent a similar process of occupation and colonization as the Vietnamese expanded their territory southward. Saigon (now Hồ Chí Minh City) has been the political and commercial center of this region since at least the 17th century. The Delta is split into sections by the various branches of the Mekong, and much of its land is filled with marshes and swamps and crisscrossed by canals.

To these lowland regions can be added three upland regions: the Việt Bắc, Tây Bắc, and Central Highlands. The Việt Bắc ("Northern Viet") comprises the provinces to the north and northeast of the Red River Delta, extending to the eastern section of the border with China. Although mountainous and traditionally inhabited by ethnic groups other than the Vietnamese, it has long been a strategically important periphery for successive Vietnamese polities. It has a few high peaks, but most of its mountains range between 600 and 700 meters (1,900 to 2,300 feet). A more recent addition to the national territory is the Tây Bắc ("Northwest") region, comprising the provinces along the Lao and western Sino–Vietnamese borders. This region was historically subject to Vietnamese, Lao, and sometimes Chinese overlordship and was only firmly attached to Vietnam under colonial rule. It is mainly mountainous in its topography, and it is home to Fansipan, the highest mountain in the country, with a height of 3,143 meters (over 10,000 feet). The Central Highlands—the long stretch of territory along Vietnam's western border with Laos and Cambodia—is made up of rugged mountains, including several peaks over 2,000 meters (6,500 feet) high, and several large plateaus. Although some of the ethnic groups in this region had frequent trade relations and (in some cases) occasional diplomatic contacts with Vietnamese rulers, the latter were never able to pacify or control more than the fringes of the highlands.

Climate

Although the average annual temperature for all of Vietnam is around 21 degrees Centigrade (70 degrees Fahrenheit), the country's geographic diversity produces considerable regional variation. Annual temperatures in Hanoi, for example, normally range from a low of 16.5 degrees Centigrade (61 degrees Fahrenheit) to a high of 28.9 (84), while in Đà Nẵng and Hồ Chí Minh City the ranges are 21.4 to 29.2 (71 to 85) and 25.7 to 28.9 (78 to 84) respectively. Seasonal change is more significant the farther north one goes, and the northern region has a definite cold season, though snowfall is almost nonexistent, except occasionally at the highest altitudes. Rainfall also varies drastically from place to place. While Hanoi and Hồ Chí Minh City have an average annual rainfall of 1.68 meters (65 inches) and 1.95 meters (76 inches) respectively, the central coastal city of Huế is inundated with 3.03 meters (118 inches). Even within the single region of the Central Highlands, annual precipitation ranges from 1.56 meters (61 inches) in Đà Lạt to 2.23 meters (87 inches) at Pleiku.

Population and Demographic Change

Vietnam has an ethnically diverse population representing all of the major language families of Southeast Asia: Austroasiatic, Austronesian, Tibeto–Burman and Tai–Kadai. The ethnic Vietnamese (Việt or Kinh) are the majority, with minorities (numbering 53 different groups, according to current classification standards) comprising 15 percent of the population. The lowland areas have populations of Khmer and Cham (whose ancestors were conquered or colonized by the Vietnamese), as well as Chinese communities. In the highland areas, steady migration from the lowland regions has shifted the demographics of upland provinces, but sizable minority populations remain, such as Tày and Nùng in the Việt Bắc; Thái and Hmong (H'mông) in the Tây Bắc; and Jarai (Gia Lai), Rhadé (Ê Đê), and Bahnar (Ba Na) in the Central Highlands.

The movement of lowland Vietnamese to highland areas during the decades since independence represents one of two major demographic changes that have taken place in Vietnam over the past half-century. (Traditionally, most Việt shunned the upland regions, which were viewed as remote and unhealthy.) The second is the growth of urban areas, particularly Hanoi and Hồ Chí Minh City. These cities were long important as political and economic centers, but postcolonial urbanization has been driven by several factors. One is the concentration of the best universities in two or three cities, and these naturally draw young Vietnamese from all parts of the country who come to pursue tertiary education and then frequently settle in urban areas after graduation rather than returning to their native provinces.

A second factor specific to South Vietnam during the war was the large-scale movement of refugees from war-torn rural areas who swelled the size of cities, such as Saigon and Đà Nẵng. Although the Socialist Republic of Vietnam government carried out resettlement policies, these efforts were relatively unsuccessful over the long run, and many people returned to the cities. Finally, with the growth of a market economy and the relaxation of restrictions on travel and residence under the "renovation" (*đổi mới*) that has taken place since the mid-1980s, there has been a consistent pattern of rural-urban migration—particularly by working-class people—in search of better employment opportunities in the cities.

Since the end of the war in 1975, the Vietnamese population has increased significantly. (The Chinese invasion of 1979 and the occupation of Cambodia, though destructive, took far fewer lives than the previous conflicts.) In 1975, the population for North and South Vietnam together stood at roughly 45 million; by 1980, this had already increased to 54 million, and the 1989 census showed 64 million. The next census a decade later recorded a figure of 76 million, and the most recent estimate (2003) stands at nearly 81 million. The trend toward urbanization is also clearly reflected; according to the 1989 census, 19.4 percent of the population lived in the cities; by 1999, this figure had increased to 23.5 percent. (It should be noted, moreover, that the number of people living as unregistered migrants in urban areas is considerable, so the 1999 figure in particular is probably low.) The United Nations Development Program estimate for 2003 is that fully one-quarter of the country's population now lives in the cities.

HISTORY

The Precolonial Kingdoms

As mentioned, the historical and geographical core of modern Vietnam was the northern Red River Delta. Vietnamese historians have combined old legends and archeological findings from this region to tell the story of a Bronze Age kingdom of Văn Lang under 18 successive generations of Hùng Kings, but, in fact, there is little concrete information about the ancestors of the Vietnamese people before they were conquered by the Chinese Han Dynasty in the second century B.C.E. The "Chinese period" of Vietnamese history, which lasted until the early 10th century C.E., indelibly stamped many aspects of Vietnamese culture with a Chinese imprint, and China remained a model and frame of reference for the Vietnamese elite through the early 20th century.

Independence from Chinese rule in the early 900s led to a chaotic century of instability characterized by a series of short-lived "dynasties" that did not survive the strongmen who established them. It was only in the early 11th century that the Lý dynasty (1010–1225) brought some degree of stability and long-term continuity. Like the Trần dynasty (1225–1400) that succeeded them, the Lý rulers worked to build a durable political structure heavily influenced by Chinese government, though Confucianism generally remained less important as an ideology and worldview than Buddhism. This situation changed with the two-decade Ming occupation (1406–27), however, which exposed the local culture to a heavy dose of Confucianism.

The Lê dynasty (1428–1788) built a stronger and more centralized government on the strength of its victory over the Chinese occupiers, but the resulting period of prosperity, unity, and territorial expansion southward lasted less than a century. By the early 1500s, the dynasty was in decline, and its temporary overthrow by the Mạc family (1527–92) began a period of civil war. The Mạc were eventually defeated, but the decades of conflict had paved the way for a new struggle between two rival families, the Trịnh and the Nguyễn. After the full restoration of the Lê in the 1590s, the Trịnh Lords dominated the kingdom ruled by the Lê emperors from Thăng Long (Hanoi); this kingdom was often referred to as *Đàng Ngoài* in Vietnamese and known to Westerners as *Tonkin*. Meanwhile, the Nguyễn Lords established an autonomous kingdom (*Đàng Trong* or Cochin China) ruled from what is now Huế, though they gave lip service to Lê suzerainty. The two Vietnamese kingdoms evolved separately over the next two centuries, though they faced similar challenges, such as coping with frequent natural disasters, developing foreign trade, and restraining the growth of Christianity being propagated by missionaries on their respective territories. After a half-decade of sporadic warfare in the 17th century, the two Vietnams maintained a relatively peaceful status quo until the 1770s, when the Tây Sơn rebellion (1771–1802) dramatically changed the political landscape and came close to unifying the Vietnamese under an entirely new dynasty. In the end, however, the Tây Sơn were defeated by the Nguyễn, who established themselves as an imperial dynasty in 1802, with their capital in Huế rather than Hanoi.

Although the Nguyễn ruled a larger expanse of territory than any previous Vietnamese dynasty, their control was often shaky. They faced threats to their power from elements still loyal to the Lê and from an unprecedented number of peasant rebellions, triggered by a constant series of floods, droughts, and other natural disasters. One visible and increasingly worrisome "enemy" in the Nguyễn rulers' eyes was Christianity, but their attempts to suppress it were generally unsuccessful and brought them into confrontation with France, whose successive post-Napoleonic regimes were increasingly interested in expanding their overseas empire. After several years of pressure, threats, and gunboat diplomacy, the French launched an initial invasion in 1858. Over the next quarter-century, they gradually conquered all of Vietnam, and, by 1884, the empire had completely lost its independence after a series of treaties that progressively signed away its territory and sovereignty to France.

Colonial Rule

Under French rule, Vietnam was divided into three parts: Tonkin, Annam, and Cochin China. These three colonies corresponded respectively to the northern, central, and southern regions described previously. Tonkin and Annam were protectorates belonging to what remained of the Vietnamese Empire, though the Nguyễn rulers and their mandarins were under tight French control and had little independent authority. Cochin China was detached from imperial rule and governed directly as a colony. The tripartite division meant that Vietnamese in the different regions did not always experience or react to colonialism in the same ways, and some of the nationalist movements that emerged were limited to specific areas. Many Vietnamese, however, saw the partition of the country as something artificial imposed on them by foreign conquest, and they thought and spoke in terms of a single "Vietnam" to be freed from French rule.

The person who ultimately articulated the clearest vision for achieving Vietnamese independence was a man known by many names; for most of his political career he was called *Nguyễn Ái Quốc* and then *Hồ Chí Minh*. Hồ was instrumental in grafting elements of Marxism-Leninism onto Vietnamese nationalism (with more than a hint of Confucianism) to mobilize his countrymen against colonialism. He was instrumental in the establishment of the Vietnamese Communist Party (soon to be renamed the *Indochinese Communist Party* or *ICP*) in 1930, and he remained the most prominent political figure in Vietnam until his death in 1969. Through the Việt Minh Front, created to draw in a wide spectrum of anti-French elements who were not Party members, Hồ and the ICP bided their time through World War II, when the colony was under both French rule and Japanese occupation. The Japanese surrender in August 1945, a few months after a coup that had taken over Indochina from the French, brought the long-awaited opportunity, and the Party made a series of power seizures known collectively as the *August Revolution*. A Democratic Republic of Vietnam (DRV) was established in September under Hồ's leadership.

The leadership of the Party-dominated DRV did not go unchallenged, either by non-Communist nationalists or by the French, who returned in force to reclaim their colony. After months of failed negotiations and bitter debates, war broke out in December 1946, and the DRV government took to the mountains and jungles to fight. By 1954, Hồ's regime proved stronger politically and militarily than the rival French-sponsored State of Vietnam under former Nguyễn Emperor Bảo Đại, and the French defeat at Điện Biên Phủ in June brought an end to colonial rule. However, the Cold War was in full swing, and American support for the Bảo Đại regime was strong enough to prevent a Communist-dominated government from controlling all of Vietnam. Instead, the Geneva Conference in July 1954 partitioned the country into two parts, with the DRV in the North and the State of Vietnam in the South.

This division was intended to be resolved by national elections within two years, but it lasted two decades.

The Vietnam War and Beyond

The period from 1954 to 1975 saw a twenty-year struggle between the anti-Communist Republic of Vietnam (successor to Bảo Đại's regime) and the DRV. The United States and its allies saw South Vietnam as a legitimate "Free World" government and supported its efforts to resist what they saw as external Communist aggression. For the DRV and many Vietnamese loyal to Hồ in the South, on the other hand, the Saigon government had no legitimacy and was merely a screen for American imperialism. The Party (now known as the *Vietnamese Workers Party*) created a National Liberation Front and a Provisional Revolutionary Government in the South, backed by large numbers of troops infiltrated from the North over the Hồ Chí Minh Trail. The political, diplomatic, and military battles raged until April 1975, when the Saigon government fell to North Vietnamese tanks.

The destructive impact of these two decades of war on all parts of Vietnam cannot be overstated. Although no fighting occurred on DRV territory, the periodic U.S. bombing campaigns did severe damage to the country's infrastructure and disrupted people's lives for months at a time, though many schools and government offices were dispersed into the countryside away from the bombs. Much of South Vietnam was devastated by ground combat, bombings, and the widespread use of napalm and other defoliants. Huge numbers of Vietnamese fled to the cities as refugees, and those who did not leave for safer quarters accounted for the large number of civilian casualties on top of millions of combat deaths. (The same was true for bombing victims in the North.) The large-scale American military presence had serious social and economic consequences, and the prolonged war on behalf of a regime to which many South Vietnamese felt little loyalty (despite the fact that many of them had little love for Communism, either) took a heavy psychological toll. All of these factors worked together to weaken the Republic of Vietnam and leave it in a highly vulnerable state after the departure of U.S. troops following the Paris Accords of early 1973.

Within a year of the fall of Saigon, the two countries were unified as the Socialist Republic of Vietnam, and Party leaders attempted to impose socialism on the South. Their efforts were hampered, however, by a brief war with China following the Vietnamese invasion and occupation of Cambodia, which was to last more than a decade. Moreover, the socialist policies that the Party viewed as essential to the country's future proved unappetizing to most Southerners and, increasingly, to many in the former DRV as well. By the mid-1980s, the Party was forced to make drastic though incremental changes to its interpretation of "socialism"; these changes became all the more important with the fall of the Soviet Union and the entire socialist bloc in Eastern Europe. Since the early 1990s, Vietnam has sought to downplay its "socialist' identity in its foreign relations (even though its leadership continues to take Marxism–Leninism seriously) and has worked hard to open up to foreign investment and to multiply its friendships in the region and elsewhere in the world.

POLITICAL, ECONOMIC, AND
SOCIAL DEVELOPMENT

Political Evolution

Vietnam, like all of its neighbors, was a monarchy throughout its history, though the structure of government and the complexity of its organs and institutions changed considerably over time. The administrative, cultural, and psychological legacy of a millennium of Chinese rule meant that even after independence in the 10th century, the Vietnamese elite tended to opt for Chinese models of government in various forms. This did not happen overnight, however, and the first decades of independence after the Chinese were characterized by almost constant conflict among successive "kings" and "emperors" from different regions who were almost certainly more like warlords than Confucian monarchs. There is little evidence of a bureaucracy or even a cohesive government during this time, and it is doubtful that any of the Vietnamese rulers were able to impose their authority throughout the territory that had so recently been under Chinese control. There was probably little in the way of an intellectual elite, and Buddhist priests seem to have been at least as important as scholar-officials when it came to advising the rulers on policymaking.

This situation only began to change with the advent of the Lý dynasty in the 11th century. Regular dynastic succession meant stability, and stability allowed gradual consolidation and expansion of the government apparatus. The important examinations began to take place (though only sporadically), which, as in China, would select men for positions in the bureaucracy; indeed, outside the imperial court, education existed essentially for this purpose alone. Vietnam began to look somewhat more like its Chinese suzerain, at least in appearance; administrative structures and titles were borrowed from China, and the Confucian classics formed a key part of the examination curriculum, though they did not yet represent the dominant ideological force that they would become in later centuries.

The general evolution in the direction of a more bureaucratic government and a more Confucian elite worldview continued over the next few centuries, but only very gradually. Most rulers through the end of the Trần dynasty (in 1400) were at least as Buddhist in their personal philosophy as they were Confucianist, and the scholar-officials who had come through the examination system, though they became larger and larger as a group, were often frustrated by the actions of their emperors who did not live up to the standards of the Chinese sage-monarchs they read about in the classics. It took the Ming occupation in the early 15th century, with its fairly tight administrative control and officially sponsored propagation of Confucian teachings, to implant these doctrines more firmly in the minds of the Vietnamese ruling class. The first century of the Lê dynasty that followed the defeat of the Chinese was in many ways a "golden age" for the Vietnamese monarchy, with several strong rulers whose thinking was grounded more thoroughly in Confucianism than in Buddhism and who worked to expand the size of the country and to strengthen the government's control over its territory.

Questions remain about the nature and effectiveness of the Vietnamese state during these early centuries of independence. Historians have tended to assume that the existence of a complex Chinese-style government apparatus and a multilayered administrative hierarchy extending from the capital down to the village guaranteed the functioning of a fairly powerful, centralized, and unified state. This assumption is open to doubt, however. The Vietnamese sociopolitical system during this time was "feudal" to some extent in that control over land and manpower in different provinces was often in the hands of powerful local interests rather than being under the authority of the central government. Localism and regionalism seem to have remained strong, though present-day historians prefer to emphasize the theme of national unity as far back as possible in their country's history.

Certainly, from the 16th century onward, unity gave way to division and conflict. The civil war between the Mạc and the Lê, and then the long-term division between the northern and southern kingdoms from 1600 until nearly 1800 meant that for a period of nearly 300 years, "Vietnam" as a geographical entity was never controlled by a single ruling family. The consequences of this division were particularly important in the territory of the southern kingdom, which expanded drastically at the expense of its Cham and Cambodian neighbors while maintaining its independence from the Lê emperors in the north. The result was a society that was more ethnically and culturally diverse than its northern counterpart and had undergone a very different historical and political experience, a fact that would have implications for future attempts to reunify the country under a single government. (It should not be forgotten that the geographical boundary between the two kingdoms was almost exactly recreated by the Demilitarized Zone, which separated North and South Vietnam between 1954 and 1975.)

When the rulers of the Nguyễn dynasty in the 19th century attempted to exercise authority over a stretch of territory larger and more diverse than any previous Vietnamese polity, they faced several important challenges. The first and most fundamental was to demonstrate their legitimacy in parts of the country that remained loyal to earlier rulers. Second, they had to deal with regional and local interests whose willingness to put the national interest before their own was problematic. Third, much of their empire consisted of a patchwork of villages that had come to enjoy considerable autonomy over the years and were determined to keep their obligations to the central government (taxes and manpower for labor and military service) to a minimum. Finally, the bureaucracy or mandarinate on which they were forced to rely to govern their subjects was frequently corrupt and oppressive, a situation that exacerbated the hardships experienced by many rural people when their livelihood was threatened by flood, drought, or disease. These challenges to the Vietnamese leadership not only had deep historical roots, they have also survived—to a large extent—into the 21st century.

Colonial rule represented an uneven mixture of continuity and discontinuity, where Vietnamese political structures were concerned. In Cochin China, direct rule meant that the French destroyed virtually all of the existing administrative system and started over. The traditional mandarinate was replaced by a more Western-style civil service, staffed by collaborators who often came from social backgrounds outside the traditional ruling elite. These collaborators came to form a new elite, and their connections to the colonial regime brought them economic advantages—notably the opportunity to acquire large landholdings—as well as power and influence. In Annam and Tonkin, the protectorate system meant that the traditional imperial structure of emperor and mandarins was left in place with relatively few changes. The continuity was superficial, however, as the intrusion of French power into the imperial system—going far beyond either the letter or the spirit of the original 1884 Patenôtre Treaty that established the final protectorate—meant that the monarchy and mandarinate alike were shorn of most of their authority and, eventually, their prestige as well. This situation produced a Vietnamese elite centered around Hanoi and Huế that was more traditional in thinking than its counterparts in Saigon and had much more in common with the precolonial ruling class but was no less closely tied to the French system that kept it in power.

One of the fundamental paradoxes of colonial rule was that although the French did their best to uphold the prestige of those Vietnamese who cooperated with them, ultimately these collaborators were undermined by becoming so closely tied to the colonial system that they were discredited and even disgraced in the eyes of many nationalists. Moreover, although the French gave lip service to the idea of "political evolution" and gradual devolution of powers toward the Vietnamese elite, any concessions in the direction of power sharing were kept to a bare minimum. The inclusion of local leaders in the Colonial Council in Saigon, for example, or the establishment of consultative assemblies in Annam and Tonkin did not lead to any significant "political evolution," and ultimately there was more vitality in the pages of the local press than in these institutions. The refusal to give into even the mildest demands for political reform meant that those nationalists who initially had some faith in French intentions ended up either marginalized and impotent as a political force (like Bùi Quang Chiêu and the Constitutionalists in Cochin China) or as frustrated symbols of patriotism (like Phan Bội Châu and Phan Chu Trinh). The final result was a polarization between loyal collaborators on one end of the political spectrum and revolutionaries on the other, with relatively little space in between.

This polarization was, over the long run, one of the key factors behind the success of Hồ Chí Minh and the Indochinese Communist Party. Communism in and of itself was not unappealing, of course; it offered a logical explanation of colonialism and its message of liberation from oppression and exploitation resonated deeply with impoverished peasants and workers. However, the Party's ability to blend anticolonial nationalism and social revolution, emphasizing one or the other depending on the audience and circumstances of a particular time and place in its struggle, meant that it could also develop a much wider base of support among patriotic Vietnamese who were less likely to benefit economically from a revolution. This was particularly true during the final months of World War II and the First Indochina War that followed it, when intellectuals, "patriotic landlords," and others who could hardly be considered as part of the proletariat in any sense of the word flocked to join the various anti-French organizations under the broad umbrella that the Party had set up in the form of the Việt Minh Front.

The period between 1946 and 1954, however, gradually produced a new kind of polarization that could not be blamed entirely on the French. Hồ and the Party (operating underground until 1951, when it reemerged as the Vietnamese Workers' Party) could be democratic when they wanted to, but once the political circumstances were in their favor, they would revert to what was essentially one-party rule. Thus, the Democratic Republic of Vietnam (DRV) during the early years of its existence followed the example of the Việt Minh by including nationalists of various political stripes. When the DRV government fled the cities for the jungle after the outbreak of war in December 1946, it was able to gradually consolidate its power over larger and larger stretches of territory, and compromise with "patriotic landlords" and others whose class background was undesirable from a Marxist point of view became less and less necessary. As Party domination of the anti-French struggle grew more obvious, many of those who had initially rallied to Hồ and the DRV reluctantly returned to the cities that remained under the control of the French-sponsored State of Vietnam.

The anti-Communist government was not a particularly palatable alternative to many Vietnamese. It was a mixed bag of individuals and parties who had little in common other than their opposition to Hồ and the Party, and there was no leader with anything approaching Hồ's prestige as a symbol of nationalism. Even Ngô Đình Diệm, who would later force the State of Vietnam to become the Republic of Vietnam (by driving Bảo Đại out of power and into permanent exile), could not compete with Hồ as a leader, despite the fact that he was the most strongly anti-French of the nationalists who were also anti-Communist. Nor did Diệm and his successors in the various military and civilian regimes that followed his assassination in 1963 have any great belief in democracy. Despite constitutions, a National Assembly, and occasional presidential elections, the South Vietnamese political system was generally only slightly less oppressive than the DRV in the North, and critics or opponents tended to end up at best as dissidents and at worst as prisoners or exiles.

The two decades of the Second Indochina War between 1954 and 1975 enabled the Party in Hanoi to consolidate its power throughout the DRV, and public criticism was suppressed after a short-lived expression of dissidence with the *Nhân Văn Giai Phẩm* affair in 1956. The victory over South Vietnam in 1975 reinforced the Party's conviction that the country's future remained with socialism, and most dissidents from the South fared little better in the reunified Socialist Republic of Vietnam than those who had actually served the Saigon regime. Although the economic reforms of *đổi mới* have helped loosen the reins of Party control in some areas, the space for political dissent remains almost nonexistent. The Party is very wary of anything that threatens its authority, and its vision of a nefarious "peaceful evolution" plot against Vietnamese socialism leads it to strike out at those advocating human rights or political pluralism, let alone a multiparty system. The question for the future is just how much longer this situation can continue, given the virtual abandonment of a socialist economy, the widespread exposure to Western culture and values, and the erosion of Party and government legitimacy caused by deep-rooted corruption.

Economic Development

French colonial rule did not drastically alter the traditional Vietnamese economy's dependence on agriculture and trade as its mainstays, but it changed the patterns and structures of this economy. Industrial development was minimal, and many consumer products were imported from elsewhere rather than manufactured locally. Trade (particularly through the port of Saigon and up and down the Red River) had been one of the main reasons for colonization in the first place, and the French maintained it as a priority as long as Indochina was in their possession. Much of the agricultural development of the colony was specifically for export purposes, especially the commodities of rice and rubber. Rice became an extremely important export, and much of the harvest in the various parts of Vietnam left the country rather than filling the stomachs of those who had grown it. Rubber, introduced by the French in various parts of Indochina, was a significant part of the colonial economy.

The economic changes associated with French rule seldom benefited the peasants. The colonial state had a considerably greater capacity to penetrate the village than its imperial predecessors, and it was thus in a position to squeeze more revenue out of those it governed. It did so through changes in the tax system as well as the use of monopolies on key products, such as rice wine. Patterns of landholding were drastically modified by the proliferation of concessions handed out to Frenchmen and Vietnamese collaborators, and many rural inhabitants were left without sufficient land to feed themselves and their families. Widespread rural poverty, indebtedness, and landlessness made the message of the Communist Party all the more attractive when it began to spread in the early 1930s, during the Great Depression.

During the early years of the Party's existence, it emphasized redistribution of private landholdings (through confiscation by force, if necessary). During the war against the French after 1946, the DRV government pursued land-reform policies that looked increasingly like those carried out by their comrades in China, with whom they had close contact. By 1954, much of the land in the rural areas under Việt Minh control had been redistributed. Some areas in the southern provinces, by contrast, were out of the Party's reach, and there remained a sizable group of wealthy landlords around Saigon and the Mekong Delta.

With the partition into North and South in 1954, the two Vietnams went in different directions in terms of economic policy. The DRV began to move toward agricultural collectivization—not as intensely or as radically as the Chinese Communist Party, for Hồ was not Mao Zedong, but at a steady pace nevertheless. Agriculture in the North was essentially collectivized by the time the war began to heat up in the early 1960s. The DRV made some progress in developing an industrial base, but its efforts in this area were seriously disrupted by the American bombings, and it was obliged to rely heavily on material aid from China, the Soviet Union, and other socialist friends.

The economy of the Republic of Vietnam was also heavily subsidized, both directly and indirectly, by American aid and the presence of hundreds of thousands of foreigners with dollars to spend. It is hard to speak of a South Vietnamese "national economy" as such because, from the late 1950s onward, increasingly large chunks of the country were outside the government's control, with economic links to the Party-led National Liberation Front. Although some farmers were able to go on peacefully growing rice with the benefit of new technology imported through American aid, many others saw their fields turn into bomb craters and often ended up as refugees in the towns and cities. There was a thriving black market and widespread network of patronage and corruption that accounted for a considerably larger share of economic activity than the country's limited industrial base.

Needless to say, the Socialist Republic of Vietnam faced a daunting task when it attempted to merge these two halves into a whole after reunification in 1976. For the first decade or so, the Party concentrated on trying to replicate the DRV's socialist experience in the South, with generally little success. Those South Vietnamese business people and entrepreneurs who had not fled the country were dismissed as capitalists who had nothing to offer a socialist Vietnam, and this was even more true for the overseas Chinese who had dominated the economy. The policies of confiscating personal assets, shutting down "capitalist" activities, and relocating urban residents in New Economic Zones to force them back into agriculture collectively took a heavy toll on the economy, and an increasingly bleak outlook in the early 1980s made it clear that something had to be changed.

The policies of đổi mới introduced at the Sixth Party Congress in 1986 (some measures had already preceded this important meeting) represented a dramatic change in direction for the Vietnamese economy. The key cornerstones of a socialist economy—cooperatives for agriculture and other production, central planning, and a series of state subsidies—were gradually dismantled, and a system based on market supply and demand and a respect for private property (including land) was gradually allowed to develop. There have been numerous fits and starts over the last two decades, but, generally speaking, the direction of change has been forward rather than backward. Vietnam has become in many ways a capitalist country, though it has done so by defining "socialism" in broader and broader terms. It now has broad-based "land usage rights" (instead of private property), a commitment to "equitization" (i.e., privatization) of state-owned enterprises, an increasing tolerance for private enterprise, a drastically improved environment for foreign investment, and even an embryonic stock market. The result is an economy that looks considerably more like the Republic of Vietnam (including the corruption and patronage) than like the DRV, despite the fact that the Communist Party is still in command.

Social Change

For most of Vietnam's history, it was a predominantly agrarian society. Although there have always been important towns and trading ports, agriculture and rural life played a significant economic and cultural role for much of the country's history. The multitiered structure of government and the opportunities for less successful graduates of the examination system to serve as teachers in villages meant that educated Vietnamese were not all concentrated in urban areas. Even for those who did take up employment and residence in the cities, psychological and social ties to their rural home villages remained strong.

This situation began to change with colonial rule, which created a critical mass of white-collar workers and intellectuals (some of them educated in France) who found rural life considerably less palatable than city life, and the term *nhà quê*, meaning a peasant or person from the countryside, took on the pejorative connotations of "hick." During the First Indochina War, there was an increasing degree of polarization between rural areas controlled by the Việt Minh revolutionaries and the cities controlled by the French and the anti-Communist State of Vietnam. This was also true of the Republic of Vietnam (South Vietnam) between 1954 and 1975, when the economic and cultural gap between city and countryside grew wider.

Post-1975 resettlement policies attempted to rectify this situation by pressuring city residents to return to the villages, but it was a difficult task to persuade urbanites to remain in the countryside attempting to eke out a living in New Economic Zones on land that was often of poor quality. The lean years of the late 1970s and early 1980s then gave way to the *đổi mới* period, which has affected different sectors of the population in different ways over the last two decades. On the one hand, the shift away from collectivized agriculture has meant that farming families have better and more diversified sources of income. On the other hand, the attractions of a more open and more Westernized urban society have proved to be a powerful draw to many Vietnamese from rural areas, as have the opportunities for more lucrative employment than farming. At the same time, the end of hostilities in Cambodia and the opening of the country to foreign investment have facilitated the growth of an industrial sector. As a result, by the beginning of the 21st century, the respective contributions of industry and agriculture to the nation's Gross Domestic Product (two-fifths and one-fifth, respectively) were the exact reverse of what they had been just a decade earlier. Many factories are concentrated in industrial zones, which tend to be closer to urban areas.

These economic changes have social consequences as well. Although agriculture remains a key component of the economy because there is a large population to be fed, village life and rural values no longer possess the strong psychological grip that they once had in Vietnamese society. Many young Vietnamese who come from the provinces to attend universities in Hanoi or Hồ Chí Minh City find that after four years of urban life, returning to their native small town or village is an unattractive prospect, not only because opportunities for interesting and lucrative employment are slim but also because they have become accustomed to a different lifestyle. More than ever, the cities are associated with prosperity, sophistication, and easier access to foreign culture.

There are some continuities, of course. Although the average marriage age is slowly rising, young men and women still face considerable familial and social pressure to tie the knot and begin having children as soon as they are financially able to do so. Urban couples are very likely to be double-income households, but even the most Yuppified young Vietnamese will be expected to produce children, and the childless couple will have a difficult time of it psychologically and socially. Women have considerably more access to educational and employment opportunities than was the case for earlier generations, but the child-bearing role remains key.

Vietnam in general remains a society in transition—from socialism to capitalism (even under another name), from isolation to integration, from constant war to a more durable peace. An increasingly large group of Vietnamese are able to benefit from these transitions and build themselves a more stable and prosperous future than anything their parents could have imagined. Others are very clearly being left behind, either because they have few skills or opportunities outside the rice fields or because they are too old or too poor to successfully navigate the shift from a "subsidy" system that guaranteed them a basic but constant level of subsistence to a "market" system in which they must fend for themselves. Still others are somewhere in between, looking enviously at the first group and wondering if they can join it while close at hand—perhaps in their own neighborhood—are stark examples of the second group. The Vietnamese as a people are proud of the resilience and flexibility that many see as part of their national character; both traits are very much in evidence as Vietnam enters the 21st century and will continue to be very much needed.

The Dictionary

– A –

A SHAU VALLEY. Pass in the **Trường Sơn** chain between **Laos** and central Vietnam. During the Vietnam War, it served as an important entry point for infiltrators coming down the **Hồ Chí Minh Trail** into the **Republic of Vietnam**. Operations by **United States** and South Vietnamese forces in the area took place in the late 1960s, but they failed to stem the tide of infiltration.

ABRAMS, CREIGHTON (1914–1974). **United States** Army general and commander of the U.S. **Military Assistance Command in Vietnam (MACV)** from 1968 to 1972. First assigned to Vietnam as a deputy to General **William C. Westmoreland** in 1967, he commanded U.S. forces in South Vietnam during the Richard Nixon administration. His primary task was to carry out Nixon's program of **Vietnamization**, according to which U.S. forces would be gradually withdrawn over a period of four years, while training South Vietnamese forces to handle their own self-defense. Following the signing of the **Paris Agreement** in 1973, he succeeded Westmoreland as Army chief of staff.

AGRICULTURE. Vietnam has traditionally been an agrarian society. Until quite recently, approximately 90 percent of the entire population consisted of peasants living off the land. Most peasants were **rice** farmers, living in the two rich river deltas, the **Red River** in the North and the **Mekong River** in the South. The cultivation of wet rice began several thousand years ago in Southeast Asia, and many archeologists believe that the Vietnamese were among the first peoples to achieve the domestication of agriculture. Throughout the tra-

21

ditional period, rice was the staple crop for the Vietnamese and the primary basis for the wealth and prosperity of the state.

Under **French** rule, agriculture became diversified, and a number of tropical cash crops such as **coffee, tea,** and natural **rubber** made their appearance. Most were grown in large plantations owned by European interests in the **Central Highlands** and adjacent areas. The production of rice and other food crops increased, but much of the increase was exported, to the profit of a new class of wealthy absentee landlords.

After the departure of the French, agricultural growth was seriously hindered by the outbreak of the Vietnam War. In both North and South, rice production stagnated, forcing both governments to import food to provide subsistence. With reunification in 1976, the **Socialist Republic of Vietnam** attempted to increase agricultural production through a combination of improved irrigation, mechanization, the increased use of fertilizers, and **collectivization**. The results were disappointing. Grain production stagnated in the years following the war and achieved only modest increases in the 1980s. With the advent of *đổi mới*, the agricultural system put in place by **collectivization** decades earlier was essentially dismantled, in terms not only of its structures but also of the principle that the state should control where farmers live or which crops they produce and in what quantities.

Today, government policy continues to emphasize agriculture (though not at the expense of other sectors of the **economy**), promoting export crops and granting incentives to farmers in an effort to increase the production of rice. The results have justified the effort. In recent years, grain production has risen significantly, making the country once again a major exporter of rice. Rubber, coffee, tea, and other cash crops have all become key export earners, and agriculture continues to account for roughly one-quarter of Vietnam's Gross Domestic Product, although that percentage is considerably lower than it was in the early years of *đổi mới*; in 1990, for instance, the figure was closer to 40 percent. *See also* SLASH-AND-BURN AGRICULTURE.

AGROVILLES (*ấp trù mật*). Program adopted by the regime of **Ngô Đình Diệm** in 1959 to regroup Vietnamese peasants into large rural settlements in the South Vietnamese countryside. The program was motivated by both economic and security concerns. Eighty agrovilles were planned for implementation by 1963, with each unit containing about 400 families moved from less-secure areas into the new centers. Smaller centers, consisting of about 100 families, were planned as clusters around larger units. Put into operation in the last half of 1959, the program was marked by **corruption**, government insensitivity, and lack of adequate funding, and soon aroused widespread criticism. The program was abandoned in 1961 and soon replaced by a new one calling for the construction of so-called **strategic hamlets** (*ấp chiến lược*). *See also* LAND REFORM.

ALESSANDRI, MARCEL (1893–1968). Major-general in the **French** Army stationed in **Indochina** during World War II. Following the Japanese coup of 9 March 1945, which abolished the French administration in Indochina, he led French troops to safety in southern **China**. He later commanded French troops in **Tonkin** against the **Việt Minh** and was dismissed from his post in 1950. *See also* JAPANESE OCCUPATION; SABATTIER, CAMILLE.

ALONG BAY AGREEMENT. *See* HẠ LONG BAY AGREEMENT.

AN DƯƠNG VƯƠNG (King An Dương). Founder of the early kingdom of **Âu Lạc** and the first figure in Vietnamese history to appear in Chinese records. In the mid-third century B.C.E., Thục Phán became the ruler of a kingdom called *Nam Cương*, based along what is now the Sino–Vietnamese frontier. In 258 B.C.E., he defeated the kingdom of **Văn Lang**, whose base of power was in the **Red River Delta**, and declared himself King An Dương (An Dương Vương) of a new state of Âu Lạc. For nearly half a century, he ruled through the local **Lạc** aristocratic class until his state was overthrown in 207 B.C.E. by Zhao Tuo (**Triệu Đà**), who set up a new kingdom of **Nam Việt**, with its capital at Canton.

Although many legends are connected with the life and reign of An Dương Vương (including the story that he came to power with the assistance of a golden tortoise that gave him a magic crossbow in order to defeat his enemies), he is considered the first truly historical figure in Vietnamese history. Recent Vietnamese scholarship has tended to downplay his "foreign" origins, suggesting plausibly that he and the inhabitants of Văn Lang were merely different subgroups of the **Bách Việt** grouping.

AN NAM CHÍ LƯỢC (*Annals of Vietnam*). An early history of Vietnam. *See also* LÊ TẮC.

ANNAM. An administrative term for Vietnam used with different meanings at different times. The term was first applied in the seventh century, when the Tang dynasty integrated several provinces of occupied Vietnam into the single protectorate of Annam. The term, meaning "pacified South" in Chinese, was offensive to patriotic Vietnamese and was dropped after independence. After the **French** conquest of Vietnam in the late 19th century, the French adopted the term to describe one of the two **protectorates** of Vietnam—along with the colony of **Cochin China** and the protectorates of **Laos** and **Cambodia**—that formed the **Indochinese Union**. This was the area of central Vietnam, also known as *Trung Bộ* or *Trung Kỳ*. Confusingly, however, the French also used the terms *Annam* and *Annamite* to refer to Vietnam as an entity and the Vietnamese as a people.

The colonial protectorate of Annam was located along the central coast of Vietnam and included all the provinces from the lower edge of the **Red River Delta** to the southern boundary of the **Central Highlands**. Although technically left under the control of the Vietnamese emperor and his imperial bureaucracy, in practice Annam was ruled by the emperor's French adviser, titled the *Résident Supérieur*, leaving the emperor with solely honorific functions. In 1949, the protectorate of Annam, along with the protectorate of Tonkin and the colony of Cochin China, was absorbed into a single **State of Vietnam**. *See also* BẢO ĐẠI.

ANNAMESE COMMUNIST PARTY (*An Nam Cộng Sản Đảng*). Short-lived Communist party formed in 1929, subsequently integrated into the **Indochinese Communist Party**. *See also* THANH NIÊN.

ANNAMESE INDEPENDENCE PARTY (*Parti Annamite de l'Indépendance*, **PAI**). Short-lived political party organized by Vietnam-

ARCHEOLOGY • 25

ese patriots living in **France** in the 1920s. The primary founder of the party was **Nguyễn Thế Truyền**, who went to Paris shortly after World War I and soon became involved in expatriate political activities. The PAI issued a public appeal for the formation of a commission to study conditions in **Indochina**, but the French ignored the suggestion, and the party disintegrated after Truyền's return to Vietnam in 1929.

ÂP BẮC, BATTLE OF. Battle between forces of the **People's Liberation Armed Forces** (PLAF, popularly known as the *Việt Cộng*) and the **Republic of Vietnam** in late December 1962. A village in Mỹ Tho province, Âp Bắc was attacked by revolutionary forces who inflicted a serious defeat on government troops before retiring. In Communist histories of the war, it marked the beginning of a new stage of battalion-level operations in the struggle in South Vietnam.

ARCHEOLOGY. Archeology in Vietnam was initiated during the colonial era, though there was frequently a lack of consensus as to the dating, interpretation, and cultural affiliations of the artifacts excavated. After 1954, archeology developed quickly in the Democratic Republic of Vietnam (DRV) (with Soviet help); there was generally less activity in the Republic of Vietnam, though a few sites were studied. DRV scholars discovered a number of important **Neolithic** and **Bronze Age** sites in the northern provinces and spent considerable time and energy exploring and analyzing them. Archeological finds, particularly those linked to the **Đông Sơn** culture, were connected to stories in ancient texts to construct a picture of Vietnamese prehistory that assumed the existence of an early Vietnamese nation even before Chinese rule.

Since the end of the Vietnam War in 1975, interest in the archeological importance of Vietnam has quickened. At the University of Hanoi, several doctoral degrees in archeology have been awarded, and numerous projects are underway involving cooperation between Vietnamese and foreign researchers. One significant postwar discovery was the remains of *Gigantopithecus* and *Homo erectus* in limestone karsts in **Hạ Long Bay**. Another area of particularly concentrated interest is the series of sites linked to the premodern **Cham** civilization. Most recently, popular interest in archeology has been stimulated by the unearthing of large quantities of artifacts in downtown **Hanoi**. *See also* BẮC SƠN CULTURE; HOÀ BÌNH CULTURE; NÚI ĐỌ CULTURE; PHÙNG NGUYÊN CULTURE.

ARCHITECTURE. During the traditional era, architectural styles in Vietnam were patterned after those in use in **China**. Pagodas and imposing official buildings, such as the imperial palace, were constructed of wood, with tile roofs. Unfortunately, little survives today. Perhaps the best-known example is the **Temple of Literature** in **Hanoi**, originally constructed in the 11th century. The dwellings of most ordinary people, however, tended to be constructed in thatch, built around a bamboo frame. Affluent Vietnamese often lived in houses built of brick or wood planking, with tile roofs. Often, they were constructed on the Chinese model, in a rectangular pattern surrounding a central courtyard. In mountain areas, ethnic minority peoples lived in thatch houses built on stilts.

After the **French** conquest in the late 19th century, official buildings were often built in French colonial style. Prominent examples are the **Bắc Bộ Palace** and the Governor-General's Palace in Hanoi and the City Hall in Hồ Chí Minh City. Many Europeans and wealthy Vietnamese lived in spacious homes built on the French colonial pattern. Housing for ordinary people, however, continued to be in the traditional pattern.

Since the end of the colonial era, architecture has tended to follow international styles. Efforts are being made in Vietnam today, however, to preserve the distinctive character of major cities such as Hanoi, **Huế**, and Hồ Chí Minh City. *See also* ONE-PILLAR PAGODA.

ARMED FORCES. *See* ARMY OF THE REPUBLIC OF VIETNAM; PEOPLE'S ARMY OF VIETNAM; PEOPLE'S LIBERATION ARMED FORCES; VIETNAMESE NATIONAL ARMY.

ARMY OF NATIONAL SALVATION (*Cứu Quốc Quân***).** Revolutionary military organization set up by Communist Party militant **Chu Văn Tấn** in the early 1940s. The army originated in the **Bắc Sơn Uprising** in the autumn of 1940, when local leaders of the **Indochinese Communist Party** (ICP) launched an insurrection against the **French** administration at the time of the brief Japanese invasion across the Sino–Vietnamese border in September. After the defeat of the rebel forces, Chu Văn Tấn led one section of the remnants into the mountains near the border and organized them into guerrilla units that created a small liberated zone at Bắc Sơn-Vũ Nhai in the border region. In early 1945, the army was merged with the Armed Propaganda Brigade created in December 1944 into a single organization—the **Vietnamese Liberation Army** under the command of **Võ Nguyên Giáp**. *See also* JAPANESE OCCUPATION.

ARMY OF THE REPUBLIC OF VIETNAM (ARVN). Established after the **Geneva Conference** of 1954, ARVN was the successor of the **Vietnamese National Army** (VNA), which had been created as a combat auxiliary force by the **French** during the **Franco–Việt Minh War**. After Geneva, the VNA was reorganized with assistance from the **United States**, which created a 342-man **Military Assistance Advisory Group** (MAAG) to provide training for the inexperienced Vietnamese. During the late 1950s, the growth of ARVN, targeted at a force level of 150,000 men by U.S. planners, was hampered by controversy over its proper role in combating the Communist-led insurgency movements.

During the Vietnam War, ARVN grew substantially in size to nearly one million men (including territorial defense forces) and, along with combat forces from the United States, carried on the fight against the revolutionary forces in South Vietnam. The role of ARVN was concentrated on the pacification effort and suppressing the activities of the southern revolutionary forces at the local level (the **People's Liberation Armed Forces**), while U.S. combat forces engaged primarily in search-and-destroy missions against the regular units of the **People's Army of Vietnam** (PAVN) from the **Democratic Republic of Vietnam**. Some outside observers were critical of this strategy, concluding that the United States was bearing the brunt of the conflict in South Vietnam. In actuality, casualties suffered by ARVN were considerably higher than those suffered by U.S. military units. A more serious issue was the fact that the ARVN was trained and equipped primarily for conventional warfare, whereas their opponents, until the final stage of the conflict, were fighting a guerrilla war.

After the departure of U.S. combat forces as a result of the **Paris Agreement** of January 1973, ARVN was given full responsibility for defending the **Republic of Vietnam** against external and internal attack. Poorly equipped by the United States as a result of cutbacks ordered by Congress, and poorly led as the result of strategical errors by President **Nguyễn Văn Thiệu** and several military commanders, ARVN was no match for the well-trained and well-equipped PAVN forces and collapsed rapidly in the face of the **Hồ Chí Minh Campaign** launched by the latter in the spring of 1975.

ASIATIC MODE OF PRODUCTION (AMP). The so-called "Asiatic Mode of Production" is a synthesis of various comments and observations on Asia found in Karl Marx's writings. Because Marx knew and wrote mainly about the West, some of his supposedly "universal" stages of social evolution are not well-suited for analyzing Asian history. Early generations of Marxist scholars cobbled together the AMP in order to help fit Asian history into a broader Marxist framework. The AMP, which is particularly intended to be an alternate to Marx's Eurocentric understanding of **"feudalism,"** postulates a state that enjoys theoretical ownership of all the land in its territory but with relatively autonomous **villages** that exercise actual control over their land through communal ownership. This model would seem to be an accurate description of Vietnam for much of its history, and some Vietnamese scholars have accepted the AMP as a relevant framework, but there is not unanimity on this issue.

ASSIMILATION. The concept of assimilation (Viet. *đồng hoá*) has become an important one in the Vietnamese understanding of their cultural history. Despite the heavy doses of **Chinese** culture, which they have absorbed over the centuries (beginning with the long **Chinese period**), they have always been proud of having maintained a separate identity along with their existence as an independent country. This is particularly the case since other ancient peoples who also came under Han Chinese domination ended up being more or less absorbed into the ethnic Chinese population. Modern Vietnamese scholars sometimes speak critically of Chinese "plots" to "assimilate" their ancestors and emphasize the resistant staying power of the Vietnamese identity in the face of such strong Chinese influences, although this point is often exaggerated for rhetorical and political purposes.

Ironically, the Vietnamese themselves have been agents of assimilation against some neighboring peoples, most notably the **Cham**. Whereas the territory inhabited by Cham-speaking people once extended from present-day Quảng Bình down to Bình Thuận, today only the southernmost part of this region still has people who consider themselves as Cham. The culture of the ethnic Vietnamese along the central coast shows clear traces of early Cham influences, but over the centuries the Cham became Vietnamese. Similarly, but peacefully earlier generations of migrants from China to Vietnam gradually became assimilated into Vietnamese culture and lost their separate ethnic identity.

ASSIMILATION (FRENCH POLICY). French colonial policy in **Indochina** and elsewhere vacillated along a spectrum of options between the two poles of assimilation and **association**. The core meaning of these terms related to the kinds of political structures that would be put in place and the degree to which the indigenous system would be remade along more Western lines. Broadly speaking, French policy in **Cochin China**, which was governed as a colony completely removed from the authority of the Vietnamese emperor in **Huế**, was based on assimilation, whereas the **protectorates** of **Annam** and **Tonkin**, where the traditional imperial structures were maintained, were more closely linked to the idea of association. Official policy during the early decades of colonial rule fluctuated between the two, however, and ultimately the most important French objectives were pacification and economic exploitation, which obviously involved more control rather than less. Assimilation such as it was, then, resulted in a system of government that was neither completely "traditional" nor truly "French" in character.

Assimilation also had cultural overtones, though generally speaking the "civilizing mission" of French colonialism did not really envision turning the Vietnamese into "French." Colonialism inevitably had a significant impact on Vietnamese culture, particularly among the urban elite who had the most contact with Europeans. It can be argued that the relatively small group of Francophiles who adopted European manners, virtually stopped using their native language, and, in some cases, acquired French citizenship, were "assimilated." This, however, was more an incidental response to the colonial experience than the result of any conscious French policy.

ASSOCIATED STATE OF VIETNAM. *See* STATE OF VIETNAM.

ASSOCIATED STATES OF INDOCHINA. The Associated States of Indochina was a structure established by the **French** in the late 1940s in an attempt to maintain control over their colony while granting a greater degree of nominal independence. Vietnam, **Cambodia**, and **Laos** were to be "Associated States" within a broader **French Union**. French President Vincent Auriol and ex-Emperor **Bảo Đại** signed the **Élysée Accords** in Paris in March 1949, an agreement that was to formalize Vietnam's status as an Associated State headed by Bảo Đại.

The French Union was meant to be an instrument of partial decolonization for France's colonial empire, but in Vietnam's case, at least, it offered few substantive concessions to nationalist aspirations for greater autonomy, let alone a clear path to independence. Bảo Đại's **State of Vietnam** thus continued to face an uphill struggle to gain legitimacy as a rival to **Hồ Chí Minh**'s **Democratic Republic of Vietnam**. In the case of Cambodia and Laos, however, where the Communist-led insurgencies represented less-significant threats to the French-backed royal governments, the Associated States provided a more concrete framework for gradual decolonization, and both countries eventually received independence under these governments. *See also* PAU CONVENTIONS.

ASSOCIATION (FRENCH POLICY). The two extremes of **French** colonial policy were **assimilation** and association, each implying a different relationship between indigenous and foreign administrative structures. Association was particularly linked to the concept of a **protectorate**, the form of government used in **Annam** and **Tonkin** but not in **Cochin China**. The imperial system was left in place in these two regions and theoretically continued to operate as before, though with French advice and guidance. In reality, however, from the earliest days of the full protectorate in 1883–1884, the French insisted on maximizing their control over the Vietnamese system, frequently pushing beyond the limits of the treaties they had signed. The monarchy was quickly reduced to a largely symbolic institution, despite French efforts to bolster its "moral authority" and prestige through face-saving rhetoric. High-ranking Vietnamese officials had little autonomy *vis-à-vis* their French counterparts, while lower-level mandarins faced few constraints in engaging in corrupt and abusive practices.

Over the long term, the policy of association eroded the legitimacy of the Vietnamese ruling elite and made them highly vulnerable targets for revolutionaries and other anticolonial nationalists. The French system maintained the visible trappings of imperial government while completely stripping it of any independent authority, and few Vietnamese were fooled. Because association linked the elite to the colonial regime and all that it stood for, it effectively prevented the development of a viable nationalist alternative to the Communist-led Revolution that could outlast French rule. (Even **Ngô Đình Diệm**, who had served in the protectorate government for several years and then dropped out of it, had to fill his government with former French collaborators.) At the same time, association served French interests insofar as it helped ensure an ample supply of local collaborators to facilitate colonial rule, but ultimately the generally low quality of many of these men served to reinforce the negative perceptions of colonialism and helped hasten its demise.

ASSOCIATION OF LIKE MINDS. *See* TÂM TÂM XÃ.

ASSOCIATION OF MARXIST STUDIES (*Hội Nghiên Cứu Chủ Nghĩa Mác ở Đông Dương*). Organization created by the **Indochinese Communist Party** (ICP) after its putative dissolution in November 1945. The purpose of the move was to persuade moderate elements in Vietnam to support the ICP-led **Việt Minh** Front in its struggle against the restoration of French colonial authority. In theory, the association was meant to provide an opportunity for individuals to study Marxist–Leninist theory after the abolition of the party. In reality, the party continued to exist in secret. The association was dissolved when the ICP reemerged as the Vietnamese Workers' Party (VWP) in early 1951.

ASSOCIATION POUR LA FORMATION INTELLECTUELLE ET MORALE DES ANNAMITES (AFIMA, *Hội Khai Trí Tiến Đức*).

Cultural society formed with official encouragement in colonial Vietnam. Established by **Phạm Quỳnh**, **Nguyễn Văn Vĩnh**, and other moderate reformists in 1922, AFIMA's aim was to promote East–West collaboration and the introduction of Western ideas and literary works into Vietnam. Many Vietnamese viewed AFIMA and its mouthpiece, the *Nam Phong* journal, as a tool of the French. *See also* LITERATURE.

ASSOCIATION OF SOUTHEAST ASIAN NATIONS (ASEAN).

Multinational organization created by five nations in Southeast Asia (Indonesia, Malaysia, Singapore, Thailand, and the Philippines) in 1967. At first, the organization restricted its activities primarily to economic and social cooperation, but after the reunification of Vietnam in 1975, it began to take on a more political function. In cooperation with **China** and several Western countries, ASEAN actively sought to bring an end to the Vietnamese occupation of **Cambodia** in the early 1980s. With the withdrawal of Vietnamese troops from Cambodia in the late 1980s, relations between ASEAN and the Indochinese countries began to improve. Vietnam was invited to join the organization in 1995, and Cambodia and **Laos** subsequently joined as well. Vietnam has become an active and enthusiastic participant, though its relations with some fellow members (such as the Philippines) have been overshadowed by overlapping claims to the **Spratly Islands**. At the same time, however, Vietnam's membership in ASEAN has enabled it to strengthen its position *vis-à-vis* China, where maritime territorial disputes are concerned. *See also* FOREIGN RELATIONS.

ATTRITION. Military strategy adopted by the **United States** to prevent a Communist takeover of South Vietnam during the mid-1960s. A leading exponent of the strategy was U.S. General **William C. Westmoreland**, commander of U.S. forces in the **Republic of Vietnam** after 1964. When President Lyndon B. Johnson began to introduce U.S. combat troops in the spring of 1965, Westmoreland formulated a three-stage strategy designed to attack and eventually eliminate Communist forces in South Vietnam. The eventual objective was to break the will of the enemy and bring about a negotiated settlement. The strategy was abandoned after the **Tet Offensive** of 1968. *See also* MILITARY ASSISTANCE COMMAND, VIETNAM.

ÂU CƠ. Wife of **Lạc Long Quân** and mythical coprogenitor of the Vietnamese race. She was a sort of fairy princess from a land in the mountains, whereas he was associated with the sea; they eventually separated and returned to their respective homes. They were said to have had a hundred sons, one of whom became the first of the **Hùng Kings**. Their descendants, the ethnic Vietnamese, have therefore been known as *con rồng cháu tiên*, or "offspring of the dragon and the fairy."

ÂU LẠC. Early kingdom in what is now northern Vietnam. In the mid-third century B.C.E., a Chinese warlord named *Thục Phán* conquered the **Bronze Age** civilization of **Văn Lang**, located in the **Red River Delta.** Assuming the title **An Dương Vương**, he set up his capital in the lowlands at **Cổ Loa**, just outside present-day **Hanoi**. Like the rulers of Văn Lang whom he had overthrown, he attempted to rule with the cooperation of the landed aristocratic class, called the "**Lạc** Lords," in the feudal ruler-vassal relationship. In 207 B.C.E., the kingdom of Âu Lạc was defeated by **Triệu Đà** (in Chinese Zhao Tuo), who set up a new state called *Nan Yue* (**Nam Việt**). Although too little is known of the kingdom of Âu Lạc to attempt to reach a definitive assessment, it has considerable significance in Vietnamese history. It might have represented the first unification of the hill peoples and the valley Lạc peoples, believed to be the ancestors of the modern lowland Vietnamese.

AUGUST REVOLUTION (*Cách Mạng Tháng Tám***).** Insurrection launched by the **Indochinese Communist Party** (ICP) in August 1945. The uprising was planned by ICP leader **Hồ Chí Minh** to take place at the point of Japanese surrender and before the return of the **French**. Responding to the appeal by the party and its front organization (the **Việt Minh**) at the **Tân Trào** Conference in mid-August, military, paramilitary, and popular forces under ICP direction took advantage of the political vacuum at the end of the war and seized control of cities, towns, and villages throughout the country. In the

North, Việt Minh authority was virtually complete, and, on 2 September, the **Democratic Republic of Vietnam** was proclaimed in **Hanoi**. In the Center, Việt Minh forces seized the imperial capital of **Huế** and forced the abdication of the reigning emperor, **Bảo Đại**. In **Cochin China** in the South, Việt Minh forces aided by non-Communist nationalist groups seized power in a bloodless coup and shared authority in a so-called **Committee of the South** (*Ủy Ban Nam Bộ*) set up in late August.

The results of the uprising were mixed. Allied occupation forces began to arrive in October, Nationalist Chinese above the 16th parallel, and British forces below. In the North, Hồ Chí Minh, provisional president of the new regime, was able to conciliate Chinese occupation authorities by offering positions in his cabinet to members of non-Communist parties such as the **Việt Nam Quốc Dân Đảng** (VNQDD) and the **Đồng Minh Hội**. But in the South, General **Douglas Gracey**, commander of the British expeditionary forces, released French prisoners and cooperated with them in driving the Việt Minh and their allies out of **Saigon**. By October, the South was back under French control.

The August Revolution was thus not an unqualified success. Within a year, negotiations to end the split between North and South broke down with the outbreak of the **Franco–Việt Minh War**. However, the August Revolution is viewed in Hanoi today as a glorious first stage in the Vietnamese revolution and, in its combination of military and political struggle, a possible model for wars of national liberation in other Third World societies. Moreover, it has acquired an iconic status as the culmination of various Vietnamese struggles against colonial rule, and the factionalism and conflicts within the anti-French groupings are downplayed in favor of an emphasis on a unified "national revolution." *See also* HO-SAINTENY AGREEMENT; JAPANESE OCCUPATION; VANGUARD YOUTH MOVEMENT.

AUSTROASIATIC. A family of languages spoken in mainland Southeast Asia since prehistoric times. Some linguists consider it to be a branch, along with **Austronesian** (spoken in maritime Southeast Asia), of an original "Austroasian" group of languages spoken throughout the region. The Austroasiatic languages spoken in Vietnam are grouped within the Mon–Khmer subfamily, which includes both Vietnamese and Khmer, as well as many of the languages spoken in the highland areas. *See also* VIETNAMESE LANGUAGE.

AUSTRONESIAN. A family of languages spoken in mainland and island Southeast Asia, as well as Taiwan; Malay/Indonesian, Javanese, and many of the languages of the Philippines are from this family. Austronesian languages in Vietnam include **Cham**, **Jarai**, and **Rhadé**. It is assumed that the first Austronesian speakers migrated to the Vietnamese coast from insular Southeast Asia; some then moved inland to the highland areas. *See also* AUSTROASIATIC.

AUTONOMOUS REPUBLIC OF COCHIN CHINA. *See* REPUBLIC OF COCHIN CHINA.

– B –

BA ĐÌNH SQUARE. Large grassy park in the northeast section of **Hanoi**. Along the edges of the park are the **National Assembly** building, the Presidential Palace (formerly the Governor-General's Palace), and the **Hồ Chí Minh Mausoleum**. It was here that **Hồ Chí Minh** read the Declaration of Independence to the people of Hanoi on 2 September 1945. Known to the French as Place **Puginier**, in commemoration of a 19th-century French bishop, it was renamed Ba Đình Square by Hồ Chí Minh in honor of three villages in Thanh Hoá province that had resisted the **French** conquest in the late 19th century. *See also* DEMOCRATIC REPUBLIC OF VIETNAM.

BÀ HUYỆN THANH QUAN. *See* NGUYỄN THỊ HINH.

BA TƠ UPRISING. A district in Quảng Ngãi in Central Vietnam. In mid-August 1945, local members of the **Việt Minh** Front launched an insurrection against **Japanese occupation** forces and formed a people's revolutionary committee in support of the **August Revolution** led by **Hồ Chí Minh**. The uprising was later suppressed by the **French**, but anticolonial sentiment in the area remained high until the end of the **Franco–Việt Minh War**. After the **Geneva Confer-**

ence temporarily divided Vietnam in half, the people of the district launched an abortive uprising against the regime of **Ngô Đình Diệm** in 1959. Throughout the Vietnam War, the people of the district retained their revolutionary character and resisted the administration of the **Republic of Vietnam**.

BÀ TRIỆU. *See* LADY TRIỆU.

BẮC BỘ (Bắc Kỳ). Vietnamese term for the northern provinces of Vietnam. During the period of **French** colonial rule, it corresponded to the provinces contained in the **protectorate** of **Tonkin**. The other regions of Vietnam are **Trung Bộ** (central) and **Nam Bộ** (southern).

BẮC BỘ PALACE (*Bắc Bộ Phủ*). Large administrative building in the colonial style constructed by the **French** in **Hanoi** in the early 20th century. Formerly, it housed the delegate of the imperial court in **Huế** to the French **protectorate** of **Tonkin**. After the **August Revolution** in 1945, it was renamed the Northern Palace (*Bắc Bộ Phủ*, "palace" here meaning a large government building, like the French *palais*) and served as an administrative office under the **Democratic Republic of Vietnam** (DRV). On 19 August 1945, supporters of the **Việt Minh** Front stormed the palace and raised the new flag of the DRV, marking the opening of the August Revolution in Hanoi. Today, it is used primarily for ceremonial purposes and as a government guest house.

BẮC SƠN CULTURE (*Văn hoá Bắc Sơn*). Prehistoric civilization of the **Neolithic** Era in what is today northern Vietnam. Bắc Sơn sites, so called because of their proximity to the Sino–Vietnamese border town of that name, date from about 8000 to 4000 B.C.E. A distinctive feature was the use of the so-called Bacsonian axe, with polished edges to facilitate cutting and scraping. Although some speculate that this technological advance was the result of an immigration of external elements into the existing **Hoà Bình** culture, Vietnamese archeologists contend that Bắc Sơn civilization emerged gradually from technological advances taking place within the Hoà Bình civilization. Bone fragments indicate that, as in Hoà Bình, the inhabitants of Bắc Sơn sites were Australoid–Melanesoid in racial composition and lived primarily in limestone caves, leading some archeologists to describe Bắc Sơn as a "late Hoabinhian" culture. *See also* ARCHAE-OLOGY.

BẮC SƠN UPRISING. Rebellion against the **French** colonial regime in the fall of 1940. In September 1940 **Japanese** troops crossed the Sino–Vietnamese border into **Tonkin** to punctuate Tokyo's demand for economic and military privileges in **French Indochina**. In the ensuing confusion, local leaders of the **Indochinese Communist Party** (ICP) launched a revolt against French authority in the area around the town of Bắc Sơn (Thái Nguyên province), an area inhabited primarily by the **Tày** and **Nùng** minorities. The French struck back and crushed the uprising, but rebel leaders, such as **Chu Văn Tấn** and **Lê Quang Ba**, turned to guerrilla warfare, establishing the Bắc Sơn-Vũ Nhai base area. Their units were eventually merged with the Vietnamese Liberation Army, formed in 1944, which later became the **People's Army of Vietnam**. *See also* VÕ NGUYÊN GIÁP.

BẠCH ĐẰNG RIVER. Site of three major naval battles fought by Vietnam against invading forces from **China** in the 10th and 13th centuries C.E. The Bạch Đằng River exits into the **Tonkin Gulf** east of modern-day **Hanoi** and was a key entry point to access the inland areas from the coast in earlier centuries. The first military campaign (938) was led by **Ngô Quyền** against the short-lived Chinese Southern Han dynasty; this victory marked the end of the **Chinese period** in Vietnamese history. The second was under **Lê Hoàn** in 980–981 against the Song dynasty, and the third was directed by **Trần Hưng Đạo**, who defeated a Mongol fleet at the same spot in 1287. The tactics adopted by the Vietnamese were the same in each case: stakes were embedded into the river bed at the mouth of the Bạch Đằng, then the enemy fleet was lured onto the stakes at high tide, sinking the ships and leading to Vietnamese victories. Some of the stakes (or possibly their replicas) can be seen at the Museum of History in Hanoi.

BÁCH VIỆT. The name *Bách Việt* is from the Chinese *Bai Yue* or "hundred Viet," an old term used by the Chinese to collectively designate the ethnic groups scattered across a wide area of what is now southern **China** and northern Vietnam. The name *Việt/*Yue itself also referred to a particular state in pre-Common Era Chinese history; the name survived as a designation for the ethnic Vietnamese after the state disappeared. The *Bai Yue* were presumably the ancestors of some of the ethnic minorities inhabiting both sides of the present-day Sino–Vietnamese border. Some Vietnamese traditions, however, have associated "Bách Việt" specifically with the hundred sons born to **Lạc Long Quân** and **Âu Cơ**.

BALANCE OF PAYMENTS. *See* TRADE.

BAN MÊ THUỘT. *See* BUÔN MÊ THUỘT.

BANKING AND FINANCE. Until the late 1980s, the banking system in Vietnam was a tool of the state in its effort to create a centrally directed socialist **economy**. At the apex of the system was the State Bank of Vietnam, with its headquarters in **Hanoi**. Under the State Bank were two subsidiaries, the Bank of Foreign Trade and the Bank for Construction and Development. At that time, the bank served primarily as a distribution center for the **State Planning** Commission and the Ministry of Finance, which periodically instructed the bank to disburse capital to various **state-owned enterprises** in accordance with government planning objectives.

Once Vietnam began the major shift to a market-oriented economy under *đổi mới*, this clearly necessitated a significant overhaul of the banking system. There were at least three important objectives. First, the banks had to begin to operate with a greater degree of efficiency and transparency while they adjusted to the changing requirements of a very different economy. Second, they had to be able to mobilize domestic savings (kept under the proverbial mattress or, more commonly, in the form of gold) to inject more liquidity into the system. Finally, they had to be able to function as viable and trustworthy institutions in the eyes of **foreign investors** for **joint ventures** and other projects.

As the result of reforms carried out in the late 1980s, the functions of the State Bank were changed, through the creation of four new semi-independent state banks with specialized functions: the Bank of Foreign Trade, which is responsible for currency transactions and the management of currency reserves, and three commercial banks, the Bank for Investment and Construction, the Bank for Agricultural Development, and the Bank for Industry and Commerce. All have branches in the major cities. The State Bank continues to perform a general supervisory function, as well as controlling the money supply and credit policies. At the same time, the number and variety of financial institutions have increased through the establishment of joint-stock banks.

Another consequence of the recent reforms was the authorization for foreign banks to set up branch offices in Vietnam. By 1995, foreign banks began to establish offices in Vietnam, and quite a number are now operating in the country; several joint venture banks have been established as well. Activities of foreign banking institutions were initially relatively limited, generally beginning with representative offices and gradually expanding the scope of their operations. At the outset, many restricted their services to short-term loans to state and joint enterprises. More recently, some have moved cautiously into medium-term transactions under urging from the government, and many are now allowed to offer retail services to individual customers.

The results of these efforts have been very mixed. Although the diversification of institutions and services has benefited many local customers, some of the banks continue to operate on shaky ground. Lending practices are not firmly established, and many state enterprises, for example, prefer to maintain their traditional status in order to obtain preferential access to credit, instead of undergoing **equitization** (a form of privatization) and facing greater competition for this access. Moreover, these firms are the source of heavy debts that remain on the books of many banks. Under the auspices of the International Monetary Fund (IMF), the Vietnamese government has been working hard to recapitalize and revitalize the larger state banks, but it is a daunting task.

The banking system also has a mixed record with Vietnamese depositors. They have often benefited from attractive interest rates to draw their savings into the bank, and the proliferation of Automatic Teller Machines and credit cards in urban areas has also been well received. The **United States** dollar and gold, however, remain the preferred mediums of exchange for larger transactions, such as the purchase of motorbikes. Nor do the occasional ripples and scandals in banking circles serve to instill deep-rooted confidence as to the stability of the system as a whole.

BẢO ĐẠI (1913–1997). Last emperor (r. 1925–1945) of the **Nguyễn dynasty** and chief of state of the **State of Vietnam** from 1949 to 1955. Born *Prince Vĩnh Thụy* in 1913, he succeeded his father **Khải Định** on the latter's death in 1925 and adopted the dynastic title *Bảo Đại* (Protector of Grandeur). During his adolescence, Bảo Đại studied in **France** while imperial duties were handled by a regency council in **Huế**, the capital of the French **Protectorate** of **Annam**. In 1932, he returned to Vietnam and formally occupied himself with the limited duties assigned by the French. Although he enjoyed a brief period of activity and minor reforms, by the mid-1930s, he was spending more and more time at his villas and hunting lodges away from the palace.

After the **Japanese** overthrow of the French colonial regime in March 1945, Bảo Đại was offered limited Vietnamese independence under Japanese protection. He accepted and named the historian **Trần Trọng Kim** as prime minister. After the defeat of Japan in August 1945, however, he was pressured to announce his abdication by the **Việt Minh**, accepting instead the innocuous position of "Supreme Adviser" to the new **Democratic Republic of Vietnam (DRV)**. For a brief period, he cooperated with the new government and its president, **Hồ Chí Minh**, but eventually concluded that his position was a mere sinecure and left for exile in Hong Kong. After the outbreak of the **Franco–Việt Minh War** in December 1946, Bảo Đại immediately became the focus of efforts by the French and anticommunist elements in Vietnam to persuade him to return as chief of state of a new Vietnamese government that would provide an alternative to Hồ's DRV. Bảo Đại attempted to use his bargaining power with the French to obtain their agreement on the creation of a united, independent, and non-Communist Vietnam. Eventually, he settled for a compromise; in the **Elysée Accords**, signed in March 1949, he agreed to an autonomous State of Vietnam as one of the **Associated States of Indochina** within the framework of the **French Union**. He returned in June to assume the office of chief of state in the new capital of **Saigon.**

Bảo Đại's compromises, which gave the French control over foreign affairs and the waging of the war against the Việt Minh, dissuaded many Vietnamese patriots from supporting his new government. Moreover, his reputation as a playboy convinced many that he lacked the capacity to lead Vietnam into independence. During its brief four years of existence, the State of Vietnam won only limited recognition at home and abroad as a legitimate representative of the national aspirations of the Vietnamese people.

The **Geneva Conference** of 1954 divided Vietnam into two *de facto* separate states: North and South. In Saigon, supporters of the French and Bảo Đại's State of Vietnam administered all of Vietnam south of the 17th parallel in preparation for national elections called for by the political accords reached at Geneva. For a year, Bảo Đại remained in power, but in 1955 his prime minister, **Ngô Đình Diệm**, held a referendum to determine who should lead South Vietnam into the future, and Bảo Đại was removed from his position. In elections widely considered fraudulent, Diệm won over 90 percent of the vote and in 1956 was elected president of the **Republic of Vietnam**. The defeat ended Bảo Đại's political career, and he spent the rest of his life in France. *See also* BẢO ĐẠI SOLUTION; HẠ LONG BAY AGREEMENT.

BẢO ĐẠI SOLUTION (Also known as *Bảo Đại Formula* or *Bảo Đại Experiment*). An effort in the late 1940s by non-Communist nationalists, aided by the **French**, to create a government under ex-Emperor **Bảo Đại** that could present the Vietnamese people with an alternative to the Communist-controlled **Democratic Republic of Vietnam** (DRV). The effort began after the opening of the **Franco–Việt Minh War** in December 1946, when the French broke off peace negotiations with the DRV. Throughout the next two years, French representatives met with Bảo Đại, then living in exile in Hong Kong, in an effort to persuade him to return to Vietnam as chief of state of an Associated State within the **French Union**. Agreement was finalized in the so-called **Elysée Accords**, signed in March 1949. *See also* HẠ LONG BAY AGREEMENT; STATE OF VIETNAM.

BẢO NINH. Pseudonym for a popular novelist in contemporary Vietnam. A veteran of the **People's Army of Vietnam** (PAVN) who

served in South Vietnam during the 1960s and 1970s and participated in the final campaign that captured the city of **Saigon**, he was
one of the first fiction writers in the postwar era to depict the horror
and pain of battle. His novel *The Sorrow of Love* (*Thân Phận của
Tình Yêu/Nỗi Buồn Chiến Tranh*) received an honorary award when
it was first published in **Hanoi** in 1991, but it was soon exposed to
severe criticism by veterans' groups, who complained that it depicted
the war in the South unpatriotically. In the novel, the protagonist survives the fighting, but he is haunted and disillusioned by the experience and highly critical of conditions in postwar Vietnam. An
English-language translation of the novel was published in the
United States under the name *The Sorrow of War*. A native of Quảng
Trị, Bảo Ninh currently lives in Hanoi. *See also* LITERATURE.

BAJARAKA. A separatist movement that broke out in the **Central
Highlands** in the late 1950s after the end of colonial rule. Its name
combined letters from the names of four major ethnic groups:
Bahnar, Jarai, Rhadé, and Kaho/Koho. The movement was launched
to protest the fact that the Central Highlands region, which had enjoyed a certain degree of autonomy under the **French** as the *Pays
Montagnards du Sud Indochinois*, was now absorbed administratively by the **Republic of Vietnam**. Although the Bajaraka as such
was short-lived and was essentially suppressed by the **Ngô Đình
Diệm** government by 1958, it provided a foundation for the more
durable **Front Uni pour la Libération des Races Opprimées**
(FULRO) movement, which appeared a few years later.

BEAU, PAUL (1857–1926). Governor-general of **Indochina** from
1902 until 1908. A lawyer and then a diplomat, Beau was appointed
to the governor-generalship in 1902. He was a believer in a policy of
"**association**" between the colonial regime and the native population
in Indochina and inaugurated a number of reforms in the area of education, including the opening of the University of Hanoi and the establishment of consultative assemblies in the **protectorates** of
Annam and **Tonkin**. His period in office was marked by the rise of
social unrest that would result in peasant riots in Central Vietnam
and a rising sense of anticolonial sentiment among intellectuals, ex-

emplified by the formation of the Tonkin Free School or **Đông Kinh Nghĩa Thục**. *See also* REVOLT OF THE SHORT HAIRS.

BẾN SÚC. Village located about 40 kilometers (25 miles) northwest of Hồ Chí Minh City that became a symbol of the failure of **United States** strategy during the Vietnam War. Located in the famous **Iron Triangle**, a **National Liberation Front** base area during the 1960, Bến Súc was razed by U.S. and South Vietnamese troops during **Operation Cedar Falls** in 1967, and its residents were relocated to other villages. The tunnel complex under the village, however, was not destroyed and continued to serve as a conduit for insurgents into the **Saigon** area. The incident was immortalized in *The Village of Ben Suc* by the journalist Jonathan Schell. *See also* WESTMORELAND, WILLIAM C.

BẾN TRE. A province in the heart of the **Mekong River Delta** that was the scene of a local uprising against the South Vietnamese government in January 1960. Renamed Kiến Hoà province by the **Republic of Vietnam**, Bến Tre had experienced rural unrest during the 1930s and became a stronghold of **Việt Minh** support during the **Franco–Việt Minh War**. In 1960, local insurgents attacked government posts and briefly established control over several villages in the province. One of the leading commanders was a woman named *Nguyễn Thị Định*, later promoted to deputy commander of the **People's Liberation Armed Forces** (PLAF). Although the insurrection was eventually suppressed, it was labeled by Communist historians in **Hanoi** as the opening of a period of "spontaneous uprisings" that unleashed the revolutionary war in South Vietnam.

BIÊN HOÀ. Small city about 30 kilometers (nearly 20 miles) north of present-day Hồ Chí Minh City. During the Vietnam War, it became one of the first **United States** military bases in the **Republic of Vietnam**. In November 1964, insurgent units attacked the base, killing several American soldiers. The Lyndon B. Johnson administration decided not to respond to the attack with force, probably because of the forthcoming presidential elections.

BILATERAL TRADE AGREEMENT (BTA). Along with normalization of relations in 1995, the bilateral **trade** agreement signed with the **United States** in 2000 was the most important development in Vietnamese–American ties since the end of the war. Although negotiations for the agreement began in 1996, the road to a BTA was long and hard, with many hurdles along the way. The pace of negotiations picked up considerably in 1999, partially thanks to the involvement of reform-minded officials like **Vũ Khoan** and **Nguyễn Tấn Dũng**, but sticking points remained over issues like the timeframe for reducing tariffs on the Vietnamese side and the degree to which certain sensitive sectors of their **economy** could be shielded from foreign investment. First a draft and then a final agreement were produced over the next few months, and the BTA was scheduled to be signed in September 1999, when the **Hanoi** government pulled back at the last minute; the final signing did not take place until July 2000.

The last-minute postponement was widely viewed as being due to several factors, both political and economic. There was widespread resistance from some influential quarters whose interests would be seriously affected by the more open market called for by the BTA. There were also objections to Washington's insistence that it would have the right to review Vietnam's normal trade status on an annual basis. A more short-term irritant was a visit by U.S. Secretary of State Madeleine Albright just after the completion of the final draft; she reportedly brought up issues like political **pluralism** and a **multiparty system**, which reminded Hanoi that there was often a political agenda behind its economic ties with Washington. It is also believed that Hanoi thought it was better not to move ahead of **China**, since Beijing's own trade agreement with the U.S. was still pending. However, the Chinese pushed ahead with their agreement both faster and more covertly than the Vietnamese had expected, and so elimination of this obstacle was facilitated by Hanoi's irritation at having been kept out of the loop by Beijing.

As with the Chinese case, the implementation of a BTA between a rich and powerful **capitalist** nation and a developing nation that is somewhere between traditional socialism and a market economy has not been easy. Disputes have already arisen over shrimp and catfish, which very quickly revealed the harsh realities of the bilateral trade relationship. However, both sides are committed to pursuing that relationship and helping it to thrive, and—as with the thorny **human**

rights issue in Vietnamese–U.S. diplomacy—such relatively minor trade spats seem unlikely to derail the BTA over the long term.

BÌNH GIA. Village about 55 kilometers (35 miles) west of present-day Hồ Chí Minh City. After the **Geneva Conference** of 1954, the village was settled by Catholic refugees from North Vietnam. In December 1964, **People's Liberation Armed Forces** (Việt Cộng) units at regimental strength attacked the area. The battle raged for several days before the insurgents withdrew. Sources in **Hanoi** later declared that the "Battle of Bình Gia" had demonstrated the failure of President John F. Kennedy's strategy of counterinsurgency and marked the coming of age of Việt Cộng forces in competing with South Vietnamese troops on even terms.

BÌNH XUYÊN. River pirates active in the **Saigon** area after World War II. Created by Lê Văn Viễn (also known as *Bảy Viễn*), an ex-convict escaped from **Poulo Condore**, the Bình Xuyên (named for a small village once used for their headquarters) preyed on river shipping along the Saigon River during the 1930s and 1940s. After World War II, they cooperated briefly with the **Việt Minh** against the French but changed sides in 1948 after several clashes with Việt Minh troops (whose leader, **Nguyễn Bình**, Viễn had known in Poulo Condore) in the region surrounding **Saigon**. That year, Viễn was made an honorary colonel by **Nguyễn Văn Xuân**, prime minister of the provisional French-sponsored Vietnamese government, and the Bình Xuyên were permitted to run the police and the gambling concession in the Chinese suburb of **Cholon**. They were eliminated in 1955 by **Ngô Đình Diệm**, as they had been among the groups mounting violent resistance against his efforts to assume control over the South after the **Geneva Conference**.

BLACK FLAGS (*Cờ Đen*). Bandit unit operating in the **Việt Bắc** region of **Tonkin** during the **French** conquest of Vietnam in the late 19th century. Led by Liu Yongfu (in Vietnamese Lưu Vĩnh Phúc), a Chinese secret society leader who fled to Vietnam in 1863, the Black Flags were primarily pirates who made their living preying on local villagers and merchants in the northern hills. When the French attempted to place Vietnam under their control in the 1870s and 1880s, the Black Flags cooperated with Vietnamese imperial forces in resisting a French takeover of the **Red River Delta** and were instrumental in the deaths of **Francis Garnier** in 1873 and **Henri Rivière** in 1882. After the establishment of the French **protectorate** in 1884, the Black Flags engaged in resistance activities in the mountains until the area was pacified at the end of the century.

BOAT PEOPLE. Refugees who fled from Vietnam by sea after the end of the Vietnam War. The exodus began in the late spring and summer of 1978 under the impact of a government decree nationalizing industry and commerce and other official measures allegedly discriminating against the **overseas Chinese** population residing in Vietnam. By 1982, over a million Vietnamese (many of whom were of Chinese extraction) had fled Vietnam to other countries in Southeast Asia. Most traveled in small boats, sometimes with the connivance of local Vietnamese authorities, who accepted bribes to ignore their departures. Some refugees later charged that the **Hanoi** regime officially permitted departures on payment of a standard fee. Thousands died at sea, from storms, hunger, or attacks by pirates.

Of those who arrived in other Southeast Asian countries, most were housed in refugee camps, and almost all have now been permanently settled in other countries outside the region. The United States continued to accept several thousand refugees each year through an Orderly Departure Program negotiated with Vietnam, but the exodus by boat gradually trickled off. *See also* OVERSEAS VIETNAMESE.

BOLLAERT, ÉMILE (1890–1978). High commissioner of French Indochina from March 1947 to October 1948. A deputy in the French National Assembly and a member of the Radical Socialist Party, Émile Bollaert was appointed to replace **Thierry d'Argenlieu** as high commissioner on 5 March 1947, slightly over two months after the beginning of the **Franco–Việt Minh War**. Bollaert attempted to adopt a relatively conciliatory attitude toward negotiations with **Hồ Chí Minh**'s **Việt Minh** while at the same time seeking to create a new government composed of non-Communist elements who would cooperate with the French against the Communist-dominated **Democratic Republic of Vietnam** (DRV).

The key to Bollaert's scheme was his ability to persuade ex-

Emperor **Bảo Đại** to return to Vietnam as chief of state of a government closely linked with **France**. Negotiations were held at **Hạ Long Bay** in the spring of 1948, but when Bảo Đại made it clear that he would not come to an agreement without a French commitment on Vietnamese unity and national independence, Bollaert resigned on 19 October 1948; he was replaced two days later by **Léon Pignon**. *See also* BẢO ĐẠI SOLUTION; HẠ LONG BAY AGREEMENT.

BORDER OFFENSIVE OF 1950. First major military offensive launched by **Việt Minh** forces in the **Franco–Việt Minh War**. Reacting to the rise to power of the Communist Party in **China**, Việt Minh leaders in the summer of 1950 planned a major campaign to wipe out French military posts along the Chinese border to open up the area for the shipment of military supplies from China. During the fall of 1950, a series of attacks launched by well-armed Việt Minh units destroyed French forces in the area and led the French high command to evacuate the entire inland border region and retreat to a single outpost at Mong Cái on the coast.

By choosing not to defend the border region, the French allowed the Việt Minh free access to southern China and virtually guaranteed France's ultimate defeat in the war. *See also* CARPENTIER, MARCEL.

BRAZZAVILLE DECLARATION. Declaration issued by the Free French government of General Charles de Gaulle on 24 March 1945. The declaration, promulgated from de Gaulle's headquarters at Brazzaville in the French Congo, stated that after the close of World War II, **France** would transform its possessions in **Indochina** into an **Indochinese Federation** within a broad **French Union** of all colonial possessions around the globe. The declaration promised that reforms would be undertaken to broaden civil liberties and political participation by French subjects in the colonies, but it emphasized that decisions on such issues as foreign affairs and national security would continue to be made by the metropolitan government. No mention was made of a right of secession from the Union or from the Indochinese Federation.

BRENIER COMMISSION. Commission set up by Emperor Napoleon III in Paris in April 1857 to study the advisability of armed intervention to establish and protect **French** commercial, missionary, and security interests in Vietnam. Not surprisingly considering the pressure applied by special interest groups representing the missionaries and traders, the commission concluded that intervention would be justified when "circumstances were opportune." Napoleon III approved an invasion project in July, and the French conquest of **Indochina** began the following year. *See also* RIGAULT DE GENOUILLY, CHARLES.

BRÉVIÉ, JULES (1880–1964). Governor-general of French **Indochina** from 1937 to 1939. A former colonial administrator in French North Africa and author of a book on Islam, Brévié was appointed to his post in Indochina by the **Popular Front** government under Léon Blum. Liberal-minded and well-meaning, Brévié attempted to apply conciliatory measures to an explosive political situation, granting political amnesties to political prisoners, liberalizing press laws, and permitting nationalist political parties to function in a legal or quasi-legal manner. These efforts were undone with the collapse of the Popular Front in **France** and the coming of war in Europe.

BRÉVIÉ LINE. A maritime border between **Cambodia** and **Cochin China** established in 1939 under Governor-General **Jules Brévié**. This line was meant to demarcate the respective waters of the two parts of French **Indochina**, but it remained a point of contention and dispute after the end of colonial rule. Cambodia claimed part of the waters and islands lying to the east of the line, and during the early months after the Communists took control in both Phnom Penh and **Saigon** in April 1975, there were clashes between their respective forces over control of the disputed area. At a deeper level, the Brévié Line partially symbolizes for Cambodians the historical loss of the **Mekong Delta** to the Vietnamese, a loss that was finalized by the borders delineated by the colonial regime.

BRONZE AGE. Period succeeding the **Neolithic Era** and marking the beginning of the Iron Age in human civilization. In Vietnam, the Bronze Age reached its apogee during the so-called **Đông Sơn** period, beginning around the eighth century B.C.E. Colonial-era **archeologists** believed that bronze-casting techniques, which resulted in the manufacturing of the famous **bronze drums** characteristic of the Đông Sơn culture, had been imported into Vietnam from **China** or even Europe. Recently, however, excavations in Indochina and Thailand have suggested that such techniques developed independently among the indigenous cultures in the area. Bronze had many uses in prehistoric Vietnam: as a source for the manufacture of such weapons as knives, axes, arrowheads, and spears; in agriculture, in the manufacture of hoes and plows; and in the production of such ritualistic implements as bronze drums. With the discovery of iron at the end of the Đông Sơn period, the use of bronze gradually declined, and it was used primarily to make household implements.

The Bronze Age has acquired tremendous importance for many Vietnamese, as Đông Sơn—symbolized by the bronze drums—has come to be seen as a flourishing Vietnamese civilization. Archeological discoveries from this period are linked to stories about the **Hùng Vương** rulers and the kingdom of **Văn Lang** to reconstruct an early Vietnamese "nation." *See also* PHÙNG NGUYÊN CULTURE.

BRONZE DRUMS. Decorated bronze musical instruments associated with the prehistoric **Đông Sơn** civilization in northern Vietnam and other areas of East and Southeast Asia. Many have been found at prehistoric sites in southern **China**, Thailand, and the **Red River** Valley in Vietnam, where more than 300 have been unearthed since the first was discovered in 1925. The drums are considered to be a sophisticated example of the art of bronze casting, manufactured from an alloy of copper and tin. Most have been engraved with human figures or geometric designs. They were apparently viewed as sacred objects by rulers who used them as musical instruments during official ceremonies to invoke rain for the harvest and to prepare for battle. In recent years, the bronze drum has become a kind of icon of Vietnamese civilization, though, in fact, similar drums can be found in numerous different cultures in the region. *See also* BRONZE AGE.

BUDDHISM. The Buddhist **religion** first entered what is now Vietnam in the early centuries C.E., brought by missionaries from India and Central Asia, so that until roughly the sixth century Buddhism among the Vietnamese was presumably Indian in form and could be considered as a kind of **Indianization**. Under the Tang dynasty (seventh–ninth centuries), however, Buddhism was primarily transmitted from **China**, and the Vietnamese were exposed to the various sects and currents of Chinese Buddhism. Pure Land Buddhism became the dominant religion in Vietnamese society.

After the end of Chinese rule in the 10th century, Vietnamese monarchs used monks as advisers, and both Buddhism and **Daoism** were influential among the elite, almost certainly more so than **Confucianism**. *Thiền*, a more philosophical form of Buddhism linked to the Chinese Chan school (known in the West by the Japanese equivalent of Zen), also became popular in the court under the **Lý** (1009–1224) and **Trần** (1224–1400) dynasties. Several Lý and Trần emperors wrote philosophical treatises on Buddhism, and the ruling class gave lavish patronage to temples.

Under the **Lê** dynasty (1428–1788), Confucianism gradually replaced Buddhism as the dominant system of thought, but Buddhism remained popular as a devotional faith in all strata of society and coexisted with Confucian beliefs rather than being replaced by them. Confucian doctrine became dominant among the ruling scholar-gentry class and the sole subject of study for the civil service examinations used for entry into the imperial bureaucracy, whereas under earlier dynasties they had incorporated elements of Buddhism and Daoism as well. Even under the strongly Confucianist rulers of the early **Nguyễn dynasty** (1802–1945), Buddhism remained a part of the worldview of most Vietnamese.

In the 20th century, Buddhism enjoyed a modest revival among intellectuals. Under the regime of **Ngô Đình Diệm**, Buddhist monks in **Huế** and **Saigon** vigorously protested alleged official favoritism toward Catholics and the vigorous repression of revolutionary forces practiced by the latter. The Diệm regime accused the Buddhist hierarchy of falling under Communist influence, but in actuality Party leaders in North Vietnam were equally suspicious of activist monks, such as Thích **Trí Quang**.

Buddhism was officially allowed under the **Democratic Republic of Vietnam**, but religious activities were severely curtailed. Reunification in 1975–1976 meant that the powerful Buddhist organizations of South Vietnam now confronted the restrictions of Party rule. A dissident Buddhist church linked to former activist elements has remained in existence, challenging the legitimacy of its officially sanctioned counterpart, and a number of monks have been arrested for suspected **dissident** activities. *See also* TRÚC LÂM.

BÙI DIỄM (1923–   ). Ambassador of the **Republic of Vietnam** (RVN) to the **United States** from 1966 to 1972. The son of a scholar who had supported the patriotic movement led by **Phan Chu Trinh**, Diễm graduated from the prestigious Thăng Long School in **Hanoi** and then studied in **France**; he later held several important posts in the RVN. During the early 1970s, he made an unsuccessful effort on behalf of President **Nguyễn Văn Thiệu** to guarantee continued U.S. support for the South Vietnamese government. He currently lives in the United States.

BÙI QUANG CHIÊU (1872–1945). Journalist and reformist political figure in colonial Vietnam. Born in a scholar-gentry family in Bến Tre, in the **Mekong River Delta**, Bùi Quang Chiêu was educated at the École Coloniale and the National Institute of Agronomy in Paris. In 1897, he returned to **Saigon** and became an agronomical engineer. In 1917, with the encouragement of Governor-General **Albert Sarraut**, he published the French-language newspaper *La Tribune Indigène*, which became a mouthpiece for an informal group of reform-minded Vietnamese in **Cochin China**, who called themselves the **Constitutionalist Party**. Its primary political goal was to increase Vietnamese participation in the political process while maintaining the **French** presence in **Indochina**.

In the mid-1920s, Chiêu became a prominent spokesperson for moderate reformist views through the publication of a new journal entitled *La Tribune Indochinoise*, which sometimes voiced cautious criticism of French policies. However, he was horrified at the violence that erupted with the **Yên Bái Revolt** and the Nghệ Tĩnh Soviets in 1930, and he subsequently became more closely identified with the colonial regime, serving as a Vietnamese member of the Supreme Council for Indochina. The Constitutionalist Party split over the issue of cooperation or resistance to the French and declined as a political force. Chiêu was assassinated shortly after the end of World War II, reportedly by order of the **Việt Minh**.

BÙI THỊ XUÂN (?—1802). A female warrior who played a prominent role in the **Tây Sơn** conflict during the late 18th and early 19th centuries. Originally from Bình Định province, she and her husband Trần Quang Diệu were both generals in the Tây Sơn forces fighting against Nguyễn Ánh (the future Emperor **Gia Long**). In the final months of the war, after the Nguyễn had recaptured their former capital of Phú Xuân (present-day **Huế**), she retreated with the Tây Sơn ruler to Nghệ An province, where she was joined by her husband and his troops. They were subsequently captured by the Nguyễn and put to death. Bùi Thị Xuân is frequently represented as riding an elephant into battle.

BÙI TÍN (1924–   ). Onetime military officer in the **People's Army of Vietnam** (PAVN) who defected to the West. Rising to the rank of colonel in the PAVN during the Vietnam War, he performed a number of important tasks on behalf of **Hanoi**'s cause. After the end of the war, he became a journalist and an editor of the Party newspaper *Nhân Dân*, but he eventually became disillusioned with the Hanoi regime and defected to **France** in 1990.

BÙI VIỆN (1841–1878). A 19th-century Vietnamese mandarin and diplomat. A native of Thái Bình, Bùi Viện was among the reformist mandarins in the court of Emperor **Tự Đức** advocating wider trade and diplomatic links with the outside world. In 1873, he was sent to Hong Kong to explore possible sources of foreign assistance against the **French**, who had already colonized the **Mekong Delta**. Viện met the **United States** Consul in Hong Kong and decided to seek American help. He traveled to the U.S. and made a tour of the country before meeting President Ulysses S. Grant in Washington. Grant was sympathetic to the Vietnamese situation but was able to make no firm commitment because Viện did not have formal letters of credence. He returned to Vietnam, obtained the proper documents, and set out again for the United States. When he reached Japan, however, he learned that American policy had changed and that Vietnam was unlikely to receive support against the French, so he returned home.

BUNKER, ELLSWORTH (1894–1984). United States Ambassador to the **Republic of Vietnam** (RVN) from 1967 until 1973. A career diplomat with earlier posts in Europe, South Asia, and Latin America, Bunker was appointed to replace **Henry Cabot Lodge** on the latter's resignation in early 1967. During his several years in **Saigon**, Bunker was a determined and unflappable advocate of continued U.S. support for the RVN. His reputation for integrity protected him from widespread criticism from antiwar groups at the end of the war. He was replaced as ambassador by **Graham Martin**.

BUÔN MÊ THUỘT (also known as *Ban Mê Thuột*). Largest city in the **Central Highlands**. Once a minority village, it grew rapidly under the **Republic of Vietnam** and by the mid-1970s was a city of about a million people. In March 1975, North Vietnamese forces attacked and occupied the city, provoking a panicky flight from the area by South Vietnamese troops. Today, it is the capital of Đắc Lắc province, the home of the Ê Đê (**Rhadé**) minority.

BỬU LỘC (?–1990). A prince in the **Nguyễn** royal house and a cousin of onetime Emperor **Bảo Đại**, Bửu Lộc went to college in **France** and after World War II became a lawyer in Paris. In 1949, he served as Bảo Đại's *chef de cabinet* and headed a delegation appointed by the latter to work out a negotiated settlement with the French that resulted in the **Elysée Accords** in March. Named high commissioner of the Associated **State of Vietnam** in June 1950, he became prime minister from January until June 1954, when he was replaced by **Ngô Đình Diệm**.

BỬU SƠN KỲ HƯƠNG. A millenarian **Buddhist** movement in southern Vietnam during the 19th century. The term is used to refer to loosely associated groups of people who followed a man named *Đoàn Minh Huyên*, known as "The Buddha Master of Western Peace" (*Phật Thầy Tây An*). The phrase *Bửu Sơn Kỳ Hương* (Strange Fragrance from the Precious Mountain) was found on amulets and also in a poem that devotees recited. Huyên's teachings were within a broad Buddhist framework but also reflected the religiously and culturally eclectic world of the **Mekong Delta**. The Bửu Sơn Kỳ Hương is regarded by the **Hoà Hảo** sect of Buddhism as a precursor of their own movement.

– C –

CÀ MAU PENINSULA. Southernmost tip of Vietnam on the Gulf of Thailand. The Cà Mau Peninsula is relatively underpopulated and covered with dense mangrove swamps. During the early stages of the Vietnam War, revolutionary forces reportedly built a revolutionary base area in the U Minh Forest, located in the center of the peninsula.

CAM RANH BAY. Site of major U.S. military base during the Vietnam War and later the location of a Soviet naval facility in the **Socialist Republic of Vietnam** (SRV). Located on the central coast about 30 kilometers (nearly 20 miles) south of the resort city of Nha Trang, Cam Ranh Bay is often described as one of the most ideally located portages in Asia. In 1905, the Russian fleet stopped at Cam Ranh on the way to a major confrontation with Japanese warships off the coast of Korea.

In early 1946, President **Hồ Chí Minh** of the **Democratic Republic of Vietnam** (DRV) offered the location to the **United States** as a naval base in return for American support for Vietnamese independence. President Harry Truman did not accept the offer, but 20 years later the administration of Lyndon Johnson constructed facilities there to accelerate the arrival of U.S. military equipment in South Vietnam. The area was used by the **Union of Soviet Socialist Republics** as a naval base after 1978, when Moscow signed a Treaty of Friendship and Cooperation with Vietnam. The Soviets had a 25-year lease to Cam Ranh beginning in 1979, and after the fall of the Soviet Union, the Russian navy maintained a considerably diminished presence there. The base was closed and returned to the Vietnamese in 2002, two years ahead of schedule. Its future is still in doubt, but it seems likely that the facilities will be used for civilian purposes rather than as a naval base.

CAMBODIA. Vietnam's neighbor immediately to the West. The Cambodian people, known as the *Khmer*, formed a variety of small polities before the establishment of a political center at Angkor in the early ninth century C.E. Angkor expanded to become the most powerful kingdom in the region; most of its rulers followed Hinduism and/ or Mahayana Buddhism, but Theravada **Buddhism** was in place by the end of the 13th century. The rise of the Thai kingdom of Ayudhya in the 14th century created a serious military and political rival for Angkor; in the mid-1400s, the Khmer ruling family reestablished itself at Phnom Penh, farther to the southeast.

Although the shift in Cambodia's power center meant closer proximity to maritime trade, the kingdom never regained its former strength. From roughly 1600 onward, its ruling class was caught in a balancing act between its more powerful neighbors, Siam and Vietnam. By the mid-19th century, their frequent political and military intervention made the prospects of "protection" from a European power attractive, and in 1863 Cambodia became a **protectorate** of **France**. After achieving initial independence under the **French Union** in 1953, it became fully independent following the **Geneva Conference** of 1954.

Throughout history, Vietnam's relations with neighboring Cambodia have been uneasy. Vietnamese attempts to establish their domination during the 18th and 19th centuries rankled deeply in Phnom Penh, but most significant was the loss of the **Mekong Delta** to Vietnamese expansion and colonization, made permanent by the **Brévié Line**, fixed under colonial rule. This legacy of enmity would have significant consequences for postcolonial relations between the two countries.

During the **Franco–Việt Minh War**, Vietnamese Communist leaders sponsored the creation of a Khmer People's Revolutionary Party (KPRP), which, along with the Pathet Lao in **Laos**, cooperated with the **Việt Minh** in the struggle against the French. This cooperation continued with the North Vietnamese forces and the **National Liberation Front** during the Second Indochina War. However, new leaders within the Communist Party of Kampuchea (CPK, which had replaced the KPRP in the early 1960s) resented Vietnamese tutelage and sought to gradually cut themselves off from their Vietnamese comrades as much as possible. When the CPK (Khmer Rouge) seized power in Phnom Penh in April 1975, the new revolutionary government under Pol Pot refused an offer by **Hanoi** to establish a "**special relationship**" with Laos and Vietnam. Clashes broke out along the Cambodian–Vietnamese border, as Democratic Kampuchea (as the new regime called itself) demanded a return of territories lost to

Vietnam in past centuries and made incursions into Vietnamese territory, which met with sharp military reprisals.

Vietnamese troops invaded Cambodia in late December 1978 and installed a new pro-Vietnamese government in Phnom Penh. When **China** and the neighboring states in Southeast Asia began to support anti-Vietnamese guerrilla forces inside the country, Hanoi eventually withdrew its occupation forces and agreed to a peace treaty that led to a coalition government composed of various groups in Phnom Penh. The Cambodian government is no longer pro-Hanoi, and in fact anti-Vietnamese sentiments are strong among many elements of the population. Most recently, the flight of ethnic minorities from Vietnam to Cambodian territory following unrest in the **Central Highlands** has been a source of tension.

CÁN BỘ. Vietnamese term meaning "cadre" currently used in the **Socialist Republic of Vietnam** (SRV). A cadre is normally a government official and may be a member of the **Vietnamese Communist Party**.

CẦN LAO PARTY (Personalist Labor Party). Clandestine political organization during the regime of **Ngô Đình Diệm** in the **Republic of Vietnam**. Created in 1955 by Diệm's brother **Ngô Đình Nhu**, the Cần Lao (full name *Cần Lao Nhân Vị Cách Mạng Đảng*, or Revolutionary Personalist Labor Party) represented the inner core of top officials and influential figures within the Diệm regime and South Vietnamese society. The Cần Lao did not function as a normal party competing for office in elections, but operated behind the scenes to influence policy and protect the interests of the Diệm regime. After the overthrow of President Diệm in 1963, a number of its members formed a new political organization, the Nhân Xã Party, which became active during the regime of **Nguyễn Văn Thiệu**. *See also* PERSONALISM.

CẦN VƯƠNG MOVEMENT (Save the King or Aid the King). Anti-**French** resistance movement in Vietnam in the late 19th century. It emerged in July 1885 at the time of the flight from the imperial capital of **Huế** by Emperor **Hàm Nghi** and his regent **Tôn Thất Thuyết**. One week later, Hàm Nghi issued an appeal entitled "Save the King" (*Cần Vương*) to mobilize popular support in an effort to drive out the French and restore Vietnamese independence.

The movement received support from Vietnamese of various walks of life throughout the country, despite the capture of Hàm Nghi in 1888. By the late 1880s, a widespread guerrilla movement led by the patriot **Phan Đình Phùng** was in operation in the central provinces. The movement lacked weapons and a coherent strategy, however, and after Phùng's death from dysentery in 1896, it collapsed. It is remembered today as one of the first organized resistance movements against French rule in Vietnam, yet one of the last movements to be focused on the monarchy before the emergence of nationalism in the 20th century.

CẢNH, PRINCE (1779–1801). Officially named *Nguyễn Phúc Cảnh*, he was the eldest son of Nguyễn Ánh, the future Emperor **Gia Long**. In 1784, during his father's struggle against the **Tây Sơn**, the young prince was sent to **France** with **Pigneau de Béhaine**, Bishop of Adran, who was intent on obtaining assistance from Paris for the Nguyễn cause. In 1787, the bishop signed a treaty on Nguyễn Ánh's behalf, which promised French aid in return for territorial and trade concessions from the Vietnamese, but various obstacles—notably the French Revolution—prevented its implementation. He and the young Prince Cảnh returned to Vietnam. Cảnh had apparently converted to **Christianity**, and he scandalized his father's entourage by refusing to pay homage to the family ancestors. Although Cảnh died too early to inherit the throne, this episode is believed to have been a factor in Gia Long's choice of **Minh Mạng** over Cảnh's son as his eventual successor. Cảnh's descendant **Cường Để** was a pretender to the throne in the 20th century.

CAO BÁ QUÁT (1809–1854). Rebel against the **Nguyễn dynasty** in 19th-century Vietnam. Born near **Hanoi** in 1809, he was talented, but although he obtained a degree in 1831, he failed to pass the metropolitan **examinations** in **Huế**. After serving in several minor posts in the bureaucracy, he was dismissed from office for rebellious behavior. He returned to his native village and took part in a local peasant uprising, popularly known as the "Locust Revolt," in which he was killed. He is still remembered as an outstanding poet and a staunch defender of the poor and oppressed.

CAO BẰNG. Province along the Sino–Vietnamese border in the **Việt Bắc** region. Long important because of its strategic location, Cao Bằng served as the last fief of the **Mạc dynasty** after they were driven out of **Hanoi** in the late 16th century. During World War II, **Việt Minh** forces created their headquarters in the mountains nearby. The area was defended by the **French** during the early stages of the **Franco–Việt Minh War** but was later taken over by the Việt Minh after the fall **Border Offensive** in 1950. This opened up the frontier region to **Chinese** assistance to the Vietnamese and hastened the eventual French defeat in **Indochina**.

CAO ĐÀI. Syncretic **religion** in 20th-century Vietnam. The religion Cao Đài, meaning "High Tower," was formally established in 1926 by Ngô Văn Chiêu, a minor functionary in the **French** colonial government. The new religion worshipped a single supreme deity but incorporated elements from a number of other major religions and ideologies, such as **Buddhism**, **Confucianism**, Islam, **Daoism**, and **Christianity**, and achieved rapid success among the urban and rural population of **Cochin China**. It established its headquarters at the city of Tây Ninh, near the **Cambodian** border, and by World War II had a membership of several hundred thousand.

During the war, Cao Đài leaders cooperated with **Japanese occupation** forces. In 1945, the movement became entangled in the struggle between the French and the **Việt Minh** Front. Some Cao Đài leaders supported the Việt Minh, but the dominant group under Pope **Phạm Công Tắc** offered qualified support to the French in an effort to preserve autonomy in areas under their control. After the **Geneva Conference** in 1954, Cao Đài leaders unsuccessfully resisted the attempt by **Ngô Đình Diệm** to consolidate his authority over South Vietnam. During the Vietnam War, they cooperated somewhat reluctantly with the **Saigon** regime against the revolutionary movement led by the **National Liberation Front** (NLF).

Since 1975, the Cao Đài Church has been permitted to function, although it has been purged of elements suspected of hostility to the revolution. It no longer possesses the autonomy it exerted under the

Saigon regime and has been subject to periodic repression by the government. The Holy See at Tây Ninh has become a popular **tourist** destination, and Cao Đài ceremonies are performed in front of crowds of visitors. *See also* HOÀ HẢO.

CAO SỸ KIÊM (also spelled *CAO SĨ KIÊM*) (1941?–). Former governor of the State Bank of Vietnam. A native of Thái Bình, Cao Sỹ Kiêm was appointed to the top post in the **banking** system in 1989. During his time in office, he oversaw a number of changes in Vietnam's financial apparatus as the country moved toward a market **economy** and worked to overhaul its banks to gain the confidence of Vietnamese depositors and **foreign investors** alike. In September 1997, however, Kiêm's reappointment as governor was voted down by the **National Assembly**; he was the only nominee in the Cabinet of incoming Prime Minister **Phan Văn Khải** to be rejected. Kiêm was sacked the following month. In November 1999, an ongoing National Assembly investigation of a large-scale **corruption** case brought formal reprimands to several top-ranking officials including Kiêm. Although graft is widespread in the ranks of the government and the **Vietnamese Communist Party**, some observers felt that Kiêm may have been a scapegoat. Whatever the case, he retained his position as deputy director of the Party Central Committee's Economic Commission, a post he had held since his tenure at the State Bank.

CAO VĂN VIÊN (1921–). General in the **Army of the Republic of Vietnam** (ARVN) and chairman of the ARVN Joint Chiefs of Staff from 1965 to 1975. Allied with **Nguyễn Khánh** and other "Young Turks" who seized power in January 1964, he later became a supporter of President **Nguyễn Văn Thiệu**. After the fall of **Saigon** in 1975, he left South Vietnam and now lives in the United States.

CAPITALISM. Modern capitalism came late to Vietnam, as to most other societies in Southeast Asia. During the traditional era, Vietnam was a predominantly agricultural society. A commercial and manufacturing sector existed, but it was dominated by immigrants from China (known in English as **"overseas Chinese"**) and was tightly controlled by the imperial court. As in neighboring **China**, commerce was viewed as a low-status occupation.

During the period of **French** control, **Indochina** was gradually linked to the international economic order. Vietnam benefited little from the experience, however, serving as the source of cheap raw materials, cash crops (such as **rice, rubber, coffee**, and **tea**), and a market for manufactured goods imported from metropolitan France. **Saigon** emerged as the most vibrant commercial and manufacturing metropolis in the country, and it was here that a growing urban bourgeoisie, dominated by the overseas Chinese in **Cholon**, began to emerge. Manufacturing was concentrated in the light industrial sector and in such areas as food processing and textiles.

After the **Geneva Conference**, a capitalist sector began to flourish in **Republic of Vietnam** under U.S. tutelage, but progress was severely impeded by the onset of the Vietnam War in the early 1960s. In the meantime, the government of the **Democratic Republic of Vietnam** (DRV) in the North nationalized most industrial and commercial establishments and began the construction of a socialist society. After the fall of Saigon in 1975, Communist leaders in **Hanoi** sought to build a Stalinist-style socialist system throughout the country, but inefficiency, **corruption**, and popular resistance led to an economic crisis in the early 1980s.

In December 1986, the **Vietnamese Communist Party** decided to launch a program of renovation (*đổi mới*) that has led to the emergence of an economic system based on a combination of capitalist and socialist characteristics (though "capitalism" itself remains a dirty word in official discourse). A vigorous private sector is tolerated, but the government seeks to guarantee the predominance of **state-owned enterprises** within the national **economy**. Results have been modestly promising, with fairly steady rates of economic growth, though hampered by a heavy-handed bureaucracy and government nervousness at foreign influence. At present, Vietnam is, in many respects, becoming a capitalist country, though officially it remains "on the road to socialism." *See also* NATIONALIZATION OF INDUSTRY AND COMMERCE.

CARAVELLE GROUP. Faction composed of politicians opposed to **Ngô Đình Diệm** in **Republic of Vietnam**. The group originated among a number of moderate political figures who petitioned the **Saigon** regime to undertake reforms in 1960. Formally known as the "Bloc for Liberty and Progress" (*Khối Tự Do Tiến Bộ*), they were popularly called the "Caravelle Group" because their manifesto was issued at the Caravelle Hotel in downtown Saigon. The petition won approval from a wide spectrum of political, religious, and social groups in South Vietnam, but it was not publicized in the local press, and Diệm broke up the group in November after an abortive coup attempt against the regime, though several members remained active in politics.

CARPENTIER, MARCEL (1895–1977). Commander in chief of the French Expeditionary Corps during the **Franco–Việt Minh War**. Appointed to the post as a successor of General Jean Valluy in September 1949, Carpentier showed excessive caution in his strategical calculations and was sacked after French forces were exposed to a major defeat in the **Border Offensive** in the fall of 1950. He was replaced in December by General **Jean de Lattre de Tassigny**.

CÁT BÀ ISLAND. Island located about 60 kilometers (35 miles) east of the port of **Hải Phòng** in the **Tonkin Gulf**. Adjacent to **Hạ Long Bay**, the island is part of the extensive limestone deposit that stretches along the coast of northern Vietnam toward the Chinese border. The island is heavily forested and contains hundreds of species of flora and fauna, some of them quite rare. Along the gulf, cliffs pockmarked with caves climb steeply skyward from pristine beaches and the blue waters. The island was used for some of the scenery in the French film *Indochine*. In 1983, the Vietnamese government declared the island a national park, and it has become a popular **tourist** destination. It can be reached by ferry or by road from Hải Phòng.

CATHOLICISM. *See* CHRISTIANITY.

CATROUX, GEORGES (1877–1969). Governor-general of French **Indochina** in 1939–1940. A career military officer, Catroux had served in civilian and military capacities in North Africa as well as Indochina. Appointed governor-general in August 1939 to succeed **Jules Brévié**, he immediately encountered the rising crisis caused by the spread of **Japanese** power in **China**. Pressured by Tokyo to grant military privileges for Japanese troops in Indochina, he first appealed to the **United States** for military assistance to resist the Japanese. When President Franklin D. Roosevelt rejected the request on the grounds that all U.S. military equipment in the Pacific was needed to strengthen American forces in the region, Catroux capitulated and agreed to the Japanese demands. For this, he was criticized by the new Vichy regime in **France** and recalled; Catroux protested but left Indochina in July. Named to replace him was Admiral **Jean Decoux**, commander of the French naval fleet in the Pacific. Catroux was a prominent supporter of Charles de Gaulle's Free French movement and later held a number of high-ranking posts with the French government. *See also* JAPANESE OCCUPATION.

CÉDILE, JEAN (1908–1984). Appointed as representative of the Free French government to **Cochin China**in the summer of 1945, Jean Cédile parachuted into Vietnam in late August. Captured by the **Japanese**, he was brought to **Saigon** and entered into negotiations with Vietnamese leaders in the **Committee of the South**. Although affable and liberal-minded, Cédile was hindered by the conditions imposed on him by the government in Paris, and no agreement was reached. In October 1946, he returned to **France**. *See also* AUGUST REVOLUTION; GRACEY, DOUGLAS.

CENSORATE (*Đô sát viện*). Modeled on the **Chinese** administrative body of the same name, the imperial censorate was responsible for evaluating the functioning of the system and the officials within it. It was composed of two chief censors and six branches (*lục khoa*) headed by senior supervisors. The censorate was considered to be an independent body that reported directly to the emperor.

CENTRAL HIGHLANDS (Tây Nguyên). Sparsely populated plateau and hill region north of the **Mekong River Delta**. Extending roughly from the 15th parallel to a point about 80 kilometers (50 miles) north of **Saigon**, it is composed of a total area of approximately 50,000 square kilometers (20,000 square miles). Most of the area consists of mountains ranging from 1,200 to 2,500 meters (4,000 to 8,000 feet) and is heavily forested. The majority of the inhabitants are **highland**

minorities, such as the **Rhadé** and the **Jarai**, who have traditionally supported themselves by **slash-and-burn** agriculture.

During the Vietnam War, the area was frequently the site of heavy fighting between revolutionary forces and **United States** and South Vietnamese troops. War planners in North Vietnam viewed the area as a strategically vital base area from which to attack lowland regions along the coast and in the **Mekong Delta**. The seizure of the Highlands by North Vietnamese forces in early 1975 was a major setback for the Saigon regime and represented the opening stage of the final victory in the South.

Since the end of the war and reunification, the Central Highlands region has undergone drastic changes, notably large-scale resettlement and free **migration** by lowland Vietnamese and other ethnic groups from different parts of the country, who are drawn by the availability of land and the chance to farm profitable crops like **coffee**. The demographic balance has shifted considerably, and there have been frequent tensions between settlers and the original inhabitants. Disputes over land rights and government restrictions on **Christianity** among the highlanders have led to several outbreaks of violence in recent years. *See also* BAJARAKA; FRONT UNIFIÉ POUR LA LIBÉRATION DES RACES OPPRIMÉES; HỒ CHÍ MINH CAMPAIGN.

CENTRAL OFFICE FOR SOUTH VIETNAM (COSVN, *Trung Ương Cục Miền Nam*). Headquarters unit for Communist revolutionary operations during the **Franco–Việt Minh War** and the Vietnam War. The office was first created in 1951 to serve as the command unit for **Việt Minh** operations in the South against the **French**, replacing the old **Committee of the South** (*Ủy Ban Nam Bộ*) that had been established at the end of World War II. In 1954, the office was abolished and replaced by a Regional Committee for the South (*Xứ Ủy Nam Bộ*) but was re-created in 1961 with the new upsurge in fighting.

COSVN was directly subordinated to the Central Committee of the Vietnamese Workers' Party (VWP) in **Hanoi**, and its top staffers, such as **Le Duẩn, Phạm Hùng**, and **Nguyễn Chí Thanh**, were leading figures in the VWP. COSVN was placed in charge of the Party's overall political and military operations in the South, and it was an important (though elusive) target of **United States** and **Army of the Republic of Vietnam** forces for much of the war. Below its central headquarters, which was located north of the Parrot's Beak inside **Cambodia**, were five regional party committees and a sixth for the **Saigon–Cholon** metropolitan area, as well as party committee and branch offices at the provincial, district, and village level. COSVN was abolished after the takeover of the South in 1975.

CERAMIC ARTS. The Vietnamese people have been shaping and baking the earth since Neolithic times. Archeologists have discovered early forms of earthenware in Vietnam that date back at least 10,000 years. Some were utilitarian and used for the holding of foods and liquids, while others were for religious or entertainment purposes. At first, they were shaped by hand and bore simple inscriptions made by the hand or a pointed stick. With the advent of the **Bronze Age** in the second millennium B.C.E. came the discovery of the potter's wheel. Decorative features also became more sophisticated, with the use of geometric designs or wavy lines, and quality was enhanced by the ability to fire objects at temperatures of over 1,000 degrees centigrade. Most of the pottery created during the Bronze Age was brownish in color and consisted of dishes, teapots, lamps, stoves, vases, and small figurines.

By the 10th century C.E., the quality of Vietnamese ceramics had improved markedly. White clay (kaolin) was fired at temperatures of over 1,800 degrees centigrade and then covered with an enamel glaze consisting of paddy husk or vegetable matter. Colors varied from brown to rice colored or a pale green similar to pieces produced during the Song era in **China**. New decorative techniques were discovered, including flowers, animals, and birds. By the 14th century, Vietnamese craftsmen had been introduced to cobalt oxide, which led to the growing popularity of blue-and-white (called by the Chinese Muslim blue) ceramic ware, first made famous by the Ming dynasty in China and eventually exported around the world. Although not as high in quality as the famous porcelains of China, Vietnamese ceramics had their own distinctive characteristics—notably the use of simple and free-flowing designs—and were prized throughout the region.

The **French** conquest in the late 19th century led to the decline of traditional ceramics and the rise of competing crafts such as lacquer-ware. Since reunification in 1976, the Vietnamese government has encouraged the revival of traditional pottery making, partly to obtain precious foreign currency through the **tourist** trade. In the process, several locations that once specialized in ceramic work, such as the **Hanoi** suburb of Bát Tràng, have resumed their activities.

CHAM. Descendants of the peoples who inhabited the kingdom or kingdoms of **Champa** in precolonial Southeast Asia who were gradually absorbed into the Vietnamese population through both peaceful expansion and warfare. The Cham speak a Malayo–Polynesian (**Austronesian**) language and have close ties to several ethnic groups in the **Central Highlands**, notably the **Jarai** or Gia Lai and **Rhadé** or Ê Đê. Their territory once stretched as far north as present-day Quảng Bình, but much of the Cham population was gradually **assimilated** by the Vietnamese. An estimated 50,000 Cham live in Vietnam today. Most are located along the central coast near the port cities of Nha Trang and Phan Rang and engage in fishing or rice farming; these Cham follow traditional beliefs (some of which have retained elements of earlier Brahmanistic practices) and/or a syncretic form of Islam. A second group living along the **Cambodian** border practices a more orthodox form of Islam.

CHAMPA. Kingdom(s) located on the central coast of Vietnam during the precolonial era, inhabited mainly by an ethnic group now called the **Cham**. The origins of Champa are generally linked to a small kingdom that appears in the **Chinese** records as **Linyi** (in Vietnamese, Lâm Ấp) in C.E. 192. Linyi is said to have been founded by rebellious elements living in the southernmost territories under Chinese rule—what is now northern central Vietnam. It broke away from Chinese control and, over the next few centuries, it absorbed Indian cultural influences moving across Southeast Asia, evolving into an Indianized polity known in Western languages as Champa. Much later, the Cham were exposed to Islam through their cultural and trade links with the Malay world, and many became Muslims, though often in a syncretic form.

After the Vietnamese became independent in the 10th century, Champa and Vietnam (then known as *Đại Việt*) became bitter rivals, with frequent border incursions and periodic full-fledged invasions by one or the other power. Vietnam gradually expanded southward with a series of acquisitions of Cham territory—occasionally peacefully but usually through warfare. Although Champa was not blessed with good agricultural land, it had a number of excellent trading ports, such as **Hội An**, which were attractive targets to the expanding Vietnamese polity. After an important territorial concession in the early 1400s, the rulers of Champa were forced to move their capital from **Indrapura** (Đồng Dương in present-day Quảng Nam) to **Vijaya**, farther south in what is now Bình Định. In 1471, Vijaya itself was captured by the Vietnamese. A small Cham kingdom survived under Vietnamese influence, though its territory continued to shrink. In the 19th century, the last remnant of Champa was formally absorbed by Vietnam.

Champa has traditionally been viewed as a single kingdom whose capital shifted among different locations up and down the coast. Recent revisionist scholarship has argued that several different polities coexisted and that one or another of them was dominant in particular periods of history. These scholars also contend that "Champa" was not merely a "Cham" entity, but that it included parts of the **Central Highlands** inhabited by other ethnic groups, some of whose leaders even took the throne in lowland power centers.

The territory of "Champa" originally stretched as far north as Quảng Bình province, but people still identifying themselves as "Cham" can only be found in the southern part of that territory. (Those living along the **Cambodian** border are descended from Cham who fled westward centuries earlier.) In much of central Vietnam, the Cham population was absorbed through intermarriage and cultural assimilation, but Cham influence can still be recognized in various ways—from music to architecture, dancing, and words in the Vietnamese language. *See also* MỸ SƠN.

CHANG FA-K'UEI. *See* ZHANG FAKUI.

CHINA. The proximity of the great neighbor China is probably the factor of greatest importance in the history of the state of Vietnam. In the second century B.C.E., much of what is now northern Vietnam was conquered by a Chinese army. For the next 1,000 years, the **Red**

River Delta and the region to its immediate south were incorporated into the Chinese Empire. During this **"Chinese period,"** the local Vietnamese culture was deeply influenced by various aspects of Chinese civilization, notably its belief system (**Buddhism, Daoism**, and **Confucianism**) and its language, as well as such basic habits as drinking tea and using chopsticks.

In 939 C.E., the Vietnamese took advantage of the collapse of the Tang dynasty to break away from northern rule, though they had to periodically mount fierce military campaigns to resist incursions from successive Chinese dynasties. The **Ming occupation** during the early 15th century—the only time when a northern invasion was successful for any significant length of time—provided another concentrated dose of Chinese influence, particularly in the form of neo-Confucianism. Even as an independent polity, Vietnam continued to borrow extensively from its powerful neighbor: political institutions, social values, literature, art, and music.

After the final **French** conquest of **Indochina** in the mid-1880s, the Qing dynasty was forced to renounce China's long tributary relationship with Vietnam. During World War II, General Chiang Kai-shek refused an offer by U.S. President Franklin D. Roosevelt to establish a postwar Chinese trusteeship in Vietnam in preparation for eventual independence, but Chinese occupation troops in northern Indochina at the close of the war intervened in Vietnamese politics to place pro-Chinese nationalist politicians in the cabinet of President **Hồ Chí Minh**.

The rise to power of the Communist Party in China was a boon to Hồ and his colleagues in their own war of national liberation. During the **Franco–Việt Minh War** and the later war in South Vietnam, the Vietnamese Communists received substantial aid and diplomatic support from China. However, China's refusal to risk a confrontation with the **United States**, and its attempts to influence Vietnamese war strategy, rankled in **Hanoi**, and after the close of the Vietnam War in 1975, relations rapidly deteriorated. Clashes along the common border and in the **South China Sea** added to the mutual hostility, as did the Vietnamese government's crackdown on the economically powerful Hoa (**overseas Chinese**) minority in the South after reunification. When Vietnamese troops invaded **Cambodia**—a country that China considered to be a friend at the time—Beijing responded in

February 1979 with a short but powerful punitive invasion of northern Vietnam.

During the next decade, Sino–Vietnamese relations were marked by bitterness and mutual distrust. With the collapse of the Union of Soviet Socialist Republics, however, Hanoi realized that it had no powerful sponsor to serve as a deterrent to Chinese intimidation and sought to improve relations. The two governments share a common distrust of Western countries and their alleged efforts to bring about the collapse of Communism and the emergence of **capitalist** systems throughout the world. The Vietnamese also see much to emulate in the Chinese Communist Party's efforts to promote economic growth without diluting its political control in a one-party system. Today, an influential faction within the Party leadership in Hanoi continues to look to China as a model and as a protector against the insistent interference of Western imperialism. Others, however, fear the emergence of a powerful and arrogant China that will seek to restore its traditional influence and domination over Vietnam and throughout Southeast Asia. A recent delineation of the land border that is alleged to have made excessive concessions to China has been criticized in Vietnam, and overlapping claims to maritime territories remain a potential source of conflict.

The relationship between China and Vietnam over the past millennium has been fraught with ambiguities, tensions, and not a few ironies. Since winning their independence in the 10th century, the Vietnamese have always asserted their identity as a separate country with its own culture and customs, often in terms of a "North–South" dichotomy. Yet these assertions have often been articulated in standard classical Chinese in texts laced with impeccably orthodox references to Chinese history and culture. Precolonial Vietnamese rulers borrowed heavily from the Chinese imperial system, both its ideology and its structure. Equally importantly, they borrowed Chinese standards of what was "civilized" or "cultured" and worked hard to maintain these standards, especially in the eyes of their northern neighbors. The Vietnamese ruling class resented being labeled as "barbarians" by the Chinese and struggled to minimize their obligations as a "vassal," yet they tended to view and treat their own neighbors (notably the **Cham**, **Cambodians**, and **Lao**) in precisely these terms. Some Vietnamese scholars are uneasy with the legacy of Sinicization and have attempted to downplay the Chinese impact on their culture and emphasize instead the success of alleged efforts to resist "assimilation" in earlier centuries. *See also* FOREIGN RELATIONS.

CHINESE PERIOD (*BẮC THUỘC*). The "Chinese period" in Vietnamese history, which lasted from the second century B.C.E. through the early 10th century C.E., was a formative period for the ethnic Vietnamese and their culture. **China**'s power during this millennium of foreign rule waxed and waned according to the strength or weakness of successive dynasties, but the influence of Chinese culture endured. The Vietnamese were exposed to **Confucianism, Buddhism**, and **Daoism**, all of which became a permanent part of their worldview to varying degrees. Chinese characters were adopted as the main writing system, and many borrowed words entered the Vietnamese language. The territory pacified by the Chinese came to constitute the borders of an independent Vietnam after the defeat at **Bạch Đằng** in 938. Present-day Vietnamese historians generally imagine a Vietnamese nation that was conquered by the Chinese and then re-emerged intact during the 10th century, but this perspective underestimates the extent to which the Chinese period was actually responsible for creating the foundations of a future Vietnam.

The dating of the exact beginning of the "Chinese period" has varied. Generally speaking, it was traditionally marked by the invasion of Han dynasty troops in the late second century B.C.E. Scholars linked to the Communist Party, however, have tended to push it back to the beginning of the century with the expansion of the kingdom of Nanyue or **Nam Việt** under the Chinese ruler Zhao Tuo or **Triệu Đà**. Most premodern Vietnamese sources considered him a "Vietnamese emperor," but recent nationalistic scholarship has labeled him a "Chinese aggressor."

CHINH PHỤ NGÂM (*Lament of a Soldier's Wife*). Famous poem written in 18th-century Vietnam. Composed in literary Chinese by Đặng Trần Côn, it was translated into colloquial Vietnamese (written in *chữ nôm*) by the poetess **Đoàn Thị Điểm**.

CHOLON (Chợ Lớn). Commercial "Chinatown" of Hồ Chí Minh City (previously known as *Saigon*). Cholon (literally "great market") originally developed as a market city inhabited primarily by **overseas Chinese** and adjacent to the citadel, which was located in what is today downtown Hồ Chí Minh City. During the Vietnam War, the population was estimated at approximately 800,000 and was noted for its restaurants, markets, and gambling establishments.

CHRISTIANITY. The Christian religion was introduced into Vietnam in the 16th century by Catholic missionaries from **France**, Portugal, and Spain. Eventually, the French became the most active through the Paris-based **Société des Missions Étrangères**, founded in 1664. Despite growing efforts to repress missionary activities by the Vietnamese authorities, the Society won many converts, and by 1700 several hundred thousand Christians lived in Vietnam. Official policy in both Vietnamese kingdoms during this period alternated between tolerance and persecution, partly depending on the whims of a particular ruler. Under some of the **Nguyễn Lords**, for example, foreign Jesuits could be found playing various roles in the royal court, as was the case in **China**. During this time, Christianity was opposed on moral and ideological grounds, meaning that it was viewed as "heterodox" in **Confucian** terms.

By the 1830s, however, the situation had changed considerably, as French missionaries in Vietnam were increasingly seen as a political threat, a perspective validated by pressure from successive French governments to allow more freedom of religion and by several incidents of gunboat diplomacy on the missionaries' behalf. Lobbying by religious interests in France also became a key factor in the drive to colonize Vietnam. After the French conquest, colonial authorities, to some extent, tolerated or even encouraged missionary efforts in the conviction that this would promote the acceptance of French rule, but many officials were free thinkers or Freemasons who had little sympathy for missionaries or the church. Some Vietnamese did convert and become collaborators with the new regime, but the bulk of the Catholic community had existed long before colonization, and there was no large-scale conversion comparable to what occurred in the Philippines or Latin America.

The Catholic community, which numbered over two million, became an important force in commerce, education, the professions, and the bureaucracy. After World War II, some Catholics supported the **Việt Minh** Front in its struggle against the French, but many distrusted the movement's Communist orientation and eventually supported the **Bảo Đại** government, formed in 1949. After the **Geneva Conference** of 1954, over 600,000 Catholics fled to the South to avoid Communist rule.

During the Vietnam War, the Catholic community in the South became a major bulwark of the **Saigon** regime in its struggle against the insurgency. Catholics were disproportionately represented among the military and civilian leadership. Relations between Catholics and **Buddhists** grew tense during the last years of the **Ngô Đình Diệm** regime, but the problem subsided somewhat under **Nguyễn Văn Thiệu**. This period also saw significant growth in the number of Protestants in South Vietnam, among both the lowland majority and the minorities of the **Central Highlands**. Government toleration of Christianity opened the door for evangelism work by foreign missionaries, and there was cooperation with the Ministry of Education to produce literacy materials and school texts in minority languages.

Since reunification, Catholics and Protestants alike have faced problems, especially those from the former South Vietnam, whose religious activities have been significantly curtailed. The Constitution of the **Socialist Republic of Vietnam** (SRV) promises freedom of religion, and there are officially recognized Catholic and Protestant Churches. However, the regime remains suspicious of the loyalty of many Christians, particularly Protestants because of their earlier ties to American missionaries. Several Vietnamese priests, nuns, and pastors have been arrested on various charges. Christian communities in the highland areas (including recent converts among the Hmong in the North) have been particularly targeted, driving many believers into underground or house churches. *See also* GIA LONG; PIGNEAU DE BEHAINE; RHODES, ALEXANDER OF.

CHU LAI (1946–). Popular novelist in contemporary Vietnam. Born in a literary family in Hải Hưng province in northern Vietnam, he has focused much of his recent writing on the difficulties of readjustment for war veterans on their return from combat. His treatment of the subject is often quite powerful, vividly portraying the growing problems of drugs and alcoholism in Vietnamese society. His novel *Soldiers' Tenements* (*Phố Nhà Binh*) was awarded the Hanoi Prize for Literature in 1994; it gives a critical view of the transition to a market economy and its impact on veterans and their families. *See also* LITERATURE.

CHỮ NÔM **("Demotic characters").** Adaptation of Chinese written characters widely used as a written form of the **Vietnamese language** in traditional Vietnam. The origins of *chữ nôm* (often called simply *nôm*) are obscure. During the long period of **Chinese** rule, all official communications and many literary works were written in literary Chinese. *Chữ nôm* probably came into use by the late eighth or early ninth centuries, although the earliest surviving examples date from the late 13th century, and was devised to provide a way to transcribe spoken Vietnamese, particularly for non-Chinese forms of poetry and other vernacular **literature**. Because many Vietnamese words had not been borrowed from Chinese, special characters had to be invented that combined elements providing meaning and phonetic value, similar to the use of special "Cantonese characters" in Hong Kong. The character *nôm* itself combined the Chinese characters for "south" and "mouth."

Until the late traditional period, *nôm* was scorned by many bureaucrats and court figures as vulgar. A few such noted writers as **Nguyễn Trãi** and **Nguyễn Bỉnh Khiêm** favored it, however. By the 18th century, it had become an accepted medium for the writing of Vietnamese verse novels. The most famous literary work written in *nôm* was **Nguyễn Du**'s *Truyện Kiều* (**Tale of Kiều**). **Nguyễn Huệ**, leader of the short-lived **Tây Sơn** dynasty, prescribed it for use by the bureaucracy, possibly for patriotic reasons, but the more orthodox **Nguyễn dynasty** (1802–1945) returned to literary Chinese. Its use eventually declined under **French** rule with the rising popularity of *quốc ngữ* ("national language"), a transliteration of spoken Vietnamese based on the Roman alphabet. *See also* SINO–VIETNAMESE.

CHU VĂN AN (?–1370). Influential scholar-official during the **Trần dynasty** in 14th-century Vietnam. A famous **Confucian** scholar and writer, Chu Văn An was selected by Emperor **Trần Minh Tông** as tutor for his son, the future ruler **Dụ Tông**. When the latter became Emperor, An appealed to him to get rid of several corrupt mandarins in the imperial administration; when the appeal was refused, An followed the classical practice of Confucian scholar-officials in **China** and resigned from office.

CHU VĂN TẤN (1908–). Veteran revolutionary leader and ranking military officer. Born in a peasant family of **Nùng** ethnic background in Thái Nguyên, Chu Văn Tấn attended the Whampoa Academy in Canton and joined the **Indochinese Communist Party** (ICP) in the early 1930s. In 1940, he took part in the abortive **Bắc Sơn Uprising** along the Chinese border. When the rebel units were defeated by combined **French** and **Japanese** forces, Chu Văn Tấn reorganized the remnants of the rebel bands into the so-called **Army of National Salvation** (*Cứu Quốc Quân*) and continued resistance activities in the **Việt Bắc** region throughout the war, becoming deputy commander of the Vietnamese Liberation Army (later the **People's Army of Vietnam**) after its formation in December 1944.

Chu Văn Tấn rose rapidly in the ranks of the ICP after the war and became a member of the Central Committee and the newly formed Revolutionary Military Committee in 1945. In 1960, he was named secretary of the Regional Bureau of the Party and commander in chief of military forces in the Việt Bắc. He also held a number of civilian positions in the government, including that of vice-president of the Standing Committee of the **National Assembly**.

After the end of the Vietnam War, Chu Văn Tấn's role declined, possibly because of suspicion of dissent from the regime's **China** policy. In 1976, he was dropped from the Central Committee, although he retained his government positions until 1979, when he was reportedly confined to house arrest.

CIVIL OPERATIONS AND REVOLUTIONARY DEVELOP- MENT SUPPORT (CORDS). *See* KOMER, ROBERT W.

*CLOCHE FÊLÉE, LA (**The Cracked Bell**).* Short-lived newspaper in colonial **Indochina**. The weekly periodical was founded in **Saigon** by the political reformer **Nguyễn An Ninh** in 1923. It had no specific ideological point of view but was outspokenly critical of many policies of the **French** colonial regime and was forced to close its doors two years later, by order of the governor of **Cochin China**. The meaning of the paper's name has never been satisfactorily explained, although some have speculated that it referred to Vietnam's state of dependency, or the author's declaration of his own lack of talent. *See also* JOURNALISM.

CLUB OF FORMER RESISTANCE FIGHTERS (*Câu Lạc Bộ Kháng Chiến Cũ*). Organization created in 1986 to seek reforms and a greater degree of **pluralism** within the Vietnamese political system. The headquarters of the organization was in Hồ Chí Minh City, and a number of prestigious Party war veterans, including **People's Liberation Armed Forces** commander **Trần Văn Trà**, were among the 4,000 members. The organization's criticism of the Party and the regime eventually aroused concern in **Hanoi**, and it was suppressed in the early 1990s after government attempts to manipulate its leadership. *See also* DISSIDENTS.

CỔ LOA. Ancient capital of the kingdom of **Âu Lạc** and major **archeological** site. In the mid-third century B.C.E., King **An Dương Vương** built a massive citadel to protect his new kingdom from its internal and external enemies. (According to legend, the local spirits were mobilized to resist him under the leadership of a giant chicken, but he defeated them with the aid of a magic crossbow made from the claw of a friendly turtle.) The citadel was called *Cổ Loa Thành*, or "old snail city," from the fact that it was composed of a series of three concentric spiraling earth ramparts to protect the inner citadel. The outer wall was eight kilometers (five miles) long and averaged four to five meters (13 to 16 feet) in height. The wall was six to 12 meters (19 to 35 feet) thick at the top, wide enough for chariot traffic, and was protected by a bamboo fence and a moat beyond it. Mounds and hills in the surrounding countryside provided a further natural defense work. During the **Chinese period**, Cổ Loa ceased to be the administrative center, but in C.E. 939, **Ngô Quyền**, the first independent Vietnamese ruler, placed his capital there; it was later relocated to **Hoa Lư**.

CƠ MẬT VIỆN (Privy Council). First council of state in the Vietnamese Empire. It was set up by Emperor **Minh Mạng** in 1834 on the pattern of a **Chinese** institution called the *Junjichu* (Military Plans Department, usually known as the *Grand Council*) during the

Qing dynasty. Composed of a few ministers drawn from such positions as board presidents, grand secretaries, high military officials, and members of the royal family, the Privy Council functioned as a confidential advisory board to assist the emperor in dealing with issues of grand strategy. It was composed of "northern" and "southern" sections that were responsible for issues dealing with the northern and southern provinces of the empire. In terms of foreign affairs, the northern section was responsible for China, the southern for relations with other Southeast Asian countries. The Cơ Mật was maintained under colonial rule but was stripped of any decision-making power independent of **French** authority.

COAL. One of the chief sources of energy in modern Vietnam. Substantial coal reserves, estimated at billions of tons, are located along the **Tonkin Gulf** northeast of the harbor port of **Hải Phòng**. During the colonial era, coal was a prime source of domestic energy use and export earnings, and by 1939 over two million tons of coal were extracted annually. Coal continued to be a major source of domestic energy use after the **Geneva Conference** and reached an output of over four million tons at the end of the Vietnam War. Since 1975, the Vietnamese government has sought to modernize coal-extraction equipment in the area. Production remained relatively stagnant for some time but began to increase significantly in the 1990s, rising from 5.9 million metric tons (6.5 million tons) in 1994 and 1995 to 18 million metric tons (19.8 million tons) in 2003, of which 35 percent was exported. *See also* ENERGY RESOURCES.

COCHIN CHINA. This name has been used in different ways at different times in Vietnamese history. During the 17th and 18th centuries, it referred to the autonomous kingdom ruled by the **Nguyễn Lords** that extended southward from the area just north of the present-day province of Quảng Trị. This region, known as *Đàng Trong* or *Nam Hà* to the Vietnamese, was generally called *Cochin China* by foreigners, whereas the kingdom to the north was referred to as *Tonkin*. The origins of the name itself are unclear, although a strong case has been made that "Cochin" is a corruption of the name *Giao Chỉ* (Chinese *Jiaozhi*), an early name for Vietnam. The "China" would then have been added to distinguish it from Cochin in India, since many early sources outside the region included the area of Vietnam in what they designated as "China."

Under **French** rule, *Cochin China* referred specifically to six provinces in the area of the **Mekong River Delta**, the region known in Vietnamese as *Nam Bộ* or *Nam Kỳ*. These provinces were seized by the French in a series of military campaigns between 1859 and 1867 and were formally ceded in the 1862 **Treaty of Saigon** and the 1874 **Treaty of Protectorate**. Cochin China was a colony under direct French rule, as opposed to the **protectorates** of **Annam** and Tonkin. After World War II, Cochin China was excluded from the new "free state" envisaged by the **Ho-Sainteny Agreement** reached in March 1946. Under the sponsorship of High Commissioner **Thierry d'Argenlieu**, native elements set up a separate **Republic of Cochin China** and requested membership in the **French Union**. In 1949, Cochin China was joined with Annam and Tonkin in the new **State of Vietnam**.

COFFEE. Since the colonial era, coffee has been a lucrative cash crop in Vietnam, with most coffee plantations being established in the **Central Highlands**. Exports went mainly to **France**. Coffee production declined significantly, however, during the long Vietnam War. After reunification in 1976, government leaders in **Hanoi** began to consider ways to promote the cultivation of coffee as a lucrative export earner, and in 1982 a state-owned Coffee Corporation was established at **Buôn Mê Thuột**, the largest city in the Central Highlands, at a time when about 5,000 hectares (12,300 acres) were under cultivation in the region.

Vietnam initially experienced a number of problems in promoting coffee exports, including a reputation for poor quality and a habit of defaulting on contracts, but in recent years it has made great headway in marketing its coffee overseas. Coffee cultivation has shot up dramatically, and the product has become one of the Vietnam's most successful cash crops, threatening to displace **rice** as the country's primary export earner. By growing year 2000–2001, 500,000 hectares (1,230,000 acres) of land were devoted to coffee production, and output that year reached 900,000 metric tons (990,000 tons), nearly all of which was exported. This figure subsequently dropped because of a global slump in prices, but in 2004 both prices and production climbed again, and exports once again topped 800,000 metric tons (880,000 tons). The coffee boom has been very much a mixed blessing for farmers who have rushed to plant coffee and then found themselves vulnerable to world market fluctuations, while the influx of **migrants** to the Central Highlands has caused considerable socioeconomic disruption.

CỞI MỞ. *See* ***ĐỔI MỚI.***

COLBY, WILLIAM (1920–1996). Station chief of the United States Central Intelligence Agency in **Saigon** during the late 1950s and early 1960s. A strong supporter of a political rather than a military approach to the war, Colby was an advocate of the pacification program and, in 1968, was named deputy director of the program of Civil Operations and Revolutionary Development Support (CORDS). He later served as director of the Phoenix Program, the objective of which was to assist Saigon's security forces in eliminating the Communist infrastructure in South Vietnam. He was named director of Central Intelligence during the Richard M. Nixon administration. *See also* KOMER, ROBERT W.; REPUBLIC OF VIETNAM.

COLLECTIVIZATION OF AGRICULTURE. For Communist leaders in the **Democratic Republic of Vietnam** (DRV), the socialist transformation of **agriculture** went through two major stages. The first stage was that of **land reform**. Beginning in the early 1950s, land belonging to the landlord class in areas controlled by the **Việt Minh** Front was redistributed to the poor. The program continued after the Party's return to **Hanoi** in 1954 and concluded in the North two years later.

The second stage, that of the collectivization of agriculture, began in 1958, with the creation of small semisocialist cooperatives (known formally as agricultural producers' cooperatives, or *nông nghiệp sản xuất hợp tác xã*) throughout the northern countryside. By 1960, over 80 percent of all farm families in the DRV were enrolled in cooperative organizations averaging fewer than 100 farm families each. During the next several years, the cooperatives increased in size (from 150 to 200 farm families) and in the level of socialist ownership. The impact of collectivization on food production, however, was disappointing, partially because there was often subtle resistance to its full implementation. Throughout the remainder of the war, the DRV was forced to rely on food imports to feed its population.

After reunification in 1975, the Hanoi regime decided to delay the building of collectives in the southern countryside in an effort to encourage an increase in grain production. The program was launched in the winter of 1977–1978, when peasants in the South were encouraged to join various types of low-level cooperative organizations (most common were so-called **production collectives** and **production solidarity teams**). Although the program was classified as voluntary, official press reports conceded that coercion was often involved at the local level, and many private farmers resisted joining the new organizations. In the early 1980s, the campaign was continued, but at a slower pace of development. In late 1986, the regime asserted that collectivization in the South had been completed "in the main," with most farmers enrolled in organizations at the semisocialist level—though this was a doubtful claim.

With the inauguration of the contract system (*khoán sản phẩm*) in the 1980s and the broader move away from orthodox socialism, the primary function of the cooperatives has been abolished, and they exist mainly as an administrative level between the farmer and the state. Although the state continues to retain ultimate ownership over the land, the extension of **land usage rights** to 20 years, with the right of inheritance and purchase or sale, has encouraged farmers to make improvements and increase the productivity of their plots. *See also* COMMUNISM.

COLLINS, J. LAWTON (1896–1987). General in the United States Army and special envoy to **Republic of Vietnam** in 1954–1955. In the fall of 1954, President Dwight D. Eisenhower sent General Collins to **Saigon** to assess the new government led by Prime Minister **Ngô Đình Diệm**. General Collins developed serious doubts as to whether Diệm was capable of handling the challenge, but the administration decided to give Diệm its full backing.

COLONIAL COUNCIL (*Conseil Colonial*). Administrative council set up by the **French** in the colony of **Cochin China** in 1880. Dominated by French colonial elements—although it did have six Vietnamese representatives chosen from wealthy natives sympathetic to the French regime—its primary function was to institute the colony's budget. Later its Vietnamese representation was increased to 10, elected by a constituency of 22,000 voters.

COLONIZATION. The **French** colonization of Vietnam spanned a period of several decades. After several abortive episodes of gunboat diplomacy in the 1840s and 1850s, intended to push for religious freedom in Vietnam (and, incidentally, open the door to French influence there), the French launched a serious military expedition in 1858. Although the effort to capture **Đà Nẵng** (Tourane) was ultimately unsuccessful, the French forces then moved southward to capture the port of **Saigon** in 1859 and three adjacent provinces two years later. The Vietnamese cession of this territory to France was confirmed in the 1862 **Treaty of Saigon**. In order to ensure security for the territory they possessed and to expand the size of the colony, the French seized the remainder of the **Mekong Delta** in 1867, though their possession of these new provinces was not formally recognized until the **Philastre Treaty** of 1874.

By the 1870s, the French had realized that the **Mekong River**—long viewed as a potential access route to China—was not going to meet their expectations, and their interest turned to the **Red River** instead. Although the adventurism of **Jean Dupuis** and **Francis Garnier** in 1873 failed to create a French presence in northern Vietnam, the Philastre Treaty the following year did open **Hanoi** and several ports to French trade and established a preliminary and rather sketchy **protectorate** over Vietnam. In the early 1880s, French forces began a conquest of the remaining Vietnamese territory, leading to the full and final loss of the country's independence through the **Patenôtre Treaty** of 1884. Pacification of the newly occupied territory took several years, but by roughly 1895 the French were fully in control.

COMINTERN (Communist International). Revolutionary organization established in Soviet Russia in 1919. For over two decades, the Comintern, with its headquarters in Moscow, directed the activities and revolutionary strategy of the Vietnamese **Communist** movement. Dozens of Vietnamese revolutionaries, including **Hồ Chí**

Minh, Trần Văn Giàu, Hà Huy Tập, **Lê Hồng Phong,** and **Trần Phú,** were trained at the organization's famous Stalin School in Moscow. The Comintern assistance and financial support were undoubtedly beneficial to the **Indochinese Communist Party** in many ways, but its advice was not always helpful. During the 1930s, Comintern strategy emphasized class struggle over national independence and urban over rural revolution. Such ideas had little relevance in Indochina and were abandoned by Hồ with the formation of the **Việt Minh** Front in 1941. The Comintern was abolished in 1943 as part of Stalin's effort to improve relations with his wartime ally, the **United States.** *See also* UNION OF SOVIET SOCIALIST REPUBLICS.

COMMISSION ON COCHIN-CHINA. *See* BRENIER COMMISSION.

COMMITTEE OF THE SOUTH (*Ủy Ban Nam Bộ*). Committee set up by the **Indochinese Communist Party** (ICP) and non-Communist nationalist parties in **Saigon** at the end of World War II. The Committee was established on 23 August 1945 as nationalist forces seized power in Saigon shortly after the surrender of **Japan,** and was designed as a means to achieve the cooperation of various anticolonial groups in seeking Vietnamese independence at the close of the war. At first, the Committee was dominated by the **Việt Minh,** the front organization of the ICP; six of its nine members were delegates from the Việt Minh, and the ICP leader **Trần Văn Giàu** was the chairman. General **Douglas Gracey,** commander of the British expeditionary forces that began to arrive in October, refused to recognize the Committee and, after riots and demonstrations broke out in Saigon, assisted the **French** in driving nationalist forces out of the city. The Committee fled from Saigon on 23 September and attempted to organize resistance in rural areas. Negotiations to find a solution were carried on throughout the remainder of the year and resulted in a preliminary agreement between **Hồ Chí Minh** and French representative **Jean Sainteny** in March 1946. *See also* AUGUST REVOLUTION; HO-SAINTENY AGREEMENT.

COMMUNAL LAND (*Công điền*). Land belonging to the **village** in traditional Vietnam. The land was managed by the village administration and periodically distributed to poor families for their temporary use. Sometimes, however, the **Council of Elders** (the leading administrative body at the village level) would permit communal land to be occupied and exploited by wealthy elements.

The concept of communal land might have been the normal form of land ownership in Vietnam prior to the **Chinese** conquest in the second century B.C.E. After Vietnamese independence in the 10th century, as much as one-third to one-half of all village land was under communal ownership. The system was frequently abused, however, as wealthy landowners often confiscated the land for their own use, a practice that was occasionally restricted by the imperial government but was often beyond the latter's control. The system gradually declined under **French** colonial rule, when landlordism and large **agricultural** concessions to individuals became commonplace. For some Marxist scholars, the significance of communal land in premodern Vietnam has been one argument in favor of the relevance of the **Asiatic Mode of Production** model to the country's history.

COMMUNISM. Communism in Vietnam has a complicated history. Originally seized upon by Nguyễn Ái Quốc (the future **Hồ Chí Minh**) and other radical intellectuals as the best tool to liberate Indochina from colonial rule, it took root among Vietnamese workers and peasants in the 1930s and remained strong despite harsh persecution from the **French**. The **Indochinese Communist Party**, founded in 1930, experienced both successes and failures over the first decade of its existence. It also suffered from internal divisions caused partly by twists and turns in **Comintern** policy coming from Moscow, particularly in terms of the relationship between the objectives of national liberation, on the one hand, and class-oriented social revolution on the other. Hồ and the group of leaders close to him sought to balance these two objectives in the struggle against the French; he was also particularly skilled at articulating revolutionary principles in a Vietnamese context, often with traditional Confucian terminology.

Yet the balance between class struggle and anticolonial nationalism within Vietnamese Communism was not easily maintained. Even during the years between the **August Revolution** of 1945 and the final withdrawal of the French in 1954, the Party fluctuated between the need to gather a wide spectrum of political and social elements under its banner through the united front strategy and the need to move toward a more egalitarian society through measures (such as **land reform**) that would inevitably target some of those elements who supported the anticolonial struggle. After 1954, the **Democratic Republic of Vietnam** moved quickly along the path of agricultural **collectivization**, following the examples of the **Union of Soviet Socialist Republics** and **China**. This process of "building socialism" was more or less tolerated by the peasantry during the anti-American struggle, but once the war was over, the consensus on socialism, particularly in **agriculture**, gradually broke down. Nor was the Party successful in implanting socialism in the former South Vietnam.

The reforms that began in the 1980s (known collectively as *đổi mới*), have to a large extent represented a long, slow dismantling of the socialist system, particularly in terms of the **economy**. Yet in order to legitimate the continued existence of a state dominated by a single Communist Party, the latter must continue to give lip service to Marxism–Leninism and to affirm that "socialism" remains the ultimate goal for Vietnam. Since Vietnam's final disentanglement from **Cambodia** around 1990 and the stabilization of its relations with China and the **United States**, the existing external threats to its security have significantly diminished. In the past, Communism in Vietnam was generally synthesized with—and sometimes subordinated to—nationalism in the context of a struggle against a common enemy. When there is no longer a foreign enemy to fight, Communism has had to stand more or less on its own as an ideology and as a system; its ability to do so over the long run will have direct consequences for the survival of the one-Party regime. *See also* INDOCHINESE COMMUNIST PARTY; VIETNAMESE COMMUNIST PARTY.

CÔN ĐẢO ISLANDS. Group of 14 islands located southeast of Vũng Tàu in the **South China Sea**. The hilly islands (the highest attains a height of 577 meters or 1,875 feet) had no permanent inhabitants during the precolonial period, but the British seized them in 1702 to prevent occupation by the **French**. The British departed after a mutiny by the local garrison and the islands were eventually claimed by

France as part of **Indochina**. The largest island in the group, Côn Sơn (**Poulo Condore**), was used by the French, and later by the government of South Vietnam, as a prison. Today, the islands have been transformed into a national park, with a total population of about 1,000 persons.

CONFUCIANISM (*Nho Giáo*). Confucianism has been an important force in Vietnamese society since the time of the **Chinese** conquest in the second century B.C.E. Introduced during the **Chinese period**, it gradually developed into the foundation for much of Vietnamese society, including its political institutions, its worldview, its educational system, its system of ethics, and even its form of family organization.

After Vietnamese independence in the 10th century C.E., Confucianism shared influence at court with **Buddhism** and **Daoism** (the so-called *tam giáo* [Ch. *sanjiao*] or "three doctrines"), also introduced from China. In the late 15th century, following the **Ming occupation**, however, Confucian doctrine became dominant at court during the reign of Emperor **Lê Thánh Tông**. From that point, it permeated the entire educated class of the country through the civil service **examination system**, the training ground of the Vietnamese **mandarinate**. Through the **scholar-gentry** class, Confucian ethics and social values, emphasizing the virtues of hierarchy, obedience, filial piety, and benevolence, gradually permeated **village** life and the minds of the Vietnamese people.

Just how much Confucian values affected the lives of the average Vietnamese is a matter of debate. Throughout the traditional period, a popular counterculture emphasizing indigenous themes and ridiculing the pomposity, pedantry, and hypocrisy of Confucian orthodoxy coexisted with official doctrine and won adherents from intellectuals and peasants alike. Still, there is no doubt that Confucianism remained the dominant ideology at court and within the bureaucracy and—through the scholar-gentry class—Confucian ethics and social values undoubtedly became a major force in village life as well. During the **Nguyễn dynasty** in the 19th century, the court actively promoted Confucian orthodoxy as the guiding doctrine of the state.

French **colonization** in the late 19th century brought an end to the ideological dominance of Confucianism in Vietnam. Under colonial rule, Western cultural values partially—though not completely—replaced those of the Sino–Vietnamese heritage. Confucianism retained a ritualistic role at the court in **Huế** and a residual half-life among conservative scholar-gentry at the village level. In the 1950s, President **Ngô Đình Diệm** attempted to revive Confucian values through the medium of his philosophy of **Personalism** in the **Republic of Vietnam**, but his efforts bore little fruit and disappeared with his death in 1963.

Still, it would be erroneous to assume that Confucian values and attitudes have disappeared. Even in contemporary Vietnam, Confucian attitudes intermingle with official Marxist–Leninist doctrine within the bureaucracy, even though Party leaders have railed against the "feudalistic" attitudes still prevalent at the village level. **Hồ Chí Minh** himself was adept at incorporating Confucian values and terminology into his revolutionary speeches and writings, a fact that is widely recognized by Marxist scholars. There has also been a rekindling of interest in Confucianism as part of the wider debate on "Asian values" and their contribution to the growth and prosperity of some Asian economies.

CÔNG THẦN. The *công thần*, or "meritorious subjects," were a group of men who supported **Lê Lợi** (the future Emperor Lê Thái Tổ) in his resistance to the **Ming occupation** of Vietnam in the early 15th century. Once he became emperor, he gave a number of rewards and privileges to these followers, some of whom were his family members and others of whom were allowed to take his family name as a sign of honor. These *công thần* came to constitute an important group during the early years of the **Lê dynasty**, and their children and grandchildren were exempted from *corvée* labor and military service.

The *công thần* soon became a faction or clique within the government, and the reign of Lê Lợi's son and successor **Thái Tông** saw a period of rivalry and conflict between those officials who had been his father's comrades-in-arms and a rising class of scholars whose numbers grew larger with implementation of regular examinations to select mandarins. Even under Lê Lợi, rivals had begun to denounce each other plotting revolt, and several loyal *công thần* were executed. The factional strife between the two groups is also believed to have been responsible for accusations of regicide against **Nguyễn Trãi** after Thái Tông's mysterious death in 1442. As Lê Lợi's followers died off, however, the new generation of scholar-officials came to dominate the court and the government.

CONSEIL SUPÉRIEUR DE L'INDOCHINE (Supreme Council of Indochina). Originally established by the governor-general of **Indochina** as an advisory body in creating the annual budget, the council later took on additional advisory responsibilities, and in 1928 Governor General **Pierre Pasquier** transformed it into the *Grand Conseil des Intérêts Économiques et Financiers de l'Indochine* (Great Council of Economic and Financial Interests in Indochina). It was abolished after World War II. *See also* FRANCE.

CONSTITUTIONALIST PARTY. Informal political organization set up in 1917 by moderate reformist elements around **Bùi Quang Chiêu**, editor of *La Tribune Indigène* and its successor *La Tribune Indochinoise*. Key concerns of the party were an expansion of representative government, equal pay for equal work in the colonial bureaucracy, and a greater role for Vietnamese in the local manufacturing and commercial economy. During the mid-1920s, the party briefly took an active role in demanding changes in French colonial policy, but many members were shocked by the violent measures adopted by anticolonial elements and, during the 1930s, it played a steadily declining role in Vietnamese politics. Both the desiderata of its white-collar membership and their generally conservative stance on social and political issues made them increasingly marginalized as the strength of more radical groups grew. *See also* NGUYỄN PHAN LONG.

CONSTITUTIONS. After the end of French colonial rule in 1954, there were two *de facto* independent governments in Vietnam, the **Republic of Vietnam** (the successor of the **State of Vietnam** set up by the French in 1949), and the **Democratic Republic of Vietnam** (DRV), first created in 1945 and renamed the **Socialist Republic of Vietnam** (SRV) in 1976. The Republic of Vietnam had two constitutions, the first promulgated by the regime of **Ngô Đình Diệm** in 1956 and the second by the regime of **Nguyễn Văn Thiệu** in 1967. Al-

though substantive differences were evident between the two constitutions, they were both based on a combination of the presidential
and the parliamentary models practiced in the West, and both paid
lip service to the concept of **pluralism** without actually putting it into
practice.

The Democratic Republic of Vietnam and its successor, the SRV,
have had four constitutions, promulgated in 1946, 1959, 1980, and
1992. The most recent version takes into account changes that had
taken place since the inauguration of the program of renovation (*đổi
mới*) six years before. Under the revised charter, references to
Marxist–Leninist principles were deleted, and the "proletarian dictatorship" was replaced by a "State of the people, from the people and
for the people," but the **Vietnamese Communist Party** remained as
"the force leading the State and society."

All the DRV and SRV constitutions have been Marxist–Leninist
in inspiration, combining elements of the Western liberal democratic
model with the Leninist concept of a dominant Communist Party ruling through the dictatorship of the proletariat. As with other **Communist** systems, each constitution was designed to reflect the state
of society at a particular stage of its development, from the national
democratic stage in 1946 to the beginnings of socialist transformation in 1959 to the effort to complete the socialization process in the
1980s. Another consistent feature is that constitutional rights and
freedoms are subordinated to specific laws rather than the law being
subordinated to the constitution.

CONTINENTAL HOTEL. Colonial-style hotel built in the early 20th
century on Rue Catinat (today, Đồng Khởi Street) in downtown **Saigon**. During the colonial era, the veranda of the hotel was a favorite
watering spot for **French** expatriates and other affluent residents of
the city. At the end of the **Franco–Việt Minh War**, it became the
scene for a number of incidents in the acclaimed novel *The Quiet
American* by the English novelist Graham Greene. During the American era, it was somewhat overshadowed by the nearby Caravelle
Hotel, popular with foreign journalists, and the Majestic Hotel, located on the Saigon River. Left unused for many years after the end
of the Vietnam War, the Continental has now been renovated for the
tourist trade. *See also* ARCHITECTURE.

CONVENTION OF 1925. Political convention signed between the French colonial government and the regency council of Vietnam after the death of Emperor **Khải Định** in 1925. According to the convention, the regency council for the new emperor, the young **Bảo Đại**, would meet under the presidency of the French *résident supérieur* in **Annam**. Virtually all political and judiciary power was placed in the hands of the latter, and only ritual functions were left as the prerogative of the emperor. The convention was abolished on September 1932 on the return of 19-year-old Bảo Đại from schooling in France, but at the time it was viewed by many as the final step in the French efforts to strip the "protected" **monarchy** of its power. *See also* PASQUIER, PIERRE; PROTECTORATE.

CORRUPTION. Corruption, graft and abuses of power are not new phenomena in Vietnam. The precolonial state, despite its promotion of "virtue," "incorruptibility," and other **Confucian** values, was constantly plagued by these problems within the **mandarinate**, especially at the lower levels, where salaries were smaller, supervision weaker, and opportunities for self-enrichment more frequent. The existence of the imperial **censorate** alleviated some of the potential for corruption, but certainly not all of it. After **colonization**, the old problems persisted, both under the **protectorates** of **Annam** and **Tonkin**, which preserved the mandarinate more or less intact, and in **Cochin China**, where **French** restructuring of the administration did not remove temptations for local officials to misuse their positions.

Between 1954 and 1975, the war in the **Republic of Vietnam** brought new opportunities to Southern officials, as black-market activities, profiteering, and smuggling became widespread. Bribery was also common for exemption from the draft, the acquisition of lucrative export–import licenses, and many other purposes. In the **Democratic Republic of Vietnam**, the **Vietnamese Communist Party** seems to have kept corruption under control during the wartime years, when in any case visible displays of ill-gotten wealth would not have been tolerated. However, Party and government **cadres** at all levels had tremendous power over those under their authority and were able to wield it in often arbitrary and unjust ways.

After reunification the situation gradually began to change, particularly in the South, where cadres from the North who flooded in to take control of the government and the economy were frequently in a position to appropriate personal property for themselves. As more and more Vietnamese began to flee the country as **boat people**, this trend brought new opportunities for the authorities to literally put gold in their pockets by accepting bribes from those desperate to leave. The move toward a market economy, which began with the implementation of *đổi mới* (renovation) in the mid-1980s, has provided fertile ground for corruption on an immense scale at all levels of the Party and government hierarchy.

The Party is all too aware of this problem and, more importantly, of the damage that such widespread corruption does to its legitimacy. It is torn between, on the one hand, recognition of the need to bring the problem under control and, on the other hand, a fundamental unwillingness to air its dirty laundry in public. (For this reason, **journalists** who attempt to investigate corruption cases are often blocked or silenced.) Since the mid-1990s, there have been more serious and more consistent efforts to improve the situation, including reprimands, dismissals, trials, and even executions of high-ranking cadres. The corruption problem is far from solved, however, as the continual flow of revelations and new scandals demonstrates all too clearly.

COUNCIL OF ELDERS (*Hội đồng kỳ mục*). Governing body in traditional Vietnamese **villages**. Normally composed of leading members of dominant families or clans in each village, the council was responsible for making key decisions affecting the village. Most of the members were members of the scholar-gentry class, and many had degrees in the civil service examinations. Meetings of the Council were held in the village community hall (*đình*) and dealt with such issues as taxation, civil affairs, local public works projects, distribution of village **communal land**, and administration of the village guardian spirit cult. A village chief (*lý trưởng* or *xã trưởng*) served as administrative officer and liaison between the council and higher levels of government.

The village council survived with some revisions into the French **colonial** era but after 1954 was replaced by other institutions in both North and South Vietnam. In the North, elected **People's Councils** (*Hội Đồng Nhân dân*) were set up at village and higher levels after the formation of the **Democratic Republic of Vietnam** (DRV) in 1945. In the South, the regime of **Ngô Đình Diệm** replaced the council with appointed councils headed by a village chief with strengthened powers and subordinate to the province chief. *See also* LOCAL GOVERNMENT.

COUNCIL OF STATE (*Hội Đồng Nhà Nước***).** Collective presidency of the **Socialist Republic of Vietnam** (SRV). It was established by the **Constitution** promulgated in 1980 and replaced the office of the presidency that existed under the Constitution of 1959. The chairman of the council served as the *de facto* chief of state of the SRV. In the revised constitution of 1992, the Council of State was replaced by a single head of state, who was to be elected by the **National Assembly** from among its members. Like other government institutions, the Council of State was considerably overshadowed by the structures of the Communist Party, and decisions from the latter's Central Committee or Politburo ultimately carried more weight. *See also* DEMOCRATIC REPUBLIC OF VIETNAM; TRƯỜNG CHINH; VÕ CHÍ CÔNG.

CỬ NHÂN. See EXAMINATION SYSTEM.

CƯỜNG ĐỂ, PRINCE (1882–1951). Member of the **Nguyễn dynastic** house who took an active role in anticolonial activities. His personal name was Nguyễn Phúc Hồng Dân; he was a descendant of Prince **Cảnh,** the first son of founding emperor **Gia Long.** He thus represented a branch of the royal family that had been bypassed at Gia Long's death in favor of **Minh Mạng,** whose descendants held the throne from then onward. Cường Đế served as the titular leader of **Phan Bội Châu**'s Modernization Society (*Duy Tân Hội*), established in 1903. For the next several decades, he was active in the resistance movement while residing in **Japan.**

During World War II, Cường Đế had links to pro-Japanese political organizations, some of which anticipated his eventual return to Vietnam. He was, in fact, considered by the Japanese as a possible replacement for the reigning Emperor **Bảo Đại,** but, in the end, they opted for continuity and maintained the latter as ruler of the "independent" Empire of Vietnam during the final months of the war.

Cường Để died in 1951 without ever returning to his homeland, though his remains were repatriated in 1957.

CURRENCY. During the precolonial period, a variety of metal-based currencies circulated in the Vietnamese **economy**, although people at the **village** level often made payments in kind, especially in **rice**. Quite a bit of metal flowed back and forth across the border with **China** because of the considerable volume of trade. Once the **French** had taken control of **Indochina**, they attempted to reduce the diversity of currencies in use and standardize the monetary system. The two most common units were the *đồng* (made from copper and zinc) and the piastre, which was the Mexican silver dollar. In 1904, the colonial regime eventually began to mint its own *đồng* and tried to maintain a stable link with the piastre, but this was easier said than done, and the two currencies coexisted with difficulty. After 10 years of very uneven results, the zinc-based *đồng* was withdrawn from circulation, and henceforth there was a single currency, which was called either "piastre" or "*đồng*," depending on which language one was using; both paper and coins were issued.

The French then spent the next two decades or so debating the question of a silver standard versus a gold standard, an issue that became particularly important with the onset of the Depression when the exchange rate between the piastre and the French franc was drastically affected. The silver standard was retained until 1930, when the currency was revalued in terms of gold, although this arrangement was, in turn, modified in 1936 and the exchange rate was fixed based on the franc instead.

When Vietnam was partitioned in two after the **Geneva Conference** of 1954, both the **Republic of Vietnam** and the **Democratic Republic of Vietnam** (DRV) maintained the *đồng* as their currency, though with different values. In the DRV, the currency was aligned to both the **United States** dollar and the ruble of the **Union of Soviet Socialist Republics**; a separate Commercial Rate was used for **trade**. In the Republic of Vietnam, the value of the currency was severely disrupted over the long term by the presence of hundreds of thousands of Americans bringing in dollars. There was a thriving black market in dollars, and the gap with the official rate (often a difference in value of 200–300 percent) was sufficient to ensure that the dollar and gold were in considerably wider use than the *đồng*.

Following the collapse of the Republic of Vietnam, a new *đồng* was introduced in the South in September 1975; all commercial transactions were suspended for a day as South Vietnamese exchanged their old currency for the new money. After formal reunification in 1976, the two halves of the new **Socialist Republic of Vietnam** maintained separate currency zones until May 1978, when a single *đồng* was introduced nationwide. Over the next few years, several different exchange rates were used for different purposes. In 1985, **Tố Hữu** (a renowned poet who had somehow ended up with the economics portfolio) and other conservative leaders forced a revaluation of the *đồng,* which caused its purchasing power to drop sharply; this error cost him his position in the government. After the inauguration of the reform program known as *đổi mới* the following year, the government gradually devalued the currency to bring the official value in line with the free-market rate. This was a slow and difficult process, however, and until the opening of official foreign exchange centers in **Hồ Chí Minh City (Saigon)** and **Hanoi** in 1991, the black market had a major impact on the currency's value, which dropped steadily against the dollar.

The *đồng*'s drop in value began to slow. By 1994, it had stabilized at nearly 11,000 to the dollar. That same year, the government attempted to maintain stability by announcing that the *đồng* should be the only currency used for most transactions (including those by **foreign investors**), but this rule had little effect. Over the next few years, there was pressure from donors and economic advisors to let the currency depreciate further to help exports, but a real devaluation did not begin until early 1998, when the *đồng* was allowed to slide 5.3 percent, which now took it to nearly 13,000. The currency's lack of convertibility and the heavy reliance on the dollar in the economy (despite repeated government attempts to impose the primacy of the *đồng*) meant that Vietnam was, to some extent, shielded from the Asian economic crisis of 1997–1998. The *đồng* has continued to depreciate, but much more slowly, and its year-on-year change has been much smaller since the late 1990s. This relative stability and government regulations notwithstanding, both the dollar and gold remain widely used, especially for more expensive purchases. *See also* BANKING AND FINANCE.

CỬU CHÂN. Ancient administrative term referring to the area corresponding to present-day Thanh Hoá and Nghệ An provinces in northern Vietnam. First used by King **Triệu Đà** of Nanyue or **Nam Việt**, it was maintained by the Han dynasty and was used by several subsequent dynasties during Chinese rule. The origins of the term are obscure, although it literally means "nine verities."

CỬU QUỐC HỘI. *See* NATIONAL SALVATION ASSOCIATIONS.

– D –

ĐÀ NẴNG (Tourane). Fourth largest city in Vietnam. Situated in a protected **naval** harbor on the central coast in the province of Quảng Nam, Đà Nẵng was long overshadowed by the nearby seaport of **Hội An** (known to European merchants as *Faifo*), a major commercial center during the 16th and 17th centuries. When the harbor at Hội An began to silt up in the 19th century, Đà Nẵng, originally known as *Cửa Hàn* (mouth of the Hàn River), emerged as the major seaport along the central coast. In 1858, **French** and Spanish fleets under Admiral **Charles Rigault de Genouilly** occupied the city in an unsuccessful effort to seize the nearby Vietnamese imperial capital at **Huế**.

During the colonial era, Đà Nẵng (called *Tourane* by the French) became a major commercial center. After the **Geneva Conference**, **Ngô Đình Diệm** renamed the city *Đà Nẵng*. It became the second largest city in the **Republic of Vietnam**. During the Vietnam War, it was the site of a major United States naval and airbase. Flooded with refugees at war's end, Đà Nẵng is today an autonomous municipality with an estimated population of nearly 750,000 people in 2003, covering an area of 80 square kilometers (30 square miles).

ĐẠI CỒ VIỆT (Great Viet). Vietnamese kingdom established by **Đinh Bộ Lĩnh** in 966. The term means "Great Viet," with the phrase *Đại Cồ* combining the Chinese and old Vietnamese terms for "great." (Some historians identify the term *Cổ* with a kind of hawk, a bird sometimes symbolizing rebellion in Vietnamese mythology.) In 1054, during the **Lý dynasty**, the name was changed to **Đại Việt**.

ĐẠI LA (Đại La Thành). Name of a citadel built during the **Chinese period** on the site of **Hanoi** at the end of the eighth century. The area of Hanoi, located just south of the **Red River** at the junction of the Đuống and the Tô Lịch Rivers, had been made into the administrative capital of the protectorate of **Annam** by the Tang dynasty in **China**. A citadel, called *Tử Thành* (in Chinese, *Zicheng*) was built to protect the area from attack. Later a larger citadel, called *La Thành* (Ch. *Luocheng*), replaced the original. In 791, La Thành citadel was repaired and strengthened by the construction of a large earth wall nearly 30 kilometers (almost 20 miles) long and over 6 meters (nearly 20 feet) high. The defense works were strengthened with bamboo hedges, watchtowers, and a surrounding moat. The name of the walled citadel was *Đại La* (in Chinese, *Daluo*). The outer wall was eventually destroyed, but the inner citadel was frequently strengthened and became the main bastion defending the imperial capital of Hanoi. Recent archeological excavations in Hanoi are expected to shed more light on this period of its history.

ĐẠI NAM (Great South). Name applied to the Vietnamese Empire during the **Nguyễn dynasty** (1802–1945). Founding emperor **Gia Long** had requested permission from **China** in 1802 to change the country's name from *Đại Việt* to *Nam Việt*. (As a vassal of China, the Vietnamese ruler had to receive investiture from the Chinese, and the title he received was linked to the country's officially authorized name.) The Qing emperor refused, however, because "Nam Việt" evoked the kingdom of the same name (Nanyue), which had existed in the third century B.C.E. and had included territory later absorbed by China; he suggested the name *Việt Nam* instead. Gia Long grudgingly accepted, but *Việt Nam* was rarely used (outside of correspondence with China) until the emergence of anticolonial nationalism. Instead, Gia Long's successor **Minh Mạng** (1820–1840) adopted the name *Đại Nam*, which was used by the imperial court until the end of the dynasty in 1945.

ĐẠI NGU (Great Yu). Term applied to the state of Vietnam under the short-lived dynasty (1400–1407) of **Hồ Quý Ly**. *Ngu* is the Vietnamese reading of the Chinese name *Yu*, which designates the dynasty established by the legendary emperors Yao and Shun, from whom Hồ Quý Ly claimed to be descended. The "crime" of choosing such a name for the country without permission was one of the reasons invoked by the Ming for invading and overthrowing Hồ.

ĐẠI VIỆT (Great Viet). Formal name of the Vietnamese Empire during the **Lý**, **Trần**, and **Lê** Dynasties from the 11th through the 18th centuries. The name, meaning "great Viet," was first adopted by **Lý Thánh Tông** in 1054, replacing the former name *Đại Cồ Việt*. This name was used by dynasties based in Hanoi through the end of the 18th century. The **Nguyễn dynasty** adopted the name *Đại Nam* in the early 1800s.

ĐẠI VIỆT PARTY. Nationalist political party in 20th-century Vietnam. Formed shortly before World War II by patriotic elements among the urban middle class in **Tonkin**, the Đại Việt Party sought assistance from the **Japanese occupation** authorities to obtain independence from **French** rule and took part with other pro-Japanese groups in a so-called United National Front established in **Cochin China** after the Japanese coup against the French administration in March 1945. The Front was superseded by the **Committee of the South** (*Ủy Ban Nam Bộ*) in August.

Plagued with internal factionalism and elitist in its membership, the party had little success in the postwar period against its main rival, the **Việt Minh** Front, and was eventually outlawed in the **Democratic Republic of Vietnam** (DRV). After the division of the country at the **Geneva Conference** in 1954, the Đại Việt resumed political activities in the **Republic of Vietnam**. Still factionalized, it became one of several parties during the 1960s.

ĐẠI VIỆT SỬ KÝ (Historical Record of Great Viet). Classic history of the Vietnamese Empire, written in the 13th century by **Lê Văn Hưu**. The original text is no longer extant, but Hưu's account and commentary were incorporated into the 15th-century *Đại Việt Sử Ký Toàn Thư* by **Ngô Sĩ Liên**. *See also* HISTORIOGRAPHY.

ĐẠI VIỆT SỬ KÝ TOÀN THƯ (*Complete Historical Record of Great Viet*). Famous history of Vietnam begun by **Lê Văn Hưu** as the *Đại Việt Sử Ký* and completed by the 15th-century historian **Ngô Sĩ Liên**. It is a chronological record of the country from its origins to the end of the 15th century. A final version was published from wood blocks in 1697. *See also* HISTORIOGRAPHY.

ĐÀLẠT. Mountain resort city in central Vietnam. Located in Lâm Đồng province in the middle of the **Central Highlands** (Tây Nguyên), Đàlạt sits at an altitude of approximately 1,500 meters (4900 feet). Because of its relatively cool climate, it became a popular resort for sweltering Europeans during the French colonial era, a practice that continued after the departure of the French, not only for affluent elements in **Saigon** society but also reportedly for the revolutionary movement, which used the mountains surrounding the city as a rehabilitation center for its own cadres.

During the Vietnam War, Đàlạt became the site of the first nuclear reactor in Vietnam and a military academy. It was also known as "the vegetable garden of Saigon," providing fruit and vegetables to the capital region in considerable quantities as well as for export. Today, the city has an estimated population of about 120,000 people.

ĐÀLẠT CONFERENCE. Conference held between **France** and the **Democratic Republic of Vietnam** (DRV) in April and May 1946. The purpose of the conference, held at the resort town of **Đàlạt**, was to discuss the terms of the **Ho-Sainteny Agreement**, reached in March, and to prepare for formal negotiations at Fontainebleau in June. The chairman of the DRV delegation was the non-Communist foreign minister **Nguyễn Tường Tam**, and only two members of the **Indochinese Communist Party** (ICP), including the Party's military strategist **Võ Nguyên Giáp**, were included in the delegation. The delegates were unable to reach an agreement on outstanding issues and adjourned without a result, but the two sides agreed to try to resolve their differences at the upcoming **Fontainebleau Conference** in June.

In early August, while negotiations at Fontainebleau were still in session, High Commissioner **Thierry d'Argenlieu** convened a second conference at Đàlạt without representatives of the DRV to discuss the formation of a proposed **Indochinese Federation**, thus attempting to sabotage the ongoing talks in France. The delegates, from **Annam, Cochin China, Laos**, and **Cambodia** agreed on the creation of a Federation under the **French Union** and denounced the DRV as unrepresentative of the Vietnamese people. D'Argenlieu's initiative achieved little beyond generating further tensions and mutual recriminations between the two sides negotiating at Fontainebleau.

DÂN CHÚNG (*The Masses*). Newspaper published by the **Indochinese Communist Party** (ICP) in the 1930s. Unofficially tolerated by the **French** colonial regime, it was closed down in August 1939 after the signing of the Nazi–Soviet pact. *See also* JOURNALISM.

ĐẢNG CỘNG SẢN ĐÔNG DƯƠNG. *See* INDOCHINESE COMMUNIST PARTY.

ĐẢNG CỘNG SẢN VIỆT NAM. *See* INDOCHINESE COMMUNIST PARTY; VIETNAMESE COMMUNIST PARTY.

ĐẢNG LAO ĐỘNG VIỆT NAM. *See* VIETNAMESE COMMUNIST PARTY.

ĐÀNG NGOÀI. The name used by the **Nguyễn Lords** to refer to the northern kingdom during the 17th and 18th centuries, as opposed to *Đàng Trong*, which designated the southern kingdom. Đàng Ngoài was called *Tonkin* by foreigners and *Bắc Hà* ("north of the river") by Vietnamese, since the Gianh River (in modern Quảng Trị) was the *de facto* border between the two kingdoms.

ĐÀNG TRONG. From around 1600 through the late 18th century, Vietnam was divided into two effectively independent kingdoms; the boundary between them came to be set at the Gianh River in present-day Quảng Trị, ironically almost the exact location of the subsequent **Demilitarized Zone** demarcated after the **Geneva Conference** of 1954. The **Nguyễn Lords** ruling in Phú Xuân (which later became **Huế**) acknowledged the nominal suzerainty of the **Lê dynasty** ruling at Thăng Long (later **Hanoi**) but opposed the authority of the **Trịnh**

Lords who dominated the Lê emperors. The Nguyễn expanded their kingdom southward through a combination of conquest and migration/colonization, absorbing the territory of **Champa** and parts of the **Mekong Delta** region of **Cambodia**. The Nguyễn kingdom, known to foreigners as **Cochin China**, was often referred to as *Đàng Trong*, which loosely translates as "the area down here"; the northern kingdom was known to the Nguyễn as *Đàng Ngoài*, "the area up there." The Lê-Trịnh government used the designations *Bắc Hà* ("north of the river") and *Nam Hà* ("south of the river").

ĐẶNG THÁI MAI (1902–1984). Respected scholar and later prominent supporter of the **Việt Minh** Front. Born in a scholar-gentry family in Nghệ An, he joined the **Tân Việt Cách Mệnh Đảng** (New Vietnamese Revolutionary Party) in the 1920s. After being sentenced to a term in prison for radical activities, he founded the Thăng Long School in **Hanoi** in 1935 and joined the **Indochinese Communist Party** (ICP). He later became a member of the Việt Minh and was appointed minister of education in the **Democratic Republic of Vietnam** government after World War II.

ĐÀO DUY ANH (1904–1988). Renowned scholar in colonial Vietnam. One of the original founders of the **Tân Việt Cách Mệnh Đảng** (New Vietnamese Revolutionary Party) in the mid-1920s, Đào Duy Anh became a teacher in **Huế** and a prominent essayist and scholar in colonial Vietnam. A vigorous advocate of Westernization but also a Marxist intellectual, he participated in an effort to broaden public knowledge by publishing a series of books on prominent Western writers and thinkers and was the author of several studies on **Confucianism** and the historical dialectic and of a widely read book on Vietnamese history, the *Outline History of Vietnamese Culture* (*Việt Nam Văn Hoá Sử Cương*).

ĐÀO DUY TỪ (1572–1634). An important scholar-official under the **Nguyễn Lords**. A native of Thanh Hoá, Đào Duy Từ was unable to go through the **examination system** because he was the son of a singer, a profession whose offspring were barred from the system. After an unpromising beginning herding buffalo for a prominent landlord, he came to the attention of a powerful provincial official and was introduced to the Nguyễn court. His intelligence and military acumen proved valuable at a time when the Nguyễn kingdom was attempting to maintain its independence against its northern rivals the **Trịnh Lords**. He is particularly well-known for his construction of walls along the kingdom's northern border, which served as its main defense perimeter until the outbreak of the **Tây Sơn** rebellion in the late 18th century. *See also* ĐÔNG HỚI.

ĐÀO DUY TÙNG (1922?–1998). A leading ideologue in the **Vietnamese Communist Party** and the **Socialist Republic of Vietnam**. Đào Duy Tùng essentially made his career in propaganda and ideological affairs, serving at different times as editor-in-chief of the important Party theoretical journal *Tạp Chí Cộng Sản* (*Communist Review*), head of the Vietnam News Agency, and director of the Institute for Research on Marxism–Leninism and Hồ Chí Minh Thought. He rose to take charge of the Party's Propaganda and Training Department and became a member of the Politburo in 1986. In 1996, prior to the Eighth Party Congress, where important leadership decisions would be made, he was thought to be a serious candidate to replace **Đỗ Mười** as secretary general of the Party, and he prepared a draft report for the Congress, which had a clearly conservative tone. Tùng is believed to have overplayed his hand, however, and both he and his protégé who collaborated on the report were removed from all Party posts when the Congress finally took place. He died not long after his fall from grace.

DAOISM (*Đạo Giáo*). Daoism or Taoism is a rather broad term that encompasses both the writings of a series of Chinese philosophers (notably Laozi and Zhuangzi, Viet. Lão Tử and Trang Tử) and a wide range of popular beliefs that have little or nothing to do with philosophy. The Vietnamese were exposed to Daoism during the **Chinese period** of their history, and it became a permanent part of their worldview in various forms. Although Daoist philosophy as such has probably never been influential in Vietnam outside a relatively small group of scholarly elite, "popular Daoism" has long resonated at all levels of society because of its strongly supernatural character. Supernatural Daoism includes the worship of the Jade Emperor (Ngọc Hoàng, Ch. Yuhuang), along with a large pantheon of spirits, as well as an interest in elixirs, amulets with magical properties, and spirit mediums.

Under the **Lý** and **Trần dynasties**, Daoism ranked with **Confucianism** and **Buddhism** as one of the "Three Religions" (*tam giáo*) to be mastered by candidates for public office taking the civil service **examination**. (This was presumably philosophical Daoism, though nothing is known about the specific subjects studied.) At the same time, historical texts suggest that during the early centuries after independence Daoist priests were common figures in the Vietnamese court, along with their Buddhist counterparts. With the increasing dominance of Confucianism from the 15th century onward, however, Daoism and Buddhism were effectively marginalized in the state ideology, though certainly not in the Vietnamese worldview as a whole. Popular Daoist practices were somewhat suspect in the government's eyes because such "heterodox" elements (from a Confucian perspective) were frequently linked to rebellions.

Daoist practices in Vietnam include both elements borrowed from China and uniquely Vietnamese components. The (originally Chinese) Jade Emperor, for example, is a less important figure than his daughter Liễu Hạnh, whose cult is widespread in Vietnam and who is a completely Vietnamese invention. Daoism's broad and flexible framework, particularly its pantheon of spirits, enables it to easily incorporate and absorb local beliefs; this is true, for instance, of the female spirits categorized as "Holy Mothers" (Thánh Mẫu, Ch. Shengmu). It should be pointed out, however, that "popular Daoism" is, in fact, an academic category imposed by scholars and that practitioners of these beliefs would probably see themselves as followers of a particular spirit and not as "Daoists" *per se. See also* RELIGION.

D'ARGENLIEU, THIERRY (1889–1964). High commissioner of French **Indochina** from August 1945 to February 1946. During his term in office, Admiral d'Argenlieu displayed an uncompromising determination to restore full French sovereignty in Indochina. In the spring of 1946, he encouraged separatist sentiment among French residents and pro-French Vietnamese in **Cochin China** to avoid a referendum as called for by the **Ho-Sainteny Agreement**. In June, he announced the establishment of a separate Autonomous **Republic**

of **Cochin China** and two months later sabotaged the negotiations at Fontainebleau by convening his own conference at Đàlạt. In February 1947, after the outbreak of the **Franco–Việt Minh** conflict, he was recalled to Paris and replaced by **Émile Bollaert**. *See also* ĐÀLẠT CONFERENCE; FONTAINEBLEAU CONFERENCE.

DE LA GRANDIÈRE, PIERRE (1807–1876). Naval officer and governor of **Cochin China** from 1863 to 1868. A career naval officer, he was appointed governor of the newly acquired **Mekong Delta** provinces in 1863. Lacking firm instructions from the **French** government in Paris, de la Grandière on his own initiative extended French influence in the area. That same year, he persuaded the King of **Cambodia** to accept a French **protectorate** over his country. In June 1867, on a slim pretext French forces seized the remaining three provinces of Cochin China (Châu Đốc, Sóc Trăng, and Vĩnh Long) from the Vietnamese. The seizure was ratified by the **Philastre Treaty**, signed in March 1874. *See also* PHAN THANH GIẢN; TỰ ĐỨC.

DE LATTRE DE TASSIGNY, JEAN (1889–1952). Commander in chief of **French** forces and high commissioner of French **Indochina** from December 1950 until December 1951. A man of enormous presence and self-esteem, de Lattre immediately charged the French effort in Indochina with a new dynamism after a disastrous campaign in autumn 1950. He blunted a major **Việt Minh** offensive on the fringes of the **Red River Delta** and eventually forced General **Võ Nguyên Giáp**, the primary Việt Minh strategist, to abandon his efforts to seize **Hanoi** during the early spring of 1951. General de Lattre then ordered the construction of a string of pillboxes (the familiar "de Lattre" line) to protect the delta from further infiltration and attack.

Although his energy and self-confidence heartened French personnel in Indochina, Việt Minh military strength continued to increase at the expense of the French, leading to the costly confrontation at Hoà Bình, on the Black River southwest of Hanoi. On the political front, his unswerving determination to maintain French dominance in Indochina hindered his effort to achieve the full cooperation of non-Communist nationalist elements in Vietnam. Stricken with cancer, de Lattre resigned from office in December 1951 and died in France a few weeks later.

ĐÊ THÁM. *See* HOÀNG HOA THÁM.

DECOUX, JEAN (1884–1963). Governor-general of French **Indochina** from 1940 to 1945. Admiral Jean Decoux, commander of the **French** Pacific Fleet, was selected by the Vichy Government to replace **Georges Catroux** as governor-general in July 1940. On arrival, he was faced with an ultimatum from Tokyo demanding free passage through Indochina for **Japanese** troops and the use of local airports. On the orders of Vichy, he agreed, and a Franco–Japanese Treaty to that effect was signed on 30 August 1940.

For the next years, Decoux followed the Vichy policy of cooperating with the Japanese in the hope of preserving French Indochina after the end of the war. At the same time, he attempted to consolidate the loyalty of the local elite by giving them more participation in the colonial government while at the same time promoting Vichyite ideology in an Indochinese context. As Charles de Gaulle grew stronger overseas, however, many officials and military officers in his administration joined the Free French movement and plotted the overthrow of the **Japanese occupation** regime. On 9 March 1945, Japan presented Decoux with an ultimatum demanding that all French military units be placed under Japanese command. A few hours later, no reply having been received, Admiral Decoux and most French personnel were placed in internment camps. Released at the end of the war, he returned to France and was tried and exonerated of the charge of collaboration. *See also POLITIQUE D'ÉGARDS.*

DEGA/DEGAR. A name that has recently come into use to refer to the upland peoples of the **Central Highlands**, often known by the French term *Montagnards*. The term has very clear political connotations, as it is used mainly by former members of the **Front Unifié pour la Libération des Races Opprimées** who have emigrated overseas and are speaking out against Vietnamese government policies in the Highlands. *See also* HIGHLAND MINORITIES.

DEMILITARIZED ZONE (DMZ). Cease-fire zone established at the **Geneva Conference** on Indochina in 1954. When conferees agreed on a partition of Vietnam between the **Democratic Republic of Vietnam (DRV)** in the North and supporters of the French and **Bảo Đại**'s **State of Vietnam** in the South, the line of demarcation was ultimately established at the 17th parallel, placing approximately half the population and territory in each zone. The DMZ was established at the Bến Hải River to prevent clashes between the two sides before a political settlement called for by the Accords. Supervision of the cease-fire agreement was vested in an **International Control Commission** composed of representatives of Canada, India, and Poland.

When the Vietnam War resumed in the early 1960s, the DMZ did not become directly involved in the fighting, although United States officials suspected that infiltration of troops from the DRV into the Republic of Vietnam took place through the zone. The bulk of troop movement, however, undoubtedly took place along the so-called **Hồ Chí Minh Trail**, a series of mountain trails across the border in **Laos.** The exception was the **Easter Offensive** of 1972, when North Vietnamese forces crossed the DMZ and captured South Vietnam's northernmost province of Quảng Trị.

DEMOCRATIC REPUBLIC OF VIETNAM (DRV) (*Việt Nam Dân Chủ Cộng Hoà*). Government established under the leadership of the **Indochinese Communist Party** after the **August Revolution** in 1945. The government was first announced on 2 September 1945, when **Hồ Chí Minh**, president of the provisional government established in mid-August by the League for the Independence of Vietnam (**Việt Minh** Front), read a declaration of independence for the new republic in its capital of **Hanoi**. It was formally established in January 1946. The DRV replaced the colonial regime and was the first independent government of Vietnam since the French conquest in the late 19th century.

At the time of its creation, the DRV was intended to be a permanent national government for Vietnam. In actuality, its authority was spotty below the 16th parallel, where French armed forces were able to restore colonial rule until the **Geneva Conference** in 1954. Although the anti-French resistance was strong in parts of central and southern Vietnam, the DRV also had to compete with such forces as the **Cao Đài** and **Hoà Hảo**. The Geneva Accords divided Vietnam into two separate regroupment zones, which, in the course of time, became de facto independent states—the DRV north of the **Demilitarized Zone** at the 17th parallel and the **Republic of Vietnam** to the south. The DRV consisted of an area totaling 409,575 square kilometers (158,750 square miles) and an estimated population of 15,903,000 (1960 census).

According to the first **constitution**, promulgated in 1946, the DRV was a parliamentary republic, with supreme authority vested in a unicameral **National Assembly** elected by all citizens over the age of 18 years. Executive power was lodged in a president, assisted by the Government Council consisting of a prime minister and other appointed ministerial officials. Below the central level, the DRV was divided into provinces, districts, and villages. At each level, governmental power was exercised by a legislative assembly, the **People's Council** (*Hội Đồng Nhân Dân*), elected by the local population, and an executive organ elected from the members of the council, the Administrative Committee (*Ủy Ban Hành Chính*). As in all Marxist–Leninist societies, the **Vietnamese Communist Party** (known from 1951 to 1976 as the Vietnamese Workers' Party) was the ruling party in the state. Two smaller parties, the **Vietnamese Socialist Party** (representing progressive intellectuals) and the **Vietnamese Democratic Party** (representing the national bourgeoisie) remained, however, but under the VWP's guidance, and a genuine **multiparty system** did not exist.

On 2 July 1976, the DRV was formally replaced with a new **Socialist Republic of Vietnam** (SRV) uniting the two zones established at the Geneva Conference into a single unitary republic under the aegis of the renamed Vietnamese Communist Party.

DEWEY, A. PETER (1917–1945). First American to be killed in Vietnam during the Vietnamese revolution. As commanding officer of the Office of Strategic Services (OSS) Project Embankment, Lieutenant Colonel Dewey was sent to **Saigon** in the late summer of 1945 to represent **United States** interests in **Cochin China** following the end of World War II. Dewey angered General **Douglas Gracey**, the commander of British expeditionary forces in Indochina, and was ordered to leave the colony. Just before his departure, he was ambushed and killed, probably by **Việt Minh** guerrillas, on 26 September 1945. *See also* AUGUST REVOLUTION.

ĐIỆN BIÊN PHỦ, BATTLE OF. Major battle fought between **French** and **Việt Minh** military forces in the spring of 1954. Điện Biên Phủ, a district capital near the **Lao** border in the **Tây Bắc** or northwestern region of Vietnam, had originally been set up by the **Nguyễn dynasty** in 1841 to consolidate the borderland and prevent bandit forays into the **Red River Delta**. The region around the town was inhabited primarily by minorities of **Thái** ethnic stock and had long been subject to influence from both Vietnamese and Lao rulers.

In November 1953, Điện Biên Phủ was occupied by French military forces in an effort by General **Henri Navarre** to prevent Việt Minh units from crossing from Vietnam into Laos to threaten the royal capital of Luang Prabang. Early in 1954, with the advice and assistance of Chinese advisers, Việt Minh strategists decided to attack the French garrison to strengthen their bargaining position at the upcoming **Geneva Conference**. The town was placed under siege in March and, after a brief attempt to overrun the French military post by frontal attack, General **Võ Nguyên Giáp** decided on a protracted approach involving massive artillery attacks from the surrounding mountains and the construction of trenches to enable Việt Minh troops to approach the fort without coming under direct French fire.

The French High Command attempted to supply its beleaguered garrison by air, but bad weather and intense Việt Minh artillery fire prevented the arrival of reinforcements and provisions in sufficient numbers, and on 6 May, the day before the Geneva Conference began to discuss the Indochina issue, the post and the surrounding town were overrun. Virtually the entire French garrison of 15,000 was killed or taken prisoner, while Việt Minh losses were estimated at more than 25,000. Whether the loss of Điện Biên Phủ itself was a major military debacle for the French is a matter of dispute, but, without doubt, it represented a severe blow to French morale and contributed to the signing of the Geneva Accords in July.

DIÊN HỒNG. A meeting held in 1284 to mobilize resistance against an impending **Mongol invasion**. Vietnam had defeated a prior incursion in 1258, and now the Mongol Yuan dynasty was making threatening noises again, demanding that Emperor **Trần Nhân Tông** support their campaign against **Champa**. The Vietnamese refused, and it was clear that they would soon be at war with **China**. The ruler's father, former Emperor **Thánh Tông** (who had earlier abdicated in favor of his son), convened a council of elders from around the country at Diên Hồng palace to obtain a consensus on resisting the Mongols. The meeting was unanimous in declaring that the Vietnamese should fight rather than cooperate, and they defeated the invasion that took place the following year.

ĐÌNH. The communal house in the traditional Vietnamese **village**. The *đình* serves both **religious** and secular functions, as the abode of the guardian spirit of the village, as well as a site for various village ceremonies and rituals during the course of the year. It was also traditionally used as the meeting hall for the local **council of elders** (*hội đồng kỳ mục*), thus representing a center of more **Confucian**-based male power, as opposed to the local **Buddhist** temple, which was frequented by laywomen.

Most *đình* were built during the period from the 16th to the 18th centuries as part of an effort to restore local law and order at the time of the civil war that followed the disintegration of the **Lê dynasty**. Many of them are renowned for the lively wood carvings representing popular scenes that have been placed along the walls of the structure. In recent years, many villages in socialist Vietnam have renovated and redecorated their *đình* as the environment for holding traditional ceremonies has been freer.

ĐINH BỘ LĨNH (923–979). A significant figure in the initial period of Vietnamese independence in the 10th century. Đinh Bộ Lĩnh was born in **Hoa Lư**, in present-day Ninh Bình at the southern edge of the **Red River Delta**. He became a local military commander during the chaotic decades after **Ngô Quyền**'s defeat of the **Chinese** and, on the death of the last Ngô ruler in 963, founded the new kingdom of **Đại Cồ Việt** (Great Viet), with its capital in his home region at Hoa Lư, far from the traditional center of Chinese power in the heart of the Delta. To consolidate his legitimacy, he married a member of the Ngô family. In 968, he adopted the title of emperor, thus emphasizing his independence from Chinese rule. Seven years later, however, he pacified the new Song dynasty by sending a tribute mission to demonstrate his fealty to the Chinese emperor.

Đinh Bộ Lĩnh energetically wielded power to build the foundations of a Vietnamese state. In 979, however, an assassin killed both him and his eldest son, Đinh Liễn, in their sleep. During the period of anarchy that followed, power was seized by **Lê Hoàn**, a general in Đinh Bộ Lĩnh's army, who subsequently took the title of emperor. Although Vietnamese sources have traditionally referred to Đinh Bộ Lĩnh and his sons as a "dynasty," it is probably more accurate to view him as one of a series of strongmen who emerged to take power in a time of instability.

ĐINH DYNASTY. *See* ĐINH BỘ LĨNH.

DISSIDENTS. The successive states that have ruled Vietnam over the centuries have had little tolerance for dissenting opinions. Under the traditional **monarchy**, the rigors of the **examination system** were expected to produce candidates for the **mandarinate**, whose intellectual and ideological views reflected **Confucian** orthodoxy as much as possible. Officials who became disenchanted with a particular ruler or with the imperial system in general normally had only two options: either to retire, like the royal tutor **Chu Văn An** in the 14th century and the great literary figure **Nguyễn Du** in the late 1700s, or to rebel, like **Cao Bá Quát** in the 19th century. Under colonial rule, the **French** regime was equally unreceptive to opposition, and nationalists like **Phan Bội Châu** and **Phan Chu Trinh** became alienated from the system shortly after they had entered it as mandarins. Although a few journalists, such as **Huỳnh Thúc Khang** or **Nguyễn Văn Vĩnh**, could criticize specific aspects of colonial policy without opposing French rule in general, those who took more radical positions, like **Nguyễn An Ninh** or Nguyễn Ái Quốc (the future **Hồ Chí Minh**) ended up either in prison or in exile.

After 1954, neither the **Democratic Republic of Vietnam** (DRV) nor the **Republic of Vietnam** allowed much space for public opposition, though the situation was marginally better in the latter than in the former. Some press criticism of the **Saigon** regime was occasionally permitted, but there was considerable censorship even so. Movements like the short-lived **Caravelle Group**, which came out against **Ngô Đình Diệm**, did not last long, and probably the most durable opposition came from activist **Buddhist** monks, such as Thích **Trí**

Quang; more peaceful critics, like his fellow monk Thích **Nhất Hạnh**, usually ended up in exile.

In the DRV, the **Vietnamese Communist Party** kept a tight lid on dissenting voices. Although there had been some degree of artistic freedom when Hồ's government was fighting the French from the jungle during the **Franco–Việt Minh War**, once the DRV was re-established in **Hanoi** and Vietnam was partitioned after the 1954 **Geneva Conference**, artists and writers were forced to toe the Party line more closely than before. The brief period of openness in 1956, known as the *Nhân Văn Giai Phẩm* affair, which saw open dissent from writers like **Phan Khôi**, lasted only a few months and resulted in a serious crackdown. From that point onward until the end of the war, both criticism and punishment were strictly internal Party affairs.

The end of the war and reunification under the **Socialist Republic of Vietnam** (SRV) brought continuance of the zero-tolerance policy of the DRV, now extended to the former South Vietnam. Many of those who had been critical of the **Saigon** government and the war, such as the Catholic priest Father Chân Tín and the well-known songwriter **Trịnh Công Sơn**, fared little better under Communist rule. Some of the Southerners who had joined the Party-led **National Liberation Front** to resist the South Vietnamese government now became severely disenchanted with the **Hanoi** regime; prominent examples were Doctor **Dương Quỳnh Hoa** and Trương Như Tảng, both of whom had held positions in the **Provisional Revolutionary Government** during the war.

The relatively greater degree of openness that has come with the *đổi mới* (renovation) period since the mid-1980s has produced a new generation of dissidents whose criticisms of the Party have earned them considerable publicity but often punishment as well. Such writers as **Dương Thu Hương**, **Nguyễn Huy Thiệp**, and **Bảo Ninh** have gained a following overseas through the translation of their works; the latter two literary figures have hovered just on the edge of dissident status with their critical views of wartime and postwar Vietnam, while Hương has been persecuted for her writings. Several intellectuals, such as **Phan Đình Diệu** and the late **Nguyễn Khắc Viện**, became disenchanted with the system that they had served, as did some prominent military figures like **Bùi Tín** and retired General Trần Độ.

The rise of the Internet has brought opportunities for cyber-dissidence, and websites set up by **overseas Vietnamese** eagerly post communications and diatribes from those inside the SRV covering everything from calls for democracy, **pluralism**, and **multiparty** rule to criticisms of official **corruption** and a recent border agreement with **China**. The government's willingness to encourage more diverse **economic** activities in the interests of growth and development has not been matched by a greater tolerance for dissent, and the possibility of any degree of political *perestroika* comparable to the final years of the **Union of Soviet Socialist Republics** seems remote.

ĐỖ MƯỜI (1916–   ). Leading official in the **Vietnamese Communist Party**. Born in a family of artisans near **Hanoi** in 1916 or 1917, Đỗ Mười joined the **Indochinese Communist Party** in the late 1930s. Imprisoned by the **French** in 1941, he escaped four years later and took part in the **August Revolution**. After the **Geneva Conference**, he was named minister of domestic trade in the **Democratic Republic of Vietnam** and became a member of the Party Central Committee. After the end of the Vietnam War and reunification, he was placed in charge of the socialist transformation of **trade** and **industry** in the former South Vietnam and became a full member of the Politburo.

In 1988, Mười replaced **Phạm Hùng** as prime minister of the **Socialist Republic of Vietnam** (SRV), and became general secretary of the Party in 1991, a post he held until his retirement in 1997. Although considered somewhat doctrinaire in his views, as Party chief he presided over a steady pace of moderate reform and was probably slightly less conservative than his successor, **Lê Khả Phiêu**. As one of the most senior leaders still alive, Mười has continued to exercise influence over Vietnam's political and economic development since his retirement. For example, in 1999 he is known to have intervened to postpone the signing of the **Bilateral Trade Agreement** with the **United States** because of resistance from opponents of the treaty.

ĐOÀN THỊ ĐIỂM (1705–1746). Noted poet in 18th-century Vietnam. One of several well-known **woman** writers under the **Lê dynasty**, Đoàn Thị Điểm was born in Bắc Ninh in 1705. She became a teacher in Hà Đông but is best known for having translated the famous poem

Chinh Phụ Ngâm (*Lament of a Soldier's Wife*) from literary Chinese into colloquial Vietnamese written in *chữ nôm* script. The work is noteworthy for pointing out the suffering and misery rather than the glory of war. It was the first Vietnamese poem to focus on the impact of war on a soldier's wife. *See also* LITERATURE.

ĐỔI MỚI. Reform program adopted by the Sixth National Congress of the **Vietnamese Communist Party** (VCP) in December 1986. Often compared with the program of perestroika launched by Soviet party chief Mikhail Gorbachev in the Union of Soviet Socialist Republics, *đổi mới* (in English translation, "renovation") has become a catchphrase for any kind of reform or change within the country. Although conceding that the *đổi mới* program was originally inspired in part by the Soviet experience, Party sources assert that it was a direct consequence of conditions in Vietnam, where stagnating economic performance and a high level of social malaise were blamed on doctrinaire policies adopted by the leadership that were aimed at rapid socialist transformation. *Đổi mới*, identified with the post-1986 leadership of General Secretary **Nguyễn Van Linh**, is designed to promote economic growth through a more flexible use of **capitalist** techniques, but the ultimate goal theoretically remains the achievement of a fully socialist society in the indefinite future.

In reality, the Party has been compelled to move steadily toward a market economy to sustain high levels of economic growth, but the ultimate commitment to socialist ideals is maintained through efforts to retain **state-owned industries** as the central feature of the Vietnamese **economy**. Even this policy, however, is weakening with the flourishing of private enterprise and **joint ventures**. Generally speaking, the Party has been more successful in maintaining political control and has made fewer significant concessions in this area. In recent years, though, dissatisfaction with **corruption** and abuses of power at the local level has led to more freedom for individuals to seek redress for such grievances and for the press to cover such problems.

Đổi mới has also included the concept of *cởi mở*, a Vietnamese term meaning "openness," a rough equivalent of the concept of *glasnost* in the former Soviet Union. Nguyễn Van Linh encouraged writers and intellectuals to voice their opinions and criticize the shortcomings of the Party and the government. Eventually, however, the criticism became too pointed, and the regime began to set limits to the freedom of speech. During the 1990s, official policy emphasized political stability along with economic reform, and criticism of Party rule or efforts to form opposition political parties are not permitted. Over the past few years, there has been a slight easing of restrictions on press reporting of corruption and other crimes by officials, but **dissident** voices are still consistently repressed.

ĐỒN ĐIỀN. **Agricultural** settlements established by the Vietnamese Empire to pacify areas recently conquered and bring them under cultivation. The system was apparently first used during the early years of the **Lê dynasty** (1428–1788) to boost production by bringing virgin lands under cultivation through incentives to private farmers, landed aristocrats, and **mandarins**. Later, it was actively utilized by the **Nguyễn Lords** in the 18th century to settle population in uninhabited frontier areas of the South, particularly the fertile **Mekong River Delta**.

At first, the settlements were composed of soldiers under the direct command of military officers. Later, the authorities began to rely increasingly on volunteers, or even on prisoners, who were established in several colonies and given their freedom once their obligations had been met. Settlers often initially received their supplies from the state and were given tax incentives to persuade them to remain on the land. Once the area had been brought under cultivation, the settlement was given official recognition as a village or a hamlet. *See also NAM TIẾN.*

DÔNG Á ĐỒNG MINH HỘI (East Asian Alliance). Multinational revolutionary organization established by Vietnamese patriot **Phan Bội Châu**. The movement was set up in **Japan** in 1908 and included members from **China**, Korea, the Philippines, and India, as well as Vietnam. It was suppressed by Japanese authorities in 1909.

DÔNG DU (Go East). Movement organized by Vietnamese patriot **Phan Bội Châu** in the early 20th century. In 1905, he decided to set up an exile headquarters in **Japan** to promote resistance activities in **French**-occupied Vietnam. A key component of this effort was to train young Vietnamese patriots in Western knowledge in preparation for the building of a modern nation as Japan had done. In the Đông Du movement, Phan Bội Châu encouraged Vietnamese youth to come to Japan to study and prepare for a national insurrection. The movement came to an end in 1908 when his exile organization was evicted from Japan, which had chosen to improve relations with the Western powers (including France) rather than to continue supporting anticolonial movements like the Đông Du.

ĐỒNG DƯƠNG. *See* INDRAPURA.

ĐÔNG DƯƠNG CỘNG SẢN ĐẢNG. *See* INDOCHINESE COMMUNIST PARTY.

ĐÔNG DƯƠNG TẠP CHÍ (*Indochina Review*). First periodical in **Tonkin** to be published entirely in *quốc ngữ* (Romanized Vietnamese). Founded by the reformist Francophile **Nguyễn Văn Vĩnh** in 1913, the review attempted to popularize Western ideas, customs, and literature among its readers. After 1919, it ceased to play a major role in the Vietnamese reform movement and became a pedagogical journal. *See also* JOURNALISM.

ĐỒNG HỚI. The capital of present-day Quảng Bình province, it was the site of a famous wall built in 1631 under the supervision of **Đào Duy Từ**. The wall was an important component of the fortifications erected by the **Nguyễn Lords** to protect their territory against the northern kingdom ruled by the **Lê dynasty** and the **Trịnh Lords**. *See also* ĐÀNG TRONG.

ĐỒNG KHÁNH (1865–1889). Emperor (r. 1885–1889) of the **Nguyễn dynasty** under the French **protectorate**. He was a nephew of Emperor **Tự Đức** and an elder brother of **Hàm Nghi**, who was raised to the throne in 1885. When the latter fled the imperial palace to launch the **Cần Vương movement** of anti-**French** resistance in July, Đồng Khánh replaced him as emperor. A docile ruler, he was dominated by the French, who extended their authority under his reign while at the same time attempting to bolster the prestige of the monarchy to buttress their rule. He died suddenly in 1889 and was succeeded by **Thành Thái**. *See also* INDOCHINESE UNION.

DÔNG KINH NGHĨA THỤC (Tonkin Free School). School founded by patriotic intellectuals in early 20th-century Vietnam. Modeled after Fukuzawa Yukichi's Keio University in **Japan**, the school was established in 1906 by the scholar and patriot Lương Văn Can. Privately financed, it aimed at introducing Western ideas into Vietnamese society. It included among its instructors and contributors such figures as Dương Bá Trạc and **Phan Chu Trinh** and promoted the use of *quốc ngữ* (Romanized Vietnamese) as the national language. It placed strong emphasis on modern subjects, such as geography, mathematics, and science.

The organization tended to follow a reformist rather than a revolutionary orientation, although advocates of the latter were involved in the school's activities. The French were suspicious of the intentions of its founders and forced it to close after a few months, accusing it of involvement with anticolonial unrest in 1908. A number of the leaders were imprisoned and sent to **Poulo Condore**.

ĐỒNG MINH HỘI (Việt Nam Cách Mệnh Đồng Minh Hội). *See* VIETNAMESE REVOLUTIONARY LEAGUE.

DÔNG SƠN CULTURE. Bronze Age civilization that flourished in the **Red River Delta** area during the first millennium B.C.E. Named for the village in Thanh Hoá province where the first artifacts were found in 1925, Đông Sơn culture is now considered the zenith of Bronze Age civilization in prehistoric Vietnam. It was characterized by the manufacture of richly decorated **bronze drums,** used as musical instruments and for ritualistic purposes. Similar drums have been found elsewhere in mainland Southeast Asia and in **China**, and it was previously believed that the technique of bronze casting had been imported into Vietnam from China or from the West. Many **archeologists** are now convinced that the technology may have developed in mainland Southeast Asia and spread from there to other societies in Asia.

According to present evidence, Đông Sơn civilization arose somewhere around the eighth century B.C.E. and Vietnamese historians link it to the semilegendary kingdom of **Văn Lang** in the Red River Valley. Đông Sơn civilization came to an end with the coming of the

Iron Age and the Chinese conquest of Vietnam at the end of the second century B.C.E.

DOUMER, PAUL (1857–1932). One of the primary architects of French **Indochina** in the late 19th century. A member of the Radical party and an ex-minister of finance, he was appointed governor-general of the new **Indochinese Union** in 1897. Doumer played a major role in fleshing out the concept of the union by providing it with a stable source of revenue in the state monopolies on salt, alcohol, and opium and by setting up central administrative offices in key areas, such as **agriculture**, civil affairs, post and telegraph, and public works. Resigning from the governor-generalship in 1902, he later became president of France and was assassinated by a Russian anarchist in 1932.

DRAMA. *See* THEATER.

DỤC ĐỨC (1852–1884). Emperor (r. 1883) under the **Nguyễn dynasty**. A nephew and adopted son of Emperor **Tự Đức**, he succeeded his uncle on the throne. However, his behavior alienated influential members of the court, and he was deposed in less than two weeks and put under house arrest; he starved to death the following year. These events opened a period of chaos following Tự Đức's death that seriously weakened the Vietnamese court precisely at the moment when it was facing the final stages of **colonization** by the **French**. *See also* NGUYỄN VĂN TƯỜNG; TÔN THẤT THUYẾT.

DƯƠNG ĐÌNH NGHỆ (also known as *Dương Diên Nghệ*). One of a series of rebel leaders who helped establish Vietnamese independence from **Chinese** rule in the early 10th century C.E. At that time, Chinese rule over its occupied territory of Vietnam had been weakened because of the collapse of the Tang dynasty in 907. In the unstable conditions, a revolt against Chinese rule was launched by **Khúc Thừa Dụ**, a local governor of the province of **Giao**. Chinese rule was temporarily restored, but rebellion continued under Dương Đình Nghệ, who seized the administrative capital of **Đại La** (present-day **Hanoi**) and controlled the **Red River Delta** for several years. He was assassinated in 937, but his family played a major role in the restora-

tion of Vietnamese independence in succeeding years. *See also* NGÔ
QUYỀN.

DƯƠNG QUỲNH HOA (1930–). A doctor and former minister in
the **Provisional Revolutionary Government of South Vietnam**
(PRG). A native of **Saigon** who trained in **France** as a pediatrician,
Dương Quỳnh Hoa returned to Vietnam shortly after its partition at
the **Geneva Conference** in 1954. Although a member of the **Vietnamese Communist Party**, she chose to stay in the South and work
for the revolution to undermine the **Ngô Đình Diệm** regime rather
than regrouping to the North as many other cadres did. She was one
of the founders of the **National Liberation Front** (NLF) in 1960,
and following the **Tết Offensive** of 1968, she joined the NLF forces
in the jungle. After the formation of the PRG (as a revolutionary alternative to the **Republic of Vietnam** government) in 1969, she
headed its Ministry of Health, Social Affairs, and Wounded Veterans
until the PRG was dissolved following the fall of Saigon in 1975.

Hoa briefly served as vice-minister of health in the **Socialist Republic of Vietnam** after reunification in 1976, but the following year
she resigned from that position as well as her Party membership to
concentrate on **health** and social issues. She became a vocal critic of
the Party's failure to adequately take care of its people and also
spoke out against the rise of problems such as child prostitution. Although she has become a kind of **dissident** in terms of her views
of Vietnam's political policies, Hoa has been threatened but never
punished for her stance. Not only is she a prominent figure in international health circles for her work, she also has impeccable revolutionary credentials for her years of service with the NLF and PRG.

DƯƠNG THU HƯƠNG (1947–). Prominent female novelist in contemporary Vietnam. A one-time member of the Communist Youth
League, Dương Thu Hương has emerged in recent years as an outspoken critic of the postwar regime in Hanoi. Her novel *Những Thiên
Đường Mù* (literally "Blind Paradises," but known in English as
Paradise of the Blind) earned popular acclaim but provoked a critical
reaction in government circles because of its vivid portrayal of nar-
row-minded and corrupt **Vietnamese Communist Party** cadres. Expelled from the Party in 1990, she was briefly arrested the following

year on the charge of smuggling a manuscript out of Vietnam. Her most recent work, translated in an English-language version as *Novel without a Name*, is a moving portrayal of the Vietnam War, as seen through the eyes of a northern soldier. Like her contemporary **Bảo Ninh**, Dương Thu Hương expresses the sense of disillusionment felt by many war veterans at the ultimate meaningless of their sacrifice and those of their comrades. Although sometimes criticized for the limits of her writing style, in her novels she creates an evocative picture of the modern Vietnamese historical experience. *See also* DISSIDENTS; LITERATURE; NGUYỄN HUY THIỆP.

DƯƠNG VĂN MINH ("Big Minh") (1916–2001). General in the **Army of the Republic of Vietnam** and a leading force in the coup d'état that overthrew President **Ngô Đình Diệm** in November 1963. Educated in **France,** Dương Văn Minh supported Diệm against the **Bình Xuyên** in 1954 and became one of the leading figures in the South Vietnamese army. Eventually, however, Diệm became suspicious of Minh's loyalty and removed him from command. In 1963, he became a leading member of the group of generals who overthrew the Diệm regime and president of the Military Revolutionary Council set up in November. Genial and plain-spoken in manner, a southerner by family background and a **Buddhist**, Big Minh was popular with the local population and well liked by most American officials, but his political capacities were limited. In January 1964, he was briefly detained in a coup led by Col. **Nguyễn Khánh**, and left for exile, though he later returned.

In the spring of 1975, Minh briefly accepted the presidency of the **Republic of Vietnam** in an unsuccessful effort to obtain conciliatory terms from **Hanoi**. He remained in Saigon after the Communist takeover and was placed in detention. He was allowed to immigrate to France in 1983 and later moved to the United States, where he spent the rest of his life. *See also* HỒ CHÍ MINH CAMPAIGN; TRẦN VĂN DÔN.

DƯƠNG VÂN NGA. A queen and queen mother in the 10th century. A member of a powerful clan in Thanh Hoá that had an important role in the turbulent decades following the end of **Chinese** rule, she became one of five wives and empresses of **Đinh Bộ Lĩnh**. After his murder in 979, he was succeeded by his young heir, with Dương Vân Nga (the boy's mother) as regent. As the country was facing military crises with both China to the north and **Champa** to the south, the court decided to replace the young emperor with **Lê Hoàn**, a leading general. Dương Vân Nga supported the deposition of her son and married the new ruler, who went on to defeat both the Chinese and the Cham. She was frequently condemned by Confucianist historians who accused her of having had an affair with Lê Hoàn and then abetted him in ending her husband's "dynasty" and establishing his own. Present-day scholars are more sympathetic, however, arguing that she supported the change in ruler because she recognized it was in the national interest.

DUPRÉ, JULES–MARIE (1813–1881). Governor of French **Cochin China** from 1871 to 1874. A career naval officer and supporter of **French** colonial expansion in Asia, Dupré sent **Francis Garnier** to **Hanoi** in 1873 to rescue the merchant-adventurer **Jean Dupuis** and extend French influence into northern Vietnam. Disavowed by the government in Paris, Dupré resigned in December 1873. The French withdrew from **Tonkin** but were granted a loose **protectorate** over the Vietnamese Empire in the **Philastre Treaty** signed in 1874. *See also* TỰ ĐỨC.

DUPUIS, JEAN (1829–1912). **French** merchant-adventurer in the mid-19th century. In 1873, he attempted to force the Vietnamese Court to open up the **Red River** as a trade route into **China**. After sailing into the Chinese province of Yunnan, he returned to **Hanoi** and made a show of force. His efforts were subsequently aided by the arrival of the French explorer and adventurer **Francis Garnier**, but Garnier was killed in fighting with Vietnamese troops, and Dupuis was forced to withdraw. *See also* DUPRÉ, JULES-MARIE.

DUY TÂN (1900–1945). Emperor (r. 1907–1916) of the **Nguyễn dynasty** under the French **protectorate**. Duy Tân, a son of Emperor **Thành Thái**, replaced his father on the throne at the age of eight when the latter was deposed by the **French** and sent in exile to the island of Réunion. Patriotic in inclination, he complained frequently about his lack of authority, and in May 1916, he fled the imperial palace in support of a revolt led by Trần Cao Vân. Apprehended two days later, he was deposed and sent to join his father in exile. He served as a commandant in the French Army during World War II and some sources claim he was considered as a possible replacement for Emperor **Bảo Đại** during the government of General Charles de Gaulle in 1945 but he was killed in an airplane crash in December.

DUY TÂN HỘI (Modernization Society). Anticolonial organization in **French**-occupied Vietnam. It was established by the Vietnamese patriot **Phan Bội Châu** in 1903 to promote an insurrection against French rule. Its goal was to evict the French and establish a constitutional monarchy under Prince **Cường Để**, a descendant of Prince **Cảnh**, a son of the founding emperor of the **Nguyễn dynasty**. The organization was replaced by a new one entitled the **Vietnamese Restoration Society** (Việt Nam Quang Phục Hội) in 1912.

– E –

EARLY LÊ DYNASTY. *See* LÊ HOÀN.

EARLY LÝ DYNASTY. *See* LÝ BÍ.

EASTER OFFENSIVE. Major military offensive launched by North Vietnamese forces in the **Republic of Vietnam** in late March 1972. Unlike the **Tet Offensive** four years earlier, the Easter Offensive took place primarily in rural areas rather than in the major cities. The attack took place in three sectors: in Quảng Trị along the **Demilitarized Zone**, in the **Central Highlands**, and along the **Cambodian** border in Bình Long. The offensive was most successful in Quảng Trị, overrunning the provincial capital and causing panic among South Vietnamese divisions defending the area. According to some sources, only the intervention of **United States** air power prevented a total collapse of Saigon's defensive position in the area. Elsewhere, South Vietnamese units generally were able to hold their positions.

Hanoi's motives in launching the offensive have been widely debated. Party leaders might have hoped that a major triumph on the battlefield would lead to a collapse of the Saigon regime. At a minimum, they undoubtedly hoped to demonstrate the failure of the American strategy of "**Vietnamization**" during a presidential election year and force U.S. concessions at the Paris peace talks. *See also* PARIS AGREEMENT.

ÉCOLE FRANÇAISE D'EXTRÊME-ORIENT (EFEO). The École Française d'Extrême-Orient was the premier **French** research institution in Southeast Asia during the colonial period. Founded in 1898 as the Archeological Mission of **Indochina**, it was renamed as the *EFEO* in 1900, following the model of similar "French Schools" in Athens and Rome and was formalized by government decree the following year. Centered in Hanoi, the EFEO was home to a wide range of scholars and amateurs with scholarly interests, and its publications (including the well-known *Bulletin*) covered topics in history, ethnology, **archeology**, linguistics, and **literature**. The EFEO's most enduring legacy was probably its work on the inscriptions, monuments, and archeological artefacts of Indochina, though many of the conclusions and theories of colonial-era scholars have been challenged in recent years. It also trained a core of local researchers in various fields. Although the EFEO closed down its work in Vietnam several years after the end of colonial rule, it returned to Hanoi in the early 1990s (and subsequently to Vientiane and Phnom Penh as well) and has once again become active in promoting French-language scholarship on the region.

ECONOMY. French rule did not leave the Vietnamese a significant legacy in terms of **industrial** development because the colonial economy gave priority to **agricultural** commodities for export, particularly **rice** and **rubber**. There was a small industrial base, mostly in the northern half of the country (which became the **Democratic Republic of Vietnam**, DRV), but even this amounted to only seven modern factories at the time of partition in 1954. Over the next few years, the DRV government worked hard on building up this base with foreign aid, mostly from the socialist bloc led by the **Union of Soviet Socialist Republics** and **China**. When the **United States** began its bombing campaigns in the mid-1960s, however, this brought the DRV's industrialization to a halt because factories were usually considered key targets and many were destroyed. Other plants were saved only by being dismantled and dispersed to different areas, resulting in a considerably diminished industrial output.

In the **Republic of Vietnam**, industrialization was minimal, as the economy tended to rely heavily on imported consumer goods rather than producing them locally. There was no shortage of wealthy Vietnamese and **overseas Chinese** with capital to invest, but their money usually went into import–export ventures, black-market operations, and speculation instead of building factories or engaging in more orthodox entrepreneurship. The growing presence of U.S. troops from the early 1960s onward, as well as the huge influx of American military and civilian aid, meant that the natural patterns of a market economy that might otherwise have encouraged the growth of light industry on a significant scale were largely absent. As under the French, the fields continued to produce rice and the plantations turned out rubber, and the facilities needed to process these commodities remained an industrial priority.

Both the North and South Vietnamese economies relied heavily on foreign subsidies, though in different ways. The DRV had begun **agricultural collectivization** soon after the final departure of the French, and by 1960 a significant proportion of the country's farmers were involved in agricultural producers' cooperatives. Because the demands of collective farming did not encourage families to produce large surpluses, once the DRV was on a war footing in the early 1960s, the government developed a subsidy and procurement system aimed at acquiring enough food to feed its military forces while ensuring a flow of basic consumer goods to its people. Peasants in cooperatives were encouraged to grow a rice surplus and turn it over to the government at low prices in exchange for consumer goods (clothes, bicycles, thermoses, etc.), most of which had come from China in the form of aid.

In South Vietnam, an important lifeline for the national economy came from the Commodity Import Program (also known as the *Commercial Import Program*), an import subsidization scheme by the United States, which also helped fund the national budget. The United States supplied dollars to the **Saigon** government as aid; it sold the dollars at a cheap rate to local importers, who then used the hard **currency** to buy foreign products, mostly luxury consumer goods. Meanwhile, the government used the income from the sale of the dollars (essentially clear profit), together with the customs revenue from the imported goods, to fund the budget for the army, police, and civil service. This system helped to keep down inflation from the extra dollars by absorbing purchasing power while also helping ensure that the South Vietnamese middle class remained more or less loyal by subsidizing a higher lifestyle for them, artificial though it was.

The drawback, of course, was that the South Vietnamese economy became increasingly dependent on this kind of aid, especially after the final departure of big-spending American troops following the 1973 **Paris Agreement**. Generally speaking, the country's economy was unnaturally dependent on foreign aid, with American funds basically bankrolling much of its budget. Between 1960 and 1974 (the last full year of the Republic's existence), total nonmilitary expenditure by South Vietnamese citizens was 114 percent of the country's Gross Domestic Product (GDP), meaning that they spent nearly 15 percent more than they produced; the difference came from U.S. aid. The scaling back of the American presence beginning with the first troop withdrawals in the early 1970s provoked a major economic crisis that helped contribute to the general deterioration of the South during the final years before the Communist victory of 1975.

One positive development in the South over the course of the war was that the power of the old landlord class had been largely broken as many wealthy landowners abandoned their property for the safety of the cities and were less and less capable of collecting rent. The Communist-led **National Liberation Front** had carried out **land reform** in areas under their control, and even the Saigon regime under **Nguyễn Văn Thiệu** had carried out a "Land to the Tiller" program, which somewhat improved the land tenure situation. Wartime shortages had brought high prices for crops for those who were still able to farm their land, and large doses of foreign development aid for agriculture, as well as increased mechanization, meant that some farmers, at least, were better off than before. Southern farmers were given easy access to fertilizer and consumer goods, such as watches and motorbikes, though whether these advantages strengthened their loyalty to a government often characterized by rapacious officials is questionable.

Peace and reunification in 1975–1976 brought long-awaited opportunities and serious challenges to the leaders of the **Vietnamese Communist Party** and the **Socialist Republic of Vietnam** (SRV). Under the leadership of General Secretary **Lê Duẩn**, who dominated policymaking from his appointment to this position in 1960 until his death in 1986, the Party moved to turn the South into a socialist economy as fast as possible. Although wisdom might well have dictated a slower pace given the dramatically different political, economic, and social conditions that the two Vietnams had experienced over the past two decades, Duẩn and those who supported him within the leadership (by no means everyone) were determined to consolidate their victory with political and economic integration.

In retrospect, the **Hanoi** government's efforts to "consolidate socialism" in the South involved many blunders, but two miscalculations in particular stand out. First, the Party pushed ahead with agricultural collectivization as it had done in the North 20 years earlier. As was just mentioned, however, changes in landholdings in South Vietnam meant that there were fewer poor or landless farmers than there had been at the beginning of the war, and certainly there was nothing like the critical mass of such people who had accepted collectivization in the DRV. Moreover, Southern farmers who had supported the revolution against the Saigon regime had been fighting partly to acquire land for themselves, not for socialist collectivization. The reversal of Party policy from the NLF's land reform (which put land into the hands of the farmers) toward collectivization (which effectively took it back) was destined to be unpopular.

The second major error involved the existing economic infrastructure in the South. The new SRV government generally did not value what industrial base there was and tended to feel that South Vietnam's economic development had been "tainted" by its association with the Americans and the despised Saigon regime. After reunification, many officials and managers left the country as refugees, and some of those who remained were put into reeducation camps, drastically shrinking the number of people with real business and management skills who might conceivably have been able to assist with economic integration. A particularly serious mistake was the decision to mount campaigns against "compradors" and other members of the bourgeoisie. Because many of these were ethnic Chinese, the attack on their economic interests not only alienated those with the most substantial financial resources and incited them to flee in droves as **boat people**, it also angered the government in Beijing and was an important factor in the breakdown of Sino–Vietnamese relations in the late 1970s.

The SRV after 1975 faced other challenges that, ironically, were posed more by peace than by war. In the former DRV territory that had experienced two decades of collectivization, socialist agriculture did not seem to have achieved what was expected of it, and a lot of Northern farmers were frustrated and ready for change. Moreover, while many people had been prepared to make sacrifices to supply food for their relatives, friends, and other compatriots who were fighting in the South, their attitude changed significantly once the war was over, and neither the short conflict with China in 1979 nor the longer military involvement in **Cambodia** beginning in 1978 could call forth the same sacrificial spirit. Economic problems multiplied through the 1980s, resulting from the limitations caused by a U.S.-led trade embargo, generally poor agricultural output, and a series of bad harvests because of natural disasters in particular. The break with China meant that the wartime flow of consumer goods had stopped, and Vietnam's industry had not begun to recover sufficiently to pick up the slack.

The Hanoi government was not blind to the problem, and, by the beginning of the 1980s, it began to effect gradual changes in agriculture, beginning with the implementation of the contract system, which gave farming households more opportunities to gain income from private sales of rice and produce. This step began a steady shift from collectively owned land to household property; this shift represented a virtually irreversible move away from a socialist agricultural system, even though theoretically there is still no private property, only **land use rights** in lieu of permanent private ownership. Today, the importance of cooperatives is still affirmed, but they function more as administrative than as economic units. These changes in the agricultural sector have driven significant growth in the production for export of commodities like **rice, coffee, tea**, and cashews. Unlike the colonial period, when quotas imposed by the government meant that farmers had to turn over their crops regardless of their own subsistence needs, the expansion of Vietnam's export market has benefited individual households, as well as the nation's GDP as a whole.

The incremental dismantling of collective agriculture is part of the broader pattern of economic reforms known as "renovation" (*đổi mới*), formally inaugurated at the Sixth Party Congress in 1986 and initiated under then-General Secretary **Nguyễn Văn Linh**. Along with the changes in agricultural policy came the gradual implementation of market structures in pricing (instead of centrally fixed prices); a much greater freedom for individuals to produce, sell, and trade on their own; and an overall shift from a centrally planned economy to one based on supply and demand. One of the most important priorities under *đổi mới* has been the move to integrate Vietnam with the global economy and to promote the country as an attractive location for **foreign investment**; the pace of these efforts has accelerated considerably over the last decade after the lifting of the last remnants of the embargo in 1994. Currently, the government's economic development policy is based on the twin buzzwords of "industrialization" and "modernization," both of which clearly assume large injections of capital from outside the country, whether in the form of investments through **joint ventures** and subsidiaries of multinational corporations or as **Overseas Development Assistance** aimed at infrastructural change.

Vietnam has made some tremendous strides in changing its economic policies and priorities, and the fairly steady growth in GDP since *đổi mới* got under way is a testimony to this fact. It has had considerable success in wooing foreign investors; between 1988 and 2004, just over 5,000 projects were initiated, representing close to $26 billion in realized capital. Joint ventures have proliferated, particularly in the **export processing zones** and more numerous industrial zones that form the cornerstone of the country's efforts to attract investors and promote industrialization. **Tourism** has proved to be a particularly lucrative sector of the economy; hotels, restaurants, and other services catering to foreigners have multiplied, with generally successful results for both GDP and the country's image abroad. (The domestic tourism market for Vietnam's own citizens has also expanded considerably in recent years with the end of internal travel restrictions and the rise in disposable income.)

There have been many bumps in the road to reform, however. The most fundamental problem, perhaps, is that many people in authority have a vested interest in the old system and would prefer to continue to profit from it without making changes in its structure. This is true, for example, of many **state-owned enterprises** whose managers are reluctant to face the risks involved with **equitization** (essentially equivalent to privatization) and prefer the status quo. At the top of the system, reform-minded junior leaders must still contend with more senior figures (often retired but still influential) who are much more ambivalent about the deeper implications of reform, feeling that much of *đổi mới* is, at best, a sacrifice of their socialist ideals and, at worst, a first step to the erosion of socialism across the board. The highly factional nature of Party leadership has meant that no reform-minded leader has demonstrated either the vision or the clout of a Deng Xiaoping in China, so that many initiatives are easily slowed down at the highest levels of government. Further problems exist at lower levels of the hierarchy, where the prevalence of bureaucracy and red tape is a frequent irritant to those involved in various kinds of economic activity. **Corruption**, too, might help to grease the wheels, but it also drains resources out of the economy.

These obstacles notwithstanding, Vietnam since the 1980s has gone far enough down the path toward a market system that there is virtually no likelihood of turning back. The benefits of *đổi mới* are clear: GDP has grown at an average annual rate of just over 6 percent since 1990. The key question for the Party and the government is how to ensure that as many as possible get a slice of the pie. Agricultural reforms not withstanding, the rural areas of the country continue to lag behind the cities in many respects, and large segments of the population remain sidelined from the opportunities for prosperity. The government has recognized that growth must also go hand-in-hand with development, and the ability to ensure that one brings the other will be crucial to the country's political, economic, and social stability in the coming years.

EDUCATION. Education has traditionally had considerable importance in Vietnamese society. During the precolonial period, the primary purpose of education was to train candidates for the imperial bureaucracy. The educational system was based on the concepts of the Chinese philosopher Confucius and was composed of **village** schools whose purpose was to train students for the civil service examinations, the traditional route into the bureaucracy. Emphasis within the **examination system** was placed on the need to inculcate young men with proper moral training and civic virtues.

After **colonization** in the late 19th century, **France** introduced Western educational values and institutions into Vietnam. Emphasis was placed on knowledge of the arts and sciences, while **Confucianism** was phased out. As in the traditional period, however, higher education was for the few. Most Vietnamese received only a rudimentary education in village schools, and literacy rates were low. The colonial regime experimented with different combinations of vernacular and French-language education; ultimately a solid knowledge of French, acquired only through many years of schooling, became the key to success.

Major advances in education occurred after the division of Vietnam into two separate states in 1954. In the South, the **Republic of Vietnam** adopted some elements of American educational philosophy but generally maintained much of the colonial school system, including the widespread use of French as a medium of instruction at upper levels, even though increasing numbers of South Vietnamese were going to the **United States** for higher education. In the North, the **Democratic Republic of Vietnam** (DRV) introduced a system based on mass education and the indoctrination of the entire population in the principles of Marxism–Leninism. After the unification of the two zones in 1975, the system in use in the North was extended throughout the entire country, as the government endeavored to use the educational system as a tool to promote the creation of an advanced socialist society. Dual emphasis was placed on technological modernization and ideological indoctrination.

Under renovation (*đổi mới*), the emphasis on ideology has, to some extent, been replaced by a focus on practical subjects to promote rapid economic development, but a lack of funding has led to a perceptible decline in quality. Teachers, unhappy at low salaries, are leaving the profession or else putting much of their time and effort into private classes to supplement their income. **University** students frequently pursue a second or third degree, both because of the relatively specialized nature of specific schools and programs and because having more than one degree makes one more marketable. Educational opportunities are broadening with the introduction of privately run schools and universities, and more Vietnamese students are being given opportunities to study overseas. *See also* SCIENCE AND TECHNOLOGY.

ÉLY, PAUL (1897–1975). General in the French Army and chief of staff during the **Geneva Conference** of 1954. In March of that year, French Prime Minister Joseph Laniel sent him to the **United States** to request aid for the beleaguered French garrison at **Điện Biên Phủ.** The response by the Dwight D. Eisenhower administration was ambiguous, leading to a misunderstanding between the two governments. When Paris formally requested assistance, the White House rejected the request. After Geneva, Ély briefly served as the senior French representative in **Saigon.**

ÉLYSÉE ACCORDS. Compromise agreement signed between the **French** government and ex-Emperor **Bảo Đại** in 1949. Signed on 8 March 1949, the accords called for French recognition of the independence of the so-called Associated **State of Vietnam** within the **French Union.** In foreign relations, Vietnamese independence was limited by its membership in the Union. Internally, Vietnamese autonomy was confirmed, except for some limitations in the judicial sphere and an agreement that Vietnam would give priority to French political and technical advisers. Vietnam would have its own military, with French forces limited to designated areas, but in practice the **Vietnamese National Army** was placed under French command for the duration of the **Franco–Việt Minh War.**

Because the autonomous **Republic of Cochin China** was technically not included within the scope of the agreement, the National Assembly in Paris authorized the creation of a territorial assembly of **Cochin China** to vote union with the State of Vietnam. It did so on 23 April. The Élysée Accords went formally into effect on 14 June with a ceremony in **Saigon**, and ratification by the French National Assembly took place on 29 January 1950. Diplomatic recognition by the **United States** came a few days later, but considerable doubt existed in the minds of many observers, both within Vietnam and on the world scene, as to whether Vietnam was yet in control of its own destiny. *See also* ASSOCIATED STATES OF INDOCHINA; BẢO ĐẠI SOLUTION; HẠ LONG BAY AGREEMENT.

ENERGY RESOURCES. Lack of sufficient energy resources has been one of the crucial problems hindering economic development in Vietnam. Although there are substantial amounts of **coal** northeast of **Hải Phòng** along the **Tonkin Gulf**, and recently discovered **oil** fields off the coast near Vũng Tàu, for many years neither source was adequately developed to promote the rapid growth of the Vietnamese **industrial** sector. Since reunification, official policy has placed increased emphasis on the development of these resources as a crucial element in the building of a modern **economy**.

Progress was slow until the late 1980s, but with the advent of reforms under *đổi mới* and particularly the growing inflow of **foreign investment**, the pace began to pick up. While the **Union of Soviet Socialist Republics** still existed, Soviet aid helped with hydroelectric and thermal power projects, and Soviet petroleum interests were heavily involved in the development of Vietnam's petroleum resources. Since the end of the Soviet Union, much of the funding for energy-related projects has had to come from other sources. (The post-socialist Russians were involved in an oil refinery project for several years but subsequently abandoned their participation in the project.)

The **Hanoi** government has been pursuing contractual relationships with various foreign companies to drill for oil in the **South China Sea**, and reserves have recently been discovered in the **Tonkin Gulf**. Exploitation of these resources, however, is seriously complicated by competing territorial claims from **China** and several Southeast Asian neighbors. Several natural gas projects are being pursued as well. Vietnam's reserves of oil and gas are currently calculated at 6.5–8.5 billion barrels and 75–100 trillion cubic feet, respectively. In 2004, petroleum production was estimated at 130 million barrels and gas production at 200 billion cubic feet.

Increasing electrical output remains an important priority, particularly given the country's rising level of industrialization. Vietnam was able to double its electricity production in less than a decade, from 15.6 billion kilowatt hours in 1995 to 33.7 billion in 2002; by 2004 this figure was just over 46 billion. Nearly half of this output was provided by hydropower, followed by coal and gas turbine production. The government continues to expand its hydropower facilities; construction on a 2400-megawatt hydroelectric plant at Sơn La on the Đà River in the northwestern region is scheduled to begin in 2005. A 500-kilovolt north–south power line commissioned in 1995 has been operating at full capacity, and a second line from **Pleiku** in the **Central Highlands** to the coastal region of **Đà Nẵng** is planned.

EQUITIZATION (*Cổ phần hoá*). "Equitization" is a quasi-privatization of **state-owned enterprises** (SOEs), which has begun to take place under the **economic** reforms known as *đổi mới* (renovation) in the **Socialist Republic of Vietnam**. The adoption of socialist economic policies by the **Democratic Republic of Vietnam** in the 1950s led to the **nationalization** of most private businesses and the establishment of SOEs. The dominant role of the state sector went virtually unquestioned until the mid-1980s, when a series of economic setbacks, together with the generally unsuccessful attempts to impose socialism onto the more **capitalist** system of the former **Republic of Vietnam**, provoked some serious rethinking of government policy. The leadership of the **Vietnamese Communist Party** concluded that the only solution was a series of reforms in the direction of a more market-oriented system.

Although dismantling or diluting the state sector would inevitably be a key component of such a policy, it was not until 1992, after reformist Prime Minister **Võ Văn Kiệt** had taken power, that a decree specifically calling for equitization was issued. Rather than being privatization in the strict sense of the term (i.e., the sale of a SOE to private investors), equitization was conceived as a restructuring of a state enterprise's ownership to attract potential investors from various sectors of the economy, including its own employees. (Most foreign observers, however, consider equitization to be privatization by another name.) It was intended not to completely separate the SOEs from the state that had spawned them, but rather to allow them to operate more efficiently and more profitably under its supervision. After a four-year pilot period, a second decree was issued in 1996 in order to speed up the process, and then a third in 1998, which provided more liberal guidelines.

Equitization has not proceeded either as quickly or as smoothly as some observers had hoped. Although there is considerable evidence that the process has indeed benefited at least some of those SOEs that actually completed it (in terms of profitability and employee salaries), the number that have done so has increased slowly. By the end of 2003, there were roughly 4,800 SOEs in operation. The government originally planned to equitize 80 percent of these by 2007, with a target of some 1,900 for 2004 (including 880 left over from 2003). In the end, however, this goal proved too ambitious, and it was expected that only about 700 of those enterprises could be successfully equitized by the end of 2004. One major obstacle has been the heavy indebtedness of many SOEs, which poses serious problems for the equitization process; nor are all directors eager to trade the benefits their companies enjoy as state-owned entities for an uncertain future as a joint stock company. A very small handful of equitized companies have listed on Vietnam's embryonic **stock market**.

EXAMINATION SYSTEM. Examination procedure for evaluating potential candidates for the imperial bureaucracy in traditional Vietnam. The civil service examinations, patterned after a similar system used in **China**, were first put into operation by the **Lý dynasty** in the 11th century. In the early centuries of its existence, the Vietnamese system tested candidates on the teachings of **Buddhism** and **Daoism** as well as those of **Confucianism** (the so-called "*tam giáo*" or "three doctrines"), but over time it became more purely Confucian in content.

At first, only members of the hereditary aristocracy were permitted to sit for the examinations and enter the ranks of officialdom. Eventually, however, the examinations were opened up to all Vietnamese men except for those convicted of crimes or engaged in proscribed occupations. The examinations took place at three levels: the *tu tài*, given annually in local centers; the *cử nhân*, given in regional cities; and the *tiến sĩ*, given triennially in the imperial palace in the capital. Students who had passed the metropolitan exam but were not considered good enough to be candidates for the *tiến sĩ* were given the title of *phó bảng*; they were eligible for employment as officials, normally at the provincial or prefectural level.

Many graduates became candidates for the imperial bureaucracy at various levels, depending on their results. Not all graduates became officials (mandarins), however; some preferred a life of scholarship or became teachers at Confucian academies established to train young Vietnamese for the examinations. Failed candidates at lower levels could return home and teach students in their **villages**. In a nation where the bureaucracy was the most respected occupation, the examinations were the primary ladder of upward mobility for aspiring young men. The system was by no means egalitarian, as **women** were excluded, and only those with sufficient leisure and financial resources were able to undergo the difficult educational process necessary to succeed in the examinations. However, it did provide the state with a bureaucracy based on merit and an exposure to Confucian political and moral philosophy.

The examination system was continued for several decades under colonial rule in order to train mandarins for the French **protectorate** but was then abolished around the time of World War I. *See also* EDUCATION; MANDARINATE.

EXPORT PROCESSING ZONES (EPZ, *Khu chế xuất*). Export Processing Zones came into existence in 1991 as a means of encouraging **foreign investment** in Vietnam. They are designated areas for the establishment of small- and medium-sized enterprises, intended to provide adequate infrastructure and financial incentives to investors that might not be easily found elsewhere in the country. So far, only a small handful of EPZ's have been established, and they have been considerably outnumbered by industrial zones (*khu công nghiệp*), which the government began to promote in 1994 and which have become the main channel for foreign investment in Vietnamese **industry**. The results have been mixed, and many of the zones are plagued by technical and management problems that have left them well below the desired rate of occupancy. However, the government is pushing ahead with these projects and they continue to be a key component of Vietnam's national development policy.

– F –

FAIFO. *See* HỘI AN.

FAMILY SYSTEM. Traditionally, the family system has been an important component of social organization in Vietnamese society. Although the nature of family life in the period prior to the **Chinese**

conquest in the second century B.C.E. is not well known, during and after Chinese rule the Vietnamese people were exposed to **Confucian** concepts of social hierarchy, such as filial piety and subordination of the wife to the husband. However, the spread of Confucian influence was slow, and its penetration into different strata of Vietnamese society was uneven. Some scholars argue that the Vietnamese were originally matriarchal, and even today the mother retains a considerable degree of authority in the family, especially where financial matters are concerned.

Although the basic unit of rural society in traditional Vietnam was the nuclear family, composed of parents and unmarried children, the extended family remained the ideal, as in neighboring China. Poor families could be assisted by their more fortunate relatives in times of hardship, whereas their sons might hope to be able to achieve a classical **education** by attending a school sponsored by wealthier members of the clan. The extended family thus acted as an informal welfare system to reduce the natural inequalities of daily existence.

The traditional family system was strongly shaken by the influence of Western concepts of individualism and sexual equality in the early 20th century. Adolescents began to resist the tradition of arranged marriages, and **women** chafed under social mores that called for obedience to their fathers and husbands. In urban areas, Western patterns of social behavior became increasingly prevalent, especially among the elite. But the traditional interpretation of the family remained strong in the countryside. The **Vietnamese Communist Party** has at times placed more emphasis on the individual than on the family as the basic unit of society, but it never attempted to destroy the family system, as was done in China during the Cultural Revolution of the 1960s. At present, as Vietnam opens up and faces the twin challenges of Western culture and undesirable moral influences, the family is seen as a key element of social stability. *See also* GIA LONG CODE; HỒNG ĐỨC CODE.

FATHERLAND FRONT (*Mặt Trận Tổ Quốc***).** Umbrella front organization in the **Socialist Republic of Vietnam** (SRV). Originally created in **Hanoi** in 1955, the Fatherland Front was the successor to the **Liên Việt Front**, established in 1951. The creation of the new front was apparently motivated by the peace agreement signed at the **Ge-**

neva Conference in 1954 and the need for the **Democratic Republic of Vietnam** to focus on new objectives, namely, the construction of socialism in North Vietnam and the peaceful reunification of the South with the North. Since that time, it has served as the umbrella organization for the various functional, ethnic, and religious mass associations that are used by the regime to mobilize support for its policies.

The Fatherland Front also served as the main front organization for the revolutionary movement in the South until December 1960, when the **National Front for the Liberation of South Vietnam** was proclaimed at a congress held at a secret location near the **Cambodian** border. The two fronts were merged in 1976 when the two zones were reunited into the SRV.

FESTIVALS. As in most **agricultural** societies, the majority of Vietnamese holidays are connected with the harvest cycle. Many were inherited from **China** during the long **Chinese period** of Vietnamese history, while others emerged after independence in the 10th century C.E. The most famous holiday in Vietnam is the traditional New Year's festival (known in Vietnamese as *Tết Nguyên Đản*). The Tết festival marks the beginning of the new year based on the lunar calendar of 355 days each year. The holiday is a period of family festivity and begins when the Kitchen God (*Táo Quân*) is sent to Heaven to report on family affairs, which hopefully will bring good fortune for the remainder of the year.

Another major holiday in Vietnam is the so-called Mid-Autumn Festival (*Tết Trung Thu*), also known as the *Moon Festival*. Also inherited from China, the Mid-Autumn Festival takes place on the 15th day of the eighth month and is marked by the lighting of colored lanterns and the eating of so-called "moon cakes" made specially for the occasion.

One annual ceremony practiced in traditional Vietnam involved the participation of the emperor. Known as the *Plowing Ritual (Lễ Tịch Điền)*, it was initiated by Emperor Lê Đại Hành (**Lê Hoàn**) in the 10th century on the basis of previous Chinese practice. The emperor plowed a furrow at the beginning of the annual harvest cycle as a symbolic act to guarantee a good harvest. Abolished under the **Trịnh Lords**, it was revived during the **Nguyễn dynasty**.

Until recently, the Party discouraged many of the traditional festivals on the grounds that they were a financial extravagance and a legacy of the **feudal** past that the regime wished to eradicate. In recent years, however, the government has been more tolerant of such practices, many of which are now viewed favorably as "popular culture," and they are thriving in rural and urban areas alike. *See also* RELIGION.

FEUDALISM. Feudalism represents one of the modes of production which, according to Marx, all societies are supposed to go through between the stage of slavery and that of **capitalism**. Vietnamese Marxists have traditionally used the term "feudal" to designate Vietnamese society through the beginnings of colonial rule. At the same time, however, scholars in various countries have raised the issue of whether Marx's concept of feudalism, rooted as it was in a particular period of European history, is applicable across the board in Asian countries. In Vietnam's case, the period of the **Trần dynasty** bore some resemblance to European feudalism, in that it saw the rise of *trang điền*, large estates owned by royal family members and nobles who controlled both land and manpower. This was an exceptional phenomenon, however, and generally speaking the model of feudalism is not a comfortable fit for much of Vietnamese history. The **Asiatic Mode of Production** represents one attempt to apply Marx's writings in an Asian context and is viewed by some Vietnamese scholars as an appropriate model for Vietnam.

FILMS. A native film industry did not begin to develop in Vietnam until the advent of independence after the **Geneva Conference** of 1954. Previously, Vietnamese artists wishing to produce a film were forced to go abroad—notably to Hong Kong—to do so. The first film produced by a Vietnamese, entitled *Field of Phantoms (Cánh Đồng Ma)* appeared in 1934. During the **Franco–Việt Minh War**, a few makeshift films, mainly newsreels and documentaries, were produced by **Việt Minh** artists in the **Việt Bắc**. In the spring of 1954, with Soviet assistance, a Vietnamese film crew produced *Vietnam on the Road to Victory*, using film footage of actual battlefield scenes at **Điện Biên Phủ**.

In March 1953, President **Hồ Chí Minh** of the **Democratic Re-**

public of Vietnam (DRV) signed a decree establishing a state enterprise for cinematography and photography. On the return of the DRV government to **Hanoi** in October 1954, the state-run Vietnamese Feature Film Studio was founded, as well as other enterprises run by the state or the People's Army to produce newsreels and documentaries. The quantity and quality of films produced during the Vietnam War, however, was limited. Among the most interesting were films produced by artists operating with **National Liberation Front** units in South Vietnam.

After reunification in 1976, film production began to increase, assisted by the creation of a College of the Cinematic Arts three years later. During the decade following the end of the war, about 10 feature films were produced annually. Themes were tightly controlled by the state and tended to focus on the heroic struggle for national unification or on the challenges of socialist construction since 1975. A few were awarded prizes at film festivals in socialist bloc countries.

In recent years, film production has increased rapidly, along with the assertion of greater independence on the part of film producers in the selection of subject matter. Recent films have displayed strong criticism of postwar conditions, even questioning the official line on the unbelievably heroic character of the struggle for national liberation. A few have even focused attention on once-hidden intimate aspects of Hồ's life. As with their literary counterparts, film producers who transcend the bounds of official approval risk government censorship or persecution. Foreign movies are now widely available in Vietnam, a development that is challenging the national film industry to produce more commercially competitive works. *See also* LITERATURE.

FONTAINEBLEAU CONFERENCE. Conference between representatives of **France** and the **Democratic Republic of Vietnam** (DRV) at the Palace of Fontainebleau in the summer of 1946. The conference was held to discuss the provisions of the **Ho-Sainteny Agreement**, reached in March. It soon became clear at Fontainebleau that the French government was not prepared to be conciliatory in key issues related to the March agreement, such as the formation of a "free state" of Vietnam and the holding of a referendum in **Cochin China** on the possible association of that colony with the DRV.

When High Commissioner **Thierry d'Argenlieu** unilaterally convened a second **Đàlạt Conference** in early August to create an **Indochinese Federation** without the participation of the DRV, the Vietnamese delegation under **Phạm Văn Đồng** despaired of an agreement and shortly thereafter left for **Hanoi**. President **Hồ Chí Minh**, in France as an observer, remained in Paris and negotiated a *modus vivendi* calling for renewed talks early the following year. Tensions increased during the fall, however, and the **Franco–Việt Minh conflict** broke out in December 1946.

FOREIGN INVESTMENT. During the Vietnam War, both Vietnams received vast amounts of **economic** assistance from their major sponsors. The physical impact in terms of nation-building was minimal, however, because of the intensity of the conflict, and much of the aid was absorbed by the day-to-day domestic needs of the two countries. The exceptions were a few **industrial** and infrastructural projects built with foreign aid, especially from the **Union of Soviet Socialist Republics** (USSR) and other socialist bloc countries in the **Democratic Republic of Vietnam**.

After the fall of the **Republic of Vietnam** in 1975, the reunified **Socialist Republic of Vietnam** hoped for substantial aid, not only from its wartime allies **China** and the USSR but also from the **United States** and other Western countries. The Vietnamese occupation of **Cambodia** and the subsequent economic embargo put paid to these hopes, however, and during the 1980s, Vietnam received only limited economic and technological assistance, mainly from the Soviet Union. Soviet aid averaged about U.S.$1 billion a year, in the form of loans or grants.

By the late 1980s, Soviet aid was beginning to dry up as the Mikhail Gorbachev leadership shifted to domestic priorities. Fortunately, Vietnam was able to establish commercial relations with a number of **capitalist** countries in Asia, although the Western embargo on trade kept major countries, such as the United States, from joining in. In late 1987, Hanoi passed a new foreign investment law that was one of the most liberal in Asia, and a number of private foreign sources began to invest in Vietnam. Although the more open economic policies associated with the reforms known as *đổi mới* (renovation) created a much more receptive environment within the country, it was

only with the lifting of the final trade embargo in 1994 that a significant inflow of foreign investment could begin. (The need to shift to
new sources of capital had become particularly urgent with the demise of the socialist bloc and its Council for Mutual Economic Assistance of which Vietnam had been a member.)

The decade since the lifting of the embargo has seen a fairly steady
increase in Foreign Direct Investment (FDI) from an increasingly
wide variety of sources. The initial wave of investment came mainly
from Asian countries, such as Taiwan, Hong Kong, South Korea, and
Singapore, but investors from the U.S., Australia, **France**, and other
Western countries were also quick to get involved. In 1995, the Hanoi
government created a new Ministry of Investment and Planning specifically to deal with what was hoped would be an ever-expanding
portfolio of projects. A number of different sectors of the economy
have been opened to foreign investors—**tourism**-related services
being a prime area of interest—and the multiplication of **export
processing zones** and particularly industrial zones along with **joint
ventures** of various sizes and shapes has brought both qualitative and
quantitative expansion of FDI.

A joint venture requires at least 30 percent of the company's legal
capital to come from the foreign partner; a 100-percent foreign-invested company is also possible. It has recently become possible—
under certain conditions—for foreign investors to put capital directly
into an existing Vietnamese entity through a Business Cooperation
Contract, rather than creating a new one through a joint venture. The
foreign investor's equity in the company under this arrangement is
capped at 30 percent, a limit that is enforced for foreigners' purchase
of shares on the **stock exchange** as well. If an investor's stake in a
company goes beyond the 30-percent mark, then the company must
be converted to a joint venture. The wholly foreign-owned company
has become increasingly popular because it avoids many of the complications involved in partnerships with Vietnamese entities.

As of the end of 2004, official government statistics gave a figure
of just over 5,000 for the number of FDI projects approved since
1988, representing nearly $26 billion of realized capital out of a total
commitment of $45 billion. Singapore was the top investor in terms
of value, followed by Taiwan, Japan, South Korea, and Hong Kong;
the United States stood at 11th place on the list. For 2004, Vietnam

received commitments of $4.1 billion in FDI, a 35-percent increase over 2003; of that figure $2.85 billion actually materialized as realized capital, a 10-percent increase over the previous year.

Although Vietnam has enthusiastically promoted itself as an investment target and has made valiant attempts to improve the regulatory climate and physical infrastructure needed for FDI, its record has been mixed. Foreign investors face many frustrations, from bureaucracy and red tape to **corruption** to troubled relations with joint-venture partners. Issues such as **land usage rights** and the need to consolidate a **rule of law** continue to pose obstacles to the growth of investment. Both opportunities and enthusiasm continue to abound despite these problems, however, and although the increase in FDI has been uneven, it continues to climb and to diversify. *See also* AGRICULTURE; BANKING AND FINANCE; FOREIGN RELATIONS; MINERAL RESOURCES; OIL; STATE PLANNING.

FOREIGN RELATIONS. For much of Vietnam's precolonial history, its rulers had two sets of relationships: **China** and everyone else. From the time of independence in the 10th century, China dominated Vietnam's foreign relations as its imperial overlord, cultural model, and most durable external threat. In dealing with this powerful neighbor, the Vietnamese assumed an explicitly subordinate role, and rulers who were "emperors" to their own people were careful to style themselves as mere "kings" in their correspondence with the Chinese court. At the same time, however, they sought to minimize Chinese expectations of their obligations as vassals and were quick to respond to military incursions or even the smallest encroachment on their territory. This policy was generally successful, and with the exception of the 20-year **Ming occupation** in the 15th century, Vietnam maintained its independence until it was **colonized** by the **French**.

Ties with other neighbors were more uneven. Vietnam was most involved with those peoples directly bordering its territory: the **Cham**, **Cambodians**, and **Lao**. From the 18th century onward, the Siamese were a constant presence on the diplomatic and military scene as well. Official chronicles portrayed these "barbarian" kingdoms as, at best, loyal vassals who "sent tribute" to Vietnam and at worst as troublemakers who "plundered" its borders and had to be "suppressed" in times of unrest. The reality was probably otherwise because for centuries these neighboring kingdoms were more or less on a par with Vietnam in terms of strength and influence. The Cham, however, began to weaken and from 1400 onward their territory was gradually absorbed by the Vietnamese. The Cambodians and Lao became caught between Vietnamese power to the east and Siamese strength to the west, beginning in the early 17th and late 18th centuries, respectively.

From the 16th century onward, the Vietnamese had contacts with Western missionaries and traders, but these were few in number, and there was no important European presence or threat until the rise of French imperialism in the mid-1800s. Although the **Nguyễn dynasty** emperors were arguably somewhat more open-minded and less insular than their Chinese counterparts, the country was not strong enough to defend itself against the concentrated force of French military might, nor could it hold its own in diplomatic negotiations. Colonial rule firmly locked the Vietnamese (along with the Cambodians and Lao) into the global French empire, and their worldview was largely a Francophone one, though small groups of nationalists did seek exile in China, **Japan**, and Siam. The first two countries in particular were influential as models for various strains of Vietnamese nationalism, and the Chinese Communist Party played an important role in supporting **Hồ Chí Minh**'s **Indochinese Communist Party** in its struggle against French rule.

After independence and the partition of Vietnam at the **Geneva Conference** in 1954, the two countries' choices of friends and enemies were determined largely by Cold War concerns. The **Republic of Vietnam**, supported diplomatically and militarily by the **United States**, was clearly linked to members of the Southeast Asia Treaty Organization and other strongly anti-Communist governments, such as South Korea and Taiwan. The **Democratic Republic of Vietnam** was tied to the socialist bloc, and most of its aid came from China, the **Union of Soviet Socialist Republics**, and the countries of Eastern Europe. It also had ties to Cuba and neutralist countries, such as Algeria. A few European nations, such as France and Sweden, which were neutral in the Vietnam conflict, maintained diplomatic relations with both **Hanoi** and **Saigon**.

With reunification and the establishment of the **Socialist Republic**

of Vietnam (SRV) in 1976, the country's foreign relations generally remained locked into a Cold War framework through the end of the 1980s. Tensions and then war with China placed Hanoi firmly within the Soviet camp, while its invasion and occupation of Cambodia in 1978–1979 pitted it against its **Association of Southeast Asian Nations** (ASEAN) neighbors, the United States, and much of Western Europe. By 1990, the fall of the USSR and the end of the Cambodian conflict drastically changed Vietnam's diplomatic priorities, and the lifting of the U.S.-led trade embargo in 1994 removed the last major hurdle to integration with the rest of the world. Since then, the SRV has sought to broaden its ties and make as many friends as possible. In particular, it has become an enthusiastic member of ASEAN and is emerging as an increasingly important voice on the regional scene.

The two most important and most complex players in Vietnamese foreign policy are the U.S. and China. With Beijing, Hanoi maintains a public face of ideological solidarity and socialist fraternity, while tensions over territorial claims and **economic** rivalry continue to bubble beneath the surface. Vietnamese–American relations, on the other hand, are steadily improving, as periodic verbal slinging matches over **human rights** and **trade** issues are ultimately less harmful to bilateral ties than the territorial disputes and border encroachments that mar the Sino–Vietnamese relationship. The Vietnamese government has pursued a wide range of diplomatic and military contacts with Washington, though it is careful to balance these developments with equally frequent initiatives directed at Beijing. An excellent example of the complex relations Hanoi has with both powers came in 1999, when Vietnam postponed the signing of a **bilateral trade agreement** with the U.S., partially out of concern for Beijing's possible displeasure, because China's own agreement with Washington was still being negotiated. Then the Chinese pushed through the Sino–American trade treaty faster than expected without informing Hanoi, and the Vietnamese scrambled to catch up.

Generally speaking, Vietnam is still learning to deal with a post-Cold War world that can no longer be neatly divided into friends who only praise and enemies who only criticize. The Hanoi government continues to grapple with the harsh reality that, unlike its former socialist allies, its trade partners and donors of **Overseas Development Assistance** are not always willing to write blank checks with no regard for its domestic policies. These changes notwithstanding, the legacy of a millennium of diplomacy and warfare remains strong, and postwar Vietnam has established itself as an important player in Asia, one that is taken increasingly seriously by Western powers as well.

FRANCE. The French first became interested in Vietnam during the 17th century, when Catholic missionaries organized under the **Société des Missions Étrangères** began to proselytize for converts among the predominantly **Buddhist** and **Confucian** Vietnamese. Such activities had some success but eventually provoked the imperial court to declare the practice of **Christianity** illegal. At the end of the 18th century, French missionary interests attempted to use persecution of the Catholic community in Vietnam as an argument to establish a French **protectorate** over the country. Such efforts did not succeed until the late 1850s, when an imperial commission sponsored by French Emperor Napoleon III approved a plan to invade Vietnam and establish a French presence in the country. By the mid-1880s, **Cochin China** had become a colony, and the remainder of the country was a French protectorate.

For half a century, French colonial officials carried out what they termed a *"mission civilisatrice"* in French **Indochina** (composed of the colony of Cochin China and the four protectorates of **Annam**, **Tonkin**, **Laos**, and **Cambodia**). Anticolonial resistance began to intensify in the 1920s, however. After World War II, the **Indochinese Communist Party**, operating through the League for the Independence of Vietnam or **Việt Minh**, seized control of the northern half of the country. France attempted to restore its authority through the application of military force, but resistance led by the Việt Minh continued, and at the **Geneva Conference** in 1954, Paris finally agreed to withdraw its military forces and grant full national independence to the country, now temporarily divided into two zones.

After the Geneva Conference, French governments attempted to maintain a degree of French economic and cultural influence in Vietnam. During the Vietnam War, France remained neutral in the conflict and frequently criticized the **United States** for its effort to resolve the problem by military force. Today, relations between France and the **Socialist Republic of Vietnam** (SRV) are increasingly cordial. The government is generally less suspicious of Paris than of Washington, and Vietnam has become an enthusiastic participant in Francophone organizations, which it sees as a counterweight to U.S. influence. *See also* ASSIMILATION; ASSOCIATION; AUGUST REVOLUTION; COLONIZATION; COMMISSION ON COCHIN-CHINA; FRENCH UNION; HO-SAINTENY AGREEMENT; INDOCHINESE UNION; PATENÔTRE TREATY; PHILASTRE TREATY; PROTECTORATE; TREATY OF SAIGON.

FRANCO–VIỆT MINH WAR. Extended conflict between the **French** colonial regime and the Communist-dominated **Việt Minh** Front after World War II, also known as the *First Indochina War*. The war began on 19 December 1946, when Việt Minh forces attacked French installations in the city of **Hanoi** and then withdrew to prepared positions in the mountains surrounding the **Red River Delta**. During most of the next several years, Việt Minh units under the command of the **Indochinese Communist Party** waged a guerrilla struggle against French forces stationed throughout Indochina. The conflict came to an end after the French public began to tire of the war and doubt the possibility of a favorable outcome. Following the French defeat at **Diện Biên Phủ**, a peace treaty was signed at the **Geneva Conference** on 21 July 1954, calling for a withdrawal of the French and the temporary division of Vietnam into two separate zones under the **Democratic Republic of Vietnam** and the **State of Vietnam**. *See also* BẢO ĐẠI; HỒ CHÍ MINH.

FREE VIETNAM. *See* REPUBLIC OF VIETNAM.

FRENCH EXPEDITIONARY FORCES (FEF). French military forces in Indochina after World War II. The first troops arrived in October 1945 under the command of General **Jacques Philippe Leclerc**, and they were immediately engaged in driving **Việt Minh** and other nationalist units from the **Saigon** metropolitan area. Later, they played the dominant role in fighting against Việt Minh troops after the outbreak of war in December 1946. All French troops were eventually withdrawn after the **Geneva Conference** of July 1954. *See also* DE LATTRE DE TASSIGNY, JEAN.

FRENCH UNION. Commonwealth-type organization set up by the **French** after World War II in an attempt to retain control over French colonial territories under a new administrative arrangement. In theory, members in the French Union possessed autonomous status, but the French government retained control over key aspects of national affairs, and there was no mention of secession from the organization *See also* BRAZZAVILLE DECLARATION; INDOCHINESE FEDERATION.

FRONT UNIFIÉ POUR LA LIBÉRATION DES RACES OPPRIMÉES (FULRO). A separatist movement for ethnic minorities in the **Central Highlands**. FULRO grew out of the **Bajaraka** movement, which was repressed by the **Ngô Đình Diệm** government in the late 1950s. Although it included highlanders who were being trained by the Central Intelligence Agency Special Forces to fight on the South Vietnamese side, FULRO was fundamentally anti-Vietnamese rather than anti-Communist, and it represented dissident elements who opposed the absorption of the Central Highlands region into the **Republic of Vietnam**. It continued to exist after the fall of South Vietnam in 1975 and there were sporadic incidents through the early 1990s, when most of the remaining FULRO elements fled to **Cambodia** and were resettled in the **United States**. These elements have maintained close links with their home region and have publicized the on-going problems that its population has faced in recent years. They have been accused of instigating outbreaks of violence in the Central Highlands in recent years. *See also* DEGA; HIGHLAND MINORITIES.

– G –

GAO PIAN (Cao Biền). Chinese general who defeated the forces of the Nanzhao kingdom in what is now northern Vietnam (then known as the *Protectorate of Annam* under Chinese rule) in the mid–ninth century. After defeating the invading army, Gao remained in Vietnam and earned the respect of the local population for his political and economic policies before his departure in 865. At the same time, however, some stories show him as being defeated by local spirits in his attempts to exert authority over Vietnamese spiritual powers. Although Gao Pian reestablished the authority of the Tang Empire in **China** over its dependency in the South, the dynasty was now in a period of steady decline, resulting in an increased degree of autonomy for local administrators in Vietnam. *See also* CHINESE PERIOD.

GARNIER, FRANCIS (1839–1873). Naval officer and adventurer who promoted **French** colonial efforts in 19th-century Vietnam. After serving as a young lieutenant in the navy, Garnier entered the French administration as inspector of indigenous affairs in the new colony of **Cochin China** in the early 1860s. Ambitious and convinced of France's destiny in Asia, Garnier organized an expedition to explore the **Mekong River** basin in 1866. The published results caught the attention of commercial interests in France.

In 1873, supported by Governor **Jules-Marie Dupré**, Garnier launched a military operation in northern Vietnam to secure the safety of the French merchant **Jean Dupuis**, who was running weapons up the **Red River** into southern **China**. On arrival in **Hanoi**, Garnier supported Dupuis's demands for the opening of the Red River to international commerce and stormed the citadel. He then attempted to extend French control over neighboring areas between Hanoi and the **Tonkin Gulf**. He died in battle on 21 December 1873.

In his brief and meteoric career, Garnier earned a reputation as one of the pioneers of French expansion in Asia. Although the French, on orders from Paris, now withdrew from **Tonkin**, the 1874 **Philastre Treaty** opened the Red River to foreign commerce and constituted the first step in establishing a French **protectorate** over the Vietnamese Empire. *See also* BLACK FLAGS; TỰ ĐỨC.

GENEVA ACCORDS. *See* GENEVA CONFERENCE.

GENEVA CONFERENCE. A major international conference attended by representatives of several nations to seek a settlement of the **Franco–Việt Minh War** in the spring of 1954. An agreement among the Great Powers to meet at Geneva had been reached at the beginning of the year. At first, the sole topic proposed for discussion had been the issue of divided Korea, but at a meeting in Berlin in January, major world leaders had agreed to raise the **Indochina** conflict for possible settlement.

The conference began to discuss the Indochinese problem on 7 May. Attending were the existing governments in Indochina (the **Democratic Republic of Vietnam** [DRV], the **State of Vietnam**, **Laos**, and **Cambodia**), the People's Republic of **China**, **France**, Great Britain, the **Union of Soviet Socialist Republics**, and the **United States**. The U.S. attended with reluctance, in the conviction that any compromise settlement could have dangerous effects on the security of the remainder of Southeast Asia.

The fall of the French garrison at **Điện Biên Phủ** on the eve of the conference cast a pall on the non-Communist delegations at the conference. At first, French representatives refused to consider major concessions to the DRV, but in June a new government under Prime Minister Pierre Mendès-France came into office on a commitment to bring the war to an end within one month. Mendès-France accepted a partition of Vietnam into two separate regroupment zones (the Communists in the North, the non-Communists and pro-French elements in the South) divided at the Bến Hải River on the 17th parallel. The zones were not to be construed as sovereign entities, however, but solely as administrative areas (to be governed by the DRV in the North and **Bảo Đại**'s State of Vietnam in the South) until the holding of reunification elections.

The issue of elections was resolved in the so-called Political Declaration, which called for consultations between representatives of the two zones one year after the signing of the Geneva Agreement. These consultations were to result in an agreement to hold national elections throughout the country one year later. The cease-fire and the carrying out of the provisions of the Political Declaration were to be supervised by an **International Control Commission** composed of representatives of Canada, India, and Poland. The cease-fire agreement was signed by representatives of the DRV and France on 21 July 1954. The Political Declaration received verbal approval from seven of the participants. The United States and the Bảo Đại government abstained, with the U.S. representative stating that Washington would not hold itself responsible for the Geneva Accords but would take no steps to disturb them.

The Geneva Conference resulted in a compromise agreement that in effect presented the DRV with half of Vietnam. The South remained under the control of non-Communist elements. France now abandoned its responsibility for Indochina and was replaced in the South by the United States. Hard-line elements on both sides were displeased, with some supporters of the **Việt Minh** expressing bitterness that their cause had been sold out by China and the Soviet Union. The United States now prepared to defend South Vietnam, as well as the independent states of Laos and Cambodia, from a further advance of Communism. The reunification elections never took place. **Ngô Đình Diệm**, successor to Bảo Đại in South Vietnam, refused to hold consultations with representatives of the DRV. By the end of the decade, the war would resume. *See also* DEMILITARIZED ZONE; REPUBLIC OF VIETNAM.

GIA ĐỊNH BÁO (*Journal of Gia Định*). First newspaper to be printed in *quốc ngữ*, the Romanized transliteration of spoken Vietnamese. Established in 1865 by the **French** colonial administration in **Saigon**, it played a major role in popularizing *quốc ngữ* in the colony of **Cochin China**. One of its editors and primary contributors was the pro-French collaborator **Trương Vĩnh Ký**. *See also* JOURNALISM.

GIA LONG (Nguyễn Ánh) (1761–1820). Founding emperor of the **Nguyễn dynasty** (1802–1945). As the last surviving ruler of the **Nguyễn Lords**, who had ruled southern Vietnam since the 16th century, Nguyễn Ánh fought a campaign for more than two decades to restore his family's power and defeat the **Tây Sơn** movement, which had overthrown them. Escaping to the marshy **Mekong Delta**, the young Nguyễn Ánh proclaimed himself king and was able to restore Nguyễn power briefly, but then he was driven out again in 1783. Taking refuge on Phú Quốc Island in the Gulf of Thailand, he accepted aid from the French Bishop of Adran, **Pigneau de Béhaine**. In 1787, he signed a treaty with **France** to restore Nguyễn power in Vietnam in return for the cession of the port of Tourane (**Đà Nẵng**) and the island of **Poulo Condore**. The promised assistance from the French court did not materialize, but Pigneau de Behaine helped organize the armed forces that eventually overthrew the Tây Sơn.

In 1802, taking the dynastic name *Gia Long*, Nguyễn Ánh declared himself founding emperor of a new dynasty—Vietnam's last—which would survive until 1945. The Nguyễn dynasty now ruled over almost all of the territory of present-day Vietnam. Once in power, Gia Long placed his capital at **Huế** and changed the name of the empire from *Đại Việt* to *Đại Nam*. He launched a number of administrative reforms and proclaimed a new penal code, known as the *Gia Long Code*. In providing a moral and ideological foundation to the empire, he imitated the **Confucian** orthodoxy of the Qing dynasty in **China**, and his legal code is seen as more closely modeled after Chinese law than previous Vietnamese codes.

Pigneau de Béhaine and other Frenchmen who had aided Nguyễn Ánh on a personal basis hoped that their country would be granted favorable commercial and missionary privileges under the new regime. Gia Long was suspicious of Western influence, however, and although he tolerated a measure of missionary activity in Vietnam, he refused to permit a substantial French commercial presence. He was also distrustful of **Christianity** after seeing his converted son Prince **Cảnh** refuse to bow before the ancestral altar. Gia Long died in 1820 at the age of 59 and was succeeded by another son, who took the imperial title of **Minh Mạng**. In the 1960s, there was a debate between scholars in **Hanoi** and **Saigon** as to whether Nguyễn Ánh or **Nguyễn Huệ** of the Tây Sơn should properly be regarded as the first ruler of a unified Vietnam after two centuries of division.

GIA LONG CODE. Penal code adopted by the **Nguyễn dynasty** in 19th-century Vietnam. Patterned after its counterpart used in Qing **China**, it was promulgated in 1815 and replaced the so-called **Hồng Đức Code** adopted by the **Lê dynasty** in the 15th century. Compared with its predecessor, it took less account of local custom and more strictly followed the Chinese model. Its fundamental objective was to maintain the power of the emperor and law and order in the social arena. Penalties were severe, and a male-oriented perspective characteristic of the Chinese system replaced the more liberal provisions of the Hồng Đức Code. The Gia Long Code continued in force under the French colonial regime until it was supported by a new one adopted in 1880. *See also* GIA LONG; LEGAL SYSTEM; WOMEN.

GIAO CHÂU. An administrative region of Vietnam under the rule of the Chinese Empire. The province (*châu*, Ch. *zhou*) of Giao was established as a unit in the third century C.E. and was located in the area of the lower **Red River Delta** in the vicinity of the present-day capital of **Hanoi**. At the time, it was the most populous province in occupied Vietnam, with an estimated total population of about 100,000 people. *See also* CHINESE PERIOD.

GIAO CHỈ. Ancient administrative term for the **Red River Delta** in northern Vietnam. The term *Giao Chi* (ch. *Jiaoehi*), which means "intertwined feet" (sometimes translated as "crossed toes"), was first introduced during the reign of **Triệu Đà** in the kingdom of Na-nyue/**Nam Việt** and might have referred to the **Chinese** view of the sleeping habits of the non-Chinese peoples of the south, who slept in communal fashion with their feet together and their heads extending outward. Giao Chỉ became one of two provinces into which the region of the Red River Delta was divided and referred to the lower region of the Red River.

Under Chinese rule from the Han dynasty onward, the term was retained as the name of one of the three provinces into which the Red River Delta was divided. The others were called *Cửu Chân* (south of the Delta) and *Nhật Nam* (south of the Hoành Sơn spur). Some scholars believe that the name *Giao Chỉ* is the source of the "Co-chin" in "**Cochin China**," arguing that the original term was corrupted by the Portuguese.

GIÓNG (sometimes spelled *DÓNG*). A legendary boy of giant size who fought off invading enemies. According to old Vietnamese texts, Gióng lived in present-day Bắc Ninh province during the prehistoric period before **Chinese** rule. He grew quite large but by the age of three he had yet to utter a single word. Then an invasion by an un-identified enemy took place, and Gióng suddenly spoke, asking for a sword and a horse. Mounting the horse, he flew up into the sky and proceeded to defeat the enemy and then disappeared. He later re-ceived the title of *Phù Đổng Thiên Vương*, which recognized him as a guardian spirit, and he is often known as *Thánh Gióng*—"Thánh" being a title given to various powerful spirits.

GRACEY, DOUGLAS (1894–1964). Commander of British Expedi-tionary Forces in **Indochina** at the close of World War II. General

Gracey sympathized with **French** plans to restore colonial rule in Indochina and assisted French forces in southern Vietnam to drive nationalist forces out of **Saigon**. His lack of sympathy for the **Việt Minh** and other Vietnamese forces was a key factor in their failure to fully consolidate their power in the southern region during the crucial weeks after the Japanese surrender. *See also* AUGUST REVOLUTION; COMMITTEE OF THE SOUTH.

GRAND CONSEIL DES INTÉRÊTS ÉCONOMIQUES ET FINANCIERS DE L'INDOCHINE (Great Council of Economic and Financial Interests in Indochina). Advisory body set up by the **French** colonial regime in **Indochina**. Established by Governor-General **Pierre Pasquier** in 1928, the council possessed limited powers connected with economic policy and the budget. Its predecessor, the *Conseil Supérieur de l'Indochine*, was established in **Cochin China** in 1887.

GROUP 559. Military organization established in the **Democratic Republic of Vietnam** (DRV) in the spring of 1959 to construct and maintain a system of trails into the **Republic of Vietnam** to facilitate the infiltration of personnel and supplies into the South. The system, which was built partly on existing trails and passed through parts of southern **Laos**, was eventually dubbed the **Hồ Chí Minh Trail**. Other units were established to create a maritime passage into the South. The name of the organization was based on the date of the original decree (May 1959), which followed shortly after the Fifteenth Plenum of the Central Committee of the Vietnamese Workers' Party (VWP). *See also* GENEVA CONFERENCE; INTERNATIONAL CONTROL COMMISSION.

– H –

HẠ LONG BAY. Coastal waterway containing a chain of scenic islands and rocky outcroppings that stretch along the **Tonkin Gulf** from just east of the port city of **Hải Phòng** toward the Chinese border. The island chain is part of an extensive limestone deposit that has been heavily eroded by wind and water, thus creating thousands of islands of various sizes, some of which have taken fantastic shapes. The bay has been a **tourist** attraction for decades and is now a popular stopping place for cruise ships sailing along the coast of Vietnam en route to Hong Kong or Singapore. *See also* CÁT BÀ ISLAND.

HẠ LONG BAY AGREEMENT (also known as *Along Bay Agreement*). Accord reached between representatives of the **French** government and ex-Emperor **Bảo Đại** of Vietnam in June 1948. According to the terms of the agreement, signed aboard a French cruiser in **Hạ Long Bay** in the **Tonkin Gulf**, Bảo Đại tentatively agreed to return to **Indochina** as soon as France agreed to the creation of a united Vietnam. The new state would be granted independence as an "Associated State" within the **French Union**, but its foreign relations would be conducted by France, and its military forces would be "available for the defense of any part of the French Union."

The agreement did not win unanimous support, either in France or among nationalist elements in Vietnam, but was finally ratified by the signing of the **Elysée Accords** on 8 March 1949. *See also* BẢO ĐẠI SOLUTION; BOLLAERT, ÉMILE; STATE OF VIETNAM.

HÀ TIÊN. Border town on the Gulf of Thailand between Vietnam and **Cambodia.** Hà Tiên was originally founded by **overseas Chinese** immigrants who had been resettled in the **Mekong Delta** after the fall of the Ming. It was governed as a sort of autonomous fief by the ethnic Chinese Mạc family, who had connections to Vietnamese, Cambodian, and Siamese rulers. Over the long run, loyalty to the Vietnamese **Nguyễn Lords** prevailed, and Hà Tiên eventually became a Vietnamese province. *See also* MẠC CỬU; MẠC THIÊN TỨ.

HẢI PHÒNG (Haiphong). Major seaport located about 115 kilometers (70 miles) southeast of **Hanoi** in North Vietnam. Located about 20 kilometers (12 miles) from the **Tonkin Gulf**, Hải Phòng first assumed significance in the late 19th century when it was transformed from a small market town into a major seaport for the **Red River Delta** by the **French**. It eventually became the second largest city in the **protectorate** of **Tonkin**.

After the **Geneva Conference** of 1954, Hải Phòng became the major seaport of the **Democratic Republic of Vietnam** and a center for cement, shipbuilding, fishing, and machine construction. Today, it is the third largest city in the **Socialist Republic of Vietnam** (SRV), with a population of nearly 1.7 million people, divided into three urban quarters and seven suburban districts. Like **Hanoi** and several other large cities, it is an autonomous municipality under the central government.

HẢI PHÒNG INCIDENT. Armed clashes between military forces of **France** and the **Democratic Republic of Vietnam** (DRV) in November 1946. The incident was triggered by a dispute over the control of Vietnamese customs in the port of **Hải Phòng** but was actually a consequence of the rising tension in Franco–Vietnamese relations since the failure of the **Fontainebleau Conference** the previous summer.

In early November, the French government, basing its action on the **Ho-Sainteny Agreement** of March 1946, announced that it would open a customs house in Hải Phòng despite a protest by DRV President **Hồ Chí Minh**. Tension rose in the city during the next few days, and when a French patrol boat seized a Chinese junk running contraband in Hải Phòng harbor, it was fired upon by Vietnamese troops on shore. On the orders of High Commissioner **Thierry d'Argenlieu**, then in Paris, the French fleet launched a massive bombardment on the native sections of the city on 23 November, killing an estimated 6,000 persons. Street riots after the incident were suppressed by French troops, but France and the DRV had taken a major step toward war.

HÀM NGHI (1872–1943). Emperor (r. 1884–1885) of the **Nguyễn dynasty** after establishment of the French **protectorate** in 1884. Brother of Emperor **Kiến Phúc**, who died after a brief reign in 1884, Hàm Nghi took the throne at the age of 12. In July 1885, he fled the capital of **Huế** with Regent **Tôn Thất Thuyết** to launch the **Cần Vương** resistance movement against French occupation. In September, he was replaced on the throne by his brother **Đồng Khánh**. Captured in November 1888, Hàm Nghi was sent to live out his life in exile in Algeria, where he died.

HANOI (*Hà Nội*). Longtime capital city of Vietnam. The city is located at the confluence of the Đuống River and the **Red River**, about 75 kilometers (45 miles) inland from the **Tonkin Gulf**. Hanoi is one of the oldest cities of Vietnam and first became the capital in the 11th century C.E. Until the early 19th century, it was called *Thăng Long* ("rising dragon") or *Kẻ Chợ* ("market town"). Located at the confluence of several rivers, the city possessed a central location, a good defensive position, and was surrounded by fertile land. The area had been inhabited since the **Bronze Age** and became a major administrative center in the seventh century, during the period of Chinese rule. A defensive citadel called *Đại La* was built there, and provided the contemporary name for the city through the end of Chinese rule.

In 1010, nearly a century after the end of the **Chinese period**, **Lý Thái Tổ**, founding emperor of the **Lý dynasty**, moved his capital there from the town of **Hoa Lư** further down in the **Red River Delta**. According to legend, the emperor saw a golden dragon rising through the clouds as he arrived at the city. In honor of that vision, he named the city *Thăng Long*. The city remained the capital of Vietnam for most of the next nine centuries. Like its model in Peking, it was divided into two parts, with an imperial city (*Hoàng Thành*) surrounded by the remainder of the city (*Kinh Thành*). Inside the imperial city was the royal palace, the forbidden city (*Cấm Thành*), surrounded by a high wall and a moat.

During the next several centuries, the name of the city was occasionally changed, from Đông Đô (Eastern Capital) under **Hồ Quý Ly** to Đông Kinh (Eastern Capital) under Emperor **Lê Lợi**, and to Thăng Thịnh under **Nguyễn Huệ** of the **Tây Sơn**. For most of the period, however, it remained Thăng Long. When the **Nguyễn dynasty** (1802–1945) moved the capital to **Huế**, Thăng Long was renamed Hanoi (Within the Rivers), the name it retains today. At the same time, it was downgraded, and the second part of its traditional name (meaning "dragon") was changed to a less imperial homonym meaning "prosperity".

In the late 19th century, Hanoi once again assumed a dominant political position when it became the headquarters of French **Indochina**. It was primarily an administrative rather than an industrial city, although it did contain a small manufacturing and commercial sector. (**Saigon**, by contrast, was the center of the colony's financial interests, while Huế remained the imperial capital.) After the **August Revolution** in 1945, Hanoi became the capital of the **Democratic Republic of Vietnam** (DRV). Driven from the city after the beginning of the **Franco–Việt Minh War** the following year, DRV leaders returned in October 1954 after the **Geneva Conference** awarded the DRV all of the territory north of the 17th Parallel. Since then, it has remained the capital of the DRV and its successor, the **Socialist Republic of Vietnam**, founded in 1976.

Hanoi today is the second largest city in Vietnam, with a population of about 900,000 in the inner city, and three million in the metropolitan area. Like Hồ Chí Minh City and several other municipalities, it is run directly by the central government. Executive power is exercised by a **People's Committee**, headed by a chairman, and by the Municipal Branch of the **Vietnamese Communist Party**. The city is divided into four urban precincts and four suburban districts, composed of slightly over 100 communities.

Hanoi has become a popular **tourist** destination, partly because of its older architectural and cultural heritage, even though the oldest sites like the **One-Pillar Pagoda** and the **Temple of Literature** are often more recent reconstructions. There are also numerous colonial structures, such as the **Bắc Bộ Palace** and numerous villas, as well as the cathedral. More recent attractions include the **Hồ Chí Minh Mausoleum** and **Hồ Chí Minh Museum**. Hanoi remains in some ways socially and culturally more conservative than Hồ Chí Minh City (formerly *Saigon*), but the gap between the two in this respect is narrowing fast.

HARKINS, PAUL (1904–?). General in the **United States** Army and commander of the U.S. **Military Assistance Advisory Group** (MAAG) in the **Republic of Vietnam** from 1962 until 1964. Harkins was strongly criticized for remaining optimistic about the situation in South Vietnam despite rising evidence to the contrary. He was replaced by General **William C. Westmoreland** in the summer of 1964. As the U.S. presence in South Vietnam increased, MAAG was replaced by a new **Military Assistance Command, Vietnam** (MACV).

HARMAND TREATY (also known as the *Treaty of Protectorate*). Treaty between **France** and the Vietnamese Empire in August 1883.

Signed by the French scholar and diplomat François Harmand a few months after the death of Captain **Henri Rivière** near **Hanoi**, it established a French **protectorate** over central and northern Vietnam. (The southern provinces had already been ceded to the French as the colony of **Cochin China**). The treaty was signed under duress as French naval forces had bombarded the entrance to the imperial capital of **Huế** a few days previously. The treaty was not formally ratified in Paris and was replaced a year later by the **Patenôtre Treaty**, signed in June 1884. The Harmand draft would have transferred several provinces from imperial Vietnam to Cochin China, but the final treaty left them within the Protectorate of **Annam**.

HEALTH AND MEDICINE. Throughout most of its history, Vietnam relied on traditional techniques, such as herbal remedies and acupuncture for the treatment of illness and disease. Acupuncture itself is believed to date back to the Neolithic Era, when it was applied with stone needles, and some of its practitioners during the era of the **Hùng Kings** became famous throughout the region. The advent of French colonial rule in the 19th century introduced the Vietnamese people to the practice of modern medicine. The new science, however, had only a limited impact on overall health conditions. While the practice of traditional techniques went into decline, the number of doctors trained in modern medicine was seriously inadequate for social needs (according to one estimate, at the end of World War II there was only one doctor for every 180,000 people in the northern provinces), and life expectancy for the average Vietnamese was less than 40 years.

After the division of the country at the **Geneva Conference** of 1954, both Vietnamese governments established programs to create a modern health program. In the **Republic of Vietnam** (RVN), modern hospitals were constructed in major cities and district capitals, while rudimentary health stations were established in 3,000 villages and hamlets throughout the RVN. Antimalarial teams carried out spraying programs around the country, benefiting about six million people, approximately 40 percent of the population. The lack of trained personnel was a serious handicap, however; in the early 1960s, there were reportedly only 600 medical doctors in South Vietnam. Half of them were assigned to the armed forces, and most of the remainder practiced in Saigon. Aid for health programs from the **United States** amounted to only slightly over 1 percent of total U.S. assistance to the RVN. Most people in rural areas, by necessity or choice, continued to rely on traditional cures.

In the North, the **Democratic Republic of Vietnam** (DRV) had set up a national service in 1945 that relied on a combination of traditional and modern techniques. After its return to **Hanoi** in 1954, the DRV attempted to establish a network of hospitals and clinics in the major cities and towns, with health-care stations at the village level. National institutes for both traditional and modern medicine were established. As in South Vietnam, the lack of adequate funds and trained personnel represented a serious problem.

As a result of efforts to encourage prevention through antimalarial programs and improved sanitation, life expectancy has risen throughout the country to over 60 years of age. But problems continue and are now exacerbated by the shift to a qualified market system. With modern medical doctors earning a salary from the state of only about U.S.$50 per month, many have resorted to moonlighting. Health care is thus a question of the patient's ability to pay. In the meantime, severe budgetary problems have forced the government to cut back on many of its social programs. Malnutrition and malaria remain serious problems in some parts of the country, and HIV/AIDS is a matter of increasing concern.

HEATH, DONALD (1894–1981). Career foreign service officer and first U.S. ambassador to Vietnam. Appointed in 1950 shortly after the Truman administration had granted diplomatic recognition to the Associated **State of Vietnam** recently created by the **Elysée Accords**, Heath became a fervent supporter of **United States** assistance to the **French** against the **Việt Minh** Front. He was replaced by General **J. Lawton Collins** in late 1954.

HIỆP HOÀ (1847–1883). Emperor of Vietnam (r. 1883) in the **Nguyễn dynasty.** A younger brother and adopted son of Emperor **Tự Đức**, he succeeded his nephew **Dục Đức** after the latter was deposed by court officials in 1883. Hiệp Hoà attempted to wrest power back from these officials, but he was not strong enough, and he, in turn, was deposed and forced to commit suicide after a reign of only four months. *See also* NGUYỄN VĂN TƯỜNG; TÔN THẤT THUYẾT.

HIGHLAND MINORITIES. Highland or upland peoples comprise about 8 percent of the total population of the **Socialist Republic of Vietnam** (SRV). The highland minorities are divided into about 50 ethnic groups, representing every major linguistic family found in Southeast Asia: Tai–Kadai, Mon–Khmer (**Austroasiatic**), Sino–Tibetan, Malayo–Polynesian (**Austronesian**), and Tibeto–Burman.

The vast majority of upland peoples live in two major geographical areas—the mountainous provinces surrounding the **Red River Delta** and the **Central Highlands**. Key groups in the northern provinces are the **Thái**, **Tày**, **Mường**, and **Nùng**. In the Central Highlands, the largest minorities are the **Rhadé** and **Jarai**. Many of these groups have traditionally lived by **slash-and-burn agriculture**, although some peoples living in the northern valley areas engage in the cultivation of wet rice.

Throughout most of Vietnamese history, the upland areas have been governed separately from the remainder of the country. During the premodern period, they were rarely under direct imperial control. During the colonial era, the **French** set up distinct administrative districts in minority regions in the northwest and the Central Highlands; that policy was continued by the **Democratic Republic of Vietnam** (DRV), which established separate autonomous zones whose elected representatives were composed of members of the chief ethnic groups in the area. This policy was not followed in the **Republic of Vietnam**, which attempted unsuccessfully to **assimilate** the mountain minorities into the general population. After the formation of the SRV, the government abolished the autonomous regions in the North and has sought to reduce the socioeconomic differences between the minorities and the majority Vietnamese. Where culture is concerned, there has been an attempt to find a tricky balance between eliminating "backward" elements and preserving enough distinctives to avoid perceptions of assimilation. *See also* TÂY BẮC; VIỆT BẮC.

HISTORIOGRAPHY. The writing of history has long been a major form of literary achievement in Vietnam. The first known historical work was the 13th-century scholar **Lê Văn Hưu**'s *History of Đại*

Việt (*Đại Việt Sử Ký*). It is no longer extant, but it served as the core of **Ngô Sĩ Liên**'s *Complete Historical Records of Đại Việt* (*Đại Việt Sử Ký Toàn Thư*). A 15th-century historian, he traced the history of the country back to semilegendary origins in the period before **Chinese** rule. These early writings were undoubtedly strongly influenced by Chinese dynastic histories, and, indeed, the writing of history in Vietnam was patterned to a considerable degree after the Chinese model, with a precise chronological treatment of events interspersed with observations by various **Confucian** scholars.

Such official history predominated until the 20th century, when a new form of historical writing influenced by the West began to take effect. Individual biographies of heroic figures from the past were one manifestation of nationalism under colonial rule. During the wartime period between 1945 and 1975, historians in both North and South Vietnam labored to produce Vietnamese translations of classical historical texts written in Chinese or *chữ nôm*. Also an outpouring of historical scholarship reflected both nationalist sentiments and (in the case of the North) Marxist ideology; the two were by no means mutually exclusive. Particularly significant were the efforts of scholars in the **Democratic Republic of Vietnam** to reconstruct Vietnam's prehistory by synthesizing **archeological** findings and stories from premodern texts.

Today, there continues to be a significant output of work by academic and amateur historians alike, as the traditional Vietnamese passion for history has not dimmed. Through the late 1980s, much of this writing was strongly patriotic and ideological in tone, but recently it has taken on a more dispassionate character. The somewhat greater openness of the *đổi mới* period has allowed the expression of a wider variety of views, as well as the reassessment of certain individuals and movements in Vietnamese history who had earlier been condemned by the Party. *See also* LÊ QUÝ ĐÔN.

HÒ CHÍ MINH (1890–1969) (also known as *Nguyễn Ái Quốc*). Assumed name of Nguyễn Tất Thành, founder of the **Vietnamese Communist Party** and long-time president of the **Democratic Republic of Vietnam** (DRV). Born *Nguyễn Sinh Cung*, the son of a scholar-official of humble means in Nghệ An, Nguyễn Tất Thành was educated at the Quốc Học (**National Academy**) in the imperial capital of **Huế**. Absorbing the highly patriotic and anticolonialist views of his father, he left Vietnam in 1911 as cook's apprentice on a French ocean liner. After several years at sea, he settled briefly in London and then at the end of World War I went to **France**.

In Paris, Thành changed his name to *Nguyễn Ái Quốc* (Nguyễn the Patriot), submitted a petition to the Allied leaders meeting at Versailles demanding Vietnamese independence, and, in 1920, became a founding member of the French Communist Party. In 1923, he was summoned to Moscow for training as an agent by the Communist International (**Comintern**) and, in December 1924, traveled to Canton in southern **China**, where he formed the first avowedly Marxist revolutionary organization in Vietnam, the Revolutionary Youth League of Vietnam (**Thanh Niên**). Charismatic, dedicated, and an effective leader, Quốc built up the league into the most prominent organization opposed to French rule in **Indochina**, and, in 1930, it was transformed under his direction into the **Indochinese Communist Party** (ICP).

Quốc was arrested by British authorities in Hong Kong in 1931, and after his release in 1933, he spent the next several years in the Soviet Union, allegedly recovering from tuberculosis. In 1938, however, he left for China, where he spent a short period at Yan'an (Yenan) the headquarters of the Chinese Communist Party. He then settled in southern China, where he restored contact with the leadership of the ICP. In 1941, at a plenary session of the Central Committee at Pác Bó, near the Sino–Vietnamese border, he declared the formation of the so-called League for the Independence of Vietnam (**Việt Minh**), an organization formed to seek Vietnamese independence from French rule and wartime **Japanese occupation**.

In August 1945, now using the new pseudonym of *Hồ Chí Minh* (roughly translated as "he who enlightens"), he led the ICP and its front organization, the **Việt Minh**, in a successful uprising to seize power in Vietnam at the moment of **Japan**'s surrender to the Allies. A **Democratic Republic of Vietnam** (DRV), with Hồ Chí Minh as president, was proclaimed in Hanoi in September. The French refused to recognize Vietnamese independence, however, and seized control of the southern provinces in the fall of 1945. Negotiations between the DRV and France resulted in a preliminary agreement in

March 1946, but further negotiations at **Fontainebleau** failed, and war broke out in December 1946.

For eight years, Hồ Chí Minh led the Việt Minh in a struggle against France and the Associated **State of Vietnam**, a rival government set up by the French in 1949 under ex-Emperor **Bảo Đại**. The Việt Minh were unable to win a clear-cut military victory, but their ability to earn public support and wage a protracted struggle undermined the French war effort, and at the **Geneva Conference** in 1954 the DRV agreed to a compromise settlement, dividing Vietnam into two de facto separate states, with the DRV in the North and supporters of the State of Vietnam in the South. Some of the more militant members of the Party resisted the compromise settlement, but Hồ Chí Minh was able to achieve majority compliance by pointing out the danger of intervention by the **United States** and the possibility of achieving total reunification of the two zones by peaceful or revolutionary means in the near future.

For the remaining 15 years of his life, Hồ Chí Minh remained president of the DRV and leader of the Party. A convinced Marxist–Leninist, he led North Vietnam toward socialism while at the same time seeking to complete unification with the South, now renamed the **Republic of Vietnam**. Although increasingly fragile in health, he was generally successful in avoiding factionalism within the party and maintained an independent position in the Sino–Soviet dispute. Although the stern policies of his regime undoubtedly alienated many Vietnamese, overall he was revered by the people of North Vietnam, who often referred to him as "Uncle Ho." He died in September 1969 at the age of 79. Since his death, his successors have attempted to use his memory as a symbol for the building of a united socialist nation. A mausoleum containing his embalmed body now stands on a main square in the capital of Hanoi. *See also* AUGUST REVOLUTION; HỒ CHÍ MINH MAUSOLEUM; HỒ CHÍ MINH MUSEUM; HO-SAINTENY AGREEMENT.

HỒ CHÍ MINH CAMPAIGN. Military offensive launched by forces of the **People's Army of Vietnam** (PAVN) in South Vietnam in the spring of 1975. Initially, the 1975 campaign, directed by Senior General **Văn Tiến Dũng**, was designed to seize territory in the **Central Highlands** in preparation for a major offensive to seize power in the

South the following year. When initial attacks resulted in unexpected success, however, in April the Politburo of the Vietnamese Workers' Party (VWP) approved an intensive effort to seize Saigon and topple the **Republic of Vietnam** before the onset of the rainy season in May.

The offensive, named for ex-president **Hồ Chí Minh** in honor of his lifelong struggle for national reunification, was a spectacular success, and North Vietnamese forces entered **Saigon** in triumph on 30 April 1975.

HỒ CHÍ MINH CITY. *See* SAIGON.

HỒ CHÍ MINH MAUSOLEUM. Built at the order of the government of the **Socialist Republic of Vietnam** (SRV) shortly after the end of the Vietnam War, the Hồ Chí Minh Mausoleum is a forbidding gray marble structure in a severe modern style that sits at the head of **Ba Đình Square** in **Hanoi**, where **Hồ Chí Minh** read the Vietnamese Declaration of Independence in early September 1945. The decision to build the mausoleum was reached in 1973 and contravened the wishes of Hồ himself, who had declared in his last testament that he wished to be cremated and have his ashes distributed in all three regions of the country. His body is on public display and is visited by thousands of Vietnamese and foreign **tourists** every year. *See also* ARCHITECTURE.

HỒ CHÍ MINH MUSEUM. Imposing museum in the modern style built in the mid-1980s in **Hanoi**. Constructed by Soviet and Eastern European architects, it is located directly behind the **Hồ Chí Minh Mausoleum** on **Ba Đình Square** in the northwest section of the city. The museum is unique in that it seeks to place the life of **Hồ Chí Minh** within the context of his times. Displays on the ground floor of the museum illustrate the stirring events of the 20th century and his own role in the course of history, albeit from a strongly ideological point of view. The museum displays include many letters and artifacts from Hồ's life. *See also* ARCHITECTURE.

HỒ CHÍ MINH TRAIL. Series of trails used by the **Democratic Republic of Vietnam** (DRV) to infiltrate men and equipment into South

Vietnam during the Vietnam War. The trail was first put into operation in 1959 as the result of a decision by DRV leaders to return to a strategy of revolutionary war in the South. Initially a fairly simple affair leading from the southern provinces of the DRV around the **Demilitarized Zone** (DMZ) into the **Republic of Vietnam**, the trail eventually developed into a complicated network of trails, paths, roads, and waterways extending down the **Trường Sơn** mountain range in southern **Laos** and **Cambodia** and was popularly known in the West as the *Hồ Chí Minh Trail*. Despite heavy bombing by the **United States** Air Force, during the height of the war in the mid-1960s, it serviced the needs of several hundred thousand regular troops of the **People's Army of Vietnam** (PAVN) operating in the South.

HÒ DYNASTY. *See* HÒ QÚY LY.

HÒ HỮU TƯỜNG (1910–1980). A political activist, writer, and **journalist** whose career spanned the colonial and postcolonial periods. After being deported from **France** in his student days for radical activities, he returned to **Cochin China** and became involved with the Vietnamese **Trotskyites**. He later said that he had abandoned Marxism and, after the partition of Vietnam in 1954, he became a professor at the Buddhist Vạn Hạnh University in **Saigon**. He was a critic of successive South Vietnamese regimes, and spent several years in prison under **Ngô Đình Diệm**. He remained in Vietnam after the fall of the **Republic of Vietnam** and in 1977 was sent to **reeducation camp**; he died on the day of his release in 1980. *See also* DISSIDENTS.

HÒ QÚY LY (Lê Qúy Ly, 1336–1407). Powerful court figure at the end of the 14th century and founder of the short-lived Hồ dynasty (1400–1407). Hồ Quý Ly was born in a family descended from Chinese immigrants that achieved prominence at court at the end of the **Trần dynasty** (1225–1400). Originally surnamed *Lê*, he was a cousin by marriage of Emperor Trần Nghệ Tông (1370–1372), who appointed him to an influential position in the imperial administration. In the 1380s, he served as a high military officer and commanded Vietnamese armed forces against **Champa**.

Ly used his position to advance his own interests and manipulated the succession until he was regent for an adolescent emperor, whom he then forced to abdicate in 1398 and shortly after assumed power himself as founder of a new Hồ dynasty. One year later, he turned the throne over to his son, Hồ Hán Thương, while retaining influence through his position as royal adviser.

Hồ Quý Ly rose to the throne in the classic manner of the usurper, seizing power during the declining years of a disintegrating dynasty into which he had married. Yet he is remembered in history not solely as a usurper but also as a progressive who attempted to resolve some of the pressing problems that had brought down the powerful Trần dynasty. During his years in power, he launched a number of reforms in the fields of civil and military administration, **education**, and finance. He also attempted to reduce the power of **feudal** lords and reduce unrest in the countryside by reforming the tax system and limiting the amount of arable land that could be held by powerful **mandarins** and the aristocracy. Land in excess was confiscated by the state and leased to landless peasants at modest rent.

Ly had the misfortune to rule at a time when the Ming dynasty was becoming increasingly powerful and expansionist. To strengthen the nation's defense, he initiated a number of military reforms and increased the size of the armed forces. In 1397, he moved the capital to Thanh Hoá province south of the flat and highly exposed **Red River Delta**. The new capital was renamed *Tây Đô* (Western Capital). But the Ming took advantage of internal resistance to his reforms and launched an invasion of Vietnam, renamed *Đại Ngu* (Great Yu), in 1407. The pretext for the attack was to restore the Trần to power, but **China**'s actual motives were undoubtedly to restore its ancient authority over Vietnam. The Ming ruler was also angry at Ly's efforts to promulgate his own interpretations of **Confucian** teachings.

Despite Ly's efforts, the Vietnamese were quickly defeated. He, his son, and other leading members of his administration were shipped off to China where, now more than 70 years of age, he was forced to serve as a common soldier. He died shortly thereafter. Vietnam returned to Chinese rule until the late 1420s. *See also* MING OCCUPATION; *TRANG ĐIỀN*.

HO-SAINTENY AGREEMENT. Preliminary agreement between France and the **Democratic Republic of Vietnam** (DRV) on 6

March 1946. The agreement was signed by President **Hồ Chí Minh** of the DRV and French representative **Jean Sainteny**. Negotiations had gotten under way the previous autumn as France and the new Vietnamese republic in **Hanoi** attempted to resolve their differences over the future of **Indochina**. According to the agreement, France would agree to recognize the DRV as a "free state" within the **French Union**, with its own "army, parliament, and finances." A referendum would be held in **Cochin China** to determine whether the people in that French colony would unite to join the new free state or make their own separate arrangement with the French. In return, Vietnam would agree to permit the restoration of a French economic and cultural presence. **Chinese** occupation forces in northern Vietnam would be replaced by a mixed Franco–Vietnamese army under French command. French troops would be permitted to provide protection for French installations in the DRV. *See also* ĐÀLẠT CONFERENCE; FONTAINEBLEAU CONFERENCE; REPUBLIC OF COCHIN CHINA.

HỒ TÙNG MẬU (1896–1951). Founding member of the **Indochinese Communist Party** (ICP) in 1930. Little is known about his early life, except that he was born in 1896 in Nghệ An. He became a founding member of the Association of Like Minds (**Tâm Tâm Xã**), established in southern **China** in 1924. From there, he entered **Hồ Chí Minh**'s Revolutionary Youth League (**Thanh Niên**) and reportedly also became a member of the Chinese Communist Party. One of Hồ's most trusted colleagues and part of the inner circle of the league in the Communist group, he headed the league after Hồ's departure from China until his arrest in December 1928. He escaped from jail in August 1929 and helped arrange the unity conference in February 1930 that led to the formation of the Indochinese Communist Party. In June 1931, he was arrested by French police in Shanghai and condemned to a life sentence at **Lao Bảo** Prison. Released in 1945, he was reportedly killed in an air attack in 1951.

HỒ XUÂN HƯƠNG. Prominent writer in 18th- and 19th-century Vietnam. Born in Nghệ An in the mid-1700s, Hồ Xuân Hương was raised in **Hanoi** (then known as *Thăng Long*) and became a noted scholar and popular writer who used irony, wit, and sarcasm to attack the ills of contemporary Vietnamese society. Once herself the concubine of a district magistrate, she reserved her most powerful attacks for the hypocrisy, the **corruption**, and the double standards practiced at court, in the **Buddhist** temples, and throughout Vietnamese society in general. Among the best-known and most controversial poets of her time, she wrote in *chữ nôm* (a system of writing transcribing spoken Vietnamese), which allowed her to incorporate sexual word-play and *doubles entendres* that would not have been possible writing in classical Chinese. She is considered one of the founders of modern Vietnamese **literature**.

HÒA BÌNH CULTURE. Prehistoric civilization of the Mesolithic or early **Neolithic Era** in northern Vietnam. Located in limestone hills near the present-day city of Hoà Bình, the site was discovered in 1927. Later, additional sites were excavated elsewhere in Vietnam. According to present evidence, Hoà Bình civilization emerged from the late Paleolithic civilization about 11,000 years ago. It is often called a "pebble culture," characterized by the emergence of a cave-dwelling society based on the use of the chipped stones made of pebbles found along the banks of streams. The most frequently found implements are pebbles whose faces have been chipped on one side only, creating an edge with a simple bevel.

Skull and bone fragments found at the site suggest that the inhabitants of Hoà Bình were of Australoid–Negroid stock and lived primarily by hunting and gathering. At later sites, there is some evidence of the cultivation of plants and pottery making. *See also* ARCHEOLOGY; BẮC SƠN CULTURE.

HÒA HẢO. Reformed Buddhist religious sect in 20th-century Vietnam. Founded by the young mystic **Huỳnh Phú Sổ** in 1939, the Hoà Hảo **religion** is an offshoot of the **Bửu Sơn Kỳ Hương** (Strange Fragrances from the Precious Mountain), a millenarian sect formed in the lower **Mekong River Delta** by Đoàn Minh Huyên (known as the "Buddha Master of the Western Peace") in the mid–19th century. It represented a synthesis of reformed **Buddhism**, folk religion, and populist social attitudes among Vietnamese peasants in the frontier region in the delta. The movement spread rapidly in the 1940s and 1950s among the rural population in Châu Đốc, Bạc Liêu, Rạch Giá, and Long Xuyên provinces, for whom it served not only as a religion but also as a means of political and social organization.

During World War II, Hoà Hảo leaders cooperated with **Japan**. After the Japanese surrender, Huỳnh Phú Sổ flirted briefly with the **Việt Minh** but soon came to see them as rivals. After his assassination by the Việt Minh in 1947, the Hoà Hảo hierarchy cooperated reluctantly with the **French**. However, relations with the French and the various Vietnamese governments that followed were uneasy, as the Hoà Hảo attempted to maintain political autonomy in the areas they controlled.

The Communist seizure of South Vietnam in 1975 brought new troubles to the Hoà Hảo. The new revolutionary regime forced the Hoà Hảo central church organization to disband and arrested several of the leaders, although private worship is permitted. Communist distrust of the Hoà Hảo was probably justified, as many Hoà Hảo have reportedly engaged in resistance activities against the **Hanoi** regime. Today, an estimated one million Hoà Hảo live in Vietnam. *See also* CAO ĐÀI.

HOA KIỀU. *See* OVERSEAS CHINESE.

HOA LƯ. Capital of an independent Vietnamese kingdom between 968 and 1009. Located on the southern edge of the **Red River Delta** in what is now Ninh Bình Province, Hoa Lư was the birthplace of **Đinh Bộ Lĩnh**. After declaring himself emperor in 968, he moved the national capital from the ancient city of **Cổ Loa** in the heart of the Red River Delta to Hoa Lư, partly for defensive reasons (it was located in a valley surrounded by low mountains and far from **China**) and partly because it was outside of the area of traditional pro-Chinese sentiment in the province of **Giao** to the North. Hoa Lư remained the capital under **Lê Hoàn**, but in 1009 **Lý Thái Tổ**, founder of the **Lý dynasty**, moved the capital back North to **Đại La**, the site of present-day **Hanoi**.

HOÀN KIẾM LAKE (Returned Sword Lake, also known as *Hồ Gươm*, "Sword Lake"). A famous lake in the center of the city of **Hanoi**. Originally called *Lục Thủy* (green water), it was once a branch of the **Red River**, which silted over as the river bed shifted.

It was renamed *Returned Sword Lake* in the 15th century because of a legend that **Lê Lợi**, the founder of the **Lê dynasty**, had drawn a sword from the lake, inhabited by a golden tortoise, to achieve his great victory over the Chinese. Later, the sword was returned to the water.

During the traditional era, the lake was larger than at present and the site of a number of princely palaces and monuments built during the **Lý** and **Trần dynasties**. The **Trịnh Lords** held naval maneuvers there for entertainment. Two small islands are currently on the lake. One, connected to the mainland by a wooden bridge, contains Ngọc Sơn Temple, originally built during the Lê dynasty and restored during the 19th century. The other contains Tortoise Tower, a symbol of the city of Hanoi. There are occasional reported sightings of a large turtle still living in the lake.

HOÀNG CAO KHẢI (1850–1933). Scholar and official in 19th-century Vietnam. A native of Hà Tĩnh, he earned an academic degree at an early age and became a mandarin in the imperial bureaucracy. After the establishment of the French **Protectorate**, he joined the colonial administration and served as Viceroy of **Tonkin** from 1888 to 1892. A believer in the French civilizing enterprise, he became one of the colonial regime's most prominent collaborators during a long and financially rewarding life. In the 1880s, in a famous exchange of letters, he attempted unsuccessfully to persuade his friend **Phan Đình Phùng**, leader of the **Cần Vương** uprising, to abandon the path of resistance to the French.

HOÀNG ĐẠO (1906–1948) (real name *Nguyễn Tường Long*). Prominent novelist in colonial Vietnam. Born Nguyễn Tường Long in 1906 in Quảng Nam, he was a younger brother of Nguyễn Tường Tam, who wrote under the name of *Nhất Linh*. After earning a law degree, he became a judicial official in Hanoi and a novelist. Under the pen name of *Hoàng Đạo*, he wrote a number of romantic novels during the interwar period, such as *Con Đường Sáng* (*Bright Road*), *Mười Điều Tâm Niệm* (*The Ten Commandments*), and *Bùn Lầy Nước Đọng* (*Slums and Huts*).

Actively interested in politics, Hoàng Đạo was one of the main theoreticians with the so-called **Tự Lực Văn Đoàn** (Self-Reliance Literary Group) and a member of the **Việt Nam Quốc Dân Đảng**. His writings reflected an admiration for Western culture but at the same time a concern over social conditions in Vietnam and an implicit dislike of the French colonial regime. He died in exile in **China** in 1948. *See also* LITERATURE.

HOÀNG DIỆU (1802–1882). A prominent mandarin under the **Nguyễn dynasty**. Originally from Quảng Nam, he held a series of high-ranking positions in the **mandarinate**. When **French** forces under **Henri Rivière** began their military campaign to occupy **Tonkin** in 1882, Hoàng Diệu was governor of **Hanoi** and the surrounding region. He led the resistance to the French attack but was unsuccessful, and the citadel was occupied. Hoàng Diệu hung himself to express his personal shame over the Vietnamese surrender.

HOÀNG HOA THÁM (Đề Thám) (1858–1913). Pirate leader and patriot in **French**-ruled Vietnam. Born *Trương Văn Thám* in a poor peasant family in Hưng Yên in the mid-19th century, Đề Thám was raised in Yên Thế, in the rugged mountains north of the **Red River Delta**. As a young man, he joined the **Black Flag** forces led by pirate leader Liu Yongfu. When the French established their **protectorates** in **Annam** and **Tonkin** in the 1880s, Đề Thám became a bandit leader of some renown, with a reputation as a Vietnamese Robin Hood, stealing from the rich to help the poor. After vainly attempting to suppress his movement, the French made a truce with him in 1893, but he began to cooperate with anticolonial elements and allegedly took part in a plot to poison the **Hanoi** military garrison planned by **Phan Bội Châu**. The French resumed their efforts to capture him, and he was assassinated by one of their agents in 1913.

HOÀNG MINH GIÁM (1904–1995). Leading member of the **Vietnamese Socialist Party** and foreign minister of the **Democratic Republic of Vietnam** (DRV) from March 1947 until April 1954, when he was replaced by **Phạm Văn Đồng**. Later, Giám served as Minister of Culture of the DRV.

HOÀNG NGỌC PHÁCH (1896–1973). Well-known romantic novelist in colonial Vietnam. Educated in the traditional Chinese style,

Hoàng Ngọc Phách became a teacher at a secondary school in **Hanoi**. In 1925, his novel entitled *Tố Tâm* took educated Vietnamese society by storm. Based on the French novel *La Dame aux Camélias*, *Tố Tâm* was a story involving the conflict between young love and family duty, with the female protagonist (whose name gives the novel its title) eventually dying of a broken heart. The novel evoked a brief rash of suicides among educated young Vietnamese **women** and inaugurated a flurry of novels on romantic themes. It was his only novel. *See also* LITERATURE.

HOÀNG QUỐC VIỆT (1905–1992). Veteran Communist Party member and labor union official in Vietnam. Born *Hà Bá Cần* in a worker family in 1905, Hoàng Quốc Việt became active in revolutionary affairs in the mid-1920s, organizing protest activities in the coal mines of **Tonkin**. After joining the **Indochinese Communist Party** (ICP) as a founding member in 1930, he was arrested by the **French** and sent to **Poulo Condore**, where he remained until his release in 1936. Thereafter, he resumed his revolutionary activities and was elected to the ICP Central Committee in 1941. After World War II, he continued as an influential member of the Party and occupied several leading positions in the **Democratic Republic of Vietnam** (DRV). Whether because of advancing age or suspected disagreement with the Party's current policies, he was dropped from the Central Committee at the Fifth National Congress in 1982.

HOÀNG VĂN HOAN (1905–1994?). Leading member of the Vietnamese Communist movement who defected to **China** in 1979. Born in Nghệ An in 1905, Hoàng Văn Hoan joined **Hồ Chí Minh**'s **Thanh Niên** Revolutionary Youth League in the late 1920s and became a founding member of the **Indochinese Communist Party** in 1930. Rising steadily in the ranks of the Party, he served as Vietnamese ambassador to the People's Republic of **China** in the early 1950s and became a member of the Politburo in 1957.

In 1957, he was dropped from his leading positions in the Party, reportedly because of his pro-Chinese views. The worsening of Sino–Vietnamese relations in the late 1970s did not help his situation. In 1979, he defected to China while on a trip abroad for medical reasons and spent the rest of his life there. He wrote a memoir that attacked his political opponents, such as **Lê Duẩn**, for having de-railed the country from the original course set by Hồ.

HOÀNG VĂN THÁI (1915–1986). Veteran Communist leader and ranking military officer in the **Socialist Republic of Vietnam** (SRV). Details about his early life are obscure, but by 1944 he had become a cadre in the newly formed Vietnamese Liberation Army. He rose rapidly through the ranks and became chief of staff to General **Võ Nguyên Giáp** at **Điện Biên Phủ** in 1954 then deputy chief of staff of the **People's Army of Vietnam** (PAVN) six years later. He saw action in South Vietnam during the last years of the war. In 1980, he was promoted to the rank of senior general and deputy minister of defense.

HOÀNG VĂN THỤ (1906–1944). Leading figure in the **Indochinese Communist Party** (ICP) before World War II. Born in Lạng Sơn of ethnic **Tày** parentage in 1906, Hoàng Văn Thụ went to **China** in 1926 to study at a training institute run by **Hồ Chí Minh**'s Revolutionary Youth League (**Thanh Niên**) and became a member of the **Indochinese Communist Party** in 1930. After setting up the first Party chapter in **Cao Bằng**, he rose rapidly in the ranks and was named to the Central Committee in 1938 and secretary of the Party's Regional Committee for **Tonkin** a year later. He was active in the **Việt Bắc** region during the war years until captured by the **French** in August 1943. He was executed in May 1944 in **Hanoi**.

HOÀNG XUÂN HÃN (1908–1996). A scholar who played an important part in the transition from a French- to a Vietnamese-language **educational** system. Trained as a mathematician and engineer in **France**, he is better known in his own country for his historical writings and for his promotion of Vietnamese as a medium of instruction. Because education in the colonial period was almost exclusively in French at the secondary and tertiary levels, the Vietnamese faced a tremendous challenge when they attempted to use their own language in the classroom in the 1940s. Hoàng Xuân Hãn helped translate scientific and technical terms into Vietnamese and, serving as minister of education in the short-lived **Trần Trọng Kim** government at the end of the **Japanese occupation**, began to implement the change to a Vietnamese-language curriculum.

Although a fervent nationalist, Hãn did not throw in his lot with either the **Democratic Republic of Vietnam** or the **State of Vietnam** during the First Indochina War in the 1950s. In 1951, he emigrated to Paris, where he remained for the rest of his life. He was one of the few prominent **overseas Vietnamese** who maintained ties with both halves of his divided homeland during the Second Indochina War. The Communist Party has praised him for his contributions to Vietnamese education.

HỘI AN. Port city in the central province of Quảng Nam. Located at the point where the Thu Bồn River meets the coast, about 30 kilometers (19 miles) south of present-day **Đà Nẵng**, the city first achieved prominence during the 17th century when it was used as a port of entry by Western commercial interests trading with the **Nguyễn Lords**. It was generally known to Western travelers as *Faifo*. First used as a port by the **Cham**, whose territory was gradually absorbed by the Vietnamese, it later housed merchants from several other countries, including Holland, **China**, and **Japan**. It declined in the 18th century when the river began to silt up and then was badly damaged during the **Tây Sơn** Rebellion. Eventually, it was replaced by Đà Nẵng as the major port in central Vietnam, but a number of old houses and temples from the traditional period remain standing. Renamed *Hội An*, it became the capital city of Quảng Nam province when independence was restored in 1954. In recent times, it has enjoyed considerable popularity as a site for **tourism** and is developing an infrastructure of hotels and other facilities at a rapid pace.

HỒNG ĐỨC CODE. Penal code adopted by the **Lê dynasty** during the reign of **Lê Thánh Tông** (1460–1497). The Hồng Đức Code, named after the dynastic period relating to Thánh Tông's reign (though there is some evidence that it might actually have been drafted a few years earlier), was promulgated in 1483. The Code consisted of 721 articles drawn together in six books. Revised in subsequent years, it remained in force until the **Gia Long Code** drafted in the 19th century. Representing a comprehensive effort to systematize the civil and criminal laws in Vietnamese society, it combined a strong **Confucian** content, borrowed from **China**, with Vietnamese practice. For example, it followed Vietnamese custom in granting certain rights to **women** not followed in Chinese society. Women possessed property rights and could have some share in their parents' inheritance. Common law marriages were recognized as valid, while wives were given the right in certain cases to divorce their husbands. With respect to land, the Hồng Đức Code attempted to provide a stronger legal basis for state ownership and followed the practice of the dynasty's founder **Lê Thái Tổ** in prescribing specific limits on the possession of land depending on the status, profession, or age of the individual. *See also* LEGAL SYSTEM.

HOPES OF YOUTH PARTY. *See* THANH NIÊN CAO VỌNG.

HSIAO WEN. *See* XIAO WEN.

HUẾ. Important city in central Vietnam and capital of the Vietnamese Empire during the **Nguyễn dynasty** (1802–1945). Located on the River of Perfume (Sông Hương), Huế (originally known as *Phù Xuân*) first assumed importance as the capital of the **Nguyễn Lords** in the 17th and 18th centuries. In 1802, Emperor **Gia Long**, founder of the Nguyễn dynasty, moved the capital there from its existing location at **Hanoi**, where his family enjoyed considerably less support. Huế remained the imperial capital until 1945, when Emperor **Bảo Đại** abdicated the throne and accepted the position of Supreme Advisor to the **Democratic Republic of Vietnam** (DRV).

Huế's imperial past is thoroughly stamped on the physical appearance of the city. The Imperial Palace and its adjacent buildings and gates (modeled after its counterpart in Beijing), surrounded by extensive battlements patterned after the style of the 17th-century French architect Vauban, lie within the city on the north side of the river. In the western suburbs, also on the north bank, is the beautiful Thiên Mụ Pagoda. In the river valley to the southwest are the tombs of several Nguyễn emperors.

Under the **Republic of Vietnam** (RVN), Huế became the capital of Thừa Thiên province and the headquarters of the politically active An Quang **Buddhist** Association, which frequently challenged the authority of the government in **Saigon**. In 1968, the city was attacked and briefly occupied by revolutionary forces during the **Tết Offensive**. During the ensuing battle for control of the city, many buildings within the Imperial City were damaged. Today, Huế is enjoying a renaissance as a cultural center and a popular site for both Vietnamese and foreign **tourists**. Its population is roughly 350,000.

HUMAN RIGHTS (*nhân quyền*). The issue of human rights has become a constant irritant in Vietnam's relations with the West, and a number of policies of the **Vietnamese Communist Party** have drawn criticism from the **United States** and the European Union. Generally speaking, the issues raised are similar to those found in **China**, particularly persecution of some **religious** groups, repression of **dissidents** (and a general intolerance of dissenting views), and a lack of **pluralism** within the political system. The government of the **Socialist Republic of Vietnam** has generally rejected such accusations. It follows China's line in defining human rights in terms of social and economic needs, maintaining that its development priorities and policies are working toward meeting these needs. It also cites the rights and liberties spelled out in the Vietnamese **constitution**, though glossing over the implications of the fact that any and all of these rights can be restricted or nullified by passing new laws because the constitution explicitly subordinates freedoms like religion and speech to the prohibitions of the **legal system**.

Not surprisingly, the **Hanoi** government tends to see criticisms of its policies as interference with its internal affairs and violations of its sovereignty. It also argues that a country like the U.S., which bears considerable responsibility for years of destructive warfare, is in no position to make such criticisms. Moreover, because the targets of repression and persecution (dissidents, **Buddhists** and **Christians** outside the officially sanctioned churches, and sects such as the **Cao Đài** and **Hoà Hảo**) are frequently viewed by the Party as part of a broader "**peaceful evolution**" plot aimed at destroying the regime, when Western governments and organizations pressure Hanoi on their behalf, it merely reinforces the belief that these individuals and groups are tools of "hostile forces" rather than genuine victims.

At the same time, however, Vietnam is faced with the reality that, in many cases, the countries that are attacking its human rights record are also important donors, and that **Overseas Development Assis-**

tance does not come without strings attached. There is also a certain recognition that part of the price for openness, integration, and a higher profile on the regional and world scene is greater outside scrutiny. Ultimately, significant long-term improvements in the human rights situation in Vietnam will have to come less from outside pressure than from internal policy changes resulting from a stronger sense of security on the government's part and a change in its definitions of what constitute "illegal" activities. *See also* FOREIGN RELATIONS.

HÙNG KINGS (Hùng Vương, Vua Hùng). A series of semilegendary rulers in prehistoric Vietnam. According to some early histories, the Hung kings ruled a kingdom called *Văn Lang* that had originally been established in the third millennium B.C.E. by the legendary hero **Lạc Long Quân**, the mythical founder of Vietnamese civilization. There were a series of 18 kings, all blessed with abnormally long lives. The last had a beautiful daughter who was courted by two suitors, Sơn Tinh (a mountain spirit) and Thủy Tinh (a water spirit). The king awarded his daughter to the former, who had arrived first with sumptuous gifts. Thủy Tinh was angry at his rejection and every year unleashes floods to punish the Vietnamese people.

Although the legend of the Hùng kings is clearly apocryphal, it has become accepted by Vietnamese (including scholars) as part of their early history. The kings and their kingdom of Văn Lang are equated with the **Bronze Age** culture of **Đông Sơn**, and they are thus seen as rulers of the first Vietnamese quasistate.

HUYỀN TRÂN, PRINCESS. A 14th-century princess of the **Trần dynasty** who was the center of an abortive attempt at marriage diplomacy between Vietnam and **Champa**. Promised in marriage to the **Cham** ruler by her father, the retired Emperor **Trần Nhân Tông**, Huyền Trân traveled to the Cham court in 1306. The agreed match had not been well-received by the Vietnamese court, and there were snide references to a Han dynasty emperor in China who had married off a princess to the barbarian Huns. Huyền Trân produced an heir for her husband but found herself widowed within two years of her arrival. As the Cham had been influenced by Indian culture, she was expected to burn herself on her husband's funeral pyre, but she was rescued by a daring official who sailed down from Thăng Long (**Hanoi**) and carried her off to safety after tricking the Cham into letting her go. Cham–Vietnamese relations were not helped by this event, particularly because two Cham districts had been ceded to Vietnam as a bride price and were not returned after her defection.

HUỲNH PHÚ SỔ (1919–1947). Founder of the millenarian **Hoà Hảo** religious sect in southern Vietnam. Born in 1919 in a rich peasant family from the village of Hoà Hảo in Châu Đốc, Sổ led a normal childhood but after an illness during adolescence went to live with a hermit who instructed him in sorcery, hypnotism, and acupuncture. In 1939, he declared himself to be a holy man and was interned at a psychiatric hospital for observation, where he allegedly converted his doctor.

After his release, Huỳnh Phú Sổ rapidly gained followers for his new reformist **Buddhist** religion known as *Hoà Hảo* (Harmony). The movement rapidly spread among the rural population in the lower **Mekong River Delta**. Anti-**French** in his political orientation, Sổ cooperated with the **Japanese occupation** authorities during World War II. In August 1945, he briefly joined forces with the **Việt Minh** against the returning French, but rivalry between the two movements rapidly intensified, and in April 1947 he was assassinated by the Việt Minh. He was succeeded by Trần Văn Soái, who rallied with most of his followers to the side of the French.

HUỲNH TẤN PHÁT (1913–1989). Leading member of the **National Liberation Front** (NLF) in South Vietnam and subsequently an official in the **Socialist Republic of Vietnam**. Born in 1913 in Mỹ Tho, Huỳnh Tấn Phát was educated in architecture at the University of Hanoi. In the 1940s, while practicing architecture in **Saigon**, he became active in political activities promoted by the **Indochinese Communist Party** (ICP).

After the partition of Vietnam at the **Geneva Conference** in 1954, Phát became a leading critic of the **Ngô Đình Diệm** regime. Arrested twice and released, he turned to clandestine activities, serving as secretary-general of the NLF, and in 1969 was named president of the **Provisional Revolutionary Government** (PRG). Following reunification and the dissolution of the PRG in 1976, he was appointed a vice-premier of the new SRV and chairman of the State Commission for Capital Construction. In 1982, he was named vice-chairman of the State Council and was relieved of his other government positions.

HUỲNH THÚC KHÁNG (1876–1947). Anticolonial journalist and scholar in French-occupied Vietnam. Trained in the traditional **examination system**, Huỳnh Thúc Kháng became involved in political activities in 1908, when he was arrested with **Phan Chu Trinh** for allegedly inciting violence during the peasant revolt in central Vietnam. After release from **Poulo Condore**, in the 1920s he turned to **journalism**, along with a brief stint in a consultative body for the Protectorate of **Annam** known as "the Chamber of People's Representatives." He was occasionally an outspoken opponent of the French colonial regime and editor of the **Huế**-based newspaper, *Tiếng Dân* (*Voice of the People*), published from 1927 to 1943. After World War II, he served a brief term as minister of the interior in the **Democratic Republic of Vietnam.**

HUỲNH TỊNH CỦA (Paulus Của) (1834–1907). Prominent linguist and writer in late 19th-century Vietnam. A Catholic, Huỳnh Tịnh Của had Francophile tendencies and became an official in the colonial administration in **Cochin China**. For the next three decades, he was a prolific writer, helping popularize *quốc ngữ*, the Romanized version of Vietnamese, and contributed frequently to the newspaper *Gia Định Báo*. *See also* TRƯƠNG VĨNH KÝ.

– I –

IA DRANG VALLEY, BATTLE OF. Major battle between **United States** combat troops and units of the **People's Army of Vietnam** (PAVN) in November 1965. Ia Drang Valley, located beneath Chu Pong Mountain near the **Cambodian** border in South Vietnam, was near one of the main entry points for infiltrators from North Vietnam. In the fall of 1961, the newly arrived U.S. First Calvary Division engaged regular PAVN forces in heavy fighting in the area, resulting in high casualties on both sides. It was the first major engagement between U.S. and North Vietnamese troops (as opposed to the southern **People's Liberation Armed Forces**).

IMPERIAL ACADEMY (*Quốc Tử Giám*). "Academy for the Children of the State," an institute set up to train officials and candidates for the bureaucracy in traditional Vietnam. The academy is said to have first been established by the **Lý dynasty** in 1076 and was located on the precincts of the **Temple of Literature** (Văn Miếu) in the imperial capital of Thăng Long (present-day **Hanoi**). Over the centuries, it underwent several changes of name and gradually broadened its selection of students beyond the original small core of princes and sons of high-ranking mandarins. After a period of decline in the 18th century, it was revived and moved to **Huế**, the new capital of the **Nguyễn dynasty**, in 1807. The original site of the academy in Hanoi is now a museum. *See also* CONFUCIANISM; EDUCATION; EXAMINATION SYSTEM.

INDIANIZATION. The phenomenon known variously as *Indianization, Hinduization*, or *Sanskritization* refers to the influence of Indian culture in Southeast Asia during the early centuries of the first millennium C.E. There are a few traces of Indian elements within the culture of the ethnic Vietnamese; the deity Indra, for example, was apparently worshipped in ceremonies for many centuries. Indian influence is clearest where **Buddhism** is concerned because that religion was first propagated among the Vietnamese by monks from India and Central Asia, and even the Chinese forms of Buddhism, which arrived later, had Indian origins. The most clearly Indianized area of present-day Vietnam, however, is the region that formerly belonged to the **Cham**, who were much more heavily exposed to Indian culture. Even today, the Indian elements in Cham culture are readily visible, as is also true of their surviving architectural monuments.

INDOCHINA. Collective term for territories under French colonial rule in 19th- and early 20th-century Southeast Asia. Originally applied to all of mainland Southeast Asia, it eventually came to refer specifically to the colony of **Cochin China** and the protectorates of **Annam**, **Tonkin**, **Laos**, and **Cambodia**, known collectively as

French Indochina. *See also* INDOCHINESE FEDERATION; IN-DOCHINESE UNION.

INDOCHINESE COMMUNIST PARTY (*Đông Dương Cộng Sản Đảng*). Short-lived Communist party formed by Vietnamese radicals in June 1929. The party was founded by northern Vietnamese members of the regional committee of **Hồ Chí Minh**'s Revolutionary Youth League of Vietnam (**Thanh Niên**), who had become convinced that the League placed insufficient emphasis on the cause of social revolution in its effort to promote the cause of national independence. The result was an organization composed primarily of urban intellectuals and functionaries rather than peasants and workers. For several months, the new party competed with the League, itself now transformed into an organization entitled the *Annamese Communist Party* (*An Nam Cộng Sản Đảng*). In February 1930, at a meeting chaired by Hồ Chí Minh and held in Hong Kong, the two factions were dissolved and merged into a new **Vietnamese Communist Party** (*Đảng Cộng Sản Việt Nam*), which subsequently returned to the original name of *ICP*, though with a slightly different name in Vietnamese.

INDOCHINESE COMMUNIST PARTY (ICP) (*Đảng Cộng Sản Đông Dương*). Communist Party founded by Vietnamese revolutionaries in 1930. The party had originally been entitled the *Vietnamese Communist Party* (*Đảng Cộng Sản Việt Nam*) at a founding meeting held in February 1930, which merged elements of three different Communist-oriented parties. However, at the first plenary session of the Party Central Committee held in October in Hong Kong, the name was changed to "Indochinese Communist Party" on the instructions of the **Comintern** in Moscow. Soviet strategists believed that the party should represent a common anticolonial struggle for all of **Indochina** rather than just the Vietnamese.

In fact, however, the ICP was dominated by ethnic Vietnamese throughout its existence, although a few **Cambodian** and **Lao** members began to join the Party in the late 1940s. Repressed by the French authorities after the Nghệ-Tĩnh Soviet revolt in 1930–1931, the ICP revived during the **Popular Front** period (1936–1938) and became the primary political organization opposed to French rule in

Vietnam. In 1939, it was again suppressed after the signing of the Nazi–Soviet Non-Aggression Pact.

In 1941, an ICP Central Committee meeting held at Pác Bó declared the formation of the League for the Independence of Vietnam, or **Việt Minh**. Although broadly nationalist in its program, the front was under firm ICP control. In August 1945, the Việt Minh seized power over most of Vietnam and declared the establishment of a provisional **Democratic Republic of Vietnam**, with **Hồ Chí Minh** as president. In the fall, the ICP declared itself abolished to strengthen the new government's appeal to moderates, although it continued to operate in secret. In February 1951, during the **Franco–Việt Minh War**, the ICP reemerged as the Vietnamese Workers' Party (VWP), while independent People's Revolutionary Parties were subsequently established in Laos and Cambodia. The change was made to satisfy rising national sensitivity among Lao and Khmer members of the ICP by equipping them with separate parties, though Vietnamese influence remained strong. The VWP oversaw the war against the **United States** and the **Republic of Vietnam**; after victory and reunification, it reverted to its original name—*Vietnamese Communist Party*—in 1976. *See also* AUGUST REVOLUTION.

INDOCHINESE CONGRESS. Popular movement promoted by the **Indochinese Communist Party** (ICP) and other anticolonial groups in the late 1930s. The movement originated with the stated intention of the **Popular Front** government under Prime Minister Léon Blum in **France** to send a governmental commission of inquiry to the French colonies to consider reforms. In Indochina, various political parties and groups attempted to solicit popular feeling in preparation for the visit. The ICP itself formed so-called "Action Committees" (*Ủy Ban Hành Động*) in offices, factories, and villages to draw up a list of popular demands for presentation to the inspection team. Concerned over the rising political unrest, the colonial authorities closed down the Action Committees. In June 1937, the French government canceled the visit of the Commission of Inquiry. *See also* BRÉVIÉ, JULES.

INDOCHINESE DEMOCRATIC FRONT (*Mặt Trận Thống Nhất Dân Chủ Đông Dương*). Front group established by the **Indochinese**

Communist Party (ICP) in 1936 as the result of changes in the revolutionary line at the Seventh Congress of the **Comintern** in Moscow. The front was designed to win the support of moderates in support of the **Popular Front** established in **France**. It was replaced in November 1939 by a new National United Indochinese Anti-Imperialist Front.

INDOCHINESE FEDERATION (*Fédération Indochinoise*). A concept announced in the **Brazzaville Declaration** issued by General Charles de Gaulle in March 1945. According to General de Gaulle's plan, the existing **Indochinese Union** would be replaced with a federation of five quasi-independent states (**Cochin China, Annam, Tonkin, Cambodia,** and **Laos**) as part of a new **French Union** planned for **France** and its colonies after the end of World War II. The federation would have a federal government presided over by a governor-general appointed in Paris and a cabinet composed of citizens of both France and the Indochinese countries. Legislative bodies in each nation would vote on taxes, the budget, and other legislation of primarily local concern. Foreign affairs and defense would be handled essentially by the French government in Paris.

The federation was briefly put in place at the second **Đàlạt Conference**, held in August 1946, but events in Indochina impeded any efforts to create a meaningful political and administration structure, and the concept was superseded with the creation of three separate **Associated States** in Vietnam, Laos, and Cambodia by the **Élysée Agreements** in March 1949. *See also* D'ARGENLIEU, THIERRY.

INDOCHINESE FEDERATION (*Liên Bang Đông Dương*). Concept developed by the **Indochinese Communist Party** (ICP) in the 1930s for the creation of a federation composed of Vietnam, **Laos,** and **Cambodia** after the eventual victory of revolutionary forces in those countries. The original idea of the federation probably came from the **Comintern**, where strategists of global revolution were convinced that social revolutions could not succeed in small states. They therefore advised Vietnamese revolutionary leaders to unite with their counterparts in Laos and Cambodia to seek liberation from French rule. For the next two decades, documents issued by the ICP periodically mentioned the possible future formation on a voluntary basis of a so-called Indochinese Federation among the three countries after the eviction of the French.

In recent years, official spokesmen for the **Socialist Republic of Vietnam** have maintained that the concept of an Indochinese Federation was explicitly abandoned at the Second National Congress of the Party in 1951, when the ICP was dissolved and subsequently divided into three parties representing the revolutionary movements in each country. At the close of the Vietnam War in 1975, the **Hanoi** regime did not attempt to resurrect the concept of a federation, but spoke instead of a **"special relationship"** among the three countries created by history and revolutionary experience. Critics charged that the "special relationship" was simply the Indochinese Federation under a new name; this argument was particularly widespread after the establishment of a pro-Vietnamese regime in Cambodia in 1979.

INDOCHINESE UNION (*Union de l'Indochine*). Administrative structure for **French** rule in **Indochina**. The union emerged from the Office of the Governor-General, which had been set up under the Ministry of Colonies in 1887. At first, the powers of the governor-general were limited to coordinating the separate activities of the governor of **Cochin China** and the *résidents supérieurs* in **Annam**, **Tonkin**, **Laos**, and **Cambodia**. Under Governor-General **Paul Doumer** (1897–1902), however, the position gained considerable stature and authority with the establishment of a number of offices and a centrally controlled budget and a major factor in the affairs of the Union. The Indochinese Union was abolished after World War II with the establishment of separate **Associated States** in Vietnam, Laos, and Cambodia. *See also* ÉLYSÉE ACCORDS.

INDRAPURA. Early **Cham** capital in central Vietnam. Located at Đồng Dương in present-day Quảng Nam, it was a capital from the ninth century until 982, when it was destroyed during a Vietnamese invasion led by **Lê Hoàn**. The Cham political center seems to have then shifted south to **Vijaya**, in modern Bình Định. Indrapura and its surrounding area were absorbed into the Vietnamese Empire during the 15th century. One of the notable characteristics of Cham art and **architecture** from Đồng Dương is the importance of Mahayana **Buddhism**, which long coexisted with elements of Hinduism in

Cham culture but was generally subordinate to it in terms of its artistic influence. Đồng Dương is exceptional for the comparatively stronger presence of Buddhist elements. *See also* INDIANIZATION.

INDUSTRY. At the time of the French conquest in the mid-19th century, Vietnam was still an essentially **agricultural** society, and industry was at a relatively primitive stage of development. The stated objective of French rule was to introduce Vietnam to modern technology, but although the French did take the initial steps to provide Vietnam with a modern transportation network, on the whole, they did little to create an industrial sector, preferring to use Vietnam as a source of raw materials and a market for French-manufactured goods.

After the **Geneva Conference** in 1954, the governments that replaced the French in the North and South did little to rectify the situation. In the North, the **Democratic Republic of Vietnam** (DRV) adopted an ambitious program of industrialization with the inauguration of the First Five-Year Plan in 1961, but lack of capital and technology, and the intensification of the war in the South, derailed plans for economic development. In the **Republic of Vietnam**, economic assistance from the **United States** and other capitalist countries led to the emergence of a modest light industrial sector based primarily on the production of consumer goods, but the lack of industrial resources and the disruption caused by the war represented insuperable obstacles to rapid industrialization.

After reunification, the **Socialist Republic of Vietnam** embarked on a major effort to promote socialist industrialization with the Second Five-Year Plan, launched in 1976. For nearly two decades, inadequate capital, lack of **energy resources**, agricultural failures, and a primitive infrastructure hindered the growth of the industrial sector, which remained based primarily on light industry. (This trend has changed, however, and some heavy industry is being developed.) Current policy emphasizes the growth of agriculture and production of consumer goods, while long-term plans for the development of energy resources, such as **coal**, **oil**, and electricity, are in the process of implementation.

Under the program of renovation (*đổi mới*), industrial production has been increasing at a rate of over 10 percent annually and now contributes roughly 40 percent of the Gross Domestic Product (GDP). (In 1990, this figure was between 20–25 percent; the industrial and agricultural sectors have thus more or less changed places in terms of their share of GDP.) Much of the success can be attributed to rising levels of **foreign investment**. One of the lingering problems, however, is the continuing existence of a number of **state-owned enterprises**, many of which are inefficient and expensive to maintain. The government has cut the number of such firms drastically, but it is determined to maintain many of the larger ones as a means of retaining state control over the "commanding heights" of the **economy**. *See also* SCIENCE AND TECHNOLOGY; STATE PLANNING.

INTERNATIONAL CONTROL COMMISSION (ICC). Supervisory commission set up by the **Geneva Conference** to oversee the cease-fire in **Indochina** in 1954. It was composed of Canada (representing the West), India (representing the neutral countries), and Poland (representing the socialist camp). The ICC was hampered by the failure of both sides to adhere to the letter of the agreement and by the inability of the delegations of the three countries themselves to agree on the definition of the issues. By the early 1960s, the Geneva Agreement, and the functions of the ICC itself, had become virtually a dead letter. *See also* DEMILITARIZED ZONE.

IRON TRIANGLE. Base area used by revolutionary armed forces in South Vietnam during the Vietnam War. The Iron Triangle was a densely forested area about 50 kilometers (30 miles) north of **Saigon** that was heavily fortified by revolutionary forces at the outset of the war. In January 1967, U.S. combat forces launched a major assault into the area to destroy enemy emplacements and the ground cover that made the area ideal for insurgency operations. The attack, known as *Operation Cedar Falls*, removed the potential threat to Saigon but incurred resentment from much of the local population, which was forcibly evacuated to transform the area into a free-fire zone.

– J –

JAPAN. The first contacts between Vietnam and Japan were primarily commercial in nature. Japanese merchants carried on active trade with Vietnam during the 16th and early 17th centuries, mainly through the port city of **Hội An** (then known to Europeans as *Faifo*), which had a thriving Japanese community, some of them Catholic converts. By midcentury, however, that trade virtually ceased, as the Tokugawa Shogunate carried out its policy of "closed country" and isolated the Japanese islands from the rest of Asia. Contacts resumed when Japan launched its drive for industrialization and modernization during the Meiji Restoration at the end of the 19th century. Many Vietnamese intellectuals, such as the revolutionary patriot **Phan Bội Châu**, turned their eyes to Japan as a model for future political and economic development and a possible staging point for the unleashing of a movement of national resistance against French rule. Japan, however, eventually decided to improve its relations with the French, and Vietnamese nationalist leaders were evicted from the country.

For many Vietnamese, admiration for Japanese achievement was tempered by uneasiness at Japan's emergence as an imperialist power. That vision became reality in 1940 when Japan demanded access to the resources of **Indochina** and the right to station troops there in preparation for an invasion of other countries in the region. Reluctantly, the **French** administration acceded to the demand, and for the bulk of World War II, Vietnam had two masters, the French administration and a **Japanese occupation** regime. Japan abruptly brought an end to French sovereignty in March 1945, and granted paper independence to the imperial government under Emperor **Bảo Đại**. That government collapsed at the moment of Japanese surrender to the Allied forces in August.

Japan was not directly involved in the Vietnam War, although it profited economically from the increased American presence in East Asia. After the war, Japan joined with the **United States** and other countries in imposing an economic embargo on the **Socialist Republic of Vietnam** (SRV) because of its 1978 invasion of **Cambodia**. By the late 1980s, however, the government was tacitly permitting Japanese business interests to operate in Vietnam. Today, with the international embargo at an end, Japan has growing trade relations with the SRV and is one of its main **foreign investors**. Japan is also an important source of **Overseas Development Assistance**, which it is generally willing to provide without accompanying pressure on **human rights** and other issues.

JAPANESE OCCUPATION. The Japanese occupation of French Indochina during World War II stands out as being significantly different in many respects from the experiences of other Southeast Asian colonies. Japanese troops entered **Indochina** beginning in late 1940 through agreements with the Vichy government in **France**, whose links with Nazi Germany made it effectively an ally of **Japan**. This relationship meant that the French were not driven from power until the very end of the occupation; rather, the colonial regime continued to function as before, though under the watchful eye of Japanese military officers. The Japanese themselves were divided as to whether they should support the status quo or encourage local nationalism and plan to eventually grant nominal independence to the Vietnamese, **Cambodians**, and **Lao**. They maintained contacts with specific groups of anti-French nationalists; among the Vietnamese these included such individuals as **Ngô Đình Diệm** and the religious sects of the **Cao Đài** and **Hoà Hảo**. Because of the uneasy coexistence with the Vichy colonial regime, even those Japanese officers and officials sympathetic to local nationalist aspirations faced constraints in providing active support for these elements.

The fall of the Vichy government and the increasingly gloomy outlook for the Japanese war effort, as well as evidence of activity by Gaullist sympathizers within Indochina, combined to push Japan to end the coexistence with the French in March 1945. The Japanese overthrew the colonial government and, over the next few weeks, granted nominal independence to the Vietnamese, Cambodian, and Lao monarchies—although "independence" in this context did not look noticeably different from the French "**protectorates**." The "Empire of Vietnam" under **Bảo Đại** and the Japanese-selected Prime Minister **Trần Trọng Kim** was given control over **Tonkin** and **Annam**, but not over **Cochin China**, which Japan felt was too strategically important to be turned over to the Vietnamese.

The new Vietnamese government faced serious challenges in trying to rule over its domain. By late 1944 and early 1945, Tonkin was facing a serious famine brought on by a combination of poor harvests, requisitions of grain by the Japanese and French, and wartime disruptions of transportation routes with Cochin China, whose **rice** supplies could have made up for what was lacking in the northern provinces. This crisis not only harmed the legitimacy of the royal government, it also provided an opportunity for the **Việt Minh** under **Hồ Chí Minh** to build up its power base in rural areas by helping to appropriate grain supplies for hungry Vietnamese. As the Japanese surrender became imminent at the end of the war, the ensuing power vacuum enabled Hồ and his **Indochinese Communist Party** to prepare for the **August Revolution,** which propelled them to power in September 1945.

Although the Vietnamese did not experience the kind of brutality at Japanese hands that characterized the occupation of other colonies, such as Malaya and Singapore, the devastating famine, caused in large part to Japanese policies, was a bitter legacy of the period. At the same time, without the disruption of French rule, which the occupation produced, the August Revolution would surely have been delayed and, perhaps, would ultimately have failed.

JARAI (also known as *Djarai* or *Gia Lai*). An ethnic group living in the **Central Highlands**. Numbering slightly over 150,000, the Jarai are one of the dominant minority peoples; they speak an **Austronesian** language related to **Cham.** Their religion is spirit worship. Administration is at the village level, and most people traditionally lived in joint family units.

In precolonial times, the Jarai accepted tributary status to the **Nguyễn dynasty** in Vietnam, and their leaders (known as the *King of Fire* and *King of Water*) were viewed by the Nguyễn as vassal rulers. After the French conquest, the Central Highlands region was granted more or less autonomous status within French **Indochina**. During the Vietnam War, the Jarai opposed **assimilation** by the **Republic of Vietnam** and were an active force in the separatist movements **Bajaraka** and **Front Unifié pour la Libération des Races Opprimées**, which fought for tribal autonomy in South Vietnam, but were also distrustful of the Hanoi-supported revolutionary movement. Since reunification, the **Socialist Republic of Vietnam** (SRV) has attempted to assimilate the highland peoples into Vietnamese society, but government policies in the Central Highlands have met with mixed results, as the severe socioeconomic changes of the post-1975 period have been highly disruptive for the Jarai and other groups. *See also* HIGHLAND MINORITIES; RHADÉ.

JOINT VENTURE (*Liên doanh*). The joint venture is a common form of **foreign investment** in Vietnam, involving the establishment of a business entity with both foreign and domestic capital; the foreign investor's share of the company's capitalization must be at least 30 percent. Alternative arrangements are the 100-percent foreign-owned company and the Business Cooperation Contract, which allows foreigners to acquire a stake in a regular Vietnamese company instead of creating a new entity. This stake is capped at 30 percent, however, and if the foreign investor's equity goes beyond that point, the company must be turned into a joint venture.

Of the some 5,000 foreign investment projects licensed since the late 1980s, 30 percent have been joint ventures, with wholly foreign-owned firms representing another two-thirds. In terms of registered capital, joint ventures accounted for over half (51 percent), while for 100 percent foreign-owned entities the figure was 36 percent. Although the joint venture has been very popular as a start-up investment vehicle, the relationship between the foreign and domestic partners is often rocky because of differing expectations, conflicting business cultures, or issues of honesty and trust. Moreover, Vietnam's Law on Foreign Investment indirectly favors wholly foreign-owned companies because its regulations for joint ventures are considerably stricter than those governing 100-percent foreign entities. (For example, it stipulates that all important decisions relating to the joint venture's operations must be unanimously approved by the management board, and therefore a single veto from one board member can bring things to a halt.) In recent years, this has led to the conversion of a number of joint ventures into wholly owned foreign companies, and the preference for the latter over the former seems likely to continue.

JOURNALISM. Newspapers and journals in the modern Western sense did not exist in Vietnam until after the French conquest in the mid-19th century. The first journal published in *quốc ngữ*, the Romanized transliteration of the Vietnamese spoken language, was the *Gia Định Báo* (*Journal of Gia Định*), issued under the auspices of the colonial government; it first appeared in **Saigon** in 1865. The first privately published *quốc ngữ* newspaper of note was the *Lục Tỉnh Tân Văn* (*News from the Six Provinces*) published in Saigon by the journalist Gilbert Chiêu. The first journal in *quốc ngữ* to be published in Tonkin was **Nguyễn Văn Vĩnh**'s *Đông Dương Tạp Chí* (*Revue Indochinoise*), which opened its doors in 1913. The 1920s and 1930s saw the publication of a number of newspapers and periodicals appearing in Vietnamese, French, or Chinese in all three regions of Vietnam.

Under the colonial regime, strict limitations were placed on the discussion of political subjects, though, generally speaking, French-language publications had more freedom than those in Vietnamese, and **Cochin China** had fewer restrictions than **Annam** and **Tonkin**. Many, like **Phạm Quỳnh**'s *Nam Phong* (*Southern Wind*), were published under official sponsorship and reflected the views of the colonial administration; those that contravened the restrictions of censorship were quickly closed down. During the period of the **Popular Front** in the late 1930s, however, controls were relaxed, and a number of new newspapers appeared, including some published by the **Indochinese Communist Party**. They were permitted to undertake cautious criticism of government policies until the approach of World War II in 1939.

After the granting of independence in 1954, journalism developed rapidly in both North and South Vietnam, although both governments imposed strict censorship on the discussion of subjects of a controversial or political nature. The **Republic of Vietnam** could make a claim to having a few independent voices in the press, but in the **Democratic Republic of Vietnam** there were few or none, with the exception of the *Nhân Văn Giai Phẩm* incident of **dissidence** in the mid-1950s. After the inauguration of the program of *đổi mới* in December 1986, General Secretary **Nguyễn Van Linh** encouraged journalists and writers to criticize the shortcomings of the government and the Communist Party, and he himself penned critical editorials under a pseudonym in the Party mouthpiece *Nhân dân* (*The People*). However, the regime continued to make it clear that criticism of the Party and the leading role of Marxism–Leninism was treasonous and subject to severe punishment by law.

The growth of a market **economy** in Vietnam has seen the flourishing of a diverse variety of publications, many of which are targeting a popular audience. A few publications, notably the highly popular weekly *Tuổi Trẻ* (*Youth*), have been testing the limits of government tolerance with investigative journalism on **corruption** and other issues with political implications. The regime continues to struggle with the need to publicize their efforts to crack down on wrong-doing by officials and the desire to carefully manage press coverage of these problems. *See also CLOCHE FÊLÉE, LA; LUTTE, LA.*

– K –

KAO P'IEN. *See* GAO PIAN.

KHẢI ĐỊNH (1882–1925). Emperor (r. 1916–1925) of the **Nguyễn dynasty** under the **French protectorate**. Born the son of Emperor **Đồng Khánh**, Khải Định replaced **Duy Tân** on the throne when the latter was sent in exile to the island of Réunion in 1916. He was generally a pliant tool of the French and was strongly criticized by the reformist **Phan Chu Trinh** for his failure to improve conditions in Vietnam. He died in November 1925 and was succeeded by his son, the young **Bảo Đại**. *See also* CONVENTION OF 1925.

KHÁI HƯNG (1898–1947). Pen name of Trần Khánh Giư, well-known romantic novelist in colonial Vietnam. Born in 1898 in a scholar-gentry family in Hải Dương, Khái Hưng attended the famous Lycée Albert Sarraut in **Hanoi**. After becoming a writer, he joined the **Tự Lực Văn Đoàn** (Self-Reliance Literary Group), established by **Nhất Linh** to promote the Westernization of Vietnamese **literature** and society. Many of his novels contained a biting critique of the emptiness and hypocrisy of the upper class in colonial Vietnam. By the late 1930s, Khái Hưng's activities moved from literature to politics. He joined the pro-Japanese **Đại Việt Party** during World War II and was assassinated, reportedly by the **Việt Minh**, in 1947.

KHAI TRÍ TIẾN ĐỨC. *See* ASSOCIATION POUR LA FORMATION INTELLECTUELLE ET MORALE DES ANNAMITES.

KHE SANH, BATTLE OF. Site of a major battle between **United States** and **People's Army of Vietnam** (PAVN) forces during the

Vietnam War. Originally a small tribal village just south of the **Demilitarized Zone** (DMZ), Khe Sanh was occupied and fortified by U.S. troops in 1967 in an effort to reduce infiltration by Communist units into South Vietnam down the **Hồ Chí Minh Trail**. Beginning in late 1967, Communist forces began to infiltrate the area, leading to a major battle in the winter of 1967–1968. The PAVN troops were unable to seize the base, but **Hanoi** had achieved its purpose in persuading U.S. commanding general **William C. Westmoreland** to send reinforcements into the area, thus opening other areas for attack. After the **Tết Offensive**, U.S. forces left the area, which was then occupied by PAVN troops.

KHMER KROM. Inhabitants of Khmer (Cambodian) descent living in southern Vietnam. Most are descendants of the original inhabitants of the lower **Mekong River Delta** before the Vietnamese colonization beginning in the 17th century. The majority are Theravada **Buddhists**. An estimated 300,000 Khmer Krom were living in the **Republic of Vietnam** at the end of the Vietnam War. Some had been trained by the Central Intelligence Agency to oppose Prince Norodom Sihanouk during his time in power in **Cambodia** (before 1970), and according to reports, some might have taken part in the Vietnamese invasion of that country in December 1978. An unknown number resettled in Cambodia after the establishment of the People's Republic of Kampuchea in January 1979, but they still constitute a sizable minority in the **Socialist Republic of Vietnam**.

KHÚC THỪA DỤ (?–907). The first of three generations of local leaders who helped provide continuity between the end of the **Chinese period** and the beginning of Vietnamese independence in the 10th century. Appointed military governor of what was then the Chinese Protectorate of **Annam** in 906, just before the collapse of the Tang dynasty, Khúc Thừa Dụ came from a powerful family in present-day Hải Dương. Although he died the following year, he was succeeded by his son, Khúc Hạo, who was, in turn, succeeded by his own son, Khúc Thừa Mỹ. The newly established Southern Han dynasty invaded in 930, putting an end to what was apparently a quarter-century of autonomy from any sort of Chinese control. The attempt to reestablish Chinese rule over the Vietnamese was short-lived, however, as military victories by **Dương Đình Nghệ** in 931 and then **Ngô Quyền** in 938 kept Southern Han power at bay. Although there is no evidence that the leaders from the Khúc family assumed royal titles, they were, to some extent, the precursors of local strong men, such as Ngô Quyền and **Đinh Bộ Lĩnh**, who did so later in the century.

KIẾN PHÚC (1869–1884). Emperor (r. 1883–1884) in the **Nguyễn dynasty.** He was the last of three young rulers who succeeded each other on the throne after the death of their adoptive father **Tự Đức.** The rapid changes of emperor were the work of two high-ranking officials, **Tôn Thất Thuyết** and **Nguyễn Văn Tường**, who were manipulating the succession during the chaotic months when the **French** imposed their **protectorate.** Kiến Phúc was forced to sign the **Patenôtre Treaty**, which finalized colonial rule over the Empire of Vietnam. Upon his death (or possibly murder) after only seven months on the throne, the French insisted on having a say in the succession process, though their choice of **Hàm Nghi** proved unwise because he rebelled the following year.

KINH. A term used to refer to the ethnic Vietnamese majority. Etymologically it is the same word as the second element of "Beijing/Peking," meaning "capital." It appears at least as early as the 17th century in a text where a distinction is being made between Chinese residents and ethnic Vietnamese. It is not clear, however, whether this term was in frequent use because texts written by the ruling elite often referred to the Vietnamese by the Chinese terms "Han people" or "Tang people" when contrasting themselves with "barbarians," such as the Cambodians, Lao, or highlanders. Under the **Democratic Republic of Vietnam** "Kinh" became a common designation for ethnic Vietnamese in academic writing, and it has gradually entered popular usage as well. Sometimes the term *Việt* is used instead, referring specifically to the Vietnamese ethnic group, as opposed to *Việt Nam*, which designates a nationality including both the Kinh and the minorities. *See also* VIETNAMESE PEOPLE.

KLOBUKOWSKI, ANTONI-WLADISLAS (1855–1934). Governor-general of French **Indochina** from 1908 until 1911. After several posts in the diplomatic service, he was appointed governor-general of Indochina at a moment when social unrest had reached a momentary peak in Vietnam with peasant riots in **Annam** and rising dissent among intellectuals. Klobukowski attempted to crack down on the unrest by closing the University of Hanoi and the advisory assembly in **Tonkin**. At the same time, he attempted to eliminate some of the root causes of the disorder by rectifying abuses in the infamous state monopolies of alcohol, opium, and salt—an effort that aroused the ire of many French residents in Indochina and led to his dismissal in 1911. *See also* ĐÔNG KINH NGHĨA THỤC.

KOMER, ROBERT W. (1921–2000). **United States** official in charge of the pacification program in the **Republic of Vietnam** during the later stages of the Lyndon B. Johnson administration, when it was known as *Civil Operations and Revolutionary Development Support* (CORDS). Later, he became involved in the Phoenix Program, a U.S.-sponsored plan to eliminate the revolutionary infrastructure in South Vietnam. After the **Tet Offensive**, Komer returned to the U.S., where, in books and articles, he became critical of the excessive emphasis on a military approach in Washington's war strategy. *See also* WESTMORELAND, WILLIAM C.

KỲ HOÀ, BATTLE OF (also known as *Chi Hòa*). Military battle during which **French** forces defeated Vietnamese troops in February 1861. When the French launched their second attack in the area of **Saigon**, General **Nguyễn Tri Phương** established a defensive bastion southwest of the city, manned by more than 20,000 Vietnamese troops. Although the French had fewer than 5,000 troops, Phương adopted a defensive strategy, and the French were victorious in two days. The French later expanded their advance into neighboring areas in the face of guerilla resistance led by **Trương Định**. *See also* TREATY OF SAIGON.

– L –

LABOR UNIONS. The Vietnamese labor movement emerged during the period of French colonial rule, when progressive intellectuals, many of whom had first become involved in labor activity in France during World War I, began to organize Vietnamese workers in large cities, such as **Hanoi, Hải Phòng, Saigon**, and the industrial city of Vinh. The first labor organization was formed in Saigon in 1920 by **Tôn Đức Thắng**, later to become a prominent member of the **Indochinese Communist Party** (ICP).

From the outset, the Party was actively involved in organizing Vietnamese workers, who numbered only about 200,000 before World War II. In 1929, a forerunner of the ICP formed local "Red Workers' Associations" to mobilize workers to support the revolution. Within a year, about 6,000 workers had become members. Although suppressed during the **Nghệ-Tĩnh Revolt**, the workers' movement revived during the **Popular Front** period in the late 1930s.

In July 1946, a few months after the founding of the **Democratic Republic of Vietnam** (DRV), the Vietnamese Confederation of Labor Unions was established in **Hanoi**. Including virtually all blue-collar workers in the DRV, the confederation reached a membership of over 400,000 by 1960 and an estimated 3.7 million members in 1983. Union activities in the **Republic of Vietnam** were less restrained and had contact with their counterparts in the **United States** and elsewhere. As in all Communist systems, the labor movement under the Hanoi government is under strict Party supervision and is meant as an instrument of control rather than as a representative of workers' interests pitted against management (because the management has traditionally been the state). With the changes brought about by *đổi mới* (renovation), however, and the rise of privately owned factories, labor strikes have become a more common occurrence, particularly in enterprises operated under foreign supervision.

LẠC. A name that occurs in several contexts with reference to the ancestors of the ethnic Vietnamese during the time just before and just after the **Chinese** conquest in the second century B.C.E. The peoples known to the Chinese as "Lạc" were primarily rice farmers who lived in lowland regions surrounding the estuary of the **Red River**. They were distinguished by their habit of chewing betel and lacquering their teeth in black. The Lạc Việt were apparently one of the ethnic groups collectively called *Bách Việt* (Baiyue) by the Chinese,

and when **An Dương Vương** conquered them in the third century
B.C.E., he named the new kingdom *Âu Lạc*.

After the beginning of the Chinese occupation, the name *Lạc* initially survived in various designations for the local elite, such as
"Lạc lords" (*Lạc hầu*) and "Lạc generals" (*Lạc tướng*). It is generally believed that this local elite collaborated with their Han dynasty
rulers and were thus able to maintain much of their authority. This
collaboration came to an end in the middle of the first century C.E.
with the revolt of the **Trưng Sisters**, whose defeat led to tighter Chinese control and the destruction of the old Lạc political system.

Some scholars have argued that the word *Hùng* in the name *Hùng
kings* is actually *Lạc*, because the characters for *Hùng* (Chin. *Xiong*)
and *Lạc* (Chin. *Luo*) are similar. The term *Lạc* was gradually replaced by the term *Việt* (Chin. *Yue*), which came to designate the
ethnic group who were the ancestors of the present-day ethnic Vietnamese (**Kinh**).

LẠC LONG QUÂN (Dragon Lord of Lạc). A legendary figure considered the mythical founder of Vietnamese civilization. According
to Vietnamese mythology, Lac Long Quân had his original home in
the sea but took as his wife **Âu Cơ**, who was of a fairy race. Âu Cơ
gave birth to 100 sons, one of whom became the first of the **Hùng
kings**, the rulers of the first Vietnamese kingdom of **Văn Lang**. The
couple eventually went their separate ways, but their children became
the progenitors of the Vietnamese race.

LẠC LORDS. *See* LẠC.

LẠC VIỆT. *See* LẠC.

LADY TRIỆU (Bà Triệu, or Triệu Âu). Famous rebel leader during
the **Chinese period** of Vietnamese history. The daughter of a village
chief, Triệu Thị Trinh—known in history as *Bà (Lady) Triệu*—was
born in the prefecture of **Cửu Chân**, in what is today Thanh Hoá.
At that time, Cửu Chân was seething with political and social unrest
because of unhappiness with Chinese occupation policies and the
presence of the aggressive state of **Lin-yi** to the south. When in C.E.
248 Lin-yi fought Chinese troops near the border of Cửu Chân, the

local population, led by Lady Triệu, erupted in revolt. After several months of battle, the rebels were suppressed, and she was killed. The memory of Lady Triệu and the revolt she inspired became famous in Vietnamese history and legend. Popular belief described her as leading her followers to battle on the back of an elephant, her three-foot breasts strapped under her armor. She is today one of the leading figures in the pantheon of Vietnamese heroes and heroines struggling against foreign invaders.

LAM SƠN UPRISING. Insurrection against Chinese occupation led by **Lê Lợi** in 1418–1427. *See also* MING OCCUPATION; NGUYỄN TRÃI.

LAND REFORM. Land reform has been a key political issue in Vietnam since the colonial era, when the commercialization of land and the development of export crops changed the economics of landholding in **Indochina.** The issue was particularly sensitive in South Vietnam, where the draining of the swamps in the **Mekong River Delta** created a new class of absentee landlords who owned an estimated half of the total irrigable land in **Cochin China.**

After the departure of the **French** in 1954, the Vietnamese governments in both the North and the South enacted land-reform legislation in an effort to resolve the inequality in landholdings in the countryside. In the **Democratic Republic of Vietnam** (DRV), a major redistribution of **agricultural** land took place in 1955 and 1956 that resulted in the transfer of land to more than half the farm families in the country. The program was marred, however, by revolutionary excesses in the form of executions of local landlords who allegedly owed "blood debts" to the people, leading in 1956 to the demotion of a number of leading figures in the Party and the government, particularly **Trường Chinh**. Two years later, the DRV introduced a new program to collectivize the countryside.

In the **Republic of Vietnam**, where inequality of landholding was more prevalent, the regime of **Ngô Đình Diệm** introduced its own land-reform program in 1956. But maximum limits on landholding were set quite high, and loopholes enabled many to evade the regulations. By the end of the decade, only about 10 percent of all eligible peasants had received land through the program. In 1969, the government of President **Nguyễn Văn Thiệu** enacted a much more comprehensive "land to the tiller" program that essentially abolished the problem of tenancy in the South.

After the fall of **Saigon** in 1975, the **Socialist Republic of Vietnam** announced that, because of the relative absence of landlordism in the southern provinces, no new land-reform program would be required. **Collectivization** of land began in the South in 1978 and had not been completed by the beginning of the Fourth Five-Year Plan in 1986. From that point onward, the government began to reverse many of its key socialist policies, and private **land-use rights** have largely replaced collective ownership. *See also* PRODUCTION COLLECTIVES; PRODUCTION SOLIDARITY TEAMS.

LAND USE RIGHTS (LUR) (*Quyền sử dụng đất*). A system currently in use in Vietnam to provide guaranteed long-term rights to land without actually instituting private property. Under the socialist system of the **Democratic Republic of Vietnam** and the early years of the **Socialist Republic of Vietnam**, private ownership was frequently either discouraged or outright forbidden, and many people's property was reduced or confiscated during the **land reform** and **collectivization** campaigns of the 1950s (and, to some extent, in the 1970s after reunification with the former **Republic of Vietnam**). With the dramatic abandonment of most of the foundations of a socialist economy in the late 1980s following the adoption of *đổi mới* (renovation), it was clear that the **Vietnamese Communist Party** would need to reverse its stand on land tenure as well. This was necessary not only to encourage farmers to grow more on land that they could truly consider as their own, but also to meet the demands of **foreign investors**, who expected guarantees that the property acquired for their projects would not suddenly be taken back.

Progress in clarifying issues of land usage has been slow and not always steady. In 1993, the government promulgated a land law that set down LUR for farmers. Rights were to be issued for 20 years, and with the possession of a Land Use Rights Certificate (essentially a title), the property could be exchanged, transferred, and bequeathed as an inheritance. Implementation of this law has been uneven, however, and many people prefer to make informal and thus unofficial transactions rather than facing the complications of obtaining certificates. Various steps have been taken to consolidate the effectiveness of LUR and to enable them to acquire more of the functions of actual private property. In 2001, for example, it was decreed that foreign **banks** could offer credit to both Vietnamese- and foreign-owned entities using LUR as security for the loan. A 2004 law set down the conditions by which LUR could be seized by a court in cases involving debt or other civil disputes.

In October 2004, the government issued a much more comprehensive Decree on the Land Law in order to consolidate and clarify the various aspects of LUR found in previous decrees and laws, notably the Land Law of 2003. Although the Law and the Decree governing its implementation have been hailed as important steps in the development of a unified system for the use and registration of land, observers have pointed out that to have the rules on paper is one thing, and to follow them consistently is quite another. Moreover, because the fundamental concept of LUR is to some extent a compromise between the people's desire for the security associated with private ownership and the reluctance of a still nominally socialist regime to institute full-fledged private property, this complex balance of pragmatism and ideology ensures that the problem of land use will remain complicated for some time to come.

LANGUAGE. Bilingualism has been a common phenomenon among Vietnamese for centuries, beginning with the **Chinese period** when, as far as is known, at least a small minority of people made the transition from an oral culture to literacy for the first time. Under Chinese rule, the local population presumably spoke their own languages (the early forms of what are now **Vietnamese, Mường,** and probably **Tày** and **Nùng**), but those who learned to read and write did so in classical Chinese, though with **Sino–Vietnamese** pronunciation. The Vietnamese elite came to pride itself on its command of the written Chinese language, which was used for official documents and many literary works well into the 20th century. Some time around the late first millennium or early second millennium of the Common Era, literate Vietnamese developed a second writing system known as *chữ nôm,* which used existing and invented Chinese characters to transliterate spoken Vietnamese. *Nôm* script coexisted with, and complemented, standard classical Chinese.

As the Vietnamese kingdom expanded and became more ethnically diverse, it incorporated speakers of other languages: **Cham**, **Cambodian**, and upland peoples such as the **Thái**. These particular languages possessed their own writing systems, but those of other groups (such as the **Jarai** and **Rhadé** in the **Central Highlands**) remained at the preliterate stage until **Christian** missionaries began to create scripts for them in the 20th century. It is likely that some members of these ethnic groups would have acquired a knowledge of Vietnamese through contacts with speakers of that language, and those holding administrative positions would probably have had to learn some written Chinese to handle official documents.

By the 17th century, sizable communities of Chinese immigrants were living under Vietnamese rule. They spoke various southern dialects, including Cantonese, Teochew, Hokkien, and Hainanese. Although these **overseas Chinese** shared a common written language with the Vietnamese, they, too, would have had to learn the local language because there is little evidence that most Vietnamese could converse in Chinese. A number of words from these Chinese dialects entered colloquial Vietnamese speech.

It is not clear how many Vietnamese bothered to learn other languages besides written Chinese; a 13th-century prince fluent in Cham is mentioned in the chronicles as an unusual figure, at least within the court. Correspondence with "barbarian" courts, such as the Siamese, **Lao**, or Cambodians, was apparently conducted in Chinese. Presumably some degree of bilingualism prevailed in border regions and other areas where more than one ethnic group coexisted, but members of the elite who acquired a command of their neighbors' languages seem to have been few and far between. This attitude has persisted through the postcolonial period, when Vietnamese have tended to take up Western or East Asian languages rather than Southeast Asian tongues.

After the **French** conquest in the 19th century, French became the main language of both government and **education**. Schools beyond the primary level used French almost exclusively, and the speech of educated Vietnamese contained heavy doses of that language; soldiers, servants, concubines, and others of lower social status spoke a kind of pidgin known as *Tây bồi* ("houseboy French"). The most Westernized among them stopped speaking their native tongue almost entirely. After independence in 1954, the **Republic of Vietnam** maintained the use of French among its more elite-oriented schools, though the system was more effectively bilingual than had been the case under colonial rule. English was also widespread because of the American presence and the large numbers of South Vietnamese being trained or educated in the **United States**. The **Democratic Republic of Vietnam**, by contrast, switched to a completely Vietnamese-language curriculum, thanks to the efforts of such educators as **Hoàng Xuân Hãn**. The study of Russian and Chinese was important because many Vietnamese were sent to **China** or the **Union of Soviet Socialist Republics** for training.

Both the North and South Vietnamese regimes promoted literacy among their ethnic minorities, and they encouraged the development of Romanized scripts and curriculum materials for the various **highland minority** languages. In the North, this project was mainly the work of academic linguists, whereas in the South the Ministry of Education relied heavily on Western missionaries to do the literacy work. Because the scripts were based on the Romanized version of Vietnamese known as *quốc ngữ*, this approach was intended to facilitate the acquisition of the national language along with literacy in minority tongues.

Since the end of the war and the reunification of the country, the study of foreign languages in the **Socialist Republic of Vietnam** has shifted with the political and diplomatic winds. During the late 1970s and 1980s, there was little official encouragement for the study of English (associated as it was with the former American enemy), and the outbreak of hostilities with China in 1978–1979 meant that Chinese virtually disappeared from the curriculum. Russian remained a key language for study until the fall of the Soviet Union and the parallel moves toward a more market-oriented economy. Since the 1990s, English has been by far the most popular foreign language, as it is viewed as an indispensable tool for business and diplomacy. French, Japanese, and Chinese are also important, though French visitors are often disappointed in the younger generation's lack of interest in their language. Closer ties with South Korea and Vietnam's neighbors in the **Association of Southeast Asian Nations** have led to the introduction of Korean, Indonesian, and Thai into some university curricula as well. *See also* FOREIGN RELATIONS.

LANSDALE, EDWARD G. (1908–1987). United States military officer and onetime Central Intelligence Agency official who played a major role in securing American support for South Vietnamese Prime Minister **Ngô Đình Diệm** in the spring of 1955. Stationed in **Saigon** following a posting in the Philippines, where he assisted President Ramon Magsaysay in suppressing the Hukbalahap guerrilla movement, Lansdale urged Washington to give Diệm its backing at a time when General **J. Lawton Collins** was expressing doubt about Diệm's viability as a leader. Later, Lansdale advised the John F. Kennedy administration on policy toward Vietnam and served as an official in the pacification program in Saigon during the late 1960s. His role in leading the struggle against Communist expansion in Asia was immortalized in Graham Greene's *The Quiet American* and the later novel *The Ugly American* by William Lederer and Eugene Burdick.

LAO BẢO. Located along the **Lao** border in Quảng Trị, Lao Bảo has become an important border crossing and has been established as a special trading zone. Under the **French** it was the site of an important prison that housed a number of Vietnamese anticolonial figures at various points in time.

LAOS. The Lao kingdom (then known as *Lane Xang*) appeared in the 14th century. Until roughly 1700, it dealt with the Vietnamese on more or less equal terms. Lane Xang was generally more oriented toward its western neighbors, all of whom were Theravada **Buddhist** kingdoms, but it did have occasional contacts with Vietnam. Not all the contacts were friendly; Emperor **Lê Thánh Tông**, for example, launched a major invasion of Lao territory in 1479, though his forces were driven back. Some of the lands along the border area between the two kingdoms, such as the Sipsong Chu Thai region (now the region known in Vietnamese as *Tây Bắc*) and what is now the Lao province of Xieng Khouang, were subject to influence and intervention from both sides.

Lane Xang fragmented into three different kingdoms at the end of the 17th century, a development that left the Lao vulnerable to intervention from their more powerful neighbors, notably the Siamese and the Vietnamese. The kingdoms of Luang Phabang and

Vientiane both paid sporadic tribute to successive Vietnamese rulers and occasionally attempted to obtain Vietnamese support either against the Siamese or against each other. Control of the Lao territories (along with **Cambodia**) was one factor in the particularly bitter Siamese–Vietnamese rivalry under the **Nguyễn dynasty** in the early 1800s.

After the colonization of Vietnam, the **French** invoked alleged Vietnamese rights of suzerainty over the Lao kingdoms to justify the extension of their own control at the expense of Siam. In 1893, after an incident of gunboat diplomacy, the Siamese were forced to sign a treaty with France ceding the territory east of the Mekong, which became French Laos. (A subsequent treaty gave away two more pieces of territory on the right bank of the river.) Laos was incorporated into French **Indochina**; a few provinces were under the "protected monarchy" of Luang Phabang, while others were under direct rule.

Colonial rule had important consequences for the long-term relationship between the Vietnamese and Lao. Significant numbers of Vietnamese immigrated to Laos (with French encouragement) to do business and work for the colonial government; the civil service, including schoolteachers, was heavily Vietnamese. Most Lao towns along the Mekong had a population that was more than half Vietnamese, and these **overseas Vietnamese** (*Việt Kiều*) communities flourished until the fall of the Royal Lao Government in 1975. It was these same communities that allowed the **Indochinese Communist Party** (ICP) to gain a foothold in Laos in the 1930s. The early years of Lao Communism were almost completely dominated by Vietnamese living in Laos and northeastern Thailand; ethnic Lao revolutionaries did not really appear until the latter years of the Second World War, and there was not a separate Lao Communist Party until the early 1950s.

From the establishment of the ICP in 1930 until the Communist victory in 1975, the Lao revolution was heavily influenced—and, many would argue, dominated—by the Vietnamese. All of the Lao Party leaders had spent time in Vietnam and spoke fluent Vietnamese, and the fighting units of the Pathet Lao (the Party-led front equivalent to the **Việt Minh**) had Vietnamese-supplied advisors and *matériel*. The Vietnamese revolutionaries saw Laos very much as their own backyard from a strategic point of view and the Lao as "fraternal comrades" in a common struggle. In the 1930s, ICP leaders forecast the eventual creation of an **Indochinese Federation** that would unite the three countries of Vietnam, Laos, and Cambodia under revolutionary leadership directed from **Hanoi**. This plan was abandoned fairly quickly, in large part because of Cambodian and Lao sensibilities, but memories of the idea have frequently been evoked by those who were distrustful of Vietnamese ambitions.

After 1975, a "**special relationship**" between Vietnam and Laos was implemented, which was expanded to include Cambodia during the 1980s, when a pro-Hanoi government was in power there. This relationship still remains, and the two governments are very close, with frequent bilateral contacts in many different fields and Lao students being given scholarships to study in Vietnam. However, with the disappearance of the original generation of revolutionaries and the emergence of a new generation of Lao leaders, there seems to be less unanimity on just how close the relationship should be. Lao students are frequently sent to Thailand, Australia, and other nonsocialist countries; at the same time, **China** has reestablished the close ties with the Party leadership that it enjoyed during the civil war between 1954 and 1975.

LATER LÊ DYNASTY. *See* LÊ DYNASTY.

LATIFUNDIA. *See* TRANG ĐIỀN.

LÊ CHIÊU TÔNG (1506–1526). Ninth emperor (r. 1516–1523) of the **Lê dynasty.** He came to the throne as a young boy at a time when the dynasty had been seriously weakened by a succession of poor rulers and political crises and the **Trần Cảo** rebellion. In 1523, he was deposed in favor of his younger brother by **Mạc Đăng Dung**, a powerful official who was soon to overthrow the dynasty, and murdered three years later.

LÊ ĐẠI HÀNH. *See* LÊ HOÀN.

LÊ DUẨN (1908–1986). Leading member of the Vietnamese Communist movement and general secretary of the Party from 1960 until his death in 1986. Lê Duẩn was born in 1908, the son of a rail clerk in Quảng Trị. He entered **Hồ Chí Minh's** Revolutionary Youth League or **Thanh Niên** in 1928 and became a founding member of the **Indochinese Communist Party** in 1930. Arrested for seditious activities in 1931, he was released five years later and rose rapidly in the ICP, becoming a member of the Central Committee in 1939.

In 1940, Duẩn was rearrested and spent the war years in **Poulo Condore** prison. Released in 1945, he served briefly under President Hồ in **Hanoi** and then was sent to the southern region, where he became secretary of the Party's **Central Office for South Vietnam** (COSVN). After the **Geneva Conference,** he remained in South Vietnam and became a vocal spokesman within Party councils for a more active effort to seek the overthrow of the **Republic of Vietnam**.

In 1957, Duẩn was recalled to Hanoi to become a member of the Politburo and *de facto* general secretary of the Party after the demotion of **Trường Chinh** in the wake of the **land reform** excesses. His position was formalized in 1960, and with Hồ Chí Minh aging and in poor health, Duẩn became the leading figure in the Party. A staunch advocate of the revolutionary effort in the South, he excelled in the art of factional politics within the Politburo and maintaining an independent Vietnamese posture in the Sino–Soviet dispute.

After 1975, however, Duẩn led the Party into an intimate relationship with the **Union of Soviet Socialist Republics** and a bitter dispute with **China**. Under his leadership, the Party encountered severe difficulties in promoting economic growth and the construction of a socialist society, leading to growing criticism of the "old men" at the top. Amid rumors of impending retirement because of poor health, he died in July 1986 and was replaced by his reputed rival Trường Chinh. Lê Duẩn has been widely perceived as a hardliner in his attitude toward political and economic reform, though this view has recently been contested by some scholars.

LÊ ĐỨC ANH (1920–). Onetime military commander and former president of the **Socialist Republic of Vietnam** (SRV). Born near the old imperial capital of **Huế** in 1920, Anh worked as a laborer as a youth and joined the **Indochinese Communist Party** in 1938. During the **Franco–Việt Minh War,** he served as a military officer in charge of militia operations. During the Vietnam War he became commander of troops stationed along the **Cambodian** border. He took charge of the invasion of Cambodia in December 1978 and later remained as commander of Vietnamese occupation troops in that country until 1985, when he returned to Vietnam with the rank of full general and membership in the Politburo. In 1987, he was named minister of defense and then, with the passage of the revised **constitution** in 1992, was made president of the SRV, a position that he held until 1997, ensuring the military a strong voice in the government.

LÊ ĐỨC THỌ (1910–1990) (real name, Phan Đình Khải). Chief Vietnamese negotiator at the Paris peace talks and leading figure in the **Vietnamese Communist Party**. Born in a scholar-gentry family in Nam Hà in 1910, Lê Đức Thọ attended the Thăng Long School in **Hanoi**, where he was reportedly taught by **Võ Nguyên Giáp**. Entering the **Indochinese Communist Party** shortly after its founding in 1930, he was arrested by the **French** and served time at **Poulo Condore** and other prisons in colonial Vietnam.

During World War II, Thọ reportedly served in the liberated zone north of the **Red River Delta**. After 1945, he served as **Lê Duẩn**'s deputy in the Party's regional bureau in South Vietnam and allegedly spent time with the revolutionary movement in **Cambodia**. He was summoned to Hanoi after the **Geneva Conference** of 1954, where he was named to the Politburo and headed the Party's Organization Department for 20 years. He came to public attention in the late 1960s as Hanoi's chief delegate to the Paris peace talks. He and Henry Kissinger jointly received the Nobel Peace Prize for negotiating the **Paris Agreement**, but he turned it down on the grounds that he had not achieved real peace in Vietnam.

After the end of the war, Thọ was a prominent member of the Party's veteran leadership and was often rumored as a possible successor to Lê Duẩn as general secretary. Then at the Sixth Party Congress in December 1986, he was dropped from the Politburo and, with **Trường Chinh** and **Phạm Văn Đồng**, was named an "adviser" to the Central Committee.

LÊ DYNASTY (1428–1788). Third great dynasty that ruled in Vietnam after independence in the 10th century, to be distinguished from the so-called Early Lê, which ruled from 980 to 1009. (The Lê dynasty is therefore sometimes referred to as the *Later Lê*). The Lê came to power in 1428, when the rebel leader **Lê Lợi** drove out the **Chinese** occupiers and established a new dynasty. He himself became emperor under the reign title *Lê Thái Tổ*. For the remainder of the 15th century, the dynasty was blessed with strong rulers and good government. During the reign of the greatest of the Lê monarchs, **Thánh Tông**, the Vietnamese Empire (then known as *Đại Việt*, or Great Viet) developed in wealth and power and expanded its territory at the expense of the neighboring kingdoms of **Champa** and **Laos**. Under Thánh Tông, the influence of **Confucian** ideology and institutions gradually replaced that of **Buddhism**, which had been dominant under the **Trần dynasty** (1225–1400).

After Thánh Tông's death, the competence of Lê rulers began to decline and in 1527, the dynasty was temporarily overthrown by **Mạc Đăng Dung**. Supporters of the Lê continued to fight for its restoration and did succeed in overthrowing the Mạc regime in 1592. The Lê monarchs were now mere figureheads, however, with political power dominated by two great families, the **Trịnh Lords** and the **Nguyễn Lords**, and the kingdom effectively split into two parts, known as *Đàng Ngoài* and *Đàng Trong*. The so-called "restored Lê dynasty" lasted until 1788, when it was overthrown by the **Tây Sơn Rebellion**. *See also* MING OCCUPATION; NGUYỄN HOÀNG; NGUYỄN KIM; TRỊNH KIỂM.

LÊ HIẾN TÔNG (1461–1504). Fifth emperor (r. 1497–1504) of the **Lê dynasty**, the son of the powerful and competent Emperor **Thánh Tông**. Hiến Tông's reign marked the end of the period of strength and prosperity that characterized Vietnam during the 15th century. His son Túc Tông succeeded him but lived less than a year, and the next ruler, Emperor **Uy Mục**, began to drag the dynasty down.

LÊ HOÀN (Lê Đại Hành) (941–1005). Founder (r. 980–1005) of the short-lived Early Lê dynasty; he is usually known as *Lê Đại Hành*, a title that means "the late or deceased emperor." Lê Hoàn, a native of the area south of the **Red River Delta**, which is now Thanh Hoá, became commander in chief of the armies of Emperor **Đinh Bộ Lĩnh**. On the latter's death in 979, the state fell into chaos because the new ruler was a child of five. A few months later, Lê Hoàn took the throne, establishing a new dynasty, and married the boy's mother, the widowed Empress **Dương Vân Nga**.

Lê Hoàn's 25-year reign was marked by foreign wars. The Song dynasty in **China** had hoped to take advantage of the instability in Vietnam by launching an invasion, but Lê Hoàn defeated the Chinese armies in 981 and obtained official Chinese recognition of Vietnamese independence. He then turned his attention to the South and waged a successful campaign against the kingdom of **Champa**, seizing some of its territory.

On the domestic scene, Lê Hoàn's reign was marked by efforts to strengthen the fragile structure of the infant Vietnamese state. He relied to a considerable degree on his sons, several of whom he appointed as governors of key provinces. Lê Hoàn died in 1005, leading to fratricidal strife among his heirs; the victor ruled as **Le Long Đĩnh** but died within a few years and was replaced by the **Lý dynasty**. Lê Hoàn is one of a succession of strongmen who rose to power in the 10th century and who established "dynasties" that did not survive them.

LÊ HỒNG PHONG (1902–1942). Prominent member of the **Indochinese Communist Party** (ICP) in the 1930s. Born *Lê Huy Doãn* in Nghệ An, he was working at an auto repair shop in **Hanoi** in 1918 when he was recruited by a member of **Phan Bội Chau**'s **Vietnamese Restoration Society** to study abroad. In 1924, he joined the radical Association of Like Minds (*Tâm Tâm Xã*) in southern China and **Hồ Chí Minh**'s Revolutionary Youth League (*Thanh Niên*) a year later. After studying at the Whampoa Academy in 1926, he was sent to the **Union of Soviet Socialist Republics** to attend aviation school and served as a liaison between the **Comintern** and the Thanh Niên leadership in **China**.

After Hồ's arrest by British police in Hong Kong in 1931, Lê Hồng Phong became the de facto leader of the ICP and the head of its Overseas Leadership Committee (*Ban Chỉ Huy Hải Ngoại*) set up in China as the provisional leading organ of the Party. In the summer of 1935, he attended the Seventh Congress of the Comintern and returned to Vietnam the following year to pass on its instructions to the newly constituted Central Committee. He was arrested by French authorities in 1940 and sent to **Poulo Condore** prison, where he died as a result of torture in 1942. *See also* NGHỆ TĨNH REVOLT.

LÊ HỒNG SƠN (also known as *Hồng Sơn*) (1899–1932). Leading revolutionary militant and founding member of the **Indochinese Communist Party** (ICP) in 1930. Born in Nghệ An, Lê Hồng Sơn (real name Lê Văn Phan) reportedly became a revolutionary in his adolescence, when he joined **Phan Bội Châu**'s **Vietnamese Restoration Society**. In 1924, he helped organize the Association of Like Minds (***Tâm Tâm Xã***) in southern **China**. One year later, he became a member of **Hồ Chí Minh**'s Revolutionary Youth League (***Thanh Niên***) and the Chinese Communist Party (CCP). In 1930, he became a member of the new ICP and, according to French sources, its liaison with the CCP. In September 1932, he was arrested by French police in the International Settlement in Shanghai. He was convicted in a French court in Vinh of assassinating two government agents during the 1920s and was executed.

LÊ KHẢ PHIÊU (1931–). Originally from Thanh Hoá, Lê Khả Phiêu spent the bulk of his career holding political positions in the **People's Army of Vietnam**, making his way up through the ranks to head the army's Political Department. He was elected to the Central Committee of the **Vietnamese Communist Party** in 1991 and then to the Politburo in 1994. A protégé of **Lê Đức Anh**, a general who served as president of the **Socialist Republic of Vietnam** from 1992 through 1997, Phiêu relied on the support of the military to attain the post of Party secretary general in 1997, thus ensuring that the outgoing president was replaced by another general in an even more powerful position.

Phiêu wielded considerable power during his tenure as secretary general, and it made him a lot of enemies. He was also severely criticized for signing a land border agreement with **China** in 1999 whose precise details were kept secret but which was widely perceived as having made too many concessions to Vietnam's northern neighbor. A diehard conservative, Phiêu met with opposition from more reform-minded elements within the Party. At the Ninth Party Congress in 2001, he was replaced by the more moderate **Nông Đức Mạnh**. On the eve of the Congress, the Politburo had recommended that

Phiêu be retained in his position, but this decision was overruled by the Central Committee.

LÊ LỢI (Lê Thái Tổ) (1385–1433). Founder (r. 1428–1433) of the Lê dynasty (1428–1788) in 15th-century Vietnam. Lê Lợi was born in 1385, the son of a wealthy landlord in Lam Sơn village, Thanh Hoá; recently some scholars have suggested that he may have been all or part ethnically **Mường**. He was successful in the civil service **examinations** and entered the imperial bureaucracy under the brief dynasty of **Hồ Qúy Ly**, which succeeded the **Trần dynasty** in 1400, but resigned after the country came under **Chinese** rule in 1407. Returning to his native village, Lê Lợi began to organize a resistance movement to overthrow the **Ming occupation** and restore Vietnamese independence. Calling himself the *Pacification King (Bình Định Vương)*, he gathered around himself several hundred close followers, including the scholar-patriot **Nguyễn Trãi**, and inaugurated a struggle for national liberation.

At first conditions were difficult, but Chinese occupation policies were harsh, and Vietnamese of many walks of life rallied to his standard. Lê Lợi's was by no means the only anti-Chinese rebel organization in Vietnam, but it gradually became the most effective movement opposed to Chinese rule. A brief truce was negotiated in 1423, but war resumed on the death of Chinese Emperor Yongle the following year, and the rebels, from their base in modern-day Nghệ An and Hà Tĩnh, gradually seized control of most of the country south of the **Red River Delta**. In 1426, they won a major battle over the Chinese west of the modern-day capital of **Hanoi**; two years later, the Ming forces evacuated Vietnam.

Lê Lợi was persuaded to accept the throne, and became founding emperor Thái Tổ of what became known as the *(Later)* **Lê dynasty**. The key problem facing his new imperial administration was to reduce the size of the great landed estates (*trang điền*) that had been owned by nobles and high mandarins under the Trần, a task begun by Hồ Quý Ly. To do so, Thái Tổ returned to the concept of the "equal field" system (*quân điền*) that had first been put into operation by the early emperors of the **Lý dynasty** (1009–1225) and set established limits on the amount of land that could be possessed by individuals, depending on their age and status. He also initiated a number of reforms in administration, civil service, military, and system of justice. Perhaps his only negative legacy was the *công thần*, a group of his loyal followers who were given special privileges and formed a powerful faction in court affairs. This problem reached a crisis point under his son **Lê Thái Tông**.

LE LONG ĐĨNH (985–1009). The third and last ruler (r. 1005–1009) of the short-lived Early Lê dynasty in the 10th century. The son of **Lê Hoàn**, Lê Long Đĩnh killed his older brother, who had succeeded their father on the throne after the latter's death in 1005. The new emperor only lived for four years, however; he reportedly suffered from various health problems, including severe hemorrhoids, which earned him the nickname *Ngọa Triều*, "[he who] holds court lying down." Whatever merits he might have had as a ruler, he is remembered mainly as a sadistic and brutal individual. When he died and was succeeded by a young son, his family was overthrown by elements loyal to Lý Công Uẩn, who established a new dynasty as **Lý Thái Tổ**. *See also* VẠN HẠNH.

LÊ LỰU (1942?–). Prolific writer of novels and short stories in contemporary Vietnam. A war veteran who spent over three decades in military service in the **People's Army of Vietnam**, Lê Lựu was born in Hải Hưng in the **Red River Delta**. During the Vietnam War, he served as a war correspondent on the **Hồ Chí Minh Trail**, and many of his writings, including a dozen novels, deal with aspects of the war or military life. His recent work, however, has shifted away from the trials of the Vietnamese nation as a whole to the problems of ordinary people. His first novel in this vein, entitled *Thời Xa Vắng* (*Times Long Past*), was awarded a prize for fiction by the Writer's Association in 1987. The work portrays the life of a scholar-gentry family from the end of the **Franco-Việt Minh conflict** to the present. *See also* LITERATURE.

LÊ MAI (1940–1996). A diplomat in the **Democratic Republic of Vietnam** (DRV) and **Socialist Republic of Vietnam** (SRV). Lê Mai was a junior member of the DRV delegation to the negotiations leading to the **Paris Agreement** of 1973. He subsequently held various diplomatic posts, including ambassador to Thailand, and rose to the rank of deputy foreign minister in the SRV. A protégé of former foreign minister **Nguyễn Cơ Thạch**, Mai achieved prominence as a key figure in the SRV's relationship with the **United States** during the years before normalization and was viewed as someone who was able to interpret American thinking to an often uncomprehending Vietnamese leadership. He led bilateral negotiations on issues related to American soldiers Missing in Action and the return of former U.S. diplomatic property in Vietnam. Mai died quite suddenly only a year after normalization took place in 1995. His death earned him an unusual and very warm eulogy during a State Department press briefing in Washington, when he was described as a "young man with a great future" and a "highly regarded diplomat and friend."

LE MYRE DE VILERS, CHARLES MARIE (1833–1918). Governor of **Cochin China** from 1879 to 1883. Although he had previously been a naval officer, he was the first civilian governor of the colony, symbolizing the consolidation of a long-term colonial regime after the initial military occupation. In 1882, he dispatched Capt. **Henri Rivière** to **Tonkin** to extend **French** influence into the area, but he was ambivalent about Rivière's belligerent actions and resigned from office when his remonstrances to Paris were rejected.

LÊ NGỌA TRIỀU. *See* LE LONG ĐỈNH.

LÊ QUANG BA. Veteran Communist Party military officer. Born in a poor ethnic **Nùng** family in Cao Bằng, Ba joined the **Indochinese Communist Party** in the early 1930s and became active in the youth movement in the **Việt Bắc** region. He became involved in military affairs during World War II and played an active role in the **August Revolution** and the **Franco–Việt Minh War**, commanding the 316th Division at the Battle of **Điện Biên Phủ**. After the **Geneva Conference**, he became active in minority nationality affairs in the **Democratic Republic of Vietnam** (DRV), and was named chairman of the State Commission of Nationalities after the end of the Vietnam War. But in the late 1970s, he was suspected of sympathy with dissident elements in minority areas and was dropped from his post in 1979. *See also* CHU VĂN TÂN; HIGHLAND MINORITIES.

LÊ QÚY ĐÔN (1726–1784). Historian of the **Lê dynasty** (1428–1788) in Vietnam. A native of Thái Bình, Lê Quý Đôn was the son of a holder of the doctorate (*tiến sĩ*) in the civil service **examinations** and an official under the Lê. He passed the metropolitan examination in 1752 and entered the **mandarinate**. As an official, he was active as a provincial governor, where he was known for his firm adherence to the principles of **Confucianism**. He strongly repressed rebellious elements but showed some sympathy for the needs of the common people, attempting to reduce bureaucratic **corruption** and inefficiency. He also served as a diplomat, leading a Vietnamese mission to the Qing court in **China** in 1761.

Đôn is best known as one of the most prominent scholars and historians of 18th-century Vietnam. Among his historical writings are *Đại Việt Thông Sử* (*A History of the Lê Dynasty*) and *Phủ Biên Tạp Lục* (*Miscellaneous Chronicles of the Pacified Frontiers*), a detailed guide to central Vietnam. His interests were encyclopedic, and he wrote in both Chinese and *chữ nôm* on such subjects as science, morality, philosophy, and agronomy. He is remembered as one of the towering intellects of late traditional Vietnam. *See also* HISTORIOGRAPHY; LITERATURE.

LÊ TẮC. Vietnamese scholar and official in the 13th century. Lê Tắc, member of a noble family dating back several hundred years, became a well-known scholar during the reign of **Trần Nhân Tông**. During the **Mongol invasions** of the 1280s, he collaborated with the invaders and after their defeat settled in **China**. While there, he wrote *An Nam Chí Lược* (*Annals of Annam*), a 20-volume history of Vietnam culled from Chinese historical records and published in 1340.

LÊ THÁI TỔ. *See* LÊ LỢI.

LÊ THÁI TÔNG (1423–1442). Second emperor (r. 1433–1442) of the **Lê dynasty**. Lê Thái Tông ascended to the throne on the death of his father, **Thái Tổ**, in 1433. Because he was only 11 years old at the time of accession, power rested in the hands of Chief Minister Lê Sát. Lê Lợi's chief adviser, **Nguyễn Trãi**, had already retired from office as a result of court intrigue, in large part the influence of *công thần*, those who had supported Lê Lợi during his resistance against the **Ming occupation**. As Thái Tông reached early maturity, he developed a reputation for debauchery. He died under mysterious circumstances in 1442 while returning from a visit to Nguyễn Trãi at the latter's retirement home at Chí Linh mountain, west of present-day **Hanoi**, and Trãi was executed for regicide.

LÊ THÀNH NGHI. Veteran Communist Party member and influential **economic** official in the **Democratic Republic of Vietnam** (DRV). Born in a worker family in Quảng Bình, Lê Thành Nghi joined the **Indochinese Communist Party** sometime in the late 1930s and was a leading economic cadre during the **Franco-Việt Minh conflict**. He became an economic specialist in the DRV, serving as minister of industry and chairman of the State Planning Commission. Identified with the Chinese model of economic development, he lost influence in the late 1970s and was dismissed in 1982 from the Politburo but maintained his position as vice-chairman of the State Council. *See also* INDUSTRY; SOCIALIST REPUBLIC OF VIETNAM; STATE PLANNING.

LÊ THÁNH TÔNG (1442–1497). Fourth and perhaps greatest emperor (r. 1460–1497) of the **Lê dynasty**. Lê Thánh Tông ascended the throne in 1460 at the age of 18, after a brief usurpation by a relative. During a reign of 37 years, he made a significant contribution to the growth and strengthening of the Vietnamese state. First and foremost he was responsible for a number of changes in the government. He reorganized the central administration, formalizing the duties of the six ministries (*Lục Bộ*) (Rites, War, Justice, Interior, Public Works, and Finance) and streamlined the operation of the civil service. He strengthened the hand of the central bureaucracy over the provincial and local administration, thus limiting the power of the landed aristocracy. He ordered a national census, a geographical survey of the entire country, and the writing of a new national history by the noted historian **Ngô Sĩ Liên**. A new penal code was promulgated—the famous **Hồng Đức code**—which systematized the rules and regulations of the state. He infused the entire system with the spirit of **Confucianism**, which, under his direction, now assumed a position of dominance over **Buddhism** in the administration and set a moral tone over the population at large.

Lê Thánh Tông also attacked the chronic problem that had plagued so many of his predecessors—the land question. Inspection of the dike system was promoted, and peasants were encouraged by various means to bring virgin land under cultivation. The government also attempted to prevent the increasing concentration of land in the hands of wealthy landlords by leveling heavy penalties for the seizure of commune land.

In the field of foreign affairs, Lê Thánh Tông presided over a significant strengthening of the armed forces and an expansion of the territory of the Vietnamese Empire at the expense of **Champa**. Continual clashes along the common border led the Vietnamese to invade Champa in 1470, resulting in the seizure of the Cham capital of Vijaya. The northern segment of the kingdom—corresponding to the modern province of Quảng Nam—was assimilated into the Vietnamese Empire and settled with military colonies (*đồn điền*). He also mounted a major invasion against **Laos**, which was eventually repelled.

Lê Thánh Tông is also known for his literary interests, and he was part of a circle of scholars and courtiers who wrote poetry. He was succeeded by his son **Hiến Tông**.

LÊ TƯƠNG DỰC (1495–1516). Eighth ruler (r. 1509–1516) of the **Lê dynasty**. He began and ended his reign in bloodshed, having killed his predecessor, **Uy Mục**. His reign was marked by continued instability and violence in the court and peasant uprisings in the countryside. The most important rebellion was launched by a pretender to the throne, **Trần Cảo**, who claimed to be a descendant of the Trần royal family. Tương Dực, known popularly as "the hog emperor" (*vua lợn*), was killed by one of his own lieutenants during the insurrection. He was succeeded by **Lê Chiêu Tông**, who managed to suppress the rebellion but was then deposed and assassinated by **Mạc Đăng Dung**, an ambitious military official who had become influential at court.

LÊ UY MỤC (1488–1509). Seventh emperor (r. 1505–1509) of the **Lê dynasty**. Lê Uy Mục quickly showed himself to be a ruthless ruler, murdering his grandmother and two of his ministers. His unpopularity led to the popular nickname given to him, the "devil king" (*vua* *quỷ*). He was assassinated by his cousin in 1509, who then seized the throne under the dynastic title of **Tương Dực**. The violence and instability provoked by these two rulers brought an end to the period of strength and prosperity that Vietnam had enjoyed during the 15th century and paved the way for the usurpation of the throne by **Mạc Đăng Dung**.

LÊ VĂN DUYỆT (1763–1832). Regional official in southern Vietnam during the 19th century. An ex-military commander who had led Nguyễn forces against the **Tây Sơn** at Qui Nhơn in 1799, Lê Văn Duyệt rose to prominence during the reign of Emperor **Gia Long**, founder of the **Nguyễn dynasty** (1802–1945). Gia Long appointed him as a kind of governor-general (effectively, a regional overlord) for the southern provinces of Vietnam; he exercised enormous power, including the authority to conduct foreign relations with Europe and other Southeast Asian nations. **Nguyễn Văn Thành**, another former commander, held a similar position in the North.

Lê Văn Duyệt was relatively sympathetic to the Western presence in Vietnam and protested when Gia Long's successor **Minh Mạng** attempted to evict **Christian** missionaries. This might have contributed to his strained relations with the new emperor, along with the fact that his strong power base in the southern provinces was a threat to the court's central authority. When Duyệt died in 1832, he was posthumously convicted of crimes and his grave desecrated, leading his adopted son, Lê Văn Khôi, to rebel. *See also* LÊ VĂN KHÔI REBELLION.

LÊ VĂN HƯU (1230–1322). Renowed historian during the **Trần dynasty** in Vietnam. Lê Văn Hưu was a gifted youngster and succeeded in the civil service examination while still at an early age, and he became a member of the prestigious Hán Lâm Academy and the National Board of History. In 1272, he wrote a comprehensive national history of the Vietnamese nation, entitled the *Đại Việt Sử Ký* (*Historical Record of Great Viet*). This dynastic history of Vietnam from the third century B.C.E. to the end of the **Lý dynasty** is no longer extant, but parts have been incorporated into the *Đại Việt Sử Ký Toàn Thư* (*Complete Historical Record of Great Viet*), written by the noted historian **Ngô Sĩ Liên** during the 15th century under the **Lê**

dynasty. Hưu's *Đại Việt Sử Ký* was written in part on the basis of an earlier work, the *Việt Chí* (*Annals of Viet*) authored by Trần Phổ, a scholar-official who served under the Trần in the mid-13th century. Although Lê Văn Hưu's work, like much historical writing in imperial Vietnam, had been officially commissioned by the court at a time when **Buddhism** remained dominant, it displays a strong **Confucian** bias. *See also* HISTORIOGRAPHY; LITERATURE.

LÊ VĂN KHÔI REBELLION. Rebellion launched by Lê Văn Khôi in southern Vietnam in 1833. Originally from a **highland minority** group (probably **Tày** or **Nùng**) in the northern province of **Cao Bằng**, Lê Văn Khôi was the adopted son of the regional warlord in the South, **Lê Văn Duyệt**. In 1833, shortly after the latter's death and posthumous humiliation by Emperor **Minh Mạng**, a major revolt broke out in the South against efforts by the court in **Huế** to curtail the region's autonomy. Khôi, leader of the rebellion, sought help from Western missionaries and the kingdom of Siam, and he proclaimed the son of Prince **Cảnh**, first son of **Emperor Gia Long** (1802–1820), as the legitimate ruler of Vietnam. Khôi died in 1834 while his fortress at **Saigon** was under siege by imperial troops. The revolt, after spreading briefly throughout the South, was suppressed the following year. *See also* NGUYỄN DYNASTY.

LEAGUE FOR THE INDEPENDENCE OF VIỆTNAM (*Việt Nam Độc lập Đồng minh Hội*). *See* VIỆT MINH.

LEAGUE FOR THE NATIONAL RESTORATION OF VIỆTNAM (*Việt Nam Phục quốc Đồng minh Hội*). *See* PHỤC QUỐC.

LEAGUE OF OPPRESSED PEOPLES OF THE WORLD (*Hội Dân tộc Bị Áp bức Thế giới*). Radical front group composed of representatives of several Asian societies formed by **Hồ Chí Minh** and other revolutionaries in southern **China** in 1925. Based in Canton, it included Koreans, Vietnamese, Indonesians, Malays, Indians, and Chinese. It was disbanded after the crackdown on Communist activities by Chiang Kai-shek's forces in 1927.

LECLERC, JACQUES PHILIPPE (1902–1947). Senior general in the **French** Army and commander of the **French Expeditionary**

Forces in **Indochina** after World War II. Leclerc, born Philippe de
Hauteclocque, joined the Free French Movement of Charles de
Gaulle during the war. He arrived in **Saigon** in October 1945 as com-
mander of French forces in Indochina and played a significant role in
reestablishing his country's authority in the colony. After the **Ho-
Sainteny preliminary agreement** in early March 1946, forces under
his command arrived in **Hanoi** to protect French interests in northern
Vietnam. He died in a plane crash in 1947.

LEFÈBVRE, (MONSIGNOR) DOMINIQUE (1810–1865). French
missionary and ecclesiastical official in Vietnam. A vigorous advocate of an activist missionary policy in Vietnam, Lefèbvre was seized
by Vietnamese authorities and sentenced to death in 1847. He was
subsequently released by order of Emperor **Thiệu Trị**, but a belligerent French naval commander used the incident as a pretext to shell
the Vietnamese port city of **Đà Nẵng**. *See also* CHRISTIANITY;
PUGINIER, PAUL-FRANÇOIS.

LEGAL SYSTEM. During the precolonial era, the Vietnamese legal
system was essentially patterned after that of neighboring
China. Like the Chinese system, it was hierarchical, punitive, com-
munitarian, rather than individualistic in assigning responsibility, and
imprecise. Minor disputes were handled within the **village** by a
neighborhood committee or the **council of elders**, while major alter-
cations were often adjudicated by the district magistrate. There was
no distinction between civil and criminal cases. In some situations,
as in the case of the **Hồng Đức Code** in the 15th century, the Vietnamese departed from Chinese experience to take account of local
traditions of slightly more sexual equality, but, for the most part, they
rigorously followed the Chinese model, as was the case with the **Gia
Long Code** promulgated by the **Nguyễn dynasty** 400 years later.

In the colonial era, the Vietnamese were introduced to Western
legal institutions. The impact was limited, however, because much of
the population continued to live under the imperial bureaucracy,
while the **French** made liberal use of traditional practices to maintain
law and order. That system was continued in the South after the **Geneva Agreement.**

In the **Democratic Republic of Vietnam** (DRV), a new legal system established by the constitution of 1959 was inspired by the Soviet model. People's courts were created at all administrative levels. Each court was assigned a judge and several "people's assessors," who played a role similar to that of the jury in the Anglo–American system. All were elected by and held accountable to the people's council at that echelon. Their decisions and actions were reviewed by the Supreme People's Court, the members of which were elected by the **National Assembly**. The National Assembly was also authorized "in certain cases" to set up special tribunals for unique cases, such as treason. The prosecuting arm of the judicial system consisted of so-called "people's organs of control" at all levels, culminating in the office of the procurator general in **Hanoi**. These organs supervised the observance of the law by all administrative offices of the state as well as by the citizenry at large. The procurate system was patterned after that of the **censorate** in traditional China and Vietnam.

In theory, the rights of defendants were adequately protected by law, as in judicial systems in the West. In fact, the system was often arbitrary, punitive, and marked by incompetence. Knowledge of the law was primitive (the first law school in Hanoi was not opened until the late 1970s) and its provisions were widely ignored. The interests of the state and the Party routinely took precedence over the rights of citizens, and the failure of the law to protect the individual was glaringly apparent in late 1975, when thousands of South Vietnamese were sent to reeducation camps without a formal trial and conviction.

The **Socialist Republic of Vietnam** attempted to alleviate some of these conditions in the 1980 **Constitution**, but provisions remained (which have been retained in the revised charter of 1992), which enabled the state to arrest and convict **dissidents**, such as writers and **journalists** whose only crime is criticism of the political system or the **Vietnamese Communist Party**. In recent years, the regime has become increasingly aware of the inadequacy of the current legal system to deal with the challenge of renovation *đổi mới* and has been attempting to bring about greater efficiency by streamlining the process and training more qualified lawyers and judges. Yet a fundamental difference remains between the Vietnamese legal system and its counterpart in the West. The assertion that the interests of the state take precedence over those of individual citizens is a legacy not only of the teachings of Marx and Lenin but of **Confucius** and the Chinese Emperor Qinshi Huangdi as well. *See also* RULE OF LAW.

LI-FOURNIER TREATY. *See* TREATY OF TIENTSIN.

LIÊN VIỆT FRONT (National United Vietnamese Front) (*Hội Liên hiệp Quốc dân Việt Nam*). Front organization set up by the **Indochinese Communist Party** (ICP) in May 1946. The front was created as a means of broadening the popular base of support for the Party and the **Democratic Republic of Vietnam**. It included several political parties and mass organizations not previously linked with the ICP's existing front organization, the **Việt Minh**. The president of the new front was the veteran nationalist **Huỳnh Thúc Kháng**; the vice-president was **Tôn Đức Thắng**, a Party member and later president of the DRV. In 1951, the Liên Việt absorbed the Việt Minh Front. In 1955, it was replaced by the **Fatherland Front** (*Mặt Trận Tổ Quốc*), which became the legal front organization in the DRV and later in the **Socialist Republic of Vietnam** as well.

LINYI (Lâm Ấp). Chinese name for an early state in what is now central Vietnam. The kingdom of Linyi (in Vietnamese, Lam Ấp) is said to have been founded in C.E. 192 in the province of **Nhật Nam**, the southernmost part of the region then under Chinese rule. It gradually slipped away from Chinese control and was increasingly subject to the cultural **Indianization** then spreading across Southeast Asia. For several centuries, it controlled an area from the Hoành Sơn Spur to the present-day city of **Đà Nẵng** and was a frequent source of conflict along the southern border of the Chinese-ruled territory. Traditionally, Linyi has been viewed as a **Cham** polity, a precursor of the later kingdoms of **Champa**, though some scholars have recently argued that it was instead inhabited by some other ethnic group more closely related to the Vietnamese.

LĨNH NAM CHÍCH QUÁI (Fantasies Selected from South of the Pass). A historical work written during the **Trần dynasty**, attributed to Trần Thế Pháp. It recounts many of the legends concerning the origins and early years of the Vietnamese people. The text was later used by the 15th-century historian **Ngô Sĩ Liên** in writing his com-

prehensive history of Vietnam, *Đại Việt Sử Ký Toàn Thư. See also*
HISTORIOGRAPHY; *VIỆT ĐIỆN U LINH TẬP.*

LITERATURE. During the traditional era, Vietnamese literature was
essentially divided into two basic forms—a classical form based on
the Chinese model and a vernacular form based on indigenous
themes and genres. Classical literature was written in literary Chinese and utilized genres popular in China, such as poetry, history,
and essays. Several famous scholars concentrated on works of **historiography**; among them were **Lê Quý Đôn, Lê Văn Hưu, Ngô Sĩ
Liên**, and **Ngô Thì Sĩ**. Vernacular literature, written in *chữ nôm*
(based on spoken Vietnamese), might have originally been expressed
in the form of poetry and essays but by the 17th and 18th centuries
began to take the form of verse or prose novels, often involving caustic commentary on the frailties of Vietnamese society. Many of Vietnam's greatest authors, such as **Nguyễn Trãi, Nguyễn Bỉnh Khiêm**,
and **Nguyễn Du**, wrote comfortably in both Chinese and *nôm*. Although the literary scene was dominated by men, several important
woman writers made a name for themselves as well, notably **Đoàn
Thị Điểm, Nguyễn Thị Hinh** (known as *Bà Huyện Thanh Quan*),
and **Hồ Xuân Hương**.

Vietnamese literature was changed irrevocably by the imposition
of colonial rule. By the 1920s, the classical style was on the decline
and increasingly replaced by a new literature based on the Western
model. Drama, poetry, and the novel, often imitating trends in the
West, were written in *quốc ngữ*, the Romanized alphabet for Vietnamese. Much of the literature from the 1920s and 1930s, especially
novels by the **Tự Lực Văn Đoàn** group, reflected the conflict between traditional values and mores and the newer influences from the
West. Several authors outside this group became prominent as well,
sometimes for a single novel: **Hoàng Ngọc Phách, Ngô Tất Tố,
Nguyễn Công Hoan**, and **Nguyễn Trọng Thuật**.

The Westernization of Vietnamese literature continued to evolve
in the **Republic of Vietnam**, formed in the South after the **Geneva
Conference** of 1954. In the North, the **Democratic Republic of
Vietnam** (DRV) brought about the emergence of a new form of literature based on the Marxist–Leninst concept of socialist realism, emphasizing the transformation of the human personality, the sacred

task of completing the Vietnamese revolution, and the building of an advanced socialist society. A brief expression of **dissident** voices in the *Nhân Văn Giai Phẩm* affair (led by **Phan Khôi**) was quickly suppressed. Such writers as **Lê Lựu** and **Nguyễn Minh Châu** were popular during the war.

In the South, a number of novelists wrote about the social and cultural impact of the war. Duyên Anh, for example, was known for his portrayals of the seamy underside of South Vietnamese society; his novels were peopled with gangsters, juvenile delinquents, and other characters who typified the social problems of **Saigon** and other urban areas. Trần Thị Nhã Ca (usually known as *Nhã Ca*) also produced many books about life in the wartime South. In addition, the colonial-era novels of the Tự Lực Văn Đoàn retained a tremendous popularity.

In 1986, with the launching of the program of renovation (*đổi mới*), the government encouraged writers to use their creative energies and imagination to criticize the inequities of the system and promote the building of a new Vietnam. Many responded with sharp attacks on official **corruption** and questioned the official patriotic interpretation of the Vietnam War, **Bảo Ninh** and **Dương Thu Hương** being prominent among them. The Party responded by suppressing its critics and arresting a number of writers on the charge of sedition, but writers in Vietnam today are engaged in creating a new form of realism outside the bounds of ideological control. Although there are still clear boundaries for what can be discussed in literature, they have generally gotten wider, and a number of authors use short stories and novels in particular as a medium of social and political critique. **Nguyễn Huy Thiệp** is the most notable example, but other writers, such as **Chu Lai**, have dealt with the issues confronting "post-socialist" Vietnam as well. *See also* NGUYỄN ĐÌNH CHIỂU; TẢN ĐÀ; TỐ HỮU.

LIU YONGFU. *See* BLACK FLAGS.

LOCAL GOVERNMENT. The administrative division of Vietnam below the central level has varied considerably over the 2,000 years of recorded history. In general, however, local administration in Vietnam has usually taken place at three main levels: province (*tinh, lộ,* *trấn*); district (*huyện, quận, châu*); and commune/**village** (*xã, thôn*) (The terminology changed over time depending on the regime). On occasion, three other levels were also used: the prefecture or *phủ* (an intermediate echelon between the province and the district), the canton or *tổng* (between the district and the commune), and the region (*bộ*) (between the central government and the province).

In the **Socialist Republic of Vietnam** (SRV), administration is at four levels: central (*trung ương*), province (*tỉnh*), district (*huyện*), and village or commune (*xã*). The village itself is often divided into smaller "natural villages" (*làng, thôn,* or *bản*) and hamlets (*xóm*). The SRV is currently divided into 58 provinces and five municipalities (**Hanoi, Hải Phòng, Đà Nẵng**, Cần Thơ, and Hồ Chí Minh City [**Saigon**]) directly subordinated to the central government. The number of provinces has fluctuated considerably since reunification. Initially, a number of them were merged into larger units, but in recent years the tendency has been to move in the opposite direction and divide larger provinces back into smaller ones.

LODGE, HENRY CABOT (1902–1985). United States ambassador to the **Republic of Vietnam** from August 1963 until June 1964, and from August 1965 until April 1967. Lodge, a veteran Republican politician from Massachusetts, was named ambassador by President John F. Kennedy just as the latter was losing patience with South Vietnamese president **Ngô Đình Diệm**, and some observers believed he was appointed specifically to handle the task of hastening Diệm's overthrow. Replaced by General **Maxwell Taylor** in the summer of 1964, he returned for a second tour one year later.

LONG, MAURICE (1866–1923). Governor-general of French **Indochina** from 1920 to 1923. A lawyer and a parliamentarian representing the Radical Socialist Party, Long increased the number of Vietnamese members in consultative assemblies in **Annam** and **Tonkin** and the local administration in **Cochin China**.

LU HAN (1891–?). Chinese military officer and warlord from Yunnan Province whose military forces were sent under the instructions of Chiang Kai-shek to occupy northern **Indochina** after the **Japanese occupation** in World War II. As commander of Chinese occupation troops, Lieutenant General Lu Han played an active role in seeking to promote the interests of non-Communist Vietnamese nationalists, such as the **Việt Nam Quốc Dân Đảng**, after the **August Revolution** brought the **Indochinese Communist Party** to power under the mantle of the **Việt Minh** Front. His troops left Indochina as a consequence of the Sino–French agreement of 28 February 1946, which called for the withdrawal of the Chinese troops in return for the abolition of **French** extraterritorial rights in southern **China.**

Although Chiang Kai-shek had rewarded Lu Han for his services by appointing him to replace Lung Yun as warlord in Yunnan, Lu defected to the Communists at the end of the Chinese Civil War.

LỤC BỘ (Six Boards). Ministries of state in precolonial Vietnam. Based on the system adopted originally by the Tang dynasty in **China**, the board system existed at least as early as the 14th century, but the full six-board structure was only consolidated in the mid-15th century under the **Lê dynasty**. It consisted of the Boards of Appointments (*Lại Bộ*), Finance (*Hộ Bộ*), Justice (*Hình Bộ*), Public works (*Công Bộ*), War (*Binh Bộ*), and Rites (*Lễ Bộ*). Operating as part of the central bureaucracy, they supervised the primary functions of the imperial government. Each was headed by a president or minister (*Thượng thư*), with two vice-presidents and two counselors. Each ministry was divided into several panels and a corps of inspection for the provinces. The term *Bộ* has remained in use for a government ministry in postcolonial Vietnam.

LỤC TỈNH TÂN VĂN (News of the Six Provinces). A newspaper published in **Saigon** during the early part of the 20th century; the name refers to the traditional administrative structure of **Cochin China**. Edited for a time by the nationalist and entrepreneur Gilbert Chiêu, *Lục Tỉnh Tân Văn* earned official displeasure by publishing articles focusing on rural economic problems. The prominent journalist **Nguyễn Văn Vĩnh** also did a stint as editor of the paper, though most of his career was made in **Tonkin**. *See also* JOURNALISM.

LUTTE, LA (The Struggle). French-language weekly newspaper published in colonial Vietnam. Published in **Cochin China** by returned students from **France**, its first issue appeared in 1933. Most of the founding members, such as **Tạ Thụ Thâu**, Trần Văn Thạch, and **Hồ Hữu Tường**, were **Trotskyites**. Several members of the **Indochinese Communist Party**, such as Nguyễn Văn Tạo and Dương Bạch Mai, also took part in the editing or contributed articles until prohibited from doing so by the **Comintern**, which opposed cooperation with the Trotskyite group. Adopting relatively moderate political views, *La Lutte* was tolerated by the French colonial regime until it was closed in 1939. *See also* JOURNALISM.

LƯU VĨNH PHÚC. *See* BLACK FLAGS.

LÝ ANH TÔNG (1136–1176). Emperor (r. 1137–1175) during the **Lý dynasty**. Lý Anh Tông was still an infant when he ascended the throne on the death of his father, Lý Thần Tông. Until reaching his maturity, power was in the hands of his mother and her lover, the court figure Đỗ Anh Vũ. His reign was generally peaceful, although rebellion broke out among **highland minorities** in the mountain areas surrounding the **Red River Delta**. It was also marked by growing trade relations with such neighboring countries in the area as **China**, Siam, **Cambodia**, and the trading states in Malaya and the Indonesian archipelago. In 1175, Anh Tông became ill and turned power over to a regent, the respected general **Tô Hiến Thành**. He died the following year at the age of 39.

LÝ BÍ (Lý Bôn) (?–548). Leader of a major revolt against **Chinese** rule in sixth-century Vietnam. Lý Bí was descended from ethnic Chinese who had fled to Vietnam at the time of the Wang Mang rebellion. Born in a family with a military background, he served as a local official in the bureaucracy of the Liang dynasty. Disappointed in his ambitions, he launched a rebellion in C.E. 542 and, despite conflict with the **Cham** to the south, was successful in overthrowing the unpopular local Chinese administration and, in 544, established an independent kingdom named *Vạn Xuân* (10,000 Springs). Lý Bi styled himself the emperor of **Nam Việt**, thus invoking the memory of the short-lived dynasty of **Triệu Đà** with the same name. The capital was probably located at Gia Ninh, near his family home at the foot of Mount Tam Đảo, northwest of **Hanoi** at the edge of the **Red River Delta**.

At first, Lý Bí's successes paralleled his ambition, and he was able to unite much of the traditional Vietnamese heartland under his rule. Then, in 545, the Liang dynasty organized a military force under the capable command of the experienced general Chen Baxian. Chen captured Lý Bí's capital, then engaged and defeated the latter's forces a few miles to the south. Lý Bí escaped but was soon killed by mountain tribesmen, and his kingdom of Vạn Xuân collapsed, although resistance to Chinese rule continued among some of his followers for several years under the leadership of **Lý Phật Tử** and **Triệu Quang Phục**. *See also* CHINESE PERIOD.

LÝ BÔN. *See* LÝ BÍ.

LÝ CAO TÔNG (1173–1210). Seventh ruler (r. 1176–1210) of the **Lý dynasty**. Lý Cao Tông ascended the throne in 1176 at the age of three. During the regency of General **Tô Hiến Thành**, his mother wished to replace him on the throne with his older brother, but General Thành's wife refused to be bribed. Cao Tông's reign was marked by social unrest and frequent rebellion. *See also* LÝ ANH TÔNG; LÝ HUỆ TÔNG.

LÝ CHIÊU HOÀNG. Last ruler (r. 1224–1225) of the **Lý dynasty**. Lý Chiêu Hoàng (proper name *Phật Kim*) was a daughter of Emperor **Lý Huệ Tông**. In 1224, her father, sickly and probably demented, decided to abdicate the throne. Lacking sons, he turned over the throne to his daughter, who was named empress, with Trần Tự Khánh, a member of the influential Trần family, serving as regent. She was then married to the eight-year old Trần Cảnh, a member of the same family. In 1225, Trần Cảnh was declared Emperor **Thái Tông** of a new **Trần dynasty** (1225–1400), and the Lý came to an end. Chiêu Hoàng reigned as Trần Thái Tông's wife for 12 years but did not produce an heir; in 1236, she was divorced in favor of her older sister.

LÝ CÔNG UẨN. *See* LÝ THÁI TỔ.

LÝ DYNASTY (1009–1225). First major dynasty after Vietnamese independence in the 10th century C.E. During the first several decades after the end of the **Chinese period**, a series of strongmen appeared who dominated the political and military scene: **Ngô Quyền, Đinh Bộ Lĩnh**, and **Lê Hoàn**. They all established short-lived "dynasties" that disappeared shortly after their deaths. It was the Lý dynasty that developed the political and social institutions (including dynastic succession) that would provide stability for the Vietnamese Empire, known after 1054 as **Đại Việt**, and place it on a firm footing for the next several hundred years.

The Lý dynasty followed a typical pattern known in Chinese history as the "dynastic cycle": foundation under a strong ruler (**Lý Thái Tổ**) and a period of peace and prosperity under competent emperors, followed by a period of decline. It was replaced by the **Trần dynasty** in the early 13th century. Generally speaking, Lý government was less structured and less centralized than its successors. It was also less **Confucian** because **Buddhism** and **Daoism** remained strong among the elite and Đại Việt had yet to institutionalize the Chinese-style **examination system**, which would ensure a steady supply of scholar-mandarins.

LÝ HUỆ TÔNG (1194–1226). Next-to-last emperor (r. 1210–1224) of the **Lý dynasty**. Lý Huệ Tông ascended the throne on the death of his father **Cao Tông** in 1210. During his reign, he was under the domination of the powerful Trần family, which had helped to restore his father to the throne after a rebellion in 1208. Huệ Tông, then the crown prince, had fled the capital with his father during the revolt and sought refuge with a member of the Trần family in what is now Thái Bình. There he met one of the daughters of his host, and on becoming emperor in 1210, took her as his queen. During the next few years, the Trần family, and particularly **Trần Thủ Độ**, a cousin of the queen, became increasingly dominant at court.

During his reign, Huệ Tông was frequently ill and suffered from periodic bouts of insanity. In 1224, he abdicated in favor of his daughter **Lý Chiêu Hoàng**, who was still a child. He retired to a monastery, but was eventually forced to commit suicide after the establishment of the new **Trần dynasty** in 1225.

LÝ NHÂN TÔNG (1066–1128). Fourth emperor (r. 1072–1128) of the **Lý dynasty**. In 1072, at the age of seven, he ascended the throne on the death of his father **Thánh Tông**. During the period of regency under the mandarin Lý Đạo Thành and his mother Ỷ Lan, two events of major significance to the future of the Vietnamese empire took place. In the capital of Thăng Long (the modern city of **Hanoi**), the first competitive civil service **examinations** for entrance into the bureaucracy were held at the **Temple of Literature** (*Văn Miếu*), established by Thánh Tông. To train candidates of noble extraction for the examinations and provide a refresher course for existing members of the **mandarinate**, an **Imperial Academy** (*Quốc Tử Giám*, literally, Institute for Sons of the State) was established in 1076 on the grounds of the Temple of Literature.

The second major event of Nhân Tông's early years on the throne was renewed war with **China**, which was won through the efforts of General **Lý Thường Kiệt**. Intermittent war also continued with **Champa**, Vietnam's perennial rival to the south. In some respects, Nhân Tông's reign continued the pattern that had been laid down by his immediate predecessors. **Buddhism** remained strong and influential, with monks prominent at court and temples possessing great landholdings like manor lords. The power of the landed aristocracy, based on the system of fiefdoms granted by the state, continued to increase.

LÝ PHẬT TỬ. A cousin of Vietnamese rebel **Lý Bí** who fought against **Chinese** rule and established a short-lived kingdom in the sixth century. His first capital was at Ô Diên, west of **Hanoi**; later it was moved to **Cổ Loa**, the ancient capital in the pre-Chinese period. Lý Phật Tử was a patron of **Buddhism**, thus his sobriquet "Son of the Buddha" (*Phật Tử*). He fought with rival leader **Triệu Quang Phục** as well as with the Chinese. In the early seventh century, his kingdom was attacked and defeated by an army sent by the rising Sui dynasty. Phật Tử surrendered and was sent to exile in the Sui capital at Chang'an.

LÝ THÁI TỔ (974–1028). Founder (r. 1010–1028) of the **Lý dynasty** (1010–1225), the first durable dynasty of independent Vietnam. Lý Thái Tổ (original name Lý Công Uẩn) was born in 974. Little is known about his family background. An orphan, he was reportedly raised in a **Buddhist** temple in what is today Bắc Ninh and became a member of the palace guard at **Hoa Lư** under Emperor **Lê Hoàn** and his successor.

After the death of the unpopular emperor **Lê Long Đĩnh** in 1009, Lý Công Uẩn seized the throne through court intrigue, with the support of a monk named *Vạn Hạnh* and declared the foundation of the Lý dynasty. One of the first actions of the new emperor, who styled himself Lý Thái Tổ, was to move the imperial capital from Hoa Lư to **Đại La**, site of the administrative center of the protectorate of **Annam** under **Chinese** rule and the location of the modern-day capital of **Hanoi.** The new capital was given the name *Thăng Long* (Soaring Dragon), in honor of the mystical dragon that the new emperor had reportedly seen rising above the city into the clouds as he first approached the city. The reasons for the move may have been both economic and political. The old capital had been located south of the **Red River Delta** in a relatively unpopulated region surrounded by mountains, suitable for defensive purposes but not for an administrative center of a growing society. Thăng Long, on the other hand, was centrally located in the heart of the Delta and the most densely populated region of the country.

During his reign of 18 years, Thái Tổ initiated a number of actions that would significantly affect the development of the new state. First, he reorganized the administration, dividing the nation into a new series of provinces, prefectures, and districts, above the historic communes at the **village** level. As a rule, leading administrators were chosen from members of the royal family, who were assigned major responsibility for maintaining security and raising revenue through taxation in the areas under their control. The emperor ardently supported Buddhism, building a number of new temples to train monks, not only for religious purposes but also to provide a literate elite to staff the growing bureaucracy. He built new dikes and irrigation canals to promote an increase in grain production and initiated new taxes to establish a stable revenue base for the state. Thái Tổ's reign provided a firm foundation for the new dynasty and set it on a path that would maintain it in power for more than two centuries, one of the longest in Vietnamese history.

LÝ THÁI TÔNG (Lý Phật Mã) (1000–1054). Second emperor (r. 1028–1054) of the **Lý dynasty.** Lý Phật Mã, crown prince under founding emperor **Lý Thái Tổ**, rose to the throne on the death of his father in 1028 after a bitter succession struggle with three of his brothers in which he was said to have been aided by a powerful mountain spirit. He continued many of the practices of his father, attempting to strengthen the state and lay the foundation for a stable and prosperous society. Determined to build a strong army to guarantee the continuity of the dynasty, he set up a system of national military conscription and created an elite guard called the *Thiên Tử Binh* (Army of the Son of Heaven) to protect the royal palace and the capital city from attacks.

In an effort to reduce the immense power possessed by princes of the blood, Thái Tông attempted to transfer authority at the provincial and prefectural level from members of the royal family to a class of professional officials selected from the landed aristocracy. To guarantee their loyalty, such administrators were granted substantial amounts of state land for exploitation and tax revenue. Although these lands remained theoretically under the ownership of the crown, in practice they were often passed on within the family. Thái Tông also attempted to strengthen the infrastructure of the state, building roads and a postal system to speed up communications. Like his father, he was an ardent **Buddhist** who relied on monks as his confidential advisers at court, yet he apparently also promoted **Confucianism** as a means of training officials.

Like most of his predecessors, Thái Tông was frequently preoccupied with foreign policy problems. The state was almost constantly at war with the state of **Champa** along the southern coast. Lands conquered from the Cham were often turned over as fiefs to high military or civilian officials or to the Buddhist church. On several occasions, Vietnamese armies were sent into the mountains north of the **Red River Delta** to quell rebellions launched by the **Nùng** ethnic group near the Chinese border. Thái Tong died in 1054 at the age of 55 and was succeeded peacefully by his son **Thánh Tông**.

LÝ THÁNH TÔNG (1023–1072). Third emperor (r. 1054–1072) of the **Lý dynasty**. Thánh Tông succeeded to the throne on the death of his father **Thái Tông** in 1054, at the age of 32. Although changing the name of the Empire from *Đại Cồ Việt* to *Đại Việt*, in general the new ruler followed the policies of his predecessors in strengthening the centralized power of the state while staunchly defending its national security from potential internal and foreign threats. **Chinese**

power along the northern border was held at bay, and attacks from **Champa** beyond the southern frontier led the emperor to launch a successful campaign in 1069, which occupied the Cham capital and seized its king. To obtain his release, the latter ceded three provinces along the central coast (comprising the contemporary provinces of Quảng Bình and Quảng Trị) to Vietnam.

Thánh Tông favored the growth of **Confucianism** as a foundation for the state, though the influence of **Buddhism** remained strong. In 1070, he ordered the construction of the **Temple of Literature** (*Văn Miếu*) for the study of Confucian philosophy and the training of officials in the capital city of Thăng Long (**Hanoi**). Thánh Tông died in 1072 and was succeeded by his elder son, the seven-year-old **Nhân Tông**.

LÝ THƯỜNG KIỆT (1030–1105). Mandarin and military commander during the **Lý dynasty**. Born in 1030 to an aristocratic family in the capital of Thăng Long (**Hanoi**), Lý Thường Kiệt served Emperor **Lý Thánh Tông** as a military officer and commanded a successful invasion of **Champa** in 1069 that resulted in major territorial concessions to the Vietnamese and the temporary cessation of the threat from the South.

In the 1070s, Kiệt commanded Vietnamese armed forces in a war with the Song dynasty in **China**. In 1075, anticipating a projected invasion of the **Red River Delta**, he launched a preemptive attack on southern China. The offensive, launched both by land and by sea, was briefly successful, resulting in the destruction of Chinese defensive positions in the frontier region, but China launched a counterattack in late 1076. Kiệt fortified the Cầu River north of **Hanoi** and was able to prevent an enemy occupation of the capital. In later years, he served as a provincial governor and died in 1105.

Lý Thường Kiệt is viewed by Vietnamese historians as one of the major figures in Vietnam's historic struggle to defend itself against Chinese domination. He is also considered to be a military strategist of considerable repute and is identified with the concept of a preemptive strike ("attacking in self-defense") against an enemy to avoid having to fight a war simultaneously in two fronts. Military strategists in contemporary Vietnam, such as General **Võ Nguyên Giáp**, acknowledge their debt to his genius.

– M –

MA YUAN (Mã Viện). Chinese military commander who suppressed the **Trưng Sisters** rebellion in C.E. 39–43 and consolidated Chinese authority over the Vietnamese. When the rebellion broke out, General Ma Yuan, who had recently put down a rebellion in Anhui in central China, was appointed commander of a force of 20,000 soldiers to suppress the revolt in Vietnam and restore Chinese rule. Advancing south along the coast, Ma defeated the Vietnamese army and had the Trưng Sisters put to death, though many stories have them committing suicide instead. He then set out to remove the potential sources of discontent by destroying the local landed nobility and replacing it with a bureaucracy staffed by officials sent from China. The administrative structure was reformed to conform with the model of the Han dynasty in China. Vietnamese territory was divided into three prefectures (**Giao Chỉ, Cửu Chân,** and **Nhật Nam**). Although Ma Yuan's role in Vietnamese history was to defeat a local rebellion and bind the territory even closer to China, he apparently earned the respect of many of the people under his charge. In later generations, many legends grew up around his memory and the prodigious feats with which he was identified, and his spirit was worshipped in some parts of Vietnam. *See also* CHINESE PERIOD.

MẠC CỬU (1655–1736). A Chinese immigrant who established his family in the **Hà Tiên** area of the **Mekong Delta**. Originally from Leizhou in Guangdong province, Mạc Cửu (Mo Jiu in Chinese) was a Ming loyalist who exiled himself from **China** after the establishment of the Qing dynasty. He made his way around Southeast Asia and settled in what was then **Cambodian** territory along the coast of the Gulf of Siam. Hà Tiên with its thriving international trade, however, became a prize piece of territory coveted by both the Siamese and the Vietnamese **Nguyễn Lords**, who were competing for domination over Cambodia. Mạc Cửu threw in his lot with the Vietnamese, and in 1708, traveled to the Nguyễn capital to officially submit to their authority. He was given an official title by the Nguyễn Lord, and Hà Tiên was gradually incorporated into the southern Vietnamese kingdom. After Mạc Cửu's death, the governorship of Hà Tiên went to his son **Mạc Thiên Tứ**. *See also* OVERSEAS CHINESE.

MẠC ĐĂNG DUNG (1483–1541). Founder (r. 1527–1530) of the **Mạc dynasty** in 16th-century Vietnam. Mạc Đăng Dung was the son of a fisherman in present-day **Hải Phòng** and claimed to be descendant of **Mạc Đĩnh Chi**, a scholar-official during the **Trần dynasty**. After becoming a military officer, Mạc Đăng Dung came to the attention of **Lê Uy Mục**, known as the "devil king," and was soon an influential figure at court. In 1516, a major rebellion led by the pretender **Trần Cảo** broke out and led to the seizure of the capital and the murder of the reigning emperor, **Lê Tương Dực**. With the help of Mạc Đăng Dung, the Lê were able to return to power but in a weakened condition. In 1527, Mạc Đăng Dung unsurped the throne and proclaimed himself emperor.

Many leading figures in the court and the bureaucracy remained loyal to the **Lê dynasty**, but Mạc Đăng Dung was able to consolidate his power in the capital of Thăng Long (**Hanoi**) and even obtained legitimation from the Ming Emperor in Beijing. In 1530, he turned the throne over to his son Mạc Đăng Doanh, while maintaining an influential role as "senior emperor" (***Thái Thượng Hoàng***), a practice that had been followed by emperors of the **Trần dynasty**. Members of the Lê family continued to struggle for a restoration of the dynasty, however, and in 1533 with the help of the loyalist mandarin **Nguyễn Kim**, Lê Trang Tông was declared the legitimate ruler, beginning a period of civil war between the Lê and the Mạc. Mạc Đăng Dung died in 1541.

MẠC ĐĨNH CHI (1280–1350). A prominent scholar-official under the **Trần dynasty**. A native of Hải Dương, he was known for his literary abilities. At one point he was sent on a diplomatic tribute mission to the Mongol (Yuan) court. Initially, he was mocked for his squat and rather unprepossessing appearance, but he quickly earned the Mongol emperor's respect for his skills in classical Chinese. He was henceforth known to the Vietnamese by the title *Lưỡng quốc Trang nguyên*, which translates as something like "laureate in two countries." Mạc Đĩnh Chi was reportedly the ancestor of **Mạc Đăng Dung**, who would provoke an extended civil war under the **Lê dynasty** in the 16th century.

MẠC DYNASTY (1527–1592). Royal dynasty established by **Mạc Đăng Dung** in 1527. A military officer and influential figure under the **Lê dynasty** in the early 16th century, he seized power during a time of political instability and declared himself founding emperor of a new Mạc dynasty. The Mạc were unable to fully consolidate their power, however, as they were not accepted by many influential elements in Vietnam, and the Lê attempted to return to power. By the early 1540s, with the help of the mandarin **Nguyễn Kim**, the Lê controlled considerable territory in central Vietnam and established their court in present-day Thanh Hoá. For the next several decades, Vietnam was divided in two. In 1592, forces loyal to the Lê seized the capital of Thăng Long (**Hanoi**) and captured the emperor, Mạc Mậu Hợp. Remnants of the Mạc family managed to retain power at **Cao Bằng** near the Chinese border until 1667.

The Mạc have traditionally been stigmatized by imperial scholars for having "usurped" the Lê throne, even temporarily. Recent scholarship, however, has recast them in a much more positive light, seeing their rise to power as a reflection of the general social, economic, and political crisis that plagued Vietnam in the early 16th century and examining their policies as attempts to redress these problems. The Mạc period was also tremendously significant in that it set the stage for the long-term division of the country between the **Trịnh Lords** and the **Nguyễn Lords**.

MẠC THIÊN TỨ (also known as *Mạc Thiên Tịch*) (1706–1780). The son of the Chinese immigrant **Mạc Cửu**, Mạc Thiên Tứ held the position of governor of **Hà Tiên** after his father's death. He remained loyal to the **Nguyễn Lords** throughout his lifetime and played a key role in the expansion of their authority over **Cambodian** territory. He also supported Nguyễn Ánh (the future Emperor **Gia Long**) in his war with the **Tây Sơn**. In addition to his efforts to develop Hà Tiên economically, Mạc Thiên Tứ is known for his poetry, particularly a set of poems about the landscapes of the region entitled *Hà Tiên Thập vịnh Tập* [*A collection of ten poems about Hà Tiên*].

MACAO CONFERENCE. First national congress of the **Indochinese Communist Party** (**ICP**), held in the Portuguese colony of Macao in March 1935. Although the ICP had been founded five years earlier, **French** security forces had suppressed the organization and killed or imprisoned most of its leaders during the abortive **Nghệ Tĩnh Revolt**

in 1930–1931. In 1934, the **Comintern** directed surviving ICP members to establish an External Direction Bureau (*Ủy Ban Hải Ngoại*) in southern **China** to direct Party affairs until the holding of a national congress. The meeting took place under the direction of **Hà Huy Tập** in March 1935, but its decision to maintain a doctrinaire position based on class conflict was immediately controverted by the Seventh Congress of the Comintern, held in Moscow that summer. In 1936, ICP member **Lê Hồng Phong** returned from the **Union of Soviet Socialist Republics** and directed the Party to adopt the new **Popular Front** strategy approved in Moscow. *See also* INDOCHINESE DEMOCRATIC FRONT.

MAI HẮC ĐẾ. *See* MAI THÚC LOAN.

MAI THÚC LOAN. Rebel leader who led a revolt against **Chinese** rule in the early eighth century. A native of the central coast near the present-day city of Hà Tĩnh, Mai Thúc Loan led a rebellion of alienated peasants, mountain tribesmen, and vagabonds against oppressive Chinese occupation in C.E. 722. The revolt was briefly successful, and after seizing most of the protectorate of **Annam**, Thúc Loan declared himself emperor. He was known as "Black Emperor Mai" (Mai Hắc Đế), probably because he came from a darker-skinned ethnic group. The Tang dynasty struck back quickly and a Chinese army put down the rebellion. Mai Thúc Loan was killed, and thousands of his followers were executed. Unrest against Chinese rule continued, however, for several years. *See also* CHINESE PERIOD.

MAN NƯƠNG. The key figure in a myth about the early period of Vietnamese **Buddhism.** An orphan staying at a Buddhist temple, she becomes pregnant when a foreign monk (from India or Central Asia) steps over her sleeping body. When a baby daughter is born, the monk takes the infant and abandons her at the root of a banyan tree. Years later, when Man Nương is an old woman, the tree blows over in a storm and begins to float away. Man Nương is the only person strong enough to pull it out of the water. She has a wood-cutter sculpt four Buddha statues out of the tree, which she names "Cloud," "Rain," "Thunder," and "Lightning." The four images were placed in a temple called *Chùa Dâu*, "Mulberry Pagoda," a very old and popular pilgrimage site in the northern province of Bắc Ninh. Man Nương's statue can still be seen in the temple; she is sometimes referred to as *Phật Mẫu*, "Buddha Mother."

MANDARINATE. Successive Vietnamese dynasties followed the **Chinese** model of government based on a hierarchy of civil and military mandarins who had achieved their rank by going through the **examination system**. These scholar-officials had to be literate in classical Chinese and they gradually came to form the backbone of the imperial government. The process was long, however, taking several centuries after the Vietnamese obtained their independence from Chinese rule. Under the short-lived "dynasties" of the 10th century and during at least the early part of the **Lý dynasty**, examinations were not held on a regular basis, and when they did take place, they included **Buddhist** and **Daoist** topics, as well as knowledge from the **Confucian** classics. Early emperors also relied on monks and priests as advisors along with Confucian-trained literati.

Under the **Trần dynasty**, the mandarinate grew larger and more regularized, but through the early 14th century, it still faced competition from powerful members of the royal family who held key positions in government. During the latter part of the century, when the royal family was declining in power and quality, the literati emerged as a more important force in government. After the **Ming occupation**, which gave large numbers of Vietnamese a Confucian education, the **Lê dynasty** both expanded the bureaucracy and adopted Confucianism as the official ideology. A bureaucratic hierarchy of mandarins was now firmly in place from the court down to the district (*huyện*) level; **village** leaders were normally not considered mandarins.

When the **French** colonized Vietnam, they abolished the traditional mandarinate in **Cochin China** but preserved it along with the **monarchy** in **Tonkin** and **Annam**. The mandarins continued to exercise their authority with varying degrees of French supervision and control. Graft and other abuses were widespread, but the French had little choice but to tolerate such practices if they were going to maintain the **protectorate** system, which enabled them to govern their colony through traditional structures with a relatively small staff of European officials. The mandarins, with their traditional dress and increasingly outmoded ideas and practices, became a target of ridicule for many Vietnamese nationalists; they were bitterly criticized by prominent figures, such as **Phan Chu Trinh** and **Nguyễn Văn Vĩnh**, who thought that their country would be better off if governed directly by the French without the monarchy and mandarinate. Mandarins and their families were also portrayed negatively in many novels of the colonial period, notably those by the group of authors known as the *Tự lực Văn đoàn*.

The **August Revolution** of 1945 brought an end to the mandarinate, and the term was no longer used for the officials of the various postcolonial Vietnamese regimes. However, some traces of its legacy can be seen in the bureaucracy and red tape, which have characterized all of these governments. *See also* SCHOLAR-GENTRY.

MARCH TO THE SOUTH. *See NAM TIẾN.*

MARTIN, GRAHAM A. (1912–1990). United States Ambassador to the **Republic of Vietnam** at the time of the fall of **Saigon** in April 1975. A career diplomat, he was appointed by President Richard Nixon to replace Ambassador **Ellsworth Bunker** in Saigon in 1973. During the final stages of the Vietnam War, Martin refused to order an early evacuation of U.S. citizens from South Vietnam in the belief that it might create panic in Saigon. He was among the last to leave the U.S. Embassy on 30 April 1975, and retired from the Department of State in 1977.

MEKONG RIVER (*Sông Cửu Long* **or "River of Nine Dragons").** 11th longest river in the world and the longest in Southeast Asia. Originating in the mountains of Tibet, the Mekong travels roughly 4,300 kilometers (2,700 miles) to its final exit into the **South China Sea** south of Hồ Chí Minh City. After entering Vietnam, it splits into several additional branches before entering the ocean, two of the best-known being the Tiền Giang and Hậu Giang.

The Mekong River is navigable from Vietnam up to a series of rapids at the **Lao–Cambodian** border. Its main importance to Vietnam, however, lies in the rich sediment that the river leaves as it empties into the sea. The entire **Mekong River Delta** has been built up over the centuries by sedimentary soil brought down from the highlands of south **China**. Originally, the Mekong figured prominently in **French** plans to colonize **Indochina** because it was believed to offer a convenient route into China. Exploration proved this assumption wrong, however, the rapids in Laos being a notable obstacle to navigation. French ambitions then focused on the **Red River**.

MEKONG RIVER DELTA. The delta region of the mighty **Mekong River** in southern Vietnam. Built up by alluvial soils brought by the river from its source in southern **China**, the Mekong Delta consists of a total of approximately 67,000 square kilometers (26,000 square miles), from the **Cà Mau Peninsula** in the South to a point south of present-day Hồ Chí Minh City (**Saigon**). Although the Delta is composed of rich sedimentary soil, until modern times it did not support a high density of population. Before 1700, when the area was controlled by **Cambodia**, human settlement was relatively sparse. Much of the land was covered with reeds, and the coastal areas were affected by tides that led to flooding by highly saline seawater. Beginning in the 17th century, the delta was colonized by the Vietnamese as part of their historic long-term process of "Southward Advance" (*Nam tiến*). Vietnamese settlers began arriving in the area, and canals were dug to improve irrigation. Later, the **French** drained much of the delta and built a series of canals and dikes, making it suitable for cultivation.

During the early 20th century, the area increased rapidly in population, as many peasants migrated to the area to work as tenant farmers on large rice fields owned by absentee landlords. An estimated 300,000 Khmer (known as **Khmer Krom**) live in the area, descendants of the original inhabitants who had lived there before arrival of the Vietnamese. Today, the Mekong River Delta is the great rice basket of Vietnam. With more than 60 percent of the total land area under cultivation, the delta produces about 30 to 40 percent of total grain production. *See also ĐỒN ĐIỀN.*

MERLIN, MARTIAL (1860–1935). Governor-general of French **Indochina** from 1923 to 1925. A former governor in French West Africa, he was relatively conservative in his views on colonial rule and initiated a number of changes in the **educational** system, strengthening elementary instruction at the expense of higher education and specifying that instruction at the basic level in the Franco–

Vietnamese system would be in Vietnamese rather than in French. The end result was to render it more difficult for young Vietnamese to advance to higher education in France. Merlin was replaced by **Alexander Varenne** in the summer of 1925.

MESSMER, PIERRE (1916–   ). French official assigned by Charles de Gaulle's government in Paris to supervise the restoration of French authority in **Indochina** after World War II. Parachuted into Vietnam in late August 1945 as commissioner of France for **Tonkin**, he was taken to **Hanoi**, but his appointment was not accepted by the new government of **Hồ Chí Minh**, and he returned to France. During the **Franco-Việt Minh conflict**, he served briefly as an adviser to High Commissioner **Émile Bollaert** in Indochina. From 1972 to 1974, he was prime minister of France. *See also* AUGUST REVOLUTION.

MÉTROPOLE HOTEL. Luxurious colonial-style hotel built by the **French** in **Hanoi** in 1911. Located directly across the street from the palace of the imperial delegate, it was the most prestigious hotel in Hanoi during the colonial period and was briefly occupied by **United States** military officials at the end of World War II. After the end of the Vietnam War, it was allowed to decay but has recently been renovated under the direction of the French Accor Hotel Management Company, and it has now been restored to its former imperial splendor. *See also* ARCHITECTURE; TOURISM.

MIDAUTUMN FESTIVAL (*Tết Trung Thu*). *See* FESTIVALS.

MIGRATION. Migration has been a long-term characteristic of Vietnamese history. During the centuries before and during Chinese rule, there seems to have been considerable movement of people from the midlands around the edge of the **Red River Delta** to the lowland heart of the delta. After independence, as the Vietnamese kingdom gradually expanded its territory southward, there was further migration to the newly conquered or annexed territories. This was particularly the case for the **Cham** and **Cambodian** territories that were settled and colonized by Vietnamese and ethnic Chinese migrants from the 17th century onward. This territory was gradually incorporated into the southern kingdom known as *Đàng Trong*, ruled by the **Nguyễn Lords.**

Until the colonial period, relatively few ethnic Vietnamese migrated from the lowlands to the upland areas, which were feared as lands of *rừng thiêng nước độc*, "spiritually potent woods and poisonous water." This began to change under French rule, as the colonial regime promoted migration from the more densely populated lowland provinces to the relatively sparsely inhabited upland regions. After independence, this migration accelerated in both the **Democratic Republic of Vietnam** and the **Republic of Vietnam**. Since reunification in 1976, the government has consistently implemented resettlement policies, particularly in the **Central Highlands**, and there has been considerable "spontaneous migration" (i.e., not under government auspices) as well.

Over the centuries, migration has had both positive and negative consequences. To some extent, it has served to relieve demographic pressures in overpopulated provinces. It has also enabled successive Vietnamese governments to extend and consolidate their control over frontier or peripheral areas. For the original inhabitants, however, influxes of migrants belonging to other ethnic groups are naturally a source of tension and conflict. This has been particularly true in the Central Highlands, where the arrival of huge numbers of ethnic Vietnamese (**Kinh**) and migrants belonging to **highland minority** groups in the northern region of the country has generated serious problems. *See also NAM TIẾN.*

MILITARY ASSISTANCE ADVISORY GROUP (MAAG). Military command established at the order of President Harry S. Truman in the **State of Vietnam** in September 1950. The goal of MAAG was to provide assistance in the training of Vietnamese armed forces in the **Vietnamese National Army**, established under **French** sponsorship a few months earlier. MAAG continued to operate after the agreement adopted at the **Geneva Conference** in 1954 and provided training for the **Army of the Republic of Vietnam**. It was replaced by the **Military Assistance Command, Vietnam**, in January 1962.

MILITARY ASSISTANCE COMMAND, VIETNAM (MACV). Military command established at the order of **United States** President John F. Kennedy in **Saigon** in January 1962. MACV replaced the **Military Assistance Advisory Group** (MAAG), which was viewed as too limited in scope to handle the rising American military presence in South Vietnam. The first commander of MACV was General **Paul Harkins**. He was succeeded in 1964 by General **William C. Westmoreland**. Under his command, MACV orchestrated the massive U.S. effort to prevent a Communist victory in the **Republic of Vietnam**.

MINERAL RESOURCES. Vietnam has a relative abundance of mineral resources, but extraction has been hindered by lack of capital and inaccessibility. During the colonial era, the French exploited plentiful supplies of **coal** along the coast of northern Vietnam, extracting small amounts of gold, silver, copper, lead, and zinc. The coal is a high-grade anthracite, and estimates measure in the billions of tons. Substantial tin reserves have been located along the Chinese border; deposits of graphite, antimony, and zinc are also to be found in various parts of the **Việt Bắc** region. There are also small deposits of apatite, bauxite, asbestos, molybdenum, manganese, phosphorite, and the high-grade kaolin clay used to manufacture porcelain. There are few ferrous minerals, except for a small amount of iron and chromium, reserves of which can be found in Thanh Hoá province south of the **Red River Delta.**

Fewer mineral deposits are located in the southern provinces, although deposits of gold, lead, and copper have been found in the central mountains, while the sandy deposits along the extensive coast are rich in silica. Molybdenum mines have been opened in Bình Thuận province. The biggest problem for the Vietnamese has been how to exploit existing reserves. In recent years, the government has opened institutes of geology and mineralogy in **Hanoi** and, with rising **foreign investment**, the prospects for the future are relatively bright. Coal production in particular has increased substantially over the past decade. *See also* ECONOMY; INDUSTRY.

MING OCCUPATION. The Ming dynasty's occupation of Vietnam in the early 15th century, lasting roughly two decades. The initial invasions of 1406–1407 were justified by the Chinese on the grounds of alleged offenses committed by **Hồ Quý Ly**, whose family had recently usurped power from the **Trần dynasty**. **China**'s actions must also, however, be understood in a broader context of Ming expansionism and cultural imperialism. The Chinese forces made quick work of the Hồ defenses and were able to suppress resistance movements led by members of the deposed Trần imperial family as well. They recruited a number of Vietnamese collaborators and proceeded with the establishment of a colonial regime—even as they continued their pacification.

Ming policy in occupied Vietnam reflected the court's preoccupation with cultural and ideological indoctrination, and they set up an extensive network of schools that promoted the neo-Confucian beliefs that constituted orthodoxy for the Chinese elite. This heavy dose of **Confucianism** influenced Vietnam's subsequent evolution, as Confucian doctrines became firmly implanted as the primary state ideology while **Buddhism** and **Daoism** generally retreated to the domain of personal spirituality. Another important cultural consequence of the occupation was the destruction and/or loss of most existing Vietnamese texts, so that few pre-1400 works remained for study by later scholars.

In 1418, an insurgency against Chinese rule began under the leadership of **Lê Lợi**. This guerrilla movement, often referred to as the *Lam Sơn Uprising* after the name of Lê Lợi's home area in Thanh Hoá, mounted an extended campaign of resistance, which ended in a Vietnamese victory by 1427. Following the defeat and departure of the Ming forces, Lê Lợi took the title Lê Thái Tổ and founded a new **Lê dynasty**.

MINH HƯƠNG. Vietnamese term for residents of Chinese descent living in Vietnam. It originally meant "Ming incense," but the second character was subsequently changed to a homonym meaning "village." Many ethnic Chinese living in traditional Vietnam were descendants of Ming loyalists who had fled **China** at the time of the Manchu conquest. Many moved into separate **villages** in relatively unpopulated areas of the southern region but later intermarried with native Vietnamese. Under the Vietnamese Empire, they were viewed as distinct from both ethnic Vietnamese (**Kinh**) and the so-called **overseas Chinese**, and gradually assimilated into the surrounding environment, although some remained in commerce and retained their Chinese customs. Often they were used by the Vietnamese court as envoys in dealings with **China**.

MINH MẠNG (1791–1840). Second emperor (r. 1820–1840) of the **Nguyễn dynasty**. Minh Mạng, second son of Emperor **Gia Long**, ascended to the throne on the latter's death in 1820. Gia Long's first son, **Prince Cảnh**, had died in 1801. Gia Long rejected Cảnh's son as his successor and chose the future Minh Mạng, the oldest son of a concubine, reportedly because of his strong character and distrust of the West. Minh Mạng's performance as ruler confirmed his father's estimate. Suspicious of the ultimate motives of Western missionaries, he reduced their presence in Vietnam and prohibited the practice of **Christianity** in the empire. He was more receptive to Western commerce, so long as it remained under strict governmental supervision.

In his internal policies, Minh Mạng was a vigorous administrator, setting up a number of new administrative offices on the Chinese model and reorganizing the empire into 31 provinces (*tỉnh*) under governors (*tuần phủ*) or governors-general (*tổng đốc*) directly subordinated to the central government. He attempted to better the economy by improving the irrigation and road network, putting new land under cultivation, and attempting to limit large landed holdings. In this, he had only moderate success and rural unrest, provoked by poor economic conditions, was a regular feature of his reign. In foreign affairs, Minh Mạng extended Vietnamese control over much of **Cambodia**, causing strained relations with Siam.

Minh Mạng died in 1840 and was succeeded by his son **Thiệu Trị**.

MODERNIZATION SOCIETY. *See* DUY TÂN HỘI.

MODUS VIVENDI. Temporary agreement reached between **Hồ Chí Minh**, president of the **Democratic Republic of Vietnam** (DRV), and the **French** government represented by Marius Moutet in September 1946. The agreement was essentially a face-saving measure after the failure of the **Fontainebleau Conference** because of French determination to hold onto as much power as possible and the equally strong Vietnamese determination to achieve as much independence as possible. It allowed Hồ to return home with something concrete in hand but did nothing to prevent the **Franco–Vietminh War**, which broke out in December.

MONARCHY. The Vietnamese monarchy underwent several important transformations over the course of its existence. The appearance of the monarchy as an institution was almost certainly related to **Chinese** political and cultural influence. Although Vietnamese sources tell of a dynasty of **Hùng Kings** ruling the kingdom of **Văn Lang** during the **Bronze Age**, it is more likely that these were tribal chiefs who were transformed into "kings" by later writers. During the "**Chinese period**," rebels against foreign rule began to use titles like *vương* (Ch. *wang*) and *đế* (Ch. *di*), suggesting that their conceptions of power and authority were coming to be at least partially articulated in Chinese terms.

After the battle of **Bạch Đằng** in 939, the 10th century saw a series of strongmen whose families rose and fell in succession: **Ngô Quyền**, **Đinh Bộ Lĩnh**, and **Lê Hoàn**. Although these men apparently assumed royal titles and were described by later scholars as founders of short-lived "dynasties," they were essentially unschooled military men who probably had little knowledge of Chinese imperial practices. By the 11th century, the **Lý dynasty** was able to establish a long-term presence with relatively stable patterns of succession, and a court culture began to develop that reflected Chinese cultural and intellectual differences. **Buddhism** and **Daoism** were almost certainly stronger than **Confucianism**, however, and the early Lý emperors seem to have relied on ties to the spirit world to strengthen their legitimacy. During this period, Vietnamese rulers began the habit of referring to themselves as "emperor" *vis-à-vis* their own people but as "king" when corresponding with their Chinese overlords, for whom there could be only one emperor.

Under the Lý and **Trần dynasties**, the monarchy had a strong Buddhist flavor, as the Vietnamese elite gave substantial patronage and rulers wrote Zen devotional and philosophical tracts rather than commentaries on classical Confucian texts. This changed with the **Ming occupation**, which shifted the ideological balance in favor of Confucianism, and the **Lê** and **Nguyễn** monarchies articulated their worldview largely in Confucian terms. After Vietnam's **colonization** by **France**, the monarchy (together with the **mandarinate**) was maintained in the **protectorates** of **Annam** and **Tonkin**, but the French stripped it of virtually all of its authority. Although the colonial regime hoped to maintain the monarchy's "moral authority" to strengthen their own position, they succeeded mainly in discrediting the last Nguyễn rulers, and when the colonial system fell, the monarchy fell with it.

MONGOL INVASIONS. A series of massive attacks launched against Vietnam and **Champa** by the Mongol (Yuan) Empire in **China** during the last half of the 13th century. The first took place in 1258, while the last two occurred during the 1280s. All were defeated because of the brilliant strategy adopted by Vietnamese military leaders and the national resistance by the Vietnamese people. The final defeat came with a naval battle at **Bạch Đằng**, which used the same strategy of stakes hidden in the water that had been deployed against the Chinese in the 10th Century. The Mongol Emperor, Kublai Khan, was preparing another invasion of Vietnam when he died in 1294. His successor accepted the Vietnamese offer of a tributary relationship, and peace was restored between the two countries until the fall of the Yuan in 1368. The victory over the Mongols strengthened the power of the ruling **Trần dynasty**, particularly the authority of several key princes within the government. *See also* TRẦN HƯNG ĐẠO; TRẦN NHÂN TÔNG.

MONTAGNARDS. Generic French term for the **highland minorities** living in French **Indochina**. During the postcolonial period, it was used in English to refer specifically to the ethnic minorities of the **Central Highlands**.

MORDANT, EUGÈNE (1885–1959). Commander of **French** troops in **Indochina** during World War II. General Mordant abandoned the Vichy cause and embraced the Free French movement in 1943. During the next months, he secretly helped to organize a Free French movement among French residents in Indochina. As a reward, Charles de Gaulle appointed him French representative in Indochina. Eventually, however, the **Japanese occupation** authorities became aware of his activities, and after the coup d'etat of 9 March 1945, which abolished French administration in Indochina, Mordant was placed in jail. He was released by Chinese occupation troops in late 1945 and returned to France.

MOUNT ĐQ CULTURE. *See* NÚI ĐQ CULTURE.

MULTI-PARTY SYSTEM (*Chế độ đa đảng*). Throughout Vietnam's modern political history, its various regimes have consistently been dominated by a single party or political grouping. The **Democratic Republic of Vietnam** (DRV), established in 1945 under the leadership of **Hồ Chí Minh**, began with the participation of several different political parties but from its inception was dominated by the **Indochinese Communist Party (ICP)**, operating through the **Việt Minh** Front. The **Chinese** occupation of northern Vietnam following the end of the **Japanese occupation** in World War II enabled non-Communist groups, such as the Vietnamese Nationalist Party (**Việt Nam Quốc Dân Đảng** or VNQDĐ) and the **Vietnamese Revolutionary League**, to get their feet in the door of the government, but this door was effectively slammed shut with the outbreak of the **Franco–Việt Minh War** in late 1946. From then onward, the ICP (which dissolved itself and later reemerged as the Vietnamese Workers' Party) had a virtual monopoly on power in the DRV; other groups, such as the **Vietnamese Democratic Party** and **Vietnamese Socialist Party**, survived as little more than windowdressing.

Political developments in the **Republic of Vietnam** between 1954 and 1975 were not fundamentally different. The **Saigon** government was controlled by a series of strongmen and military juntas, the most prominent leaders being **Ngô Đình Diệm, Nguyễn Cao Kỳ**, and **Nguyễn Văn Thiệu**. Although pre-1954 movements, such as the VNQDĐ and **Đại Việt Party**, existed, they played a relatively minor role, and the occasional elections held in South Vietnam did not produce a genuine multiparty system.

The **Vietnamese Communist Party**'s grip on power has been firm since reunification and the establishment of the **Socialist Republic of Vietnam** in 1976, and the entire political system, is predicated on the assumption that the Party is the sole legitimate representative of the people's interests. With the advent of reforms (known as *đổi mới*) since the mid-1980s, and particularly since the fall of socialist regimes in Europe, some Vietnamese have dared to talk openly of the idea of a multiparty system in their country. Such talk is consistently and firmly quashed by the **Hanoi** government, however, and those who articulate this idea are treated as **dissidents** or worse. The Party, like its counterparts in **China** and **Laos**, is determined to maintain its monopoly on political power for the foreseeable future, and even the most general discussion of a multiparty system is construed as an attack on that monopoly. *See also* COMMUNISM; PEACEFUL EVOLUTION; PLURALISM.

MUNICIPAL THEATER (*Nhà Hát Lớn*). Ornate opera house built in the **French** colonial style in the early 20th century in **Hanoi**. Because of its size and central location, the Municipal Theater played a central role in many of the events of the **August Revolution** of 1945. It was there, on 19 August, that spokesmen for the **Việt Minh** Front called on the populace to rise up against **Japanese occupation** troops and declare their independence. It was there, too, that **Hồ Chí Minh** announced to assembled crowds the signing of the preliminary **Hồ-Sainteny Agreement** of 6 March 1946. And it was there that the first **National Assembly** of the **Democratic Republic of Vietnam** (DRV) convened after its election in January 1946. *See also* ARCHITECTURE.

MƯỜNG. A **highland minority** group in Vietnam. Numbering approximately 700,000 in population, the Mường live primarily in the hilly provinces south of **Hanoi** at the bottom of the **Red River Delta**, although smaller numbers inhabit the neighboring provinces of Sơn La, Vĩnh Phúc, Phú Thọ, and Thanh Hoá. In terms of background and language, the Mường are closely related to the ethnic Vietnamese (**kinh**), and some historians speculate that the original separation of the two peoples took place in the first millennium C.E. Like the neighboring **Thái** peoples, the Mường lived until recently under a feudal sociopolitical structure, with a single noble family possessing jurisdiction over several villages (the term *Mường* is, in fact, a Thái word for several villages under a single ruler).

MUS, PAUL (1902–1969). Prominent French scholar on the history and culture of Vietnam who briefly served as an intermediary between the **French** government and the **Democratic Republic of**

Vietnam (DRV) led by **Hồ Chí Minh**. In April 1947, while Mus was serving as the personal adviser to French High Commissioner for Indochina **Émile Bollaert**, the latter ordered him to undertake a mission to **Việt Minh** headquarters in the **Việt Bắc** to negotiate with Hồ over a possible cessation of hostilities. Although Mus was personally somewhat sympathetic to Vietnamese aspirations for national independence, the peace terms that he carried with him amounted to little less than surrender to the French. In a much-quoted response, **Hồ Chí Minh** remarked to Mus, "In the **French Union**, there is no place for cowards. If I accepted these terms, I should be one." Mus returned to **Saigon** empty-handed.

In later years, Paul Mus gained respect as one of the most knowledgeable Western scholars on the history and culture of modern Vietnam. His *Viêt-Nam: Sociologie d'une guerre* (*Vietnam: Sociology of a War*) has become a classic study of the dynamics of the Vietnamese revolution. *See also* FRANCO–VIỆT MINH WAR.

MUSIC. Traditional music in Vietnam reflects a variety of influences from within the region. Chinese influence is reflected in the adoption of the five-tone scale and the use of instruments such as the three-stringed guitar (*tam huyền*, Ch. *sanxian*) or the two-stringed violin (*nhị*; in Chinese, *erhu*). From the neighboring **Cham** came Indian-style dancing and percussion, such as the use of the rice drum. As in **China**, music and verse were often closely tied together, as in *chèo* and *tuồng* **theater** and the uniquely Vietnamese *ca dao* (a form of lyrical folk song performed without any instrumental accompaniment).

Western music began to elbow aside the traditional forms during the colonial era and reached a peak in South Vietnam after the **Geneva Conference**, when rock music from the **United States** attained a high degree of popularity among the young, hence the name *nhạc trẻ* (youth music). As in the West, locally composed songs often contained a political edge, reflecting the malaise of a generation maturing in a society ripped asunder by war. Performers such as **Trịnh Công Sơn** became role models in Vietnam, just like their counterparts in Europe and North America.

In the **Democratic Republic of Vietnam**, Communist leaders called for the emergence of a new musical tradition that would supplement the message of patriotism and self-sacrifice promoted by the regime. The traditional *ca dao* form was given a new purpose with the addition of lyrics extolling the virtues of socialism and national reunification. After the end of the Vietnam War, however, Western music began to spread to the North through records and tapes. Since the launching of *đổi mới* in 1986, it has achieved great popularity among young people throughout the country. There has also been a resurgence of pre-1975 popular music in the former South Vietnam.

On the surface, musical expression in contemporary Vietnam lacks the political connotations of rebellion that it has often possessed in the West. Still, conservative Party leaders are concerned—probably with some justification—that the influence of Western music encourages attitudes of laziness, hedonism, and a shirking of obligations that are dangerous fare to a new generation of Vietnamese. They are equally ambivalent about locally produced rock music and occasionally criticize the quality of the music and the lifestyles of those who perform it.

MỸ SƠN. Cham archeological site in central Vietnam. Located in a mountain valley about 60 kilometers (35 miles) southwest of the city of **Đà Nẵng**, Mỹ Sơn was a sacred site of the **Cham** people. To Mỹ Sơn were brought the trophies of Cham wars for dedication to the Hindu god Shiva. The site, which measures about 1,000 meters (3,250 feet) wide and 2,000 meters (6,500 feet) long, consists of about 70 buildings in various stages of decay. Construction was in red brick, with ornate doorways in carved stone. The earliest structures date from the fourth century C.E. and the latest from the 12th century. The site was severely damaged in 1969 as the result of **United States** bombing raids but is now gradually being restored with the aid of foreign funding and expertise. *See also* ARCHITEC-TURE; INDIANIZATION; INDRAPURA.

– N –

NAM BỘ (also known as *Nam Kỳ*). Term used by the Vietnamese to refer to the southernmost provinces around **Saigon** and in the **Mekong Delta**. During the period of **French** rule, this region constituted the colony of **Cochin China**. The other main regions of Vietnam are **Trung Bộ** (central) and **Bắc Bộ** (northern).

NAM KỲ UPRISING (*Nam Kỳ Khởi Nghĩa*). Abortive revolt launched by the **Cochin China** branch of the **Indochinese Communist Party** (ICP) in 1940. Taking advantage of political unrest caused by troop call-ups, peasant discontent in the **Mekong Delta** provinces, and the growing international crisis in the Pacific, the ICP's Regional Committee for Cochin China (*Ủy Ban Nam Bộ*) planned an insurrection in the Mekong region in the fall of 1940. The Party Central Committee, holding its Seventh Plenum in **Tonkin**, advised a postponement, but emissaries sent to the South were captured by the **French**, and the revolt broke out on schedule in late November. Although the rebels were briefly successful in a few areas, the French counterattack was successful, and the revolt was quickly suppressed. In the process, the local ICP apparatus was virtually destroyed.

*NAM PHONG (**Southern Wind**).* Literary journal published by the journalist and scholar **Phạm Quỳnh** in the 20th century. The journal, established in **Tonkin** in 1917, was sponsored by the **French** colonial regime to channel Vietnamese literary nationalism into the relatively innocuous arena of cultural reform. The journal published articles in three languages (French, Vietnamese, and Chinese) on various literary subjects, but it was best known for its popularization of *quốc ngữ* (the Roman transliteration of Vietnamese) as the dominant form of literary expression in modern Vietnam. It published more than 200 issues and finally closed its doors in December 1934. *See also* JOURNALISM; LITERATURE; NGUYỄN TRỌNG THUẬT.

NAM TIẾN ("**March to the South**" or "**Southward Advance**"). Vietnam's historic expansion southward from the **Red River Delta** to the Gulf of Thailand. The process began after Vietnamese independence in the 10th century C.E. For the next several centuries, the Vietnamese Empire and its neighbors to the South, the **Cham**, clashed periodically in a struggle for control over territories along the central coast. Vietnam obtained control over several parcels of Cham territory, though their attempts at pacification and integration of these lands were not always successful over the short term.

After the absorption of the Cham territories, Vietnam continued its expansion southward into areas of the **Mekong River Delta** controlled by the **Cambodian** kingdom, which was both weaker and smaller than the former Angkor Empire. After achieving the military conquest of a particular area, the Vietnamese established colonial settlements (*đồn điền*) composed of soldiers or peasants resettled from the North and usually under military command. Once the security of the area had been achieved, the settlements would be turned over to civilian leadership. Settlement of the Delta area was a gradual process lasting from the 17th through the 19th centuries.

The *Nam tiến* has traditionally been viewed as a linear process and is frequently mapped out with a series of lines showing the successive dates at which Vietnam's southern borders reached particular geographical points. It is important to understand, however, that these stages of conquest did not always mean complete pacification or integration into a Vietnamese state. Moreover, some scholars have challenged the very existence of the *Nam tiến* as a single and linear historical phenomenon, arguing that it should be understood as a series of different developments (both military conquest and peaceful settlement), rather than the steady expansion of a single nation. Historians under **Hanoi** governments, too, have been reluctant to use the term as it is a reminder of the fact that the Vietnamese people were not always the victims of foreign aggression but engaged in expansionism and **assimilation** themselves at their neighbors' expense. Conversely, Southern-based scholars have generally been quite proud of the *Nam tiến* as an important part of their own region's history.

NAM VIỆT (Nanyue). Early kingdom created in the late third century B.C.E. by the **Chinese** adventurer **Triệu Đà**. Triệu Đà (in Chinese, Zhao Tuo) was a military commander charged by the Qin Empire to occupy newly conquered areas in southern China. When the Emperor Qinshi Huangdi died in 206 B.C.E., his empire disintegrated, and Triệu Đà declared himself ruler of the new state of Nanyue ("Southern Viet," Viet. Nam Việt), with his capital at Canton (Guangzhou). For several years, Triệu Đà received tribute from the state of **Âu Lạc**, located to the south in the **Red River Delta**, while he attempted to secure his independence from the newly created Han dynasty in northern China. Eventually, however, his relations with the Han court improved, and he attacked and defeated Âu Lạc and incorporated its territory into Nanyue, thus expanding his kingdom well across the present-day Sino–Vietnamese border.

In 111 B.C.E., however, Nanyue was conquered by the Han, and its entire territory incorporated into the Chinese Empire. After independence in the 10th century, the term *Nam Việt* occasionally reappeared in the titles of various rulers. In the early 19th century, Emperor **Gia Long** of the newly established **Nguyễn dynasty** briefly considered reviving the term and requested the Chinese to approve the change of his country's name. The idea was vetoed by the Manchu emperor, however, apparently because it evoked a kingdom that had included territory in what was now China. The Qing ruler inverted the terms and renamed the Vietnamese kingdom as "**Việt Nam**," but the Nguyễn rulers preferred to use their own creation of "**Đại Nam**."

NANYUE. *See* NAM VIỆT.

NATIONAL ACADEMY (*Quốc Học***).** Prestigious secondary school set up in 1896 in the imperial capital of **Huế** to train future bureaucrats. The school was seen as a replacement for the **Imperial Academy** (*Quốc Tử Giám*), which for centuries had instructed students in the **Confucian** classics. The school was run by **French** administrators, and the curriculum focused on Western learning. A number of future political leaders attended the institute, including **Hồ Chí Minh** and **Ngô Đình Diệm**. It remains in operation as a school today, though under a different name. *See also* EDUCATION.

NATIONAL ASSEMBLY (*Quốc Hội***).** Supreme legislative body of the **Socialist Republic of Vietnam** (SRV). Originally established by decree in November 1945 and confirmed in the Constitution of 1946, it has been retained by the later **constitutions** promulgated in 1959, 1980, and 1992. It is a unicameral assembly whose members are reelected by universal suffrage on the basis of one deputy for every 10,000 voters in urban areas and one per 30,000 in the countryside. In theory, the National Assembly is the sovereign power in the state. In actuality, for much of its existence it played a role similar to legislative assemblies in other Marxist–Leninist societies, serving as a rubber stamp to ratify decisions already taken by the **Vietnamese Communist Party** leadership and the executive branch.

In recent years, however, it has attained a greater degree of influence of autonomy within the political system. The number of candidates for office has increased, and delegates play a larger role in selecting key government officials and in formulating key policy decisions; some sessions are shown on television, including questioning of government ministers. Several important leaders, such as **Nông Đức Mạnh**, have held positions in the National Assembly during their rise to power. There are currently over 500 seats in the assembly, about evenly divided between the northern and the southern provinces. In the 1997 elections, "self-nominated" candidates (those who had not been specifically chosen by the Party or its affiliates) could participate for the first time. *See also* DEMOCRATIC REPUBLIC OF VIETNAM.

NATIONAL COUNCIL FOR RECONCILIATION AND CONCORD (NCRC). Subgovernmental body established by the **Paris Agreement** of January 1973 to bring about a political settlement in Vietnam. For years, the **Democratic Republic of Vietnam** (DRV) had demanded the resignation of the government of President **Nguyễn Văn Thiệu** as a condition for a peace agreement in South Vietnam. The **United States** had refused to abandon the **Saigon** regime. In the fall of 1972, the two sides agreed to create the NCRC as an administrative body to implement the terms of the peace agreement eventually signed the following January. Representatives of the **Republic of Vietnam**, the **Provisional Revolutionary Government** (PRG), and the neutralist "third force" in the South were to be represented on the council with the task of implementing the agreement and carrying out future elections in South Vietnam. After its creation, however, the parties were unable to reach agreement, and the war resumed.

NATIONAL DEFENSE GUARD (*Vệ Quốc Quân*). New name for the **Vietnamese Liberation Army** (VLA) adopted during the fall of 1945 to alleviate problems with the Chinese occupation forces. The VLA had been established by order of **Hồ Chí Minh** in December 1944. With the opening of hostilities between the **Việt Minh** Front and the **French** in mid-December 1946, the guard was renamed once again as the **People's Army of Vietnam** (*Quân Đội Nhân Dân Việt Nam*). *See also* VÕ NGUYÊN GIÁP.

NATIONAL FRONT FOR THE LIBERATION OF SOUTH VIỆT-NAM (NLF) (*Mặt Trận Dân Tộc Giải Phóng Miền Nam*). Revolutionary front organization established on the territory of the **Republic of Vietnam**. Usually referred to as the *National Liberation Front* (NLF), it was created in December 1960 at a secret location near the **Cambodian** border. Composed of South Vietnamese citizens from a wide variety of backgrounds, it was organized under the sponsorship of the Vietnam Workers Party (the **Vietnamese Communist Party**) in the **Democratic Republic of Vietnam** (DRV) to mobilize popular sentiment against the regime of **Ngô Đình Diệm** in **Saigon**. Like its predecessor, the League for the Independence of Vietnam (**Việt Minh**), the program of the NLF stressed relatively uncontroversial objectives, such as democratic freedoms, peace, and land reform to appeal to moderate sentiment in the South. There was no reference to socialism or to the Front's links with the Party and the DRV, and references to national reunification with the North were vague, indicating that the process would be peaceful and take place over a number of years.

Structurally, the NLF was directed by an elected central committee and a presidium. At the grassroots level, it functioned through a series of mass associations for peasants, workers, writers and artists, women, students, and so forth. In the mid-1960s, membership in the Front and its mass organizations was estimated in the millions. It continued to function until the end of the Vietnam War in 1975, but it was effectively superseded by the **Provisional Revolutionary Government** (PRG) of South Vietnam, created in 1969. After national reunification in 1975, the NLF was merged into the **Fatherland Front** (*Mặt Trận Tổ Quốc*), its counterpart in the North. Although some of its leaders, such as **Nguyễn Hữu Thọ**, continued to serve in the government of the **Socialist Republic of Vietnam**, others, such as **Dương Quỳnh Hoa**, became disenchanted with the new regime.

NATIONAL LIBERATION COMMITTEE (*Uỷ Ban Giải Phóng Dân Tộc*). Committee established at the **Tân Trào** Conference of

Việt Minh representatives in mid-August 1945 in preparation for the **August Revolution**. **Hồ Chí Minh** was named chairman of the five-person committee. After the successful uprising in **Hanoi**, the National Liberation Committee was transformed into a provisional government, which, in turn, became the **Democratic Republic of Vietnam**.

NATIONAL SALVATION ARMY (*Cứu Quốc Quân*). Name of the guerrilla forces organized under the direction of the **Việt Minh** Front after the abortive **Bắc Sơn Uprising** in September 1940. Commander of the army was the minority leader **Chu Văn Tấn**. For three years, the National Salvation Army operated in the mountainous areas of the **Việt Bắc**. In December 1944, it was merged with other Việt Minh units under **Võ Nguyên Giáp** into the new Vietnamese Liberation Army, which later became the **People's Army of Vietnam**.

NATIONAL SALVATION ASSOCIATIONS (*Cứu Quốc Hội*). Mass organizations set up by the **Indochinese Communist Party** as a component of its struggle against the **French** and the **Japanese occupation** forces during World War II. Associations were established representing various ethnic, functional, and religious groups in Vietnam under the overall umbrella of the League for the Independence of Vietnam or **Việt Minh**. After 1954, the so-called *cứu quốc* were simply called *mass associations*.

NATIONALIZATION OF INDUSTRY AND COMMERCE. In accordance with Marxist–Leninist doctrine, it has been the intention of **Vietnamese Communist Party** leaders to put all industry and commerce in Vietnam under state or community control as part of a broad program to build a socialist and ultimately a Communist society. During the late 1950s, heavy industry and most natural resources were placed under state control in the **Democratic Republic of Vietnam** (DRV), although a small private commercial and manufacturing center, mainly composed of **overseas Chinese**, was tolerated in large cities, such as **Hanoi** and **Hải Phòng**.

After reunification in 1975, Party leaders nationalized major industries and utilities in the former **Republic of Vietnam** but permitted a small private sector until March 1978, when a government decree announced the nationalization of all industry and commerce above the family level throughout the country. The measure, probably undertaken to undercut the growing economic power and influences of the Chinese community in Hồ Chí Minh City (previously known as *Saigon*), aroused widespread resentment and led to the flight abroad of thousands of urban residents during the next few years.

Since the mid-1980s, the Party has abandoned the effort to create an entirely socialist economy in the area of manufacturing and trade and has tolerated the emergence of a vigorous private sector. Some of the more inefficient **state-owned enterprises** have been privatized (**"equitized"**) or dismantled, and a number of **joint ventures** have been established with **foreign investors** or firms. The government remains determined, however, to retain essential control over key sectors in the economy, and for the more diehard Marxists among the leadership, a strong state sector is a *sine qua non* of socialism. Equitization is moving ahead in fits and starts, but of the thousands of state firms that existed when the program of renovation (*đổi mới*) was launched, a large number still remain. *See also* BANKING AND FINANCE; INDUSTRY; STATE PLANNING.

NAVARRE, HENRI (1898–1983). Commander in chief of French expeditionary forces in **Indochina** from May 1953 until July 1954. General Navarre was appointed to the post as a replacement for General **Raoul Salan** as a means of placating the Dwight D. Eisenhower administration in the **United States**, which was demanding a more forceful prosecution of the war on the part of the French. Navarre produced an ambitious three-stage plan to clean out pockets of **Việt Minh** control in central and southern Vietnam and then launch a major military offensive in the spring and summer of 1954 to destroy Việt Minh positions in the North.

The Eisenhower administration gave its approval to the so-called Navarre Plan and increased U.S. aid to the French to assist in the war effort. However, the French government, under growing pressure from public opinion to bring the unpopular war to an end, did not send sufficient reinforcements or equipment to Indochina, and the Navarre Plan was never fully put into effect. After their disastrous defeat at **Điện Biên Phủ** in the spring of 1954, the French accepted a compromise settlement at the **Geneva Conference** in July.

NAVARRE PLAN. *See* NAVARRE, HENRI.

NEOLITHIC ERA. The final stage of the Stone Age characterized by the development of sophisticated stone tools and domestication of **agriculture**. It is the general view of archeologists that in Vietnam the Neolithic Era commenced with the development of agriculture during the Hoabinhian period about 11,000 years ago, thus somewhat earlier than the arrival of the New Stone Age civilization elsewhere in Asia and in the West. By the third millennium B.C.E., the use of stone tools coexisted with the appearance of bronze technology. The Neolithic Era gave way to the **Bronze Age** with the rise of the advanced **Đông Sơn** culture sometime around roughly the eighth century B.C.E. *See also* ARCHEOLOGY; HOÀ BÌNH CULTURE.

NEW ECONOMIC ZONES (NEZ, *Khu Kinh Tế Mới*). Agricultural settlements established by the **Socialist Republic of Vietnam** (SRV) to relieve the refugee problem in the cities after the Vietnam War. The concept had originated in the **Democratic Republic of Vietnam** in the 1960s when **economic** planners promoted the construction of centers at the district level to combine both agricultural and manufacturing activities. Although hampered by war requirements and the reluctance of many Vietnamese to leave their native **villages**, nearly one million peasants had been resettled from the crowded **Red River Delta** to underpopulated areas in the mountains by the end of the war.

In 1975, the **Hanoi** regime revived the concept in an effort to resettle the three million refugees who had fled the southern countryside to settle in refugee camps in the major cities during the last years of the war. So-called "New Economic Zones" were hurriedly set up in the **Central Highlands** and other sparsely populated regions in the South. Recruits were provided with seeds, farm tools, building materials, and food for several months. Most of the land was held in common, but each family received a private plot to cultivate vegetables or fruit for its own use.

The aim of the program was to place nearly two million people in the new settlements as part of a major resettlement program that would result in the transfer of 10 million Vietnamese from crowded regions into less-populated areas. Between 1976 and 1980, more than one million people were sent to the NEZs. Recruitment was intended to be voluntary, but there were persistent reports of coercion, and the zones soon earned a bad reputation for poor preparation and unattractive conditions. Many people gradually slipped away and returned to the cities or else **migrated** to more desirable territory as freedom of movement gradually increased. NEZs are still in existence today, mainly in the upland areas, but the policy is being implemented on a smaller scale and with more attention to the complications and sensitivities involved in resettling migrants from the lowlands. To some extent, the original purpose of NEZs has been effectively nullified by the widespread spontaneous migration, which has taken place outside government control.

NEW SOCIETY GROUP (*Tân Xã Hội Đoàn*). Informal legislative group that functioned in the **Republic of Vietnam** in the late 1960s and early 1970s. Loosely identified with General **Dương Văn (Big) Minh** and the **Buddhist** movement in South Vietnam, the group served as a potential source of opposition to the government of President **Nguyễn Văn Thiệu**, but never evolved into a major political party.

NEW VIETNAMESE REVOLUTIONARY PARTY. *See* TÂN VIỆT CÁCH MỆNH ĐẢNG.

NGHỆ TĨNH REVOLT. Major uprising against **French** colonial rule in central Vietnam in 1930–1931. The unrest began in early 1930 with factory strikes and riots throughout the country on **rubber** plantations in **Cochin China**. By late spring, peasants in the northern-central provinces of Nghệ An and Hà Tĩnh began to demonstrate against high taxes and **corruption** in the **mandarin**. The unrest was encouraged by activists of the newly formed **Indochinese Communist Party** (ICP) (known until October as the *Vietnamese Communist Party*) but was provoked to a considerable degree by poor economic and social conditions, exacerbated by the Great Depression. During the summer and fall of 1930, angry peasants in the central provinces seized power in the villages and set up local peasant associations (known as *soviets*) that reduced rents and taxes and, in some instances, confiscated land and punished unpopular landlords. ICP leaders, caught by surprise by the violence of the revolt, supported the rebels but attempted to limit the damage to their own apparatus.

The French reacted swiftly and, by spring 1931, the revolt—which had never spread effectively beyond the two provinces known collectively as *Nghệ-Tĩnh*—had been suppressed. In the process, several Communist leaders were captured, and the Party's local organization was virtually destroyed. The revolt had thus been disastrous for the Party over the short term but had demonstrated the potential power of the rural masses, a lesson that would be learned and applied after World War II.

NGÔ ĐÌNH DIỆM (1901–1963). Prime minister of the **State of Vietnam** and then president of the **Republic of Vietnam** from 1954 until 1963. Born in a family of **mandarins** with court connections in the imperial capital of **Huế** in 1901, Ngo Đình Diệm attended the prestigious **National Academy** (*Quốc học*) and then took a law degree at the University of Hanoi. He entered imperial service under Emperor **Khải Định** and was eventually appointed minister of the interior under the government of Emperor **Bảo Đại** in 1933, but he resigned shortly thereafter in protest against French policy.

For several years, Diệm was inactive in politics. In late 1945, he refused an offer by **Hồ Chí Minh** to collaborate with the **Việt Minh**. A fervent Catholic, he was as opposed to Communism as he was to **French** colonialism, and he was further angered by the Việt Minh assassination of his brother Ngô Đình Khôi, governor of Quảng Ngãi province. Over the next few years, he traveled between the **United States**, Europe, and Asia, making contacts and building up his own support base for an eventual bid for power.

In the early 1950s, Diệm came to the attention of U.S. officials as a potential leader of a free Vietnam. As a Catholic and an anti-French patriot, his credentials were appealing to Washington, but many doubted his political acumen. In the summer of 1954, Bảo Đại appointed him prime minister of the State of Vietnam just as the **Geneva Conference** was coming to a close. After Geneva and the partition of the country, Diệm moved rapidly to consolidate his power in the south, eliminating the **Bình Xuyên**, cowing the religious sects, and removing Bảo Đại's supporters from positions of influence in his government. In 1955, he rigged a referendum that led to the resignation of Bảo Đại and his own election as president of a new **Republic of Vietnam.**

Diệm eventually won full support from the United States, which hoped to use him to transform South Vietnam into a viable, anti-Communist, democratic society. He had several weaknesses, however. He had authoritarian instincts and alienated key groups in South Vietnamese society. He was beholden to his primary supporters, the Catholic community and the wealthy landed classes, and failed to carry through on a promised **land reform** program. By 1959, social and political unrest, backed by the Communist regime in North Vietnam, was on the rise.

In 1961, President John F. Kennedy reaffirmed American support for South Vietnam but pressured Diệm to introduce reforms in the hope of reducing internal discontent. Diệm agreed but, in subsequent months, ignored U.S. advice, cracking down on **Buddhist** critics concerned over his increasing tendency to favor Catholics. In 1963, Buddhist demonstrations erupted, leading to police reprisals and an outcry of criticism in the West. When discontented military officers secretly sought U.S. approval for a coup to overthrow the Diệm regime, the Kennedy administration approved. On 1 November 1963, coup leaders seized key installations in the capital of **Saigon**. Diệm was captured with his brother **Ngô Đình Nhu** and assassinated the following day. Although Kennedy was reportedly horrified at the murder, Washington quickly indicated its approval of the new military government under the leadership of General **Dương Văn (Big) Minh.**

The Diệm regime has inspired controversy among scholars and close observers of the Vietnam War. Some argue that Diệm was the only strong anti-Communist leader in South Vietnam and that his overthrow guaranteed an eventual Communist takeover. Others counter that Diệm was the source of the problem, inciting the very dissent that led to his own downfall. He has frequently been viewed as a creation and puppet of the United States, but recent scholarship using archival records has demonstrated that this was not the case. It is certainly true, however, that American support for Diệm's anti-Communist regime, particularly his decision not to follow through with the nationwide elections called for by the Geneva Agreements, set Vietnam on a course that neither its own leaders nor those of the United States would be able to reverse.

NGÔ ĐÌNH NHU (1910–1963). Brother of **Ngô Đình Diệm** and minister of the interior under his regime (1955–1963). The son of Ngô Đình Khả, an influential **mandarin** at the imperial court, Nhu was educated in **France** and eventually became active as an organizer of the Catholic **labor union** movement, the Vietnamese Federation of Christian Workers. After the rise to power of his older brother Diệm in 1954, Nhu became the driving force behind the regime. Although officially serving in the influential post of minister of the interior, it was as an adviser and the organizer of Diệm's secret **Cần Lao Party** that Nhu exercised enormous influence behind the scenes in **Saigon**. Widely viewed as manipulative and feared for his tactics in ridding the regime of its enemies, Nhu (along with his wife, **Trần Lệ Xuân**, generally known as *Madame Nhu*) came to be seen by **United States** officials as a prime source of Diệm's unpopularity. In 1963, the John F. Kennedy administration privately demanded that he be removed as Diệm's chief adviser. When the latter refused, Washington signaled its approval for the military coup that overthrew the regime on 1 November 1963. The next day, Nhu and Diệm were executed by supporters of the coup group. *See also* PERSONALISM.

NGÔ ĐÌNH NHU, MADAME. *See* TRẦN LỆ XUÂN.

NGÔ ĐỨC KẾ (1879–1929). Journalist and scholar in colonial Vietnam. A **Confucian** scholar and editor of the Hanoi review *Hữu Thanh*, Ngô Đức Kế, in the early 1920s, waged a literary war with the Francophile journalist and writer **Phạm Quỳnh** over the relative merits of the *Tale of Kiều* (*Truyện Kiều*) as a symbol of Vietnamese nationalism. Where Phạm Quỳnh had argued that so long as *Truyện Kiều* survived, Vietnamese national identity still existed regardless of Vietnam's political status, Ngô Đức Kế countered that the **Vietnamese language** and **literature** would not survive unless the nation survived.

NGÔ DYNASTY. *See* NGÔ QUYÊN.

NGÔ QUANG TRƯƠNG (1929–). General in the **Army of the Republic of Vietnam** (ARVN). Born during the colonial era, he joined ARVN during the 1950s and rose rapidly in the ranks. In the spring of 1972, he was the commander of IV Corps, in the **Mekong River Delta**, but was ordered north to stiffen South Vietnamese resistance against the North Vietnamese **Easter Offensive**. His energy and talent were instrumental in preventing panic and a possible serious reverse for the **Saigon** regime. In 1975, he was serving as commander of I Corps (the northern provinces of the **Republic of Vietnam**) when the final **Hồ Chí Minh Campaign** was unleashed. Ordered by President **Nguyễn Văn Thiệu** to evacuate all ARVN forces from the region, he attempted to carry out the task by an orderly means, but the retreat degenerated into a rout. After the fall of Saigon on 30 April, he resettled in the **United States**.

NGÔ QUYÊN (899–944). Rebel leader who helped consolidate Vietnamese independence from Chinese rule in the 10th century. Ngô Quyền, son of a provincial official and a native of the western **Red River Delta** near **Mount Tản Viên**, became a military commander and a son-in-law of **Dương Đình Nghệ**, who had seized power in the unstable conditions following the collapse of the Tang dynasty in **China**. After Nghệ was assassinated in 937, Quyền launched an attack on the troops loyal to the assassin and a Chinese army that supported them. At the mouth of the **Bạch Đằng River**, at the entrance to the **Tonkin Gulf**, he won a major victory by sinking wooden poles into the mud at the mouth of the river. When the tide fell, the Chinese fleet was impaled on the poles and destroyed. After his victory, he declared himself king of the independent kingdom of **Nam Việt**, with its new capital at **Cổ Loa**, the ancient capital of Vietnam before the **Chinese period**. Quyền died in 944, leading to a period of political instability, which ended only with the rise to power of **Đinh Bộ Lĩnh**.

Although Ngô Quyền had restored Vietnamese independence after a thousand years of Chinese domination, later Vietnamese historians were generally reluctant to consider him the true founder of Vietnamese independence because he had only claimed the title of "king" rather than "emperor." They did, however, view his reign as the beginning of a short-lived "dynasty," even though he should more properly be understood as the first of a series of regional strongmen who dominated the scene during the 10th century.

NGÔ SĨ LIÊN. Noted Vietnamese historian during the 15th century. A member of the Bureau of History, Ngô Sĩ Liên participated in an examination of historical records during the early years of the reign of Emperor **Lê Thánh Tông**. He later compiled a comprehensive history of the Vietnamese nation from its origins to the **Lê dynasty**, *Đại Việt Sử Ký Toàn Thư* (*Complete Historical Record of Great Viet*), published in 1479. The book made use of **Lê Văn Hưu**'s *Đại Việt Sử Ký* written in the 13th century, as well as Phan Phu Tien's *Đại Việt Sử Ký Tục Biên* (*Supplementary Compilation of the Historical Records of Great Viet*), which had carried Hưu's narrative history from the **Trần dynasty** to the founding of the Lê in 1428. Later, Ngô Sĩ Liên's work was periodically revised and became recognized as the official imperial history of the state of Vietnam. *See also* CONFUCIANISM; HISTORIOGRAPHY; LITERATURE.

NGÔ TẤT TỐ (1894–1954). Novelist of the 1930s whose writings in the realist style criticized **feudal** society in colonial Vietnam. He also attempted to make Vietnamese history and traditional **literature** available to the average Vietnamese by publishing *quốc ngữ* (Romanized Vietnamese) translations of extant historical works dating back to the **Lý dynasty**.

NGÔ THÌ NHẬM (also known as *Ngô Thời Nhậm*) (1746–1803). Scholar and official in late 18th-century Vietnam. He was born in 1746 in a prominent **scholar-gentry** family from Hà Đông province, which produced generations of literati, known collectively as the *Ngô gia Văn phái* (Ngo family literary group). Ngô Thì Nhậm was a gifted student, passing his doctoral examination at the relatively young age of 30. Serving in the **mandarinate** during the declining years of the **Lê dynasty**, he later became a supporter of the **Tây Sơn** leader **Nguyễn Huệ**, whom he served as a diplomat and an official. He was put to death shortly after the **Nguyễn dynasty** came to power in 1802.

NGÔ THÌ SĨ (1726–1780). Scholar and official in late 18th-century Vietnam. A member of the same gifted family as **Ngô Thì Nhậm**, he held **mandarinal** posts in various different provinces and traveled widely outside the scope of his work as well. He wrote several literary travelogues as well as the important historical work *Việt Sử Tiêu Án (Discussion of Vietnamese History)*, which incorporated his comments on various historical developments. Because Ngô Thì Sĩ died before the **Tây Sơn** conflict reached the northern kingdom, where he served the **Lê dynasty**, he did not have to choose sides, as other family members did in the second half of the 1780s. *See also* HISTORIOGRAPHY; LITERATURE.

NGUYỄN ÁI QUỐC. *See* HỒ CHÍ MINH.

NGUYỄN AN NINH (1900–1943). Influential **journalist** and patriotic activist in early 20th-century colonial Vietnam. Nguyễn An Ninh was born in 1900 near **Saigon**. His father was a scholar who had participated in the anti-French **Cần Vương** (Save the King) movement before the turn of the century. Nguyễn An Ninh was educated in **French** schools and then studied law in Paris. He returned to **Cochin China** in 1922 and immediately became engaged in political activities, publishing a newspaper entitled *La Cloche Fêlée* and giving speeches critical of the colonial regime.

Although he repudiated revolutionary violence and admired the teachings of Mahatma Gandhi and Rabindranath Tagore, his fiery speeches galvanized the emotions of many young intellectuals in Cochin China, loosely organized under the name "The Hopes of Youth" (**Thanh Niên Cao Vọng**), and earned the distrust of the colonial government. He was arrested and briefly imprisoned for his outspoken criticism of France in March 1926. On his release, Ninh began to agitate among rural villagers in the **Mekong River Delta** and developed a mystical streak. Once again, his organization was dispersed. In the 1930s, he began to collaborate with the **Indochinese Communist Party**, although he himself never became a member. He was a frequent contributor to the newspaper *La Lutte (The Struggle)* published by Party members and **Trotskyites** in Saigon.

In September 1937, Nguyễn An Ninh was arrested and sentenced to five years in prison. He died on **Poulo Condore** Island, allegedly of torture, in 1943.

NGUYỄN ÁNH. *See* GIA LONG.

NGUYỄN BÌNH (1906–1951). Prominent commander of **Việt Minh** forces in **Cochin China** during the **Franco-Việt Minh** conflict. A native of Hưng Yên and a onetime member of the Vietnamese Nationalist Party (*Việt Nam Quốc Dân Đảng*), Nguyễn Bình (real name *Nguyễn Phương Thảo*) became acquainted with Communism during the early 1930s while in prison on **Poulo Condore** Island. After his release, he spent several years in **China** but returned to Vietnam sometime around the **August Revolution.** In the next months, his military talents became recognized, and after military service in the North he was sent to replace **Trần Văn Giàu** as commander of Việt Minh forces in the South.

Energetic and passionate, Nguyễn Bình was portrayed by the **French** as a fearful and effective adversary, but his cruelty and fanaticism antagonized many, and he often ignored directives from the Party leadership in the **Việt Bắc.** Sometime in 1951, he was dismissed from his post and recalled to the North, ostensibly because of the failure of a major offensive the previous year. En route to the Việt Bắc, he was killed in an ambush inside **Cambodia;** rumors persist that he was assassinated at the orders of the Party.

NGUYỄN BỈNH KHIÊM (1491–1585). Scholar and writer in 16th-century Vietnam. His father was a **mandarin**, and he too served as an official in the **Mạc dynasty** and then, disgusted at the high level of **corruption** within the bureaucracy and at court, resigned his office in 1542 to become a teacher and a poet. For much of the remainder of his life he lived at his famous retreat, Bạch Vân Âm (Hermitage of the White Cloud) in Hải Dương, where he became renowned for his prophecies and was visited by a number of prominent political figures of his day, including **Trịnh Kiểm** and **Nguyễn Hoàng**, the respective founders of the Trịnh and Nguyễn ruling families. He reportedly counseled Nguyễn Hoàng to seek his fortune at the southernmost reaches of the empire; Hoàng followed this advice and established his own kingdom, known as **Đàng Trong.**

A noted **Confucianist**, Nguyễn Binh Khiêm represented the tradition of resigning from office and living a life of seclusion rather than becoming involved in a corrupt society. He wrote more than a thousand poems, many about the beauty of nature and the ironies of life, in both *chữ nôm* and Chinese. *See also* LITERATURE.

NGUYỄN CAO KỲ (1930–). Flamboyant Vietnamese air force officer and vice-president of the **Republic of Vietnam** from 1967 to 1971. A Northerner by origin, Nguyễn Cao Kỳ chose a military career after graduation from high school and rose to the rank of air force colonel under the regime of President **Ngô Đình Diệm**. In January 1964, Kỳ participated in the "Young Turk" rebellion that put General **Nguyễn Khánh** in power as chairman of the Military Revolutionary Council. He played an active role in the factional struggles that followed and, in June 1965, joined with fellow Young Turk **Nguyễn Văn Thiệu** in overthrowing the weak regime. In 1967, Kỳ was elected vice-president on a ticket led by Thiệu that took office after the approval of a new constitution. Kỳ's relations with President Thiệu declined, however, and after being disqualified from running for president in the 1971 elections, he retired from politics. With the Communist takeover of **Saigon**, he fled to the **United States** as a refugee. In 2004, he made a highly publicized trip to Vietnam—the first since his departure in 1975.

NGUYỄN CHÁNH THI (1923–). Influential military commander of the **Army of the Republic of Vietnam** (ARVN) during the Vietnam War. Nguyễn Chánh Thi had come into national prominence in the mid-1950s, when he had assisted **Ngô Đình Diệm** in suppressing his rivals among the religious sects and the **Bình Xuyên**, a bandit group that controlled vice operations in **Saigon**. As a **Buddhist**, however, he eventually began to resent Diệm's alleged favoritism toward Vietnamese Catholics. After taking part in an abortive coup against Diệm in 1960, he fled briefly to **Cambodia**. He returned after Diệm's overthrow and took part in the Young Turk movement that came to power in 1964. Posted to **Huế**, he eventually joined Buddhist elements in that city in opposing the policies of the government, now under **Nguyễn Cao Kỳ** and **Nguyễn Văn Thiệu**. When his supporters were defeated in an insurrection in **Đà Nẵng** launched in 1966, he went into exile in the **United States**. *See also* REPUBLIC OF VIETNAM.

NGUYỄN CHÍ THANH (1914–1967). Senior general in the **People's Army of Vietnam** (PAVN) during the Vietnam War. Nguyễn Chí Thanh was born in a poor peasant family in Thừa Thiên. He became active in revolutionary activities in the mid-1930s and a member of the **Indochinese Communist Party** in 1937. In August 1945, he attended the **Tân Trào** Conference and was named to the Party Central Committee. Thanh rose rapidly in the ranks of the PAVN and was head of its Political Department in 1950. During the Vietnam War, he was placed in charge of military operations in South Vietnam, where he recommended an activist policy of big unit warfare against **United States** military forces. His strategy was criticized by **Võ Nguyên Giáp** for the high casualties incurred, and a more modest approach was adopted. He is said to have died either of a heart attack or from a U.S. bombing raid in July 1967 while formulating initial plans for the **Tết Offensive**, though some sources have suggested that his death was linked to political developments within the **Vietnamese Communist Party**.

NGUYỄN CƠ THẠCH (1923–1998). Former foreign minister of the **Socialist Republic of Vietnam** (SRV). Born in a peasant family in northern Vietnam, Nguyễn Cơ Thạch entered revolutionary activities in the late 1930s and was jailed by the **French**. In 1954, he served as a staff officer in the **People's Army of Vietnam** (PAVN) at **Điện Biên Phủ**, but he made his career as a diplomat. After Geneva, he entered the Ministry of Foreign Affairs; in 1980 he replaced the veteran **Nguyễn Duy Trinh** as minister of foreign affairs and in 1982 became the first career diplomat to join the Politburo. Knowledgeable about the West and regarded as a moderate in domestic affairs, he was considered a prime candidate for future leadership in the SRV, but in 1991 he was dismissed and replaced by **Nguyễn Mạnh Cầm**. Thạch's "fall" is generally attributed to his antagonism toward **China**, which was in the process of reestablishing normal ties with the SRV at the time of his dismissal.

NGUYỄN CÔNG HOAN (1903–1977). Well-known realistic novelist in colonial Vietnam. Beginning as a teacher in Hải Dương, Nguyễn

Cong Hoan came to public attention in the late 1930s as a novelist dealing with serious social themes concerning the life of poor villagers and the **corruption** and arrogance of officialdom. Among his most famous works were *Cô Giáo Minh* (*School Teacher Minh*) and *Lá Ngọc Cánh Vàng* (*Leaves of Jade, Branches of Gold*). *See also* LITERATURE.

NGUYỄN CÔNG TRỨ (1778–1858). Noted scholar and **mandarin** under the early **Nguyễn dynasty**. Born the son of a mandarin from Hà Tĩnh who held a high position under the **Lê dynasty**, Nguyễn Công Trứ encountered difficulties with the civil service **examinations** and did not enter officialdom until the relatively advanced age of 41. From that point, he rose rapidly in the bureaucracy, becoming a provincial governor, governor-general, and eventually, minister of war under the Nguyễn. He was particularly known for overseeing land reclamation efforts, which created large stretches of habitable land along the coast of the **Red River Delta** in present-day Thái Bình and Ninh Bình. Trứ was equally well known as the author of poems satirizing hypocrisy, social climbing, and other foibles of human nature, many of which he shared. After retiring from office in 1848, he volunteered to participate in the struggle against the French but died shortly after their initial invasion. *See also* LITERATURE.

NGUYỄN ĐÌNH CHIỂU (1822–1888). Scholar and poet in 19th-century Vietnam. Blind from childhood, Nguyễn Đình Chiểu taught school in his home province of Gia Định until the **French** conquest of **Cochin China**. He then resigned and moved to Bến Tre, where he began to write poetry; the primary theme of his writing was that of patriotism and resistance to foreign rule. He composed a funeral ovation for Trương Công Định, the military commander who fought against French troops. His most famous work, entitled *Lục Vân Tiên*, is both a moral essay and a pastiche of life in 19th-century Vietnam. *See also* LITERATURE.

NGUYỄN DU (1765–1820). Well-known Vietnamese writer and author of a classic verse novel. Born in a family of scholars and officials in Hà Tĩnh in 1765, he grew up during the turbulent years of the **Tây Sơn** Rebellion, which broke out in 1771 and resulted in the formation of a new, though short-lived dynasty, in 1789. His family supported the declining **Lê dynasty**, and Nguyễn Du did not enter officialdom until the overthrow of the Tây Sơn and and rise of the **Nguyễn dynasty** in 1802. He served as a provincial official and a diplomat on a mission to the Qing court in Peking. He eventually became vice-president of the Board of Rites in **Huế** and died by 1820.

It is as an author and commentator on social conditions in Lê dynasty Vietnam that Nguyễn Du's reputation rests. Although he wrote a number of poems in Chinese, he is best known for his famous vernacular poem (written in *chữ nôm*), *Truyện Kiều* (*The Tale of Kiều*), a classic, which quickly became a favorite of his countrymen and has been widely praised as the greatest work in Vietnamese **literature**.

NGUYỄN DUY TRINH (1910–1985). Leading member of the Vietnamese Communist movement and onetime foreign minister of the **Democratic Republic of Vietnam** (DRV). Nguyễn Duy Trinh became involved in anticolonial activities while a student of **Trần Phú** at a secondary school in the provincial capital of Vinh. He joined the **Indochinese Communist Party** and was arrested for taking part in the **Nghệ Tĩnh Revolt**. Trinh was released from prison in August 1945 and took part in the **August Revolution** in **Huế**. After the **Geneva Conference**, he was called to **Hanoi,** where he was elevated to the Party Politburo and served as director of the State Planning Commission. In 1965, he replaced **Phạm Văn Đồng** as minister of foreign affairs. He resigned in 1980, reportedly for health reasons, and was dropped from the Politburo two years later, allegedly for his earlier failure to anticipate the Chinese border invasion in February 1979.

NGUYỄN DY NIÊN (1935–). Minister for foreign affairs of the **Socialist Republic of Vietnam**. A native of Thanh Hoá, Nguyễn Dy Niên is unusual among top Vietnamese leaders for having been educated in English and in a country outside the main socialist bloc. He was sent to Banaras Hindu University in India as a result of an agreement between **Hồ Chí Minh** and Indian Prime Minister Jawaharlal Nehru. A career diplomat, Niên held a number of posts in the Foreign Ministry during the 1980s and 1990s, including the presidency of the National Commission of the United Nations Economic, Scientific and Cultural Organization (UNESCO) and the National Committee for **Overseas Vietnamese**. In 1992, he was elected to the Central Committee of the **Vietnamese Communist Party**. After many years as deputy foreign minister, he succeeded **Nguyễn Mạnh Cầm** as minister in 2000. Although he has not had as high a profile as Cầm or **Nguyễn Cơ Thạch**, he has presided over a steady expansion of Vietnam's **foreign relations**, which has generally proceeded smoothly thanks to the groundwork laid by his predecessors, notably in terms of the normalization of ties with **China** and **United States** in the 1990s.

NGUYỄN DYNASTY (1802–1945). Last imperial dynasty in Vietnam, founded by Nguyễn Ánh (Emperor **Gia Long**) in 1802. The origins of Nguyễn political influence date back to the 16th century when the powerful mandarin **Nguyễn Kim** assisted the **Lê dynasty** to restore its control over the Vietnamese throne, which had been usurped by the **Mạc**. Under the restored Lê the Nguyễn family, known as the *Nguyễn Lords*, controlled the South (known as *Đàng Trong*) under the nominal authority of the Lê, whose rulers in Thăng Long (**Hanoi**) were dominated by the **Trịnh Lords**, the bitter rivals of the Nguyễn. In the late 1700s, the Nguyễn were driven from the power by the **Tây Sơn**, but a member of the house, Prince Nguyễn Ánh eventually defeated the latter and founded a full-fledged imperial dynasty.

The Nguyễn were generally a conservative dynasty, ruling in **Huế** according to **Confucian** precepts and often imitating Qing practices in **China**, notably in their **Gia Long Code** of laws and in the architecture of their imperial city. Their rule tended to be repressive, and the first several decades were marked by intermittent rural unrest. The dynasty's problems were compounded by French ambitions to establish their political and economic influence in Southeast Asia. The court's efforts to fend off the challenge were ineffective and, in 1884, the empire was transformed into a French **protectorate**, the **Mekong Delta** having already been ceded to **France** as the colony of **Cochin China**.

During the next half century, the Nguyễn emperors were essentially puppets of the French colonial regime. The last emperor, **Bảo Đại**, ruled until March 1945 when **Japanese occupation** forces granted him a spurious independence. When Japan surrendered to the Allies in August, **Việt Minh** forces seized power and persuaded Bảo Đại to abdicate, bringing the dynasty to an end. Since 1945, all Vietnamese governments have been republics, except for the French-sponsored **State of Vietnam**, which had a rather ambiguous status with Bảo Đại as chief of state.

The Nguyễn were long vilified by many historians, Marxist and non-Marxist alike, for their allegedly reactionary outlook on government and trade and particularly their concessions to, and defeat by, the French. They have recently undergone a significant rehabilitation, however, and even Party historians have praise for their achievements in strengthening centralized government and their efforts to stamp out **corruption**. *See also* MONARCHY; PATENÔTRE TREATY.

NGUYỄN GIA THIỀU (1741–1798). Renowed poet in late 18th-century Vietnam. Born in a mandarin family, he was the author of *Cung Oán Ngâm* (*Lament of an odalisque*), the story of a beautiful woman forced to live in a royal harem. *See also* LITERATURE.

NGUYỄN HẢI THẦN (1879–1955). Non-Communist nationalist figure in colonial Vietnam. Originally named *Võ Hải Thu*, the son of a **mandarin** in Hà Đông, he joined **Phan Bội Châu**'s movement to overthrow **French** rule and later lived for many years in **China**. During World War II, he cooperated with Chinese Nationalist General **Zhang Fakui** in setting up the **Vietnamese Revolutionary League** (Đồng Minh Hội), a non-Communist front organization designed to achieve Chinese objectives in French **Indochina**. After World War II, Thần returned to Vietnam and served briefly as vice-president in **Hồ Chí Minh**'s **Democratic Republic of Vietnam**. Dissatisfied with the extent of Communist domination over the government, he resigned and returned to China.

NGUYỄN HOÀNG (1524–1613). Influential political figure in the 16th century and first of the **Nguyễn Lords** lineage. Nguyễn Hoàng was the son of the noted mandarin **Nguyễn Kim**. When Kim supported the restoration of the **Lê dynasty** against the usurper **Mạc Đăng Dung** and his successors, Hoàng became a military commander of the Lê armed forces and helped build a resistance base and capital in the family's native Thanh Hoá, south of the **Red River Delta**. However, Hoàng felt threatened by his powerful brother-in-law **Trịnh Kiểm**, who, according to rumor, had poisoned Hoàng's older brother in an effort to increase his own political influence.

In 1558, Hoàng sought and received an appointment as governor of the southern provinces of Thuận Hoá and Quảng Nam, which, at the time, were frontier areas very much at the periphery of the Vietnamese Empire. In succeeding years, he consolidated his power in that region while helping Trịnh Kiểm and his successor Trịnh Tùng conquer the Mạc in the North. After the Mạc were driven out of the capital of Thăng Long (present-day **Hanoi**) in 1592, Hoàng returned to his southern fief. As the restored Lê court was now dominated by the Trịnh, he preferred to keep his geographical and political distance. Under his descendants, known collectively as the *Nguyễn Lords*, the southern territories (known as *Đàng Trong*) evolved into an autonomous kingdom that gave only nominal recognition to Lê suzerainty. *See also* MẠC DYNASTY; TRỊNH LORDS.

NGUYỄN HUỆ (1753–1792). Leader of the **Tây Sơn** and founder of a short-lived dynasty in the late 18th century. Nguyễn Huệ was the second of three brothers from the village of Tây Sơn in what is now Bình Định. In the early 1770s, the brothers, led by the eldest Nguyễn Nhạc, revolted against the rule of the **Nguyễn Lords**. Their Tây Sơn movement went on to drive the Nguyễn from the power and then turned on the **Lê dynasty** and **Trịnh Lords** ruling in the North as well. Nguyễn Huệ seized the imperial capital of Thăng Long (**Hanoi**) in July 1786.

At first, Nguyễn Huệ kept his campaign slogan and recognized the legitimacy of the aged ruler, **Lê Hiển Tông**, who gave him Princess Ngọc Hân in marriage. When Hiển Tông died in late 1786, the throne passed to his grandson Lê Chiêu Thống, who called on Chinese assistance to restore the power of the dynasty and drive out the Tây Sơn. When Chinese troops entered Vietnam in late 1788 and occupied Thăng Long, Nguyễn Huệ declared himself Emperor Quang Trung and launched an attack that drove out the Chinese forces after the battle of Đống Đa (now located inside the city limits of Hanoi) in early 1789.

After his victory, Emperor Quang Trung maintained his capital in

Thăng Long and offered tribute to **China**. He also moved vigorously to strengthen the state, reorganizing the military, promoting land reform, and stimulating trade relations with the West. The uniquely Vietnamese writing system *chữ nôm* replaced classical Chinese as the official language at court and in the civil service examinations. Quang Trung died suddenly in 1792 at age 39 and was succeeded by his 10-year-old son, who took the reign name *Cảnh Thịnh*. The young emperor was unable to prevent the outbreak of internal dissention within the regime, which weakened it politically and militarily at a time when Nguyễn influence was on the rise in the **Mekong Delta** region. Quang Trung's premature death is seen as a crucial factor in the ultimate defeat of the Tây Sơn. *See also* GIA LONG.

NGUYỄN HỮU THỌ (1910–1996). Leading figure in the **National Liberation Front** (NLF) in the **Republic of Vietnam** and a high-ranking official in the **Socialist Republic of Vietnam** (SRV). Born the son of an official in Vĩnh Long in 1910, Nguyễn Hữu Thọ studied in **France** and became a lawyer in **Cochin China** in the 1930s. A member of the French Socialist Party, he joined the **Việt Minh** in the late 1940s and took part in anti-American and anti-French activities in **Saigon**. After the **Geneva Conference** in 1954, he became vice-chairman of the Saigon Peace Committee. Arrested by the regime of **Ngô Đình Diệm**, Thọ served seven years in prison, and on his release in 1961, he became a leading figure in the NLF. After the formation of the **Provisional Revolutionary Government** (PRG) in 1969, he was chairman of its advisory council. After reunification and the dissolution of the PRG in 1976, he was named vice-president of the SRV and served briefly as acting president on the death of **Tôn Đức Thắng**.

NGUYỄN HUY THIỆP (1950–). Popular fiction writer in contemporary Vietnam. Nguyễn Huy Thiệp was born in **Hanoi** in 1950 but spent most of his childhood in the **Việt Bắc** region. Returning to Hanoi at the age of 10, he completed high school and attended teacher's college. After graduation, he began to teach history but eventually turned to fiction writing. He first came to national prominence in 1988 when he wrote three controversial short stories in the literary magazine *Văn Nghệ*. The pieces were highly praised in the intellectual community but subjected to harsh criticism for their realistic and sometimes critical portrayal of patriotic figures and of contemporary conditions in Vietnam. Despite official harassment, in 1990 Thiệp was elected to membership in the prestigious Writer's Association. Some of his writings have been translated into English under the title *The General Retires and Other Stories. See also* LITERATURE.

NGUYỄN KHẮC HIẾU. *See* TẢN ĐÀ.

NGUYỄN KHẮC VIỆN (1915–1997). Prominent intellectual and writer in socialist Vietnam. The son of a court official in the imperial capital of **Huế**, Nguyễn Khắc Viện received his baccalaureate at a colonial school in **Indochina** and then entered the University of Hanoi to study for a career in medicine. When World War II began, he was enrolled in a medical school in **France**. By now, however, his political views had gradually drifted toward the left. Following the war, he decided to return to Vietnam and join the **Indochinese Communist Party**. Later, he returned to France for treatment of tuberculosis. There, he became interested in **literature** and history and began to write on a variety of subjects for French-language journals.

In 1963, Viện returned to the **Democratic Republic of Vietnam** (DRV), where he continued to write and became an editor of a number of English- and French-language periodicals published in the DRV, including *Vietnamese Studies* and *Vietnam Courier*. After the end of the Vietnam War, although still a member of the **Vietnamese Communist Party**, he became increasingly critical of the official suppression of criticism in his country and claimed that with the Party dominating every aspect of life, the **Fatherland Front** had become a façade. In 1981, he distributed a very critical letter to various leaders, but this initiative did not earn him the punishment that he would have faced if he had publicly attacked government policies. *See also* DISSIDENTS.

NGUYỄN KHÁNH (1927–). South Vietnamese military officer and head of the "Young Turks" movement that took power in **Saigon** in January 1964. Born of a modest background in the North, Nguyễn Khánh became a career military officer and rose rapidly in the ranks after the **Geneva Conference** in 1954, becoming deputy chief of staff under the regime of President **Ngô Đình Diệm**. In January 1964, he led a coup organized by younger military officers against the senior officers under General **Dương Văn Minh** that had removed Diệm from power.

Khánh and his "Young Turks"—middle-ranking military officers, such as **Nguyễn Chánh Thi**, **Nguyễn Văn Thiệu**, and **Nguyễn Cao Kỳ**—were younger than the generation that had overthrown Diệm and were inclined to favor the Americans over the French. They lacked political experience, however, and suffered from factionalism in their ranks. Khánh was ousted from power in February 1965. *See also* TRẦN VĂN HƯƠNG.

NGUYỄN KIM (1467–1545). Court official who fought to restore the **Lê dynasty** to power in the 16th century. A native of Thanh Hoá, he was related to the Lê royal family by marriage and supported their struggle for reinstatement when power was usurped by **Mạc Đăng Dung** in 1527. After 1533, he supported Emperor Lê Trang Tông, who had declared himself the legitimate ruler of Vietnam while living in exile in **Laos**. By the early 1540s, supporters of the Lê established their court in Thanh Hoá and continued to fight the Mạc. In 1545, Nguyễn Kim died, allegedly poisoned by the Mạc. His son **Nguyễn Hoàng** continued to serve the Lê restorationist cause but established his own fief at the southern periphery of the Vietnamese Empire, which he and his descendants transformed into an autonomous kingdom. *See also* ĐÀNG TRONG; NGUYỄN LORDS; TRỊNH KIỂM.

NGUYỄN LORDS (*Chúa Nguyễn*). Powerful aristocratic family and predecessors of the **Nguyễn dynasty** (1802–1945). The family rose to prominence in the 16th century, when an influential mandarin, **Nguyễn Kim**, supported the restoration of the **Lê dynasty** against the new dynasty established in 1527 by **Mạc Đăng Dung**. After Kim's death, his family continued to support the restoration of the Lê but worried over the domination of his son-in-law **Trịnh Kiểm**. Kim's son **Nguyễn Hoàng** feared assassination at the hands of his ambitious brother-in-law and sought appointment as governor of the southern region of Vietnam. The two cooperated to achieve the overthrow of the Mạc in 1592, but the split between Kiểm and Hoàng led, in later years, to the civil war between the two families; the **Trịnh Lords** nominally served but actually controlled the restored Lê in the North, while the Nguyễn ruled an autonomous kingdom in the South (known as *Đàng Trong* or *Cochin China*) from their capital in the region of present-day **Huế**.

Under Nguyễn rule, Vietnamese boundaries gradually extended toward the south at the expense of their **Cham** and **Cambodian** neighbors. They gradually absorbed what remained of **Champa** and extended their control over much of the Cambodian territory of the **Mekong Delta**. The **Tây Sơn** rebellion of 1771 temporarily drove them from power, but Nguyễn Ánh, a member of the family, mounted what became a 30-year campaign of resistance. In 1802, he defeated the Tây Sơn, and proclaimed the establishment of the Nguyễn dynasty as Emperor **Gia Long**. *See also NAM TIẾN.*

NGUYỄN LƯƠNG BẰNG (1904–1979). Early member of the **Indochinese Communist Party**. The son of an impoverished scholar in Hải Dương, Nguyễn Lương Bằng joined **Hồ Chí Minh**'s Revolutionary Youth League or **Thanh Niên** while working as a seaman on a French ship in the mid-1920s. Arrested for seditious activities in 1930, he spent several years in prison and ended up at the famous Sơn La prison in **Tonkin**. He escaped in 1943 and joined Việt Minh leaders in the **Việt Bắc**. After taking part in the **August Revolution**, Bằng was named director of the National Bank of Vietnam. Later, he was elected a vice-president of the **Democratic Republic of Vietnam** (DRV).

NGUYỄN MẠNH CẦM (1929–). Former foreign minister of the **Socialist Republic of Vietnam** (SRV). He joined the **Indochinese Communist Party** in 1946, one year after the **August Revolution**. After diplomatic training, he became a foreign service officer and in the early 1980s was named vice-minister of foreign trade. A few years later, he became SRV ambassador to the **Union of Soviet Socialist Republics**. In 1991 he replaced **Nguyễn Cơ Thạch** as foreign minister, a post he held for several years before becoming deputy prime minister.

NGUYỄN MINH CHÂU (1930–1989). Sometimes described as Vietnam's best-loved novelist, Nguyễn Minh Châu was a writer of both novels and short stories. His treatment of the life experiences and sufferings of the Vietnamese people during the bitter struggles of the Vietnamese revolution are often moving, and his sharp eye in the portrayal of human character marks him as distinctive in an era when writers in North Vietnam were urged to focus on the fate of the Vietnamese nation. Perhaps his most famous book is a collection of short stories entitled *Người Đàn Bà trên Chuyến Tàu Tốc Hành* (*Woman on an Express Train*), published in 1983. *See also* LITERATURE.

NGUYỄN PHAN LONG (1889–1960). Reformist political figure in early 20th-century Vietnam. Born in **Hanoi** in 1889, he returned to his father's home region of **Cochin China** and, after taking employment as a customs official, became a **journalist**, founding his own newspaper, *L'Echo Annamite*, in 1920. For several years, he cooperated with **Bùi Quang Chiêu** in the moderate reformist **Constitutionalist Party**, based in **Saigon**. In 1925, he presented a famous list of demands for reform (*Cahier des Voeux Annamites*) to Governor-General **Alexander Varenne**. By the 1930s, the two had parted political company because Long disagreed with Chiêu's close relationship with the **French**. In 1949, he was named foreign minister in the first government of the **State of Vietnam** under Chief of State **Bảo Đại**. Becoming prime minister in January 1950, he was forced out by the French two months later, after attempting to obtain direct economic assistance from the **United States**.

NGUYỄN SƠN (1910–1956). Prominent member of the **Indochinese Communist Party**. Born *Võ Nguyên Thủy* in a patriotic scholar-gentry family in Hải Dương, Nguyễn Sơn joined the revolutionary movement in the late 1920s and studied at the Whampoa Academy in Canton. After his training program was concluded, he remained in **China**, where he joined the Chinese Communist Party and took part in the Long March. He returned to Vietnam from Yan'an after the **August Revolution** and was named commander of the **Việt Minh**'s Fourth War Zone. During his years in China, however, he had developed strongly Maoist views, and when Việt Minh leaders began to seek Chinese assistance, Nguyễn Sơn opposed the idea and advocated a Maoist policy of self-reliance. He was dismissed from his command in 1949 and left for China. He returned to the **Democratic**

Republic of Vietnam (DRV) in 1955 and died shortly after, reportedly of a heart attack.

NGUYỄN TẤN DŨNG (1949–). Deputy prime minister of the **Socialist Republic of Vietnam**. Born in **Cà Mau** at the tip of the Mekong Delta, Nguyễn Tấn Dũng apparently grew up in North Vietnam, where he served in the **People's Army of Vietnam** and studied law. After a stint at the **Vietnamese Communist Party**'s Nguyễn Ái Quốc Advanced Studies School, he returned to his native province (then called *Kiến Giang*), where he held a succession of Party positions until 1995, when he was called to Hanoi to assume the post of deputy minister of the interior. In 1996, Dũng was elected to the party's Politburo, one of the youngest members ever to achieve this important status. The following year, he was appointed deputy prime minister and chairman of the government's Finance and Currency Council, a combination of posts that gave him considerable authority over the country's **economy**. In May 1998, he briefly held the position of acting governor of the State Bank after the sacking of **Cao Sỹ Kiêm**, but later that year he relinquished that post to concentrate on his broader economic portfolio. Dũng has long been considered one of the bright stars in the Party and government hierarchy. His influence and intervention during negotiations leading to the 2000 **Bilateral Trade Agreement** with the **United States** are known to have helped achieve a successful outcome.

NGUYỄN THÁI HỌC (1904–1930). Radical Vietnamese patriot and founder of the Vietnamese Nationalist Party (**Việt Nam Quốc Dân Đảng**). Born in a peasant family in Vĩnh Yên in the **Red River Delta** in 1902, Nguyễn Thái Học studied education and commerce in **Hanoi**. At first, he was inclined toward moderate reform, but when his letter to Governor-General **Alexander Varenne** was ignored, his political persuasions turned more radical. Using a publishing firm as a front, Học founded a new political party, the Viet Nam Quốc Dân Đảng, usually known as *VNQDĐ*, in the fall of 1927. The new party was modeled after Sun Yat-sen's political party of the same name, the Chinese Nationalist Party (Guomindang), and had as its objective a violent revolution to overthrow **French** rule and restore Vietnamese independence. Học was arrested and executed after the **Yên Bái** mutiny of February 1930.

NGUYỄN THẾ TRUYỀN (1898–1969). Prominent political figure in colonial Vietnam. Born in 1898 in Nam Định, Nguyễn Thế Truyền went to Paris in 1920 and was soon involved in radical political activities connected with the journal *Le Paria* and the Intercolonial Union, a front organization of the French Communist Party (PCF) composed of radical exiles from **French** colonies in Asia and Africa. An engineer by profession, he became a member of the PCF's Colonial Section and headed the Union after **Hồ Chí Minh**'s departure for Moscow in 1923. In 1926, he set up a new Vietnamese-language journal, *Việt Nam Hồn* (*Soul of Vietnam*), and organized a new political party among Vietnamese expatriates in Paris called the ***Annamese Independence Party*** (*Parti Annamite de l'Indépendance*). The party dissolved after his return to Vietnam in the late 1920s. By the 1940s, he had abandoned radical activities and supported the **Bảo Đại** government in 1949. He died in **Saigon** in September 1969.

NGUYỄN THỊ BÌNH (1927–   ). Most prominent **woman** member of the Vietnamese Communist Party and official in the **Socialist Republic of Vietnam** (SRV). Born in **Bến Tre** Province in the **Mekong Delta**, she became an active member of the **National Liberation Front** during the early 1960s and, in 1969, she was named foreign minister of the **Provisional Revolutionary Government** (PRG). She soon became well known as the chief representative of the PRG in the peace talks. In 1976, she was appointed minister of education in the SRV. She was promoted to the Central Committee of the **Vietnamese Communist Party** in 1982 and subsequently became the country's vice-president until her retirement in 2002. *See also* PARIS AGREEMENT.

NGUYỄN THỊ ĐỊNH (1920–1992). Prominent member of the **People's Liberation Armed Forces** (PLAF) and later an official in the **Vietnamese Communist Party** and the **Socialist Republic of Vietnam** (SRV). Born in a poor peasant household in **Bến Tre** in the heart of the **Mekong River Delta**, she became active in the revolutionary movement at the time of the **Nam Kỳ Uprising** in November

1940. Her husband died in prison on **Poulo Condore** after being arrested after the insurrection. She was one of the leaders in the "spontaneous uprising" that broke out at Bến Tre in January 1960 and was later named deputy commander of the PLAF. She recounted her experiences in an autobiographical account entitled *Không Có Đường Nào Khác* (*No Other Road to Take*). In December 1976, she was elected to the Central Committee of the Party.

NGUYỄN THỊ HINH. A prominent poetess of the 19th century. She is generally referred to as *Bà Huyện Thanh Quan*, meaning "the wife of the district official of Thanh Quan," which was located in Thái Bình province. Her literary abilities earned her a position as a palace tutor for imperial concubines and princesses under Emperor **Minh Mạng**.

NGUYỄN THỊ MINH KHAI (1910–1941). Prominent **woman** revolutionary and leading member of the **Indochinese Communist Party** (ICP) in colonial Vietnam. Born the daughter of a railway clerk in Nghệ, Nguyễn Thị Minh Khai attended school in the provincial capital of Vinh and there became involved in anticolonial activities. Joining the **Tân Việt Cách Mệnh Đảng**, she became a member of the ICP in the early 1930s and reportedly married **Hồ Chí Minh** while serving as his assistant in Hong Kong, though Party sources are silent on this. Her sister married another colleague, **Võ Nguyên Giáp.**

Minh Khai was arrested in 1931 by British police in Hong Kong; after release, she attended the Seventh Congress of the **Comintern**, held in Moscow in 1935. At some point, she apparently split from Hồ and married **Lê Hồng Phong**, then a leading member of the Party. Returning to Vietnam a few months later, she was named Secretary of the ICP Municipal Committee in **Saigon**. She was captured by **French** authorities in July 1940 and executed a year later. She is now considered one of the heroic figures of the Vietnamese revolution, but any intimate relationship with Hồ continues to be denied in official circles.

NGUYỄN TRÃI (1380–1442). Famous scholar and statesman in early 15th-century Vietnam. Nguyễn Trãi was the son of Nguyễn Phi

Khanh, a prominent scholar-official. Trãi passed his doctoral examination in 1400 at the age of 20 and entered into the **mandarinate**
under the new dynasty founded the same year by **Hồ Quý Ly**. When
Chinese forces occupied Vietnam in 1407, Trãi refused to collaborate with the new regime and was placed under house arrest in Thăng
Long (**Hanoi**). His father was sent to China, where he died. When
Lê Lợi raised the standard of revolt against the **Ming occupation** in
1418, Trãi escaped from confinement and became his closest advisor
and the primary strategist of his victory over the Chinese in 1428.

In his numerous writings, Trãi stressed the importance of political
struggle, "winning hearts and minds" ("it is better to conquer hearts
than citadels"), stratagems, protracted struggle, the use of negotiations to mislead the enemy, and the need to choose the right opportunity to strike for victory. Many of his military works, such as *Quân
Trung Từ Mệnh Tập* (*Writings Composed in the Army*), have become
classics of Vietnamese literature. *Bình Ngô Đại Cáo* (*Proclamation
on Defeating the Wu* [i.e., the Ming]), written after victory, became
a timeless assertion of Vietnamese independence.

After victory in 1428, Trãi served the new emperor as a high official in the bureaucracy. As a staunch **Confucianist**, he emphasized
the importance of such values as integrity, righteousness, and purity
of purpose. Such high moral standards frequently aroused resentment
and jealousy among his colleagues in the faction-rent bureaucracy
and even aroused the suspicion of Emperor Lê Thái Tổ (Lê Lợi) himself. He retired after the death of Thái Tổ and the accession of the
latter's son **Lê Thái Tông**. When the emperor died mysteriously in
1442 after a short visit to Trãi's retirement home, he was accused of
regicide and executed along with his entire family. Twenty years
later, his name was rehabilitated by Emperor **Lê Thánh Tông**.

Nguyễn Trãi is viewed in modern Vietnam as one of the truly great
figures in Vietnamese history. His ideas on formulating a strategy
to defeat the Ming were not only respected and admired, they were
consciously imitated by leading strategists of the **Vietnamese Communist Party** in their own struggle for national liberation and unification. Although not all of his writings have survived, he is
considered one of the foremost writers in Vietnamese history and a
pioneer in the use of *chữ nôm*, the written form of the spoken Vietnamese language. Above all, his integrity, his sense of loyalty and

human-heartedness, representing the best elements of Confucian humanism, have won him the respect and admiration of generations of Vietnamese. *See also* CÔNG THẦN; LÊ DYNASTY; LITERATURE.

NGUYỄN TRI PHƯƠNG (1799–1873). Vietnamese military commander under the **Nguyễn dynasty**. Born *Nguyễn Văn Chương* in Thừa Thiên, Nguyễn Tri Phuong was commander of Vietnamese troops in **Cochin China** at the time of the **French** attack on the area in 1859–1860. Although larger than that of its adversary, his army was defeated by the French in February 1861 at the Battle of **Chí Hoà** (Kỳ Hoà) near **Saigon**. After the victory, the French gradually extended their control over the neighboring provinces of Biên Hoà, Gia Định, and Định Tường. In November 1873, as military commander in **Tonkin**, Phương received an ultimatum from the French adventurer **Francis Garnier** demanding the surrender of **Hanoi**. When he refused, Garnier attacked the citadel. When the bastion was taken, Phuong starved himself to death.

NGUYỄN TRỌNG THUẬT (1883–1940). Vietnamese novelist in the early 20th century. Born in 1883 in a **scholar-gentry** family, Nguyễn Trọng Thuật received a Confucian education and remained all his life an admirer of **Confucianism** and **Buddhism**. A frequent contributor to **Phạm Quỳnh**'s literary journal *Nam Phong* and to the Buddhist journal *Đuốc Tuệ* (*Torch of Illumination*), he wrote a novel entitled *Quả Dưa Đỏ* (*The Watermelon*) in 1926 that achieved a widespread, if brief, popularity. Based loosely on Daniel Defoe's Robinson Crusoe, it was an escapist adventure novel exemplifying the traditional Confucian virtues of loyalty and self-sacrifice and was understandably praised by the colonial regime. In 1932, Nguyễn Trọng Thuật replaced Phạm Quỳnh as editor of *Nam Phong*. *See also* LITERATURE.

NGUYỄN TRƯỜNG TỘ (1828–1871). Reformist intellectual in 19th-century Vietnam. A native of Nghệ An, Nguyễn Trường Tộ was born in a **scholar-gentry** family that had converted to **Christianity**. Prohibited from taking the civil service **examinations** because of his religion, he spent time overseas and became an admirer of Western culture. On his return to Vietnam in 1861, he served the court in negotiations with the **French** after the latter's seizure of the southern provinces.

After the **Treaty of Saigon** in 1862, Tộ submitted several petitions to the court suggesting reforms that were needed to prevent the collapse of the empire. His suggestions ran the gamut from politics to education and economic reform, including the separation of powers, educational reform, the sending of students abroad, and the modernization of **agriculture** and **industry**. It was Tộ's belief that Vietnam needed to conciliate France to buy time for self-strengthening, and Emperor **Tự Đức** was initially receptive to at least the spirit of his proposals, but ultimately they were voted down by more conservative **mandarins**. Tộ died of illness in 1871.

NGUYỄN TƯỜNG TAM. *See* NHẤT LINH.

NGUYỄN VĂN BÌNH (1911–1995). Roman Catholic archbishop to Vietnam after reunification in 1975. Monsignor Bình had served as a bishop in South Vietnam for 40 years, first in Cần Thơ and later in **Saigon**. After reunification, he urged all Vietnamese Catholics to give their loyalty to the new regime in **Hanoi** and cooperated in the creation of a progovernment Solidarity Committee of Patriotic Vietnamese Catholics. *See also* CHRISTIANITY; RELIGION.

NGUYỄN VĂN CAO (also known as *Văn Cao*) (1922–1995). Vietnamese composer who authored the national anthem of the **Democratic Republic of Vietnam** (DRV). Entitled *Tiến Quân Ca* (*Marching Forward*) and composed in 1944, it was later selected as the national anthem. Van Cao was also the author of a number of other songs during his long career. *See also* MUSIC.

NGUYỄN VĂN CỪ (1912–1941). General secretary of the **Indochinese Communist Party** (ICP) in the late 1930s. A native of Bắc Ninh, Nguyễn Văn Cừ (also known by his pseudonym of *Tri Cương*) joined the revolutionary movement in the late 1920s. After a period in prison on **Poulo Condore**, he was released and took part in united front activities in **Tonkin**. Elected to the ICP Central Committee, he became general secretary of the Party in March 1938. In November

1939, shortly after the colonial government had cracked down on ICP activities because of the signing of the Nazi–Soviet Pact, Cừ convened a meeting of the Central Committee near **Saigon**. The session decided to initiate preparations for a general uprising to seize power from the **French**. The following January, however, he was arrested and condemned to death. He was executed in 1941. *See also* NAM KỲ UPRISING.

NGUYỄN VĂN HUYÊN (1908–1975). A prominent scholar and **education** official in the **Democratic Republic of Vietnam** (DRV). Nguyễn Văn Huyên was trained by the **École Française d'Extrême-Orient** during the colonial period and published several important works of anthropology and ethnology. After the **August Revolution**, he served as Education Minister for the new DRV regime and was active in governmental affairs and international educational exchange.

NGUYỄN VĂN LINH (1915–1998) (real name *Nguyễn Văn Cực*). Former general secretary of the **Vietnamese Communist Party** (VCP). Born near Hanoi, Nguyễn Van Linh was brought up in southern Vietnam, where he joined the revolutionary movement as an adolescent and was arrested for political activities in 1930. Released from prison in 1936, he took part in **Indochinese Communist Party** operations in Hải Phòng and then **Cochin China**. He was rearrested in 1941 and spent the war years in **Poulo Condore** prison. After World War II, Linh served under **Lê Duẩn** in the Party apparatus in the South (under the pseudonym *Mười Cực*) and was director of the **Central Office for South Vietnam** (COSVN) from 1961 until his replacement by General **Nguyễn Chí Thanh** in 1964. He remained as deputy to Thanh and later to Thanh's successor **Phạm Hùng** until the end of the war.

In 1976, Linh was raised to Politburo rank and headed the Party Committee for Hồ Chí Minh City (the new name for **Saigon**). In 1978, he was dismissed, reportedly because of his failure to carry out the Party's plans for socialist transformation in the South. At the Fifth National Congress of the Party, held in March 1982, he lost his Politburo seat, but shortly thereafter he returned as Party chief in Hồ Chí Minh City and was quietly reinstated to the Politburo in 1985.

At the Sixth National Party Congress in December 1986, Linh was named general secretary to replace the aging **Trường Chinh**. As general secretary, he pushed reforms to stimulate the stagnant Vietnamese **economy** and is generally credited with having overseen the launching of *đổi mới* (renovation). Beginning in May 1987, he published a series of articles entitled "To Be Done Immediately" in the Party newspaper *Nhân Dân* with his initials as the byline. Linh retired from his position in 1991, after a five-year term that had seen significant economic reform but considerably less relaxation of political control than had been anticipated at the beginning of his tenure.

NGUYỄN VĂN SÂM (?–1947). Moderate political figure in colonial Vietnam. A **journalist** and editor of the Vietnamese-language newspaper *Đuốc Nhà Nam* [*Torch of the South*], Nguyễn Văn Sâm became active in politics with the moderate reformist **Constitutionalist Party**. In 1936, he took part in activities to promote an **Indochinese Congress** movement to present a list of demands to the **Popular Front** government in **France**. In August 1945, he was named imperial delegate for **Cochin China** shortly before the **Japanese** surrender and the abdication of Emperor **Bảo Đại**. After World War II, Sâm became active in the movement to persuade Bảo Đại to return to Vietnam as chief of state in an Associated State in the **French Union**. He was assassinated, apparently by the **Việt Minh**, in October 1947. *See also* BẢO ĐẠI SOLUTION.

NGUYỄN VĂN TÂM (1895–?). Prime minister of the **State of Vietnam** from June 1952 until December 1953. A native of Tây Ninh, Tâm became a **French** citizen and served in several official positions within the colonial administration before and after World War II. As a police official, he became noted for his vigorous suppression of the **Nam Kỳ Uprising** in November 1940, which earned him the sobriquet "the tiger of Cay Lai." After the formation of the State of Vietnam, Tâm served under Prime Minister **Trần Văn Hữu** as minister of the interior and, after November 1951, as governor of **Tonkin**. He succeeded Hữu as prime minister in the summer of 1952. During his stay in office, he attempted to promote **land reform** and a democratization of the political process, but widespread official **corruption** undermined such efforts and led to his severe defeat in national elections held in January 1953. Tâm belatedly attempted to win nationalist support by demanding increased autonomy within the **French Union** but won little support from either patriotic elements or the French and was asked to resign from office in December. *See also* BẢO ĐẠI SOLUTION.

NGUYỄN VĂN TẠO (1908–1970). Prominent member of the **Indochinese Communist Party** (ICP) and official in the **Democratic Republic of Vietnam** (DRV). Born in **Cochin China** in 1908, Nguyễn Văn Tạo joined the revolutionary movement while a student at the Lýcée Chasseloup-Laubat in **Saigon**, where he helped arrange student demonstrations at the time of the funeral of the patriotic intellectual **Phan Chu Trinh**. Expelled from school, he went to **France** and joined the French Communist Party (PCF). In 1928, he attended the Sixth Congress of the **Comintern** as a representative of the PCF and spoke before a session of the congress on conditions in **Indochina**. Deported from France in 1931, he returned to Indochina and was involved in ICP activities in Saigon. Arrested in 1939, he was released in 1945 and took part in the **August Revolution**. Later, he was elected to the **National Assembly** and served as minister of labor of the DRV.

NGUYỄN VĂN THÀNH (1757–1817). A powerful military officer and **mandarin** under the **Nguyễn dynasty**. As a young man, he followed his father into the service of Nguyễn Ánh (the future Emperor **Gia Long**) in his fight against the **Tây Sơn**. After the Nguyễn victory and the founding of a new imperial dynasty, Thành was made governor of the northern provinces, which he ruled as a sort of autonomous warlord from **Hanoi**; his counterpart for the **Mekong Delta** region was **Lê Văn Duyệt**. Thành participated in the drafting of the new legal code known as the *Gia Long Code*. His power and influence created enemies, and they seized on some playful poetry written by his son as evidence of an alleged plot against the emperor. Gia Long was persuaded that his former companion-in-arms had now turned rebel and beheaded him, while his son was forced to commit suicide. The position of Thành and Duyệt as regional overlords was a phenomenon of Gia Long's reign, which was eliminated by the centralization that took place under his son **Minh Mạng**.

NGUYỄN VĂN THIỆU (1923–2001). President of the **Republic of Vietnam** from 1967–1975. Born to a family of farmers and fishermen in Ninh Thuận, Nguyễn Van Thiệu served briefly with the **Việt Minh** forces after World War II but later left the revolutionary movement and joined the **Vietnamese National Army**, organized by the **French** to serve as the official armed forces of the Associated **State of Vietnam**. After service as a combat officer during the **Franco–Việt Minh War**, Thiệu was named superintendent of the National Military Academy in 1956 and later assumed command of the Fifth Division of the **Army of the Republic of Vietnam** (ARVN).

After the overthrow of the regime of President **Ngô Đình Diệm** in November 1963, Thiệu, now a general, became involved in politics. In June 1965, he was a member of the "Young Turk" movement, led by **Nguyễn Khánh**, that overthrew the civilian government in Saigon and was named chairman of the military-dominated National Leadership Committee. During the next several months, he shared power with General **Nguyễn Cao Kỳ**, a fellow Young Turk. In September 1967, he was elected president under a new **constitution**; Kỳ served as his vice-president. During the next four years, he attempted with only moderate success to bring political stability to South Vietnam and progress in the war against revolutionary forces. He did issue a **land reform** decree entitled "land to the tiller" that severely reduced the inequality of landholdings that had characterized **agriculture** in South Vietnam since the colonial period.

In 1971, Thiệu was reelected president, for a second four-year term. Technically, he was unopposed, although it was widely believed that other potential candidates were persuaded not to run by the **United States** Mission in **Saigon**. During his second term, he unsuccessfully resisted the American decision to sign the **Paris Agreement** in January 1973. President Richard M. Nixon promised to provide adequate military assistance to provide for the defense of South Vietnam, but when the **Democratic Republic of Vietnam** (DRV) launched a major military offensive against the South in early 1975, Nixon's successor, Gerald Ford, was unable to persuade the U.S. Congress to increase aid to the Saigon regime. After several serious military reverses, Thiệu decided to abandon the entire northern half of the country to revolutionary forces. The decision led to panic, and in late April, a few days before North Vietnamese entered Saigon in triumph, Thiệu left South Vietnam for exile. Angry at the American government, he spent many years in Great Britain, but eventually moved to the U. S., where he died. *See also* HỒ CHÍ MINH CAMPAIGN.

NGUYỄN VĂN THINH (1884–1946). Moderate political figure and president of the abortive **Republic of Cochin China** in 1946. A medical doctor by profession, Nguyễn Van Thinh joined the **Constitutionalist Party** in 1926 and then founded his own party, the Đảng Dân Chủ (Democratic Party), in 1937. After World War II, he supported the **French**-sponsored movement for Cochinchinese autonomy and was named the president of the new "republic" in 1946. Discouraged at his failure to achieve credibility for his government, he committed suicide in November 1946.

NGUYỄN VĂN TƯỜNG (1824–1886). A powerful **mandarin** under the **Nguyễn dynasty**. Nguyễn Văn Tường is known mainly for his role in the political turmoil that followed the death of Emperor **Tự Đức** in 1883, when Tường and **Tôn Thất Thuyết** enthroned and killed a succession of rulers. He initially worked with Thuyết to launch the **Cần Vương** rebellion in support of the young Emperor **Hàm Nghi**, but soon broke with the movement and returned to **French**-occupied **Huế** with other members of the royal family who chose safety over resistance. However, the French did not enlist him as a collaborator, exiling him instead to Tahiti, where he died shortly afterward.

NGUYỄN VĂN VĨNH (1882–1936). Journalist and reformist political figure in colonial Vietnam. Born in Hà Đông in 1882, Nguyễn Văn Vĩnh attended interpreter's school in Hanoi and entered the colonial administration, where he served in Lao Cái, **Hải Phòng**, Bắc Ninh, and **Hanoi**. Becoming a journalist, he founded *Đông Dương Tạp chí* (*Revue Indochinoise*) in 1913. Through its pages, he attempted to popularize Western ideas, institutions, and customs.

Vĩnh was a tremendous admirer of France and things French and did everything he could to promote them among his countrymen, including translating Western literature and making deprecating remarks about what he saw as the more backward and undesirable aspects of his own culture. He had little respect for the Vietnamese **monarchy** and **mandarinate** that had been maintained under the colonial **protectorate**, and he attacked these traditional institutions in a bitter public debate with the royalist **Phạm Quỳnh**. During the final years of his life, he published two newspapers in Hanoi—*Annam Nouveau* and *Trung Bắc Tân Văn* (*Annam-Tonkin News*)—which were a forum for his political views.

NGUYỄN VĂN XUÂN. Prime minister in the provisional government established by the French in 1948. Educated in **France**, Nguyễn Văn Xuân became a French citizen and a career officer in the French Army. After World War II, he became involved in the separatist movement in **Cochin China** and was named vice-president and minister of national defense in the **Republic of Cochin China** government under Doctor **Nguyễn Văn Thinh**. He became head of the government, which he renamed the *Provisional Government of South Vietnam*, in October 1947. His efforts to win nationalist support foundered on his reputation as a Cochinchinese separatist. After failing to achieve significant concessions from the French, he resigned as president after the return of **Bảo Đại** in June of 1949. After the **Geneva Conference** of 1954, Xuân and other pro-French politicians made an unsuccessful attempt to prevent the ascendance of **Ngô Đình Diệm** to power in South Vietnam. *See also* BẢO ĐẠI SOLUTION.

NGUYỄN XUÂN 'N (1825–1889). Anti-French resistance leader in late 19th-century Vietnam. A poet and a scholar-official from Nghệ An, Nguyễn Xuân ôn resigned from the bureaucracy to respond to Emperor **Hàm Nghi**'s "**Cần Vương**" appeal in July 1885 and commanded guerrilla forces in central Vietnam until his capture in 1887. He died in prison in 1889.

NHÂN DÂN (*The People*). The official newspaper of the **Vietnamese Communist Party**. *Nhân Dân* began publication after the Party leadership returned to **Hanoi** in October 1954 at the end of the **Franco-Việt Minh War** and has continued uninterrupted to the present. Articles in *Nhân Dân* are considered authoritative because of the newspaper's direct link with the Party. *See also* JOURNALISM.

NHÂN VĂN GIAI PHẨM. The names of two literary publications (meaning "Humanities" and "Masterpieces" respectively) from the **Democratic Republic of Vietnam** (DRV), used as shorthand to refer to an outbreak of **dissidence** in the 1950s. During the early years after the end of **French** rule, there was considerable dissatisfaction among DRV intellectuals and artists about the Party's heavy-handed political line on their work. These grievances were manifested in a series of publications in 1956–1957, spearheaded by **Phan Khôi** and other literary and artistic figures. The publications criticized the Party line on arts and **literature**, provoking considerable debate before they were shut down and many of their contributors arrested. The *Nhân Văn Giai Phẩm* affair, which is often compared to the contemporary "Hundred Flowers" movement in **China**, was the last serious expression of dissent in socialist Vietnam for several decades. Only with *đổi mới* have writers and artists begun once again to push the boundaries of what is accepted by the Party.

NHẤT HẠNH, THÍCH (1926–   ). A prominent monk and peace activist. Born *Nguyễn Xuân Bảo*, he became involved in **Buddhist** opposition to the **Ngô Đình Diệm** regime in the **Republic of Vietnam** in the 1960s. (*Nhất Hạnh* is the name he has used since ordination, while *Thích* is a title for Vietnamese monks based on the Buddha's name.) However, he found himself at odds with his fellow monks who were involved in demonstrations and violent confrontations with the government and established his own retreat center to pursue a more peaceful course of action. He was teaching in the **United States** when Diệm was overthrown in November 1963 and then returned to South Vietnam. Thích Nhất Hạnh promoted education and social activism among Buddhist youth through his ideas of "Engaged Buddhism." In 1967, he left for an overseas trip to promote peace in his country, efforts for which he was branded a traitor by the military regime in **Saigon**. He has remained in exile ever since and has established several meditation centers in the West, where he has a wide network of supporters. Thích Nhất Hạnh visited his homeland for the first time in January 2005. *See also* DISSIDENTS.

NHẤT LINH (1906–1963) (Nguyễn Tường Tam). Well-known novelist and founder of the Self-Reliance Literary Group (**Tự Lực Văn**

Đoàn) in colonial Vietnam. Born Nguyễn Tường Tam in 1906, Nhất Linh studied painting in Hanoi and science in Paris. Returning to Vietnam in 1930, with his younger brother Nguyễn Tường Long (**Hoàng Đạo**), he founded the Self-Reliance Literary Group, a collection of writers anxious to Westernize Vietnamese literature.

During the next few years, he wrote a number of celebrated novels, including *Đôi Bạn* (*Friends*), *Đoạn Tuyệt* (*Rupture*), and *Lạnh Lùng* (*Coldness*). Romantic in style, they reflected an implicit mood of rebellion and individualism against the accumulated evils in modern Vietnamese society. In the late 1930s Nhất Linh became actively involved in politics, joining the Vietnamese Nationalist Party (**Việt Nam Quốc Dân Đảng**) and spending World War II in exile in **China**. After the war, he served briefly as minister of foreign affairs in the **Democratic Republic of Vietnam**. In the spring of 1946, however, he left suddenly for China and joined the anti-Communist national United Front set up in Hong Kong. He later withdrew from the Front to protest against what he considered the pro-French attitudes of other members of the organization. He moved to South Vietnam after the **Geneva Conference** in 1954. Arrested by the **Ngô Đình Diệm** regime in 1960, he committed suicide in 1963, reportedly in protest against Diệm's policies. *See also* LITERATURE.

NHẬT NAM. Administrative term used to refer to one of several provinces in occupied Vietnam during the **Chinese period**. The term referred to an area along the **South China Sea** coast comprising the modern-day provinces of Nghệ An and Hà Tĩnh. During the early centuries of Chinese rule, the area was a relatively peripheral frontier region and the site of a number of rebellions. Chinese control of this southernmost region was always problematic; by the end of the fifth century, it had been lost to the emerging polity of **Linyi**.

NỘI CÁC (**Grand Secretariat**). Influential administrative body in 19th-century Vietnam. Known in English as the *Grand Secretariat*, the *Nội Các* (in Chinese, *Neige*) was established in 1829 and, like much of the imperial administration under the **Nguyễn dynasty**, was based on the **Chinese** model. It functioned as an intermediary between the emperor and the ministers of the Six Boards (*Lục Bộ*), and was composed of four "Grand Secretaries," a number of lesser officials, and six sections comprising Finances, Interior, Justice, Rites, War, and Public Works. The term was subsequently used for "Cabinet" in some Vietnamese governments.

NOLTING, FREDERICK E. (1911–1989). Career foreign service officer and **United States** ambassador to the **Republic of Vietnam** (RVN) during the John F. Kennedy administration. In January 1961, while he was posted in Europe as U.S. representative to the North Atlantic Treaty Organization headquarters, Kennedy appointed him ambassador to **Saigon** to replace Eldridge Durbrow, whose usefulness as U.S. envoy had been damaged by his poor relations with President **Ngô Đình Diệm**. Nolting avidly supported Diệm during his tour in Saigon, and vocally defended him when a debate broke out in Washington on whether to support a coup by South Vietnamese military officers in the summer of 1963. He was replaced by **Henry Cabot Lodge** in July, presumably because the White House felt that he was not the appropriate vehicle to "get tough with Diệm."

NÔNG ĐỨC MẠNH (1940–). General secretary of the **Vietnamese Communist Party**. Nông Đức Mạnh, an ethnic **Tày** from Bắc Can province, was trained in forestry in the **Union of Soviet Socialist Republics** and then served in various professional capacities until he was assigned to provincial administrative and Party posts in the 1980s. He became a member of the Party Central Committee in 1986 and was appointed chairman of the **National Assembly** in 1992, presiding over the legislature's transition to a more active role after years of rubber stamping. In 1998, he became a member of the Party Politburo and was elected general secretary at the 9th Party Congress in 2001, holding the highest-ranking position ever achieved by an ethnic minority. His rise to power represents the emergence of a new generation of Vietnamese leaders who did not participate in the Revolution against the **French**, and his designation to replace **Lê Khả Phiêu** as general secretary was perceived as a victory for reformist elements within the Party. *See also* PHAN VĂN KHẢI; TRẦN ĐỨC LƯƠNG.

NORTH VIETNAMESE ARMY (NVA). *See* PEOPLE'S ARMY OF VIETNAM.

NỮ GIỚI CHUNG (**Women's Bell**). A short-lived newspaper published in 1918, the first such publication specifically targeting **woman** readers. Edited by **Sương Nguyệt Anh**, a prominent poetess, *Nữ Giới Chung* aimed to acquire a female readership throughout colonial Vietnam. However, the number of women who had been taught to read the Romanized *quốc ngữ* script in which the paper was published was still quite small, and the publication failed to get off the ground. *See also* JOURNALISM.

NÚI ĐỌ CULTURE. Prehistoric site located in the northern province of Thanh Hoá, discovered by Vietnamese **archeologists** in November 1960. Located on a slight elevation about 15 meters (50 feet) above surrounding rice fields, the Núi Đọ find was a clear indication of a Paleolithic culture in mainland Southeast Asia, thus indicating that prehistoric humans inhabited this area as early as 500,000 years ago. Artifacts found at the site included chipped cutters and scrapers and hand axes. *See also* HOÀ BÌNH CULTURE; SƠN VI CULTURE.

NÙNG. A **highland minority** group related to the **Tày**, who live in the northeastern provinces along the **Chinese** border. The ancestors of the Nùng lived in southern China but migrated to Vietnam after the defeat of a rebellion by their people under the Song dynasty in the 11th century. The Nùng speak a Tai language and practice wet-rice **agriculture**. Like the Tày, they have been more heavily influenced by Vietnamese culture than the **Thái** in the northwestern region. During the Vietnamese Revolution, many Nùng joined the **Việt Minh** movement, and several became leading members of the Communist Party. At the same time, however, large numbers fled to South Vietnam after the partition at the **Geneva Conference** in 1954 and resettled in the **Central Highlands**. Today, approximately 600,000 Nùng live in the **Socialist Republic of Vietnam** (SRV).

– O –

ÓC EO. An ancient seaport on the western coast of the **Cà Mau** Peninsula in the **Mekong Delta**. During the early Common Era, ó Eo was located on the trade route between East Asia and the Indian Ocean that crossed southern **Indochina** to the Isthmus of Kra. Archeologists have found Indian and Roman coins at the site, which is the most important such site in the Delta. The port eventually declined when a new route developed farther to the south through the Straits of Malacca. Ó Eo was most probably associated with what is broadly known as *pre-Angkorean Cambodia*; although it was long believed to have been part of a powerful kingdom called *Funan*, more likely it was linked to one of several smaller power centers.

OIL. Since the reunification of the country in 1976, the **Socialist Republic of Vietnam** (SRV) has placed considerable emphasis on the development of oil production as a source of domestic energy and export earnings. In recent years, substantial oil reserves have been discovered off the southern coast in the **South China Sea** (and in the **Tonkin Gulf** in 2004), and the government in **Hanoi** has signed contracts with a number of foreign oil firms to engage in extraction and further exploration. Anxious to obtain a larger share of the profits of rising oil exports, the Vietnamese government has begun to construct the infrastructure and facilities necessary to support an oil industry. For 2004, the estimated output of oil was 130 million barrels; total offshore reserves are currently calculated at between 6.5 and 8.5 billion barrels.

A major obstacle is the ongoing territorial disputes over the **Paracel** and **Spratly** Islands and the surrounding waters, as well as the Tonkin Gulf, which means that any contract signed by the Vietnamese government for the exploration or exploitation of oil reserves in the contested areas is automatically challenged by one or more of its neighbors. Since the mid-1990s, Hanoi has been signing contracts with various foreign companies to go ahead with exploration and drilling in the South China Sea. A large refinery is being completed at Dung Quat in Quảng Ngãi and a second one is planned for Thanh Hoá province. The Dung Quất project has been plagued with funding and feasibility issues that have added to the challenges facing Vietnam in attempting to develop its petroleum industry. *See also* ENERGY RESOURCES; FOREIGN INVESTMENT; TRADE.

ONE-PILLAR PAGODA (*Chùa Một Cột*). A famous pagoda set on a single pillar in the city of **Hanoi**. Said to have been built in the 11th century by Emperor **Lý Thái Tông**, it was originally part of a larger **Buddhist** complex called the Diên Hựu (Prolonging Life) Temple. According to popular belief, Thái Tông dreamed of a Bodhisattva seated on a lotus flower who invited him to join him in conversation. To commemorate the dream, the emperor built the pagoda on the model of a lotus flower. Until its destruction, the temple was used by the **Lý dynasty** rulers to worship the Buddha. The pagoda itself was destroyed by the **French** in 1954 and has been rebuilt by the current government. It is one of the symbols of Hanoi. *See also* ARCHITEC-TURE.

OPERATION ATTLEBORO. *See* ZONE C.

OPERATION CEDAR FALLS. *See* IRON TRIANGLE.

OVERSEAS CHINESE (*Hoa Kiều*). Ethnic Chinese residing in Vietnam. Chinese have been immigrating to Vietnam for centuries; large groups, for example, resettled there after the fall of the Ming dynasty in **China** in the 17th century. Most Chinese immigrants or their descendents became assimilated into Vietnamese society over time, and the term *Hoa Kiều* (now just 'Hoa') has been used for those that are still considered as a separate, unassimilated ethnic group. Most overseas Chinese historically went into trade or manufacturing, although some became miners, longshoremen, or fishermen.

For centuries, the more recent Chinese immigrants who maintained their own language and customs were viewed as a distinct group in Vietnamese society, separate from the more assimilated **Minh Hương**. The **Nguyễn dynasty** dealt with them as a separate social unit, placing them in so-called "congregations" (*bang*) according to their dialect group, with their own leaders, schools, and other social institutions. This practice was retained under **French** colonial rule. After independence in 1954, the governments of both North and South Vietnam attempted to integrate the overseas Chinese into the broader community. In the **Democratic Republic of Vietnam** (DRV), they were permitted to retain their own customs, schools, and nationality, but by agreement with the People's Republic of China, were encouraged voluntarily to seek Vietnamese citizenship. In the **Republic of Vietnam**, they were similarly permitted to remain legally distinct, but the regime of **Ngô Đình Diệm** pressured them to become citizens. In both societies, most were in commerce and manufacturing. Overseas Chinese interests reportedly controlled nearly 90 percent of the **banking** and import–export trade in the South Vietnamese capital of **Saigon**.

After 1975, the **Socialist Republic of Vietnam** (SRV) viewed the overseas Chinese with some suspicion because of their cultural and political ties with China and their **capitalist** habits. In 1978, when the **Hanoi** regime announced the nationalization of all property above the family level, thousands of ethnic Chinese crossed the northern border on foot or fled as **boat people** to other countries in the region, fearing that the government was attempting to eliminate them. Government policy toward these Chinese communities became a serious source of tension between Hanoi and Beijing and one of the factors leading to the Chinese invasion of 1979.

For those remaining in Vietnam (approximately one million), the problem of assimilation into Vietnamese society remains unresolved. In recent years, however, improved relations with China as well as a drastic change in official attitudes toward business have meant that the perception of the Hoa community is more favorable, and their historical role in Vietnam's **economic** development has been recognized. The only remaining large concentration of overseas Chinese is in Hồ Chí Minh City, where they are concentrated in the area of **Chợ Lớn**.

OVERSEAS DEVELOPMENT ASSISTANCE (ODA). Vietnam's decision to open up its **economy** and implement profound structural reforms beginning in the mid-1980s, combined with the fall of socialist regimes in the **Union of Soviet Socialist Republics** and elsewhere in Eastern Europe, meant that foreign aid from a wide variety of sources became increasingly crucial for the country's economy. During the early years of the *đổi mới* (renovation) period, however, much of the potential flow of ODA was blocked by the trade embargo enforced by the **United States** and other countries, and even with the 1991 normalization of relations with **China** (once an important source of aid), the **Socialist Republic of Vietnam** (SRV) still faced a significant shortage of donors. With the progressive dismantling of the embargo, however (the last barriers came down in 1994), Vietnam was on track to become a major recipient of development assistance.

ODA grew quickly; disbursements rose from just over $200 million in 1993 to a peak of $1.6 billion in 2000 and then dropped slightly over the next few years. **Japan** has become the largest single donor, followed by the World Bank and the Asian Development Bank. The SRV has relied heavily on assistance from these multilateral donors, as well as the International Monetary Fund (IMF), though aid from the latter was suspended for several years in the 1990s because of its dissatisfaction over the slow pace of Vietnamese reforms. Generally speaking, most donors are now relatively satisfied with the government's efforts at economic restructuring, though foot-dragging in reforms of the state sector (notably **equitization** of **state-owned enterprises**) is a constant complaint. The Vietnamese government has, at times, been irritated by the conditionality of various kinds that comes attached to multilateral aid (as well as the criticism of **human rights** and other issues put forth by some donors), and it is likely that some of the remaining old guard among the **Vietnamese Communist Party** leadership have mixed feelings about accepting handouts from what they still privately view as the **capitalist** world. However, the government is pragmatic enough to recognize that the world has changed since the days when it could get by almost completely on aid from "fraternal socialist" allies, and it has made considerable progress in its cooperation with donors on all sides. On certain issues, it is willing to sacrifice aid for the sake of sovereignty, however, as witnessed by its refusal to accept IMF demands for an independent audit of its foreign exchange reserves, which led to another cutoff in IMF lending in April 2004. *See also* FOREIGN RELATIONS.

OVERSEAS VIETNAMESE (*Việt Kiều*). Although there were apparently small communities of Vietnamese **Christians** in Siam as early as the 17th century, Vietnamese did not begin to settle outside their country in significant numbers until the colonial period. Some were deported to other parts of the **French** empire as convicts or labor conscripts; many more emigrated to **Cambodia** and **Laos**, where the common administrative framework of colonial **Indochina** enabled them to resettle with few obstacles. As traders and merchants, they became a powerful economic force in these two neighbors, and they came to form a large proportion of the civil service bureaucracy there as well. A number of revolutionaries and other exiles settled in northeastern Siam. Meanwhile, Vietnamese traveled to France in large numbers as soldiers, laborers, and students.

With the rise of the **Indochinese Communist Party** (ICP) in the 1930s, Vietnamese Communists in Siam, Cambodia, and Laos played a crucial role in the propagation of revolutionary doctrine throughout Indochina. Indeed, during the early years of ICP activities in Cambodia and Laos, the movement was comprised almost exclusively of ethnic Vietnamese. After the **August Revolution** of 1945, supporters of **Hồ Chí Minh** and the **Democratic Republic of Vietnam** (DRV) formed a solid core of the Vietnamese community in France, though nationalists of other political colorings moved there as well.

France was home to the largest overseas Vietnamese community until 1975, when the massive outpouring of refugees after the fall of the **Republic of Vietnam** sent thousands of people to countries like the **United States**, Canada, Australia, and West Germany. France took in large numbers of refugees as well, and the strong anti-Communist sentiments of these new arrivals created tensions and divisions with some of those who had immigrated earlier but remained sympathetic to Hồ and the DRV (now the **Socialist Republic of Vietnam**). In other Western countries, by contrast, the overseas Vietnamese communities were dominated by the anti-Communist refugees, and those who held other views rarely dared to express them.

At present, the overseas Vietnamese number more than a million and constitute large, well-established communities in many countries. Many of them have returned to Vietnam for visits or to do business, and their relationship with the **Hanoi** government remains ambiguous. On the one hand, they are publicly welcomed and encouraged to maintain close ties with their "homeland" and to invest their capital there. On the other, they are often viewed with suspicion as potentially subversive because there are anti-Communist activists in every large overseas Vietnamese community around the world. They are often envied and resented by others in Vietnam for their prosperity and for the opportunities they enjoyed by leaving the country. In terms of their psychological and legal status, they occupy a "grey area" somewhere between full-fledged Vietnamese citizens and foreigners born and raised overseas. Many foreign companies have hired overseas Vietnamese to oversee their operations in Vietnam, but with mixed results because the returnees might not easily fit back into life there after many years abroad.

Since 1990, the ranks of the overseas Vietnamese have been swelled by the thousands of people who were studying or working in the **Union of Soviet Socialist Republics** and other East European countries when the socialist bloc fell and have elected to stay there long-term. Although they are in some respects "subversive" for having witnessed first-hand the demise of socialism in Vietnam's former allies, they are generally of less concern to the government than those who fled to **capitalist** countries. Like their compatriots elsewhere in the world, these Vietnamese also represent an important source of foreign exchange for the country through the sizable remittances they send home to their relatives, which topped $3 billion in 2004. *See also* BOAT PEOPLE.

– P –

PALLU, FRANÇOIS (1626–1684). Apostolic delegate appointed by the Vatican in 1658 to oversee Catholic missionary activities in the northern Vietnamese kingdom known to the West as *Tonkin*. Although he never actually went to Vietnam, Pallu was the driving force behind the establishment of the **Société des Missions Étrangères** (Society of Foreign Missions), which played a crucial role in the history of Vietnamese Catholicism. Together with Bishop Pierre Lambert de la Motte, who was his counterpart for **Cochin China** (the southern kingdom), he laid the foundations for the long-term French mission presence among the Vietnamese. Pallu solicited the support of French commercial interests in the missionary effort to promote a French presence in mainland Southeast Asia. Because of opposition to **Christianity** by Vietnamese officials, the Asian headquarters of the society and a seminary were established in Siam, where it was also active in the missionary effort. Later, Pallu spent time in the Philippines, where he was arrested by the Spanish. He returned to

Siam and then went to **China**, where he died. *See also* RHODES, ALEXANDER DE.

PARACEL ISLANDS (*Quần Đảo Hoàng Sa*). A cluster of small islands in the **South China Sea**. Located about 300 kilometers (190 miles) east of the central Vietnamese coast, the islands were only sporadically occupied by traders and pirates from several neighboring nations during the traditional period. During the colonial era, the **French** claimed the islands, and a small enterprise to extract guano (used in the manufacture of phosphate fertilizer) was established there. In 1951, several of the islands were seized by the People's Republic of **China**, which claimed that they had been historically Chinese. In the 1960s, a few islands were occupied by the **Republic of Vietnam**, but the South Vietnamese were driven out by Chinese forces in 1974. Spokesmen for the **Democratic Republic of Vietnam** (DRV) protested the action, claiming that the islands had been Vietnamese since traditional times. The dispute is one of several territorial issues currently dividing China and Vietnam. The islands themselves have relatively little intrinsic importance, but their owner can state a claim to control over the surrounding territorial seas, reported to hold extensive **oil** reserves. *See also* SPRATLY ISLANDS.

PARIA, LE (The Pariah). Newspaper founded by **Hồ Chí Minh** in Paris in early 1920s. *Le Paria* was designed to focus on the evils of the **French** colonial system in Asia and Africa and to promote interest in social revolution; the first issue appeared in April 1922. For several months, Hồ (then known as *Nguyễn Ái Quốc*) not only served as editor but also wrote many of the articles and distributed the newspaper on the streets. After Hồ's departure for Moscow in 1923, *Le Paria* declined in popularity, but survived through 37 issues until 1926. The publication of this newspaper demonstrated Hồ's ability to look at his country's problems in the wider context of the worldwide anticolonial struggle. *See also* JOURNALISM.

PARIS AGREEMENT. Treaty signed by the **Democratic Republic of Vietnam** (DRV), the **Republic of Vietnam** (RVN), the **Provisional Revolutionary Government** of South Vietnam (PRG), and the **United States** on 27 January 1973. The agreement, reached after four years of negotiations, which began in late 1968, brought the Vietnam War temporarily to an end. It called for the removal of U.S. troops from South Vietnam and a cease-fire in place by the armed forces of the RVN and the PRG. It made no reference to the presence of South Vietnam of nearly 200,000 troops of the **People's Army of Vietnam (PAVN)**, which had infiltrated from the DRV.

The Paris Agreement also made provisions for a political settlement of the war. The PRG and the RVN were instructed to set up a so-called **National Council of Reconciliation and Concord** (NCRC) to organize "free and democratic general elections" to elect a new government in South Vietnam. In the meantime, the existing government of **Nguyễn Văn Thiệu** remained in office in **Saigon**. The Agreement did not end the war, only the direct involvement of U.S. troops. Arrangements for the formation of the NCRC broke down, and clashes between forces of the Saigon regime and the PRG took place throughout the country. In early 1975, North Vietnamese forces launched the **Hồ Chí Minh Campaign** against the South, leading to the seizure of Saigon by PAVN units on 30 April 1975.

PASQUIER, PIERRE (1877–1934). Governor-general of French **Indochina** from 1928–1934. A graduate of the Colonial School in Paris, he was appointed governor-general of Indochina in 1928 after extended service in the colony. Although he was knowledgeable about Vietnamese affairs and author of a popular history of Vietnam in French, his efforts to improve conditions in Indochina were hindered both by resistance from **French** commercial interests and by Vietnamese radicals, whose activities culminated in the **Yên Bái Mutiny** and the **Nghệ Tĩnh** Revolt in 1930. Pasquier was influential in the efforts to promote the young emperor **Bảo Đại** as a modern ruler who blended Eastern and Western values. His death in a plane crash in January 1934 is almost certainly one of the reasons why Bảo Đại's role began to decline.

PATENÔTRE TREATY. Treaty signed between **France** and the Vietnamese Empire in June 1884. It replaced the **Harmand Treaty** negotiated by François Harmand in August 1883. Like its predecessor, it granted France a **protectorate** with extensive rights to represent Vietnam in foreign affairs and oversee internal policy. (The main difference between the two versions was that the Harmand document transferred the southern part of the royal empire to direct French rule in **Cochin China**). The emperor remained the legitimate ruler but with sharply reduced power. The new agreement also provided France with increased authority in northern Vietnam, henceforth to be known as *Tonkin*. It was negotiated by the Vietnamese court official **Nguyễn Văn Tường**, regent during the minority of Emperor **Kiến Phúc**, and the French diplomat Jules Patenôtre.

The Patenôtre Treaty became both the legal basis for French rule in **Annam** and Tonkin and the symbol for the protectorate. Many French actions, such as insisting that they had the right to approve the selection of a new emperor, violated both the letter and the spirit of the treaty (and thus of the protectorate as a system of government). Royalists, such as **Phạm Quỳnh** in the 1920s and 1930s, called for a stricter adherence to the treaty, which would have shifted the balance of power somewhat in favor of the **monarchy** and the **mandarinate**. The French refusal to make any concessions in this respect was one of the factors that dampened and even extinguished loyalty to the monarchy among many Vietnamese nationalists. The treaty was abolished on 12 March 1945, when Emperor **Bảo Đại** declared Vietnamese independence, and there was no attempt to restore it with the reimposition of French rule after the war.

PAU CONVENTIONS. A series of agreements dealing with **French** relations with the **Associated States of Indochina** and signed at Pau, France, on 27 November 1950. The **Élysée Accords** of 8 March 1949 had stipulated the holding of interstate conferences to work out arrangements governing communications, foreign trade and customs, immigration control, economic planning, and finances. As a result of the conventions, a series of interstate agencies consisting of representatives of all four countries was set up to handle the "common services" formerly handled by the high commissariat of the **Indochinese Union**. Included in the convention was an agreement on a monetary and customs union for all the countries concerned. *See also* BẢO ĐẠI SOLUTION; STATE OF VIETNAM.

PEACEFUL EVOLUTION (*Diễn biến hoà bình*). "Peaceful evolution" is a term used by the **Vietnamese Communist Party** to refer collectively to all attempts by external and internal enemies to subvert or overthrow the socialist system in Vietnam. The term was apparently originally culled from a speech by Under Secretary of State Averell Harriman during the Lyndon B. Johnson Administration in 1964. The idea of "peaceful evolution" as a threat to socialism was popularized by the **Chinese** Communist Party and then picked up by the Vietnamese and **Lao** Parties as well. It has remained a more operative concept in the latter two countries than in China, reflecting their greater sense of insecurity. Peaceful evolution became a particularly potent threat in the eyes of Vietnamese leaders after the fall of the **Union of Soviet Socialist Republics** and other socialist bloc countries in Eastern Europe, which they saw as the result of political, cultural, and moral subversion initiated and supported from outside the Iron Curtain. Today, the term is a catch-all for anything perceived as ideologically threatening by the Vietnamese government, ranging from pressure on **human rights** to undesirable imports from Western culture to evangelical **Christianity**. *See also* MULTIPARTY SYSTEM; PLURALISM.

PEOPLE'S ARMY OF VIETNAM (PAVN) (*Quân Đội Nhân Dân Việt Nam*). Army of the **Socialist Republic of Vietnam** (SRV). The army was created at a conference of the **Indochinese Communist Party** in the northern highlands on 15 May 1945. It was formed from a union of the **Army of National Salvation** (*Cứu Quốc Quân*), the Armed Propaganda Brigade (founded December 1944), and other revolutionary forces preparing for an insurrection against **French** and **Japanese occupation** forces at the end of World War II. Originally known as the *Vietnamese Liberation Army* (*Việt Nam Giải Phóng Quân*), the PAVN bore the brunt of the fighting against the French during the **Franco-Việt Minh War**. Later, it played an active role in promoting the revolutionary war in South Vietnam and was the dominant force in the final "**Hồ Chí Minh Campaign**" that conquered the **Saigon** regime on April 1975. Beginning as an ill-equipped armed force relying predominantly on guerrilla tactics against stronger adversaries, it was eventually transformed through experience and Soviet military assistance into one of the most powerful and modern armies in the world.

After 1975, the PAVN took part in peacetime reconstruction and the occupation of South Vietnam until 1978, when it played a dominant role in the Vietnamese invasion of neighboring **Cambodia**. Two months later, it bolstered local forces in defending the northern border against a **Chinese** invasion. During the mid-1980s, more than 150,000 Vietnamese troops served as an occupying force in Cambodia, but they were withdrawn by the end of decade. During the 1990s, the size of the PAVN declined with the return of peacetime conditions. Today, the PAVN is estimated at slightly under 400,000 men and women; an additional three million serve in the reserves, and one million in local militia units. In recent years, the army has taken part in a number of construction projects and runs a number of profitable economic enterprises, though there have been occasional attempts to streamline and reduce its business activities.

The armed forces in Vietnam are under strict control of the **Vietnamese Communist Party** through the Central Military Committee, a body under the Central Committee, and so-called "Military Councils" at various echelons of the army. However, senior military officers have always played an influential role in the Party and are consistently represented in the Politburo. A general, **Lê Đức Anh**, served as president of the **Socialist Republic of Vietnam**, though normally the top Party and government positions are reserved for civilians.

PEOPLE'S COMMITTEE (*Ủy Ban Nhân Dân*). Executive body at the local level in the **Socialist Republic of Vietnam** (SRV). It belongs to the state apparatus, as opposed to the structure of the **Vietnamese Communist Party**. *See also* LOCAL GOVERNMENT; PEOPLE'S COUNCIL.

PEOPLE'S COUNCIL (*Hội Đồng Nhân Dân*). Legislative body at lower echelons in the **Socialist Republic of Vietnam** (SRV). Originally created in the **Democratic Republic of Vietnam** (DRV) as a result of the **Constitution** of 1946, People's Councils exist at all levels below the central level as the supreme legislative organ of authority. They are elected by all adult residents at each echelon and are responsible for local administration. A **People's Committee** (*Ủy Ban Nhân Dân*) is elected by the People's Council at each level to handle executive duties in the interim between meetings of the council.

In some respects, the functions of People's Councils resemble those of local administrative bodies in Western democracies. Constitutional provisions theoretically protect the right of councils to question decisions taken by other government organs at each level, and government regulations severely limit **Vietnamese Communist Party** membership in the councils. In practice, the People's Councils (as in other Marxist–Leninist systems) have served essentially as an instrument of the state in the effort to build an advanced socialist society. Since *đổi mới* (renovation), however, they have gained increasing autonomy and have begun to more vigorously advocate the interests of their constituents. *See also* LOCAL GOVERNMENT.

PEOPLE'S LIBERATION ARMED FORCES (PLAF) (*Nhân Dân Giải Phóng Quân*). Formal name for the armed forces of the revolutionary movement in South Vietnam during the Vietnam War. Commonly known in the West as the *Việt Cộng* (a pejorative term first applied by the regime of **Ngô Đình Diệm**), the People's Liberation Armed Forces came into existence at a secret military conference held near **Saigon** in February 1961. The new PLAF merged armed units formerly operating independently in the lower **Mekong River Delta** and the **Central Highlands** and was placed under the operation of the **Central Office of South Vietnam** (COSVN), the southern branch office of the Central Committee of the Vietnamese Workers' Party in **Hanoi**.

The PLAF was organized on the three-tiered basis used earlier in the **Franco–Việt Minh War**, with fully armed regular units under the command of COSVN or regional military command. Below that level were full-time guerrillas organized in companies and operating under provincial or district command, and the village militia, part-time troops used in combat villages for local defense. At first, the PLAF was composed almost entirely of troops recruited within South Vietnam and supplemented by a small number of trained officers and advisers infiltrated from the North. Until 1965, the PLAF carried the primary burden of fighting against the troops of the Saigon regime, but beginning in the mid-1960s, units of the **People's Army of Vietnam (PAVN)** infiltrated from North Vietnam played a larger role in the war, and the PLAF occupied a more subsidiary role. During the **Tết Offensive** in 1968, however, the PLAF bore the brunt of the fighting and suffered heavy casualties, a development that shifted the burden of combat back to the PAVN. It had not fully recovered as an effective fighting organization when the war came to end.

PEOPLE'S REVOLUTIONARY PARTY OF VIETNAM (PRP) (*Đảng Nhân Dân Cách Mạng Việt Nam*). Southern branch organization of the Vietnamese Workers' Party (VWP) set up in the **Republic of Vietnam** in 1962. Although supposedly an independent "revolutionary party of the working class in South Vietnam," the People's Revolutionary Party was in fact directly subordinate to the VWP, through the **Central Office of South Vietnam** (COSVN). It was Marxist–Leninist in orientation and was merged with the parent VWP in the North in 1976 under the new name *Vietnamese Communist Party* (*Đảng Cộng Sản Việt Nam*).

PERSONALISM (*Thuyết Nhân Vị*). Philosophical creed adopted by the **Ngô Đình Diệm** regime in the **Republic of Vietnam** from 1954 to 1963. A blend of the Western concept of individual freedom and the **Confucian** emphasis on community responsibility, the philosophy of Personalism represented an attempt to create a living philosophy for the Vietnamese people that would avoid the extremes of Marxist collectivism and Western materialistic hedonism alike. Personalism in the Vietnamese context was articulated mainly by Diệm's brother **Ngô Đình Nhu**. The European source of his ideas was the Catholic existentialism of Jacques Maritain and Emmanuel Mounier, which promoted a spirit of personal dignity without the egotism characteristic of much of Western capitalist society. To many South Vietnamese, it was a confusing ideology that displayed little departure from traditional Confucian morality and obedience to authority. It achieved little popularity within Vietnamese society at large, and its influence was limited to the inner circle of the regime within Nhu's **Cần Lao** (Personalist Labor) **Party**.

PETERSON, DOUGLAS "PETE." The first **United States** ambassador to the **Socialist Republic of Vietnam** (SRV) after normalization of relations in 1995. A former prisoner-of-war in **Hanoi** for six-and-a-half-years, "Pete" Peterson had served in the U.S. Air Force during the war and was shot down in 1966. His nomination for the ambassadorship to the SRV came after he had served several terms in Congress. Although President Bill Clinton's designation of a former P.O.W. as ambassador to the country where he had once been held prisoner met with very mixed reactions, Peterson acquitted himself admirably in the post, which he held from 1997 through 2001. He made a high-profile visit to the place where he had been shot down and was reunited with the man who had made sure that he was handed over safely to the authorities after his capture rather than suffering at the hands of angry villagers. During his tenure as ambassador, Peterson was a constant voice of Vietnamese–American reconciliation.

PHẠM CÔNG TÁC (1890–1959). Pope of the **Cao Đài** religion in South Vietnam from 1935 until 1955. He joined the Cao Đài movement while serving as a customs official in **Saigon** in the 1920s. On the death of the first "Temporal Pope" Lê Văn Trung, Phạm Công Tác succeeded him as head of the church in 1935. Under his leadership, the Cao Đài became more directly involved in political and social causes. The movement grew rapidly in both urban and rural areas in **Cochin China**, leading to an unsuccessful **French** attempt to suppress it in the early 1940s. Tác himself was exiled to the Comoros Islands in 1941.

He returned from exile in August 1946 and resumed direct authority over the Cao Đài movement. At first, he supported the French against the **Việt Minh** but eventually adopted a neutralist position during the ensuing **Franco–Việt Minh War**, while supporting the return of **Bảo Đại** as chief of state of a new Vietnamese government. After the **Geneva Conference**, he opposed the rise to power of **Ngô Đình Diệm**. In October 1955, Diệm's troops occupied the Cao Đài capital at Tây Ninh and deposed him. Tác fled to **Cambodia**, where he died several years later.

PHẠM HỒNG THÁI (1893–1924). Radical political figure in the early 20th century. The son of an educational administrator who had once supported the anti-French **Cần Vương** movement, Phạm Hồng Thái was born in 1893 in the province of Nghệ An. He left school at a relatively early age to work in a factory, where he first took part in radical activities. In 1923, he joined with such other radicals as **Lê**

Hồng Phong and Hồ Tùng Mậu in forming a radical political party in Canton, **China**, with the name of *Tâm Tâm Xã* (Association of Like Minds). The aim of the group was to promote a general uprising against **French** rule.

In June 1924, Thái made an attempt to assassinate French Governor-General **Martial Merlin** while the latter was attending an official banquet in Shamian, the international settlement in Canton. The attempt was unsuccessful, and Thái drowned while trying to escape. His act was commemorated by **Phan Bội Châu** in a pamphlet published later that year. Many members of the *Tâm Tâm Xã*, including Phong and Mậu, later became founding members of the **Indochinese Communist Party**.

PHẠM HÙNG (1912–1988) (real name *Phạm Văn Thiện*). Veteran member of the **Vietnamese Communist Party**. Born in a scholar-gentry family in Vĩnh Long, Phạm Hùng became a founding member of the **Indochinese Communist Party** in 1930. Arrested in 1931, he was imprisoned in **Poulo Condore** until the end of World War II. During the **Franco–Việt Minh** conflict, he served as deputy to **Lê Duẩn** in the Party's branch office in the South. In 1955, he was summoned to **Hanoi** and raised to Politburo rank two years later.

In 1967, Phạm Hùng (using the *nom de guerre* Bảy Cường) returned to South Vietnam as a replacement for General **Nguyễn Chí Thanh** as chief of the **Central Office for South Vietnam** (COSVN) and the party's branch organization in the South, the **People's Revolutionary Party**. After the end of the war, Hùng returned to Hanoi and became the fourth-ranking member of the Politburo; he was named minister of the interior in 1979. He was replaced in early 1987, but, in June, he was appointed chairman of the Council of Ministers (equivalent to premier) to replace the veteran **Phạm Văn Đồng**, who had retired. He died shortly thereafter.

PHẠM NGỌC THẠCH (1906–1968). **Việt Minh** sympathizer and progressive figure in colonial Vietnam. A doctor by profession, Thạch formed the so-called **Vanguard Youth** (*Thanh Niên Tiên Phong*) movement in **Cochin China** near the end of World War II. Although the movement was formed under Japanese sponsorship, Thạch was a secret Việt Minh supporter and used the movement to mobilize participation in the popular uprising that seized power in **Saigon** in late August 1945. He became a member of the Việt Minh **Committee of the South** (*Ủy Ban Nam Bộ*) under the presidency of **Trần Văn Giàu** and later was appointed minister of health in the new **Democratic Republic of Vietnam** (DRV). He reportedly died of malaria while serving in South Vietnam in the 1960s. *See also* AUGUST REVOLUTION; JAPANESE OCCUPATION.

PHẠM QUỲNH (1892–1945). Leading literary figure and Francophile in early 20th-century Vietnam. The son of a village scholar in Hải Dương, Phạm Quỳnh was educated at the School of Interpreters, where he learned French and Chinese, and at the **École Française d'Extrême-Orient**, a **French**-run research institute in **Hanoi**. He entered **journalism** in 1913 as a writer with **Nguyễn Văn Vĩnh**'s *Đông Dương Tạp Chí* (*Revue Indochinoise*). In 1917, he founded a new journal entitled *Nam Phong* (Southern Wind), which was officially subsidized by the colonial regime and meant to promote political and cultural collaboration with the French. The new journal published articles on various literary subjects in three languages (French, Chinese, and Vietnamese), but Quỳnh's primary objective was to popularize the use of *quốc ngữ*, the Romanized form of written Vietnamese, as the national literary language.

Phạm Quỳnh's political views made him a controversial figure on the colonial scene. Traditionalist and pro-French in his political preferences, he favored a careful synthesis of Western and **Confucian** values based on a continued French presence in Vietnam. He was a convinced royalist, and he bitterly debated the virtues of the **monarchy** and **mandarinate** with Nguyễn Văn Vĩnh, who believed that the imperial system should be done away with. By the 1930s, Quỳnh was increasingly active in politics, serving as minister of education and then director of the cabinet in **Huế** under Emperor **Bảo Đại**. Members of the traditional elite often viewed him as a *parvenu*, however, and his extremely conservative views alienated him from many nationalists. Dismissed from power after the Japanese coup d'état in March 1945, he was assassinated in August by the **Việt Minh**.

PHẠM VĂN ĐÔNG (1906–2000). Leading member of the **Vietnamese Communist Party** and prime minister of the **Socialist Republic**

of Vietnam (SRV). Born in 1906 in a **mandarin** family in Quảng Ngãi, Phạm Văn Đồng was educated at the **National Academy** (*Quốc Học*) in **Huế**. He went to Canton in 1926 and joined the Revolutionary Youth League or **Thanh Niên**. After attending the Whampoa Academy, he returned to Vietnam and served as a member of the league's regional committee in the South. In 1931, he was arrested and imprisoned in **Poulo Condore** until granted an amnesty in 1937.

During the next several years, he was involved in party work in southern China under the alias Lin Baijie (Lâm Bá Kiệt) and became one of **Hồ Chí Minh**'s top lieutenants during World War II. Named minister of finance of the **Democratic Republic of Vietnam** (DRV) in 1946, he became minister of foreign affairs in 1954 and prime minister the following year. He was elected to the Party Politburo in 1951.

As prime minister for more than 30 years, Phạm Văn Đồng gained a reputation as an effective administrator and a conciliatory figure who could reconcile divergent opinions within the Party and government leadership. He was generally considered to be a moderate in internal affairs and neutral in the Sino–Soviet dispute. He resigned from the Politburo because of "advanced age and ill health" at the Sixth Party Congress in December 1986 and was replaced as prime minister by **Phạm Hùng** in June 1987. He continued to play an advisory role in retirement as one of the most senior leaders still alive. *See also* INDOCHINESE COMMUNIST PARTY.

PHAN BÁ VÀNH (?—1827). The leader of a major peasant rebellion during the early years of the **Nguyễn dynasty**. Following a serious famine in several provinces of the **Red River Delta** in the early 1820s, Phan Bá Vành, who was a native of Thái Bình, appeared as the leader of a serious peasant rebellion around 1825. He styled himself king and led a force of several thousand men to attack towns and villages up and down the coastal region. It took the imperial government considerable time and effort to capture him and suppress his rebellion. Revolts such as that of Phan Bá Vành became a frequent phenomenon under the Nguyễn in the decades before French **colonization**.

PHAN BỘI CHÂU (1867–1940). Leading figure in the anticolonial movement in the early 20th century. Born in a **scholar-gentry** family in Nghệ An, Phan Bội Châu showed a quick mind as a youth and earned a second-class degree in the metropolitan **examinations** in 1900. He appeared destined to pursue a career in the **mandarinate**, but his patriotic instincts led him in a different direction. In 1903, he formed a revolutionary organization called the *Duy Tân Hội* (Modernization Society) under the titular leadership of Prince **Cường Để**, a member of the Nguyễn ruling house. Two years later, he established his headquarters in **Japan**, where he wrote patriotic tracts designed to stir anti-**French** sentiments among the general population and encouraged young Vietnamese to flee abroad and join his exile organization.

In 1908, Phan Bội Châu was ordered to leave Japan, forcing him to turn to **China**, where Sun Yat-sen's Revolutionary Alliance (*Tongmenghui*) was attempting to overthrow the tottering Qing dynasty. In 1912, he transformed the Modernization Society into a new organization, the **Vietnamese Restoration Society** (*Việt Nam Quang Phục Hội*), modeled after Sun Yat-sen's own Republican Party. The new organization had little more success than its predecessor, and several attempted uprisings in Vietnam failed. Phan Bội Châu himself was briefly imprisoned in China. On his release in 1917, he appeared temporarily discouraged at the prospects of victory, writing a pamphlet entitled "On Franco–Vietnamese Collaboration" (*Pháp-Việt Đề Huề Luận*) that suggested the possibility of reconciliation with the colonial regime.

In 1925, Phan Bội Châu was seized by French agents while passing through the International Settlement in Shanghai. Brought under guard to **Hanoi**, he was tried and convicted of treason. He spent the remainder of his life in house arrest in **Huế** and died in 1940, one of the most respected patriots in modern Vietnam. Although his frequent ideological shifts and failed organizational strategies meant that he ultimately had few concrete accomplishments in opposing French rule, his symbolic significance as a consistently anticolonial figure was considerable. A small museum is located at his grave in Huế.

PHAN CHU TRINH (1872–1926). Leading reformist figure in the early 20th century. Phan Chu Trinh was born in Quảng Nam, the son of a military officer. He received a traditional **Confucian** education and earned his degree in 1901. His father, a supporter of the **Cần Vương** (Save the King) movement, was assassinated by one of his colleagues on suspicion of treason. Phan Chu Trinh accepted a minor job with the imperial Ministry of Rites but was soon involved in political activities, sending a famous public letter to **French** Governor-General **Paul Beau** in 1906 in which he appealed to Beau to live up to the French civilizing mission in Vietnam by reforming its society along Western lines. He also became involved in the so-called Tonkin Free School (*Đông Kinh Nghĩa Thục*), a private institution financed by patriotic elements to introduce Western ideas into Vietnamese society. Phan Chu Trinh was convinced that Vietnam's primary enemy was not the French but its own antiquated **feudal** government. He became bitterly opposed to the **mandarin** system of which he was a product, and he wrote an article sharply attacking Emperor **Khải Định**.

Phan Chu Trinh was imprisoned in 1908 for allegedly supporting peasant demonstrations (popularly known as the "**Revolt of the Short Hairs**") in **Annam**, though, in fact, the accusations seem to have been a convenient excuse for arresting him and shutting down the Tonkin Free School. After spending time on **Poulo Condore**, he was sent to live in exile in **France**, where he supported himself as a photo retoucher and contributed occasionally to the patriotic cause with writings on contemporary issues. In 1925, he was permitted to return to Vietnam, and he died in **Saigon** the following year. His funeral became the occasion of a fervent expression of patriotic fervor throughout all three parts of colonial Vietnam.

Phan Chu Trinh is often contrasted with **Phan Bội Châu** as representing the nonviolent reformist wing of the patriotic movement in early 20th-century Vietnam, while Châu represented the path of revolutionary violence. Although Party historians have been ambivalent about him because he did not take a consistently strong anticolonial position, he is still recognized as an important nationalist figure in his time. *See* MONARCHY; PROTECTORATE.

PHAN ĐÌNH DIỆU (1937–). Prominent mathematician and **dissident** in contemporary Vietnam. Born in Hà Tĩnh, Phan Đình Diệu studied mathematics at the University of Hanoi and then took postgraduate studies in the **Union of Soviet Socialist Republics**. After his return to Vietnam, he was elected a member of the **National Assembly** in 1976 and was appointed director of the Computer Science Institute. During the 1980s, he became chairman of the National Center for Scientific Research, but when he began to speak out publicly in favor of an abandonment of Marxist–Leninist ideology as the guiding doctrine of the **Socialist Republic of Vietnam**, he was dropped from his position. *See also* SCIENCE AND TECHNOLOGY.

PHAN ĐÌNH PHÙNG (1847–1895). Anti-**French** resistance leader in the late 19th century. Raised in a scholar-official family from Hà Tĩnh, Phan Đình Phùng showed talent at an early age and received a doctorate (*tiến sĩ*) in the civil service **examinations** given in 1877. He served in the Imperial Censorate, where he was noted for his integrity and was briefly imprisoned in 1883 for refusing to sanction a successor to the deceased emperor **Tự Đức** not designated by the emperor himself.

When Emperor **Hàm Nghi** issued his famous **Cần Vương** (Save the King) appeal in July 1885, Phùng responded and launched a revolt in his native Hà Tĩnh. The movement quickly spread to neighboring provinces and lasted several years, despite numerous appeals to Phùng from colleagues who had chosen to collaborate with the French, and despite the desecration of his ancestral plot by the colonial regime. The movement was a nuisance to the French, but the rebels lacked weapons and central direction from the puppet court in **Huế**, and shortly after he died of dysentery in December 1895, it collapsed. Today, Phan Đình Phùng is viewed as one of the great patriots in the struggle for Vietnamese independence.

PHAN HUY CHÚ (1782–1840). A prominent scholar and **mandarin** under the **Nguyễn dynasty**. Member of a Nghệ Tĩnh family, which turned out generations of **scholar-gentry**, he served in the imperial administration and was sent on diplomatic missions to **China** and to Batavia in the Dutch East Indies. He is best known for his authorship of *Lịch Triều Hiến Chương Loại Chí* (*A Reference Book of the Institutions of Successive Dynasties*), an encyclopedia of Vietnamese history and government. *See also* HISTORIOGRAPHY.

PHAN HUY QUÁT (1901–1975). Nationalist party leader and onetime civilian prime minister of the **Republic of Vietnam (RVN)**. A member of the **Đại Việt Party**, Phan Huy Quát was active in South Viet-namese politics throughout the post–World War II era. In the spring of 1965, General **Nguyễn Khánh** appointed him prime minister just at the moment when the **United States** was about to increase its pres-ence in South Vietnam. His government was overthrown by a mili-tary junta led by Colonel **Nguyễn Cao Kỳ** in June. Quát was reportedly executed by the new revolutionary regime after the fall of **Saigon** in 1975. *See also* PHAN KHẮC SỬU.

PHAN KHẮC SỬU (1905–1970). Political figure and chief of state of the **Republic of Vietnam** from October 1964 until June 1965. An agricultural engineer by profession and a nominal member of the **Cao Đài** sect, Phan Khắc Sửu was chosen chief of state in a civilian government placed in office by General **Nguyễn Khánh** in the fall of 1964; **Phan Huy Quát** later joined this government as well. Sửu's government was unable to gain a grip on the nation's complicated problems and was overthrown by a military coup led by **Nguyễn Cao Kỳ** and **Nguyễn Văn Thiệu** in June 1965.

PHAN KHÔI (1887–1960). Progressive scholar, intellectual, and eventual **dissident** in the 20th century. Educated in the traditional **Confucian** system, Phan Khôi, in a long career devoted to scholar-ship and **journalism**, became a renowned critic and commentator on the cultural scene. Through his etymological analyses, he contributed significantly to the development of *quốc ngữ* as a serviceable Viet-namese national language. He became involved in a highly publi-cized polemic in 1930 with the scholar **Trần Trọng Kim** over the latter's effort to synthesize traditional Confucian values with those of the modern West. In Phan Khôi's view, the key to forming a new national culture was value, not whether it conformed to "national es-sence." Phan Khôi remained in the **Democratic Republic of Viet-nam** (DRV) after the **Geneva Conference** and was publicly critical of the regime over the lack of freedom and democracy. He was one of the key figures in the *Nhân Văn Giai Phẩm* affair, the brief flour-ishing of literary dissent in the DRV in 1956–1957; his involvement with this movement ended his professional career, and he died only a few years later. *See also* LITERATURE.

PHAN THANH GIẢN (1796–1867). Vietnamese official who signed the **Treaty of Saigon** with the **French** in June 1862. Born the son of a minor government official in Bến Tre in 1796, Phan Thanh Giản earned a doctorate in the civil service **examinations** in 1826 and entered the imperial **mandarinate**. He served as a military commander in Quảng Nam and later was named governor of Quảng Nam and Bình Định provinces; he also served as deputy chief of a diplomatic mission to **China**.

In 1862, Giản was appointed plenipotentiary to negotiate a peace treaty with **France** following the disastrous defeat by French forces at Kỳ Hoa. In the Treaty of Saigon signed in June, he accepted the loss of three provinces around **Saigon** and the opening of the remainder of Vietnam to French commercial and missionary activity. A year later, he was sent to Paris on an unsuccessful mission to persuade the French to return their newly acquired territory. In 1865, Giản was appointed viceroy of the remaining three provinces of **Cochin China**. When the local French commander attacked and seized the provinces in June 1867, he assumed personal responsibility for the humiliation and committed suicide. *See also* DE LA GRANDIÈRE, PIERRE; TỰ ĐỨC.

PHAN VĂN KHẢI (1933–). Prime minister of the **Socialist Republic of Vietnam** (SRV). Born near what is now Hồ Chí Minh City (then **Saigon**), Phan Văn Khải joined revolutionary organizations as a teenager and regrouped to the North after the partition of Vietnam at the **Geneva Conference** in 1954. He subsequently pursued studies in economics in the **Union of Soviet Socialist Republics**, returning to the **Democratic Republic of Vietnam** to serve in the State Planning Committee. He also did a stint in a government unit that planned for economic reunification with the South. With the end of the war and the establishment of the SRV, Khải returned to his home region and held a series of increasingly important positions in the Hồ Chí Minh City municipal government until 1989, when he shifted back to **Hanoi** with appointments in the central government. He rose to the position of deputy prime minister before becoming prime minister in 1997 following the Eighth Party Congress. Although not a powerful political presence, he is viewed as a moderate who will help advance Vietnam along the path of reform. Like **Võ Văn Kiệt**, an earlier prime minister, Khải represents a faction whose power base lies mainly in the government, as opposed to the **Vietnamese Communist Party** or **People's Army of Vietnam**.

PHAN XÍCH LONG REBELLION. Revolt against the **French** colonial regime in early 20th-century Vietnam. The leader, Phan Xích Long (real name *Phan Phát Sanh*, 1893–1916), was the son of a **Saigon** merchant who became involved in messianistic activities near the **Cambodian** border. In March 1913, taking advantage of widespread unrest caused by high taxes and corvée labor in the **Mekong River Delta** area, he planned an uprising to seize power in Saigon but was arrested by the French and the revolt proved abortive. Three years later, his supporters launched a new insurrection aimed at freeing him from prison, and a number of disturbances broke out in Saigon metropolitan area. The French repressed the uprising with severity, and the ringleaders were executed.

PHILASTRE, PAUL (1837–1902). French diplomat and naval officer who negotiated the 1874 **Philastre Treaty** between **France** and Vietnam. He was also known for his translations of Vietnamese laws, notably the **Hồng Đức Code** and **Gia Long Code**. *See also* DUPRÉ, JULES-MARIE; GARNIER, FRANCIS.

PHILASTRE TREATY. Treaty between **France** and Vietnam signed on 15 March 1874. After the occupation of **Tonkin** by **Francis Garnier** and the latter's death in battle in December 1873, the French government decided to evacuate its troops from the area and seek a settlement. The agreement was negotiated by **Paul Philastre**, who opposed an aggressive French policy in Asia. According to the terms of the agreement, the **Nguyễn dynasty**, fearful of a new military action, recognized full French sovereignty over all six provinces of **Cochin China**. (The **Treaty of Saigon** signed in 1862 had ceded three of these provinces, and the French occupied the other three in 1867.) The **Red River** was opened to international commerce; French consular offices were to be opened in **Hanoi**, **Hải Phòng**, and Qui Nhơn. Vietnam promised that its foreign policy would conform with that of France.

However, the treaty served more to create new tensions between the two sides than it did to resolve them. The next decade was a constant tug-of-war between French representatives trying to assert what they perceived as their rights under the "**protectorate**" established by the 1874 treaty and the Court of **Tự Đức**, which was determined to concede as little as possible. French dissatisfaction with what they had gained through the Philastre Treaty was a major factor in their decision to invade and **colonize** the remainder of Vietnam in 1883–1884. The protectorate established by the 1884 **Patenôtre Treaty** was considerably harsher than the relatively mild relationship formalized in 1874. *See also* DUPRÉ, JULES-MARIE.

PHÓ BẢNG. See EXAMINATION SYSTEM.

PHỤ NỮ TÂN VĂN (*Women's News*). Weekly periodical devoted to **women**'s concerns published in **Saigon** under the French colonial regime. First published in May 1929 by Madame Nguyễn Đức Nhuận, the wife of a prominent businessman, it reflected a rising concern for women's rights among the Western-educated middle class in the major cities. At its peak, it reached a weekly circulation of 8,500 copies and became a formidable rival for *Nam Phong*, the literary journal published by conservative journalist **Phạm Quỳnh**. Written in a fluid and precise modern style, it helped to advance the cause of *quốc ngữ* as the national language of Vietnam. Politically, it reflected the vacillating attitude of its primary leadership—the Vietnamese bourgeoisie—craving independence but fearing social revolution. In the end, it was closed by the colonial regime in December 1934. *See also* JOURNALISM.

PHỤC QUỐC (*Việt Nam Phục Quốc Đồng Minh Hội*) (**League for the National Restoration of Vietnam**). Pro-**Japanese** political party formed by Prince **Cường Để** at the beginning of World War II. The party, often called *Phục Quốc*, was composed of anti-**French** nationalist groups living in exile in southern **China** and was probably a successor to **Phan Bội Châu**'s **Việt Nam Quang Phục Hội**, formed in 1912. It first saw action during the brief Japanese invasion on the Sino–Vietnamese border in September 1940. During the war, it joined with such other groups as the **Cao Đài** in a broad alliance under Japanese sponsorship and based in Vietnam. The organization

314 • PHÙNG HƯNG

collapsed when Japan surrendered in August 1945. *See also* JAPA-
NESE OCCUPATION.

PHÙNG HƯNG. Vietnamese military leader who rebelled against the
Chinese in the eighth century. Son of a leading local figure of the
western edge of the **Red River Delta**, Phùng Hưng became commander of a military garrison to guard the protectorate of **Annam**
from rebel attacks by tribal groups in the mountains to the west.
When the local administration virtually disintegrated, reflecting instability within the Tang dynasty in **China**, his personal influence
rapidly increased. In the early 780s, Phùng Hưng seized the capital
of La Thành (on the site of present-day **Hanoi**) and ruled the protectorate until his death in 789. In later centuries, Phùng Hưng's prodigious physical strength and allegedly superhuman capacities made
him a folk hero in Vietnam. *See also* CHINESE PERIOD.

PHÙNG NGUYÊN CULTURE. A Neolithic culture in prehistoric
Vietnam. Named for a site in the mountains north of the **Red River
Delta** uncovered in 1958, Phùng Nguyên culture flourished at the end
of the third millennium B.C.E. and was characterized by the use of
polished stone implements and decorated pottery. The **economy** was
based on **slash-and-burn agriculture** and animal husbandry, and
dwellings were constructed of wood and bamboo and placed on stilts.
Phùng Nguyên culture is often considered the earliest stage of the
Bronze Age in Vietnam. *See also* ARCHEOLOGY; ĐÔNG SƠN
CULTURE; NEOLITHIC ERA.

**PIGNEAU DE BÉHAINE, PIERRE-JOSEPH (1741–1799) (Bishop
of Adran).** French bishop and adventurer who helped prepare the
way for the establishment of the **Nguyễn dynasty**. In 1766, the
young Pigneau de Béhaine was sent to Asia as a missionary by the
French **Société des Missions Étrangères de Paris** (Society of Foreign Missions). For more than two years, he served as head of a Catholic seminary in **Hà Tiên** along the Gulf of Thailand. Forced to flee
by official persecution, he went to Malacca and was eventually sent
to India as Bishop of Adran.

In 1775, Pigneau returned to Hà Tiên, where he met Nguyễn Ánh,
scion of the Nguyễn house, which had just been driven from Gia

Định (**Saigon**) by the **Tây Sơn** Rebellion. From that point, Pigneau dedicated himself to restoring Nguyễn Ánh to the throne as the rightful ruler of Vietnam and hopefully obtaining concessions for **France** in the process. In 1787, he arranged a visit to Paris with the young Prince **Cảnh**; a treaty was signed with the French court, providing for assistance against the Tây Sơn in return for French occupation of the port of Tourane (**Đà Nẵng**) and the island of **Poulo Condore**. France did not live up to the terms of the treaty, but Pigneau helped build up the Nguyễn armed forces on his own initiative, undoubtedly hoping that after his restoration to power, the latter would grant commercial and missionary privileges to the French.

In 1801, Nguyễn Ánh completed his defeat of the Tây Sơn and founded a new Nguyễn dynasty in **Huế** as Emperor **Gia Long**. Pigneau did not live to see the triumph of his protégé, however; he died of dysentery at the siege of Qui Nhơn in 1799. *See also* NGUYỄN HUỆ; NGUYỄN LORDS.

PIGNON, LÉON (1908–1976). French high commissioner in **Indochina** from October 1948 until December 1950. A career official in the colonial civil service, Pignon was commissioner of **Cambodia** at the time of his appointment. Earlier, he had served as counselor to High Commissioner **Thierry d'Argenlieu** shortly after the end of World War II and shared the latter's anti-Communist sentiments and dedication to the preservation of a French colonial presence in Indochina.

As high commissioner, Pignon followed the path traced by his predecessor, **Émile Bollaert**, and presided over the completion of arrangements for the establishment of a **State of Vietnam** under Chief of State (and ex-Emperor) **Bảo Đại**. The new state was intended to provide the Vietnamese with an alternative to **Hồ Chí Minh**'s **Democratic Republic of Vietnam** (DRV), now fighting a protracted struggle against French forces in Indochina. He was replaced as high commissioner by General **de Lattre de Tassigny** in December 1950. *See also* BẢO ĐẠI SOLUTION; ÉLYSÉE ACCORDS; HẠ LONG BAY AGREEMENT.

PLEIKU (Play Cu, Playku). City in the **Central Highlands** and capital of Gia Lai Province. Pleiku was the site of a highly publicized attack by **People's Liberation Armed Forces** Việt Cộng forces on a **United States** Special Forces camp in February 1965. When the incident was reported in Washington, the Lyndon B. Johnson administration decided to use the attack as a pretext to increase U.S. pressure on the **Democratic Republic of Vietnam** (DRV). Johnson thereupon launched bombing raids over North Vietnam and introduced the first U.S. combat troops into the **Republic of Vietnam**.

PLURALISM (*Thuyết đa nguyên*). Along with a **multiparty system**, "pluralism" remains one of the ideas toward which the **Vietnamese Communist Party** has remained most consistently hostile. In a Vietnamese context, the term refers to the tolerance of a wider spectrum of political thinking and ideology than is currently acceptable to the Party. As long as Vietnam remains a "socialist" country, Marxism–Leninism and **Hồ Chí Minh**'s thought must—in theory, at least—remain its ideological foundation. Although **economic** reform is actively promoted within the broader framework of "renovation" or *đổi mới*, for example, it cannot be described as "**capitalism**," which is anathema for true believers in Marxism and would be implicitly linked to ideologically incorrect ideas. **Education** maintains a strong ideological component to inculcate Party teachings in students' minds, though the effectiveness of this policy is rapidly diminishing, particularly with the increasing access to nonofficial sources of information over the Internet and the large numbers of Vietnamese who are going abroad for study and training. *Democracy* is an acceptable term, but only as it is defined by the Party, and Western interpretations of the term are linked to the undesirable phenomenon of pluralism. *See also* COMMUNISM; PEACEFUL EVOLUTION.

POLITICAL PARTIES. *See* MULTIPARTY SYSTEM; VIETNAMESE COMMUNIST PARTY.

POLITIQUE D'ÉGARDS (**Policy of consideration**). A feature of **French** colonial policy under more liberal-minded officials. By the 1930s, some of the more perceptive French policymakers were aware that the treatment of their subjects in **Indochina**, particularly those serving in official posts, left much to be desired. Driven partially by sensitivity for the feelings of those they ruled but more by concern for their loyalty, some colonial officials emphasized the need to show more consideration and respect, particularly for collaborators. The *politique d'égards* remained operative through the governor-generalship of the pro-Vichy Admiral **Jean Decoux** during the **Japanese Occupation**. Entrenched French attitudes toward their Indochinese subjects were difficult to change, however, and, in any case, whatever "consideration" might have been shown was not matched by a corresponding devolution of responsibility or authority into the hands of local officials. The *politique d'égards* seems to have remained largely a dead letter. *See also* ASSIMILATION; ASSOCIATION; PROTECTORATE.

POPULAR FRONT. Period of relative liberalization in pre–World War II colonial **Indochina**. The period was opened with the formation of a coalition government in **France** led by the Socialist Party under Premier Léon Blum in May 1936. The new government promised to appoint a commission to look into conditions in the French colonies and to recommend necessary reforms. The colonial regime introduced a number of measures in Indochina to improve conditions, including a more liberal attitude toward the freedom of speech and organization, and a new labor code, but rising popular agitation made local authorities nervous. Eventually, the projected visit of an inspection commission to Indochina was canceled. The Popular Front government came to an end in 1939. Its most significant impact was probably in **Cochin China**, where the liberalized atmosphere allowed leftist elements, notably **Trotskyites**, to openly participate in local politics, though for a brief time only. *See also* BREVIÉ, JULES; INDOCHINESE COMMUNIST PARTY; INDOCHINESE CONGRESS.

POPULATION. Rapid population growth is a fact of life in most **rice**-growing societies, and Vietnam is no exception. In 1995, the population of the **Socialist Republic of Vietnam** (SRV) was estimated at approximately 73 million, an increase of more than 24 million since the end of the Vietnam War in 1975. By 2003, the estimated population figure was 80.7 million; one-quarter of Vietnamese were now living in urban areas.

Until recently, Party leaders in the SRV had expressed little public concern over the potential implications of rapid population growth. As early as 1963, the **Hanoi** regime had set up a Committee for Family Planning, but little was achieved during the war. By the early 1980s, however, the program was promoted with an increased sense of urgency. At the Fifth National Congress of the **Vietnamese Communist Party** in 1982, the Party announced its intention of reducing the growth rate from 2.4 percent to 1.7 percent by 1985.

Progress has been slow, hindered by popular resistance and lackadaisical enforcement by cadres, in contrast to the fairly draconian methods imposed in **China**. Unofficial estimates suggest, however, that the annual rate of increase declined in the mid-1990s to about 2.2 percent, and the figure for 2003 was 1.18 percent. *See also* HIGHLAND PEOPLES; VIETNAMESE PEOPLE.

POPULATION RESETTLEMENT. *See* MIGRATION; NEW ECONOMIC ZONES.

POULO CONDORE (Côn Sơn Island). A small island in the **South China Sea** about 80 kilometers (50 miles) off the coast of southern Vietnam, part of the **Côn Đảo** group of islands. Essentially uninhabited in precolonial times, it was transformed into a penitentiary for Vietnamese political prisoners during the **French** colonial regime. Many members of anticolonial parties, including the **Indochinese Communist Party** (ICP), spent time there, transforming the prison (in the words of Communist leaders) into "schools of Bolshevism"; prisoners were hardened by their brutal treatment, and many left convinced supporters of the ICP.

After the **Geneva Conference** of 1954, the island continued to be used as a prison by the **Republic of Vietnam**, leading to charges by critics in Vietnam and abroad that the regime was mistreating its prisoners in so-called "tiger cages" unfit for human habitation. Under the current government of the **Socialist Republic of Vietnam** (SRV), the island has become a national park.

PRODUCTION COLLECTIVES (*Tập thể sản xuất*). Low-level collective organization used by the **Socialist Republic of Vietnam** (SRV) as a transitional stage to full **collectivization of agriculture**. Production collectives are small cooperative organizations in which the basic means of production are collectively owned, and the peasants within the collective are divided into teams to produce according to plan. The production collective is normally smaller than the usual collective (formally known as an *agricultural producers' cooperative*) and consists of 60 to 70 farm families working on a cultivated area of 30 to 35 hectares (74 to 86 acres).

After reunification production collectives, along with the more primitive "**production solidarity teams**" were adopted in the southern provinces (the former **Republic of Vietnam**) in the late 1970s as a means of introducing private farmers to the collective concept. In the early 1980s, about 85 percent of the farm population in southern Vietnam was enrolled in approximately 40,000 production collectives. With the advent of *đổi mới* and the virtual abandonment of socialist agriculture, however, these measures were nullified.

PRODUCTION SOLIDARITY TEAMS. Early form of collective organization used by the **Socialist Republic of Vietnam** (SRV) as a transitional stage to full **collectivization of agriculture**. The production solidarity team (also known as a *work exchange team*) is a first stage in the collective process. Private farmers at the hamlet level establish contractual relations with the authorities on production goals, but the means of production (land, machinery, and draft animals) are not collectively owned. Teams are usually composed of 50 to 60 farm families on a cultivated area of 30 to 40 hectares (74 to 99 acres).

The SRV adopted the concept in the southern provinces as a means of achieving full collectivization of the land by the end of the Second Five-Year Plan in 1980. It was used in conjunction with the more prevalent **production collectives** and was utilized in areas where private farmers were likely to be particularly resistant to collectivization.

PROTECTORATE. The form of government established by the **French** over what remained of the Empire of Vietnam after its provinces in **Cochin China** had been detached and set up as a colony under direct rule. The protectorate was successively established between 1874 and 1884 by the **Philastre**, **Harmand**, and **Patenôtre** Treaties. (Protectorates were also established in **Cambodia** in 1863 and **Laos** in 1893.) **Tonkin** and **Annam** were still ruled by the "protected monarchs" of the **Nguyễn dynasty**.

In theory, the protectorate limited French authority to specifically though broadly defined areas, with power in other matters remaining in the hands of the rulers. In reality, however, right from the beginning the French fought to wrestle as much power as they possibly could out of Vietnamese hands, leaving the Nguyễn emperors little more than ceremonial and symbolic responsibilities. France believed that by maintaining what it saw as the "moral authority" of the emperors while wielding the actual political authority itself, it could channel popular loyalty to the colonial regime through the traditional government. Few Vietnamese were fooled, however, and the **monarchy** and **mandarinate** gradually lost most or all of their prestige. Ultimately, French "protection" was a major reason for opposition to—and the eventual elimination of—the imperial system. (In Cambodia and Laos, by contrast, the transition from protected monarchy to an independent one was relatively smooth.) *See also* ASSIMILATION; ASSOCIATION.

PROTESTANTISM. *See* CHRISTIANITY.

PROVISIONAL GOVERNMENT OF VIETNAM. *See* DEMOCRATIC REPUBLIC OF VIETNAM.

PROVISIONAL REVOLUTIONARY GOVERNMENT OF SOUTH VIETNAM (PRG) (*Chính Phủ Cách Mạng Lâm Thời Miền Nam Việt Nam*). Alternative administration set up in May 1969 by revolutionary forces operating in South Vietnam. Formally known as the *Provisional Revolutionary Government of the Republic of South Vietnam*, it was intended to provide a legitimate revolutionary alternative to the **Republic of Vietnam (RVN)**, with its capital in **Saigon**. Leading figures in the PRG were **Huỳnh Tấn Phát** and **Nguyễn Hữu Thọ**, both active in the **National Liberation Front**, Hanoi's front organization that had been established in December 1960. The PRG was recognized by the **Democratic Republic of Vietnam** (DRV) and several other socialist countries as the legitimate government of South Vietnam and was represented as a legal entity in the Paris peace talks. After the fall of Saigon in 1975, the

PRG was abolished with the reunification of North and South Vietnam into a single **Socialist Republic of Vietnam** (SRV).

PUGINIER, PAUL-FRANÇOIS (1835–1892). A **Catholic** bishop and missionary in northern Vietnam. Puginier arrived in Vietnam in 1858, the same year that the French began the first stage of their campaign to colonize Indochina. He served in **Tonkin** for more than 30 years and was a strong voice in favor of French colonization of the entire country. *See also* CHRISTIANITY.

– Q –

QUẬN. Administrative term for prefecture in ancient Vietnam. The term, equivalent to the Chinese *jun*, was used during the **Chinese period**. It is presently used to refer to a district in large municipalities, such as **Hanoi** or Hồ Chí Minh City (**Saigon**). *See also* LOCAL GOVERNMENT.

QUANG TRUNG. *See* NGUYỄN HUỆ.

QUỐC HỌC. *See* NATIONAL ACADEMY.

QUỐC NGỮ. Romanized written form of the **Vietnamese language**. *Quốc ngữ* (meaning "national language") was invented by **Christian** missionaries in the 17th century as a tool for teaching scripture to Vietnamese converts. At that time, the official written language of government and much of Vietnamese **literature** was classical Chinese, but a separate script based on Chinese characters, known as *chữ nôm*, was used to transcribe spoken Vietnamese. Until the time of colonization, *quốc ngữ* was used exclusively by missionaries and converts, and a corpus of religious texts using the new script was produced over the centuries.

In the late 19th century, *quốc ngữ* was popularized by **French** authorities in the colony of **Cochin China** and subsequently in the **protectorates** of **Annam** and **Tonkin** as well. From the French perspective, not only did *quốc ngữ* facilitate literacy in Vietnamese, it also served to break the psychological and cultural links to **China** represented by the use of characters. At first the innovation was resisted by conservative intellectuals, but in the early 20th century reformist figures like **Phan Chu Trinh** began to see its value as a replacement for the cumbersome writing systems based on characters. Many nationalist scholars trained in the Chinese classics, however, never really became comfortable writing in *quốc ngữ*—even though they recognized its value. Eventually, its convenience and simplicity overcame the alleged aesthetic and near-sacred qualities of Chinese characters and gained wide acceptance throughout Vietnam.

In 1924, *quốc ngữ* was established as a primary tool of instruction at the elementary level throughout colonial Vietnam. The **Indochinese Communist Party** worked hard to propagate knowledge of the script as a tool for teaching literacy. After the division of the country in 1954, the governments in both the North and the South used *quốc ngữ* as their national script. As a writing system, it suffers from certain eccentricities in that it reflects a rendering of 17th-century Vietnamese pronunciation based on certain spelling conventions of European languages, and even orthographic changes made since it was first invented have not solved this problem. Moreover, no major dialect of Vietnamese has all of the phonetic distinctions implied by its spelling. **Hồ Chí Minh** and other early Communist leaders experimented with orthographic reforms, such as introducing the letters "z" and "f," but these changes were not maintained over the long term.

QUỐC TỬ GIÁM. *See* IMPERIAL ACADEMY.

– R –

RED EARTH (*đất đỏ*). A term used to describe certain regions of Vietnam because of the color of the soil. It is particularly associated with the areas along the eastern edge of the **Mekong Delta** on both sides of the **Cambodian** border and the western edge of the **Central Highlands**, where the **French** established huge **rubber** plantations after introducing the crop. Workers were recruited and shipped to these plantations from impoverished regions in **Tonkin** and **Annam**.

Working conditions on the plantations were often deplorable and death rates high.

RED RIVER (Hồng Hà, Sông Hồng or Sông Cái). Second major river in Vietnam. Originating in Yunnan Province in southern **China** (where it is called the *Yuanjiang*), the Red River flows over 1,100 kilometers (700 miles) in a southeasterly direction into the **Tonkin Gulf**. Of that distance, 505 kilometers (313 miles) lie within the territory of Vietnam. Its primary tributaries are the Đà (Black) and Lô Rivers.

RED RIVER DELTA. Delta in northern Vietnam. The delta region was built up over centuries by the deposit of alluvial soils brought down the **Red River** from its source in southern **China**. Surrounded by mountains to the north and west, the delta consists of a total area of nearly 15,000 square kilometers (5,800 square miles) and has exerted a formative influence on the history of the **Vietnamese people**. It was on its fringes that the ethnic Vietnamese first emerged as a distinct people, and it remained the heartland of their culture as well as the center of political power after independence from China in the 10th century C.E. Although other political and cultural centers have emerged, **Hanoi** remains the most important of all.

The importance of the delta in Vietnamese history is essentially **economic**. Here, on the rich sedimentary soils left by the river on its passage to the sea, the early Vietnamese mastered the cultivation of wet **rice**, the staple food of their diet. The Red River was also a constant threat, however, as sediment gradually built up in the bed underneath and led to disastrous floods that destroyed crops and often caused widespread starvation. To protect their rice fields from flooding, Vietnamese peasants built dikes along the banks that often reached heights of greater than 6 meters (20 feet), while the river bed itself is often several feet above the surrounding riceland. During the Vietnam War, some **United States** strategists proposed the bombing of the dikes as a means of destroying the North Vietnamese economy and forcing the Hanoi regime to abandon its effort to bring about national reunification.

REEDUCATION CAMPS. Detainment centers established by the **Hanoi** regime in the former **Republic of Vietnam** after the Vietnam

War. After the seizure of **Saigon** by North Vietnamese forces in April 1975, a new revolutionary administration was established in the South. All individuals suspected of possible hostility to the new regime were instructed to report to reeducation camps for ideological indoctrination and possible reassignment. According to official sources, over one million South Vietnamese required reeducation in some form. The majority received a short period of indoctrination and then were released; the remainder were sent to work camps for longer periods of time. According to critics of the regime, several hundred thousand South Vietnamese were housed in these camps, often under intolerable conditions. Official sources in Hanoi insist that most have been released, and knowledgeable observers estimate that currently only a few hundred prisoners are still detained; it is probable that they have now been absorbed into the national penal system.

REFUGEES. *See* BOAT PEOPLE; OVERSEAS VIETNAMESE.

RELIGION. Before the Common Era, the religious beliefs of the Vietnamese people were most probably restricted to animism and forms of magic. Even today, belief in the existence of nature deities and the spirits of the deceased is widely prevalent and constitutes the core of the Vietnamese worldview. "Great tradition" religions and philosophies began to arrive during the **"Chinese period"** in the first millennium C.E. Some, like **Daoism** and **Confucianism**, undoubtedly came from **China. Buddhism** was initially introduced by traveling monks from India and Central Asia but from roughly the sixth century onward also came mainly from China. As a result, the Vietnamese belief system came to incorporate all of these elements to different degrees.

After national independence in the 10th century, the state provided official sponsorship to all three religions—Confucianism, Buddhism, and Daoism, known collectively as *tam giáo đồng nguyên* ("three religions from the same source"). Students studying for the civil service **examinations** were expected to master key classical works from all three of them. Buddhism and Daoism remained strong at the official level until the **Ming occupation** of the early 15th century, an event that considerably strengthened the position of Confucianism as a state ideology. Meanwhile, syncretic forms of Islam and Brahmanism survived among the **Cham** in the central provinces. Catholic **Christianity** arrived with the first Europeans in the 16th and 17th centuries and is still widely practiced today; Protestantism began to take root during the colonial period.

In general, Vietnam has been tolerant of peoples of different faiths, although persecution of Christianity was a major factor in provoking the French invasion in the late 19th century. Religious conflicts between Catholics and Buddhists led to political instability during the 1960s in the **Republic of Vietnam**. Today, the **Socialist Republic of Vietnam** (SRV) officially proclaims freedom of religion in its **constitution**. However, this freedom is subordinated to the law so that in practice the activities of religious groups are seriously restricted by various regulations. This is particularly true of such sects as the **Cao Đài** and **Hoà Hảo**, which have a tradition of stubborn autonomy and anti-Communist sentiments, and of Protestantism, which is linked in the government's mind to the **United States**. Generally speaking, the Party remains wary of religion as a possible tool of the so-called **peaceful evolution** targeting socialism in Vietnam. *See also* SOCIÉTÉ DES MISSIONS ÉTRANGÈRES.

REPUBLIC OF COCHIN CHINA. Autonomous "free state" within the **Indochinese Federation** created by the **French** in June 1946. According to the preliminary **Ho-Sainteny Agreement** reached between **Hồ Chí Minh** and French representative **Jean Sainteny** in March 1946, the **protectorates** of **Annam** and **Tonkin** would be recognized by the French as a "free state" within the **French Union**. In a separate clause, a referendum was to be held in the colony of **Cochin China** to permit the people of that colony to decide whether to associate themselves with the new "free state" to the north. Outraged by the possibility that the French might lose Cochin China, colonial elements led by the new High Commissioner **Thierry d'Argenlieu** established a separate Republic of Cochin China that was formally recognized by France as a "free republic" in June. Dr. **Nguyễn Văn Thinh** was chosen president of the provisional government of the republic, but he committed suicide in November over the failure of the new republic to receive recognition either from the **Democratic Re-**

public of Vietnam (DRV) in the North or from the French, who treated it as a tool in their negotiations with Hồ Chí Minh.

Although Cochin China had been colonized earlier than, and experienced a different political evolution from, the rest of Vietnam, few Vietnamese supported the idea of long-term separation from the Northern and Central regions. For two years, the autonomous republic lived a shadow existence as a cat's-paw for French efforts to restore their authority in Indochina. It was formally abolished in March 1949 with the signing of the **Elysée Accords** that created a united **State of Vietnam**. A Territorial Assembly of Cochin China voted for union with the new entity under Chief of State **Bảo Đại** on 23 April. *See also* ĐÀLẠT CONFERENCE; FONTAINEBLEAU CONFERENCE.

REPUBLIC OF VIETNAM (RVN) (*Việt Nam Cộng Hoà*). Formal name for the government in South Vietnam after the **Geneva Conference** established two separate administrative entities in North and South in 1954. The Republic of Vietnam, formally inaugurated on 23 October 1955, was administratively the successor of the **State of Vietnam** established within the **French Union** in 1949. Its first chief of state, ex-Emperor **Bảo Đại**, had served in the same capacity before 1954, but he was defeated in a referendum orchestrated by Prime Minister **Ngô Đình Diệm**, who then became president under a new **constitution** approved in 1956. The political structure established by the 1956 constitution combined the parliamentary and the presidential systems, with a strong president presiding over a unicameral **National Assembly**. After the overthrow of Diệm by a military coup in 1963, South Vietnam came under military rule until 1967, when a new constitution was approved by President General **Nguyễn Văn Thiệu**. The form of government was essentially retained, although in practice there were a number of dissimilarities.

The Republic of Vietnam consisted of a territory composed of 173,809 square kilometers (67,376 square miles) and was divided into 43 provinces (*tỉnh*) stretching from the **Demilitarized Zone** at the 17th parallel to the southern tip of the **Cà Mau** Peninsula. The total population rose from about 13 million in 1954 to nearly 25 million in the mid-1970s. The Republic of Vietnam was abolished on 30 April 1975, with the inauguration of a new provisional regime in Sai-

gon. The following July, South and North Vietnam were united into a single **Socialist Republic of Vietnam** (SRV). *See also* PROVISIONAL REVOLUTIONARY GOVERNMENT.

REVOLT OF THE SHORT HAIRS. Peasant tax revolt in early 20th-century Vietnam, so called because many participants cut their hair short as a symbol of protest against the system. It began in Quảng Nam in March 1908 and eventually spread southward to Quảng Ngãi and Bình Định, with some unrest among students in the imperial capital at **Huế**. The **French** repressed the revolt with severity and one of the leaders, Trần Quý Cáp, was executed. *See also* PHAN CHU TRINH.

REVOLUTIONARY YOUTH LEAGUE OF VIETNAM. *See* THANH NIÊN.

RHADÉ (Ê Đê). **Highland minority** people living in the **Central Highlands**. They number about 150,000 people today, and inhabit an area stretching from eastern **Cambodia** to the inland sections of Phú Yên and Khánh Hoà. Most live in the province of Đắk Lắk (recently divided into two with the creation of a new Đắc Nông province). The Rhadé are **Austronesian** speakers who probably migrated into Southeast Asia well before the Common Era. Their language is related to **Cham**, and most practice spirit worship, although some converted to **Christianity** in the 20th century. Society is matrilinear, and **slash-and-burn** has traditionally been the main form of **agriculture**.

Like several other minority groups in the Highlands, the Rhadé have traditionally resisted assimilation into Vietnamese society. Many were active in the **Front Uni pour la Libération des Races Opprimées** (FULRO) that opposed the integrationist policies followed by both the **Republic of Vietnam** and the present-day government based in **Hanoi**. *See also* BAJARAKA; JARAI; SABATIER, LÉOPOLD.

RHODES, ALEXANDRE DE (1591–1660). French missionary involved in the propagation of **Christianity** in 17th-century Vietnam. A native of the papal city of Avignon in southern France, he arrived in **Hanoi** as a Jesuit missionary in 1627. At first, he had considerable success in converting **mandarins** and aristocrats of the **Lê dynasty** to Roman Catholicism. Eventually, his activities aroused suspicion among **Confucianist** elements convinced of the radical character of the Western doctrine, and he was expelled from Vietnam in 1630.

For the remainder of his life, Alexander of Rhodes worked indefatigably to promote the missionary effort in Vietnam. He wrote a Portuguese–Latin–Vietnamese dictionary and helped devise a Romanized transliteration of the Vietnamese spoken language (thereafter known as *quốc ngữ*) to facilitate the training of local priests in Christian teachings. Between 1640 and 1645, he was based in the Portuguese colony of Macao, from which he undertook a number of short trips to Vietnam to promote missionary work there. Eventually, he became exasperated at the failure of the Vatican bureaucracy to increase church activities in Vietnam and prevailed on the church hierarchy in France to form a **Société des Missions Étrangères** to undertake the operation. He died on a mission to Persia in 1660.

RICE CULTURE. Since prehistoric times, rice has been the primary crop in Vietnam. During the traditional period, up to 90 percent of the population was engaged in wet-rice **agriculture**, with the bulk of production centered in the rice bowls of the **Red River** and the **Mekong River Deltas**. Until recently, historians had assumed that the cultivation of rice was brought to Vietnam from **China**, where irrigated agriculture was introduced in the Yellow River Valley several thousand years ago. During the past few years, however, archeologists have uncovered evidence of the domestication of wild rice on sloped terraces in the midlands or mountain valleys northwest of the Red River Delta as early as 4000 B.C.E., and perhaps earlier. Although the precise date of its first appearance has not yet been established, it is probably safe to say that the peoples of the Red River region were among the first in Asia to cultivate rice.

As the ancestors of the **Vietnamese people** moved down from the midlands to settle in the delta during the prehistoric era, they began to cultivate rice in the plains. At first, irrigation took place by tidal action, and dikes were built solely to prevent flooding. Later, dikes and canals became part of an extensive irrigation system throughout the region. Since then, rice culture has developed into the primary

economic activity of the Vietnamese, spreading along the central coast and into the rich delta of the Mekong River to the south. The basic social units of the Vietnamese state—the **village** (*xã* or *thôn*) and the family/household (*gia* or *hộ*)—developed around the requirements of the harvest cycle. Rice culture has also strongly influenced the mores and political attitudes and institutions of the Vietnamese, placing supreme importance on the virtues of cooperation, hard work, and sacrifice of individual needs to those of the broader community.

During the colonial era, rice production expanded when vast lands in the Mekong River Delta were opened to cultivation, and rice exports became one of the prime export earners in Indochina. During the Vietnam War, however, production was stagnant because of the disruption in the countryside. Recently, rice production has recovered, and Vietnam is now the third-largest exporter of rice in the world. The structural changes in the country's economy have reduced agriculture's share in the Gross Domestic Product to slightly over one-fifth, but rural areas—which remain primarily agricultural—still account for three-fourths of the Vietnamese population. Currently, a total of 1.2 million hectares (2.9 million acres) of land is devoted to growing rice, and exports in 2004 were expected to reach 3.9 million metric tons (4.3 million tons). *See also* BALANCE OF PAYMENTS; SLASH-AND-BURN AGRICULTURE.

RIGAULT DE GENOUILLY, CHARLES (1807–1873). Naval commander in the **French** Pacific fleet who directed the attack on Vietnam in 1858. Captain Rigault de Genouilly had taken part in a bombardment of Vietnamese ships in **Đà Nẵng** harbor in March 1847. In November 1857, now promoted to admiral and in charge of the Pacific fleet, he was instructed by the French government to seize the city with the aid of Spanish warships. The attack was launched in August 1858 and at first succeeded. But malarial conditions and local resistance prevented a projected advance to the imperial capital of Huế, and he abandoned Đà Nẵng and moved farther south, where he captured the citadel of **Saigon** in February 1859. He returned to Đà Nẵng for a second attempt in April but had no more success and resigned from his command. He later became minister of the Navy and Colonies in Paris. *See also* COLONIZATION.

RIVIÈRE, HENRI (1827–1883). French military officer prominent in the seizure of **Tonkin** in the 1880s. A naval officer, Rivière in early 1882 was ordered by **Le Myre de Vilers**, the governor of **Cochin China**, to undertake a military operation designed to increase French political influence in northern Vietnam. On his own initiative, Rivière stormed the **Hanoi** citadel and assumed authority in the city. He was killed in May 1883 in a skirmish with Vietnamese troops and **Black Flag** units under the command of Liu Yongfu. *See also* HOÀNG DIỆU.

RUBBER. One of the primary export crops in Vietnam. The tree *Heveas brasiliensis*, from which natural rubber has traditionally been produced, is native not to Southeast Asia but to the Amazon River basin in Brazil. In the late 19th century, **French** naturalists brought seedlings to their colony of **Indochina**, and by the end of the century, extensive rubber plantations had been founded in the so-called *"terre rouge"* (**red earth**) area of **Cochin China** and eastern **Cambodia**. Most of the plantations were owned by French interests and farmed by Vietnamese laborers recruited for the task, sometimes lured by false descriptions of life on the plantations. Living conditions were frequently atrocious, so strikes by plantation workers were a common occurrence before World War II and death rates were high. But rubber became a major export earner in French Indochina, with exports rising to 60,000 tons in 1938.

Today, the Vietnamese government has revived the export of rubber as a major source of foreign currency, and domestic demand is increasing as well. As of 2004, Vietnam was the world's sixth-largest producer and fourth-largest exporter of the commodity. That year, the total area under cultivation was 450,000 hectares (1.1 million acres) of plantations; the government's objective is to increase this figure to 700,000 hectares (1.73 million acres) by 2010. Total production of rubber in 2004 was roughly 400,000 metric tons (440,000 tons), of which some 375,000 metric tons (412,500 tons) were exported.

RULE OF LAW (*Nhà nước pháp quyền***).** The concept that Vietnamese society at all levels should be governed as much as possible in conformance with a solid legal framework rather than by Party fiat or the whim of individual officials. Over the past few years, the **Vietnamese Communist Party** has gradually (and sometimes grudgingly) come to recognize that **economic** reform and broad-based effective national development require a firm and **legal system**. Although the **Socialist Republic of Vietnam** and its predecessor, the **Democratic Republic of Vietnam**, have had no shortage of laws, from the **constitution** down to local regulations, it has frequently been all too easy for these laws to be bypassed by those with the power to do so. Since the advent of *đổi mới* (renovation) in the mid-1980s, changing attitudes on the part of Vietnamese citizens and the very clear and vocal expectations of **foreign investors** have shown the need for deep-seated structural and philosophical reforms of the legal system. This agenda is known collectively in English as the "rule of law" and in Vietnamese as *"nhà nước pháp quyền,"* which translates as something like "state ruled by law."

Efforts to implement a rule of law are operating at several levels. The role of the **National Assembly**, once essentially a rubber-stamp legislature, has been considerably expanded and toughened, particularly during the tenure of **Nông Đức Mạnh** (now Party general secretary) as its chairman in the 1990s. A series of important laws have been promulgated over the past decade: for example, a Civil Code (which took effect in 1996), an Enterprise Law (2000), and a Land Law (2004). At the same time, several foreign organizations, including the United Nations Development Program, are offering aid to the Vietnamese government in areas such as "public administration reform," "rule of law and access to justice," and "parliamentary development," under the broader heading of "democratic governance." A particular priority is strengthening legislative institutions across the board, from the National Assembly down to the **People's Councils** at the local level.

A key assumption of the "rule of law" agenda—though it is not explicitly stated—is that the various organs of the government need to be strengthened to lessen the potential of Party interference in their work, as the blurring of the line of authority between the Party and the state has long been a problem in Vietnam. This will be acceptable to the Party to the extent that its ultimate authority over the political process is not diluted, and "democratic" in this context should not be understood in a Western sense of political **pluralism** or a **multi-**

party system. Rather, it means that both the Party and the state exercise their authority in conformity with the law, with fewer abuses and opportunities for **corruption**, both of which pose increasingly serious threats to the prestige of the Party.

RUSSIA. *See* UNION OF SOVIET SOCIALIST REPUBLICS.

– S –

SABATIER, LÉOPOLD (1877-?). An influential and controversial colonial official in the early 20th century. Posted to the **Central Highlands**, which were more or less under direct **French** control rather than being administered by the Vietnamese government of **Annam**, Sabatier fell in love with the **Rhadé** people and produced several ethnographic works on their **language** and culture. He came to see himself as an advocate for the **highland minorities**, known to the French as **Montagnards**. Although he wanted to ensure that the highlanders were loyal to the colonial regime, he also sought to protect them from excessive immigration by lowland Vietnamese and Europeans. Sabatier's stance on this issue, however, flew in the face of other, more powerful colonial interests wishing to open up the Central Highlands for cultivation of **rubber** and other products. His career as a colonial official ended in the late 1920s, but his concerns for the negative impact of economic exploitation and **migration** by outsiders into the Central Highlands proved all too well-founded; unrest began in the region in the 1930s and has never completely ended.

SABATTIER, CAMILLE ANGE GABRIEL (1892–1966). Military commander of **French** forces in **Tonkin** during World War II. After the **Japanese occupation** authorities abolished the French colonial regime in March 1945, General Sabattier led 2,000 French troops through the mountains to safety in southern **China**.

SAIGON (Sài Gòn) (now known as *Hồ Chí Minh City*). Major commercial and industrial center in southern Vietnam and, before 1975, capital of the **Republic of Vietnam.** At the time of the Vietnamese expansion into the **Mekong River Delta**, Saigon was a small trading post on what is known today as the *Saigon River*, controlled by the kingdom of **Cambodia**. During the next two centuries, the area was settled by Vietnamese farmers and Chinese traders, and the **Nguyễn Lords** built a citadel on the site of modern Saigon, calling it *Gia Định* (the term *Saigon* was originally used specifically for the area of present-day **Chợ Lớn**). The year 1698 is now recognized as the "founding" of Saigon as a Vietnamese town, although it had been a Cambodian settlement and customs station long before that.

After the **French** conquest of the southern provinces in 1860, Saigon became the capital and commercial center of the colony of **Cochin China**. Surrounded by the relatively rich lands of the South, the city became the residence of an affluent class of Westernized Vietnamese bourgeoisie. After World War II, Saigon and its surrounding area were re-occupied by the French, while the northern provinces were controlled by **Hồ Chí Minh**'s **Democratic Republic of Vietnam** (DRV). In 1949, Saigon became the administrative seat of the **State of Vietnam** (usually referred to as the **Bảo Đại** government). After the **Geneva Conference**, it became the capital of the Republic of Vietnam.

During the next 20 years, Saigon was exposed to a heavy dose of **United States** cultural and economic influence. Flagrant wealth coexisted with grinding poverty, and the city as a whole vibrated with a pervasive sense of permanent political instability. In February 1968, the local apparatus of the **National Liberation Front** (NLF) attempted to provoke a general uprising in Saigon as a counterpoint to the **Tết Offensive** in the countryside. As a whole, the local population did not respond, although the occupation by suicide squads of key installations, including the ground floor of the U.S. embassy, had a significant impact on U.S. public opinion.

With the capture of Saigon on 30 April 1975 by North Vietnamese forces, the South joined the Vietnamese revolution and was purged of the "poisonous weeds" of bourgeois **capitalism**. As a symbol of the dawning new era, the city was renamed *Hồ Chí Minh City* (*Thành Phố Hồ Chí Minh*). With the changed political atmosphere since the late 1980s, however, it has become increasingly common for Vietnamese to refer to it by its old name, all the more as it has regained its position as an important economic and financial center.

In terms of population, Hồ Chí Minh City is currently the largest city in Vietnam, with approximately 3.9 million people, though this figure is constantly growing with **migration** from rural areas. Like other major municipalities in the country, Hồ Chí Minh City is administered directly by the central government in **Hanoi**. The **Vietnamese Communist Party**, the ruling party in the SRV, is represented by a Municipal Branch, headed by a chairman, who is a leading member of the Party.

Since the integration of North and South, Hồ Chí Minh City has represented a persistent challenge to the Party leadership in Hanoi. "Bourgeois" attitudes and practices have survived among the population despite vigorous efforts by the regime to stamp them out. Efforts to eliminate **capitalism** and create a dominant state sector had little success and led to a high degree of malaise among local residents, many of whom had little trust in the socialist system. Current policy since the launching of *đổi mới* in the mid-1980s has allowed the city to take more initiative and make use of its distinctive history and resources; it currently ranks as the leading **industrial** and commercial center in Vietnam and the home of much of the nation's technological expertise, as well as its embryonic **stock market**. Almost all leaders considered as reformers have cut their political teeth in Hồ Chí Minh City, from the now-retired **Nguyễn Văn Linh** and **Võ Văn Kiệt** to rising stars **Nguyễn Tấn Dũng** and **Trương Tấn Sang**.

Being a much younger city than Hanoi, Hồ Chí Minh City does not have the same **architectural** heritage. Many of its prominent buildings date from the colonial era, such as the Cathedral, the **Continental Hotel**, and the building that houses the Municipal **People's Committee**. It has become important as a **tourist** destination in its own right and as a jumping-off place for travelers leaving for other parts of the country.

SAIGON UPRISING. *See* NAM KỲ UPRISING.

SAINTENY, JEAN (1907–1978). French representative in **Indochina** at the close of World War II. A son-in-law of ex-Governor-General **Albert Sarraut** and an international banker with experience in Indochina, Jean Sainteny supported General Charles de Gaulle's Free French movement during World War II and was sent to southern **China** in 1944 to represent Free French interests in the area as the war came to an end. In August 1945, he went to **Hanoi** as French commissioner for the **protectorates** of **Annam** and **Tonkin** and negotiated with **Hồ Chí Minh**, president of the **Democratic Republic of Vietnam** (DRV), to resolve mutual differences over postwar Indochina. In March 1946, the two signed a preliminary **Ho-Sainteny Agreement** recognizing the DRV as a "free state" in the **French Union**. The agreement broke down, leading to war in December 1946. In the fall of 1954, Sainteny served briefly as senior French representative to the DRV.

SALAN, RAOUL (1899–1984). **French** general and commander of French forces in **Indochina** in 1952–1953. A much-decorated veteran of both world wars, General Salan arrived in Indochina in 1952 as a replacement for the popular and dynamic general **Jean de Lattre de Tassigny,** who had died of cancer a few months previously. Unlike de Lattre, Salan adopted a cautious strategy that sought to protect territories under French control rather than to win the struggle against the **Việt Minh** Front. At the insistence of the **United States**, Paris replaced Salan with General **Henri Navarre** in the spring of 1954. *See also* FRANCO-VIỆT MINH WAR.

SARRAUT, ALBERT (1872–1962). Prominent **French** official and two-time governor-general in early 20th-century **Indochina**. Born in Bordeaux, Sarraut became a journalist and a Radical Socialist deputy in the French National Assembly. In 1911, he was named governor-general of Indochina. A firm believer in the French civilizing mission in Indochina, on his arrival Sarraut promised a new era of Franco–Vietnamese collaboration. After returning to France in 1914 on the grounds of ill health, he was reappointed for a second term in 1916. During his two terms in office, he inaugurated a number of reforms in the political and social arenas, setting up a new system of **education** based on a two-track system and setting up provincial assemblies in **Annam** and **Tonkin.**

Sarraut returned to France in 1919 and served as minister of colonies from 1920 to 1924. He served as prime minister of the French government in two cabinets during the 1930s.

SCHOLAR-GENTRY (*Văn thân*). English-language term for officials and other members of the local elite in traditional Vietnam. Membership, at least in theory, was not based on the right of birth but on merit, meaning success in the civil service **examinations**, the route to entrance into the prestigious imperial bureaucracy. In fact, usually a relatively direct relationship existed among education, official status, and wealth, since for the most part, only the affluent landed class possessed the resources to provide a classical **Confucian** education to its children. In turn, officialdom provided an opportunity to accumulate wealth through the purchase of land, the primary source of wealth in traditional Vietnam.

Not all who passed the examinations became members of the bureaucracy, and not all officials became landlords. This category included scholars who had not reached a sufficiently highpoint in the examinations to obtain positions in the **mandarinate** and returned to become teachers in their home **villages**, which made them part of the local elite. These local scholars could sometimes become rebels, while at other times they led their neighbors in resisting foreign invaders. *See also* SCHOLARS' UPRISING.

SCHOLARS' UPRISING (*Văn Thân Khởi Nghĩa*). A violent political movement led by scholars in Nghệ An in the late 19th century. They were angered at favoritism allegedly shown to Catholic converts as the result of **French** pressure on the imperial court in **Huế**, as well as the court's concessions and surrender of **Cochin China** to France during the 1860s. This was also the time of the **Philastre Treaty**, which increased French influence over Vietnam. In March 1874, a group of scholars led by Trần Tấn and Đặng Như Mai mobilized support for demonstrations that erupted throughout the provinces of Nghệ An and Hà Tĩnh. The riots focused on **Catholic** converts, hundreds of whom were killed by crowds acting under the slogan "Defeat the Westerners and exterminate the heretics [Catholics]." The movement was suppressed by imperial troops the following year, but it demonstrated the level of resentment felt by the ruling elite toward Emperor **Tự Đức** and his court. *See also* NGUYỄN DYNASTY.

SCIENCE AND TECHNOLOGY. With the end of the Vietnam War in 1975, the **Vietnamese Communist Party** (VCP) for the first time in a generation could turn its attention to domestic problems. A key to resolving those problems was to carry out a revolution in science and technology that could help to erase the damage of three decades of war and over half a century of colonial rule. As testimony to the Party's recognition of the importance of the challenge, it was listed as one of three major tasks in the first postwar five-year plan approved by the Fourth Congress in December 1976. During the next few years, an Institute of Science was established, and subsidiary institutes were created for research and development in all aspects of the social and physical sciences.

A decade later, few of these bright hopes had been brought to realization. Lack of capital and technological assistance from abroad was undoubtedly a factor. However, the regime compounded its problems by adopting a foreign policy that resulted in war with **Cambodia** and **China**, rising military expenditures, and the flight of many of the nation's most talented citizens abroad during the late 1970s. In the mid-1980s, Vietnam earned the dubious categorization of being one of the poorest countries in Asia. The advent of the new program of renovation (*đổi mới*) promised to bring about a reversal of these trends and introduce Vietnamese society to the global economic marketplace. During the next decade, Vietnam gradually began to enter the technological age. Computers and credit cards began to make their appearance. By the early 1990s, owners of personal computers in Vietnam obtained access to the Internet, and state and private enterprises throughout the country clamored to join the technological revolution.

At this juncture, however, Vietnam still has a long way to go. There remains a serious shortage of skilled technicians, forcing many companies to import specialists from abroad. Programs are under way to retrain conservative bureaucrats accustomed to handling things in the old way. Still, knowledgeable experts estimate that it will take an investment of over U.S.$1 billion to bring Vietnam abreast of technological investments taking place elsewhere in the region. Modernization has become a key buzzword, and the government is now actively encouraging the spread of technology. The Internet has become very popular with young people in particular, though the government has established firewalls to block access to politically and morally "undesirable" sites. *See also* EDUCATION; FOREIGN INVESTMENT; INDUSTRY.

SCULPTURE. The earliest forms of sculpture in Vietnam date back to the late **Neolithic Era**, when unknown artisans produced primitive figurines depicting animals, human beings, and local deities. More sophisticated forms of sculpture began to develop during the **Bronze Age** and the centuries immediately following the Chinese conquest of the **Red River Delta** in the late first millennium B.C.E. Unfortunately, little of that art survives today.

The period following independence from **Chinese** rule in the 10th century C.E. saw a rapid rise in the quality and quantity of Vietnamese sculpture. Much of it was undoubtedly a consequence of the popularity of **Buddhism** during the **Lý** and **Trần dynasties**. Statues of the Buddha, carved in stone or wood, were often highly stylized and followed Chinese models, but some of the few surviving examples display an impressive level of technique and a sophisticated degree of characterization.

After the 15th century, sculpture began to decline somewhat in popularity, as Buddhism was gradually replaced by **Confucianism** as the foremost ideology of the state. During the **Lê dynasty** and the period of civil war that brought it to an end, the primary form of creativity was in the form of wooden relief carvings and statuary on temples or village communal houses (*đình*). Unlike the early period, the sculpture produced in this period was strongly influenced by folk art, featuring vigorous lines and rural themes close to the lives of the common people.

The **French** conquest and the importation of Western influence completed the decline of traditional sculpture in Vietnam. During the 20th century, popular styles created in wood, terra cotta, or metal, predominate, although some traditional sculpture continues to be produced, primarily for the **tourist** trade. *See also* CERAMIC ARTS.

SĨ NHIẾP (Shi Xie). A local official under **Chinese** rule in the second century C.E. Sĩ Nhiếp came from an ethnic Chinese family whose ancestors had immigrated to the **Red River Delta** area in the first century. His father was prefect of **Nhật Nam** at the southern limits of Chinese-ruled territory, and he himself became prefect of the delta area of **Giao Chỉ** during the 1800s. He and his family governed the region during the turbulent years spanning the fall of the Han dynasty and the rise of the Jin. This phenomenon of local elite collaborating with the Chinese but governing without them when the opportunity arose was to become a frequent pattern during the **Chinese period** of Vietnamese history.

Sĩ Nhiếp is supposed to have had considerable scholarly abilities and is associated with the spread of Chinese culture among the Vietnamese he governed. (He was reportedly so pedagogically gifted that he continued to teach and lecture from beyond the grave, and his voice could be heard ringing out from his tomb.) Later Vietnamese sources gave him the informal title of "Sĩ Vương" (King Sĩ) because he personified the ideals of a **Confucian** monarch and because he was the *de facto* ruler of his subjects during the dynastic transition.

SINO–VIETNAMESE. A term used to describe the vocabulary and writing system borrowed from Chinese. Although Vietnamese is an **Austroasiatic** language unrelated to Chinese, the centuries of direct rule and indirect cultural contact left it with a heavy Chinese imprint. Vietnamese contains numerous Chinese borrowings, even for fairly basic vocabulary items, as well as many of the grammatical conjunctions used to structure sentences. For much of Vietnam's history during and after the **Chinese period**, classical Chinese was the standard written language, though the characters were pronounced out loud in Vietnamese. (The pronunciation of these characters was derived from Chinese, as is the case with Japanese and Korean, but is generally no longer intelligible to Chinese speakers.) The term "Sino–Vietnamese" is sometimes used to refer to the readings of these characters, as well as to the texts written by Vietnamese in the Chinese language, as opposed to those in *chữ nôm*, which transcribes spoken Vietnamese. It can also refer to Chinese lexical borrowings in the **Vietnamese language**.

SIX BOARDS. *See LỤC BỘ.*

SLASH-AND-BURN AGRICULTURE. A form of **agriculture** traditionally practiced by many **highland minorities** in Vietnam, also known as *swidden*. (In Vietnamese the formal term, borrowed from Chinese, is *đao canh hoả chủng*, but it is more commonly referred to as *làm rẫy*, as opposed to *làm ruộng* for wet-rice farming.) Slash-and-burn agriculture predominates at higher altitudes, where irrigation is difficult or impossible. It involves cutting down and burning the vegetation on a parcel of land, which then becomes the field (rẫy), with the ash serving to provide nutrients. Slash-and-burn involves a cycle of using fields and then leaving them fallow for several years.

Modern governments in Southeast Asia have generally been hostile toward slash-and-burn and have undertaken measures to force highland minorities to change their style of agriculture. In Vietnam. this has involved a program known as *định canh định cư,* "fixed cultivation and settled residence"; the name is somewhat misleading because most groups practicing slash-and-burn already have permanent **villages**, even though they rotate the use of fields. Over the past few years, there has been considerable debate over the merits and demerits of this system of agriculture in Vietnam and elsewhere. Advocates for the upland peoples argue that the practice of slash-and-burn is not inherently harmful to the environment provided that the fields have sufficient time to lie fallow and become arable once more. They contend that the very real problem of deforestation faced by Vietnam and its neighbors is caused more by the influx of outsiders into the upland regions and to illegal logging and that the minorities are scapegoats being unfairly targeted for their traditional cultivation methods. *See also* MIGRATION; RICE CULTURE.

SLAVERY. The existence of slaves in early Vietnamese society has been a topic of much debate among historians. According to the Marxist view of social evolution, there must have been a "slave stage" in every society's history at some point in time. Some Party historians have dutifully followed this line and posited the existence of slaves in the **Bronze Age** based on certain images found on **bronze drums**, but more specifically on the assumption that there had to have been slaves because Marx said so. In recent years, however, less doctrinaire interpretations have tended to leave the existence of a "slave society" open to question.

There is certainly evidence of various forms of bondage in earlier centuries, particularly under the **Lý** and **Trần dynasties** between the 11th and 15th centuries. However, the precise meaning of the various terms used to refer to these people is far from clear, and it is very possible that they were more like serfs than slaves. On the other hand, it is evident that several of the **highland minorities** traditionally possessed and traded in slaves, and this practice was still widespread when the **French** arrived in the late 19th century. *See also* ASIATIC MODE OF PRODUCTION; FEUDALISM.

SOCIAL PROBLEMS. With the conquest of the South in the spring of 1975, leaders in **Hanoi** faced the future with a full dose of optimism. At the Fourth **Vietnamese Communist Party** Congress a year later, they launched their first postwar five-year plan aimed at laying the foundations of a socialist society throughout the country by the end of the decade. Not least as a factor in their self-confidence was the conviction that the Vietnamese people—steeled in war and led by the disciplined ranks of the Party—would follow the regime in the postwar era in its effort to win the fruits of the revolution.

As it turned out, this supreme confidence was somewhat misplaced. Within a decade, a sense of disillusionment had risen to alarming levels in Vietnamese society, and public trust in the ability of the country's veteran leaders was rapidly ebbing. Unemployment levels were high, and malnutrition was rampant; the Party's ability to discipline itself had seriously eroded, leading to growing complaints of **corruption** within the ranks. Within the population as a whole, a growing sense of malaise among wide groups of society was palpable, and even within the ranks of the Party and the governmental bureaucracy, complaints were voiced that the nation's veteran leaders were no longer able to deal with the burgeoning problems of Vietnamese society.

Part of the problem was a natural letdown after the decades of war and sacrifice. Part, too, was a consequence of the foreign policy crises that engulfed the nation in war with both **Cambodia** and **China** before the end of the decade. The regime contributed to its own difficulties by adopting a doctrinaire approach toward the building of a fully socialist society that ignored the popular weariness with decades of war and the wide distrust of Party leadership within the population in the South. By the early 1980s, the signs of distress were clear. With unemployment levels rising rapidly, alienation and cynicism on the part of the younger generation were becoming chronic. Official corruption eroded the fragile sense of trust and undoubtedly played into the hands of **dissident** elements who called for a new generation of leaders or even an end to Party rule.

Such conditions were a factor in the Party's decision to launch the program of renovation (*đổi mới*) at the Sixth National Congress in December 1986. The economic consequences of that decision are self-evident because the overall standard of living of the population has improved markedly in the last two decades. At the same time, though, the rising prosperity, materialism, and exposure to foreign ideas that renovation has entailed have also brought some undesirable by-products, collectively known as "social evils" (*tệ nạn xã hội*). Drug addiction and alcoholism are on the rise, prostitution is running rampant in the urban areas, and AIDS has made its appearance. With government funding of **education** and **health** on the decline, health care is slipping and the number of young people attending school has dropped to alarming levels. Although many of these problems are occurring primarily in the major cities, conditions in rural areas are, in some respects, even more serious. Underemployment in the countryside is high, causing considerable **migration** of laborers to the urban areas, and a substantial proportion of the rural population is living near or under the poverty line.

In the end, rising prosperity will alleviate some of these problems, but others are a natural and perhaps inevitable consequence of the modernization process. As such, they represent a serious challenge to a government and a Party determined to bring about **economic** development without the accompanying problems of social and political instability.

SOCIALIST REPUBLIC OF VIETNAM (SRV) (*Cộng Hoà Xã Hội Chủ Nghĩa Việt Nam*). Successor to the **Democratic Republic of Vietnam** (DRV) and current name of the country. The SRV came into existence on 2 July 1976, approximately 14 months after the seizure of **Saigon** by revolutionary forces and the fall of the government of South Vietnam. The new republic united the two separate states— the DRV in the North and the **Republic of Vietnam** in the South— which had existed since the **Geneva Conference** of 1954. Like its predecessor, the SRV is officially a Marxist–Leninist state, ruled by the **Vietnamese Communist Party** (the new name for the Vietnamese Workers' Party, adopted in December 1976). It inherited the political and administrative system already in existence in the North, which was now extended to the entire country. The capital remained in **Hanoi**, and a new one-house **National Assembly**, consisting of 492 members elected from both North and South, was elected in April 1976. A new **constitution** promulgated in 1980 introduced a number of minor changes in the political system, notably the establishment of a collective presidency, known as the *Council of State* (*Hội Đồng Nhà Nước*). This was replaced by the 1992 constitution, however, which structured the government around a president, prime minister, and cabinet/council of ministers.

The total land area of the SRV is roughly 331,000 square kilometers (145,800 square miles). It consists of 58 provinces (including the Vũng Tàu-Côn Đảo Special Zone) and five municipalities directly subordinate to the central government (Hanoi, Hồ Chí Minh City, **Hải Phòng**, **Đà Nẵng**, and Cần Thơ). The population was estimated at approximately 81 million in 2003.

SOCIÉTÉ DES MISSIONS ÉTRANGÈRES DE PARIS (Society of Foreign Missions).

French-run organization for the promotion of Roman Catholicism in Asia set up in the 17th century. The society was primarily the result of the efforts of the French Jesuit **Alexandre de Rhodes**, who was an active force in the spread of **Christianity** to Vietnam beginning in 1627. When the Vatican was reluctant to promote missionary efforts in Vietnam against the opposition of Portugal, Alexander turned to the French church and was able to find financial support for a new organization established in France. The Society was formally established in Paris in 1664, representing both missionary and commercial interests ambitious to find a new outlet for French activities in Asia.

During the next few years, the Society was actively involved in missionary efforts in Southeast Asia but encountered opposition from other forces within the church and eventually concentrated its activities in Vietnam, where official antagonism made the society's operations increasingly difficult. Despite such opposition, the Society was relatively successful in promoting Christianity among the Vietnamese population, and there were an estimated 450,000 Christian converts in Vietnam by the mid-19th century. In recent years, the opening of the mission archives in France has provided a rich new source of information for historians. *See also* PIGNEAU DE BÉHAINE.

SƠN VỊ CULTURE. Prehistoric culture dating from the late Paleolithic period whose core area is the hilly region of Vĩnh Phúc and Phú Thọ. Discovered by Vietnamese **archeologists** in 1968, it is generally considered to predate the more advanced **Hoà Bình** culture into which it might have evolved. Chipped pebbles found at Sơn Vị sites are technologically less advanced than the tools found at sites dating from the Hoà Bình era. Carbon-14 methods date the Sơn Vị sites at approximately 12,000 years ago, placing the culture in the Pleistocene or late Paleolithic era. *See also* NÚI ĐỌ CULTURE.

SOUTH CHINA SEA (Biển Đông). The body of water known in English as the *South China Sea* has always played a key role in the Vietnamese economy. **Trade** has been an essential part of Vietnam's history since early times, and much of it has moved in and out of the country's ports scattered up and down the coast. At the same time, the long coastline creates a certain vulnerability where Vietnam's defense is concerned. Although its traditional enemy, **China**, tended to opt for invasions over the land border, naval intrusions could not be ruled out, as the famous battles of **Bạch Đằng** demonstrate, and the various stages of **colonization** by the **French** in the 19th century generally began with naval attacks or, at the very least, landings by troops transported on ships.

Although Vietnam has not faced an invasion of its coast in many years, the South China Sea remains of tremendous strategic importance. The **Paracel** and **Spratly** island chains, which **Hanoi** claims as its own territory, are the subject of disputes with China, Taiwan, Malaysia, Indonesia, and the Philippines. The latter three countries are fellow members of the **Association of Southeast Asian Nations**, and Vietnam's membership in this organization has somewhat attenuated the potential for clashes with those particular neighbors, while Taiwan seems unlikely to project its power strongly enough to take on the Vietnamese. The main threat to what Vietnam sees as its territorial sovereignty in the Sea comes from the Chinese, a threat that is made more concrete by persistent tensions along the land border and in the **Tonkin Gulf**. Vietnamese sensitivities over this issue are clearly demonstrated by the fact that official English-language publications normally refer to "the Eastern Sea" (a translation of the Vietnamese name), thus consciously avoiding the semantic connection with China.

Along with the need to uphold claims to sovereignty, of course, the South China Sea is valuable for its reserves of **oil**. The various claimants have separately moved ahead with commitments for exploration and exploitation of these reserves in the particular zones under their control, always to the accompaniment of squawks of protest from the other claimants. This situation seems likely to continue as long as the overlapping maritime claims are not resolved; whether the resolution will be peaceful or violent remains to be seen.

SOVIET–VIETNAMESE TREATY OF FRIENDSHIP AND CO-OPERATION. Treaty between the **Socialist Republic of Vietnam** (SRV) and the **Union of Soviet Socialist Republics** signed on 3 November 1978. It was scheduled to run for 25 years and called for mutual consultations in case of a military attack on either party. The treaty was apparently requested by Vietnam to deter **China** from taking action in response to a planned Vietnamese invasion of **Cambodia** but it failed to prevent the Chinese 'punitive infasion' of 1979. In an unpublished annex, the SRV reportedly agreed to provide the USSR with the use of port and air base facilities in Vietnam. The treaty expired prematurely with the collapse of the Soviet Union.

SPECIAL RELATIONS/RELATIONSHIP (*Quan hệ đặc biệt*). An arrangement designed by Communist leaders in Vietnam to replace the **Indochinese Federation**, a concept originally elaborated in the 1930s. Sometime in the 1950s or 1960s, Vietnam dropped the idea of a future Indochinese Federation, probably because of heightened nationalist sensitivities among party members in neighboring **Laos** and **Cambodia**. As the Vietnam War came to an end, official sources in **Hanoi** began to speak of the creation of a "special relationship" among the revolutionary governments of the three countries, which tacitly abandoned the concept of a tight union. Although the leaders of the new Lao People's Democratic Republic accepted this relationship, the Khmer Rouge regime in Democratic Kampuchea did not.

After the Vietnamese occupation of Cambodia in 1979 and the establishment of the People's Republic of Kampuchea, the bilateral special relationship became trilateral and involved the establishment of close links among the three countries in the political, economic, military, social, cultural, and diplomatic fields. Because of its size and historical experience, Vietnam was the dominant force in the arrangement. After the creation of a coalition government in Phnom Penh in 1991, however, the special relationship lost much of its cohesion and became more or less bilateral again, involving only Laos. *See also* INDOCHINESE COMMUNIST PARTY; VIETNAMESE COMMUNIST PARTY.

SPRATLY ISLANDS (*Quần Đảo Trường Sa*). Scattered small islands in the **South China Sea**, consisting of hundreds of tiny sand spits and coral reefs stretching over several hundred square miles between southern **China**, the Philippines, the island of Borneo, and mainland Southeast Asia. The Spratlys were rarely occupied before the present century; **France** laid claim to the islands in 1933 and put a small meteorological station on one of the largest. Since World War II, several of the islands have been claimed or occupied by most of the nations in the vicinity, including the Philippines, the Republic of China, the People's Republic of China (PRC), Malaysia, the **Republic of Vietnam,** and recently the **Socialist Republic of Vietnam** (SRV). **Hanoi** has presented historical evidence to support its claim to ownership over the islands, but this claim has been disputed by China, and a number of small-scale clashes have occurred between forces of several claimants.

As with the **Paracel Islands** to the north, the primary importance of the Spratlys is not the islands themselves but the surrounding seas, which reportedly contain substantial **oil** reserves.

STATE OF VIETNAM. Semi-independent state established within the **French Union** in 1949. The Associated State of Vietnam came into being as the result of negotiations between ex-Emperor **Bảo Đại** and representatives of the **French** government in 1947 and 1948. The agreement was finalized by the so-called **Élysée Accords** signed on 8 March 1949. According to the agreement, the new state, along with its counterparts in **Cambodia** and **Laos**, had some of the attributes of an independent government. In some key areas, however, the independence of these **Associated States of Indochina** was limited by membership in the French Union. In practice, major decisions related to foreign affairs and the conduct of the **Franco–Việt Minh War** continued to be made by the French. The State of Vietnam did not receive broad support from nationalist elements inside the country, but it was formally recognized in February 1950 by the **United States** and several of its allies.

The Associated States came to an end as the result of the **Geneva Conference**, which divided Vietnam temporarily into two separate regroupment zones in the North and the South. Many members of the State of Vietnam government continued to serve of the **Republic of Vietnam**, which was set up after 1954 in **Saigon**. Bảo Đại himself, however, was removed from power by his Prime Minister **Ngô Đình Diệm**, who became President of the Republic. *See also* BẢO ĐẠI SOLUTION.

STATE-OWNED ENTERPRISE (SOE, *Doanh nghiệp nhà nước*). Originally the core of the socialist **economy** of the **Democratic Republic of Vietnam** and its successor, the **Socialist Republic of Vietnam**, the state-owned enterprise has become somewhat of an albatross around the government's neck as Vietnam makes the transition to a market-oriented system. At the ideological and conceptual levels, it is difficult for the older generation of leaders steeped in Marxism to accept the significant restructuring—let alone the dismantling—of such a crucial element of socialism. (For this reason, the alternative "private sector" is officially referred to as the "nonstate sector" or *khu vực ngoài quốc doanh.*) At the practical level, tinkering with thousands of state-owned entities is a daunting task—especially when not all the consequences can be clearly calculated.

The process of **equitization** (*cổ phần hoá*) of SOEs officially began with a government decree in 1992 and has proceeded in fits and starts since then. (The government took the initial step of merging many enterprises and closing others so that the original number of roughly 12,000 state firms was halved by 1994.) The purpose of equitization is not so much to sell off an SOE to private investors as to recapitalize it as a joint stock company or other entity by attracting investment from various sources. Although there have been some success stories in terms of SOEs that have been sufficiently restructured to operate at a profit, retain their original workforce, raise employees' salaries, and even list on Vietnam's **stock market**, there have also been many difficulties along the way. SOEs, for example, have traditionally enjoyed preferential access to land and credit and more favorable export quotas and tax rates; the prospect of losing these benefits obviously reduces the attraction of equitization for directors and managers. There are also serious problems involved with assessing the value of a state firm's assets, particularly its land, and with the resolution of its liabilities after it has been equitized. Nor is it a certainty that a restructured SOE will need or be able to afford all of its previous workforce.

These disincentives to equitization have not prevented the government from moving ahead with its **equitization** program, but they have significantly slowed down its progress. Ambitious annual targets of 1,000 or more successfully equitized SOEs have not been met, and the figures are constantly being scaled downward. The current plan is to complete the equitization of all but 1,000 SOEs by 2007, with the remaining firms continuing to operate under state management. In 2004, the government announced that it would limit the latter to only 20 or so categories of business (such as utilities, publishing, and aviation), which are considered undesirable targets for any degree of privatization. Generally speaking, the dismantling of the state sector as a direct reversal of the original **nationalization** associated with socialist economics is probably an irreversible trend, but the path to a vigorous private sector (no matter what it is called) is a long and rocky one.

STATE PLANNING. Since the inception of the **Democratic Republic of Vietnam** (DRV) in 1945, Communist leaders have been advocates of the concept of a planned economy. When party leaders returned to **Hanoi** after the end of the **Franco–Việt Minh War** in 1954, they established a state planning commission and in 1958 embarked on their first multiyear state plan, a three-year plan to lay the first foundations of a socialist society. **Agriculture** was **collectivized**, and key **industrial** and commercial firms were placed under state ownership.

In 1961, the first five-year plan (1961–1965) was inaugurated. The objective was to begin the process of socialist industrialization, but the Vietnam War intervened, and the plan was eventually replaced by a series of one-year plans. Long-term planning resumed in 1976, with the second five-year plan (1976–1980) designed to build the foundations of socialism throughout the entire country. The achievements of the second plan were limited, primarily because of lack of capital and managerial inefficiency, but a third plan was put in place at the **Vietnamese Communist Party**'s Fifth National Congress in 1982. When it, too, had only limited success, in December 1986 Party leaders tacitly abandoned the concept and, with the program of renovation (*đổi mới*), moved toward the establishment of a market-based socialist economy.

With economic reforms proceeding apace, notably the expansion of the private sector and the increasingly important role of market forces, the scope of central planning is becoming more restricted. Government plans still exist, but they tend to focus more on specific issues, such as poverty reduction or general economic development. In 1996, for example, the State Planning Commission announced the inauguration of a new five-year plan to bring about a revolution in **science and technology** by the end of the decade. *See also* NATIONALIZATION OF INDUSTRY AND COMMERCE.

STOCK MARKET. The stock market in the **Socialist Republic of Vietnam** is very much a product of the 21st century, the first stock exchange (officially known as the *Securities Transaction Center, Trung Tâm Giao Dịch Chứng Khoán*) having opened in Hồ Chí Minh City in July 2000 after several years of planning, trials, and false starts. At the time of its opening, only two companies were listed; by early 2005, this number had increased to 26, with a total market capitalization of roughly $125 million. The market has been slow to acquire momentum due to a general lack of confidence in its fundamentals; for example, firms listing on the Stock Exchange are not subject to the kinds of requirements in terms of accounting standards and transparency that most **foreign investors** expect. However, the number of foreign and Vietnamese investors is on the rise, and investment funds outside the country are beginning to pay it some attention.

Almost all the firms listed on the Stock Exchange are former **state-owned enterprises** that have undergone restructuring of their capital through **equitization**. Only a small proportion of these firms have been willing to hazard a listing on the market, however. There are expectations that the number of equitized companies seeking listings will increase as the market develops momentum and demonstrates its viability as a potential source of capital for these firms. Currently foreign-invested companies are not allowed to list on the exchange, reflecting a broader government ambivalence regarding the double-edged sword of relying on foreign capital, a point driven home very clearly by the experience of its Asian neighbors in the 1997–1998 financial crisis. Even for those Vietnamese companies whose stock can be purchased by foreign investors, the latter's share is limited to 30 percent (up from an earlier limit of 20 percent until July 2003), and the authorities keep a careful watch to ensure that this cap is not exceeded. A second stock exchange was opened in Hanoi in March 2005.

STRATEGIC HAMLETS (*Ấp chiến lược*). Program adopted by the **Ngô Đình Diệm** government during the Vietnam War to improve security in the countryside. The program began in 1962 at the suggestion of the John F. Kennedy administration, which hoped that the concept, successfully put in operation by the British in Malaya, could be reproduced in the **Republic of Vietnam**. Smaller than the so-called **Agrovilles** (*khu trú mật*), which had been created in 1959, the Strategic Hamlets were to be built, where possible, on the basis of existing **villages** and hamlets in rural areas. The new hamlets were to be provided with funds to help build schools, wells, and clinics and were expected to provide for their own security.

United States officials suggested that the program initially be adopted only in secure areas to enhance confidence and popular support for the concept, but the Diệm regime opted to promote the program with a greater sense of urgency and organized many hamlets in contested areas, where revolutionary activity was high. The results were mixed. Although the hamlets created severe problems for the **National Liberation Front** and **People's Liberation Armed Forces** (popularly known as the *Việt Cộng*), persistent efforts resulted in the destruction or takeover of many of them. Moreover, the usual problems of **corruption** and mismanagement plagued the program and led to its widespread unpopularity, as did the frequently coercive measures used to achieve resettlement of unwilling peasants. By the mid-1960s, the program was virtually moribund.

SƯƠNG NGUYỆT ANH (1864–1921). A female writer and editor in the early 20th century. Her real name was *Nguyễn Thị Khuê*, but she was best known by her *nom de plume Sương Nguyệt Anh*. (*Sương* was a title used by widows). The daughter of the famous poet **Nguyễn Đình Chiểu**, she was a poetess in her own right who became the editor of *Nữ Giới Chung* (*Women's Bell*), the first publication specifically targeting **women** readers. Although the newspaper, which appeared in 1918, lasted less than a year before folding, it represented an important step in the development of Vietnamese **journalism** and in the evolution of women's status under colonial rule.

– T –

TẠ QUANG BỬU (1920–1986). Prominent nationalist politician and later an official in the **Democratic Republic of Vietnam** (DRV). Educated in Europe, Bửu returned to **Indochina** and during World War II taught mathematics and the English language in **Huế**. His first political involvement came in 1944, when he directed a Vietnamese Boy Scout movement sponsored by the Vichy regime of Governor-General **Jean Decoux** and became a member of the pro-**Japanese Đại Việt Party**. In August 1945, however, he joined the **Việt Minh** Front and in March 1946 was named vice-minister of national defense in the DRV. After the **Geneva Conference** of 1954, Bửu became a professor of science at the University of Hanoi and vice-chairman of the State Commission for **Science and Technology**. From 1965 to 1976, he was minister of Vocational Universities and Secondary Schools. *See also* EDUCATION.

TẠ THU THÂU (1905–1945). Prominent member of the **Trotskyite** faction in colonial Vietnam. The son of a poor carpenter, Tạ Thu Thâu was a follower of **Nguyễn An Ninh** in **Saigon** during the early 1920s. While studying in Paris, he joined **Nguyễn Thế Truyền**'s **Annamese Independence Party**, and then embraced Trotskyism. Evicted from France in 1930 for his political activities, he returned to Vietnam and joined the Trotskyite journal in Saigon, *La Lutte* (*The Struggle*). For the next several years, he was an active force in the Trotskyite movement, and on the **journalistic** scene. The **Indochinese Communist Party** bitterly opposed Trotskyism, however, and Thâu was assassinated by the **Việt Minh** in late 1945.

TALE OF KIÈU (*Truyện Kiều*, also known as *Kim Vân Kiều* after the names of its three main characters). Classic poem written by Vietnamese author **Nguyễn Du** in the early 19th century. Generally considered to be the greatest literary work written in the Vietnamese language, the *Tale of Kiều* is based on a Chinese love story and relates the story of a beautiful and intelligent young woman who sells herself as a concubine while remaining true to her real lover. Underlying the narrative plot is a powerful criticism of the greed, hypocrisy, and viciousness of contemporary **Confucian** society in Vietnam. The dramatic plot, as well as the beauty and the delicacy of the language, have made this 3,254-line poem the favorite literary work of millions of Vietnamese. As with such characters as Falstaff, Shylock, or Scrooge in the English-speaking world, several of its characters have become synonyms for certain personality types in Vietnamese society.

In the 1920s, the *Tale of Kiều* became the centerpiece of a literary controversy between supporters and opponents of **French** rule in colonial Vietnam. The debate between the conservative **Phạm Quỳnh** and the anticolonial **Ngô Đức Kế** centered around just which values of the beloved story were most significant for Vietnamese, as well as the question of just how their national culture was to survive under foreign rule. *See also* LITERATURE.

TÂM TÂM XÃ (Association of Like Minds). Radical political party organized among Vietnamese exiles in southern **China** in 1923. Founded by several Vietnamese patriots, such as **Hồ Tùng Mậu, Lê Hồng Phong**, and **Phạm Hồng Thái**, it was originally connected with **Phan Bội Châu**'s **Vietnamese Restoration Society** (Việt Nam Quang Phục Hội), established in Canton in 1912. Leaders of the association broke away from Châu's organization in 1923, apparently convinced that it was insufficiently activist.

The program of the Tâm Tâm Xã was relatively simple. Believing, like the French revolutionary Auguste Blanqui, that disputes over ideology were divisive, the party's leaders concentrated on uniting all resistance elements through a program of assassination and propaganda for a general uprising to overthrow the colonial regime in Vietnam. The association apparently sponsored an abortive effort by Phạm Hồng Thái to assassinate French Governor-General **Martial Merlin** in Canton. Many members subsequently joined the Revolutionary Youth League of Vietnam or **Thanh Niên.**

TẢN ĐÀ (1888–1939). Pen name of Nguyễn Khắc Hiếu, a popular Vietnamese poet during the early 20th century. Born in Sơn Tây, Tản Đà received a classical education and unsuccessfully took the regional civil service **examination** in 1912. Becoming a **journalist**, he worked for **Nguyễn Văn Vĩnh**'s *Đông Dương Tạp Chí* and then established his own journal, *An-Nam.* During his active life, Tản Đà became famous as a poet, writing in the modern idiom of *quốc ngữ* but evoking traditional **Confucian** themes that still appealed to conservative elements within the population. He also wrote moral primers designed to preserve traditional virtues in a rapidly changing society. Yet Tản Đà also stated publicly that the Vietnamese needed the **French** to assist them in adjusting to the challenges of the modern world. After his journal ceased publication in 1933, he retired to his native village, where he supported himself by fortune-telling until his death a few years later. *See also* LITERATURE.

TÂN TRÀO. A village in the border area of the northern provinces of Tuyên Quang and Thái Nguyên, originally called *Kim Lung.* Located in a region inhabited by the ethnic **Tày** minority, the village (renamed *Tân Trào*, "new trend") became an important base of operations for the **Việt Minh** and served as the capital of the **Việt Bắc** liberated zone. The important Tân Trào Conference, composed of delegates from localities throughout the country, was held on 13–15 August 1945 to launch the **August Revolution.** Prior to the opening of the conference, a plenary session of the Central Committee of the **Indochinese Communist Party** convened to prepare a response to the imminent surrender of **Japan.** On hearing of the Japanese surrender on 14 August, the Central Committee instructed the Việt Minh conference to declare a nationwide uprising to liberate Vietnam and

create an independent republic. *See also* JAPANESE OCCUPA-
TION.

TẢN VIÊN MOUNTAIN. A sacred mountain in northern Vietnam, located near the point where the **Red River** leaves the mountains and
enters the delta, about 30 kilometers (20 miles) northwest of **Hanoi**.
According to legend, it was the home of the Mountain Spirit (Sơn
Tinh), a powerful being who protected the city of Thăng Long,
present-day **Hanoi**. Sơn Tinh won a competition with his rival Water
Spirit (Thủy Tinh) for the hand of a princess during the reign of the
Hùng Kings. The defeated Water Spirit expressed his anger by causing floods. The spirit of Tản Viên is considered one of the most powerful in the Vietnamese pantheon.

**TÂN VIỆT CÁCH MỆNH ĐẢNG (New Vietnamese Revolutionary
Party).** Radical political party founded by anticolonial Vietnamese
in 1920s. Originally known as the *Phục Việt* (Revive Vietnam) party,
it was composed of **Hanoi** intellectuals and released prisoners, along
with some workers and students. Prominent members included **Đào
Duy Anh**, Tôn Quang Phiệt, and **Đặng Thái Mai**. The party went
through a number of name changes, settling on Tân Việt Cách Mệnh
Đảng in 1928, with its headquarters at Vinh in Nghệ An.

The overall aim of the party was to restore Vietnamese independence, but party leaders disagreed over whether to use the tactics of
reformation or violence. It cooperated as well as competed with **Hồ
Chí Minh**'s Revolutionary Youth League (**Thanh Niên**) for followers, but eventually the latter became dominant. In early 1930, the Tân
Việt merged with the Thanh Niên into a new **Vietnamese Communist Party**, which would soon change its name to the *Indochinese
Communist Party*.

TAOISM. *See* DAOISM.

TẬP CHÍ CỘNG SẢN (*Communist Review*). Official monthly journal
of the **Vietnamese Communist Party** (VCP). Articles in the journal
deal primarily with political or economic topics, often from a theoretical perspective, and have an official character because of the direct
link with the Party. Its predecessor, *Học Tập (Study)*, began publica-

tion in 1954; the name was changed after the shift in the nomenclature of the Party in 1986. *See* JOURNALISM.

TÀY. An ethnic minority in northern Vietnam who speak a Tai **language**. Known as the *Thổ* under the **French**, the Tày are numerically the largest **highland minority** group in Vietnam, with a total population of nearly 900,000. Related to the **Thái** and more closely to the **Nùng** in terms of ethnic background and language, their original habitat was probably the region straddling the Sino–Vietnamese border. Today, they live in the mountain provinces north of the **Red River Delta**, stretching northeast to the **Chinese** border.

Like most highland peoples in Vietnam, the Tày reside primarily in rural **villages** (*bản*) where they practice wet-**rice** agriculture. Political authority traditionally rested in a hereditary nobility, headed by a noble known by the Vietnamese title *thổ ty*, who typically ruled several villages and had the right to allocate lands to his kin. Most Tày are spirit worshipers, although some have incorporated Mahayana **Buddhism** or **Confucianism** as the result of contact with the lowland Vietnamese. (The Tày have been more exposed to Vietnamese culture than many minorities, and this influence is reflected in both their culture and their language.)

During the Vietnamese Revolution, the Tày were actively enlisted into the **Việt Minh**, led by **Hồ Chí Minh**, and many Tày reached high positions in the **Vietnamese Communist Party**. During the tensions with **China** in the late 1970s, however, active propagandizing by Beijing targeting the Tày and other minorities reportedly led to some official distrust of their loyalty. *See also* VIỆT BẮC.

TÀY BẮC. The Tày Bắc ("Northwest") region includes the provinces of Lào Cai, Lai Châu, **Điện Biên**, and Sơn La. Dominated by the Black and White **Thái** ethnic minorities, it was historically a separate entity known as *Sip Song Chu Thai* ("Twelve Thai States" or "Twelve Thai Lords"). The Sip Song Chu Thai was a loose federation of small polities that variously paid tribute to Vietnamese, **Lao**, and **Chinese** overlords. **French** colonial rule eventually attached it to **Tonkin**, so that it became a permanent part of Vietnam despite its strong ethnic, cultural, and historical ties to Laos.

In 1955, the **Democratic Republic of Vietnam** (DRV) established the Tai-Meo Autonomous Region to provide some degree of local self-government to **highland minorities** in the area, along the lines of similar administrative units in China. ("Tai" was the French spelling of "Thai," while "Meo" referred to the Hmong, who are scattered throughout the Tây Bắc region.) It was renamed the *Tây Bắc Autonomous Region* (*Khu Tự Trị Tây Bắc*) in 1961. A second autonomous zone, called the *Việt Bắc* Autonomous Region, was created northeast of the **Red River Delta**. The Tây Bắc Autonomous Region contained a total of 2.5 million people and had 60 representatives in the **National Assembly**. The region was abolished after the end of the Vietnam War and replaced by regular provinces. It has considerable strategic importance because of its proximity to Laos and China, and has now become a popular **tourist** destination as well.

TÂY SƠN. A major rebellion that shook Vietnam throughout the final decades of the 18th century. The rebellion originated in rural unrest that affected wide areas of the southern kingdom under the rule of the **Nguyễn Lords** in the 1760s and early 1770s. In 1771, three brothers from the village of Tây Sơn (Western Mountain) in modern-day Bình Định raised the standard of revolt against the **corruption** and misrule of the Nguyễn government and called for the distribution of land to the poor. The rebellion won broad support from peasants, townspeople, local members of the **scholar-gentry**, and upland minorities; it drove the Nguyễn out of their capital of Phú Xuân (now **Huế**) in 1775. The Nguyễn fled to the **Mekong Delta** region of Gia Định, where Nguyễn Ánh (the future Emperor **Gia Long**) assumed leadership of the anti-Tây Sơn struggle.

The Tây Sơn concentrated on fighting the Nguyễn for the next decade and, by 1785, had almost completely driven them from Vietnamese territory. Tây Sơn armies then attacked and defeated the **Trịnh Lords** in the North, eventually bringing down the **Lê dynasty** as well. In 1788, the last ruler of the Lê was deposed and the leading Tây Sơn brother, **Nguyễn Huệ**, ascended to the throne as Emperor Quang Trung. The new dynasty began to decline after his death in 1792, however, and the revived Nguyễn forces gradually gained the upper hand. Over the next ten years, Nguyễn Ánh gradually fought his way northward (with the help of a handful of French mercenaries). By 1802, he had defeated the Tây Sơn and established his family as an imperial dynasty.

The Tây Sơn movement looms large in Vietnamese history as the most important of its kind, comparable in scale and violence to the Taiping Rebellion in **China**. Marxist historians have generally hailed it as a genuine peasant rebellion, the closest thing to a real revolution that Vietnam ever experienced before the revolution led by the **Indochinese Communist Party**. The Tây Sơn were lionized, while Nguyễn Ánh was vilified for having defeated it with foreign assistance. Recently, however, Vietnamese scholars have begun to recognize that the differences between the Tây Sơn and Nguyễn were not so black and white and that when the former were established as a short-lived dynasty, they did not behave so terribly differently from other "**feudal**" regimes.

TÂY VU. Administrative and territorial term for an ancient district in Vietnam. Located in the lower **Red River Delta** around the city of **Cổ Loa**, not far from present-day **Hanoi**, Tây Vu became an administrative district during the **Âu Lạc** and **Nam Việt** periods. The area was one of considerable political importance and had been the site of heavy fighting in early struggles against **Chinese** occupation. After the **Trưng Sisters'** rebellion in 39–43 C.E., General **Ma Yuan** divided Tây Vu into two separate administrative units.

TAYLOR, MAXWELL (1901–1987). United States Ambassador to the **Republic of Vietnam** from August 1964 until August 1965. In 1961, he was sent to **Saigon** by the incoming John F. Kennedy administration to assess the situation in South Vietnam and provide advice on future U.S. policy. His suggestions to send two divisions of American combat troops to stiffen Vietnamese resolve, however, was rejected. After serving as chairman of the Joint Chiefs of Staff under Kennedy, he was appointed ambassador to Saigon in August 1964 in the hope of improving the performance of the military junta under **Nguyễn Khánh**. Taylor was replaced by **Henry Cabot Lodge** the following summer.

TEA. The origins of tea cultivation in Vietnam are unknown. Tea was grown in small quantities during the pre-colonial period, and, as in

China, tea drinking served as a sign of hospitality. Tea cultivation began to expand during the period of French rule. The first tea plantations were founded in Phú Thọ and Thái Nguyên in **Tonkin** in the 1920s, and soon other plantations appeared in the **Central Highlands**, where the climate and the red basaltic soil were particularly favorable for the plants. Tea exports reached 2,446 tons in 1940. Today, tea is produced on farms and plantations in several northern provinces and in parts of the Central Highlands; an area of roughly 120,000 hectares (nearly 300,000 acres) is devoted to tea cultivation. In 2004, the country exported 95,000 metric tons (105,000 tons) of processed tea out of approximately 120,000 metric tons (130,000 tons) produced. Vietnam ranks fifth among the world's tea producers and eighth as a tea exporter.

TEMPLE OF LITERATURE (*Văn Miếu*). Historical site in **Hanoi**. The temple, which has altars dedicated to Confucius and his disciples, is said to have first been opened during the reign of Emperor **Lý Thánh Tông** in the 11th century. It was the site of the metropolitan level of the civil service **examinations** during much of the traditional era and stone tablets were erected at the temple to honor the successful candidates. It also housed the **Imperial Academy** (*Quốc tử giám*), used to train potential candidates and imperial officials in **Confucian** doctrine. In recent years, with the growth of the domestic and foreign **tourist** industry, the Temple of Literature has become one Hanoi's most important sites for visitors. *See also* EDUCATION.

TÉT (*Tết Nguyên Đán*). *See* FESTIVALS.

TÉT OFFENSIVE. Major military offensive and general uprising launched by the revolutionary forces in South Vietnam during the traditional Tết New Year holiday in early 1968. The offensive was planned by **Hanoi** military strategists in an effort to shake the stability of the **Saigon** regime and undermine public support for the war effort in the **United States**. It began during the Tết holidays on January 31 with a series of major attacks on the capital of Saigon and other cities and towns throughout South Vietnam. It concluded with smaller thrusts (often called *Mini-Tet*) on urban areas later in the year.

Most of the troops involved in the offensive were members of the southern **People's Liberation Armed Forces (PLAF)**, although regular forces of the **People's Army of Vietnam (PAVN)** took part in an extended attack on the old imperial capital of **Huế**, which they occupied for two weeks. The offensive resulted in heavy casualties for the revolutionary forces and did not achieve its maximum objective of provoking general uprisings in the big cities leading to the collapse of the Saigon regime. Even so, televised reports of the offensive—notably the seizure of the ground floor of the U.S. Embassy in Saigon by a PLAF sapper team—seriously undermined public confidence in the war effort in the United States and led eventually to the reduction of American force levels in South Vietnam. Moreover, the serious casualties inflicted on the forces of the mainly Southern PLAF meant that the PAVN had to bear an increasing share of the military burden through the rest of the war.

THÁI. Highland minority living in the mountainous provinces of northwestern Vietnam (**Tây Bắc**), known to the **French** as *Tai*. The Thái are numerically the third largest tribal minority in the country. Related to the **Tày** and **Nùng** peoples to the northeast of the **Red River Delta**, as well as a number of other Tai-speaking peoples scattered across the northern tier of mainland Southeast Asia, the Thái live close to what was probably the original homeland of the various Tai groups along the Sino–Vietnamese border.

The Thái people are subdivided into separate groups according to the color of the blouses worn by the women; the most common are the Black Thái and White Thái. The Thái were given extensive autonomy during the colonial era, and many of their leaders cooperated with the French during the **Franco–Việt Minh War**. This was particularly true of the White Thái, who had been close to the colonial regime; the Black Thái tended to be more sympathetic to the **Việt Minh**. The strategically important site of **Điện Biên Phủ** was located in Thái territory. After the **Geneva Conference** in 1954, the government of the **Democratic Republic of Vietnam** (DRV) attempted to win their allegiance by turning several provinces inhabited by the Thái into an autonomous region, though this was subsequently abolished.

THÁI NGUYÊN UPRISING. Rebellion against **French** rule launched during World War I. The revolt was led by Lương Ngọc Quyến, son of Lương Văn Can, one of the founders of the **Đong Kinh Nghĩa Thục** (Tonkin Free School). The uprising broke out at a military garrison in the capital of Thái Nguyên province in **Tonkin** in August 1917. The French counterattacked, but many of the rebels were able to retreat into the mountains, where they were soon captured.

THÁI THƯỢNG HOÀNG **(Senior Emperor).** Royal title adopted during the **Trần dynasty** to designate a position established to guarantee an orderly succession on the imperial throne. Under the preceding **Lý dynasty**, court intrigues over the transition to a new emperor had frequently led to political instability. The system was first adopted by the founding Trần ruler, **Trần Thái Tông**, who retired from office while still politically active, to serve as a royal adviser to the crown prince, who now ascended to the throne. The system functioned well until the middle of the 14th century, when the quality of rulers began to disintegrate. The title briefly reappeared under the **Mạc dynasty** in the 16th century.

THĂNG LONG. *See* HANOI.

THANH NIÊN (*Việt Nam Thanh Niên Cách Mệnh Đồng Chí Hội,* **Revolutionary Youth League of Vietnam**). Early Vietnamese revolutionary organization founded by **Hồ Chí Minh** in southern **China** in 1925. The league was the first avowedly Marxist–Leninist political organization in Vietnam and was apparently established on the instructions of the Communist International (**Comintern**) in Moscow. Hồ Chí Minh, a Comintern agent then using the name *Nguyễn Ái Quốc*, did not feel that the level of political sophistication and ideological awareness within the Vietnamese radical movement justified a formal Communist party. He did set up a core organization of six dedicated members within the League, called the *Thanh Niên Cộng Sản Đoàn* (Communist Youth Group), to serve as the nucleus of a future party. The headquarters of the League was set up in Canton to avoid **French** repression.

The League's objectives were broadly focused on national independence and social revolution, but the former issue received more emphasis to win the support of anticolonial elements throughout Vietnam. This concentration on nationalism earned the league considerable popularity. By the late 1920s, it had recruited more than 1,000 members, many of whom had gone through training in Marxism–Leninism in Canton. However, the muted emphasis on social revolution led to a split in the league after Hồ Chí Minh's departure for Europe in 1927, and at the First National Congress of the League, held in Hong Kong in May 1929, radical elements stalked out of the conference to found their own **Indochinese Communist Party** (*Đông Dương Cộng Sản Đảng*). Remaining members of the league then changed the name of the organization to *Annamese Communist Party* (*An Nam Cộng Sản Đảng*).

In February 1930, at the behest of the Comintern, Hồ Chí Minh united the two factions, along with remnants of the *Tân Việt Cách Mệnh Đảng* (New Vietnamese Revolutionary Party) into a new **Vietnamese Communist Party** (*Đảng Cộng Sản Việt Nam*). In October, the name was changed to *Indochinese Communist Party* (*Đảng Cộng Sản Đông Dương*).

***THANH NIÊN** (Youth)*. Weekly newspaper published by **Hồ Chí Minh**'s Revolutionary Youth League or **Thanh Niên** in the 1920s. Printed in Canton, it was smuggled to **Indochina** for distribution and first appeared in June 1925. The articles, many of which were written anonymously by Hồ until his departure from **China** in 1927, promoted both national independence and the need for a social revolution led by a Communist party. *Thanh Niên* ceased publication in May 1930 after 208 issues, shortly after the founding of what would become the **Indochinese Communist Party**. *See also* JOURNALISM.

THANH NIÊN CAO VỌNG (Hopes of Youth). Short-lived political movement in early 20th-century Vietnam. The inspiration of the group was the progressive **Saigon** intellectual **Nguyễn An Ninh** (1900–1943), who hoped to spur the **French** to grant reforms and eventually grant independence to the Vietnamese. Ninh's speeches and writings attracted considerable support among patriotic intellectuals throughout **Cochin China**, who adopted as a name for their informal group the title of one of his most famous political speeches.

Ninh did not wish to organize a formal political party, which in any
event was illegal, and the organization collapsed after his arrest in
1926. It might have inspired the formation of a second party, the
Youth Party (*Đảng Thanh Niên*), formed by such radical intellectuals as **Trần Huy Liệu**, in **Saigon** in late 1925.

THÀNH THÁI (1879–1954). Emperor (r. 1889–1907) of the **Nguyễn
dynasty** under the French **Protectorate**. A son of Emperor **Dục Đức**,
who reigned briefly in 1883, Thành Thái succeeded Emperor **Đồng
Khánh** on the latter's death in 1889. Sensitive and intelligent, he resented **French** domination over his country and was deposed on suspicion of conspiracy in 1907. French archival records portray him as
an unstable and sadistic youth, but his deposition and exile have
earned him a place in the pantheon of Vietnamese nationalist heroes.
Exiled to the island of Réunion for more than 40 years, he was permitted to return to Vietnam shortly before his death.

THEATER. The theater has a long tradition in Vietnam. The origins
of popular theater are probably to be found in ceremonies performed
at **festivals** that reflected **religious** beliefs or marked the harvest
cycle. Out of this tradition emerged *chèo*, a form of popular opera
based on folk tales that makes liberal use of music and dance to inspire and entertain the audience. Serious theater, called *tuồng*, was
probably imported from **China** during the long centuries of Chinese
rule. Originally performed at court, *tuồng* performances also contained singing and dancing, but the action was more stylized and ceremonial in nature, and a moral message (such as loyalty to the
monarch) was often embedded in the thematic material.

In the early 20th century, both *chèo* and *tuồng* declined in popularity and were replaced by "reform" (*cải lương*) opera, which originated in southern Vietnam and reflected Western influence in its
choice of topical themes and modern melodies. Chinese opera also
became increasingly prevalent. Western dramatic works were occasionally performed during the colonial period, but they did not
achieve great popularity.

The existence of traditional theater represented a knotty challenge
to the cultural czars of the **Democratic Republic of Vietnam**
(DRV). Ideological hardliners, sometimes influenced by Maoist

trends in China, criticized traditional drama as feudalistic and attempted to eradicate its influence among the population, while reform theater was dismissed because of its ties to the colonial era. During the 1960s and 1970s, dramatic works produced in the DRV reflected the concept of "socialist realism" originally developed during the Stalinist era in the **Union of Soviet Socialist Republics**, promoting values and activities important to the needs of the state, such as patriotism and commitment to the ideals of socialism. Dramatic troops were sent on tours through South Vietnam to entertain the soldiers and cadres of the **People's Liberation Armed Forces (PLAF)** and inspire them to greater feats of courage and self-sacrifice.

Since the end of the war, the government has encouraged the revival of traditional theater in Vietnam, and professional companies have been formed to perform popular and classical theater to audiences throughout the country. Many contemporary dramatists are turning once again to topical themes as a means of expressing their views on events of the day. Many of their works are laced with satire, as writers attempt to use their pens to criticize the shortcomings of the government and the party. *See also* LITERATURE.

THIỆU TRỊ (1807–1847). Third emperor (r. 1840–1847) of the **Nguyễn dynasty**. Thiệu Trị reigned at a time when the French challenge to Vietnamese independence was growing increasingly insistent. Like his father **Minh Mạng**, Thiệu Trị was poetic and intellectually curious and cautiously attempted to learn from the West, but he was often hindered by a cumbersome and xenophobic bureaucracy. He attempted to resolve the continuing dispute over the presence of **French** missionaries in Vietnam, but his efforts were sabotaged by a brutal French bombardment of **Đà Nẵng** in 1847. He died shortly afterward. One of his positive accomplishments was the decision to withdraw Vietnamese troops from **Cambodia** after an extended period of occupation and attempted assimilation.

THỤC PHÁN. *See* AN DƯƠNG VƯƠNG.

TIẾN SĨ. See EXAMINATION SYSTEM.

TÔ HIỂN THÀNH (?–1179). Military leader and court figure during the **Lý dynasty**. Tô Hiển Thành, a respected military commander and

strategist under Emperor **Lý Anh Tông**, served as regent during the
infancy of Emperor **Lý Cao Tông** (1178–1210).

TÔ HỮU (1920–2002). Revolutionary poet and prominent political
figure in the **Socialist Republic of Vietnam** (SRV). Born *Nguyễn
Kim Thành* near **Huế**, Tô Hữu became active in revolutionary work
in the 1930s and gained a reputation as the most prominent poet of
the Vietnamese revolution. He also became a key figure in Party control over **literary** and artistic activities and was in the front line of
official repression directed at **dissidents**, such as those involved in
the ***Nhân Văn Giai Phẩm*** affair. He served in a variety of posts in
the **Democratic Republic of Vietnam** (DRV) and was a member of
the Central Committee of the **Vietnamese Communist Party**.

Tô Hữu was named vice-premier in 1980; he was active in ideological and **economic** work and was identified with the conservative
faction under **Trường Chinh** that promoted rapid socialist transformation in the South. It is generally recognized that he was not
successful in handling the economic portfolio, however, and his reputation suffered because of the failure to achieve a stable **currency**.
He was dropped from the Politburo at the reformist-oriented Sixth
Party Congress in December 1986, which formally inaugurated the
period of *đổi mới* (renovation).

TÔN ĐỨC THẮNG (1888–1980). Veteran member of the **Vietnam-
ese Communist Party** and president of the **Democratic Republic of
Vietnam** (DRV). Born in 1888 in a poor peasant family in Long
Xuyên in the **Mekong Delta**, Tôn Đức Thắng became a mechanic in
Saigon and later joined the **French** navy. He participated in a 1918
uprising by French sailors in the Black Sea and in 1920 returned to
Saigon, where he formed the first workers' organization in French
Indochina. Joining **Hồ Chí Minh**'s Revolutionary Youth League
(Thanh Niên), he was arrested for revolutionary activities in 1919,
and imprisoned in **Poulo Condore** until 1945.

After World War II, Thắng was named inspector general for political and administrative affairs and president of the Standing Committee of the **National Assembly**. In 1960, he became vice-president of
the DRV. He succeeded **Hồ Chí Minh** as president after the latter's

death in 1969, though given his advanced age this post was largely ceremonial.

TÔN THẤT THUYẾT (1835–1913). Anti-**French** resistance leader in the 19th century. After the **Patenôtre Treaty** in 1884 established French control over the Vietnamese Empire, Tôn Thất Thuyết, an influential court official and member of the **Nguyễn** royal family, fled with the young Emperor **Hàm Nghi** in the hope of launching a nationwide revolt against French rule. Seeking refuge in the mountains north of **Huế**, Thuyết and Hàm Nghi issued an appeal entitled "Save the King" (**Cần Vương**) to the Vietnamese people. In 1886, Thuyết went to **China** to seek arms and support from the Qing dynasty. Hàm Nghi was captured in 1888, and the movement gradually declined. Despite his involvement with patriotic resistance, Thuyết's reputation is mixed because his political maneuvering and making and unmaking of emperors (**Dục Đức**, **Hiệp Hoà**, and **Kiến Phúc**) after the death of **Tự Đức** seriously weakened the court precisely at the time it was facing a new round of French aggression. *See also* NGUYỄN VĂN TƯỜNG.

TÔN THỌ TƯỜNG (1825–1877). Reformist and supporter of collaboration with the **French** in the 19th century. Descended from a family of **scholar-gentry**, Tôn Thọ Tường failed in his examination but became influential while serving as an intermediary between the French and the court in 1862 during the negotiations led by **Phan Thanh Giản**. He was named a prefect by the French and served in the colonial administration until his death.

TONKIN. One of three regions of Vietnam under French colonial rule. In 1884, the **Patenôtre Treaty** signed between **France** and the **Nguyễn dynasty** declared a **protectorate** over what remained of the Vietnamese Empire. (The southernmost provinces of Vietnam had already been transformed into the French colony of **Cochin China** by the treaties of 1862 and 1874.) France divided the protectorate into two parts, **Annam** (the central provinces) and Tonkin (the **Red River Delta**, from the Chinese border to the province of Thanh Hoá). During the period between 1600 and 1800, when there were two separate Vietnamese kingdoms, *Tonkin* was also used by foreigners to refer to the northern kingdom (**Đàng Ngoài**) under the **Lê dynasty** and **Trịnh Lords**. **Đàng Trong**, the southern kingdom under the **Nguyễn Lords** was known as *Cochin China*.

The name *Tonkin* is adapted from the term *Đông Kinh* (Eastern capital), a name sometimes used for **Hanoi**. It was usually referred to by the Vietnamese as *Bắc Bộ* or *Bắc Kỳ* (Northern region). Annam and Tonkin were both French protectorates and remained part of the Empire of Vietnam. Imperial authority over the northern provinces was theoretical, however, as the French governed Tonkin even more directly than they did Annam. The emperor was initially permitted to maintain a viceroy (*kinh lược*) in Hanoi, but, in 1897, the French abolished the position and transferred its authority to the *Résident Supérieur*, the French official responsible for Tonkin.

Tonkin was included with Annam and Cochin China in the **State of Vietnam** created by the Elysee Accords in 1949. Although the term is no longer used today, a regional identity is still associated with the northern provinces as opposed to the central and southern regions.

TONKIN FREE SCHOOL. *See* ĐÔNG KINH NGHĨA THỤC.

TONKIN GULF (Vịnh Bắc Bộ). Body of water off the coast of northern Vietnam. A part of the **South China Sea**, the Tonkin Gulf is bounded on the east by Hainan Island, on the north by **China**'s Guangdong Province, and on the west by the coast of Vietnam. Traditionally considered part of the open sea, in recent years the Tonkin Gulf has been the scene of a growing rivalry between China and Vietnam as both attempt to validate their claim to the mineral resources lying under the sea bed in the area. In 1964, it was the site of a well-publicized clash between naval forces of the **Democratic Republic of Vietnam** and the **United States**. *See also* PARACEL ISLANDS; TONKIN GULF INCIDENTS.

TONKIN GULF INCIDENTS. Two alleged clashes between naval craft of the **Democratic Republic of Vietnam** (DRV) and the **United States** in August 1964. The administration of Lyndon Johnson contended that Vietnamese ships fired on two U.S. destroyers, the *Maddox* and the *C. Turner Joy*, without provocation and in the open sea. According to the United States, a second incident took place a few days later. The Johnson administration retaliated by launching air strikes against North Vietnamese cities and seeking a resolution from Congress authorizing the White House to take appropriate military measures to protect U.S. security interests in the area.

Further investigation revealed that the two U.S. warships operating near the North Vietnamese coast were monitoring Vietnamese radar capabilities in the area. The Hanoi regime might have identified the presence of the U.S. ships with South Vietnamese guerrilla operations on the nearby coast. The second incident probably never occurred, although it is still a matter of debate among scholars whether it was a genuine false alarm or a complete fabrication by the American military. *See also* TONKIN GULF RESOLUTION.

TONKIN GULF RESOLUTION. A resolution passed by the **United States** Congress authorizing President Lyndon Johnson to take necessary measures to protect American security interests in the area of mainland Southeast Asia. Approved by a near-unanimous vote, it later became controversial because many Americans criticized the broad powers it granted the president to make war without consulting Congress. The resolution was passed after two alleged incidents involving U.S. and North Vietnamese warships in the **Tonkin Gulf**. *See also* TONKIN GULF INCIDENTS.

TOURISM. Technically speaking, tourism in Vietnam is not a product of our day. Stelae dating back several centuries and found in various parts of Vietnam contain inscriptions that describe scenic spots and famous historical sites, undoubtedly serving as an attraction to the traveler. Scholar-officials serving under various dynasties wrote travelogues and poetry about the sites they visited as well. Modern tourism began in Vietnam during the colonial era. Travelers from Europe and the **United States**, as well as from elsewhere in Asia, began to travel to French **Indochina** to see the architectural ruins at Angkor Wat, the imperial city of **Huế**, and vestiges of the **Cham** civilization in the central provinces of **Annam**. Others frequented the beaches at Vũng Tàu, Nha Trang, and Tourane (**Đà Nẵng**) or visited the mountain city of **Đàlạt** in the **Central Highlands** to escape the tropical heat of the lowlands.

Tourism declined drastically during the long years of civil conflict after World War II, but it has begun to revive with the removal of the embargo and the gradual opening of Vietnam to foreign travelers. In the last few years, the Vietnamese government has made a concerted effort to improve its facilities as a means of attracting tourists and earning precious hard currencies. In addition to renovations taking place in famous hotels like the **Métropole** in **Hanoi** and the **Continental** in Hồ Chí Minh City (**Saigon**), other luxury hotels have been built in both cities. Golf courses have been constructed, and beach facilities improved along the coast. Vietnam Airlines has upgraded its fleet of modern airplanes, and key airports are being renovated to improve service. International service on foreign airlines into the major cities of Hanoi and Hồ Chí Minh City has increased rapidly, and a number of cruise lines now sail up and down the coast of the **South China Sea** en route to Hong Kong or Singapore, stopping at **Cát Bà Island** and **Hạ Long Bay**.

Vietnamese tourism is very much a growth industry, despite some obstacles. Lack of hotel space in some places limits the number of arrivals, while the sometimes primitive rail and road structure can make travel a challenge. However, the private and state sectors alike are working hard to make improvements in these areas, and the number of tourists is increasing steadily. The beauty of the country and its rich history represent an appealing combination, and tourism has become a major industry in Vietnam. Between 1994 and 2003, tourism's share of Gross Domestic Product doubled, reaching 3.5 percent. In 2003, the number of foreign tourists coming to Vietnam was roughly 2.7 million; visitors from **China** headed the list, followed by those from the United States. *See also* TRANSPORTATION AND COMMUNICATIONS.

TRADE. Vietnam's trade patterns have shifted dramatically over the past 15 years. The implementation of *đổi mới* (renovation) beginning in the mid-1980s initiated the change to a market-oriented **economy**, but it took a series of events over the next few years to move the country's trade relations away from their previous reliance on the Council for Mutual Economic Assistance (CMEA) under the leadership of the **Union of Soviet Socialist Republics** and other socialist bloc countries. First, the fall of the European socialist regimes meant that the CMEA became a dead letter, and the new governments in these countries had little motivation to maintain the **Socialist Republic of Vietnam** (SRV) as a privileged trading partner. Second, the restoration of normal ties with **China** after 15 years of tension and intermittent clashes generated an important flow of bilateral trade, including a significant volume of smuggling. Finally, the gradual lifting of the trade embargo led by the **United States** (completely removed by 1994) and the subsequent normalization of relations with Washington opened another important door.

Since the 1990s, the SRV has made diplomatic and economic integration with the rest of the world a top priority, and its pool of trade partners has been considerably diversified. The country has put great effort and expense into developing an export market, both for traditional commodities such as **rice, rubber**, and **coffee** (all of which were important exports under **French** colonial rule) and for a whole range of consumer goods (notably clothing, shoes, and electronics). Although the **agricultural** products are being produced and exported largely by domestic companies, the consumer products mainly flow out of the factories set up in **export processing zones** and industrial zones by **joint ventures** and other **foreign investment** projects. **Oil** and aquatic products, such as shrimp, have become major exports as well.

The lifting of the trade embargo had a major impact on Vietnam's trade flow, and its exports doubled from $7.2 billion to $14.3 billion during the five-year period from 1996 to 2000. After a brief slowdown, export growth took off again, and official statistics give a figure of $19.9 billion for 2003. Imports have also ballooned, however, with significant increases in cars and motorbikes, as well as steel for construction and other products to support the country's **industrialization**. For 2003, imports reached nearly $25 billion, creating a trade deficit of $5 billion, nearly 13 percent of Vietnam's Gross Domestic Product; in 2004, the deficit increased by another 9 percent. This deficit is likely to remain large, given consumer demand for imported products (only some of which can be manufactured inside the country) and the wide range of items needed for industrial and infrastructural growth.

On the positive side, Vietnam continues to multiply its trade relationships; its major partners include the United States, **Japan**, Australia, China, Singapore, South Korea, Germany, and the United Kingdom. For 2004, China and Japan were expected to be among the top three partners for both imports and exports in terms of dollar value; Singapore headed the list of import sources, while the U.S. was the top market for Vietnamese exports. The SRV's membership in the **Association of Southeast Asian Nations** and the Asia-Pacific Economic Cooperation organization, as well as other regional and international groupings, has enabled it to acquire more experience in dealing with international trade issues. Vietnam has signed a number of **bilateral trade agreements**, the most important being those with the U.S., China, and India. Currently, its most important priority in terms of trade is to join the World Trade Organization, and negotiations to this end are ongoing. *See also* FOREIGN RELATIONS.

TRÂN ANH TÔNG (1276–1320). Fourth emperor (r. 1293–1314) of the **Trần dynasty**. Trần Anh Tông succeeded his father **Nhân Tông** as emperor in 1293 when the latter retired from office to serve the new ruler as adviser with the title *Thái Thượng Hoàng*. Anh Tông's reign was a generally peaceful one. The **Mongol invasions** had come to an end with the death of Emperor Kublai Khan in 1294, and the intermittent wars with **Champa** had been succeeded by a period of peace marked by the marriage in 1306 of the emperor's daughter Princess **Huyền Trân** to the Cham king in return for the transfer of two districts of his territory to the Vietnamese, although this thaw in relations was short-lived. Trần Anh Tông abdicated in 1314 in favor of his son, who ruled as Emperor **Minh Tông**, and served as *Thái Thượng Hoàng* until his death in 1320.

TRÂN BẠCH ĐẰNG (1926?–   ). Leading member of the revolutionary movement in South Vietnam during the Vietnam War. A native southerner, Trần Bạch Đằng joined the **Việt Minh** movement during the **Franco-Việt Minh War**. In 1961, he organized the Youth Liberation Association, one of the key components of the **National Liberation Front**. Four years later, he became **Võ Văn Kiệt**'s assistant with the Communist Party's underground Municipal Committee in **Saigon.** At the end of the war, however, he came under suspicion for his outspoken views on the performance of the Party's work among laborers in the city.

After the Vietnam War, Đằng underwent ideological remolding at the Nguyễn Ái Quốc Institute in **Hanoi** and was selected as a leading official of the **Fatherland Front** in Hồ Chí Minh City. With the inauguration of *đổi mới* in December 1986, his star was on the rise, and he became a close associate of General Secretary **Nguyễn Văn Linh**. He has maintained an active role as a **journalist** and commentator. *See also* VIETNAMESE COMMUNIST PARTY.

TRẦN CẢO (or Trần Cao). A 16th-century official who rebelled against the **Lê dynasty**, claiming to be a descendant of the **Trần dynasty** royal family. His revolt, which broke out in 1516, was symptomatic of the political, economic, and social malaise associated with the decline of the Lê after a century in power. Although Trần Cảo's rebellion was successfully repressed, it provided the opportunity for an ambitious military officer named *Mạc Đăng Dung* to make a name for himself; he subsequently overthrew the Lê and established his own dynasty. *See also* LÊ UY MỤC.

TRẦN DỤ TÔNG (1336–1369). Seventh emperor (r. 1341–1369) of the **Trần dynasty**. The son of Emperor **Trần Minh Tông**, Dụ Tông succeeded his older brother on the latter's death. His reign was marked by financial extravagance and official **corruption** in a time of climatic disaster and pestilence. Yet when one of his officials, the **Confucian** scholar **Chu Văn An**, appealed to the emperor for an end to official malfeasance, the appeal was ignored. Internal difficulties resulted in a more perilous situation in foreign affairs. **China**, in the throes of the collapse of the Yuan (Mongol) dynasty, was pacified by tribute, but **Champa** took advantage of Vietnamese weaknesses and launched repeated attacks over the southern frontier.

Dụ Tông died without issue in 1369. After a court intrigue, he was succeeded by his brother, the inept Nghệ Tông, who allowed the mandarin **Hồ Quý Ly** to become dominant at court. By the end of the century, Hồ Quý Ly was powerful enough to overthrow the dynasty that he had served. Dụ Tông was one of a succession of weak rulers who marked the decline of the Trần.

TRẦN ĐỨC LƯƠNG (1937–). President of the **Socialist Republic of Vietnam** (SRV). Born in the central province of Quảng Ngãi, Trần

Đức Lương was one of the large number of Vietnamese loyal to **Hồ Chí Minh** who regrouped in the **Democratic Republic of Vietnam** after the country's partition at the **Geneva Conference** in 1954, rather than remaining in what became the **Republic of Vietnam**. Although he joined the **Vietnamese Communist Party** (then called the *Vietnamese Workers' Party*) in 1959, he made his career as a geologist and his official Party posts were limited to cells and committees within academic and professional units until he received formal political training in the mid-1970s. Over the next decade, Lương held various different low-level posts and became a member of the **National Assembly**. Between 1987 and 1997, he rose higher within the ranks of the Party and government, perhaps because the changes taking place under "renovation" (*đổi mới*) opened doors for loyal Party members with technical skills but little or no revolutionary experience. In 1996, he was appointed to the Party Politburo, and, in 1997, he was elected president of the SRV.

TRẦN DUỆ TÔNG (1336–1377). Ninth emperor (r. 1372–1377) of the **Trần dynasty**. Trần Duệ Tông succeeded his brother **Nghệ Tông** when the latter abdicated in 1372 during the course of a Cham invasion. The 1370s saw the worst trouble with **Champa** in Vietnam's history, and Cham forces several times penetrated as far as the capital at Thăng Long (**Hanoi**), which was unprecedented. Duệ Tông was determined to even the score by personally mounting an invasion against the powerful Cham ruler known to the Vietnamese as *Chế Bồng Nga*. Against the counsel of his advisors, he set out for war and was killed in battle in 1377. His death and the Vietnamese inability to repel the Cham invasions were symptomatic of the Trần dynasty's decline.

TRẦN DYNASTY (1225–1400). Second major dynasty in Vietnamese history. The Trần family, who were originally fishermen, rose to a position of power at court during the declining years of the preceding **Lý dynasty**. In 1225, the powerful court figure **Trần Thủ Độ** took advantage of the weakening of the Lý to place a member of his own family on the throne as the first emperor of the new Trần dynasty.

The Trần are best known for their staunch defense of Vietnamese independence against the **Mongol invasions** by the Yuan dynasty in the 13th century. Through the outstanding leadership of **Trần Hưng Đạo** and other leaders, the Trần were able to defeat the most powerful military force in Asia on three separate occasions, while simultaneously extending Vietnamese territory to the south at the expense of neighboring **Champa**. These victories strengthened the position of powerful Trần princes within the imperial government, to some extent at the expense of the scholar-officials who made up the **mandarinate**.

Two centuries of Trần rule also had a significant impact on the internal development of the Vietnamese Empire. The Trần continued the process of extending the centralized power of the state through a series of administrative reforms that strengthened the bureaucracy. To avoid imperial succession crises, many Trần emperors abdicated in favor of adult sons, taking the title of *Thái Thượng Hoàng* (Senior Emperor). The rulers were assisted in some measure by the adoption of **Confucian** institutions and values, which became increasingly influential, although the Trần emperors themselves remained heavily influenced by **Buddhist** teachings. Economic growth was promoted through the expansion of trade and manufacturing and the extension of land under cultivation through territorial expansion and the expansion of the irrigation networks.

Like the Lý before them, however, the Trần fell victim to a series of weak rulers that led in the 14th century to the decline and ultimately the overthrow of the dynasty. They contributed to their own downfall by their failure to resolve the land problem. Under the Trần, landholding was increasingly concentrated in the hands of royal family members, nobles, and powerful mandarins, who received land from the court and often seized private lands belonging to individual peasants or rural **villages**. Some of the fiefdoms (*trang điền*) consisted of thousands of peasants, most of whom were serfs or **slaves**. Growing landlessness (created by land seizures and a growing population) and high taxes led to a rising incidence of peasant rebellion during the mid–14th century.

In the long run, the Trần dynasty was unable to avoid the fate of its predecessor. After a series of competent if not brilliant rulers, the dynasty gradually lost its momentum during the 14th century and did not survive into the next. The Trần had sought to preserve their position by intermarriage; early emperors always married princesses from their own family. However, this presumably did little good to the family's bloodline and is probably one factor in the declining quality of Trần rulers from the 1340s onward. Moreover, at some point, the Trần violated this practice and allowed an outsider, **Hồ Quý Ly**, to marry into their family. Just as their ancestors had feared, he used his connection to rise to power and overthrow the dynasty at the end of the 14th century.

TRẦN HIỆN ĐẾ (Trần Phế Đế) (1361–1388). Tenth emperor (r. 1377–1388) of the **Trần dynasty.** Trần Hiện Đế ascended to the throne on the death of his predecessor, **Duệ Tông**, in battle. His was a troubled reign. Externally, Vietnam was involved in war with **Champa** and a strained relationship with the rising power of the Ming dynasty in **China**. Internally, the court was rife with intrigue, one faction supporting ex-emperor **Nghệ Tông**, now serving as senior emperor (*Thái Thượng Hoàng*) since his abdication in 1372, and another **Hồ Quý Ly**, a high-ranking mandarin and a cousin by marriage of Nghệ Tông. As a result of scheming at court, Hồ Quy Ly persuaded Nghệ Tông to replace Hiện Đế as emperor with the retired emperor's own son, **Thuận Tông**. He was then assassinated and has come to be known in history as *Trần Phế Đế* ("deposed emperor").

TRẦN HIẾN TÔNG (1319?–1341). Sixth emperor (r. 1329–1341) of the **Trần dynasty.** Hiến Tông succeeded his father, **Minh Tông**, as emperor in 1329, but the latter remained dominant at court through his position as senior emperor (*Thái Thượng Hoàng*). Hiến Tông died in 1341 at the age of 23 without having produced an heir.

TRẦN HƯNG ĐẠO (Trần Quốc Tuấn) (1226–1300). Famous general who defeated two **Mongol invasions** in the late 13th century. A prince of the **Trần dynasty**, in 1287 he was appointed commander-in-chief of the Vietnamese armed forces in the face of the growing threat of another invasion. Asked by Emperor **Trần Nhân Tông** whether Vietnam should appease the Mongols rather than fight, Hưng Đạo replied with a famous declaration in which he appealed to his sovereign and to the population at large for a policy of national resistance.

When the Mongol army invaded in 1285, Hưng Đạo carried out a brilliant defense that resulted in a massive victory over the Mongol forces. After initially giving ground and allowing the numerically larger enemy troops to occupy the **Red River Delta**, he inaugurated a policy of guerrilla warfare and scorched-earth tactics, and then he launched a major counteroffensive that liberated the capital city of Thăng Long (**Hanoi**), won a major battle at Tây Kết, and drove the Mongol forces back into **China**.

In 1287, the Mongols mounted another attack. Hưng Đạo continued the same tactics, avoiding a pitched battle until the enemy had occupied the capital and then launching a series of attacks that culminated at the mouth of the **Bạch Đằng River**, where, in early 1288, he repeated the feat of **Ngô Quyền** more than 300 years earlier, sinking metal-tipped stakes into the river that impaled the ships of the Mongol fleet as they sailed into the river at high tide. The defeat led to the evacuation of the enemy armed forces and the end of the last Mongol threat to Vietnamese independence. Hưng Đạo died in 1300, at the age of 87. A temple, which still exists, was built at Kiếp Bạc, his final home in what is today Hải Dương Province.

Trần Hưng Đạo is viewed today as one of the truly great military strategists in Vietnamese history. His use of guerrilla warfare to harass a more powerful enemy became a model for revolutionary military planners of the 20th century as they sought to devise a strategy to defeat the powerful armed forces of **France** and the **United States**. His emphasis on the importance of national unity, with the entire nation fighting as one, was cited by Communist leaders as they attempted to mobilize the population of North Vietnam in the struggle to reunify the North with the South. His peroration of resistance to the invaders and his book on military strategy, entitled *Essentials of Military Art* (*Bình Thư Yếu Lược*), have become classics of Vietnamese **literature**. At the same time, his spirit is considered to be one of the most potent in the Vietnamese pantheon and is worshipped by many people. The cult dedicated to him is one of the prominent features of Vietnamese popular **religion** that has not been borrowed from China.

TRẦN HUY LIỆU (1901–1969). Prominent member of the **Indochinese Communist Party** (ICP), later a historian in the **Democratic Republic of Vietnam**. A native southerner, Trần Huy Liệu became active in the nationalist movement in **Saigon** in the mid-1920s. Once a member of the short-lived **Youth Party** and the Vietnamese Nationalist Party (**Việt Nam Quốc Dân Đảng**), he switched to **Hồ Chí Minh**'s Revolutionary Youth League (**Thanh Niên**) at the end of the decade. A journalist by training, he published articles in ICP-affiliated newspapers in **Tonkin** during the **Popular Front** period in the mid-1930s. In 1945, he was named minister of propaganda in the new government established during the **August Revolution**. At the end of August, he led a delegation to **Huế** to accept the abdication of Emperor **Bảo Đại**. After 1954, Trần Huy Liệu became a prominent historian, writing several lengthy histories of the anti-**French** resistance movement in Vietnam. *See also* JOURNALISM.

TRẦN LỆ XUÂN (Madame Ngô Đình Nhu) (1924–   ). Wife of **Ngô Đình Nhu** and self-styled "first lady" of the **Ngô Đình Diệm** regime in the **Republic of Vietnam** because Diệm (her brother-in-law) was a bachelor. A daughter of Trần Văn Chương, Vietnamese ambassador to the **United States** during the 1950s, and educated in **Hanoi** and **Saigon**, she married Nhu shortly after graduation from the *lycée*. A woman of immense energy and intensity, she became a figure of considerable importance—and controversy—under the Diệm regime. She was active in promoting Catholic causes, the struggle against Communism, and the fortunes of the Diệm regime itself, and she was the guiding spirit behind the Women's Solidarity Movement, an anti-Communist paramilitary organization established in South Vietnam after the **Geneva Conference.**

Known to foreigners as the "dragon lady" for her influence and steely determination, she was considered by critics as an evil force within the Diệm regime and a key source of its unpopularity among non-Catholics in the population. Her sarcastic use of the term "barbeque" to describe the self-immolations by **Buddhist** monks protesting the regime was a particular source of enmity both in South Vietnam and abroad. Since the assassination of her husband and brother-in-law in 1963, she has lived in Europe.

TRẦN MINH TÔNG (1301?–1358). Fifth emperor (r. 1314–1329) of the **Trần dynasty** in the 14th century. He succeeded to the throne in 1314, when his father **Anh Tông**, in accordance with dynastic custom, abdicated. His reign was a relatively peaceful one, marked only by a brief war with **Champa** in 1318, resulting in the seizure of the Cham capital.

According to Vietnamese historians, Minh Tông was somewhat of an innovator. He issued a decree prohibiting the traditional practice of tattooing in the Vietnamese armed forces—a practice that had been made famous in the previous century when soldiers fighting under **Trần Hưng Đạo** had tattooed themselves with the phrase "death to the Mongols" (*sát Thát*). After his retirement in 1329, he played an active role as adviser to the throne during the reign of two of his sons, **Hiến Tông** and **Dụ Tông**, until his death in 1358. He seems to have been the last of the strong, capable emperors before the Trần dynastic line went into decline during the last half-century of its existence. However, he was sometimes overly sanguine about conditions in his kingdom—an attitude that **Confucian** scholars in later times blamed on his **Buddhist** outlook on life.

TRẦN NGHỆ TÔNG (1321–1395). Eighth emperor (r. 1370–1372) of the **Trần dynasty**. Nghệ Tông took the throne after a brief usurpation by a man who was not a blood relative of the imperial clan, but he only reigned for a brief time before abdicating, apparently overcome with fear at the dramatic **Cham** invasion of 1371. He remained an influential figure at court after abdication and frequently conspired to affect policy, eventually intervening to place his own son, **Thuận Tông**, on the throne. His influence, however, was insufficient to check the rising power of an ambitious official named *Hồ Quý Ly*, who overthrew the Trần within a few years of Nghệ Tông's death. *See also* TRẦN HIỆN ĐẾ.

TRẦN NHÂN TÔNG (1258–1308). Third emperor (r. 1278–1293) of the **Trần dynasty** in late 13th-century Vietnam. Trần Nhân Tông succeeded his father **Trần Thánh Tông** as emperor in 1278. His reign was marked, above all, by war with the Mongol Yuan dynasty in **China**. His predecessor had attempted to placate the Mongols by adopting a conciliatory attitude toward their demands and accepting tribute status with the emperor in Beijing. By the late 1270s, the Mongols had seized all of southern China from the remnants of the Song dynasty and continued their southward expansion with an attack on the kingdom of **Champa**, south of Vietnam on the central coast. When the Cham government took to the hills to continue guerrilla warfare against the invaders, Kublai Khan demanded the right of passage for Mongol troops through Đại Việt. When the Vietnamese refused, the Yuan launched an invasion that resulted in the seizure of most of the **Red River Delta** and the occupation of the capital of Thăng Long (modern-day **Hanoi**). Supported by the outstanding generalship of **Trần Hưng Đạo**, Nhân Tông rallied the population behind a defensive effort that defeated the Mongols and forced the withdrawal of their forces from China. A final attack in 1287–1288 was defeated as well, at the battle of **Bạch Đằng**. Nhân Tông sought negotiations and offered to recognize Chinese suzerainty, but Kublai Khan was reportedly planning a new invasion of Vietnam when he died.

Nhân Tông is perhaps best-known for his role as a patron of Vietnamese **Buddhism**. He wrote a number of essays and poems on Buddhist themes and was also the patron of the **Trúc Lâm** sect; after his abdication, he became a monk. During a visit to holy sites in Champa, he proposed the idea of a marriage alliance through the "gift" of his daughter **Huyền Trân**. *See also* MONGOL INVASIONS.

TRẦN PHẾ ĐẾ. *See* TRẦN HIỆN ĐẾ.

TRẦN PHÚ (1904–1931). Founding member of the **Indochinese Communist Party** (ICP) in 1930. Born in Quảng Ngãi, the son of a district official, Trần Phú attended the **National Academy** in **Huế** and after graduation became a teacher in Vinh. In the mid-1920s, he became a member of the New Vietnamese Revolutionary Party (**Tân Việt Cách Mệnh Đảng**). Sent to Canton in 1926 to discuss a merger with **Hồ Chí Minh**'s Revolutionary Youth League (**Thanh Niên**), he defected to the latter.

As a promising member of the League, Phú was sent to the **Union of Soviet Socialist Repulics**in 1927 to study at the Stalin School (Communist University for Toilers of the East). In early 1930, he returned to Vietnam and in October was chosen as general secretary of the newly formed ICP and a member of its three-man presidium. He was arrested by French police in April 1931 after attending the party's second plenum in **Saigon**. He died in prison in September of torture or tuberculosis.

TRẦN QUANG KHẢI (1241–1294). Prince and military leader who fought against **Mongol invasions** in the late 13th century. Trần Quang Khải, a son of Emperor **Trần Thái Tông** (r. 1225–1258), commanded Vietnamese military forces in the South, near the border of **Champa**. In 1285, Mongol troops, fresh from a successful military campaign against the Cham, launched an attack through the present-day region of Nghệ An—Hà Tĩnh. Trần Quang Khải was unable to prevent the Mongol advance and retreated northward, but eventually his force joined with those of **Trần Hưng Đạo** to defeat the Mongol armies and drive them out of Vietnam.

TRẦN QUỐC PAGODA (*Chùa Trần Quốc*). A famous pagoda in **Hanoi**. Originally called the *Khai Quốc Pagoda*, it was first built in the fifth century C.E. on the banks of the **Red River** near the present-day city of Hanoi. Later, it was moved to a peninsula on the **West Lake** on the northern edge of the city and renamed the Trần Quốc Pagoda. During the **Lý dynasty**, it housed a **Buddhist** monastery.

TRẦN QUỐC TUẤN. *See* TRẦN HƯNG ĐẠO.

TRẦN THÁI TÔNG (1218–1277). First emperor (r. 1225–1258) of the **Trần dynasty**. Trần Thái Tông (proper name *Trần Cảnh*) ascended the throne at age seven in 1225, through the influence of the powerful Trần family, which had been dominant at court during the final years of the **Lý dynasty**. During his youth, the dynasty was under the influence of his scheming uncle **Trần Thủ Độ**. In 1236, Thủ Độ forced the young emperor to abandon his wife, who was childless, in favor of her older sister, who was already married to another member of the family and already pregnant. In protest, Thái Tông, a fervent **Buddhist**, fled the capital and sought refuge at a Thiền (Zen) monastery on nearby Mount Yên Tử, but his uncle cajoled him into returning to the palace, and he reigned for 20 more years.

The reign of Thái Tông was marked by the further centralization and regularization of the Vietnamese state. Through the influence of

Thủ Độ, who remained a dominant figure at court until his death in 1264, a number of administrative reforms were introduced. The civil service **examination system** (based on the "three doctrines"— Buddhism, **Confucianism**, and **Daoism**) was extended, a national system of taxation and several new bureaucratic institutions were established, and a penal code was promulgated. Thái Tông also attempted to resolve the continuing problem of imperial succession by introducing a new system whereby the emperor retired from the throne while still active to serve the new emperor with the title of *Thái Thượng Hoàng* (senior emporer).

Thái Tông's three decades on the throne were also a period of active Vietnamese involvement in regional affairs. In the early 1250s, the empire fought a new war with **Champa** to the south. Although that campaign was a striking success, a new and more ominous threat now appeared on the horizon in the form of the rise of the Mongol Empire in **China**. In 1257, Kublai Khan demanded that Đại Việt grant passage to Mongol troops through Vietnamese territory to attack the Southern Sung, but Thái Tông refused. A Mongol army invaded the **Red River Delta** and briefly occupied the capital at Thăng Long (modern-day **Hanoi**), but disease, the weather, and Vietnamese attacks forced them to retreat.

In 1258, Thái Tông abdicated the throne in favor of his son, who became Emperor **Thánh Tông**; this abdication in favor of a successor became a regular practice of the Trần dynasty. He served his son as senior emperor for 19 more years and died at the age of sixty. *See also* MONGOL INVASIONS.

TRẦN THÁNH TỒNG (1240–1290). Second emperor (r. 1258–1278) of the **Trần dynasty**. Thánh Tông rose to the throne in 1258 when his father, **Thái Tông**, abdicated to become senior emperor (*Thái Thượng Hoàng*). Unlike the previous period, which had been marked by war with **Champa** and a **Mongol invasion** of the **Red River Delta** in 1257, Thánh Tông's reign was a relatively peaceful one. Although pressure on the northern border from the Yuan (Mongol) dynasty continued, he followed a policy of conciliation, accepting the role of tribute status with the Mongol emperor, and was able to avoid war with **China**. In preparation for a possible attack from the North, however, he strengthened the armed forces and enforced national conscription to create a peacetime army of over 100,000 men.

In domestic affairs, Thánh Tông essentially continued the policy of his father, promoting the centralization of government and the rationalization of administration. A massive program to open virgin lands to cultivation through the construction of dikes was put in operation. The new lands were then turned into estates (*trang điền*) owned by great noble and **mandarin** families and farmed by peasants whose social and legal position resembled those of serfs in feudal Europe. Although the land policy might have had economic benefits for the state, it led to the creation of powerful autonomous fiefdoms that would later undermine the power of the **monarchy** and a rising level of social unrest in the countryside.

In 1278, Thánh Tông followed the model of his father and retired from the throne in place of his son, who became Emperor **Nhân Tông**. He remained influential as *Thái Thượng Hoàng* until his death.

TRẦN THIỆN KHIÊM (1925–). General in the **Army of the Republic of Vietnam** and leading official in the **Saigon** regime. Khiêm joined other disgruntled generals in overthrowing the regime of President **Ngô Đình Diệm** in November 1963. Appointed minister of defense under **Nguyễn Khánh**, he later served as ambassador to the **United States** and prime minister of the **Republic of Vietnam** from 1969 to 1975. He fled the country in April 1975 and is reportedly living in **France**.

TRẦN THỦ ĐỘ (1194–1264). Powerful political figure in the 13th century and founder of the **Trần dynasty** (1225–1400), though he himself did not reign. Trần Thủ Độ was a cousin of Trần Thị, wife of Emperor **Lý Huệ Tông** and an influential member of the Trần family, which had helped restore Emperor Lý Cao Tông to power after a rebellion in 1208. In 1225, Huệ Tông abdicated in favor of his daughter, **Lý Chiêu Hoàng**. Thủ Độ, now a lover of ex-queen Trần Thị, arranged a marriage between the young empress and his nephew, the seven-year old Trần Cảnh, who became founding Emperor **Trần Thái Tông** of the new dynasty. Thủ Độ then arranged for the death of remaining members of the Lý family, including the retired ex-emperor Huệ Tông.

During the next several decades, Thủ Độ remained a dominant figure at the Trần court. When Lý Chiêu Hoàng failed to produce an heir, he arranged for her to be replaced as wife of Emperor Thái Tông by her older sister. His Machiavellian scheming caused widespread outrage and led to rebellion by other influential figures at court, whom he pacified by providing them with state land or official titles. He also used his influence to achieve administrative reforms to strengthen the Trần dynasty, promulgating a new penal code and setting forth new regulations on hiring and promotions within the bureaucracy.

TRẦN THUẬN TÔNG (1377?–1398). Eleventh emperor (r. 1388–1398) of the **Trần dynasty**. A son of the retired emperor **Nghệ Tông**, Thuận Tông was elevated to the throne by his father as a replacement for his cousin **Hiện Đế** at a time when court politics were seriously destabilized by the powerful official **Hồ Quý Ly**. Thuận Tông was subsequently removed from power and assassinated at the order of Quý Ly; he was succeeded by his son, Emperor Thiếu Đế. Quý Ly deposed Thiếu Đế in 1400, bringing the Trần dynasty to an end.

TRẦN TRỌNG KIM (1883–1953). Conservative historian and politician in colonial Vietnam. Born in Hà Tĩnh, Trần Trọng Kim was educated at the École Coloniale in **France** and returned to Vietnam in 1911. He began his professional career by writing elementary school textbooks on **Confucian** ethics and philosophy. In the 1920s, he published two major volumes on Asian history and civilization, *Nho Giáo* (*Confucianism*) and *Việt Nam Sử Lược* (*Outline History of Vietnam*). Kim's attempt to preserve and interpret Confucianism for his contemporaries provoked a literary war with such critics as **Phan Khôi**, who argued that traditional Confucian culture had little value in 20th-century Vietnam. Trần Trọng Kim was briefly prime minister of Vietnam after the **Japanese** coup d'etat, which overthrew the French colonial administration in March 1945. His government resigned with the defeat of Japan in August. His history textbook remained in use in the **Republic of Vietnam** until 1975. *See also* AUGUST REVOLUTION; BẢO ĐẠI; JAPANESE OCCUPATION; LITERATURE.

TRẦN VĂN ĐÔN (1917–   ). General in the **Army of the Republic of Vietnam** and participant in the coup that overthrew President **Ngô Đình Diệm** in 1963. Born and raised in **France**, Trần Văn Đôn was trained in economics and then joined the French Army at the outbreak of World War II. Respected for his competence and integrity, he rose rapidly in rank and was appointed Army Chief of Staff by Diệm, whom he had supported during the latter's rise to power after the **Geneva Conference** in 1954. He eventually lost Diệm's confidence, however, and was deprived of his command. In 1963, he joined the "coup group" that overthrew the Diệm regime and briefly served as minister of defense. Arrested in early 1964 by General **Nguyễn Khánh** on the suspicion of dealings with neutralist elements in France, General Đôn retired from active service and eventually settled in the **United States**.

TRẦN VĂN GIÀU (1911–   ). Leading Communist militant and prominent historian in Vietnam. Born in a village south of **Saigon**, Trần Văn Giàu received his education in **France**, where he entered radical activities and was recruited to study at the Stalin School in Moscow. After completing a two-year program, he was sent back to Vietnam to help reconstruct the **Indochinese Communist Party** (ICP) after its virtual destruction during the **Nghệ Tĩnh Revolt**.

For the next several years, Giàu directed the ICP apparatus in **Cochin China**, where he began to display the independence in thought and action that made him one of the most powerful, if undisciplined, members of the party. Arrested in 1935 and sent to **Poulo Condore**, he was apparently in jail at the time of the disastrous uprising in Cochin China in November 1940 (the so-called **Nam Kỳ Uprising**) that resulted in the arrests of several of its top operatives.

Immediately after World War II, Trần Văn Giàu led the party's activities in the South and was briefly chairman of the Committee for the South (*Ủy Ban Nam Bộ*) during the **August Revolution**. But his harsh methods of operation were considered unsuitable by Party leaders in **Hanoi**, and he was replaced in 1946 by **Nguyễn Bình**. Trần Văn Giàu later became a historian and has published a number of major works on the history of the Communist Party and the Vietnamese Revolution.

TRẦN VĂN HƯƠNG (1902–1982). Civilian political figure and briefly president of the **Republic of Vietnam** prior to the Communist takeover in 1975. A native of **Cochin China**, Trần Văn Hương was a schoolteacher who had gone into politics and became the mayor of **Saigon** under the regime of **Ngô Đình Diệm**. A critic of Diệm, he became briefly prominent after the latter's overthrow when he was named prime minister under the elderly politician **Phan Khắc Sửu** in a civilian government established by General **Nguyễn Khánh** in the fall of 1964. He was replaced by **Phan Huy Quát** a few months later.

In 1971, after the resignation of **Nguyễn Cao Kỳ** as vice-president of the Second Republic established by the 1967 constitution, Hương replaced him. In late April 1975, Hương was named president when **Nguyễn Văn Thiệu** resigned on the eve of the fall of Saigon. Communist leaders refused to deal with him, however, and he was replaced a few days later with General **Duong Văn (Big) Minh**, who finally surrendered power. *See also* HỒ CHÍ MINH CAMPAIGN.

TRẦN VĂN HỮU (1896–1984). Prime minister of the **State of Vietnam** from May 1950 until June of 1952. A wealthy landlord and a **French** citizen, Trần Văn Hữu was trained as an agricultural engineer and served as an official in the French Department of Agriculture after World War I. Amassing considerable wealth as a landlord, he became active in the movement to restore ex-Emperor **Bảo Đại** to power in the late 1940s and was rewarded with the governorship of **Cochin China** in 1949. In May 1950, he was appointed to replace **Nguyễn Phan Long** as prime minister. Although as governor Hữu had vigorously defended Cochinchinese separatism, as prime minister he attempted to broaden Vietnamese autonomy within the **French Union**. Like his predecessor Long, he eventually turned to the **United States** as a means of applying pressure on the French. His gamble was not successful, and he was dismissed from office in June 1952. *See also* ASSOCIATED STATES OF INDOCHINA; BẢO ĐẠI SOLUTION; REPUBLIC OF COCHIN CHINA.

TRẦN VĂN TRÀ (1918–1996). Veteran Communist leader and military commander in Vietnam. Born in Quảng Ngãi, Trần Văn Trà became involved in anticolonial activities while working as a railroad laborer in the 1930s. Arrested in 1939, he was released from prison in March 1945 and became a leading figure in the **Ba Tơ Uprising** launched in Quảng Ngãi that month.

During the **Franco–Việt Minh War**, Trần Văn Trà served as a military commander with **Việt Minh** forces in **Cochin China** and political officer of the **Saigon-Chợ Lớn** zone. After the **Geneva Conference**, he was reassigned as deputy chief of staff of the **People's Army of Vietnam (PAVN)**. He returned to the South at the beginning of the Second Indochina War as a ranking military officer, chairman of the Central Military Commission of the **Central Office for South Vietnam** (COSVN), and commander of the **People's Liberation Armed Forces**.

After the end of the war in 1975, he briefly headed the Military Management Committee in Saigon and became a member of the Central Committee of the **Vietnamese Communist Party** the following year and vice-minister of defense of the **Socialist Republic of Vietnam** (SRV). He was dropped from all his party and government positions in 1982, reportedly because of policy criticisms that appeared in his memoirs, which are also believed to have emphasized the wartime role of his Southern troops to an extent that displeased officers in **Hanoi**.

TRANG ĐIỀN. A form of land tenure that appeared under the **Trần dynasty** in the 13th century. Sometimes referred to by the Latin term "latifundia," *trang điền* were private estates owned primarily by members of the royal family. Initially the growth of these estates served to promote the cultivation of arable land and also provided a home and settled employment for the people who farmed the land. (Although it has been suggested that these men and their families were **slaves**, it is more likely that they were serfs.) Over time, however, the *trang điền* came to represent land and manpower that were out of central government control because the **feudal** nature of Vietnamese society at the time meant that the princes who owned them—often only distantly related to the ruling monarch—could treat them as more or less autonomous fiefs. When times got bad and it became more difficult for the peasants on these estates to make a living, they sometimes took to roaming the countryside as vagrants and bandits.

As the Trần dynasty went into decline from the mid-14th century onward, the *trang điền* became a manifestation of the court's loss of control over its territory. When **Hồ Quý Ly** began his rise to power, eventually overthrowing the dynasty, one of his most important accomplishments was the gradual reversal of this fragmentation of control and the reconsolidation of the court's hold over its territory. Although individuals continued to own tracts of land (sometimes quite large) under subsequent dynasties, the phenomenon of the *trang điền* in the form it took under the Trần disappeared.

TRANSPORT AND COMMUNICATIONS. In the traditional era, most of the transport of goods and people in Vietnam was by water, on barges or sampans that plied the vast network of rivers and canals that threaded through the two major river valleys. The only major highway was the "Mandarin Road" (what later became Colonial and then National Route 1), which stretched down the coast from **Hanoi** to the **Mekong River Delta** in the South. The more affluent could take that lengthy journey by palanquin (sedan chair) or by sea, but for most Vietnamese, even the most lengthy voyage was usually on foot.

During the colonial era, the **French** built a system of metaled roads to connect the major cities and a rail line that linked **Hanoi** and **Saigon** and the **Red River Delta** with the **Chinese** border. At the time, the road system was reputed to be the best in Southeast Asia. Radio, the telegraph, and the telephone were also introduced. Such innovations, however, were primarily for the affluent. Outside the cities, they had little impact on the lives of Vietnamese peasants, still isolated behind the bamboo hedges in their native villages.

After the division of the country at the **Geneva Conference** in 1954, the road system underwent further development in the **Republic of Vietnam**, and regular airline service was instituted to link all the major cities. With **United States** assistance, radio and eventually television service was gradually improved, and most villages had access to telephone or telegraph facilities. But with the advent of war in the early 1960s, communications between major urban centers were badly disrupted by the fighting in the countryside. For several years the rail service that had once extended from the imperial capital of **Huế** to Saigon was virtually eliminated.

The situation was even worse in the **Democratic Republic of**

Vietnam, where inadequate government revenues and heavy bombing of main arteries and rail lines by U.S. B-52 raids combined to make the transportation of persons and goods increasingly difficult. By the end of the war, most of the major routes had been severely damaged, and the country's fleet of vintage Soviet-built buses and trucks that were virtually the only means of wheeled transportation outside of the bicycle were becoming increasingly decrepit.

Little was accomplished in the first years following national reunification, except for the building of two new bridges over the **Red River** at Hanoi to supplement the old Paul Doumer Bridge, which had been heavily damaged during the war. Route 1 remained full of bomb craters and potholes and the state-run airline service operated with a fleet of aging Soviet passenger planes and primitive safety equipment. Because of a lack of radio equipment and a shortage of electrical power, relatively few villages outside the heavily populated river deltas received radio broadcasts. The vast majority of Vietnamese still traveled by water or on foot.

In recent years, the situation has gradually improved. A program of highway repair has been under way and new roads and highways are being constructed or planned to link different parts of the country. Vietnam Airlines has purchased a number of foreign passenger airliners to replace the Soviet-built Ilyushins, which combined inadequate safety features and lack of creature comforts to make every flight an adventure, and air service has been considerably expanded to include popular **tourist** destinations. The government has begun to import automobiles from overseas, and assembly plants for Japanese and U.S. vehicles are in operation. A traffic jam in Hanoi is no longer just a tangle of pedestrians and bicycles because motorbikes and automobiles flood the roads. Handphones are ubiquitous in the cities and Internet access is widespread. *See also* FOREIGN INVESTMENT; INDUSTRY.

TREATY OF 1874. *See* PHILASTRE TREATY.

TREATY OF PROTECTORATE (1883). *See* HARMAND TREATY.

TREATY OF PROTECTORATE (1884). *See* PATENÔTRE TREATY.

TREATY OF SAIGON. Peace treaty signed between Vietnam and **France** in June 1862. The treaty was negotiated after a series of military victories won by French forces in the southern provinces of Vietnam. The Vietnamese court ceded three provinces in the **Mekong Delta** to France (Biên Hoà, Định Tường, and Gia Định), as well as the island of **Poulo Condore**, and Vietnam was required to pay a large indemnity. Three ports were opened to French commerce, and French missionaries were permitted to propagate their faith on Vietnamese soil. The treaty had been negotiated on behalf of Emperor **Tự Đức** by the mandarin **Phan Thanh Giản**. The **Philastre Treaty**, signed in March 1874, formally ceded the remaining Mekong Delta provinces to the French, though they had, in fact, been occupied since 1867. *See also* COCHIN CHINA; KỲ HOÀ, BATTLE OF; NGUYỄN TRI PHƯƠNG; TRƯƠNG ĐỊNH.

TREATY OF TIENTSIN (TIANJIN) (1885). Treaty signed between **China** and **France** in June 1885. An earlier (May 1884) agreement between the Chinese plenipotentiary Li Hongzhang and French representative François Fournier had provided initial Chinese recognition of the French **protectorate** over Vietnam. China renounced its suzerainty over Vietnam and agreed to withdraw its troops, which had been sent at the request of Emperor **Tự Đức** to help resist French attacks in the **Red River Delta**. Clashes broke out between the two sides, however, leading to a resumption of war and the signing of a second and final Treaty of Tientsin in June 1885.

TREATY OF VERSAILLES. Treaty signed between **France** and Nguyễn Ánh, pretender to the Vietnamese throne and future Emperor **Gia Long**, in November 1787. **Pigneau de Béhaine**, French Bishop of Adran, had promised to assist Nguyễn Ánh, a prince of the family of the deposed **Nguyễn Lords**, in return for future French privileges in Vietnam. France agreed to provide Nguyễn Ánh with naval craft, troops, and financial support for the latter's effort to defeat the **Tây Sơn**, now in power in Vietnam. In return, Nguyễn Ánh promised to grant commercial and missionary rights to France along with the cession of the city of **Đà Nẵng** and the island of **Poulo Condore** to France. Accompanied by Nguyễn Ánh's son Prince **Cảnh**, the bishop signed the treaty on his behalf. In the end, France failed to live up to its commitments, but the Nguyễn were later vilified by Communist historians for having made this commitment with the future colonial power, even though the treaty did almost nothing to strengthen French influence in Vietnam.

TRÍ QUANG, THÍCH (1922–). Buddhist monk and prominent critic of the South Vietnamese regime during the Vietnam War. Born in Quảng Bình of a rich peasant father, Thích Trí Quang sympathized with the **Việt Minh** movement during the **Franco–Việt Minh conflict** but eventually decided on a religious life and entered a Buddhist monastery. In 1955 he was elected president of the Buddhist Association of Central Vietnam, with its capital in **Huế**. During the 1960s, he became an outspoken critic of the regime of **Ngô Đình Diệm** and its successors in **Saigon** and called for a peace settlement and a neutralized South Vietnam. Spokespersons for the Saigon government claimed that he had Communist leanings, but actually his activities were viewed with equal suspicion by **Hanoi**, which in private reports criticized his "petty bourgeois mentality."

After the end of the Vietnam War, he retreated from politics but was briefly arrested in 1982 on the charge of supporting Buddhist **dissidents**. The tradition of Buddhist activism and dissidence that he and his fellow monks initiated in the 1960s remains a potentially potent force in the **Socialist Republic of Vietnam**. *See also* NGUYỄN VĂN THIỆU; NHẤT HẠNH, THÍCH; REPUBLIC OF VIETNAM; UNITED BUDDHIST ASSOCIATION.

TRIBAL MINORITIES. *See* HIGHLAND MINORITIES.

TRIBUNE INDOCHINOISE. A French-language newspaper published in **Saigon** between 1926–1942 by **Bùi Quang Chiêu** and other leaders of the moderate nationalist group known as the *Constitutionalist Party*. A successor to Chiêu's earlier *Tribune Indigène*, the *Tribune Indochinoise* was a moderate but often caustic publication that was critical of specific **French** policies without questioning the ultimate rationale for colonial rule. The relatively lighter press censorship in **Cochin China**, particularly for French-language publications whose readership was much smaller, enabled the *Tribune Indochinoise* to criticize colonial policy. During the early 1930s, for example, it supported royalists in **Huế** in their calls for more power to be given to Emperor **Bảo Đại**, newly returned from France. *See also* JOURNALISM.

TRIỆU ĐÀ (Zhao Tuo). Founder of the kingdom of Nanyue (**Nam Việt**) in the late third century B.C.E. Of **Chinese** ethnic background, Zhao Tuo (Triệu Đà in Vietnamese) was a commander in the army of the first emperor of the Qin dynasty (Qinshi Huangdi) who established his own kingdom with its capital in present-day Guangzhou (Canton). The new state exacted tribute from **Âu Lạc**, a kingdom located in the **Red River Delta**. In 178 B.C.E., however, his armies conquered the area and assimilated it into his kingdom. After seizing control of the delta, Triệu Đà reportedly married a Vietnamese wife and ruled the area through the local aristocratic lords, resisting further attempts by the Han dynasty in China to conquer the territory.

Traditionally, Triệu Đà was viewed as a "Vietnamese king" despite his Chinese origins, and numerous writers over the centuries routinely mentioned him in lists of Vietnamese rulers. Some scholars bemoaned the fact that the territory of Nam Việt north of what became the Sino–Vietnamese border had been "lost" to China after the end of his dynasty. Historians affiliated with the Communist Party, however, have taken a harder line and viewed him as a "Chinese ruler" whose conquest of Âu Lạc was an act of aggression against the Vietnamese and marked the beginning of the "**Chinese period**" in Vietnam's history.

TRIỆU QUANG PHỤC. A sixth-century rebel against **Chinese** rule. Originally a follower of **Lý Bí**, who initiated a rebellion against the Liang dynasty during the **Chinese period**, Triệu Quang Phục assumed leadership of the movement shortly before Lý Bí's death. However, he had to contend with the rival force of **Lý Phật Tử**, a blood relative of his former leader, and they came to govern over separate fiefs, having called a truce after fighting each other without a clear victory for either side. Eventually, both leaders were defeated by the new Sui dynasty at the end of the century. Triệu Quang Phục is frequently known by the title *Triệu Việt Vương*.

TRIỆU VIỆT VƯƠNG. *See* TRIỆU QUANG PHỤC.

TRỊNH CÔNG SƠN (1939–2001). One of the most prominent Vietnamese musicians in the 20th century. He became famous under the

Republic of Vietnam government for his haunting, plaintive songs, many of which were explicitly antiwar, and was often referred to as Vietnam's Bob Dylan. As an advocate of peace, he was harassed by the South Vietnamese government, but because he emphasized the conflict as a civil war (albeit with foreign backing) rather than a case of American aggression against the Vietnamese revolution, his views were criticized by the **Vietnamese Communist Party** as well, and he spent several years in a **reeducation camp** after the fall of the South Vietnamese regime in 1975. Upon his release, he chose to remain in Vietnam rather than emigrate as many of his fellow artists had done. During the 1980s and 1990s, he was able to resume his singing career but was only permitted to perform romantic **music**, not the songs about the war, which were "politically incorrect." His music was known and loved by the younger generation of Vietnamese at the time of his death.

TRỊNH KIỂM (?–1570). Political figure of the 16th century and first of the **Trịnh Lords**. A native of Thanh Hoá of obscure but apparently humble origins, Trịnh Kiểm married a daughter of **Nguyễn Kim**, a noted mandarin who supported the restoration of the **Lê dynasty** after the usurpation of power by **Mạc Đăng Dung**. After Kim's death in 1545, Kiểm became the dominant figure in a movement to put the Lê back in power in the capital of **Thăng Long** (present-day **Hanoi**). His main potential rival for influence was his brother-in-law **Nguyễn Hoàng**, whom he agreed to appoint governor of Quảng Nam and Thuận Hoá, at that time a barely pacified region at the southern periphery of the Vietnamese kingdom.

Kiểm commanded the Lê armed forces, which defeated the Mạc on several occasions and carved out a resistance base in Thanh Hoá. He reportedly considered seizing power in his own name but, on being advised against it by the noted scholar and oracle **Nguyễn Bỉnh Khiêm**, satisfied himself with being the power behind the throne. He died in 1570, but his descendants, known as the *Trịnh Lords*, coruled with the Lê emperors through the end of the 18th century.

TRỊNH LORDS (*Chúa Trịnh*). Powerful family that dominated the political scene during the last half of the **Lê dynasty**. The Trịnh arose during the mid-16th century, when the Lê had been overthrown by **Mạc Đăng Dung**, who established a new dynasty in the capital of Thăng Long (present-day **Hanoi**). With the aid of **Trịnh Kiểm**, the Lê drove out the Mạc and returned to Thăng Long in 1592. However, the restored dynasty was now dependent on Kiểm's successors, known as the *Trịnh Lords*, who became the dominant force at court. The Trịnh were nominally subordinate to the Lê emperors but in fact held much of the power in their hands. The relationship between a particular Trịnh Lord and his emperor depended very much on the personality and ambitions of the two men and ranged from coopera-tion to antagonism; especially powerful Trịnh Lords were not above doing away with one ruler and replacing him with another. They also set up a set of administrative offices directly under their control that duplicated the *Lục Bộ* or Six Boards of the imperial government.

The Trịnh, however, never controlled what had once been the southern part of the empire, which was now ruled as an autonomous kingdom by their main rivals, the "**Nguyễn Lords**," descendants of **Nguyễn Hoàng**, a brother-in-law of Trịnh Kiểm who had become governor of Thuận Hoá and Quảng Nam in 1588. Intermittent civil war between the two kingdoms (**Đàng Ngoài** and **Đàng Trong**) began in the 17th century and continued until the overthrow of both families, along with the Lê dynasty, by the **Tây Sơn** Rebellion in the 1780s.

TROTSKYITES. Radical wing of the revolutionary movement in co-lonial Vietnam. The faction originated among Vietnamese intellectu-als studying in **France** in the late 1920s, some connected with the shortlived **Annamese Independence Party** (PAI), organized by **Nguyễn Thế Truyền**. On their return to Vietnam in the early 1930s, many Trotskyite leaders like **Tạ Thu Thâu**, **Hồ Hữu Tường**, and Phạm Văn Hùm played a significant role on the political scene, mainly in the **Cochinchinese** capital of **Saigon**, where the Trotsky-ites published a popular newspaper, *La Lutte*, and ran candidates in several local elections.

Trotskyite activities involved them in competition with their Sta-linist rivals in the **Indochinese Communist Party**, whom they ac-cused of betraying the interests of revolution by their united front activities. In 1937, the **Comintern** prohibited any cooperation between the two groups, and despite their shared commitment to violent anticolonial struggle, they remained divided by ideological differences. Despite inner splits within the movement, the Trotskyites remained active in Vietnam until the post–World War II period, when they were essentially eliminated as a political force by the **Việt Minh**. *See also* POPULAR FRONT.

TRÚC LÂM. A sect of Vietnamese **Buddhism** established in the early 14th century by former Emperor **Trần Nhân Tông**. Centered around the Yên Tử pagoda in Hải Dương, which had been associated with the Trần imperial family for several generations, Trúc Lâm ("Bamboo Forest") was one of many sects that appeared and disappeared over the centuries, usually linked to a particular temple and lineage of monks. It flourished under the patronage of the ruling elite for several decades but gradually faded away as a specific sect with the fall of the **Trần dynasty**. However, the name of Trúc Lâm still resonates with practitioners of Vietnamese Zen (*Thiền*), some of whom consider themselves as adherents to its tradition.

TRUNG BỘ (Central Vietnam, also known as *Trung Kỳ*). Vietnamese term for the provinces along the central coast of Vietnam extending from Thanh Hoá at the southern edge of the **Red River Delta** down to Bình Thuận to the north of the **Mekong Delta**. Under French colonial rule, the central region was known as *the protectorate of Annam*. People from the Central region (known colloquially as *miền Trung*) have distinctive accents, and certain elements of popular culture show traces of the **Cham** who originally inhabited much of this stretch of territory. The area around **Huế**, the former imperial capital, has its own linguistic and cultural characteristics.

TRƯNG SISTERS (Hai Bà Trưng). Sisters who led a rebellion against **Chinese** rule in Vietnam in the first century C.E. The revolt was caused by the attempt of Chinese administrators to raise taxes and consolidate their control over the **Lạc** Lords, the indigenous landed aristocracy. The two sisters, Trưng Trắc and Trưng Nhị, were the daughters of a Lạc lord from **Tây Vu**, on the **Red River** northwest of the modern capital of **Hanoi**. Trưng Trắc, the elder, had married Thi Sách, a landed aristocrat from nearby Chu Diên. When in

C.E. 39, Thi Sách complained about exactions demanded by the Chinese prefect Su Ding, he was arrested and apparently put to death. In revenge, Trắc, supported by her younger sister, raised the flag of rebellion. Revolt quickly swept through all of the Chinese-occupied territory, with participation by both aristocrats and peasants, and Su Ding fled to China. Trắc was declared queen and set up a royal government at Mê Linh, seat of the Vietnamese kingdom during the Âu Lạc period.

China, however, returned the attack, sending the veteran military commander **Ma Yuan** to pacify the territory and return it to Chinese rule. In C.E. 41, Trắc, now abandoned by most of her followers, was defeated, captured, and, with Nhị, put to death (popular mythology holds that they committed suicide or died in battle). Although the Trưng Sisters' rebellion ended in failure, the two later became cult figures in the pantheon of heroic patriots struggling to win Vietnamese independence. The failure of their revolt ushered in a new phase in the **Chinese period** as the Han dynasty cracked down on the local elite, which had been collaborating with them until the rebellion.

TRƯỜNG CHINH (1907–1988) (real name *Đặng Xuân Khu*). Veteran member of the **Vietnamese Communist Party** and chief of state of the **Socialist Republic of Vietnam** (SRV) from 1981–1987. Born in an illustrious **scholar-gentry** family in Nam Định, Trường Chinh received a baccalaureate at the Lýcée Albert Sarraut in **Hanoi**. After briefly embarking on a teaching career, he joined **Hồ Chí Minh**'s Revolutionary League or **Thanh Niên** and in 1930 its successor, the **Indochinese Communist Party** (ICP). Arrested that same year, he served six years in Sơn La prison until his release in 1936. During the **Popular Front** period, he served the party in Hanoi as a journalist and was named chairman of the **Tonkin** Regional Committee of the ICP in 1940.

In 1941, Trường Chinh was formally elected general secretary of the ICP and became one of the leading figures in the Party. Considered an admirer of the **Chinese** revolution (Trường Chinh, his revolutionary alias, means "Long March"), he became a leading ideologist and advocate of the use of Chinese revolutionary strategy in Vietnam. In 1956, however, he was dropped from his position as general secretary because of criticism of the **land reform** campaign; it is often argued that his dismissal was meant to assuage widespread dissatisfaction with the excesses of the campaign and to deflect criticism from Hồ.

Trường Chinh retained his seat on the Politburo, however, and was an influential force in the party leadership throughout the Vietnam War. Generally considered a hardliner in domestic matters, he reportedly opposed **Le Duẩn**'s emphasis on winning the war in the South. In 1981, he was named chairman of the new **Council of State** established as a collective presidency under the 1980 **Constitution** and he was viewed as the leading figure in the faction that opposed granting **capitalist** incentives to promote **economic** growth in the SRV. On the death of Le Duẩn in July 1986, Trường Chinh replaced him as general secretary of the Party, but resigned at the Sixth Party Congress in December. He was replaced as chairman of the State Council in June 1987 but served as an adviser to the Party Politburo until his death the following year.

TRƯƠNG ĐỊNH (Trương Công Định) (1820–1864). Military commander of Vietnamese forces resisting the French **colonization** of **Cochin China** in the early 1860s. Born in present-day Quảng Nam, he was the son of a career military officer, who was appointed commander of royal troops in Gia Định near **Saigon**. After his father's death, he remained in the area to marry a woman from a wealthy local family. When the threat of French invasion loomed in the late 1850s, he helped organize military settlements and became deputy commander of militia forces in the region.

After taking part in the Battle of **Kỳ Hoà** (February 1861), Trương Định withdrew his forces south of Saigon, where he launched a prolonged guerrilla resistance against French occupation. Ordered to desist by the imperial court after the **Treaty of Saigon** in June 1862, he refused and continued the struggle. Wounded in battle in August 1864, he committed suicide. *See also* NGUYỄN TRI PHƯƠNG.

TRƯƠNG MỸ HOA (1945–). Vice-president of the **Socialist Republic of Vietnam** (SRV). A student activist during her high school days in the **Republic of Vietnam**, she was arrested in 1964 by the South Vietnamese government and spent the next 11 years in prison, including the notorious "tiger cages" of **Côn Đảo**. After the Communist victory in the South, she served for more than a decade in various leadership positions in the **Vietnamese Communist Party** in Hồ Chí Minh City. Beginning in 1987, she assumed a series of high-ranking positions in the national **Women's Union** and was elected to the Party's Central Committee. In 1994, she became vice-president of the **National Assembly**. In 2002, she replaced **Nguyễn Thị Bình** as vice-president of the SRV.

TRƯỜNG SƠN (Annamese Cordillera). Mountain chain along the western border of Vietnam. Known in the West as the *Annamese Cordillera*, the Trường Sơn ("long mountains") stretch for more than 1,200 kilometers (750 miles) in a north-south direction from slightly below the **Red River Delta** to the southern slopes of the **Central Highlands** north of Hồ Chí Minh City. Along much of its length, the range forms the border between Vietnam and its neighbors to the west, **Laos** and **Cambodia**. The highest mountains in the Trường Sơn rise over 2,500 meters (8,100 feet) in height.

TRƯƠNG TẤN SANG (1953–   ). Head of the Economic Commission of the **Vietnamese Communist Party**. A southerner from Long An, Trương Tấn Sang rose to prominence during his tenure as head of the Party in Hồ Chí Minh City between 1996 and 2000; he joined the Party Politburo the same year that he assumed the top municipal position in the important southern city. By the late 1990s, he was reportedly being considered as a possible successor to **Lê Khả Phiêu** as Party general secretary, but instead he was called to Hanoi in 2000 to serve as director of the Economic Commission, an important post that reflected his success in handling **economic** and other matters in Hồ Chí Minh City. He was one of several Party leaders from the southern region who were viewed to be competent young reformists; another member of this group was **Nguyễn Tấn Dũng**.

In 2003, Sang's reputation was marred by an official reprimand from the Party's Central Committee in connection with the massive "Năm Cam" **corruption** scandal that had emerged as a serious blot on the Party's record. Although it is not clear whether Sang was directly involved, he was criticized for committing "personnel errors" and for having failed to properly investigate the activities of those involved in the corruption case during his time in Hồ Chí Minh City.

He has retained his headship of the Economic Commission, however, and his career does not seem to have been derailed.

TRƯƠNG VĨNH KÝ (Pétrus Ký) (1837–1898). Pro-**French** official and scholar in 19th-century Vietnam. Born the son of a Catholic military official (*Pétrus* was his baptismal name), Trương Vĩnh Ký attended a missionary school in Penang and in 1863 served as an interpreter in the delegation of **Phan Thanh Giản** in Paris. Convinced of the benefits of French rule, he later became an official in the colonial administration, a teacher at the Collège des Interprètes in **Saigon**, and editor of the Vietnamese-language newspaper *Gia Định Báo*, the first newspaper to be published in the Romanized *quốc ngữ* script. Although fluent in several Western languages, he placed great importance on his own language and promoted the study of Vietnamese **literature**, history, and culture, along with the propagation of the *quốc ngữ* writing system. He was the first of a series of collaborator scholar-journalists who emerged under colonial rule; other prominent examples were **Huỳnh Tịnh Của, Nguyễn Văn Vĩnh**, and **Phạm Quỳnh**. *See also* JOURNALISM.

TỰ ĐỨC (1829–1883). Fourth emperor (r. 1847–1883) of the **Nguyễn dynasty**. Tự Đức ascended the throne on the death of his father, **Thiệu Trị**, as the result of a court intrigue against his older brother Hồng Bảo, who later plotted to reclaim his right to the throne and died in prison. It was a difficult time for the Vietnamese Empire, and Tự Đức, sickly and pessimistic by nature, was unequal to the task. Internal rebellion in the mid-1850s was followed by an attack by **France** in 1858, the first stage of colonization. After a brief effort to drive out the invaders, Tự Đức became resigned to French domination of his country, which, by a series of treaties, eventually became a French **protectorate** in 1884, shortly after his death.

At the last, Tự Đức attempted to resist, calling on the Qing dynasty for assistance against a French invasion of northern Vietnam in 1882, but it was really too late. The court was badly divided between advocates of peace and of resistance, leading to a succession crisis; he was sterile as a result of smallpox and thus left no heir. He was succeeded by his nephew **Dục Đức**, who reigned for only three days and was replaced by his (Dục Đức's) uncle **Hiệp Hoà**, who died shortly thereafter, and then by **Kiến Phúc**, a cousin. This rapid succession of rulers was the work of two powerful regents, **Tôn Thất Thuyết** and **Nguyễn Văn Tường**, and proved to be a fatal sequence of events given French military pressure at the time.

History has not always been kind to Tự Đức, who has often been vilified for his weakness and vacillation in dealing with domestic and foreign policy crises. Some historians, however, have recognized that he was to some extent symptomatic of deeper problems that plagued the dynasty through much of the century before colonization, which were at least as harmful as his own character flaws. He is also acknowledged for his literary skills.

TỰ LỰC VĂN ĐOÀN (Self-Reliant Literary Group). Literary organization established by Vietnamese writers in the early 1930s. Established by the romantic novelists **Nhất Linh** (Nguyễn Tường Tam) and **Khái Hưng** (Trần Khánh Giư) in 1932, the organizers of Tự Lực Văn Đoàn intended to promote the Westernization of Vietnamese **literature** and society as a whole. Novels written by members of the group, who also included Nhất Linh's brother Nguyễn Tường Long (pen name *Hoàng Đạo*) and Hồ Trọng Hiếu, were romantic in style and consciously avoided the literary allusions and pretentiousness of earlier **Confucian** writers. Many expressed a strong concern over social conditions and the legacy of **feudal** society in colonial Vietnam but tended to promote an attitude of individual rebellion toward traditional moral values, rather than one of organized resistance to political authority.

Mouthpiece for the group was the newspaper *Phong Hoá* (*Manners*), replaced in 1935 by *Ngày Nay* (*These Days*), while many of its novels were issued by its own publishing house, Đời Này. The group gradually lost influence in the late 1930s as the romantic style of writing gave way to a more realistic approach adopted by a new group of writers influenced by Marxism, and many members of Tự Lực Văn Đoàn became involved in politics during World War II. Their work reflects the emotional and psychological preoccupations of a generation of young Vietnamese whose exposure to Western culture in varying degrees led them to doubt and question many aspects of their traditional Confucian culture. The novels of Tự Lực Văn Đoàn authors were extremely popular in South Vietnam after the end of the colonial rule. The **Vietnamese Communist Party** long banned them, but, in recent years, they have reappeared on the shelves of bookstores around Vietnam.

TU TÀI. See EXAMINATION SYSTEM.

TỬ THÀNH (Ch. Zicheng). An early name for the city of **Hanoi** during the period of Chinese rule. *See also* ĐẠI LA.

– U –

UNION OF SOVIET SOCIALIST REPUBLICS (USSR). The first contact between Vietnam and the new Soviet state in Russia probably took place in 1923, when the revolutionary **Hồ Chí Minh**—then known under a different pseudonym of *Nguyễn Ái Quốc*—was invited to Moscow to study Marxism at the famous Stalin School, which had been recently established by the **Comintern** to train revolutionaries in Asian countries. Late the following year, Hồ went to Canton to work in the local Comintern headquarters and promote the creation of the first openly Marxist–Leninist movement in colonial **Indochina.**

Five years later, the **Indochinese Communist Party** (ICP) was founded in Hong Kong. During the next several years, the fledgling party received financial assistance and strategical guidance from Moscow. Several dozen party members received training at the Stalin School and returned to Indochina. Soviet advice was not always useful—the Comintern discouraged the theme of national independence and urged attention to the small Vietnamese working class rather than to peasants—but party leaders remained loyal to Moscow, and when World War II began, the ICP had become a major force in the anticolonialist movement.

At the end of the war, Hồ Chí Minh's **Việt Minh** Front came to power in **Hanoi.** Hồ appealed to the victorious Allies, including the USSR, for diplomatic recognition, but none responded. The refusal of the **United States** was caused partly by a reluctance to irritate the **French.** Ironically, Moscow refused for the same reason because Joseph Stalin was still hoping that the French Communist Party would win national elections and come to power in Paris.

When the **Franco–Việt Minh War** began in December 1946, then, Hồ and his colleagues fought alone. Three years later, the Communists came to power in **China**, and the new government in Beijing granted diplomatic recognition to Hồ's **Democratic Republic of Vietnam** (DRV). Two weeks later, Moscow followed suit. China backed up its diplomatic ties with military assistance, but the Soviet Union did not because Stalin argued that the revolution in Indochina would be a Chinese responsibility. Moscow's indifference was once again displayed in 1954, when Soviet representatives gave only modest support to DRV demands for the seating of representatives of the **Cambodian** and **Lao** Communist parties at the **Geneva Conference**. In the end, the proposal was rejected.

During the late 1950s, a new Soviet leadership under Nikita Khrushchev provided the DRV with limited **economic** assistance, but Khrushchev vehemently argued against actions that might lead to a resumption of revolutionary war. China, now on a collision course with the USSR over the latter's global strategy of peaceful coexistence, supported Hanoi in its contention that, in some cases, violent revolution was necessary to destroy the power of the imperialists. Vietnamese leaders in Hanoi were reluctant to irritate Moscow, however, and sought to maintain good relations with both parties.

By the early 1960s, Hanoi had become convinced of the need to return to a policy of violence to complete reunification and leaned increasingly toward China. Pro-Soviet elements in the DRV were persecuted for "revisionism" and removed from the Party. The overthrow of Khrushchev in October 1964 led to a more activist Soviet policy in Southeast Asia, however, and, in 1965, Soviet–Vietnamese relations began to improve. For the remainder of the war, Moscow agreed to satisfy Vietnamese military requirements, while Hanoi promised in return that the war in Indochina would not get out of hand and lead to a great power confrontation. The Vietnamese attempted to maintain a neutral position in the Sino–Soviet dispute because China provided considerable aid to the DRV as well.

The end of the Vietnam War in 1975 led to a decisive shift in Vietnamese foreign policy. As relations with China deteriorated rapidly because of rivalry over influence in Southeast Asia and a bitter territorial dispute. Hanoi turned increasingly toward Moscow, declaring that the relationship with the USSR was a "foundation stone" of Vietnamese foreign policy. In 1978, when the situation in Cambodia led China and Vietnam to the brink of war, the Vietnamese signed a treaty of alliance with the Soviet Union as a possible deterrent against a Chinese attack. The treaty did not require Soviet action in the event of a Sino–Vietnamese conflict, but over the long run it undoubtedly served as a restraining factor on Beijing, though the latter went ahead with its punitive invasion in 1979.

During the 1980s, Hanoi attempted to use Soviet support as a means of countering Chinese actions in Southeast Asia and maintaining its "**special relationship**" with Laos and Cambodia. In return, it permitted the USSR to maintain a substantial military presence in Vietnam, notably at the one-time U.S. naval base at **Cam Ranh** Bay. In the late 1980s, Moscow became anxious to improve relations with the **United States**, and counseled the Vietnamese to adopt a less confrontational policy in the region. With the collapse of the USSR in 1991, Hanoi lost its most powerful friend and found itself compelled to seek an improvement in relations with Washington and Beijing. It also found itself saddled with a very large debt, which led to several years of haggling over repayment and the actual valuation (because of fluctuations in the value of the ruble). Russia initially assessed the figure to be repaid at $11 billion, but subsequently 85 percent of this debt was forgiven, and Hanoi committed itself to a long-term repayment of less than $2 billion, only 10 percent of which would be in hard **currency**.

Today, Vietnamese relations with Russia remain friendly, but the historical Soviet–Vietnamese relationship, based on *realpolitik* and ideology, is a thing of the past. Hanoi and Moscow have political, economic, and military ties—Vietnam continues to purchase Russian planes, ships, and other military hardware, for example. Russia's role as a **foreign investor** in Vietnam has been less successful, however; it initially committed itself to participation in the country's first **oil** refinery project at Dung Quất but subsequently withdrew from the deal because of viability questions and other issues. Another demonstration of the changed strategic relationship between the two countries came in 2002 with the closure of the Russian naval base at **Cam Ranh Bay**, two years before the actual expiration of Moscow's lease.

In 2004, bilateral **trade** was roughly $800 million, a 30 percent increase from the previous year; Vietnamese exports to Russia accounted for one-fifth of this figure.

UNITED FRONT FOR THE LIBERATION OF OPPRESSED PEOPLES. *See* FRONT UNI POUR LA LIBÉRATION DES RACES OPPRIMÉES (FULRO).

UNITED STATES. The first contacts between the United States and Vietnam took place in the early 19th century, when U.S. merchant ships began to visit the area in search of trade opportunities. In 1832, the American trader Edmund Roberts attempted unsuccessfully to negotiate a trade agreement with the imperial court in **Huế**. His effort reportedly aborted because of his refusal to kowtow to Emperor **Minh Mạng**; later efforts to open commercial relations similarly failed. The Vietnamese envoy **Bùi Viện** was involved with abortive attempts to seek American support against the **French**.

After the French conquest of **Indochina**, trade between the area and the outside world began to increase, and in the 1920s Vietnam was linked to the West Coast of the United States by a regular steamship service. By the 1930s, the United States opened a consular office in **Saigon**, and trade between the two countries began to increase. Exports to the United States (much of it natural **rubber**) reached an annual total of over U.S.$10 million in 1939, amounting to more than 10 percent of Indochina's total exports.

The rising level of **trade** was symbolic of growing U.S. interest in the region as a whole as a source for vital natural resources. The **Japanese occupation** of Indochina in 1940 and 1941 inspired a U.S. protest and indirectly triggered Washington's involvement in the Pacific War. During World War II, President Franklin D. Roosevelt privately indicated his determination to prevent the restoration of French sovereignty at the end of hostilities, but after Roosevelt's death, Harry Truman abandoned the effort, on condition that Paris grant an increased measure of self-government to the peoples of the area.

In 1950, with fears of Communist expansion in Asia rapidly ascending, the Truman administration granted diplomatic recognition to the **State of Vietnam** and extended economic and military assistance to the French in their struggle with the **Việt Minh**. When

France decided to negotiate a withdrawal in 1954, however, President Dwight D. Eisenhower rejected the introduction of U.S. combat forces to continue the war. Following the **Geneva Conference** in July, the White House decided to provide economic and military assistance to the new regime under **Ngô Đình Diệm** in the South.

During the next several years, U.S. support of Diệm continued, as popular resistance to his rule, actively supported by the **Democratic Republic of Vietnam** (DRV) in the North, intensified. In November 1963, the John F. Kennedy administration gave its blessing to a military coup that overthrew Diệm and led to his assassination. A change of leaders was insufficient to reverse the deterioration of the U.S. client state in **Saigon**, however. In 1965, President Lyndon Johnson introduced U.S. combat forces to prevent the imminent collapse of the South Vietnamese government. After four years of heavy fighting, however, victory remained elusive, and Washington agreed to begin peace negotiations. Johnson's successor Richard M. Nixon continued the negotiations and gradually withdrew U.S. troops while seeking to strengthen Saigon's armed forces. In January 1973, the United States signed the **Paris Agreement** calling for the final withdrawal of all combat troops. Two years later, the **Republic of Vietnam** fell to a Communist offensive.

After the end of the Vietnam War, the United States briefly attempted to establish diplomatic relations with the **Socialist Republic of Vietnam**, but talks were derailed because of Cold War antagonisms and the failure of Vietnam to account for the fate of U.S. troops killed or captured during the war. For years, the United States joined with **China** and other nations in the region to place an economic embargo on trade with Vietnam following its invasion and occupation of **Cambodia** in 1978–1979. By the early 1990s, however, regional conditions had changed, and Hanoi had agreed to cooperate on resolving the problem of Americans missing in action (MIAs) in Vietnam.

In 1995, President Bill Clinton agreed to reopen diplomatic and commercial relations between the two countries, and the relationship has developed rapidly on both fronts. Clinton himself made a hugely successful visit to the country in 2000, shortly before the end of his term in office. Vietnam remains suspicious of American strategic intentions and resentful of Washington's criticisms of **human rights** issues, but this has not prevented increasingly frequent official exchanges between the two countries. After protracted negotiations, a **bilateral trade agreement** was signed in 2000, and the U.S. has become an important trading partner, despite disputes over shrimp and catfish imports from Vietnam. Americans constitute the second largest group of **tourists** visiting Vietnam, after those from China.

Generally speaking, the younger generation of Vietnamese do not share their elders' anti-American sentiments and are much more sympathetic toward the U.S. and its culture than they are toward China. Even though the latter is officially portrayed as a fraternal socialist country, many elements in the government and the military are interested in developing ties with the U.S. as a counterweight. In 2003, Vietnamese Defense Minister Phạm Văn Trà made an official visit to the U.S., and an American warship docked in Vietnam for the first time since the end of the war. Although Washington and Hanoi are unlikely to be forming an alliance any time soon, the pace of commercial and diplomatic exchanges augurs well for the building of a more solid and stable relationship.

UNIVERSITIES. Before the **French** conquest, higher **education** in Vietnam was essentially limited to training in the **Confucian** classics for the **examination system**, which was the gateway to an official career. The *locus classicus* of such study was the **Imperial Academy** (*Quốc Tử Giám*) in **Hanoi**, where aspiring students underwent lengthy training in Confucian (and sometimes **Buddhist** and **Daoist**) works in the hope of eventual appointment to a position in the mandarinate.

The concept of a modern university education was introduced into Vietnam in the early 20th century, when the French colonial administration founded the University of Hanoi to provide an opportunity for young Vietnamese to receive higher education in a Western curriculum. Unfortunately, the university was closed a short while later after a series of events frightened French officials, who were concerned about the rising force of nationalism. It was reopened by the reformist Governor-General **Albert Sarraut** in 1917 and contained schools of medicine and law and a teachers' college.

When Vietnam was divided at the **Geneva Conference** in 1954, the University of Hanoi was the only institute of higher learning in the entire country. The new government in the **Republic of Vietnam** immediately set out to remedy the situation, and by the end of the decade, three new universities had been established in **Saigon, Đàlạt,** and **Huế**. By the mid-1960s, 12,000 students were attending courses at the university level, with most of them in Saigon. Many of the more brilliant students, however, went abroad to study.

In the North, the **Democratic Republic of Vietnam** placed the University of Hanoi under new direction and opened a number of new technical institutes. Promising students went to universities in **China**, the **Union of Soviet Socialist Republics**, or Eastern European countries, most of them in the fields of the applied sciences. The system suffered from a lack of funding and a rigid and bureaucratic approach to learning. After the conquest of Saigon in 1975, the regime inherited the university system in South Vietnam and immediately attempted to bring it into line with the principles being applied in the North. Ideological retraining programs, official distrust of those with a bourgeois class background, low salaries, and poor facilities led many professors to abandon their careers or flee abroad.

In 1993, the government attempted to reorganize the system of higher education, amalgamating the proliferating number of colleges and technical institutes into several major centers, including the National University of Hanoi and other universities in Huế, Thái Nguyên, **Đà Nẵng**, and Hồ Chí Minh City. Smaller institutes are located in provincial capitals. The curriculum was also broadened and given additional flexibility. In the 2004–2005 academic year, an estimated 1.32 million students were taking courses at the postsecondary level; just over half of these were full-time, and just hnder half of these were women. There were some 47,000 teachers, of whom 19,000 were women.

Still, problems continue to pose an obstacle to the government's plan to improve the system of higher education. Funding remains seriously inadequate, and the training of the staff and faculty is often poor. A relatively small percent of all instructors possess the doctorate. Suspicion of ideologically unorthodox ideas persists, and tertiary education continues to rely heavily on rote learning and examinations. The government has recognized the need for more diversity and has allowed the establishment of private and semiprivate colleges, which are significantly changing the face of Vietnamese higher education.

– V –

VĂN CAO. *See* NGUYỄN VĂN CAO.

VẠN HẠNH (?–1018). A prominent monk and court advisor in the late 10th and early 11th centuries. His role in Vietnamese history reflects the importance of **Buddhist** and **Daoist** clergy as political and spiritual advisors during the period before emperors could draw on the expertise of a critical mass of **Confucian**-trained scholars. Vạn Hạnh served Emperor Lê Đại Hành (**Lê Hoàn**) but then helped bring his short-lived "dynasty" to an end after the death of his son **Lê Long Đĩnh**. The monk "discovered" a prophecy engraved in a tree trunk, which predicted the coming to power of a new **Lý dynasty**; coincidentally, he had connections to a court official named *Lý Công Uẩn*. With the support of Vạn Hạnh (and probably other members of the clerical elite), Lý Công Uẩn took power after Lê Long Đĩnh's death and established a new dynasty as *Emperor* **Lý Thái Tổ**.

VĂN LANG. The name for what is believed to be an early Vietnamese kingdom at the dawn of the historical era. It was supposedly founded in the **Red River Delta** some time during the first millennium B.C.E. and lasted until its eventual destruction in the late third century B.C.E. by the military adventurer Thục Phán, who ruled as *An Dương Vương* over a new kingdom in the area named *Âu Lạc*. **French** scholars believed that the kingdom of Văn Lang was a legend invented by Vietnamese historians to explain and embellish the origins of their civilization, but precolonial sources treated it as a real entity and depicted a kingdom extending over a large area of what is now Vietnam. In recent years, Vietnamese historians and **archeologists** have linked Văn Lang to the **Bronze Age** culture known as *Đông Sơn* and to the legends of the rulers called the *Hùng Kings*. Văn Lang is therefore considered to be an "embryonic" or "proto-" state, marking the origins of the Vietnamese nation. Despite the considerable archeological evidence for a civilization during the Bronze Age, however, actual proof of the existence of a "state" or "nation" ruled by "kings" is scanty.

***VĂN THÂN* REBELLION.** *See* SCHOLARS' UPRISING.

VĂN TIẾN DŨNG (1917–2002). Senior general in the **People's Army of Vietnam (PAVN)** and leading political figure in the **Socialist Republic of Vietnam** (SRV). Born in Hà Đông in a poor peasant family, Văn Tiến Dũng worked in a **French**-owned textile factory in the 1930s and joined the **Indochinese Communist Party** in 1937. Arrested twice, he escaped both times and was named secretary of the Party's Regional Committee for **Tonkin** in 1944.

During the **Franco–Việt Minh War**, Dũng rose rapidly in the ranks of the PAVN and was elected to the Party Central Committee in 1951. He attained full Politburo rank in 1972. He was sent to the South in 1974 to command North Vietnamese forces during the so-called **Hồ Chí Minh Campaign**, which resulted in the seizure of **Saigon** the following spring. In 1980, he was appointed minister of defense and played an active role in directing the Vietnamese invasion of **Cambodia** in 1979. He was reportedly criticized, however, for his autocratic leadership style and was dropped from the Politburo and his position at the Ministry of Defense in December 1986.

VANGUARD YOUTH MOVEMENT (*Thanh Niên Tiền Phong*). Quasi-revolutionary youth movement in colonial Vietnam. The movement was established under Japanese sponsorship during World War II by Dr. **Phạm Ngọc Thạch**, a secret supporter of the Communist-dominated **Việt Minh**. Resembling the Boy Scouts, it recruited followers in schools, factories, and rural villages. By the end of the war, it had more than one million members in virtually every province in **Cochin China**. In August 1945, radical elements within the movement were organized into paramilitary units that participated in the take-over of **Saigon** at the moment of Japanese surrender. *See also* AUGUST REVOLUTION; JAPANESE OCCUPATION.

VANN, JOHN PAUL (1924–1972). **United States** military officer who served as an adviser in the **Republic of Vietnam** in the early 1960s and later returned to play a prominent role in the pacification program, then known as *Civil Operations and Revolutionary Development Support* (CORDS). Vann first came to public attention when he criticized the performance of **Army of the Republic of Vietnam** troops at the battle of **Ấp Bắc** in December 1962. Later, he was outspoken in his criticism of the strategy applied by the U.S. in the Vietnam War. He died in a helicopter crash in June 1972. His career later became the subject of Neil Sheehan's prize-winning *A Bright Shining Lie*, published in 1988. *See also* WESTMORELAND, WILLIAM C.

VARENNE, ALEXANDER (1870–1946). Governor-general of French **Indochina** from 1925 to 1928. A member of the French Socialist Party and a deputy in the **National Assembly**, Varenne was appointed governor-general of Indochina in 1925. His liberal views led him to undertake a number of reforms to reduce the rising level of discontent in Vietnam. Shortly after his arrival, he granted clemency to **Phan Bội Châu**, the revolutionary patriot who had just been sentenced to death in **Hanoi**. He followed up that symbolic act by promising reforms in the areas of **education**, civil rights, and local administration, and implied that at some future date the **French** would grant Vietnam independence.

Varenne's statements aroused a storm of criticism among French residents in Indochina, and he was forced to back down on a number of his pledges. He did achieve several changes in social and administrative policy, setting up a regional assembly in **Annam** and offices to inspect labor conditions and expand rural credit. He resigned from office in January 1928.

VIỆT BẮC. Vietnamese term meaning "northern Vietnam" for the mountainous provinces to the north and northeast of the **Red River Delta**. A traditional refuge for bandits and rebels, the Việt Bắc was used by the **Việt Minh** as a liberation base area during World War II and the **Franco–Việt Minh conflict** that followed. The region comprises an area of roughly 36,000 square kilometers (14,000 square miles) and includes the present-day provinces of Hà Giang, **Cao Bằng**, Bắc Thái, Lạng Son, and Tuyên Quang. Traditionally, it was inhabited predominantly by **highland minorities**, notably the **Tày** and **Nùng**, and the support of these groups was an important factor in the success of the Revolution. After 1954, a Việt Bắc Autonomous

Region was created northeast of the **Red River Delta** as part of the **Democratic Republic of Vietnam**. This autonomous zone, modelled along the lines of ethnic minority regions in **China**, was abolished with reunification and the creation of the **Socialist Republic of Vietnam**. *See also* TÂY BẮC.

VIỆT CỘNG (Vietnamese Communists). Popular name in the West for the **National Liberation Front** and **People's Liberation Armed Forces (PLAF)** in South Vietnam. The term was originally applied by the regime of President **Ngô Đình Diệm**.

VIỆT ĐIỆN U LINH TẬP (Compilation of the Departed Spirits in the Realm of Việt). A collection of myths and legends, originally written in the 14th century. Authored by a scholar-official named *Lý Tế Xuyên*, the *Việt Điện U Linh Tập* gathered together various stories about historical, semihistorical, and completely mythical individuals from Vietnamese history. Like the *Lĩnh Nam Chích Quái*, it provides an important historical and cultural perspective that is less orthodox and less Confucian than the standard chronicles.

VIỆT KIỀU. *See* OVERSEAS VIETNAMESE.

VIỆT MINH (*Việt Nam Độc Lập Đồng Minh***, League for Vietnamese Independence).** Front organization set up by the **Indochinese Communist Party** (ICP) during World War II. It was founded at the suggestion of **Hồ Chí Minh** at the Eighth Plenum of the ICP Central Committee meeting at **Pác Bó** in **Tonkin** in May 1941. The Việt Minh was a broad front organization under ICP leadership designed to win popular support for national independence and social and economic reform, with branch committees set up at province, district, and **village** levels in virtually all areas of Vietnam. At the same time, so-called **national salvation associations** (*cứu quốc hội*), a form of mass association for such functional groups as workers, peasants, **women**, students, writers, artists, and **religious** organizations were also organized under the broad rubric of the League.

After the **August Revolution** and the establishment of the **Democratic Republic of Vietnam**, the Party used the Việt Minh and its attendant mass associations as the vehicle to achieve broad mass support in the struggle against the **French**. In 1951, it was merged into a larger **Liên Việt Front** in an effort to win increased support from moderate elements. The term *Việt Minh*, however, was still commonly applied to the movement and its supporters, and the organization is viewed as a classic case of a Communist-front organization in wars of national liberation.

VIỆT NAM. The formal name of the country of Vietnam since 1945. The term *Việt* (Chin. **Yue**) was originally the name of a state in what is now southern **China** and was also used by the Chinese to designate a number of different non-Han peoples in that region and in present-day northern Vietnam; they were collectively known as the *Bách Việt* (Ch. *Baiyue*). Over time, the name came to be used specifically for the ethnic Vietnamese (**Kinh**), although a homonym (with a different Chinese character) is still used to refer to the Cantonese. The term *Nam* is the Vietnamese reading of the Chinese character *nan*, "south." Because Vietnamese is a monosyllabic language, the Vietnamese separate the two words into *Việt Nam*; most Westerners, however, refer to the country by the single word *Vietnam*.

In 1802, Emperor **Gia Long**, founder of the new **Nguyễn dynasty**, requested permission from China to change the country's name to *Nam Việt*. The Qing court refused, however, since this name evoked an ancient kingdom that had included territory now part of China. Gia Long's kingdom was given the new name *Việt Nam* instead, but the Nguyễn preferred to coin a different new name: *Đại Nam*. This term was generally used within the country until the colonial period, when it came to be employed less and less outside the imperial court. As Vietnamese nationalism developed, the term *Việt Nam* became popular and was the natural choice for **Hồ Chí Minh**'s independent government in 1945: the **Democratic Republic of Vietnam.**

VIỆT NAM CÁCH MỆNH ĐỒNG MINH HỘI. *See* VIETNAMESE REVOLUTIONARY LEAGUE.

VIỆT NAM ĐỘC LẬP ĐỒNG MINH. *See* VIỆT MINH.

VIỆT NAM GIẢI PHÓNG ĐỒNG MINH. *See* VIETNAMESE LIBERATION LEAGUE.

VIỆT NAM GIẢI PHÓNG QUÂN. *See* PEOPLE'S ARMY OF VIETNAM.

VIỆT NAM PHỤC QUỐC ĐỒNG MINH HỘI. *See* PHỤC QUỐC.

VIỆT NAM QUANG PHỤC HỘI. *See* VIETNAMESE RESTORATION SOCIETY.

VIỆT NAM QUỐC DÂN ĐẢNG (Vietnamese Nationalist Party). Radical political party in colonial Vietnam, usually known by its initials as VNQDĐ. The party was organized in the fall of 1927 by a number of radical intellectuals and merchants linked to the Nam Đông Thư Xá bookstore in **Hanoi**. The party was modeled and named after Sun Yat-sen's *Guomindang* (Nationalist Party) in **China**, then under the control of Chiang Kai-Shek. (*Quốc Dân Đảng* is the Vietnamese reading of the characters for *Guomindang*). Its goal was to promote a violent uprising to evict the **French** regime and establish a democratic republic in Vietnam. The party's social and economic goals were rudimentary, and most members were not sympathetic to Marxism. It took the significant step of recruiting followers among Vietnamese soldiers in the colonial army and militias, however—a group generally ignored at the time by Communist organizers.

In February 1930, the VNQDĐ, under the leadership of **Nguyễn Thái Học**, launched an insurrection at **Yên Bái** and several other military posts in **Tonkin**, but poor coordination and the reluctance of many of the troops to support the uprising led to disaster. Most of the party's leaders were captured and executed. From that time on, the VNQDĐ lived a shadow existence as an exile organization in southern China and was effectively eliminated as a possible rival to the nascent **Indochinese Communist Party**. At the end of World War II, a number of VNQDĐ elements returned to Vietnam with the Chinese occupation forces tasked to disarm the **Japanese**. The Chinese generals (**Lu Han** and **Xiao Wen**) exerted pressure on **Hồ Chí Minh**'s new **Democratic Republic of Vietnam** government to include representatives of the VNQDĐ in the government. However, there was considerable tension between these pro-Chinese nationalists and those associated with Hồ's **Việt Minh** Front. Armed clashes took place with the Communists, and in the summer and fall of 1946, many members of the VNQDĐ were arrested or fled into exile. After 1954, the VNQDĐ became one of several minor political parties in South Vietnam.

VIỆT NAM THANH NIÊN CÁCH MỆNH ĐỒNG CHÍ HỘI. *See* THANH NIÊN.

VIETMINH FRONT. *See* VIỆT MINH.

VIETNAMESE COMMUNIST PARTY (*Đảng Cộng Sản Việt Nam*). Current name of the ruling party in the **Socialist Republic of Vietnam** (SRV). The name was adopted at the Fourth National Congress of the party in December 1976 to replace the previous name, *Vietnamese Workers' Party* (VWP, *Đảng Lao Động Việt Nam*). Formally established in 1951, the VWP was the successor to the **Indochinese Communist Party** (ICP, *Đảng Cộng Sản Đông Dương*), founded under the leadership of **Hồ Chí Minh** in 1930. The ICP initiated the revolution against **French** rule and then officially dissolved itself shortly after the foundation of the **Democratic Republic of Vietnam** (DRV) in 1945. It functioned covertly for the next few years and then reemerged as the VWP in 1951, prior to the establishment of separate **Cambodian** and **Lao** parties.

The VWP played the dominant role in the DRV after Vietnam's partition at the **Geneva Conference** in July 1954. Its first general secretary, **Trường Chinh**, was dismissed in 1956 and replaced by President **Hồ Chí Minh. Lê Duẩn** succeeded to the post in September 1960 and held it until his death in 1986. The VWP was renamed the **Vietnamese Communist Party** (VCP) at its Sixth Congress in December 1976 after reunification of the North and the South into the **Socialist Republic of Vietnam.**

The new VCP created in 1976 included past members of both the VWP and the so-called **People's Revolutionary Party of Vietnam** (*Đảng Nhân Dân Cách Mạng Việt Nam*), created as a branch of the VWP in South Vietnam in 1962. It remains the ruling party in the SRV, with a total membership of nearly 2.7 million. The supreme body of the Party is the National Party Congress (*Đại Hội*), which meets approximately every five years. Delegates to the National Congress, elected by Party branches at lower echelons, approve major policy decisions, and elect a Central Committee (*Ban Chấp Hành Trung Ương*) that functions in the intervals between the National Congresses. The Central Committee, which holds plenary sessions twice a year to approve key decisions by Party leaders, elects a Politburo (*Bộ Chính Trị*) that serves as the ruling body of the Party. Currently, the Politburo has 15 members and the entire Central Committee has 150. At the Ninth Party Congress in 2001, the powerful Standing Committee of the Politburo was replaced by a Secretariat.

Much of the history of the ICP, VWP, and VCP can be structured around the successive Party Congresses. The most important leadership changes and policy decisions are generally made at these events; policies are then finetuned at the periodic plenums of the Central Committee elected at the previous Congress. The Sixth Party Congress of 1986, for example, laid the foundations for the changes known as *đổi mới* (renovation) and installed the reform-minded **Nguyễn Văn Linh** as general secretary. The Eighth Congress a decade later ushered in the retirement of a whole generation of leaders, notably the venerable **Đỗ Mười**, who had replaced Linh in 1991. Typically, these retirements were not actually finalized at the Congress itself and only took place several months afterward, reflecting the jockeying for power and negotiating among factional interests that characterize most important Party meetings.

One long-term issue for the VCP since the inception of the DRV has been the relationship between the Party and the state or government. The Party clearly dominates the government system; the prime minister, for example, is a member of the Politburo but is outranked by the general secretary of the Party. At the provincial and subprovincial levels, the Party Branch is normally more powerful than the corresponding **People's Committee**. In recent years, there has been talk of making a clearer separation between Party and State powers or functions, but it seems unlikely that the VCP's authority will be significantly diluted in the foreseeable future.

After Lê Duẩn's extended tenure, the general secretaryship of the VCP became a short-term position, and so far the trend has been to replace the incumbent at or shortly after each Party Congress. Thus, in 1997, after the Eighth Congress, Mười was succeeded by **Lê Khả**

Phiêu, a hardliner who represented the **People's Army of Vietnam**, whose influence must be counterbalanced by other factions (personal, regional, and ideological) within the Party and government. Phiêu came to power along with **Trần Đức Lương** as president and **Phan Văn Khải** as prime minister. The three men represented a transition to a postwar generation of leaders who had not held top political or military positions before 1975. Phiêu was in turn replaced by **Nông Đức Mạnh** in 2001, following the Ninth Party Congress. Mạnh, Lương, and Khải are viewed as moderates whose more professional and even technocratic backgrounds leave them better equipped than some of their predecessors to oversee Vietnam's transition to a market **economy**.

At the same time, however, none of these younger leaders enjoys the prestige or clout of the more senior generation, now either dead or retired. They are confronted with the ongoing problem of **corruption** within the Party's ranks and the broader question of how to maintain its legitimacy in a society where socialism seems less and less relevant. At present, talk of democracy, political **pluralism**, and the possibility of a **multiparty system** is still confined largely to a handful of **dissidents**, but the potential for more deep-rooted opposition—already signaled by protests over abuses by local officials and land disputes—is clearly there.

VIETNAMESE DEMOCRATIC PARTY (*Đảng Dân Chủ Việt Nam*). One of two small non-Communist political parties in the **Socialist Republic of Vietnam** (SRV). Created on 30 June 1944 as part of the **Việt Minh** Front, the Democratic Party plays a largely ceremonial role in contemporary Vietnam as a representative of patriotic intellectuals and a symbol of the coalition of classes under the **Vietnamese Communist Party** that is leading Vietnam through the so-called "national people's democratic revolution" to socialism. *See also* VIETNAMESE SOCIALIST PARTY.

VIETNAMESE LANGUAGE. Language spoken by the ethnic Vietnamese (**Kinh**), the majority population in modern Vietnam. Together with the **Mường** language, to which it is most closely related, it is classified in the Việt–Mường group of the Mon–Khmer subfamily of the **Austroasiatic** language family. Mon–Khmer languages are spoken by many of the original inhabitants of Southeast Asia. Vietnamese shows its Mon–Khmer roots in its grammatical structure and in some of its basic vocabulary, but it has a heavy overlay of **Sino–Vietnamese** borrowings as a result of centuries of contact with the **Chinese** language and culture. There are also Tai and **Austronesian** elements in the language as well.

Vietnamese spelling, which is based on the *quốc ngữ* Romanized script created by European missionaries and local converts in the 17th century, reflects the variations in pronunciation found around the country and does not correspond exactly to any one dialect. The language can be broadly grouped into Northern, Central, and Southern dialects, though there are considerable variations within these regions. Each dialect has a distinctive accent (including tonal patterns) and a number of local words. The mass media have contributed to some extent to the standardization of the language. However, even today, two uneducated Vietnamese from very distant parts of the country would still encounter some communication problems. *See also* VIETNAMESE PEOPLE.

VIETNAMESE LIBERATION ARMY. *See* PEOPLE'S ARMY OF VIETNAM.

VIETNAMESE LIBERATION LEAGUE (*Việt Nam Giải Phóng Đồng Minh*). Front organization set up by **Hồ Chí Minh** in southern **China** in 1941. Established at Jingxi near the Sino–Vietnamese border, it was designed to unite the various anti-**French** nationalist organizations under the overall leadership of the **Indochinese Communist Party**. The ICP's role was to be disguised, however, and a non-Communist, Hồ Ngọc Lãm, was named chairman.

For the next few months, the league trained cadres in southern China for the patriotic cause. After Hồ Chí Minh's arrest by Chinese authorities in 1942, however, the league was taken over by non-Communists, who expelled the ICP members, and it virtually disintegrated. In 1942, its remaining members were incorporated into a new front organization under Chinese sponsorship, the **Vietnamese Revolutionary League** (*Đồng Minh Hội*). *See also* VIỆT MINH.

VIETNAMESE NATIONAL ARMY (VNA). Armed forces of the **State of Vietnam** set up in the fall of 1950. According to the **Élysée**

Accords of March 1949, the new Associated State was to have its own national army, which would cooperate with **French** expeditionary forces in the spreading conflict with **Hồ Chí Minh**'s **Việt Minh**. The concept had originated in a military conference held at Cap St. Jacques (Vũng Tàu) early in the year, and the final military agreement was signed on 8 December 1950.

According to arrangements reached between the two countries, Chief of State **Bảo Đại** was designated Supreme Commander of the Army, but he was responsible to the French High Command in **Indochina**. During the next three years, the VNA gradually grew into a fighting force of nearly 200,000 men. Constant bickering marked its growth, however. The French government, dubious about its fighting capacity and suspicious that it could provide the Vietnamese with the temptation to turn against French forces in Indochina, was stingy in providing trained personnel and modern equipment, and it used the VNA primarily for pacification operations. The **United States** viewed the VNA as an important vehicle for leading Vietnam toward independence and pressured the French to permit U.S. advisers to provide training to Vietnamese troops. When the **Franco–Việt Minh War** came to an end in 1954, the army had not lived up to the expectations of any of its sponsors. After the **Geneva Conference**, the VNA was replaced by a new **Army of the Republic of Vietnam** (ARVN), created by the **Saigon** regime.

VIETNAMESE NATIONALIST PARTY. *See* VIỆT NAM QUỐC DÂN ĐẢNG.

VIETNAMESE PEOPLE. Majority population of the modern state of Vietnam. Known as *ethnic Vietnamese* (Việt or **Kinh**), they comprise today about 90 percent of the total population of the country. The ancestors of the present-day Vietnamese were among the peoples straddling both sides of the present-day border between **China** and Vietnam; the Chinese referred to them collectively as *Baiyue* (Viet. *Bách Việt*) The **Vietnamese language** shows influences from several different language families, and early myths and legends also suggest movement and contact among different groups. Gradually, the **Red River Delta** came to be seen as the political, geographical, and cultural homeland of the ethnic Vietnamese, though the somewhat higher midlands region has been as important as the lowland areas. Eventually, the Vietnamese people began to expand south, settling along the central coast of modern Vietnam (usually after conquest and pacification), the **Mekong River Delta**, and, to a lesser extent, the highland regions. Today, the Vietnamese are numerically dominant in all lowland regions of modern Vietnam, and **migration** over the last few decades has dramatically shifted the demographic balance in upland provinces traditionally dominated by **highland minorities**. *See also NAM TIẾN.*

VIETNAMESE RESTORATION SOCIETY (*Việt Nam Quang Phục Hội*) (**also known as** *Restoration Society*). Anti-French political organization established by the patriot **Phan Bội Châu** in 1912. Unlike its predecessor, the monarchist Modernization Society (*Duy Tân Hội*), its program called for the establishment of an independent Vietnamese republic patterned after the plans of Sun Yat-sen's Nationalist Party (*Guomindang*) in **China**. It is likely that Châu founded the new party to win the sympathy of Sun Yat-sen and his colleagues in China, where Châu was living in exile.

The Vietnamese Restoration Society launched several unsuccessful revolts in succeeding years, gradually declining into an ineffective nationalist organization in exile during the 1920s and 1930s. It underwent a brief resurgence before World War II when it was reorganized under the name of the *Việt Nam Phục Quốc Đồng Minh Hội* (Alliance for the Restoration of Vietnam) or *Phục Quốc* led by Prince **Cường Để**.

VIETNAMESE REVOLUTIONARY LEAGUE (*Việt Nam Cách Mệnh Đồng Minh Hội* or *Đồng Minh Hội*). Vietnamese nationalist organization founded under **Chinese** sponsorship in August 1942. Founded at Liuzhou in southern China, it included a number of Vietnamese nationalist parties and factions, including the *Việt Nam Quốc Dân Đảng*, the so-called *Phục Quốc*, and members of a previous front organization called the **Vietnamese Liberation League** (*Việt Nam Giải Phóng Đồng Minh Hội*), set up in 1941 by **Hồ Chí Minh**. The Đồng Minh Hội was the brainchild of Chinese Nationalist General **Zhang Fakui**, who hoped to use it as a vehicle for obtaining intelligence on **Japanese** troop movements in **Indochina**, and perhaps as the basis for a pro-Chinese political organization following the end of the war.

Led by **Nguyễn Hải Thần**, an ex-follower of **Phan Bội Châu**, the Đồng Minh Hội specifically excluded the **Indochinese Communist Party**, and it competed with Hồ's **Việt Minh** for support during the remainder of World War II. After the end of the war in August 1945, members of the Đồng Minh Hội were briefly included in the government organized by Hồ in **Hanoi**, mainly because of pressure from the Chinese occupying forces. They were later expelled, as Hồ tightened his control over the government. *See also* AUGUST REVOLUTION; JAPANESE OCCUPATION.

VIETNAMESE REVOLUTIONARY YOUTH LEAGUE. *See* THANH NIÊN.

VIETNAMESE SOCIALIST PARTY (*Đảng Xã Hội Việt Nam***).** One of the non-Communist political parties in contemporary Vietnam. A successor of the French Socialist Party, active in pre–World War II **Indochina**, it was formally created in 1946, shortly after the establishment of the **Democratic Republic of Vietnam** (DRV). Ideologically linked to social democratic parties elsewhere in the world, the party plays a negligible political role in a country dominated by the ruling **Vietnamese Communist Party** and serves, along with the small **Vietnamese Democratic Party**, to provide a ceremonial basis for the regime's claim to lead a "united front" of progressive classes of the final goal of Communism.

VIETNAMESE WORKERS' PARTY. *See* VIETNAMESE COMMUNIST PARTY.

VIETNAMIZATION. Strategy adopted by President Richard Nixon in 1969 to seek an end to **United States** involvement in the Vietnam War. Coming into office at a time of rising domestic opposition to the war, Nixon devised a plan to withdraw U.S. troops from the **Republic of Vietnam** on a gradual basis while simultaneously strengthening its armed forces. According to Nixon's schedule, the last U.S. combat forces would be withdrawn in June 1972, just before the November presidential elections. "Vietnamization" took place roughly on schedule, but the final withdrawal occurred as a result of the **Paris Agreement**, signed in January 1973. *See also* ARMY OF THE REPUBLIC OF VIETNAM.

VIJAYA. One of the political centers for the **Cham** people in what is now central Vietnam, located in present-day Bình Định province. Over the centuries the capital was frequently attacked and conquered by Vietnamese, Mongol, and Khmer armed forces and was finally seized by the Vietnamese in 1471. After that point, the power center for what remained of the Cham kingdom shifted farther south. *See* INDRAPURA; LÊ THÁNH TÔNG.

VILLAGE. Basic administrative unit in Vietnam. There were actually three levels of **local government** in traditional Vietnam: the commune (*xã*), the natural village (*thôn* or *làng*), and the hamlet (*ấp* or *xóm*). The commune—the name that came to be used by the **French** based on a somewhat analogous structure in their own country—was the largest and possessed the most extensive administrative apparatus; below the commune was the natural village. Many villages were themselves often divided into smaller hamlets. A typical commune would contain about 5,000 inhabitants and incorporate two or three villages and several hamlets.

In the pre-colonial period, the village was fairly autonomous and was only indirectly linked to the central government, a fact that has led some Marxist historians to apply the model of the **Asiatic Mode of Production** to premodern Vietnamese society. Village affairs were administered by a **council of elders** (*hội đồng kỳ mục*) composed of leading members of the dominant families, including scholars and retired **mandarins**. The council was assisted by a village chief (*xã trưởng* or *lý trưởng*) subordinate to its authority who served as village executive officer and liaison with higher government echelons. The village had certain obligations toward the government, namely payment of taxes and the provision of manpower for military forces and *corvée* labor. Government mandarins largely depended on the leadership of a village to provide accurate figures on the number of men living there, which determined the amount of tax to be paid and the number of people to be levied. Local leaders thus had considerable motivation to "cook the books" in order to minimize their obligations, and when the French had established colonial rule, they found huge discrepancies in the records being kept by village authorities.

In the **Republic of Vietnam**, the position of village chief was raised in importance, and the chief reported directly to higher levels of administration. Today the village remains the basic governmental unit in the **Socialist Republic of Vietnam** (SRV), but the position of village chief as such no longer exists. Local administration is handled by a **People's Council** (*Hội Đồng Nhân Dân*) elected by adult residents of the village and a **People's Committee** (*Ủy Ban Nhân Dân*) that handles executive functions.

VÕ CHÍ CÔNG (1912–). Leading figure in the **Vietnamese Communist Party** (VCP) and former chief of state of the **Socialist Republic of Vietnam** (SRV). Born near **Đà Nẵng** in 1912, Võ Chí Công became active in the **Indochinese Communist Party** in the 1930s. After imprisonment in World War II, he served in a number of Party and government posts in the **Democratic Republic of Vietnam**, rising to Politburo ranking in 1961, and was a leading member of the Party's apparatus in the South during the Vietnam War. Known as an ally of General Secretary **Lê Duẩn**, he rose to the number three ranking in the Politburo after the end of the war and in July 1987 was named chief of state to replace **Trường Chinh**, who served in that position until 1992. In recent years, Võ Chí Cong has reportedly supported reformist efforts to provide incentives to promote **economic** growth in the SRV.

VÕ NGUYÊN GIÁP (1910?–). Senior general in the **People's Army of Vietnam (PAVN)** and leading figure in the **Socialist Republic of Vietnam** (SRV). Born in a peasant family with reported **scholar-gentry** connections in Quảng Bình, Võ Nguyên Giáp attended the **National Academy** (*Quốc Học*) in the imperial capital of **Huế**. In the mid-1920s, he joined the **Tân Việt Cách Mệnh Đảng** (New Vietnamese Revolutionary Party) and participated in demonstrations following the death of the Vietnamese patriot **Phan Chu Trinh**, leading to his expulsion from school. In 1930, he joined the new **Indochinese Communist Party** and was immediately arrested. Released in 1932, he graduated from the University of Hanoi in law and taught history at the Thăng Long school in **Hanoi**, where he married Nguyễn Thị Quang Thái, sister of the prominent female revolutionary **Nguyễn Thị Minh Khai**; both women were arrested and executed by the **French** in the early 1940s.

During the **Popular Front** period, Giáp worked as a journalist in Huế and coauthored a short pamphlet entitled "The Peasant Question" with fellow ICP member **Trường Chinh**. During World War II, he became a chief lieutenant of **Hồ Chí Minh** in the **Việt Minh** movement and, in 1944, was named commander of the Armed Propaganda Brigade, the predecessor of the **Vietnamese Liberation Army**. After World War II, he became the chief military strategist in the party and advocate of the concept of "people's war," which borrowed loosely from Maoist techniques in **China**. He was one of the commanders responsible for the Vietnamese victory at **Điện Biên Phủ**.

During the Vietnam War, Giáp was a leading member of the Party Politburo and attained the highest ranking of senior general in the PAVN. Although serving as minister of defense in the **Democratic Republic of Vietnam** (DRV) and widely viewed in the West as the prime architect of Vietnamese revolutionary strategy in the South, he was actually replaced as chief strategist by his colleague and reported rival, General **Nguyễn Chí Thanh**, of whose aggressive tactics Giáp did not fully approve. His involvement in the final **Hồ Chí Minh Campaign** is often overshadowed by that of General **Văn Tiến Dũng**.

Despite his important military role, Giáp has several times fallen victim to internal Party politics. After the end of the war in 1975, he was reduced to the role of elder statesman, losing his position as minister of defense and was dropped from the Politburo at the Fifth Party Congress in March 1982. The reasons for his decline have been widely rumored but never clarified. In recent years, he has become active in promoting **science and technology** in the SRV. Despite his marginalization from the government, he remains an extremely popular and respected figure among Vietnamese.

VÕ THỊ THẮNG (1948?–   ). Director general of the Vietnam National Administration of Tourism. A native of Long An in the **Mekong Delta**, Võ Thị Thắng was a student activist involved with antigovernment activities in the **Republic of Vietnam**. Following the **Tết Offensive**, she was sentenced to 20 years of hard labor. A picture of her smiling defiantly before her incarceration was widely circulated. After the fall of the South Vietnamese government, Thắng held positions in the **Vietnamese Communist Party**'s youth and **women**'s organizations. She was subsequently appointed to her current post, which has become a high-profile position given the significance of **tourism** as a source of income and as a way to bolster the country's image in the world. Thắng is a member of the Party Central Committee and the **National Assembly,** and she heads the Vietnam–Cuba Friendship Association, which oversees one of **Hanoi**'s oldest and warmest friendships.

VÕ VĂN KIỆT (1922–   ). Leading reformist figure in the **Socialist Republic of Vietnam** (SRV). Born in an educated family in Cần Thơ in 1922, Võ Văn Kiệt entered revolutionary activities in **Saigon** in the early 1940s. After World War II, he was a leading member of the Party apparatus in South Vietnam and secretary of the Saigon Municipal Party Committee in the last years of the Vietnam War.

After the seizure of Saigon in 1975, Kiệt was appointed chairman of the city's **People's Committee**. When **Nguyễn Văn Linh** was called to **Hanoi** in 1976 to take charge of the trade union movement, Kiệt succeeded him as chairman of the Hồ Chí Minh City Party Branch. He remained in that position until 1982 and gained a reputation as a moderate who emphasized **economic** growth over ideological purity. In 1982, he was elected a full member of the Politburo and was appointed vice-chairman of the Council of Ministers in **Hanoi**. In March 1988, he was appointed acting prime minister on the death of **Phạm Hùng** but was defeated in an election to fill that post at the **National Assembly** meeting in June. He served as prime minister from 1991–1997 and is considered a leading member of the reformist faction in the Party leadership.

VŨ HỒNG KHANH (1899?–1993). Nationalist leader who competed with **Hồ Chí Minh's Indochinese Communist Party** for power in **Hanoi** after World War II. A prominent member of the **Việt Nam Quốc Dân Đảng** (Vietnamese Nationalist Party) who had spent most of World War II in southern **China**, he returned to **Indochina** in the early fall of 1945 in the hopes of using the support of Chinese occupation forces to organize a non-Communist government in Hanoi. However, Hồ Chí Minh, president of the provisional government that became the **Democratic Republic of Vietnam**, was able to retain his office by offering nationalist parties a number of seats in the new **National Assembly** elected in January 1946.

In June, with relations between Hồ's government and the nationalist parties rapidly deteriorating after the departure of the Chinese troops, Khanh left for the Chinese border, where he remained with a group of his followers, for several months. In 1952, he settled in **Saigon**, where he served as minister of youth and sports in **Bảo Đại**'s new **State of Vietnam**. He remained in South Vietnam after the **Geneva Conference** of 1954 and ran unsuccessfully for president of the **Republic of Vietnam** in 1967. Despite his advanced age, he spent several years in **reeducation camps** after the fall of South Vietnam in 1975.

VŨ KHOAN. Deputy prime minister and minister of **trade** in the **Socialist Republic of Vietnam**. Vũ Khoan made his career in the Ministry of Foreign Affairs, including a stint in the Vietnamese Embassy in the **Union of Soviet Socialist Republics**. In 1990, he became deputy foreign minister with responsibility for Asian matters, a post he held through the end of the decade. He was appointed as minister of trade in 2000 and added the deputy prime minister's portfolio in 2002. Khoan's involvement with international trade has been highly visible, particularly in the growing commercial relationship with the **United States** following the signing of the **Bilateral Trade Agreement** in 2000, which he helped negotiate. In December 2003, he led a large trade delegation on an extended visit to the U.S.

– W –

WATER PUPPETS. Traditional form of entertainment in the **Red River Delta**. Puppets placed on the surface of a sheet of water are manipulated by artists situated behind the background stage scenery, usually consisting of a pavilion. Performances consist mainly of one-act plays based on familiar folk tales or excerpts from traditional operatic works. This form of entertainment has existed for centuries in rice-growing areas in the Red River Delta and is currently a popular **tourist** attraction in **Hanoi** and other major cities. *See also* DRAMA.

WEST LAKE (*Tây Hồ, Hồ Tây*). Scenic lake in the northern suburbs of Hanoi. Originally a part of the **Red River**, the lake appeared when the river changed course because of sediments deposited in the delta region. The lake, now measuring about 600 hectares (1500 acres) in size, is widely used for water sports by the residents of the city. Along its banks are restaurants, hotels, and the private homes of leading members of the **Vietnamese Communist Party**.

WESTMORELAND, WILLIAM C. (1914–). General in the **United States** Army and commander of the U.S. **Military Assistance Command in Vietnam** (MACV) from 1964–1968. Under General Westmoreland's command, the American troop presence in the **Republic of Vietnam** increased from about 22,000 on his arrival to 525,000 in mid-1968, and its position from an advisory role to the full combat role in the Vietnam War. During that period, U.S. troops played a major part in combat operations in Vietnam, carrying out search-and-destroy operations against North Vietnamese regular forces (**People's Army of Vietnam**) while South Vietnamese units of the **Army of the Republic of Vietnam** concentrated on the pacification effort in the countryside. Westmoreland was replaced by General **Creighton Abrams** in July 1968.

WOMEN. As in most Asian societies, women played a relatively subordinate role in traditional Vietnam. Some evidence indicates that in early Vietnamese society women had a strong part in family and local affairs, as indicated by the presence on the historical stage of prominent female rebels such as the **Trưng Sisters** and **Bà Triệu**. After the centuries-long "**Chinese period**," traditional **Confucian** attitudes gradually took precedence. At least in terms of official policy, as entry into the imperial bureaucracy was restricted to males, the place of women was assumed to be in the home, and the women who played a visible political or military role are few: **Dương Vân Nga, Ỷ Lan**, and **Bùi Thị Xuân**. A residue of pre-Chinese practice survived, however, in the **Hồng Đức Code** passed in the 15th century, which appears to have given women greater legal rights than those possessed by their counterparts in Confucian **China**, though the extent to which this became a reality is unclear.

Behind such official restrictions, women nonetheless often played an active part in Vietnamese society, led by such role models as the poetess **Hồ Xuân Hương**, who used irony and sarcasm to criticize the failings of male-dominated society in 18th-century Vietnam. She represented a kind of Vietnamese woman who was independent from, and scornful of, Confucian ideals. It is, in fact, difficult to know just how deeply these patriarchal ideals penetrated Vietnamese society because women at the **village** level in particular are believed to have had an important economic role that would have been in conflict with the subordination to men assumed by Confucian patterns of social organization. At the upper levels of society, however, it is fairly clear that Confucianized relationships came to exert considerable influence.

Under **French** colonial rule, Vietnamese women began to press for an extension of their rights. Beacon of this effort was the Saigon-based periodical **Phụ Nữ Tân Văn** (*Women's News*), published by middle-class women intellectuals during the late 1920s and early 1930s. (Its predecessor, the **Nữ Giới Chung** or *Women's Bell* was less successful.) A number of issues relating to women, notably changing values in the areas of romance and family, were portrayed in the novels of the **Tự Lực Văn Đoàn**.

The **Democratic Republic of Vietnam** (DRV), established in September 1945, promised sexual equality, a guarantee that has been incorporated into the **Constitution** promulgated in 1980. In fact, women played an active role in many areas of Vietnamese society under the DRV, including the struggle for national liberation, where women formed a so-called "long-haired army" to carry provisions to the men at the front. **Nguyễn Thị Định** was a prominent commander in the Southern **People's Liberation Armed Forces**. The **National Liberation Front** and **Provisional Revolutionary Government** also included several high-ranking women, notably **Nguyễn Thị Bình** and **Dương Quỳnh Hoa**.

Women in the **Socialist Republic of Vietnam** (SRV) today are active in many areas of Vietnamese life, and several have served in the government at the cabinet level. Their position in the ruling **Viet-**

namese **Communist Party** remains a subordinate one, however, and only one woman has held even a brief membership in the Politburo. Conversely, the SRV has had two consecutive female vice-presidents, Bình and **Trương Mỹ Hoa**, both of them Southerners. (The latter, like government tourism director **Võ Thị Thắng**, was a political prisoner in the **Republic of Vietnam**.) Official sources concede that male-chauvinist attitudes continue to prevail in many areas of Vietnamese society, and the benefits for women of the *đổi mới* reforms of the last two decades have been mixed. *See also* ĐOÀN THỊ ĐIỂM; DƯƠNG THU HƯƠNG; SƯƠNG NGUYỆT ANH.

– X –

XIAO WEN (1892–?). General in the Nationalist **Chinese** Army and a senior member of the Chinese occupation command in **Indochina** after World War II. A native of Guangdong in southern China, in 1943, Xiao was appointed as deputy to General **Zhang Fakui**, commander of Chongqing (Chungking)'s Fourth War Zone with its headquarters in Liuzhou, Guangxi. In that capacity Xiao met **Hồ Chí Minh**, recently released from Zhang's jail to organize anti-**Japanese** forces in southern China to assist a Chinese invasion of **Indochina**. After serving as political adviser to the Vietnamese nationalist groups in the area, he was ordered by Chinese leader Chiang Kai-shek to command Chinese occupation troops in northern Indochina at the close of the war.

Arriving in **Hanoi** in the fall of 1945, General Xiao attempted to pressure Hồ, now president of the Provisional Government of Vietnam (later the **Democratic Republic of Vietnam**), to broaden his government to include non-Communist nationalists. In late February 1946, he and his troops returned to China as part of an agreement with **France**. He remained in China after the Communist takeover in 1949.

– Y –

Ỷ LAN (?–1117). A concubine and later queen mother under the **Lý dynasty**. The wife of Emperor **Lý Thánh Tông** and mother of **Lý**

Nhân Tông, she is one of the few **women** in premodern Vietnamese history to be attributed an overly political role. She reportedly acted as regent while her husband led a military campaign against the **Cham**, and her competent management of national affairs is said to have inspired him to keep fighting and snatch victory from the jaws of defeat. She is also known for having put to death her main rival and a large number of female attendants in order to ensure the succession of her own son when Thánh Tông died. She appears to have built up her own faction of powerful officials that maintained a tight grip on court affairs during her son Nhân Tông's minority.

YÊN BÁI MUTINY. Insurrection launched by the Vietnamese Nationalist Party (**Việt Nam Quốc Dân Đảng** or VNQDĐ) against **French** rule in February 1930. The revolt, planned by VNQDĐ leader **Nguyễn Thái Học**, erupted at Yên Bái (frequently spelled *Yên Báy*) and several other military posts in **Tonkin**. However, poor coordination and lack of support by local troops doomed the uprising, and it was crushed within a few days. Học and several other party leaders were caught by the French and executed. The suppression of the Yên Bái uprising effectively eliminated the VNQDĐ as a revolutionary force, thus removing a potential rival to the **Indochinese Communist Party**.

YOUTH PARTY (*Đảng Thanh Niên*). Short-lived political party formed by **Saigon** intellectuals around **Trần Huy Liệu** in late 1925. It was established at a time of rising effervescence but limited political experience within the nascent nationalist movement in **Cochin China**. The party had no specific platform or strategy beyond a vague desire to promote the establishment of a constitution in Cochin China and was dispersed by the colonial regime within a few months. Trần Huy Liệu would later become a member of the **Indochinese Communist Party**. *See also* NGUYỄN AN NINH.

YUE (Việt). Generic name used by early Chinese to describe proto-Chinese peoples living in coastal regions south of the Yangzi River in **China**; the Vietnamese equivalent is *Việt*. During the so-called Warring States (480–222 B.C.E.) period, Yue was a state in the coastal region south of the Yangzi River Delta. After the disappearance of the state, the name survived in the Chinese term *Baiyue* or "Hundred Yue" (Viet. *Bách Việt*), applied to other non-Chinese peoples living in southern China and mainland Southeast Asia. In the third century B.C.E., part of this region was conquered by **Triệu Đà** (Zhao Tuo) and absorbed into a larger state called *Nanyue* or *Nam Việt*.

After the conquest of the **Red River** region by the Han dynasty, Chinese sources began to refer to the peoples of the area as the *Luoyue* (Lạc Việt, "Yue people of **Lạc**"). Eventually, the term *Yue/Việt* came to describe the ethnic Vietnamese (**Kinh**). After the end of Chinese rule in the 10th century, Vietnamese monarchs used the term as the formal title for their country, as in **Đại Cồ Việt**, **Đại Việt**, and **Việt Nam**. *See also* VIETNAMESE PEOPLE.

– Z –

ZHANG FAKUI (1896–?). General in the Nationalist **Chinese** Army and commander of the Fourth War Zone in southern China during World War II. In that capacity, Zhang discovered that **Hồ Chí Minh**, a political prisoner in one of his prisons, was actually a senior member of the Vietnamese Communist movement. Zhang released Hồ from jail in September 1943, partly on the instructions of Chiang Kai-shek but also in the belief that the Vietnamese revolutionary could help organize Vietnamese nationalist elements in support of a planned Chinese invasion of northern Indochina near the end of the war. Hồ became active in the **Vietnamese Revolutionary League**, an exile organization formed at Zhang's behest, and returned to **Indochina** in September 1944. After the Chinese Communist victory on the mainland in 1949, Zhang left for Hong Kong and then settled for the remainder of his life in the **United States**. *See also* XIAO WEN.

ZHAO TUO. *See* TRIỆU ĐÀ.

ZONE C. Base area used by revolutionary forces in South Vietnam during the Vietnam War. Located in Tây Ninh province adjacent to the **Cambodian** border, Zone C was used by the **People's Liberation Armed Forces (PLAF)** as a staging area for operations near

Saigon and was the site of the movement's headquarters, the **Central Office for South Vietnam** (COSVN), after 1961. The area was ideal because of its heavy jungle cover and its location adjacent to the sanctuary of eastern Cambodia. In April 1966, United States forces launched Operation Attleboro into the area in an effort to wipe out PLAF fortifications and seize COSVN. The operation probably inflicted severe damage on the revolutionary infrastructure in South Vietnam but did not capture COSVN, which retreated across the border into Cambodia. *See* IRON TRIANGLE; ZONE D.

ZONE D. Communist redoubt about 50 kilometers (30 miles) northeast of **Saigon**. Located in a heavily forested area not far from Biên Hoà, Zone D became a major revolutionary base area during the late 1950s. **United States** and **Army of the Republic of Vietnam** armed forces entered the area on several occasions during the height of the Vietnam War but were unable to prevent enemy units from using it as a base for operations near the capital city. *See* IRON TRIANGLE; ZONE C.

Appendix A

A Brief Outline History of Vietnam

I. *Archeological Cultures*
  Paleolithic Era (?–10,000 B.C.E.)
    Núi Đọ Culture
    Sơn Vị Culture (?–9000 B.C.E.)
  Mesolithic Era
    Hoà Bình Culture (9000–7000 B.C.E.)
  Neolithic Era
    Bắc Sơn Culture (7000–3000 B.C.E.)
  Bronze Age
    Phùng Nguyên Culture (2500 B.C.E.–1500 B.C.E.)
    Đông Sơn Culture (1600 B.C.E.–2nd century B.C.E.)

II. *Prehistory and Protohistory*
  Kingdom of Văn Lang (Hùng Kings) (~9th century B.C.E.–258 B.C.E.)
    Capital: Phong Châu
  Kingdom of Âu Lạc (258 B.C.E.–207 B.C.E.) (Founder: An Dương Vương)
    Capital: Cổ Loa
  Kingdom of Nam Việt (207 B.C.E.–111 B.C.E.) (Founder: Triệu Đà)
    Capital: Canton (Guangzhou)

III. The "Chinese Period"
    Western Han dynasty (111 B.C.E.–C.E. 23)
    Eastern Han dynasty (C.E. 23–39)
    Trưng Sisters Rebellion (Vietnamese) (C.E. 39–43)
    Eastern Han (43–220)
    Three Kingdoms (221–263)
    Western Jin (265–316)
    Eastern Jin (317–419)
    Southern Dynasties (420–589)
    Early Lý "Dynasty" (Vietnamese) (6th century) (Founder: Lý Bí)
        Kingdom: Vạn Xuân. Capital: Gia Ninh
    Sui (589–618)
    Tang (618–907)
    Five Dynasties Period (907–939)

IV. Transition to Independence
    Ngô Quyền (939–945)
        Kingdom: Nam Việt. Capital: Cổ Loa
    Period of 12 Warlords (965–968)
    Đinh Bộ Lĩnh (968–980)
        Kingdom: Đại Cồ Việt. Capital: Hoa Lư
    Lê Hoàn (980–1009)
        Kingdom: Đại Cồ Việt. Capital: Hoa Lư

V. Dynastic Rule
    Lý Dynasty (1009–1225) (Founder: Lý Công Uẩn)
        Kingdom: Đại Cồ Việt. (1009–1054): Đại Việt (1054–1225)
        Capital: Thăng Long (Hanoi)
    Trần Dynasty (1225–1400) (Founder: Trần Thủ Độ)
        Kingdom: Đại Việt. Capital: Thăng Long (Hanoi)
    Hồ Dynasty (1400–1407) (Founder: Hồ Quý Ly)
        Kingdom: Đại Ngu. Capital: Tây Đô
    Period of Ming Occupation (1407–1428)
        Name: An Nam. Capital: Đông Quan (Hanoi)
    Later Lê Dynasty (1428–1527) (Founder: Lê Lợi)
        Kingdom: Đại Viet. Capital: Thăng Long (Hanoi)
    Mac Dynasty (1527–1592) (Founder: Mạc Đăng Dung)
        Kingdom: Đại Việt. Capital: Đông Kinh (Hanoi)

Trịnh–Nguyễn Period (1592–1788)
Northern Kingdom (Lê Emperors, Trịnh Lords) Capital: Thăng Long (Hanoi)
Southern Kingdom (Nguyễn Lords) Capital: Phú Xuân (Huế)
Tây Sơn Dynasty (1788–1802) (Founder: Nguyễn Huệ/Quang Trung)
Kingdom: Đại Việt. Capital: Huế and Thăng Long (Hanoi)
Nguyễn Dynasty (1802–1945) (Founder: Nguyễn Ánh)
Kingdom: Đại Việt (1802–1838) Đại Nam (1838–1945). Capital: Huế

VI. *Period of French Colonial Rule*
French Indochina (1884–1945)
Protectorates of Tonkin and Annam; Colony of Cochin China
Capitals: Hanoi (Tonkin, Indochina); Huế (Annam); Saigon (Cochin China)
Democratic Republic of Vietnam (1945–1976) (Founder: Hồ Chí Minh)
Capital: Hanoi
Autonomous Republic of Cochin China (1946–1949)
Capital: Saigon
Associated State of Vietnam (1949–1954) (Founder: Bảo Đại)
Capital: Saigon

VII. *Period of Independence*
Republic of Vietnam (1955–1975) (Founder: Ngô Đình Diệm)
Capital: Saigon
Democratic Republic of Vietnam (1945–1976) (Founder: Hồ Chí Minh)
Capital: Hanoi
Socialist Republic of Vietnam (1976–present)
Capital: Hanoi

Appendix B

Rulers of Vietnamese Kingdoms, 10th–19th Centuries

Note: Rulers who did not survive into adulthood or who were too ephemeral to have had any impact are omitted from this list. When rulers are commonly known to history by both their personal name and an imperial title, the first is indicated in parentheses. All dates given are reign dates.

10th Century
Ngô Quyền (939–44)
Đinh Tiên Hoàng (Đinh Bộ Lĩnh) (963–79)
Lê Đại Hành (Lê Hoàn) (980–1005)
Lê Ngọa Triều (Lê Long Đĩnh) (1005–09)

Lý Dynasty
Lý Thái Tổ (Lý Công Uẩn) (1010–28)
Lý Thái Tông (Lý Phật Mã) (1028–54)
Lý Thánh Tông (1054–72)
Lý Nhân Tông (1072–1128)
Lý Thần Tông (1128–37)
Lý Anh Tông (1137–75)
Lý Cao Tông (1176–1210)

Lý Huệ Tông (1210–24)
Lý Chiêu Hoàng (empress) (1224–25)

Trần Dynasty
Trần Thái Tông (1225–58)
Trần Thánh Tông (1258–78)
Trần Nhân Tông (1278–93)
Trần Anh Tông (1293–1314)
Trần Minh Tông (1314–29)
Trần Hiến Tông (1329–41)
Trần Dụ Tông (1341–69)
Trần Nghệ Tông (1370–72)
Trần Duệ Tông (1372–77)
Trần Phế Đế (1377–88)
Trần Thuận Tông (1388–98)
Trần Thiếu Đế (1398–1400)

Hồ Dynasty
Hồ Quý Ly (1400)
Hồ Hán Thương (1401–07)

Lê Dynasty
Lê Thái Tổ (Lê Lợi) (1428–33)
Lê Thái Tông (1433–42)
Lê Nhân Tông (1442–59)
Lê Thánh Tông (1460–97)
Lê Hiển Tông (1497–1504)
Lê Uy Mục (1505–09)
Lê Tương Dực (1509–16)
Lê Chiêu Tông (1516–23)
Lê Cung Hoàng (1523–27)

(during Mạc interregnum and civil war)
Lê Trang Tông (1533–48)
Lê Trung Tông (1548–56)
Lê Anh Tông (1556–73)
Lê Thế Tông (1573–99)
Lê Kính Tông (1600–19)

Lê Thần Tông (1619–43, 1649–62)
Lê Chân Tông (1643–49)
Lê Huyền Tông (1663–71)
Lê Gia Tông (1671–75)
Lê Hy Tông (1675–1704)
Lê Dụ Tông (1704–28)
Lê Phế Đế (1728–32)
Lê Thuần Tông (1732–35)
Lê Ý Tông (1735–40)
Lê Hiến Tông (1740–86)
Lê Chiêu Thống (1787–89)

Mạc Dynasty
Mạc Thái Tổ (Mạc Đăng Dung) (1527–30)
Mạc Thái Tông (Mạc Đăng Doanh) (1530–40)
Mạc Hiến Tông (Mạc Phú Hải) (1540–46)
Mạc Tuyên Tông (Mạc Phúc Nguyên) (1546–64)

(ruler without imperial titles)
Mạc Mậu Hợp (1564–92)

Trịnh Lords (ruled as viceroys under later Lê emperors)
Trịnh Kiểm (1545–70)
Trịnh Tùng (1570–1623)
Trịnh Tráng (1623–57)
Trịnh Tạc (1657–82)
Trịnh Căn (1682–1709)
Trịnh Cương (1709–29)
Trịnh Giang (1729–40)
Trịnh Doanh (1740–67)
Trịnh Sâm (1767–82)
Trịnh Khải (1782–86)
Trịnh Bồng (1786–87)

Nguyễn Lords (ruled autonomous southern kingdom known as Đàng Trong)
Nguyễn Hoàng (1600–13)
Sãi Vương (Nguyễn Phúc Nguyên) (1613–35)

Thượng Vương (Nguyễn Phúc Lan) (1635–48)
Hiền Vương (Nguyễn Phúc Tần) (1648–87)
Nghĩa Vương (Nguyễn Phúc Trăn) (1687–91)
Minh Vương (Nguyễn Phúc Chu) (1691–1725)
Ninh Vương (Nguyễn Phúc Trú) (1725–38)
Võ Vương (Nguyễn Phúc Khoát) (1738–65)
Định Vương (Nguyễn Phúc Thuần) (1765–77)

Tây Sơn Rulers
Trung Ương Hoàng Đế (Nguyễn Nhạc) (1778–93)
Quang Trung (Nguyễn Huệ) (1788–92)
Cảnh Thịnh (Nguyễn Quang Toản) (1792–1802)

Nguyễn Dynasty (Independent)
Gia Long (1802–20)
Minh Mạng (1820–40)
Thiệu Trị (1840–47)
Tự Đức (1847–83)
Dục Đức (1883)
Hiệp Hoà (1883)
Kiến Phúc (1883–84)

Appendix C
Emperors and Governors under Colonial Rule

Nguyễn Dynasty ("Protected Rulers")
Hàm Nghi (1884–85)
Đồng Khánh (1885–89)
Thành Thái (1889–1907)
Duy Tân (1907–16)
Khải Định (1916–25)
Bảo Đại (1925–45)

French Colonial Officials
Note: Interim and acting governors are excluded.

Governors of Cochin China and Indochina
Pierre de la Grandière (1863–68)
Marie–Gustave Ohier (1868–69)
Alphonse de Cornulier–Lucinière (1870–71)
Marie–Jules Dupré (1871–73)
Victor Auguste Duperré (1874–77)
Louis Lafont (1877–79)
Charles Le Myre de Vilers (1879–82)
Charles Thomson (1882–85)
Charles Begin (1885–86)
Charles–Louis Filippini (1886–87)

Governors-General of Indochina
Ernest Constans (1887–88)
Étienne Richaud (1888–89)
Jules Piquet (1889–91)
Jean de Lanessan (1891–94)
Armand Rousseau (1895–96)
Paul Doumer (1897–1902)
Paul Beau (1902–07)
Antony Klobukowski (1908–10)
Albert Sarraut (1911–14, 1917–19)
Ernest Roume (1915–16)
Maurice Long (1920–22)
Martial Merlin (1922–25)
Alexandre Varenne (1925–28)
Pierre Pasquier (1928–34)
René Robin (1934–36)
Jules Brévié (1936–39)
Georges Catroux (1939–40)
Jean Decoux (1940–45)

High Commissioners for Indochina
Thierry d'Argenlieu (1945–47)
Émile Bollaert (1947–48)
Léon Pignon (1948–50)
Jean de Lattre de Tassigny (1950–52)
Jean Letourneau (1952–53)

Commissioners General for Indochina
Jean Letourneau (1953)
Maurice Dejean (1953–54)
Paul Ély (1954–55)
Henri Hoppenot (1955–56)

Associated State of Vietnam

Chief of State
Bảo Đại (1949–55)

Prime Ministers
Bảo Đại (1949–50)
Nguyễn Phan Long (1950)
Trần Văn Hưu (1950–52)
Nguyễn Văn Tam (1952–53)
Bửu Lộc (1954)
Ngô Đình Diệm (1954–55)

Appendix D
Leaders of Independent Vietnamese Governments

Democratic Republic of Vietnam

Presidents
Hồ Chí Minh (1945–69)
Tôn Đức Thắng (1969–76)

Premier
Phạm Văn Đồng (1955–76)

Republic of Vietnam

First Republic
Ngô Đình Diệm (1955–63) (President)

Military Juntas and Military-Backed Governments
Dương Văn Minh (1963–64) (Chief of State)
Nguyễn Khánh (1964–65) (Prime Minister, then President)
Phan Khắc Sửu (1964–65) (Chief of State under Nguyễn Khánh)
Trần Văn Hương (1964–65) (Prime Minister under Nguyễn Khánh)
Phan Huy Quát (Feb.–June 1965) (Prime Minister)

Nguyễn Văn Thiệu (1965–67) (Chief of State)
Nguyễn Cao Kỳ (1965–67) (Prime Minister)

Second Republic
(Presidents)
Nguyễn Văn Thiệu (1967–75)
Trần Văn Hương (21–28 April 1975)
Dương Văn Minh (28–30 April 1975)

(Vice-Presidents)
Nguyễn Cao Kỳ (1967– 71)
Trần Văn Hương (1971–75)

(Prime Ministers)
Nguyễn Văn Lộc (1967–68)
Trần Văn Hương (1968–69)
Trần Thiện Khiêm (1969–75)
Nguyễn Bá Cẩn (14–23 April 1975)
Vũ Văn Mậu (23–30 April 1975)

Provisional Revolutionary Government of South Vietnam
Huỳnh Tân Phát (1969–76) President

Socialist Republic of Vietnam

Presidents/Chairman of Council of State/Chiefs of State
Tôn Đức Thắng (1976–80)
Trường Chinh (1981–87)
Võ Chí Công (1987–92)
Lê Đức Anh (1992–1997)
Trần Đức Lương (1997–)

Premiers
Phạm Văn Đồng (1976–87)
Phạm Hùng (1987–88)
Võ Văn Kiệt (1988)
Đỗ Mười (1988–91)
Võ Văn Kiệt (1991–97)
Phan Văn Khải (1997–)

Appendix E
Communist Party General Secretaries

Indochinese Communist Party
Trần Phú (1930–31)
(interim period of disruption with no formally chosen General Secretary)
Lê Hồng Phong (1935–36)
Hà Huy Tập (1936–38)
Nguyễn Văn Cừ (1938–40)
Trường Chinh (1940–51)

Vietnamese Workers' Party
Trường Chinh (1951–56)
Hồ Chí Minh (1956–60) (concurrent with position of Party Chairman, 1951–69)
Lê Duẩn (1960–76) ("First Secretary")

Vietnamese Communist Party
Lê Duẩn (1976–86) ("General Secretary")
Nguyễn Văn Linh (1986–91)
Đỗ Mười (1991–97)
Lê Khả Phiêu (1997–2001)
Nông Đức Mạnh (2001–)

Appendix F
Population of Vietnam (Yearly Estimates)

1802 4 million
1840 5 million
1880 7 million
1926 16.3 million (Tonkin 6.6 million; Annam 5.5 million; Cochin China; 4 million)
1936 18.6 million (Tonkin 7.8 million; Annam 5.6 million; Cochin China 4.6 million)
1945 25 million (North 14 million; South 11 million)
1960 30 million (North 16 million; South 14 million)
1970 38.3 million (North 21.3 million; South 17 million)
1974 44.3 million (North 23.8 million; South 20.5 million) (DRV estimate)
      46.7 million (North 24 million; South 22.7 million) (US estimate)
1976 49 million (North 24.6 million; South 24.4 million) (SRV estimate)
      49.1 million (North 26 million; South 24.3 million) (US estimate)
1979 52.7 million (North 27.4 million; South 25.3 million) (SRV estimate)
      52.5 million (North 26 million; South 26.5 million) (US estimate)

1980   53.9 million (North 28 million; South 25.9 million) (SRV estimate)

1981   54.9 million (North 28.6 million; South 26.3 million) (SRV estimate)

        54.9 million (North 27 million; South 27.9 million) (US estimate)

1982   56.2 million (North 29.2 million; South 27 million) (SRV estimate)

        56.2 million (North 27.6 million; South 28.6 million) (US estimate)

1983   57.6 million (North 28.2 million; South 29.4 million) (US estimate)

1986   62 million (SRV estimate)

1989   64 million

1992   71 million

1995   74.6 million (estimate)

1999   76,3 million (census)

2003   80.7 million (estimate)

Sources: *Vietnam Courier* (October 1983); U.S. Department of Commerce, Bureau of the Census, *The Population of Vietnam*, Series P–95, No. 77 (Issued October 1985), SRV Bureau of Statistics.

Appendix G

Population Distribution According to Province and Municipality (official 1999 census statistics)

Municipality	Population
Hanoi	2,672,100
Hồ Chí Minh City	5,037,200
Hải Phòng	1,673,000
Đà Nẵng	684,100

Province	Population
Cao Bằng	490,700
Hà Giang	602,700
Tuyên Quang	675,100
Lạng Sơn	704,700
Lai Châu (a)	588,700
Hoà Bình	757,600
Bắc Kạn	275,300
Thái Nguyên	1,046,200
Lào Cai	594,600
Sơn La	881,400
Vĩnh Phúc	1,092,000
Phú Thọ	1,261,500
Yên Bái	679,700

	Population
Bắc Giang	1,492,200
Bắc Ninh	941,400
Quảng Ninh	1,004,500
Hà Tây	2,386,800
Hải Dương	1,649,800
Hưng Yên	1,068,700
Thái Bình	1,785,600
Hà Nam	791,600
Nam Định	1,888,400
Ninh Bình	884,100
Thanh Hoá	3,467,600
Nghệ An	2,858,300
Hà Tĩnh	1,269,000
Quảng Bình	793,900
Quảng Trị	573,300
Thừa Thiên–Huế	1,045,100
Quảng Nam	1,372,400
Quảng Ngãi	1,190,000
Bình Định	1,461,100
Phú Yên	787,000

Khánh Hoà	1,031,300	An Giang	2,049,000
Ninh Thuận	505,200	Tiền Giang	1,605,100
Bình Thuận	1,047,000	Bến Tre	1,296,900
Bà Rịa – Vũng Tàu	800,600	Vĩnh Long	1,010,500
Gia Lai	971,900	Cần Thơ/Hậu	
Kon Tum	314,000	Giang (c)	1,811,100
Đắk Lắk (b)	1,776,300	Trà Vinh	965,000
Lâm Đồng	996,200	Kiên Giang	1,494,400
Bình Phước	653,600	Sóc Trăng	1,173,800
Tây Ninh	965,200	Bạc Liêu	736,300
Bình Dương	716,400	Cà Mau	1,119,300
Đồng Nai	1,989,500		
Long An	1,306,200	Total	76,327,900
Đồng Tháp	1,565,000		

(a) Since the 1999 census, Lai Châu has been divided into Lai Châu and Điện Biên provinces.

(b) Since the 1999 census, Đắk Lắk has been divided into Đắk Lắk and Đắn Nông provinces.

(c) Since the 1999 census, Cần Thơ province has been divided into Cần Thơ municipality and Hậu Giang province.

Source: *Số Liệu Thống Kê Kinh Tế—Xã Hội Việt Nam 1975–2000/ Statistical Data of Việt Nam Socio–Economy [sic] 1975–2000* (Hanoi: NXB Thống Kê, 2000)

Appendix H

Population by Ethnic Background
(1979 estimates)

Vietnamese	46,065,000	Dao	317,000
Hoa (Chinese)	935,000	Gia rai (Jarai)	184,000
Tày	901,000	Ê đê (Rhadé)	141,000
Thái	767,000	Ba na (Bahnar)	100,000
Khmer	717,000	Chàm	77,000
Mường	686,000	Sán Chay	77,000
Nùng	560,000	Xơ đăng (Sedang)	73,000
Hmông	411,000	Cơ ho	70,000

Source: *Statistical Data 1930–1984*, published by the SRV Statistics General Department, Statistics Publishing House, Hanoi (translated in Joint Publications Research Service–SEA 86,108).

(No more recent breakdown of the population by ethnic group could be found for the third edition of this dictionary.)

Appendix I
Key Social and Economic Indicators

Annual population growth rate:	1.18% (2003)
GDP per capita:	US $485 (2003)
Real GDP growth rate:	7.24% (2003)
Foreign debt (% of GDP)	40% (2003)
Principal exports:	Crude oil, garments and textiles, sea products, footwear, rice, coffee
Electricity production	46 billion kilowatt hours (2004)
Rice production	36 million tons (2005 est.)
Coffee production	794,000 tons (2004 est.)
Petroleum production	130 million barrels (2004)
Life expectancy at birth:	65.5 years (men); 70.1 years (women) (2001)
Adult literacy rate:	91% (2002)
Poverty rate (national standard)	12% (2002)
Poverty rate (international standard)	29% (2002)
Human development index (out of 175 countries):	109 (2003)

Main sources: *Far Eastern Economic Review Asia Yearbook;* UNDP Vietnam Website: http://www.undp.org.vn/undp/fact/base.htm (accessed 14 November 2004).

Bibliography

The bibliography that appears here reflects the evolution of Western knowledge about and interest in Vietnamese history and society. Most of the classical works written about the traditional era in Vietnam were written by French scholars during the colonial period. The first comprehensive history of precolonial Vietnam written in English was Joseph Buttinger's *The Smaller Dragon*. Although it is now somewhat out of date, it still serves as a useful introduction to the history of Vietnam, especially as it was understood by many Westerners involved in the country during the Cold War. Since the end of the war, several new narrative histories of Vietnam have appeared: Thomas Hodgkin's *Vietnam: The Revolutionary Path*; Stanley Karnow's *Vietnam: A History*; and Oscar Chapuis, *A History of Vietnam: From Hong Bang to Tu Duc*. D. R. SarDesai has published a general history that has appeared under various titles; the most recent edition is *Vietnam, Past and Present*.

Unfortunately, there are still relatively few book-length studies of the precolonial period. Important studies include Keith W. Taylor's *The Birth of Vietnam*, which carries history up to the 10th century, and Li Tana, *Nguyễn Cochinchina: Southern Vietnam in the Seventeenth and Eighteenth Centuries*. Alexander B. Woodside's *Vietnam and the Chinese Model* and Yoshiharu Tsuboï, *L'Empire viêtnamien face à la France et à la Chine* are richly detailed studies of the 19th century. Victor Lieberman's *Strange Parallels: Southeast Asia in Global Context* has an excellent discussion of precolonial Vietnam.

Books on the French colonial era are available in much greater abundance. The most-detailed general treatment in English remains Joseph Buttinger's massive *Vietnam: The Dragon Embattled*, in two volumes. For a critical view of the effects of colonial policy on the Vietnamese economy, see Martin Murray's *The Development of Capitalism in Colonial Indochina (1870–1940)*. A French interpretation, more sympathetic to the colonial enterprise, is Charles Robequain's *The Economic Development of French Indochina*. Another provocative study, which focuses on changes taking place at the village level, is Samuel L. Popkin's *The Rational Peasant*; a rival view on the same issue is James C. Scott's *The Moral Economy of the Peasant*. Also see Mark McLeod's short but informative *The Vietnamese Response to French Intervention, 1862–1874*. An important recent study is Peter Zinoman, *The Colonial Bastille: A History of Imprisonment in Vietnam, 1862–1940*.

Much of the recent scholarly literature on French colonialism has understandably focused on the origins of the Vietnamese resistance movement. The first and, in many ways, still the best account is David G. Marr's *Vietnamese Anticolonialism, 1885–1925*. Other useful studies are Huynh Kim Khanh's *Vietnamese Communism, 1925–1945*, John T. McAlister's *Vietnam: The Origins of Revolution*, and William J. Duiker's *The Rise of Nationalism in Vietnam, 1900–1941*. David Marr's *Vietnam 1945: The Quest for Power* is an excellent study of the events leading up to the August Revolution. A number of French-language works are mentioned in the bibliography.

Impressive studies of intellectual trends during the later colonial period include Hue-Tam Ho Tai's *Radicalism and the Origins of the Vietnamese Revolution* and Shawn McHale's *Print and Power: Confucianism, Communism, and Buddhism in the Making of Modern Vietnam*. For the effects of colonial rule on Vietnamese culture, see David G. Marr's *Vietnamese Tradition on Trial 1925–1945*. Another useful work, which focuses on the Vietnamese sense of community, is Alexander B. Woodside's *Community and Revolution in Vietnam*. Neil Jamieson's *Understanding Vietnam* traces political and cultural developments during the colonial and postcolonial periods with a heavy emphasis on literature.

The period of the August Revolution and the Franco-Việt Minh War or First Indochina War (1945–1954) has been the subject of considerable attention from both French- and English-speaking specialists. A personal account of the origins of the war is Archimedes Patti's *Why Vietnam: Prelude to America's Albatross*. For still useful, though somewhat dated, general surveys, see Ellen J. Hammer's *The Struggle for Indochina, 1940–1954* or Donald Lancaster's *The Emancipation of French Indochina*. Arthur Dommen's *The Indochinese Experience of the French and the Americans* provides a detailed account of the First and Second Indochina Wars. The best overall accounts in French are still Philippe Devillers's *Histoire du Vietnam de 1940 à 1952* and Paul Mus's insightful *Viet-Nam: Sociologie d'une guerre*. Stein Tønnesson's *The Outbreak of War in Indochina, 1946* is an excellent study of the beginning of the conflict.

The Franco–Việt Minh war itself is chronicled in Edgar O'Ballance, *The Indo-China War, 1945–1954* and Bernard B. Fall's dramatic accounts, *Street without Joy: Indochina at War, 1946–1954* and *Hell in a Very Small Place*. This period, of course, marked the beginning of Great Power involvement in the Indochina conflict. The origins of the U.S. role in Vietnam are beginning to attract scholarly attention because of the release of public documents relating to the period. Mark Bradley, *Imagining Vietnam and America: The Making of Postcolonial Vietnam, 1919–1950* is a unique contribution to this topic. On the Chinese side, see King C. Chen's *Vietnam and China, 1938–1954*; Francois Joyaux's fascinating *La Chine et le règlement du premier conflit d'Indochine*; and Qiang Zhai, *China & the Vietnam Wars, 1950–1975*. Jacques de Folin's *Indochine 1940–1955: La fin d'un rêve*, provides the perspective of a French diplomat who participated in the Geneva Conference of

1954. Another useful account is the magisterial *Histoire de la guerre d'Indochine* by General Yves Gras.

On the Geneva Conference of 1954, three classic studies are Robert F. Randle's *Geneva 1954: The Settlement of the Indochina War*, Melvin Gurtov's *The First Vietnam Crisis*, and Jean Lacouture's *La fin d'une guerre: Indochine 1954*. A newer study, providing a British perspective, is James Cable's *The Geneva Conference of 1954 on Indochina*. Documentation on the U.S. role at Geneva is provided in *Foreign Relations of the United States (1952–1954)*, vol. 16.

Books about what is known to Americans as the Vietnam War and its immediate antecedents make up the vast bulk of the books and materials on Vietnam in most U.S. libraries. Little indeed about the war has escaped close scrutiny. A number of comprehensive narrative histories of the war have appeared in recent years, including Marilyn B. Young, *The Vietnam Wars, 1945–1990* and George D. Moss, *Vietnam: An American Ordeal*, but Stanley Karnow's *Vietnam: A History* is still unsurpassed in scope and dramatic power. An ambitious attempt to place the war in critical perspective is Gabriel Kolko's *Anatomy of a War: Vietnam, the United States, and the Modern Historical Experience*. For a short, balanced account of the war, see William S. Turley's *The Second Indochina War: A Short Political and Military History*. William Duiker, *Sacred War: Nationalism and Revolution in a Divided Vietnam* emphasizes the Vietnamese perspective. The massive *Our Vietnam: The War, 1954–1975* by Arthur J. Langguth assembles many narratives from all the various sides in the conflict.

Most of what has been written about the war in the English language deals with the American role in the conflict. George Herring's *America's Longest War: The United States in Vietnam, 1950–1975* provides a useful general survey. A more thematic account is Paul M. Kattenburg's *The Vietnam Trauma in American Foreign Policy, 1945–1975*. John W. Lewis and George M. Kahin, *The United States in Vietnam* is also a useful account, although its assumptions about the independence of the revolutionary movement in the South are now somewhat dated. More recent attempts to place the American role in the broader perspective of postwar foreign policy include George M. Kahin's *Intervention: How America Became Involved in Vietnam* and William J. Duiker's *U.S. Containment Policy and the Conflict in Indochina*. For a highly controversial personal account by a participant, see Robert S. McNamara's *In Retrospect: The Tragedy and Lessons of Vietnam*. The late R. B. Smith's ambitious *International History of the Vietnam War* covers the period through 1966.

A number of specialized studies have been done on particular incidents or issues connected with the war, many of them written by participants in the decision-making process. Among the most useful are Roger Hilsman's *To Move a Nation*; Townsend Hoopes, *The Limits of Intervention*; Chester Cooper, *The Lost Crusade*; and Leslie Gelb and Richard Betts, *The Irony of Vietnam: The System Worked*. For the attempt to "win hearts and minds," see Robert Komer, *Bureaucracy at War* and Edward G. Lansdale, *In the Midst of Wars*.

A number of good journalistic accounts of the war are available. The first to attract major public attention were Malcolm Browne's *The New Face of War* and
David Halberstam's *The Making of a Quagmire*. Halberstam followed up with his
best-selling *The Best and the Brightest*, a devastating critique of the failure of leading figures in the Kennedy and the Johnson administrations to come to grips with
the realities of the war. Equally well known was Frances Fitzgerald's *Fire in the
Lake*. Awarded the Pulitzer Prize, *Fire in the Lake* summed up the feelings of many
Americans who had now become convinced that the war could not be won at an
acceptable price.

There have been several scholarly studies of U.S. policy at the height of the war.
Two of the better ones are Herbert Schandler's *The Unmaking of a President: Lyndon Johnson and Vietnam* and Wallace J. Thies, *When Governments Collide*. Other
studies of the Johnson era include Larry Berman's provocative *Planning a Tragedy:
The Americanization of the War in Vietnam*, George C. Herring's *LBJ and Vietnam:
A Different Kind of War*, and Brian VanDeMark's *Into the Quagmire: Lyndon Johnson and the Escalation of the Vietnam War*. The Kennedy era remains controversial,
and John M. Newman's contention in *JFK and Vietnam: Deception, Intrigue, and
the Struggle for Power* that Kennedy was prepared to abandon the effort in Southeast Asia is disputed by many seasoned observers.

The primary documentary source on the U.S. role in the war is still *The Pentagon
Papers*, currently available in several versions. The most accessible is the so-called
Senator Gravel edition, published by Beacon Press in 1971. A second version, published in 12 volumes by the U.S. Government Printing Office, is less well organized
and quite difficult to use. The Office of the Historian in the Department of State
has issued several of the post-1954 volumes in the series entitled *Foreign Relations
of the United States*. Additional useful information on Vietnam, most of it declassified documents, is available in the records of the National Security Council, as well
as State Department Central Files and CIA Research Reports, all published in microform collections by University Publications of America. The Indochina Archives
from Berkeley have been published in microform by University Microfilms International.

Several American universities have important collections on Vietnam. Cornell's
Echols Collection on Southeast Asia remains one of the best in the world, and substantial holdings can be found at Yale, Harvard, Hawaii, and other universities with
Southeast Asia programs. Texas Tech University has a large Vietnam Archive project focusing on the American side of the war, which includes the personal collection of the late Douglas Pike. The Indochina Archive, which Pike had overseen at
Berkeley, continues to operate as well. Also important for researchers, of course,
are the holdings of the Presidential Papers libraries of the various U.S. presidents
involved in the conflict.

The Vietnamese side of the war has not been as exhaustively researched, but a
number of useful sources exist. For contemporary studies of the Ngô Đình Diệm
regime, see Robert Scigliano's *South Vietnam: Nation under Stress* and Wesley

Fishel's *Problems of Freedom: South Vietnam since Independence*, as well as Bernard B. Fall, *The Two Vietnams*. An important new study is Philip Catton's *Diem's Final Failure: Prelude to America's War in Vietnam*. A number of senior figures in the South Vietnamese regime have recorded their accounts of the war. Most notable are Nguyễn Cao Kỳ's *Twenty Years and Twenty Days* and *Buddha's Child: My Fight to Save Vietnam*; Bùi Diêm's *In the Jaws of History*, and Trần Văn Đôn's *Our Endless War*. A fascinating inside account of the National Liberation Front in South Vietnam is Trương Như Tảng's *A Viet Cong Memoir*.

The Communist side has been dealt with in a number of studies, including James P. Harrison's *The Endless War: Fifty Years of Struggle in Vietnam* and William J. Duiker's *The Communist Road to Power in Vietnam*. A classic study on the revolutionary movement in the South is Douglas Pike's *The Viet Cong*, followed up by his *War, Peace, and the Viet Cong*. David Elliott has recently published his massive two-volume *The Vietnamese War: Revolution and Social Change in the Mekong Delta, 1930–1975*.

Hanoi's military leaders have themselves written extensively about the war. Several of Võ Nguyên Giáp's strategical writings are available in English, including *People's War, People's Army* and *Banner of People's War: The Party's Military Line*. Trường Chinh's own early strategical writings are compiled in *Primer for Revolt*. Other key figures who wrote about the war were Gen. Văn Tiến Dũng, whose account of the final campaign in 1975 is translated in *Our Great Spring Victory* and Trần Văn Trà, part of whose memoirs appear in *Vietnam: History of the B2-Bulwark Theater, vol. 5*. (The latter source is particularly interesting because it contains information critical of Hanoi's strategy. Not surprisingly, Trà was relieved of his official posts, and his book is no longer available in Vietnam.) For official DRV accounts of the war, see *Anti-U.S. Resistance War for National Salvation, 1954–1975: Military Events*, translated by *Joint Publications Research Service*, 80,968 (June 3, 1982); and *Victory in Vietnam, The Official History of the People's Army of Vietnam, 1954–1975*, translated by Merle Pribbenow.

Hanoi's relations with its allies have been the subject of some scholarship in the West. The Vietnamese role in the Sino–Soviet dispute was analyzed in Donald Zagoria's *The Vietnam Triangle*, and William R. Smyser's *The Independent Vietnamese*. For a highly critical view of Hanoi from an academic Cold Warrior, see P. J. Honey's *Communism in North Vietnam: Its Role in the Sino–Soviet Dispute*.

Documentary sources on the war published in North Vietnam are relatively rare, and scholars have been forced to rely to a considerable degree on captured documents, many of them available in microfilm in the United States. Among the most useful are the so-called *Race Documents*, a collection of material deposited by Jeffrey Race with the Center for Research Libraries in Chicago; two collections of Viet Cong documents compiled by Douglas Pike, and a selection entitled "Communist Vietnamese Publications" issued by the Library of Congress in Washington, D.C. A large collection of captured documents compiled by the U.S. Air Force has recently been placed in the National Archives, but search facilities for the material are cumbersome, and it might be some time before the material can be exhaustively researched. The Virtual Vietnam Archive at Texas Tech University is an important resource.

The end of the war was dramatically portrayed in a number of accounts, notably Frank Snepp's *Decent Interval* and Tiziano Terzani's *Giai-Phong: The Fall and Liberation of Saigon*. Also see Alan Dawson, *55 Days: The Fall of South Vietnam*, and Stephen T. Hosmer et al. (eds.), *The Fall of South Vietnam: Statements by Military and Civilian Leaders*. The latter source chronicles the charge by South Vietnamese figures that the fall of Saigon lies at least partly at the feet of the United States for failing to provide adequate support to its ally at the supreme moment of crisis.

Retrospective accounts of the war have been appearing with increasing regularity. Richard Nixon recorded his views in *No More Vietnams*. Justification for the U.S. effort is provided by Norman Podhoretz in *Why We Were in Vietnam*. A more analytical account is Timothy J. Lomperis' *The War Everyone Lost—and Won*. For a critical assessment of the military strategy adopted by the United States in Vietnam, see Harry G. Summers' *On Strategy: A Critical Analysis of the Vietnam War*.

After the end of the war, interest in Vietnam temporarily declined, but a number of books appeared during the 1980s that chronicled Hanoi's difficulties in coping with postwar challenges. Three general studies dealing with the internal situation were Nguyen Van Canh's *Vietnam under Communism 1975–1982*, Robert Shaplen's *Bitter Victory*, and William J. Duiker's *Vietnam since the Fall of Saigon*. Neil Sheehan's *After the War Was Over: Hanoi and Saigon* lacks substance but is written with the author's usual flair.

On Hanoi's postwar entanglements with Cambodia and China, see David W. P. Elliott (ed.), *The Third Indochina Conflict*; Nayan Chanda, *Brother Enemy: The War after the War*; Grant Evans and Kelvin Rowley, *Red Brotherhood at War: Vietnam, Cambodia, and Laos since 1975*; Robert S. Ross, *The Indochina Tangle: China's Vietnam Policy, 1975–1979*; and Stephen J. Morris, *Why Vietnam Invaded Cambodia: Political Culture and the Causes of War*. Moscow's role in Indochina is analyzed in Douglas Pike's *Vietnam and the Soviet Union: Anatomy of an Alliance*.

In the years since the first two editions of this historical dictionary appeared, a number of changes have taken place in Vietnam. The *đổi mới* reform program that was initiated at the Sixth Party Congress in 1986 has continued to gather momentum, inciting some observers to predict that the country could become the next "little tiger" to emerge in the region, though fits and starts in structural reforms and persistent issues of red tape and corruption continue to cause problems. Changes on the political scene have been slower to appear, as the Communist Party stubbornly resists demands that it share power with other political forces in the country. In foreign affairs, the collapse of the USSR has deprived Hanoi of its closest alley and forced Vietnamese leaders to seek other ways of guaranteeing national security, notably by improving relations with China and the United States and embracing its neighbors in ASEAN.

We have tried to take account of these factors in selecting bibliographical items for the third edition of this book. Increasing access to Vietnam by foreign researchers means that there is a growing body of scholarship based on first-hand observation and fieldwork, as well as more informed analysis from outside the country. Gareth Porter's *Vietnam: The Politics of Bureaucratic Socialism*, examines the nature of the political culture in the SRV; Lewis M. Stern, in *Renovating the Communist Party: Nguyen Van Linh and the Programme for Organizational Reform*, investigates the impact of the program of đổi mới. Carlyle Thayer's *The People's Army under Doi Moi* is one of the first studies to analyze the role of the armed forces since the end of the war.

A number of recent books have focused attention on the changes taking place in the economic arena. For a broad perspective, see Per Ronas and Orjan Sjoberg's *Socio-Economic Development in Vietnam: The Agenda for the 1990s* and William S. Turley and Mark Selden in *Renovating Vietnamese Society: Doi Moi in Comparative Perspective*. In *Postwar Vietnam: Dilemmas in Socialist Development*, editors David G. Marr and Christine P. White have selected articles on a number of separate topics dealing with economic and social issues as they appeared at the very outset of đổi mới. Also see Adam Fforde's *The Agrarian Question in North Vietnam, 1974–1979*, which provides the context for understanding subsequent agricultural reforms. Benedict Kerkvliet, *The Power of Everyday Politics*, looks at the same issue in a longer time frame. Important edited volumes on current developments that have appeared in recent years include Anita Chan et al., *Transforming Asian Socialism: China and Vietnam Compared* and Hy Văn Lương (ed.), *Postwar Vietnam: Dynamics of a Transforming Society*.

Vietnam's changing foreign relations have been chronicled in several useful studies. Frank Frost's *Vietnam's Foreign Relations: Dynamics of Change* takes a comprehensive look at the evolution of Hanoi's foreign policy as the region emerged from the Cold War. In *Second Chance: The United States and Indochina in the 1990s*, Frederick Z. Brown traces the early stages in the gradual improvement of relations between the SRV and the United States, though his study preceded the actual normalization by several years. More recent overviews can be found in Carlyle Thayer and Ramses Amer (eds.), *Vietnamese Foreign Policy in Transition* and James Morley and Masashi Nishihara (eds.), *Vietnam Joins the World*.

Vietnamese culture has yet to be exposed to the critical attention that is now being applied in the fields of politics and economics, but several recent studies have focused on various aspects of Vietnamese art, architecture, ceramics, and music. A growing number of Vietnamese novels and short stories have now been translated into English. These items are listed in the bibliography.

With the growth of the Internet, an increasingly large number of important primary sources are available online; only a few can be mentioned here. Texas Tech University offers the Virtual Vietnam Archive at archive.vietnam.ttu.edu/virtual archive. Some of the volumes in the *Foreign Relations of the United States* series that relate to the Vietnam War are available online at www.state.gov/www/

about_state/history/frus.html. Some important recent translations of wartime documents are available through the International Cold War History Project at cwihp .si.edu. Information and resources about contemporary Vietnam can be found at the Vietnam Studies Internet Resource Center at www.vstudies.org. Most Vietnamese government ministries now have English-language websites. More websites are mentioned at the end of the bibliography.

I. History
A. General Works

Buttinger, Joseph. *The Smaller Dragon*. New York: Praeger, 1958.
———. *Vietnam: The Dragon Embattled*. 2 vols. New York: Praeger, 1967.
———. *Vietnam: A Political History*. New York: Praeger, 1968.
Chesneaux, Jean. *Contribution à l'histoire de la nation viêtnamienne*. Paris: Plon, 1955.
———. *The Vietnamese Nation: Contribution to a History*, trans. Malcolm Salmon. Sydney: Current Book Distributors, 1966.
Duiker, William J. *Vietnam: Revolution in Transition*. Revised ed. Boulder, Colo.: Westview, 1996.
Hammer, Ellen J. *Vietnam Yesterday and Today*. New York: Holt, Rinehart & Winson, 1966.
Hodgkin, Thomas. *Vietnam: The Revolutionary Path*. New York: St. Martin's, 1981.
Jamieson, Neil L. *Understanding Vietnam*. Berkeley, Calif.: University of California Press, 1993.
Karnow, Stanley. *Vietnam: A History*. New York: Penguin, 1997.
Lê Thành Khôi. *Le Viêt-Nam: Histoire et civilisation*. Paris: Minuit, 1955.
———. *Histoire du Vietnam des origines à 1858*. Paris: Sudestasie, 1987.

Masson, André. *Histoire du Vietnam*. Paris: Presses Universitaires de France, 1960.

Nguyễn Khắc Viện. *Vietnam: A Long History*. Hanoi: Thế Giới, 1993.

Nguyễn Khắc Viện, and Hữu Ngọc (eds.). *From Saigon to Ho Chi Minh City: A Path of 300 Years*. Hanoi: Thế Giới, 1998.

Nguyễn Phút Tần. *A Modern History of Vietnam, 1802–1954*. Saigon: Khai Trí, 1964.

Papin, Philippe. *Histoire de Hanoi*. Paris: Fayard, 2001.

——. *Viêt-Nam. Parcours d'une nation*. Paris: Belin, 2003.

Pelley, Patricia M. *Postcolonial Vietnam: New Histories of the National Past*. Durham, N.C.: Duke University Press, 2002.

Pham Kim Vinh. *Vietnam: A Comprehensive History*. Fountain Valley, Calif.: Pham Kim Vinh Research Institute, n.d.

Ruscio, Alain. *Viet Nam, l'histoire, la terre, les hommes*. Paris: L'Harmattan, 1989.

SarDesai, D. R. *Vietnam, Past and Present*. 3d ed. Boulder, Colo.: Westview, 1998.

Smith, Ralph B. *Vietnam and the West*. London: Heinemann, 1968.

Taylor, Keith. "Surface Orientations in Vietnam: Beyond Histories of Nation and Region," *Journal of Asian Studies*, 57, 4 (1998): 949–78.

Taylor, Keith W., and John K. Whitmore (eds.). *Essays into Vietnamese Pasts*. Ithaca, N.Y.: Cornell Southeast Asia Program, 1995.

Vella, Walter (ed.). *Aspects of Vietnamese History*. Honolulu: University of Hawaii Press, 1973.

B. Precolonial Period

Ancient Town of Hội An: International Symposium Held in Đànẵng. Hanoi: Thế Giới, 1993.

Barrow, John. *A Voyage to Cochinchina, in the years 1792 and 1793*. Kuala Lumpur: Oxford University Press, 1975 reprint.

Chapuis, Oscar. *A History of Vietnam: From Hong Bang to Tu Duc*. Westport, Conn.: Greenwood Press, 1995.

Chen, Chingho. *Historical Notes on Hoi-An*. Carbondale, Ill.: Southern Illinois University Center for Vietnamese Studies, 1973.

Choi, Byung Wook. *Southern Vietnam under the Reign of Ming Mang (1820–1841): Central Policies and Local Response*. Ithaca, N.Y.: Cornell Southeast Asia Program, 2004.

Cotter, Michael G. "Towards a Social History of the Vietnamese Southward Movement." *Journal of Southeast Asian History*, 9, 1 (March 1968).

Crawfurd, John. *Journal of an Embassy to the Courts of Siam and Cochinchina*. 2 vols. Kuala Lumpur: Oxford University Press, 1968 reprint.

Duteil, Jean-Pierre. *L'ombre des nuages. Histoire et civilisation du Vietnam au temps des Lê et au début de la dynastie des Nguyễn (1427–1819)*. Paris: Éditions Argument, 1997.

Dutton, George. "The Tay Son Uprising: Society and Rebellion in Late Eighteenth-Century Vietnam, 1771–1802." Ph.D. diss., University of Washington, 2001.

Forest, Alain. *Les missionnaires français au Tonkin et au Siam (XVIIe–XVIIIe siè-cles): Analyse comparée d'un relatif succès et d'un échec certain.* 3 vols. Paris: L'Harmattan, 2000.

Hinton, Harold. *China's Relations with Burma and Vietnam.* New York: Institute of Pacific Relations, 1958.

Holmgren, Jennifer. *Chinese Colonisation of Northern Vietnam: Administrative Geography and Political Development in the Tong King Delta.* Canberra: Australian University Press, 1980.

Hữu Ngọc. *Dictionary of Traditional Vietnam.* Hanoi: Thế Giới, 1992.

Kelley, Liam C. *Beyond the Bronze Pillar: Envoy Poetry and the Sino–Vietnamese Relationship.* Manoa: University of Hawaii Press, 2005.

Lamb, Alistair. *The Mandarin Road to Old Hue.* London: Chatto & Windus, 1970.

Lamb, Helen. *Vietnam's Will to Live: Resistance to Foreign Aggression from Early Times through the Nineteenth Century.* New York: Monthly Review Press, 1972.

Langlet, Philippe. *L'ancienne historiographie d'état au Vietnam.* 2 vols. Paris: École Française d'Extrême-Orient, 1985–1992.

Li, Tana. *Nguyễn Cochinchina: Southern Vietnam in the Seventeenth and Eighteenth Centuries.* Ithaca, N.Y.: Cornell Southeast Asia Program, 1998.

Li, Tana, and Anthony Reid (eds.). *Southern Vietnam under the Nguyen: Documents on the Economic History of Cochinchina (Dang Trong), 1602–1777.* Singapore: Institute of Southeast Asian Studies, 1993.

Lieberman, Victor. *Strange Parallels: Southeast Asia in Global Context, c. 800–1830. Volume 1: Integration on the Mainland.* New York: Cambridge University Press, 2003.

Logan, William S. *Hanoi: Biography of a City.* Sydney: University of New South Wales Press, 2000.

McLeod, Mark W. *The Vietnamese Response to French Intervention, 1862–1874.* New York: Praeger, 1991.

Manguin, Pierre-Yves. *Les Nguyen, Macau et le Portugal.* Paris: École Française d'Extrême-Orient, 1984.

———. *Les Portugais sur les côtes du Viet-Nam et du Campa.* Paris: École Française d'Extrême-Orient, 1972.

Mantienne, Frédéric. *Monseigneur Pigneau de Béhaine, Évêque d'Adran, dignitaire de Cochinchine.* Paris: Églises d'Asie, 1999.

———. *Les relations politiques et commerciales entre la France et la péninsule indochinoise: XVIIe siècle.* Paris: Indes Savantes, 2001.

Maspéro, Georges. *Le royaume de Champa.* Paris: G. van Oest, 1928.

Miyakawa, Hisayuki. "The Confucianization of South China." In *The Confucian Persuasion,* ed. Arthur F. Wright. Stanford, Calif.: Stanford University Press, 1960.

Ngô Kim Chung, and Nguyễn Đức Nghinh. *Propriété privée et propriété collective dans l'ancien Vietnam.* Paris: L'Harmattan, 1987.

Nguyễn Khắc Viện. *Traditional Vietnam: Some Historical Stages.* Vietnam Studies 21. Hanoi: Foreign Language Press, no date.

Nguyen Thanh Nha. *Tableau économique du Vietnam aux XVIIe et XVIIIe siècles.* Paris: Cujas, 1970.

Nguyen Tu Cuong. *Zen in Medieval Vietnam: A Study and Translation of* Thiền Uyển Tập Anh. Honolulu: University of Hawaii Press, 1997.

Nguyễn Vĩnh Phúc. *Hanoi: Past and Present.* Hanoi: Thế Giới, 2001.

Phố Hiến, the Centre of International Commerce in the XVIIth–XVIIIth Centuries. Hanoi: Thế Giới, 1994.

Po Dharma. *Le Panduranga (Campa) 1802–1835. Ses rapports avec le Vietnam.* 2 vols. Paris: École Française d'Extrême-Orient, 1987.

Poisson, Emmanuel. *Mandarins et subalternes au nord du Viêt-Nam: Une bureau-cratie à l'épreuve, 1820–1918.* Paris: Maisonneuve & Larose, 2004.

Sokolov, Anatoly A. *Traditsionnyi Vietnam* [Traditional Vietnam]. Moscow: Institute of Oriental Studies, 1993.

Taylor, Keith W. *The Birth of Vietnam.* Berkeley, Calif.: University of California Press, 1983.

———. "The Rise of Dai Viet and the Establishment of Thang Long." In *Explorations in Early Southeast Asian History: The Origins of Southeast Asian State-craft,* ed. Kenneth R. Hall, and John K. Whitmore. Ann Arbor, Mich.: Michigan Papers on South and Southeast Asia, 1976.

Tran, Nhung Tuyet. "Vietnamese Women at the Crossroads: Gender, and Society in Early Modern Đại Việt." Ph.D. diss., University of California/Los Angeles, 2004.

Tsuboï, Yoshiharu. *L'Empire viêtnamien face à la France et à la Chine.* Paris: L'Harmattan, 1987.

Vietnamese Studies 56. *The Confucian Scholar in Vietnamese History.* Hanoi: Foreign Languages Press, 1979.

——— 48. *Hanoi: From the Origins to the 19th Century.* Vol. 1. Hanoi: Foreign Languages Press, 1977.

Wheeler, Charles. "Cross-Cultural Trade and Trans-Regional Networks in the Port of Hoi An: Maritime Vietnam in the Early Modern Era." Ph.D. diss., Yale University, 2001.

White, John. *A Voyage to Cochin China.* Kuala Lumpur: Oxford University Press, 1972 reprint.

Whitmore, John K. "The Development of Lê Government in 15th Century Vietnam." Ph.D. diss., Cornell University, 1968.

———. *Vietnam, Hồ Quý Ly, and the Ming.* New Haven, Conn.: Yale University Southeast Asian Studies, 1985.

Wiens, Herold J. *Han Chinese Expansion in South China.* Hamden, Conn.: Shoe String, 1970.

Wolters, O. W. "Historians and Emperors in Vietnam and China: Comments Arising Out of Le Van Huu's History, Presented to the Tran Court in 1272." In *Per-*

ceptions of the Past in Southeast Asia, ed. Anthony Reid and David G. Marr. Singapore: Heineman, 1979.

————. "On Telling a Story of Vietnam in the Thirteenth and Fourteenth Centuries." *Journal of Southeast Asian Studies* 26, no. 1 (1995): 63–74.

————. *Two Essays on Đại-Việt in the Fourteenth Century.* New Haven, Conn.: Yale University Council on Southeast Asia Studies, 1988.

Woodside, Alexander B. "Early Ming Expansionism (1406–1427): China's Abortive Conquest of Vietnam." *Harvard Papers on China* 17 (1963).

————. *Vietnam and the Chinese Model.* Cambridge, Mass.: Harvard University Press, 1988.

Yang Baoyun. *Contribution à l'histoire de la principauté des Nguyên au Vietnam méridional (1600–1775).* Geneva: Éditions Olizane, 1992.

Yu, Insun. *Law and Society in Seventeenth and Eighteenth Century Vietnam.* Seoul: Korea University Asiatic Research Centre, 1990.

C. Colonial Period

Adams, Nina S. "The Meaning of Pacification: Thanh Hoa under French Rule, 1865–1908." Ph.D. diss., Yale University, 1978.

Artaud, Dénise, and Lawrence Kaplan (eds.) *Diên Biên Phu, l'Alliance atlantique et la défense du Sud-Est asiatique.* Lyon: La Manufacture, 1989.

Azeau, Henri. *Ho Chi Minh, dernière chance: La conférence franco–vietnamienne de Fontainebleau, 1946.* Paris: Flammarion, 1968.

Betts, R. F. *Assimilation and Association in French Colonial Theory, 1890–1914.* New York: Columbia University Press, 1961.

Bodard, Lucien. *The Quicksand War: Prelude to Vietnam,* trans. Patrick O'Brien. Boston: Little, Brown, 1967.

Bousquet, Gisèle, and Pierre Brocheux (eds.). *Viêt Nam Exposé: French Scholarship on Twentieth-Century Vietnamese Society.* Ann Arbor, Mich.: University of Michigan Press, 2002.

Brocheux, Pierre (ed.). *L'Asie du Sud-Est. Révoltes, réformes, révolutions.* Lille: Presses Universitaires de Lille, 1981.

Brocheux, Pierre, and Daniel Hémery. *Indochine: La colonisation ambiguë 1858–1954.* Paris: La Découverte, 2001.

Cable, James. *The Geneva Conference of 1954 on Indochina.* New York: St. Martin's, 1986.

Cady, John T. *The Roots of French Imperialism in Eastern Asia.* Ithaca, N.Y.: Cornell University Press, 1954.

Cao Huy Thuan. *Les missionnaires et la politique coloniale française au Vietnam (1857–1914).* New Haven, Conn.: Yale University Southeast Asia Studies, 1990.

Catroux, Georges. *Deux actes du drame indochinois.* Paris: Plon, 1959.

Chapuis, Oscar. *The Last Emperors of Vietnam: From Tu Duc to Bao Dai.* Westport, Conn.: Greenwood Press, 2000.

Chen, King C. *Vietnam and China, 1938–1954*. Princeton, N.J.: Princeton University Press, 1969.

Chesneaux, Jean (ed.). *Tradition et révolution au Vietnam*. Paris: Anthropos, 1971.

Cole, Allan B. (ed.). *Conflict in Indochina and International Repercussions: A Documentary History*. Ithaca, N.Y.: Cornell University Press, 1956.

Cooper, Nicola. *France in Indochina. Colonial Encounters*. Oxford: Berg, 2001.

Dalloz, Jacques. *La guerre d'Indochine, 1945–1954*. Paris: Seuil, 1987.

D'Argenlieu, Thierry. *Chroniques d'Indochine*. Paris: Albin Michel, 1985.

Decoux, Jean. *A la barre de l'Indochine: Histoire de mon Gouvernement-général, 1940–1945*. Paris: Plon, 1952.

De Folin, Jacques. *Indochine 1940–1955: La fin d'un rêve*. Paris: Perrin, 1993.

Demariaux, Jean-Claude. *Les secrets des Îles Poulo-Condore: le grand bagne indochinois*. Paris: J. Peyronnet, 1956.

Devillers, Philippe. *Français et Annamites. Partenaires ou ennemis? 1856–1902*. Paris: Denoël, 1998.

———. *Histoire du Vietnam de 1940 à 1952*. Paris: Seuil, 1952.

———. *Paris, Saigon, Hanoi, les archives de la guerre, 1944–1947*. Paris: Gallimard/Julliard, 1988.

Dorgelès, Roland. *Sur la Route Mandarine*. Paris: Kailash, 1995 reprint.

Dorsenne, Jean. *Faudra-t-il évacuer l'Indochine?* Paris: Nouvelles Sociétés d'Editions, 1932.

Doyon, Jacques. *Les soldats blancs de Ho Chi Minh*. Paris: Fayard, 1973.

Duiker, William J. *The Rise of Nationalism in Vietnam, 1900–1941*. Ithaca, N.Y.: Cornell University Press, 1976.

Elliott, Duong Van Mai. *The Sacred Willow: Four Generations in the Life of a Vietnamese Family*. New York: Oxford University Press, 1999.

Elsbree, Willard E. *Japan's Role in Southeast Asian Nationalist Movements*. Cambridge, Mass.: Harvard University Press, 1953.

Ély, Paul. *L'Indochine dans la tourmente*. Paris: Plon, 1964.

Ennis, Thomas E. *French Policy and Developments in Indochina*. Chicago: University of Chicago Press, 1936.

Fall, Bernard B. *Hell in a Very Small Place: The Siege of Dien-Bien-Phu*. New York: Lippincott, 1967.

———. *Street without Joy: Indochina at War, 1946–1954*. Harrisburg, Penn.: Stackpole, 1961.

Fourniau, Charles. *Annam-Tonkin (1885–1896). Lettrés et paysans viêtnamiens face à la conquête coloniale*. Paris: L'Harmattan, 1989.

———. *Vietnam, domination coloniale et résistance nationale (1858–1914)*. Paris: Indes Savantes, 2001.

Fourniau, Charles et al. *Le contact colonial franco–viêtnamien. Le premier demi-siècle (1858–1911)*. Aix-en-Provence: Publications de l'Université de Provence, 1999.

Francini, Philippe (ed.). *Saigon 1925–1945: De la belle colonie à l'éclosion révolutionnaire ou la fin des dieux blancs*. Paris: Éditions Autrement, 1992.

Garros, Georges. *Forceries humaines*. Paris: André Delpeuch, 1926.

Gomane, Jean-Pierre. *L'exploration du Mékong: La Mission Doudart de Lagrée-Francis Garnier (1866–1868)*. Paris: L'Harmattan, 1995.

Goscha, Christopher. *Thailand and the Southeast Asian Networks of the Vietnamese Revolution, 1885–1954*. Richmond, UK: Curzon Press, 1999.

———. *Vietnam or Indochina? Contesting Concepts of Space in Vietnamese Nationalism, 1887–1954*. Copenhagen: Nordic Institute of Asian Studies, 1995.

Gran, Guy. "Vietnam, and the Capitalist Route to Modernity: Village Cochinchina 1880–1940." Ph.D. diss., University of Wisconsin, 1975.

Gras, Yves. *Histoire de la guerre d'Indochine*. Paris: Denoël, 1992.

Gunn, Geoffrey. *Political Struggles in Laos (1930–1954): Vietnamese Communist Power and the Lao Struggle for National Independence*. Bangkok: Eds. Duang Kamol, 1988.

Gurtov, Melvin. *The First Vietnam Crisis*. New York: Columbia University Press, 1967.

Hammer, Ellen J. *The Struggle for Indochina, 1940–1955*. Stanford, Calif.: Stanford University Press, 1955.

Hémery, Daniel. *Révolutionnaires viêtnamiens et pouvoir colonial en Indochine*. Paris: Maspéro, 1975.

Hue-Tam Ho Tai. *Radicalism and the Origins of the Vietnamese Revolution*. Cambridge, Mass.: Harvard University Press, 1992.

Huynh Kim Khanh. "The August Revolution Reinterpreted." *Journal of Asian Studies* 30, 4 (August 1971).

Institut Charles de Gaulle. *De Gaulle et l'Indochine, 1940–1946*. Paris: Plon, 1982.

Irving, Ronald. *The First Indochina War: French and American Policy, 1945–1954*. London, 1975.

Isoart, Paul. *L'Indochine française, 1940–1945*. Paris: Presses Universitaires de France, 1982.

———. *Le phénomène national viêtnamien*. Paris: Librairie Générale de Droit et de Jurisprudence, 1961.

Jennings, Eric. *Vichy in the Tropics: Pétain's National Revolution in Madagascar, Guadeloupe, and Indochina. 1940–1944*. Stanford, Calif.: Stanford University Press, 2001.

Joyaux, François. *La Chine et le règlement du premier conflit d'Indochine: Genève, 1954*. Paris: Sorbonne, 1979.

Lacouture, Jean, and Phillippe Devillers. *La fin d'une guerre: Indochine 1954*. Paris: Seuil, 1960.

Lancaster, Donald. *The Emancipation of French Indochina*. London: Oxford University Press, 1961.

Langlois, Walter G. *Andre Malraux: The Indochina Adventure*. New York: Praeger, 1965.

Laniel, Joseph. *Le drame indochinois: de Dien-Bien-Phu au pari de Genève*. Paris: Plon, 1957.

Lê, Nicole-Dominique. *Les missions étrangères et la pénétration française au Viet Nam*. Paris: Mouton, 1975.

Lin Hua. *Chiang Kai-shek, De Gaulle contre Hô Chi Minh. Viêt-Nam 1945–1946*. Paris: L'Harmattan, 1994.

Lockhart, Bruce M. *The End of the Vietnamese Monarchy*. New Haven, Conn.: Yale Southeast Asian Studies, 1993.

Marr, David G. *Vietnam 1945: The Quest for Power*. Berkeley, Calif.: University of California Press, 1995.

———. *Vietnamese Anticolonialism, 1885–1925*. Berkeley, Calif.: University of California Press, 1971.

———. *Vietnamese Tradition on Trial, 1925–1945*. Berkeley, Calif.: University of California Press, 1985.

McAleavy, Henry. *Black Flags in Vietnam*. New York: Macmillan, 1968.

McAlister, John T., Jr. *Vietnam: The Origins of Revolution*. New York: Harper & Row, 1970.

McAlister, John T., Jr., and Paul Mus. *The Vietnamese and Their Revolution*. New York: Harper & Row, 1970.

McConnell, B. Scott. *Leftward Journey: The Education of Vietnamese Students in France, 1919–1939*. New Brunswick, N.J.: Transaction, 1989.

McHale, Shawn Frederick. *Print and Power: Confucianism, Communism, and Buddhism in the Making of Modern Vietnam*. Honolulu: University of Hawaii Press, 2004.

McLeod, Mark. *The Vietnamese Response to French Intervention, 1862–1874*. New York: Praeger, 1991.

Meyer, Charles. *La vie quotidienne des Français en Indochine, 1860–1910*. Paris: Hachette, 1985.

Mkhitarian, Suron A. *Rabochii klass i Natsional'no-Osvoboditel'noe Dvizhenie vo Vietname*. Moscow, 1967.

Monnais-Rousselot, Laurence. *Médecine et colonisation. L'aventure indochinoise, 1860–1939*. Paris: CNRS, 1999.

Morlat, Patrice. *Les affaires politiques de l'Indochine (1895–1923). Les grands commis du savoir au pouvoir*. Paris: L'Harmattan, 1995.

———. *La répression coloniale au Vietnam (1908–1940)*. Paris: L'Harmattan, 1990.

Mus, Paul. *Viêt-Nam sociologie d'une guerre*. Paris: Seuil, 1952.

Navarre, Henri. *Agonie de l'Indochine (1953–1954)*. Paris: Plon, 1956.

Ngo Van. *Au pays de la cloche fêlée. Tribulations d'un Cochinchinois à l'époque coloniale*. Paris: L'Insomniaque, 2000.

———. *Viet Nam 1920–1945. Révolution et contre-révolution sous la domination coloniale*. Paris: L'Insomniaque, 1996.

Ngo Vinh Long. *Before the Revolution*. Cambridge, Mass.: MIT Press, 1973.

————. "Peasant Revolutionary Struggles in Vietnam in the 1930s." Ph.D. diss., Harvard University, 1978.

Nguyễn Đình Hoà. *From the City Inside the Red River: A Cultural Memoir of Mid-Century Vietnam.* Jefferson, N.C.: McFarland, 1999.

Nguyễn Duy Thành. *My Four Years with the Viet Minh.* Bombay: Democratic Research Service, 1950.

Nguyên Thê Anh. *Monarchie et fait colonial au Viet-Nam (1875–1925): Le crépuscule d'un ordre traditionnel.* Paris: L'Harmattan, 1992.

Nguyen Van Ky. *La société viêtnamienne face à la modernité. Le Tonkin de la fin du XIXe siècle à la Seconde Guerre Mondiale.* Paris: L'Harmattan, 1995.

Nguyen Van Phong. *La société viêtnamienne de 1882 à 1902.* Paris: Presses Universitaires de France, 1971.

Nordell, John R., Jr. *The Undetected Enemy: French and American Miscalculations at Dien Bien Phu.* College Station, Tex.: Texas A&M Press, 1995.

Norindr, Panivong. *Phantasmatic Indochina: French Colonial Ideology in Architecture, Film and Literature.* Durham, N.C.: Duke University Press, 1996.

O'Ballance, Edgar. *The Indo-China War, 1945–1954: A Study in Guerrilla Warfare.* London: Faber & Faber, 1964.

Ognetov, I. A. "Komintern i revoliutsionnoe dvizhenie vo Vietname." *Komintern i Vostok* [Comintern, and the East]. Moscow, 1969.

Osborne, Milton. *The French Presence in Cochinchina and Cambodia.* Ithaca, N.Y.: Cornell University Press, 1969.

Patti, Archimedes. *Why Vietnam: Prelude to America's Albatross.* Berkeley, Calif.: University of California Press, 1980.

Phan Thien Chau. "Transitional Nationalism in Vietnam, 1903–1931." Ph.D. diss., Denver University, 1965.

Porter, Gareth. "Imperialism and Social Structure in Twentieth-Century Vietnam." Ph.D. diss., Cornell University, 1976.

————. "Proletariat and Peasantry in Early Vietnamese Communism." *Asian Thought and Society.* (3) (December 1976).

Randle, Robert F. *Geneva 1954: The Settlement of the Indochina War.* Princeton, N.J.: Princeton University Press, 1969.

Roy, Jules. *The Battle of Dien Bien Phu*, trans. Robert Baldrich. New York: Harper & Row, 1965.

Ruscio, Alain. *1945–1954: Le mémoire du siècle: La guerre française d'Indochine.* Paris: Complexe, 1991.

————. *Les communistes français et la guerre d'Indochine, 1944–1954.* Paris: L'Harmattan, 1985.

————. *Dien Bien Phu, la fin d'une illusion.* Paris: L'Harmattan, 1986.

Sainteny, Jean. *Histoire d'une paix manquée: Indochine 1945–1947.* Paris: Dumont, 1953.

Shipway, Martin. *The Road to War. France and Vietnam, 1944–1947.* Providence, R.I.: Berghahn Books, 1996.

Shiraishi, Takashi, and Motoo Furuta (eds.). *Indochina in the 1940s and 1950s: Translation of Contemporary Japanese Scholarship on Southeast Asia.* Ithaca, N.Y.: Cornell Southeast Asia Program, 1992.

Short, Anthony. *The Origins of the Vietnam War.* London: Longmans, 1989.

Simpson, Howard R. *Dien Bien Phu: The Epic Battle America Forgot.* Riverside, N.J.: Macmillan, 1994.

Starobin, Joseph R. *Eyewitness in Indochina.* New York: Cameron & Kahn, 1954.

Taboulet, Georges. *La geste française en Indochine.* 2 vols. Paris: Adrien-Maisonneuve, 1955–1956.

Tanham, George K. *Communist Revolutionary Warfare: The Vietminh in Indochina.* New York: Praeger, 1961.

Tertrais, Hugues. *La piastre et le fusil: Le coût de la guerre de l'Indochine, 1945–1954.* Paris: Comité pour l'Histoire Économique de la France, 2002.

Thévenet, Amédée (ed.). *La guerre d'Indochine, racontée par ceux qui l'ont vécue, 1945–1954.* Paris: France-Empire, 2001.

Thompson, Virginia. *French Indochina.* New York: Octagon, 1968.

Tønneson, Stein. *The Outbreak of War in Indochina, 1946.* Oslo: International Peace Research Institute, 1984.

———. *The Vietnamese Revolution of 1945: Roosevelt, Ho Chi Minh and de Gaulle in a World at War.* Thousand Oaks, Calif.: Sage, 1991.

Trần Huy Liệu. *Les Soviets du Nghe-Tinh de 1930–1931 au Viet-Nam.* Hanoi: Foreign Languages Press, 1960.

Trần Mỹ-Vân. *A Vietnamese Scholar in Anguish: Nguyễn Khuyến and the Decline of the Confucian Order, 1884–1909.* Singapore: Journal of Southeast Asian Studies, 1992.

———. *A Vietnamese Royal Exile in Japan: Prince Cuòng Đế (1882–1951).* London: Routledge, 2005.

Trinh Van Thao. *Vietnam, du confucianisme au communisme. Un essai d'itinéraire intellectuel.* Paris: L'Harmattan, 1990.

Truong Buu Lam. *Colonialism Experienced: Vietnamese Writings on Colonialism, 1900–1931.* Ann Arbor, Mich.: University of Michigan Press, 2000.

———. *Patterns of Vietnamese Response to Foreign Intervention, 1858–1900.* New Haven, Conn.: Yale University Southeast Asia Studies, 1967.

Tuck, Patrick. *French Catholic Missionaries and the Politics of Imperialism in Vietnam, 1857–1914. A Documentary Survey.* Liverpool: Liverpool University Press, 1987.

Valette, Jacques. *La guerre d'Indochine, 1945–1954.* Paris: A. Colin, 1994.

———. *Indochine 1940–1945. Français contre Japonais.* Paris: SEDES, 1993.

Vann, Michael G. "White City on the Red River: Race, Power, and Culture in French Colonial Hanoi, 1872–1954." Ph.D. diss., University of California/Santa Cruz, 1999.

Viollis, André. *Indochine S.O.S.* Paris: Gallimard, 1935.

Vo Duc Hanh. *La place du catholicisme dans les relations entre la France et le Viet Nam de 1870 à 1886*. 3 vols. 2nd ed. Berne: Peter Lang, 1993.

Zinoman, Peter. *The Colonial Bastille: A History of Imprisonment in Vietnam, 1862–1940*. Berkeley, Calif.: University of California Press, 2001.

D. Republic of Vietnam

Brown, Weldon A. *Prelude to Disaster*. Port Washington, N.Y.: National University Publications, 1975.

Carver, George. "The Real Revolution in South Vietnam." *Foreign Affairs* 43 (April 1965).

Catton, Philip E. *Diem's Final Failure: Prelude to America's War in Vietnam*. Lawrence, Kans.: University Press of Kansas, 2002.

Fall, Bernard B. *Last Reflections on a War*. New York: Doubleday, 1967.

———. *The Two Vietnams*. New York: Praeger, 1967.

———. *Vietnam Witness, 1953–1966*. New York: Praeger, 1966.

Fishel, Wesley R. (ed.). *Problems of Freedom: South Vietnam Since Independence*. New York: Free Press of Glencoe, 1961.

Greene, Graham. *The Quiet American*. New York: Viking, 1956.

Halberstam, David. *The Making of a Quagmire*. New York: Random House, 1965.

Hunt, Richard. *Pacification: The American Struggle for Vietnam's Hearts and Minds*. Boulder, Colo.: Westview, 1995.

Joiner, Charles A. *The Politics of Massacre*. Philadelphia: Temple University Press, 1974.

Lacouture, Jean. *Vietnam: Between Two Truces*, trans. Konrad Kellen and Joel Carmichael. New York: Random House, 1966.

Lindholm, Richard W. (ed.). *Viet-Nam: The First Five Years*. East Lansing, Mich.: Michigan State University, 1957.

Maneli, Mieczyslaw. *War of the Vanquished*. New York: Harper & Row, 1971.

Mechlin, John. *Mission in Torment*. New York: Doubleday, 1965.

Nguyen Tien Hung, and Jerrold L. Schecter. *The Palace File*. New York: Harper & Row, 1986.

Nighswonger, William A. *Rural Pacification in Vietnam*. New York: Praeger, 1966.

Osborne, Milton E. *Strategic Hamlets in South Vietnam*. Ithaca, N.Y.: Cornell University Southeast Asia Program, 1965.

Race, Jeffrey. *War Comes to Long An*. Berkeley, Calif.: University of California Press, 1972.

Scigliano, Robert. *South Vietnam: Nation under Stress*. Boston: Houghton Mifflin, 1963.

Smith, Harvey H. et al. *Area Handbook for South Vietnam*. Washington, D.C.: Government Printing Office, 1967.

E. Democratic Republic of Vietnam

Boudarel, Georges, and Nguyen Van Ky. *Hanoi: City of the Rising Dragon*, trans. Claire Duiker. Lanham, Md.: Rowman & Littlefield, 2002.

Burchett, Wilfred G. *Vietnam North: A First-Hand Report*. New York: International Publishers, 1967.

DeCaro, *Rhetoric of Revolt: Ho Chi Minh's Discourse for Revolution*. Westport, Conn.: Praeger, 2003.

Fall, Bernard B. "North Vietnam: A Profile." *Problems of Communism* (July–August 1965).

———. *The Two Vietnams*. New York: Praeger, 1967.

———. *The Vietminh Regime*. Ithaca, N.Y.: Cornell University Press, 1954.

Giebel, Christoph. *Imagined Ancestries of Vietnamese Communism: Ton Duc Thang and the Politics of History and Memory*. Seattle: University of Washington Press, 2004.

Goscha, Christopher, and Benoît de Tréglodé. *Naissance d'un état-parti: Le Viet Nam depuis 1945/The Birth of a Party-State: Vietnam since 1945*. Paris: Les Indes Savantes, 2004.

Hardy, Andrew. *Red Hills: Migrants and the State in the Highlands of Vietnam*. Copenhagen: Nordic Institute of Asian Studies, 2003.

Hoang Van Chi. *From Colonialism to Communism*. New York: Praeger, 1964.

Honey, P. J. *Communism in North Vietnam: Its Role in the Sino-Soviet Dispute*. Cambridge, Mass.: MIT Press, 1963.

———(ed.). *North Vietnam Today: Profile of a Communist Satellite*. New York: Praeger, 1962.

Nhu Phong, "Intellectuals, Writers, and Artists." *China Quarterly* 9 (January–March 1962).

Ninh, Kim. *A World Transformed: The Politics of Culture in Revolutionary Vietnam, 1945–1965*. Ann Arbor, Mich.: University of Michigan Press, 2002.

Porter, Gareth. *The Myth of the Bloodbath: North Vietnam's Land Reform Reconsidered*. Ithaca, N.Y.: Cornell University Southeast Asian Series, 1972.

Salisbury, Harrison E. *Behind the Lines—Hanoi*. New York: Harper & Row, 1967.

Smith, Ralph B. "The Work of the Provisional Government of Vietnam, August–December 1945." *Modern Asian Studies* 12, 4 (1978).

Thai Quang Trung. *Collective Leadership and Factionalism: An Essay on Ho Chi Minh's Legacy*. Singapore: Institute of Southeast Asian Studies, 1985.

Tréglodé, Benoît de. *Héros et révolution au Viêtnam*. Paris: L'Harmattan, 2001.

Turley, William S. (ed.). *Vietnamese Communism in Comparative Perspective*. Boulder, Colo.: Westview, 1980.

U.S. Department of State. *Who's Who in North Vietnam*. Washington, D.C.: Government Printing Office, 1972.

Van Dyke, Jon M. *North Vietnam's Strategy for Survival*. Palo Alto, Calif.: Pacific Books, 1972.

Weiss, Peter. *Notes on the Cultural Life of the D.R.V.* New York: Dell, 1970.

F. Second Indochina War
1. General

Anderson, David L. *The Columbia Guide to the Vietnam War*. New York: Columbia University Press, 2002.

Bain, Chester A. *The Roots of Conflict.* Englewood Cliffs, N.J.: Prentice-Hall, 1967.

Browne, Malcolm W. *The New Face of War.* Indianapolis: Bobbs-Merrill, 1965.

Cao Van Vien, and Dong Van Khuyen. *Reflections on the Vietnam War.* Washington, D.C.: Center for Military History, 1980.

Critchfield, Richard. *The Long Charade: Political Subversion in the Vietnam War.* New York: Harcourt, Brace, & World, 1968.

Elliott, Paul. *Vietnam: Conflict and Controversy.* London: Arms and Armour, 1996.

Emerson, Gloria. *Winners and Losers.* New York: Random, 1976.

Ford, Ronnie. *Tet 1968: Understanding the Surprise.* Portland, Ore.: F. Cass, 1995.

Gilbert, Marc Jason (ed.). *The Vietnam War: Teaching Approaches and Resources.* Westport, Conn.: Greenwood, 1991.

Hall, Mitchell. *The Vietnam War.* New York: Longman, 1999.

Hammer, Ellen J. *A Death in November: America in Vietnam, 1963.* New York: Oxford University Press, 1987.

Harrison, James P. *The Endless War: Fifty Years of Struggle in Vietnam.* New York: Free Press of Glencoe, 1982.

Head, William, and Lawrence Grinter. *Looking Back on the Vietnam War: A 1990s Perspective on the Decisions, Combat and Legacies.* Westport, Conn.: Praeger, 1993.

Herr, Michael. *Dispatches.* New York: Knopf, 1977.

Hixson, Walter (ed.). *The Roots of the Vietnam War.* New York: Garland, 2000.

Isaacs, Arnold R. *Without Honor: Defeat in Vietnam and Cambodia.* Baltimore: Johns Hopkins University Press, 1983.

Just, Ward. *To What End: Report from Vietnam.* Boston: Houghton Mifflin, 1968.

Langguth, Arthur J. *Our Vietnam: The War, 1954–1975.* New York: Simon & Schuster, 2000.

Le Ly Hayslip, with Jay Wurts. *When Heaven and Earth Changed Places.* New York: Penguin, 1990.

Leslie, Jacques. *The Mark: A War Correspondent's Memoir of Vietnam and Cambodia.* New York: Four Walls Eight Windows, 1995.

Lomperis, Timothy J. *The War Everyone Lost—and Won.* Baton Rouge, La.: Louisiana State University Press, 1984.

Lowe, Peter (ed.). *The Vietnam War.* Basingstoke, Hants.: Macmillan, 1998.

Luce, Donald, and Summer, John. *Viet Nam: The Unheard Voices.* Ithaca, N.Y.: Cornell University Press, 1969.

Ly Qui Chung (ed.). *Between Two Fires: The Unheard Voices of Vietnam.* New York: Praeger, 1970.

McNamara, Robert. *In Retrospect: The Tragedy and Lessons of Vietnam.* New York: Times Books, 1995.

Melling, Phil, and Jon Roper (eds.). *America, France, and Vietnam: Cultural History and Ideas of Conflict.* Brookefield, Vt.: Gower Pub., 1991.

Millet, Allan (ed.). *A Short History of the Vietnam War.* Bloomington, Ind.: Indiana University Press, 1978.

Moïse, Edwin E. *Historical Dictionary of the Vietnam War.* 3 vols. Basingstoke, Hants: Macmillan, 1983–1991.

Moss, George. *Vietnam: An American Ordeal*. Upper Saddle River, N.J.: Prentice Hall, 2002.

Nalty, Bernard (ed.). *The Vietnam War: The History of America's Conflict in Southeast Asia*. New York: Smithmark, 1996.

Neu, Charles (ed.). *After Vietnam: Legacies of a Lost War*. Baltimore: Johns Hopkins University Press.

Oberdorfer, Don. *Tet!* New York: Doubleday, 1971.

Olson, James S., and Randy Roberts. *Where the Domino Fell: America and Vietnam, 1945 to 1995*. 2nd ed. New York: St. Martin's Press, 1996.

Podhoretz, Norman. *Why We Were in Vietnam*. New York: Simon & Schuster, 1982.

Sheehan, Susan. *Ten Vietnamese*. New York: Knopf, 1967.

Smith, R. B. *International History of the Vietnam War*. 3 vols. Basingstoke, Hants: Macmillan, 1983–1991.

Starr, Jerold M. (ed.). *The Lessons of the Vietnam War*. Pittsburgh: Center for Social Studies Education, 1996.

Sully, François (ed.). *Voices from Vietnam*. New York: Praeger, 1971.

Summers, Harry G. *Historical Atlas of the Vietnam War*. Boston: Houghton Mifflin, 1995.

Swain, Jon. *River of Time*. New York: Thomas Dunne, 1997.

Thompson, Robert. *Defeating Communist Insurgency: Experiences from Malaya*. London: 1967.

———. *No Exit from Vietnam*. New York: McKay, 1969.

Tran Van Don. *Our Endless War*. San Rafael, Calif.: Presidio, 1978.

Tucker, Spencer. *Vietnam*. London: UCL Press, 1999.

———. (ed.). *Encyclopedia of the Vietnam War: A Political, Social and Military History*. New York: Oxford University Press, 2000.

Turley, William S. *The Second Indochina War: A Short Political and Military History*. Boulder, Colo.: Westview, 1986.

Werner, Jayne, and Luu Doan Huynh (eds.). *The Vietnam War: Vietnamese and American Perspectives*. Armonk, N.J.: Sharpe, 1993.

West, Richard. *War and Peace in Vietnam*. London: Sinclair-Stevenson, 1995.

Winters, Francis X. *The Year of the Hare: America in Vietnam, January 25, 1963–February 15, 1964*. Athens, Ga.: University of Georgia Press, 1997.

Young, Marilyn B. *The Vietnam Wars, 1945–1990*. New York: HarperCollins, 1991.

2. The Revolutionary Side

An, Tai Sung. *The Vietnam War*. Madison, N.J.: Fairleigh Dickinson University Press, 1998.

———. *The Village War: Vietnamese Communist Revolutionary Activities in Dinh Tuong Province, 1960–1964*. Columbia, Mo.: University of Missouri Press, 1973.

Ang Cheng Guan. *The Vietnam War from the Other Side: The Vietnamese Communists' Perspective*. London: RoutledgeCurzon, 2002.

Berman, Paul. *Revolutionary Organization*. Lexington, Mass.: Heath, 1974.

Brigham, Robert K. *Guerrilla Diplomacy: The NLF's Foreign Relations and the Vietnam War*. Ithaca, N.Y.: Cornell University Press, 1998.

Burchett, Wilfred. *My Visit to the Liberated Zones of South Vietnam*. Hanoi: Foreign Languages Press, 1966.

———. *Vietnam: Inside Story of the Guerrilla War*. New York: International Publishers, 1965.

———. *Vietnam Will Win*. New York: International Publishers, 1969.

Chanoff, David, and Doan Van Toai. *Portrait of the Enemy*. New York: Random House, 1986.

Colvin, John. *Giap—Volcano under Snow: Vietnam's Celebrated General Giap*. New York: Soho Press, 1996.

Duiker, William J. *The Communist Road to Power in Vietnam*. 2nd ed. Boulder, Colo.: Westview, 1996.

———. *Sacred War: Nationalism and Revolution in a Divided Vietnam*. New York: McGraw-Hill, 1995.

Elliott, David W. P. *NLF–DRV Strategy in the 1972 Spring Offensive*. Ithaca, N.Y.: Cornell University IREA Project, 1974.

———. *The Vietnamese War: Revolution and Social Change in the Mekong Delta, 1930–1975*. 2 vols. Armonk, N.Y.: M.E. Sharpe, 2003.

Fitzgerald, Frances. *Fire in the Lake*. New York: Vintage, 1972.

Gilbert, Marc Jason (ed.). *Why the North Won the Vietnam War*. New York: Palgrave, 2002.

Hess, Martha. *Then the Americans Came: Voices from Vietnam*. New York: Four Walls Eight Windows, 1993.

Hoàng Quốc Việt. *A Heroic People: Memoirs from the Revolution*. Hanoi: Foreign Languages Press, 1965.

———. *Récits de la résistance viêtnamienne*. Hanoi: Foreign Languages Press, 1966.

Langer, Paul, and Joseph J. Zasloff. *North Vietnam and the Pathet Lao: Partners in the Struggle for Laos*. Cambridge, Mass.: Harvard University Press, 1970.

Lanning, Michael Lee, and Dann Cragg. *Inside the VC and the NVA: The Real Story of North Vietnam's Armed Forces*. 2nd ed. New York: Ballantine, 1992.

Lansdale, Edward G. "Vietnam: Do We Understand Revolution?" *Foreign Affairs* 43 (October 1964) 75–86.

Leites, Nathan. *The Viet Cong Style of Politics*. Rand Corporation Report RM-5487. Santa Monica, Calif.: Rand Corporation, 1969.

Lockhart, Greg. *Nation in Arms: Origins of the People's Army of Vietnam*. Wellington, NZ: Allen & Unwin, 1989.

Nguyễn Khắc Viện. *Tradition and Revolution in Vietnam*. Berkeley, Calif.: Indochina Resources Center, 1974.

Nguyễn Thị Dinh. *No Other Road to Take*, trans. Mai Elliott. Ithaca, N.Y.: Cornell University Southeast Asia Program, 1976.

Pike, Douglas. *The Viet Cong.* Cambridge, Mass.: MIT Press, 1966.
———. *War, Peace, and the Viet Cong.* Cambridge, Mass.: MIT Press, 1969.
Post, Ken. *Revolution, Socialism, and Nationalism in Vietnam.* 4 vols. Aldershot, UK: Dartmouth, 1989.
Rand Corporation. *Interviews Concerning the National Liberation Front for South Vietnam.* Rand Corporation Documents Series FD & G. Santa Monica, Calif.: Rand.
Rousset, Pierre. *Communisme et nationalisme viêtnamien.* Paris: Galilée, 1978.
Thayer, Carlyle. *War by Other Means: National Liberation and Revolution in Vietnam, 1954–60.* Sydney: Allen & Unwin, 1989.
Trần Văn Trà. *Vietnam: History of the Bulwark B2 Theater. Vol. 5.* Joint Publications Research Service, Southeast Asia Report 1247.
Truong Nhu Tang. *A Vietcong Memoir: An Inside Account of the Vietnam War and Its Aftermath.* San Diego, Calif.: Harcourt Brace Jovanovich, 1985.
Trường Sơn. "The Failure of Special War (1961–1965)." *Vietnamese Studies* 11. Hanoi: Foreign Languages Press, 1967.
Turner, Karen G. with Phan Thanh Hao. *Even the Women Must Fight: Memories of War from North Vietnam.* New York: Wiley, 1998.
Victory in Vietnam: The Official History of the People's Army of Vietnam, 1954–1975, trans. Merle Pribbenow. Lawrence, Kans.: University Press of Kansas, 2002.
Warner, Denis. *Certain Victory: How Hanoi Won the War.* Kansas City: Sheed Andrews & McMeed, 1977.
Woodside, Alexander B. *Community and Revolution in Vietnam.* Boston: Houghton Mifflin, 1976.
Zasloff, Joseph J. *Origins of the Insurgency in South Vietnam, 1954–1960: The Role of the Southern Vietminh Cadres.* Rand Corporation Collection, RM 5163/ Z ISA/ARPA, May 1968.

3. U.S. Involvement

Allen, George W. *None So Blind: A Personal Account of the Intelligence Failure in Vietnam.* Chicago: Ivan R. Dee, 2001.
Anderson, David L. (ed.). *Shadow on the White House: Presidents and the Vietnam War, 1954–1975.* Manhattan, Kans.: University of Kansas Press, 1994.
———. *Trapped by Success: The Eisenhower Administration and Vietnam, 1953–1961.* New York: Columbia University Press, 1991.
Ball, George W. *The Past Has Another Pattern.* New York: Norton, 1982.
Bator, Victor. *Vietnam: A Diplomatic Tragedy.* New York: Faber & Faber, 1967.
Berman, Larry. *Planning a Tragedy.* New York: Norton, 1972.
Beschloss, Michael (ed.). *Taking Charge: The Johnson White House Tapes, 1963–1964.* New York: Simon and Schuster, 1997.
Blair, Anne. *Lodge in Vietnam: A Patriot Abroad.* New Haven, Conn.: Yale University Press, 1995.

Blum, Robert M. *Drawing the Line: The Origins of the American Containment Policy in Asia.* New York: Norton, 1982.

Bradley, Mark. *Imagining Vietnam and America: The Making of Postcolonial Vietnam, 1919–1950.* Chapel Hill, N.C.: University of North Carolina Press, 2000.

Braestrup, Peter. *Big Story: How the American Press and Television Reported and Interpreted the Crisis of Tet 1968 in Vietnam and Washington.* 3rd ed. Novato, Cal. Presido, 1994.

Brown, Weldon A. *The Last Chopper: The Denouement of the American Role in Vietnam, 1963–1975.* Port Washington, N.Y.: Kennikat Press, 1976.

Chomsky, Noam. *At War with Asia.* New York: Random House, 1970.

Cobb, William W., Jr. *The American Foundation Myth in Vietnam: Reigning Paradigms and Raining Bombs.* Lanham, Md.: University Press of America, 1998.

Colby, William. *Lost Victory: A Firsthand Account of America's Sixteen-Year Involvement in Vietnam.* Chicago: Contemporary Books, 1989.

Cooper, Chester. *The Lost Crusade.* New York: Dodd, Mead, 1970.

Daum, Andreas, Lloyd Gardner, and Wilfried Mausbach (eds.). *America, the Vietnam War, and the World: Comparative and International Perspectives.* New York: Cambridge University Press, 2003.

DeGroot, Gerard. *A Noble Cause? America and the Vietnam War.* Harlow, UK: Longman, 2000.

Donaldson, Gary. *America at War since 1945: Politics and Diplomacy in Korea, Vietnam, and the Gulf War.* Westport, Conn.: Praeger, 1996.

Doyle, Robert C. *Voices from Captivity.* Lawrence, Kans.: University Press of Kansas, 1994.

Duiker, William J. *U.S. Containment Policy and the Conflict in Indochina.* Stanford, Calif.: Stanford University Press, 1994.

Ernst, John. *Forging a Fateful Alliance: Michigan State University and the Vietnam War.* East Lansing, Mich.: Michigan State University Press, 1998.

Freedman, Lawrence. *Kennedy's Wars: Berlin, Cuba, Laos, and Vietnam.* New York: Oxford University Press, 2000.

Galluci, Robert. *Neither Peace nor Honor: The Politics of American Military Policy in Vietnam.* Baltimore: Johns Hopkins University Press, 1975.

Gardner, Lloyd, and Ted Gittinger (eds.). *Vietnam: The Early Decisions.* Austin, Tex.: University of Texas Press, 1997.

Gelb, Leslie, and Richard Betts. *The Irony of Vietnam: The System Worked.* Washington, D.C.: Brookings Institution, 1979.

Gibbons, William C. *The U.S. Government and the Vietnam War.* 2 vols. Princeton, N.J.: Princeton University Press, 1986.

Gittinger, Ted (ed.). *The Johnson Years: A Vietnam Roundtable.* Austin, Tex.: LBJ School of Public Affairs, 1993.

Goulden, Joseph. *Truth is the First Casualty: The Gulf of Tonkin Affair.* Chicago: Rand McNally, 1969.

Halberstam, David. *The Best and the Brightest.* New York: Random House, 1969.

Hamilton, Donald W. *The Art of Insurgency: American Military Policy and the Failure of Strategy in Southeast Asia.* Westport, Conn.: Praeger, 1998.

Hatcher, Patrick. *The Suicide of an Elite: American Internationalists and Vietnam.* Stanford, Calif.: Stanford University Press, 1990.

Hayes, Samuel P. (ed.). *The Beginning of American Aid to Southeast Asia: The Griffin Mission of 1950.* Lexington, Mass.: Prentice-Hall, 1971.

Herring, George. *America's Longest War: The United States in Vietnam, 1950–1975.* 3rd ed. New York: McGraw-Hill, 1979.

———. *LBJ and Vietnam: A Different Kind of War.* Austin, Tex.: University of Texas Press, 1994.

Hess, Gary R. *Vietnam and the United States: Origins and Legacy of War.* New York: Twayne Publishers, 1998.

Hilsman, Roger. *To Move a Nation.* New York: Doubleday, 1969.

Hixson, Walter (ed.). *Leadership and Diplomacy in the Vietnam War.* New York: Garland, 2000.

Hoopes, Townsend. *The Limits of Intervention.* New York: David McKay, 1969.

Hunt, Michael H. *Lyndon Johnson's War: America's Cold War Crusade in Vietnam, 1945–1968.* New York: Hill and Wang, 1996.

Jones, Howard. *Death of a Generation: How the Assassinations of Diem and JFK Prolonged the Vietnam War.* New York: Oxford University Press, 2003.

Kahin, George M. *Intervention: How America Became Involved in Vietnam.* New York: Knopf, 1986.

Kahin, George M., and John W. Lewis. *The United States in Vietnam.* New York: Delta, 1967.

Kaiser, David E. *American Tragedy: Kennedy, Johnson, and the Origins of the Vietnam War.* Cambridge, Mass.: Belknap/Harvard University Press, 2000.

Kattenburg, Paul M. *The Vietnam Trauma in American Foreign Policy, 1945–1975.* New Brunswick, N.J.: Transaction Books, 1980.

Kenny, Henry J. *The American Role in Vietnam and East Asia.* New York: Praeger, 1984.

Kimball, Jeffrey. *Nixon's Vietnam War.* Lawrence, Kans.: University Press of Kansas, 1998.

———. *The Vietnam War Files: Uncovering the Secret History of Nixon-Era Strategy.* Lawrence, Kans.: University Press of Kansas, 2004.

Kissinger, Henry. *Crisis: The Anatomy of Two Major Foreign Policy Crises.* New York: Simon & Schuster, 2003.

Kolko, Gabriel. *Anatomy of a War: Vietnam, the United States, and the Modern Historical Experience.* New York: Pantheon, 1985.

Komer, Robert. *Bureaucracy at War.* Boulder, Colo.: Westview, 1985.

Lansdale, Edward G. *In the Midst of Wars: An American's Mission to Southeast Asia.* New York: Harper & Row, 1972.

Lederer, William J. *Our Own Worst Enemy.* New York: Norton, 1968.

Lewy, Guenter. *America in Vietnam.* New York: Oxford University Press, 1978.

Lodge, Henry Cabot. *The Storm Has Many Eyes*. New York: Norton, 1973.

Logevall, Frederick. *Choosing War: The Lost Chance for Peace and the Escalation of War in Vietnam*. Berkeley, Calif.: University of California Press, 1999.

Mann, Robert. *A Grand Delusion: America's Descent into Vietnam*. New York: Basic Books, 2001.

McConnell, Malcolm. *Inside Hanoi's Secret Archives: Solving the MIA Mystery*. New York: Simon & Schuster, 1994.

McNamara, Robert, James G. Blight, Robert K. Brigham. *Argument without End: In Search of Answers to the Vietnam Tragedy*. New York: Public Affairs, 1999.

Metzner, Edward. *More than a Soldier's War: Pacification in Vietnam*. College Station, Tex.: Texas A&M, 1995.

Moise, Edwin E. *Tonkin Gulf and the Escalation of the Vietnam War*. Chapel Hill, N.C.: University of North Carolina Press, 1996.

Montgomery, John D. *The Politics of Foreign Aid: American Experience in Southeast Asia*. New York: Praeger, 1962.

Morgan, Joseph G. *The Vietnam Lobby: The American Friends of Vietnam, 1955–1975*. Chapel Hill, N.C.: University of North Carolina Press, 1997.

Newman, John M. *JFK and Vietnam: Deception, Intrigue, and the Struggle for Power*. New York: Warner Books, 1992.

Nixon, Richard. *No More Vietnams*. New York: Arbor House, 1985.

Olson, Gregory Allen. *Mansfield and Vietnam: A Study in Rhetorical Adaptation*. East Lansing, Mich.: Michigan State University Press, 1995.

Pfeffer, Richard M. (ed.). *No More Vietnams? The War and the Future of American Foreign Policy*. New York: Harper & Row, 1968.

Podhoretz, Norman. *Why We Were in Vietnam*. New York: Simon and Schuster, 1982.

Poole, Peter. *Eight Presidents and Indochina*. New York: Krieger, 1978.

Prados, John. *The Hidden History of the Vietnam War*. Chicago: Ivan R. Dee, 1995.

Rochester, Stuart, and Frederick Kiley. *Honor Bound: American Prisoners of War in Southeast Asia, 1961–1973*. Annapolis, Md.: Naval Institute Press, 1998.

Rotter, Andrew. *The Path to Vietnam: Origins of the American Commitment to Southeast Asia*. Ithaca, N.Y.: Cornell University Press, 1987.

Schandler, Herbert. *The Unmaking of a President: Lyndon Johnson and Vietnam*. Princeton, N.J.: Princeton University Press, 1977.

Scheer, Robert. *How the United States Got Involved in Vietnam*. Santa Barbara, Calif.: Center for the Study of Democratic Institutions, 1965.

Schlesinger, Arthur M., Jr. *The Bitter Heritage: Vietnam and American Democracy, 1941–1966*. Boston: Houghton Mifflin, 1967.

Schulzinger, Robert D. *A Time for War: The United States and Vietnam, 1941–1975*. New York: Oxford University Press, 1997.

Schwartz, Thomas A. *Lyndon Johnson and Europe: In the Shadow of Vietnam*. Cambridge, Mass.: Harvard University Press, 2003.

Shaplen, Robert. *The Lost Revolution: The U.S. in Vietnam, 1946–1966.* New York: Harper & Row, 1966.

———. *The Road from War, 1965–1970.* New York: Harper & Row, 1970.

Shawcross, William. *Sideshow: Kissinger, Nixon, and the Destruction of Cambodia.* New York: Simon & Schuster, 1979.

Showalter, Dennis E. *An American Dilemma: Vietnam, 1964–1973.* Chicago: Imprint, 1993.

Thies, Wallace J. *When Governments Collide.* Berkeley, Calif.: University of California Press, 1980.

VanDeMark, Brian. *Into the Quagmire: Lyndon Johnson and the Escalation of the Vietnam War.* New York: Oxford University Press, 1991.

Werner, Jayne, and David Hunt (eds.). *The American War in Vietnam.* Ithaca, N.Y.: Cornell Southeast Asia Program, 1993.

Windchy, Eugene. *Tonkin Gulf.* Garden City, N.Y.: 1971.

Woods, Randall Bennett. *J. William Fulbright, Vietnam, and the Search for a Cold War Foreign Policy.* New York: Cambridge University Press, 1998.

Wyatt, Clarence. *Paper Soldiers: The American Press and the Vietnam War.* New York: Norton, 1993.

Zinn, Howard. *The Logic of Withdrawal.* Boston: Beacon, 1967.

4. Involvement by Other Countries

Ang Cheng Guan, *Vietnamese Communists' Relations with China and the Second Indochina Conflict, 1956–1962.* Jefferson, N.C.: McFarland, 1997.

Bloomfield, L. P. *The United Nations and Vietnam.* New York: 1968.

Burstall, Terry. *Vietnam: The Australian Dilemma.* St. Lucia, Qld: University of Queensland Press, 1993.

Doyle, Jeff, Jeffrey Grey, and Peter Pierce. *Australia's Vietnam War.* College Station, Tex.: Texas A & M Press, 2002.

Frankum, Robert Bruce. *The United States and Australia in Vietnam, 1954–1968: Silent Partners.* Lewiston, N.Y.: Edwin Mellon Press, 2001.

Frost, Frank. *Australia's War in Vietnam.* Sydney: Allen & Unwin, 1987.

Gurtov, Melvin. *China and Southeast Asia: The Politics of Survival.* Baltimore: Johns Hopkins University Press, 1971.

King, Peter (ed.). *Australia's Vietnam: Australia in the Second Indochina War.* Sydney: Allen & Unwin, 1983.

McLane, Charles B. *Soviet Strategies in Southeast Asia.* Princeton, N.J.: Princeton University Press, 1966.

McNeill, Ian. *To Long Tan: Australian Army and the Vietnam War, 1950–1966.* St. Leonards, NSW: Allen & Unwin, 1993.

McVey, Ruth T. *The Calcutta Conference and the Southeast Asian Uprisings.* Ithaca, N.Y.: Cornell Modern Indonesia Project, 1958.

Ministry of Foreign Affairs, Socialist Republic of Vietnam. *The Truth about Viet-*

namo–Chinese Relations over the Past Thirty Years. Hanoi: Ministry of Foreign Affairs, 1979.

Murphy, John. *Harvest of Fear: A History of Australia's Vietnam War*. Boulder, Colo.: Westview, 1994.

Sar Desai, D. R. *Indian Foreign Policy in Cambodia, Laos, and Vietnam, 1947–1964*. Berkeley, Calif.: University of California Press, 1968.

Smyser, William R. *The Independent Vietnamese*. Athens, Ohio: Ohio University Center for International Studies, 1980.

Taylor, Jay. *China and Southeast Asia*. New York: Praeger, 1976.

Zagoria, Donald. *Vietnam Triangle*. New York: Pegasus, 1972.

Zasloff, Joseph J. *The Role of the Sanctuary: Communist China's Support to the Vietminh, 1945–1954*. Santa Monica, Calif.: Rand, 1967.

Zhai, Qiang. *China & the Vietnam Wars, 1950–1975*. Chapel Hill, N.C.: University of North Carolina Press, 2000.

5. Negotiations Process

Goodman, Allan. *The Lost Peace*. Stanford, Calif.: Hoover Institution Press, 1978.

Herring, George C. (ed.). *The Secret Diplomacy of the Vietnam War: The Negotiating Volumes of the Pentagon Papers*. Austin, Tex.: University of Texas Press, 1983.

Huntington, Samuel. "The Bases of Accommodation." *Foreign Affairs* 46 (July 1968): 642–656.

Kissinger, Henry. *Ending the Vietnam War: A Personal History of America's Involvement in and Extrication from the Vietnam War*. New York: Simon & Schuster, 2003.

———. "Viet Nam Negotiations." *Foreign Affairs* 47 (January 1969): 211–234.

Lưu Văn Lôi, and Nguyễn Anh Vũ. *Lê Đức Thọ–Kissinger Negotiations in Paris*. Hanoi: Thế Giới, 1996.

Porter, Gareth. *A Peace Denied*. Bloomington, Ind.: Indiana University Press, 1975.

West, Richard. *War and Peace in Vietnam*. London: Sinclair-Stevenson, 1995.

6. End of the War

Cao Văn Viên. *The Final Collapse*. Washington, D.C.: Government Printing Office, 1983.

Dawson, Alan. *55 Days: The Fall of South Vietnam*. Upper Saddle River, N.J.: Prentice-Hall, 1977.

Hoàng Văn Thái. *How South Vietnam Was Liberated (Memoirs)*. Hanoi: Thế Giới, 1996.

Hosmer, Stephen T., Konrad Kellen, and Brian M. Jenkins. *The Fall of South Vietnam: Statements by Military and Civilian Leaders*. New York: Crane, Russak, 1980.

• BIBLIOGRAPHY

McKelvey, Robert S. *A Gift of Barbed Wire: America's Allies Abandoned in South Vietnam*. Seattle, Wash.: University of Washington Press, 2002.

Snepp, Frank. *Decent Interval*. New York: Random House, 1977.

Terzani, Tiziano. *Giai Phong: The Fall and Liberation of Saigon*. New York: St. Martin's, 1976.

Văn Tiến Dũng. *Our Great Spring Victory*. New York: Monthly Review Press, 1977.

Warner, Denis. *Not with Guns Alone*. London: Hutchinson, 1977.

7. The Military War

Air War Study Group. *The Air War in Indochina*. Boston: Beacon, 1972.

Bergerud, Eric M. *The Dynamics of Defeat: The Vietnam War in Hau Nghia Province*. Boulder, Colo.: Westview, 1991.

Cable, Larry. *Conflict of Myths: The Development of American Counterinsurgency Doctrine and the Vietnam War*. New York and London: New York University Press, 1986.

Clodfelter, Micheal. *Vietnam in Military Statistics: A History of the Indochina Wars, 1772–1991*. Jefferson, N.C.: McFarland & Co., 1995.

Conboy, Kenneth J., and Dale Andradé. *Spies and Commandos: How America Lost the Secret War in Vietnam*. Lawrence, Kans.: University of Kansas Press, 2000.

Cutler, Thomas. *Brown Water, Black Berets: Coastal and Riverine Warfare in Vietnam*. Annapolis, Md.: Naval Institute Press, 2000.

Davidson, Phillip. *Vietnam at War: The History, 1946–1975*. Novato, Calif.: Presidio Press, 1988.

Eschmann, Karl J. *Linebacker: The Untold Story of the Air Raids over North Vietnam*. New York: Ivy Books, 1993.

Hixson, Walter L. (ed.). *Military Aspects of the Vietnam Conflict*. New York: Garland, 2000.

Hoang Ngoc Luong. *The General Offensive of 1968–1969*. Washington, D.C.: Center for Military History, 1981.

Humphries, James F. *Through the Valley: Vietnam 1967–1968*. Boulder, Colo.: L. Rienner, 1999.

Kelly, Francis J. *The Green Berets in Vietnam, 1961–1971*. New York: Macmillan, 1991.

Kinnard, Douglas. *The War Managers*. Hanover, N.H.: University Press of New England, 1977.

Littauer, Raphael, and Walter N. Uphoff (eds.). *The Air War in Indochina*. Boston: Beacon, 1972.

Lomperis, Timothy J. *From People's War to People's Rule: Insurgency, Intervention, and the Lessons of Vietnam*. Chapel Hill, N.C.: University of North Carolina Press, 1996.

Marshall, S. L. A. *Battles in the Monsoon: Campaigning in the Central Highlands*. New York: William Morrow & Co. 1967.

McNamara, Francis T. *Escape with Honor: My Last Hours in Vietnam*. Washington, D.C.: Brassey's, 1997.

Moore, Harold G., and Joseph Galloway. *We Were Soldiers Once . . . and Young*. New York: HarperCollins, 1992.

Moyar, Mark. *Phoenix and the Birds of Prey: The CIA's Secret Campaign to Destroy the Viet Cong*. Annapolis, Md.: Naval Institute Press, 1997.

Murphy, Edward F. *Semper Fi—Vietnam: From Da Nang to the DMZ: Marine Corps Campaigns, 1965–1975*. Novato, Calif.: Presidio, 1997.

Pisor, Robert. *The End of the Line: The Siege of Khe Sanh*. New York: Norton, 1982.

Prados, John. *Valley of Decision: The Siege of Khe Sanh*. Boston: Houghton Mifflin, 1991.

Rogers, Bernard. *Cedar Falls, Junction City: A Turning Point*. Washington, D.C.: Government Printing Office, 1974.

Schell, Johathan. *The Military Half: An Account of Destruction in Quang Ngai and Quang Tin*. New York: Random House, 1968.

———. *The Village of Ben Suc*. New York: Random House, 1967.

Serong, Brigadier, F. B. "The 1972 Easter Offensive." *Southeast Asian Perspectives* 10 (Summer 1974).

Sharp, Ulysses S. Grant. *Strategy for Defeat: Vietnam in Retrospect*. San Rafael, Calif.: Presidio, 1978.

Smith, Warner. *Covert Warrior: Fighting the CIA's War in Southeast Asia and China, 1965–1967*. Novato, Calif.: Presidio, 1996.

Spector, Ronald H. *Advice and Support: The Early Years: The U.S. Army in Vietnam*. Washington, D.C.: Center for Military History, 1983.

———. *After Tet: The Bloodiest Year in Vietnam*. New York: Free Press, 1993.

Stevens, Richard L. *Mission on the Ho Chi Minh Trail: Nature, Myth and War in Vietnam*. Norman, Okla.: University of Oklahoma Press, 1995.

Summers, Harry G. *On Strategy: A Critical Analysis of the Vietnam War*. Novato, Calif.: Presidio, 1982.

Taylor, Maxwell D. *Swords and Plowshares*. New York: Norton, 1972.

Tilford, Earl H. *Setup: What the Air Force Did in Vietnam and Why*. Maxwell AFB, Ala.: Air University Press, 1991.

Trường Sơn. *Five Lessons of a Great Victory (Winter 1966–Spring 1977)*. Hanoi: Foreign Languages Press, 1967.

Trullinger, James W. *Village at War: An Account of Conflict in Vietnam*. Stanford, Calif.: Stanford University Press, 1994.

U.S. Marines in Vietnam. 5 vols. Washington, D.C.: U.S. Marine Corps, 1990–1991.

Walt, Lewis W. *Strange War, Strange Strategy: A General's Report on Vietnam*. New York: Funk & Wagnall's, 1970.

Westmoreland, William. *A Soldier Reports*. Garden City, N.Y.: Doubleday, 1976.

Willbanks, Col. James H. *Thiet Giap! The Battle of An Loc, April 1972*. Fort Leavenworth, Kans.: U.S. Army Command and Staff College, 1993.

8. Collections of Articles or Documents

Boettiger, John (ed.). *Vietnam and American Foreign Policy*. Boston: Heath, 1968.

Cameron, Allan W. *Viet-Nam Crisis: A Documentary History*. Ithaca, N.Y.: Cornell University Press, 1971.

Communist Vietnamese Publications. A microfilm series issued by the Library of Congress, Washington, D.C.

Fishel, Wesley (ed.). *Vietnam: Anatomy of a Conflict*. Itasca, Ill.: Peacock, 1968.

Gettleman, Marvin E., H. Bruce Franklin, Jane Franklin, and Marilyn B. Young (eds.). *Vietnam and America: A Documented History*. New York: Grove, 1990.

Gettleman, Marvin E. (ed.). *Vietnam: History, Documents, and Opinions*. New York: Fawcett, 1965.

Lake, Anthony (ed.). *The Legacy of Vietnam*. New York: New York University, 1976.

McGarvey, Patrick (ed.). *Visions of Victory: Selected Communist Military Writings, 1964–1968*. Stanford, Calif.: Hoover Institution Press, 1969.

McMahon, Robert J. (ed.). *Major Problems in the History of the Vietnam War*. 2nd ed. Lexington, Mass.: Heath, 1995.

Pike, Douglas. *Catalog of Viet Cong Documents. Series 2*. Cornell University Library (February 1969).

———. *Documents of the NLFSVN*. Series microfilmed at MIT (1967).

Porter, Gareth (ed.). *Vietnam: The Definitive Documentation of Human Decisions*. 2 vols. New York: New American Library, 1981.

Race Documents. A collection of materials deposited by Jeffrey Race with the Center for Research Libraries, Chicago.

Raskin, Marcus G., and Bernard B. Fall. *The Viet-Nam Reader: Articles and Documents on American Foreign Policy and the Viet-Nam Crisis*. New York: Vintage, 1965.

Schlight, John (ed.). *The Second Indochina War Symposium: Papers and Commentary*. Washington, D.C.: Center for Military History, 1986.

G. Socialist Republic of Vietnam

Beresford, Melanie. *Vietnam: Politics, Economics, and Society*. London: Pinter Publishers, 1988.

Borton, Lady. *After Sorrow: An American among the Vietnamese*. New York: Viking, 1995.

Doan Van Toai, and David Chanoff. *The Vietnamese Gulag*. New York: Simon & Schuster, 1985.

Duiker, William J. *Vietnam since the Fall of Saigon*. Athens, Ohio: Ohio University Monographs in International Studies, 1989.

Gough, Kathleen. *Political Economy in Vietnam.* Meerut, India: Archana, 1990.

Grant, Bruce. *The Boat People: An "Age" Investigation.* Harmondsworth, UK: Penguin, 1979.

Hiebert, Murray. *Vietnam Notebook.* Hong Kong: Review, 1993.

Ho-Tai, Hue-Tam (ed.). *The Country of Memory: Remaking the Past in Late Socialist Vietnam.* Berkeley, Calif.: University of California Press, 2001.

Huynh Sanh Thong (ed.). *To Be Made Over: Tales of Socialist Reeducation in Vietnam.* New Haven, Conn.: Yale Center for International and Area Studies, 1988.

Kolko, Gabriel. *Vietnam: Anatomy of a Peace.* London: Routledge, 1997.

Lacouture, Jean, and Simone Lacouture. *Vietnam: Voyage à travers une victoire.* Paris: Seuil, 1976.

Mai Thu Van. *Vietnam: Un peuple, des voix.* Paris: Pierre Horay, 1983.

Nguyen Duc Nhuan et al. *Le Viet Nam post-révolutionnaire: Population. Économie. Société.* Paris: L'Harmattan, 1987.

Nguyen Long (with Harry Kendall). *After Saigon Fell: Daily Life under the Vietnamese Communists.* Berkeley, Calif.: University of California Institute of East Asian Studies, 1981.

Nguyen Ngoc Huy. *Vietnam under Communist Rule.* Washington, D.C.: George Mason University, 1982.

Nguyen Van Canh. *Vietnam under Communism, 1975–1982.* Stanford, Calif.: Hoover Institution Press, 1983.

Nugent, Nicholas. *Vietnam: The Second Revolution.* Brighton, UK: In Print, 1996.

Sagan, Ginetta, and Stephen Denny. *Violations of Human Rights in the Socialist Republic of Vietnam.* Atherton, Calif.: Aurora Foundation, 1983.

Shaplen, Robert. *Bitter Victory.* New York: Harper & Row, 1986.

Sheehan, Neil. *After the War Was Over: Hanoi and Saigon.* New York: Vintage, 1992.

Thai Quang Trung (ed.). *Vietnam Today: Assessing the New Trends.* New York: Crane Russak, 1990.

II. Politics and Government

A. Government and Institutions

Abuza, Zachary. *Renovating Politics in Contemporary Vietnam.* Boulder, Colo.: Lynne Rienner Publishers, 2001.

Boudarel, Georges et al. *La bureaucratie au Vietnam.* Paris: L'Harmattan, 1983.

Dang Phong, and Melanie Beresford. *Authority Relations and Economic Decision-Making in Vietnam: An Historical Perspective.* Copenhagen: Nordic Institute of Asian Studies, 1998.

Donnell, John C. "Politics in South Vietnam: Doctrines and Authority in Conflict." Ph.D. dissertation, University of California, 1964.

Donnell, John C., and Charles A. Joiner. *Electoral Politics in South Vietnam.* Lexington, Mass.: Heath, 1974.

Dorsey, John T. "Bureaucracy and Political Development in Vietnam." In *Bureaucracy and Political Development*, ed. Joseph LaPolombara. Princeton, N.J.: Princeton University Press, 1963.

Duncanson, Dennis. *Government and Revolution in Vietnam*. London: Oxford University Press, 1968.

Elliott, David W. P. "Institutionalizing the Revolution: Vietnam's Search for a Model of Development." In *Vietnamese Communism in Comparative Perspective*, ed. William S. Turley. Boulder, Colo.: Westview, 1980.

―――. "Revolutionary Reintegration: A Comparison of the Foundations of Post-Liberation Political Systems in North Vietnam and China." Ph.D. dissertation, Cornell University, 1976.

Goodman, Allan E. *Politics in War: The Bases of Political Community in South Vietnam*. Cambridge, Mass.: Harvard University Press, 1973.

Jumper, Roy. "Mandarin Bureaucracy and Politics in South Vietnam." *Pacific Affairs* 30 (March 1957): 47–58.

Kahin, George M. *Government and Politics of Southeast Asia*. Ithaca, N.Y.: Cornell University Press, 1964.

Kerkvliet, Benedict, Russell H. K. Heng, and David W. H. Koh (eds.). *Getting Organized in Vietnam: Moving in and around the Socialist State*. Singapore: Institute of Southeast Asian Studies, 2003.

Mus, Paul. "The Role of the Village in Vietnamese Politics." *Pacific Affairs* 23 (September 1949): 265–271.

Nghiem Dang. *Vietnam: Politics and Public Administration*. Honolulu: East-West Center Press, 1966.

Nguyen Thai. "The Government of Men in the Republic of Vietnam." Ph.D. dissertation, Michigan State University, 1962.

Osborne, Milton E. "The Vietnamese Perception of the Identity of the State." *Australian Outlook* 23 (April 1969).

Pham The Hung. "Village Government in Vietnam, 968–1954." Ph.D. dissertation, Southern Illinois University at Carbondale, 1972.

Porter, Gareth. *Vietnam: The Politics of Bureaucratic Socialism*. Ithaca, N.Y.: Cornell University Press, 1993.

Sacks, I. Milton. "Restructuring the Government in South Vietnam." *Asian Survey* 7 (August 1967).

Stern, Lewis M. *Renovating the Vietnamese Communist Party: Nguyen Van Linh and the Programme for Organizational Reform, 1987–1991*. Singapore: Institute of Southeast Asian Studies, 1993.

Wurfel, David. "The Saigon Political Elite: Focus on Four Cabinets." *Asian Survey* 7 (August 1967).

B. Constitution and Law

Carley, Francis J. "The President in the Constitution of the Republic of Vietnam." *Pacific Affairs* 34 (Summer 1961).

Devereux, Robert. "South Vietnam's New Constitutional Structure." *Asian Survey* 8 (August 1968).

Durand, Bernard, Philippe Langlet, and Chanh Tam Nguyen (eds.). *Histoire de la codification juridique au Vietnam/Lịch sử điển chế pháp luật ở Việt Nam*. Montpellier: Université de Montpellier, 2001.

Falk, Richard A. *The Vietnam War and International Law*. 4 vols. Princeton, N.J.: Princeton University Press, 1967–1976.

Falk, Richard A., Gabriel Kolko, and Robert Jay Lifton (eds.). *Crimes of War: After Songmy*. New York: Random House, 1971.

Fall, Bernard B. "North Viet-Nam's New Constitution and Government." *Pacific Affairs* 33 (September 1960): 282–289.

Fforde, Adam. "Law and Socialist Agricultural Development in Vietnam: the Statute for APCs." *Review of Socialist Law* 10 (1984).

Grant, J. A. C. "The Vietnamese Constitution of 1956." *American Political Science Review* 52 (June 1958) 437–462.

Nguyen Ngoc Huy, and Ta Van Tai. *The Lê Code: Law in Traditional Vietnam*, 3 vols. Athens, Ohio: Ohio University Press, 1987.

The Socialist Republic of Vietnam: Constitution, 1992. Hanoi: Foreign Languages Publishing House, 1992.

A Survey of Vietnam's Legal Framework in Transition. Washington, D.C.: The World Bank, 1994.

Ta Van Tai. "Protection of Women's Civil Rights in Traditional Vietnam: A Comparison of the Code of the Le Dynasty (1428–1788) with Chinese Codes." In *Law and the State in Traditional East Asia: Six Studies on the Sources of East Asian Law*, ed. Brian McKnight. Honolulu: University of Hawaii Press, 1987.

Thayer, Carlyle, and David G. Marr (eds.). *Vietnam and the Rule of Law*. Canberra: Australian National University, 1993.

Vietnam: Juridical Bases, Present Opportunities, Prospects. Hanoi: Thế Giới, 1994.

C. Political Parties

Anh Vân, and Jacqueline Roussel. *An Outline History of the Vietnam Workers' Party*. Hanoi: Foreign Languages Press, 1970.

———. *Mouvements nationaux et lutte des classes du Vietnam*. Paris: Réamur, n.d.

Cook, Megan. *The Constitutionalist Party in Cochin China: The Years of Decline, 1930–1942*. Clayton, Vic.: Monash University Centre of Southeast Asian Studies, 1977.

Dabezies, Pierre. "Forces politiques au Vietnam." Master's thesis, University of Bordeaux, 1955.

Duiker, William J. *The Comintern and Vietnamese Communism*. Athens, Ohio: Ohio University Southeast Asia Program, 1975.

———. "The Revolutionary Youth League: Cradle of Communism in Vietnam." *China Quarterly* 53 (July–September 1972).

Engelbert, Thomas, and Christopher Goscha. *Falling out of Touch: A Study on Vietnamese Communist Policy towards an Emerging Cambodian Communist Movement, 1930–1975.* Clayton, Vic.: Monash University Centre of Southeast Asian Studies, 1995.

Hémery, Daniel. *Révolutionnaires viêtnamiens et pouvoir colonial en Indochine. Communistes, trotskystes, nationalistes à Saigon de 1932 à 1937.* Paris: Maspéro, 1975.

History of the August Revolution. Hanoi: Foreign Language Press, 1972.

Huynh Kim Khanh. *Vietnamese Communism, 1925–1945.* Ithaca, N.Y.: Cornell University Press, 1982.

Ngo Van. *Revolutionaries They Could Not Break: The Fight for the Fourth International in Indochina 1930–1945.* London: Index Books, 1995.

Nguyễn Ngọc Huy. *Political Parties in Vietnam.* Saigon: Vietnamese Council on Foreign Relations, 1971.

Pike, Douglas. *A History of Vietnamese Communism, 1925–1978.* Stanford, Calif.: Hoover Institution Press, 1978.

Rousset, Pierre. *Le Parti Communiste Vietnamien.* Paris: Maspéro, 1975.

Sacks, I. Milton. "Communism, and Nationalism in Vietnam, 1918–1946." Ph.D. dissertation, Yale University, 1960.

———. "Marxism in Vietnam." In *Marxism in Southeast Asia*, ed. Frank Trager. Stanford, Calif.: Stanford University Press, 1959.

Scigliano, Robert G. "Political Parties in South Vietnam under the Republic." *Pacific Affairs* 33 (December 1960): 327–346.

Smith, Ralph B. "Bui Quang Chieu and the Constitutionalist Party in French Cochin China." *Modern Asian Studies* 3 (April 1969): 131–150.

Thompson, Virginia, and Richard Adloff. *The Left Wing in Southeast Asia.* New York: Sloane, 1950.

Turner, Robert F. *Vietnamese Communism: Its Origins and Development.* Stanford, Calif.: Hoover Institution Press, 1975.

D. Armed Forces

Collins, J. Lawton. *The Development and Training of the South Vietnamese Army, 1950–1972.* Washington, D.C.: U.S. Gov't Printing Office, 1975.

Pike, Douglas. *PAVN: The People's Army of Vietnam.* Novato, Cal.: Presidio, 1986.

———. "The People's Army of Vietnam." In *The Armed Forces in Contemporary Asian Societies*, ed. Edward A. Olsen and Stephen Jurika. Boulder, Colo.: Westview, 1986.

Thayer, Carlyle A. *The Vietnam People's Army under Doi Moi.* Singapore: Institute of Southeast Asian Studies, 1994.

Turley, William S. "Army, Party, and Society in the Democratic Republic of Vietnam." Ph.D. dissertation, University of Washington, 1972.

E. Biographies and Memoirs

Bao Dai. *Le dragon d'Annam.* Paris: Plon, 1980.

Boudarel, Georges. *Giap.* Paris: Atlas, 1977.

Boudarel, Georges (tr.). "Phan Bội Châu: Mémoires." *France-Asie* 22 (3rd–4th Trimestre, 1968).

Bouscaren, Anthony T. *The Last of the Mandarins: Diem of Vietnam.* Pittsburgh: Duquesne University Press, 1965.

Brocheux, Pierre. *Hồ Chí Minh.* Paris: Presses de Sciences Politiques, 2000.

Bui Diem, with David Chanoff. *In the Jaws of History.* Boston: Houghton Mifflin, 1987.

Bùi Tín. *Following Ho Chi Minh: Memoirs of a North Vietnamese Colonel.* Honolulu: University of Hawaii Press, 1995.

Chack, Paul. *Hoang Tham: Pirate.* Paris: Éditions de France, 1933.

Chu Văn Tấn. *Reminiscences on the Army for National Salvation,* trans. Mai Elliott. Ithaca, N.Y.: Cornell University Southeast Asia Program, 1974.

Commission for Research on Party History. *Ho Chi Minh.* Hanoi: Thế Giới, 1995.

Das, S. R. Mohan. *Ho Chi Minh: Nationalist or Soviet Agent?* Bombay: Democratic Research Service, 1951.

Duiker, William S. *Ho Chi Minh.* New York: Hyperion, 2000.

Fenn, Charles. *Ho Chi Minh: A Biographical Introduction.* London: Studio Vista, 1973.

Figuères, Léo, and Charles Fourniau. *Ho Chi Minh: Notre camarade.* Paris: Éditions Sociales, 1970.

Gaspard, Thu Trang. *Ho Chi Minh à Paris (1917–1923).* Paris: L'Harmattan, 1992.

Halberstam, David. *Ho.* New York: Random House, 1971.

Hémery, Daniel. *Hô Chi Minh. De l'Indochine au Vietnam.* Paris: Gallimard, 1990.

Hoài Thanh et al. *Uncle Ho.* Hanoi: Foreign Languages Press, 1962.

Hoàng Văn Hoan. *A Drop in the Ocean.* Beijing: Foreign Language Publishing House, 1988.

Kobelev, Evgenyi. *Ho Chi Minh.* New York: Progress, 1989.

Lacouture, Jean. *Ho Chi Minh: A Political Biography,* trans. Peter Wiles. New York: Random House, 1968.

Macdonald, Peter. *Giap: Victor in Vietnam.* New York: Norton, 1993.

Neumann-Hoditz, Reinhold. *Portrait of Ho Chi Minh.* New York: Herder, 1972.

Nguyen Cao Ky, *Buddha's Child: My Fight to Save Vietnam.* New York: St. Martin's Press, 2002.

———. *Twenty Years and Twenty Days.* New York: Stein & Day, 1976.

Nguyen Khac Huyen. *Vision Accomplished?* New York: Collier, 1971.

Nguyễn Khanh Toàn et al. *Avec l'Oncle Ho.* Hanoi: Foreign Languages Press, 1972.

O'Neill, Robert. *General Giap: Politician and Strategist.* New York: Praeger, 1969.

Phạm Văn Đồng et al. *President Ho Chi Minh.* Hanoi: Foreign Languages Press, 1960.

Quinn-Judge, Sophie. *Ho Chi Minh: The Missing Years 1919–1941.* London: Hurst & Company, 2003.

Rageau, Christiane P. *Ho Chi Minh.* Paris: Éditions Universitaires, 1970.

Sainteny, Jean. *Ho Chi Minh and his Vietnam.* Chicago: Cowles, 1971.

Sheehan, Neil. *A Bright Shining Lie: John Paul Vann and America in Vietnam.* New York: Random House, 1988.

Sihanouk, Norodom. *My War with the CIA.* Baltimore: Pantheon, 1973.

Trần Dân Tiến. *Glimpses of the Life of Ho Chi Minh.* Hanoi: Foreign Languages Press, 1958.

Trường Chinh. *President Ho Chi Minh.* Hanoi: Foreign Languages Press, 1966.

Warner, Denis. *The Last Confucian.* New York: Macmillan, 1963.

F. *International Politics and Foreign Policy*

Brown, Frederick Z. *Second Chance: The United States and Indochina in the 1990s.* New York: Council on Foreign Relations Press, 1989.

Burchett, Wilfred. *The China—Cambodia—Vietnam Triangle.* New York: Vanguard, 1979.

Chanda, Nayan. *Brother Enemy: The War after the War.* New York: Harcourt Brace Jovanovich, 1986.

Chang Pao-min. *The Sino-Vietnamese Territorial Dispute.* New York: Praeger, 1985.

Chen, King C. *China's War with Vietnam, 1979.* Stanford, Calif.: Hoover Institution, 1987.

Chomsky, Noam, and Edward Herman. *After the Cataclysm: Postwar Indochina and the Reconstruction of Imperial Ideology.* Montreal: Black Rose Books, 1979.

Duiker, William J. *China and Vietnam: The Roots of Conflict.* Berkeley, Calif.: University of California Institute of East Asian Studies, 1986.

Elliott, David W. P. (ed.). *The Third Indochina Conflict.* Boulder, Colo.: Westview, 1981.

Evans, Grant, and Kelvin Rowley. *Red Brotherhood at War.* Rev. ed. London: Verso, 1990.

Fifield, Russell. *The Diplomacy of Southeast Asia, 1945–1958.* New York: Harper & Row, 1958.

Frost, Frank. *Vietnam's Foreign Relations: Dynamics of Change.* Singapore: Institute of Southeast Asian Studies, 1993.

Gilks, Anne. *The Breakdown of the Sino–Vietnamese Alliance, 1970–1979.* Berkeley, Calif.: University of California Center for Chinese Studies, 1992.

Hurst, Steven. *The Carter Administration and Vietnam.* New York: St. Martin's, 1996.

Lawson, Eugene K. *The Sino–Vietnamese Conflict.* New York: Praeger, 1984.

Morley, James, and Masashi Nishihara. *Vietnam Joins the World.* Armonk, N.Y.: M.E. Sharpe, 1997.

Morris, Stephen J. *Why Vietnam Invaded Cambodia: Political Culture and the Causes of War*. Stanford, Calif.: Stanford University Press, 1999.

Pike, Douglas. *Vietnam and the Soviet Union: Anatomy of an Alliance*. Boulder, Colo.: Westview, 1987.

Poole, Peter A. "Vietnam: Focus of Regional Conflict." *International Security Review* 7(2) (Summer 1982).

Porter, Gareth. "Hanoi's Strategic Perspective and the Sino–Vietnamese Conflict." *Pacific Affairs* 57 (Spring 1984).

Ross, Robert A. *The Indochina Tangle: China's Vietnam Policy, 1975–1979*. New York: Columbia University Press, 1988.

Thayer, Carlyle, and Ramses Amer (eds.). *Vietnamese Foreign Policy in Transition*. Singapore: ISEAS, 1999.

Ton That Thien. *The Foreign Politics of the Communist Party of Vietnam: A Study of Communist Tactics*. New York: C. Russak. 1989.

Turley, William S. (ed.). *Confrontation or Coexistence: The Future of ASEAN–Vietnam Relations*. Bangkok: Institute of Security and International Studies, 1985.

Turley, William S., and Jeffrey Race. "The Third Indochina War." *Foreign Policy* 38 (Spring 1980): 92–116.

Van der Kroef, Justus. "The South China Sea: Competing Claims and Strategic Conflict." *International Security Review* 73 (Fall 1982).

G. Collected Writings

Fall, Bernard B. *Ho Chi Minh on Revolution*. New York: Praeger, 1960.

Hồ Chí Minh. *Prison Diary*. Hanoi: Foreign Languages Press, 1966.

———. *Selected Works*. 4 vols. Hanoi: Foreign Languages Press, 1961–1962.

———. *Selected Writings*. Hanoi: Foreign Languages Press, 1977.

Lê Duẩn. *On the Right of Collective Mastery*. Hanoi: Foreign Languages Press, 1980.

———. *Some Questions Concerning the International Tasks of Our Party*. Peking: Foreign Languages Press, 1964.

———. *The Vietnamese Revolution: Fundamental Problems, Essential Tasks*. New York: International Publishers, 1971.

Marr, David G. *Reflections from Captivity: Phan Boi Chau and Ho Chi Minh*. Athens: Ohio University Southeast Asia Translation Series, 1978.

Nguyễn Văn Linh. *Vietnam Urgent Problems*. Hanoi: Foreign Languages Publishing House, 1988.

Phạm Văn Đồng. *Some Cultural Problems*. Hanoi: Foreign Languages Press, 1981.

Stettler, Russell (ed.). *The Military Art of People's War*. New York: Monthly Review Press, 1970.

Tran Van Dinh (ed.). *This Nation and Socialism Are One: Selected Writings of Le Duan*. Chicago: Vanguard Books, 1976.

Trường Chinh. *The August Revolution*. Hanoi: Foreign Languages Press, 1958.
————. *Primer for Revolt: The Communist Takeover in Vietnam*. New York: Praeger, 1963.
————. *The Resistance Will Win*. Hanoi: Foreign Languages Press, 1960.
————. *Selected Writings*. Hanoi: Foreign Languages Press, 1977.
Trường Chinh, and Võ Nguyên Giáp. *The Peasant Question (1937–1938)*, trans. Christine Pelzer White. Ithaca, N.Y.: Cornell University Southeast Asia Program, 1974.
Võ Nguyên Giáp. *Banner of People's War: The Party's Military Line*. New York: 1970.
————. *Big Victory, Great Task*. New York: Praeger, 1968.
————. *Dien Bien Phu*. Hanoi: Foreign Languages Press, 1974.
————. *People's War, People's Army*. New York: Praeger, 1962.

III. Society
A. Anthropology and Ethnography

Bertrand, Gabrielle. *Le peuple de la jungle. Hommes, bêtes et légendes du pays Moï*. Paris: Je Sers, 1952.
Boulbet, Jean. *Pays de Maa', domaine des génies (Nggar Maa', nggar yaang)*. Paris: École Française d'Extrême-Orient, 1967.
————. *Paysans de la forêt*. Paris: Publications de l'École Française d'Extrême-Orient, 1975.
Bourotte, Bernard. *History of the Mountain People of Southern Indochina up to 1945*. Washington: USAID translation, 1967.
Cadière, Léopold et al. *Vietnamese Ethnographic Papers*. New Haven, Conn.: Human Relations Area Files, 1953.
Condominas, Georges. *L'exotique est quotidien*. Paris: Plon, 1965.
————. *We Have Eaten the Forest*. New York: Kodansha, 1994.
Đặng Nghiêm Vạn. *Ethnological and Religious Problems in Vietnam*. Hanoi: Social Sciences Publishing House, 1998.
Đặng Nghiêm Vạn et al. *Ethnic Minorities in Vietnam*. Hanoi: Thế Giới, 1993.
Doling, Tim. *North East Vietnam: Mountains and Ethnic Minorities*. Hanoi: Thế Giới, 2000.
Dournes, Jacques. *Coordonnées: Structures jörai familiales et sociales*. Paris: Institut d'Ethnologie, 1972.
————. *Pötao: Une théorie du pouvoir chez les Indochinois Jörai*. Paris: Flammarion, 1977.
Embree, John F. *Ethnic Groups of Northern Southeast Asia*. New Haven, Conn.: Yale University Press, 1950.
Gourou, Pierre. *The Peasant in the Tonkin Delta: A Study of Human Geography*, 2 vols. New Haven, Conn.: Human Relations Area Files, 1955.
Gregerson, Marilyn, J. "The Ethnic Minorities of Vietnam." *Southeast Asia: An International Quarterly* 2 (Winter 1972).

Guilleminet, Paul. *Coutumier de la tribu Bahnar, des Sedang et des Jarai de la Province de Kontum.* Hanoi: École Française d'Extrême-Orient, 1952.

Hautecloque-Howe, Anne de. *Les Rhadés. Une société de droit maternel.* Paris: Éditions du CNRS, 1987.

Hickey, Gerald C. *Free in the Forest.* New Haven, Conn.: Yale University Press, 1982.

———. *The Highland People of South Vietnam: Social and Economic Development.* Santa Monica, Calif.: Rand, 1967.

———. *Kingdom in the Morning Mist.* Philadelphia: University of Pennsylvania Press, 1988.

———. *Shattered World: Adaptation and Survival among Vietnam's Highland Peoples during the Vietnam War.* Philadelphia: University of Pennsylvania Press, 1993.

———. *Sons of the Mountains.* New Haven, Conn.: Yale University Press, 1982.

Jamieson, Neil, Le Trong Cuc, and A. Terry Rambo. *The Development Crisis in Vietnam's Mountains.* Honolulu: East-West Center, 1998.

Janse, Olov R. T. *The Peoples of French Indochina.* Washington, D.C.: Smithsonian Institution, 1944.

Kahin, George M. "Minorities in the Democratic Republic of Vietnam." *Asian Survey* 12 (July 1972).

Kunstadter, Peter (ed.). *Southeast Asian Tribes, Minorities, and Nations.* 2 vols. Princeton, N.J.: Princeton University Press, 1967.

Lafont, Pierre-Bernard. *Toloi Djuat: Coutumier de la tribu Jarai.* Paris: École Française d'Extrême-Orient, 1963.

Le Bar, Frank M. et al. *Ethnic Groups of Mainland Southeast Asia.* New Haven, Conn.: Human Relations Area Files, 1964.

Maurice, Albert-Marie. *Croyances et pratiques religieuses des Montagnards du Centre-Vietnam.* Paris: L'Harmattan, 2002.

———. *Les Mnong des Hauts-Plateaux (Centre-Vietnam).* Paris: L'Harmattan, 1993.

Mole, Robert L. *The Montagnards of South Vietnam.* Tokyo: Tuttle, 1970.

Nguyễn Khắc Viện (ed.). *Ethnographic Data.* Vietnamese Studies 32. Hanoi: Foreign Languages Press, 1972.

———. *Mountain Regions and National Minorities in the Democratic Republic of Vietnam.* Vietnamese Studies 15. Hanoi: Foreign Languages Press, 1968.

Provencher, Ronald. *Mainland Southeast Asia: An Anthropological Perspective.* Pacific Palasades, Calif.: Goodyear, 1975.

Purcell, Victor W. *The Chinese in Southeast Asia.* London: Oxford University Press, 1951.

Rambo, A. Terry, Robert Reed, Le Trong Cuc, and Michael DiGregorio. *The Challenge of Highland Development of Vietnam.* Honolulu: East-West Center, 1995.

Salemink, Oscar. *The Ethnography of Vietnam's Central Highlanders: A Historical Contextualization, 1850–1900.* London and New York: RoutledgeCurzon, 2003.

Schrock, Joan L. et al. (eds.). *Minority Groups in the Republic of Vietnam.* Washington, D.C.: Government Printing Office, 1967.

Stern, Lewis M. "The Overseas Chinese in the Socialist Republic of Vietnam." *Asian Survey* 25 (May 1985).

Tran Khanh. *The Ethnic Chinese and Economic Development in Vietnam.* Singapore: Institute of Southeast Asian Studies, 1993.

B. Archeology

Archeological Data. Vietnamese Studies 46. Hanoi: n.d.

Davidson, Jeremy H. C. S. "Archeology in Northern Vietnam since 1954." In *Early Southeast Asia: Essays in Archeology, History, and Historical Geography,* ed. Ralph B. Smith and William Watson. New York: Oxford University Press, 1979.

Hà Văn Tấn, "Nouvelles recherches préhistoriques et protohistoriques au Vietnam." *Bulletin de l'École Française d'Extrême-Orient* 68 (1980).

Janse, Olov R. *Archeological Research in Indo-China.* Cambridge, Mass.: Harvard University Press, 1947.

Malleret, Louis. *L'archéologie du delta du Mekong.* 4 vols. Paris: École Française d'Extrême-Orient, 1959.

C. Education

Anonymous. *The Struggle against Illiteracy in Vietnam.* Hanoi: Foreign Languages Press, 1959.

Education in the DRV. Vietnamese Studies 5. Hanoi: Foreign Languages Press, 1965.

General Education in the DRV. Vietnamese Studies 30. Hanoi: Foreign Languages Press, 1971.

Kelly, Gail P. "Colonial Schools in Vietnam: Policy, and Practice." In *Education and Colonialism,* ed. Phillip G. Altbach and Gail P. Kelly. New York: Longmans, 1978.

———. "Franco–Vietnamese Schools, 1918–1938." Ph.D. dissertation, University of Wisconsin, Madison, 1975.

———. *French Colonial Education: Essays on Vietnam and West Africa,* ed. David H. Kelly. New York: AMS Press, 2000.

Phạm Minh Hắc (ed.). *Education in Vietnam: Situation, Issues, Policies.* Hanoi: Ministry of Education, 1993.

Pike, Edgar. "Problems of Education in Vietnam." In *Problems of Freedom: South Vietnam since Independence,* ed. Wesley Fishel. New York: Free Press of Glencoe, 1961.

Sloper, David, and Le Thac Can. *Higher Education in Vietnam: Change and Response.* New York: St. Martin's, 1995.

Tongas, Gérard. "Indoctrination Replaces Education." *China Quarterly* 9 (January–March 1962).

Trần Văn Nhung. *Vietnam Education and Training Directory.* Hanoi: Educational Publishers, 1995.

Trinh Van Thao. *L'école française en Indochine.* Paris: Karthala, 1995.

Vu Tam Ich. *A Historical Survey of Educational Developments in Vietnam.* Lexington, Ky.: University of Kentucky, 1959.

Woodside, Alexander B. "Problems of Education in the Vietnamese and Chinese Revolutions." *Pacific Affairs* (Winter 1976–1977).

D. Religion

Adriano di St. Thecla. *Opusculum de Sectis apud Sinenses et Tunkinenses (A Small Treatise on the Sects among the Chinese and Tonkinese: A Study of Religion in China and North Vietnam in the Eighteenth Century),* tr. Olga Dror. Ithaca, N.Y.: Cornell Southeast Asia Program, 2002.

Cadière, Leopold M. *Croyances et pratiques réligieuses des Vietnamiens.* Saigon: Imprimerie Nouvelle d'Extrême-Orient, 1958.

Do Thien. *Vietnamese Supernaturalism: Views from the Southern Region.* London and New York: Routledge, 2003.

Dumoutier, Gustave. *Annamese Religions* (translation of *Les cultes annamites*). New Haven, Conn.: Human Relations Area Files, 1955.

Durand, Maurice. *Technique et panthéon des médiums viêtnamiens.* Paris: École Française d'Extrême-Orient, 1989.

Fall, Bernard B. "The Political-Religious Sects of Viet-Nam." *Pacific Affairs* 28 (September 1955).

Gheddo, Pierre. *The Cross and the Bo Tree: Catholics and Buddhists in Vietnam.* New York: Twin Circle, 1970.

Gobron, Gabriel. *History and Philosophy of Caodaism,* trans. Pham Xuan Thai. Saigon: Tứ Hải, 1950.

Hà Văn Tấn. *Buddhist Temples in Vietnam.* Hanoi: Social Sciences Publishers, 1992.

Ho-Tai, Hue-Tam. *Millenarianism and Peasant Politics in Vietnam.* Cambridge, Mass.: Harvard University Press, 1983.

Malarney, Shaun Kingsley. *Culture, Ritual and Revolution in Vietnam.* London: RoutledgeCurzon, 2002.

Marr, David G. "Church and State in Vietnam." *Indochina Issues* 47 (April 1987).

McLane, John R. "Archaic Movements and Revolution in Southern Vietnam." In *National Liberation: Revolution in the Third World,* ed. Norman Miller and Roderick Aya. New York: Free Press, 1971.

Nguyễn Tài Thư. *History of Buddhism in Vietnam.* Hanoi: Thế Giới, 1992.

Taylor, Philip. *Goddess on the Rise: Pilgrimage and Popular Religion in Vietnam.* Honolulu: University of Hawaii, 2004.

Oliver, Victor L. *Cao Dai Spiritism: A Study of Religion in Vietnamese Society.* Leiden: Brill, 1976.

Robadey, Jean-Louis, Jeffrey Micklos, and Anne Himmelfarb. *Vietnam: Free Market Captive Conscience: A Puebla Institute Report on Religious Repression.* Washington, D.C.: Puebla Institute, 1994.
Schecter, Jerrold. *The New Face of Buddha: Buddhism and Political Power in Southeast Asia.* New York: Coward, 1967.
Nhat Hanh, Thich. *Vietnam: Lotus in a Sea of Fire.* New York: Hill & Wang, 1967.
Tran Thi Lien. *Les catholiques viêtnamiens pendant la guerre d'indépendance (1945–1954).* Paris: L'Harmattan, 2001.
Tran Van Giap. "Le Bouddhisme en Annam des origines au XIIIe siècle." *Bulletin de l'Ecole Francaise d'Extreme Orient* 32 (1932).
Werner, Jayne. *Peasant Politics and Religious Sectarianism: Peasant and Priest in the Cao Dai in Vietnam.* New Haven, Conn.: Yale Southeast Asia Studies, 1981.
———. "Vietnamese Communism and Religious Sectarianism." In *Vietnamese Communism in Comparative Perspective,* ed. William S. Turley. Boulder, Colo.: Westview, 1980.

E. Sociology

Banister, Judith. *Vietnam Population Dynamics and Prospects.* Berkeley, Calif.: Institute of East Asian Studies, 1993.
Công Huyền Tôn Nữ Thị Nha Trang. "The Traditional Roles of Women as Reflected in Oral and Written Vietnamese Literature." Ph.D. dissertation, University of California, Berkeley, 1973.
Coulet, Georges. *Les sociétés secrètes en terre d'Annam.* Paris: Ardin, 1926.
Demarest, Andre. *La formation des classes sociales en pays annamite.* Lyon: Ferreol, 1935.
Desbarats, Jacqueline. "Population Relocation Programs in Socialist Vietnam: Economic Rationale or Class Struggle." *Indochina Reports* (Singapore) (April–June 1987).
Drummond, Lisa, and Mandy Thomas (eds.). *Consuming Urban Culture in Contemporary Vietnam.* London and New York: Routledge, 2003.
Eisen, Arlene. *Women and Revolution in Vietnam.* London: Zed Books, 1984.
Goodman, Allan E., and Lawrence M. Franks. "The Dynamics of Migration to Saigon, 1964–1972." *Pacific Affairs* 48 (Summer 1975).
Gourou, Pierre. *Les paysans du delta tonkinois: Étude de géographie humaine.* Paris: Éditions d'Art et d'Histoire, 1936.
Haines, David W. "Vietnamese Kinship, Gender Roles, and Societal Diversity: Some Lessons from Research on Refugees." *Vietnam Forum* 8 (Summer–Fall 1986).
Hendry, James B. *The Small World of Khanh Hau.* Chicago: Aldine, 1964.
Hickey, Gerald C. "Social Systems of Northern Vietnam." Ph.D. diss., University of Chicago, 1958.
———. *Village in Vietnam.* New Haven, Conn.: Yale University Press, 1964.

Hoskins, Marilyn W., and Eleanor Shepherd. *Life in a Vietnamese Urban Quarter.* Carbondale, Ill.: Southern Illinois University Press, 1971.

Jamieson, Neil. "The Traditional Family in Vietnam" and "The Traditional Village in Vietnam." *Vietnam Forum* 7 (Summer–Fall 1986) and 8 (Winter–Spring 1986).

Kleinen, John. *Facing the Future, Reviving the Past: A Study of Social Change in a Northern Vietnamese Village.* Singapore: Institute of Southeast Asian Studies, 1999.

Lê Thi, and Đỗ Thị Bình (eds.). *Ten Years of Progress, Vietnamese Women from 1985 to 1995.* Hanoi: Phụ Nữ, 1997.

Mai Thị Tu, and Lê Thị Nhâm Tuyết. *Women in Viet Nam.* Hanoi: Foreign Languages Press, 1978.

Ngo Vinh Long, and Nguyen Hoi Chan. *Vietnamese Women in Society and Revolution.* 3 vols. Cambridge, Mass.: Vietnamese Resource Center, 1974.

Popkin, Samuel. *The Rational Peasant: The Political Economy of Rural Society in Vietnam.* Berkeley, Calif.: University of California Press, 1979.

Scott, James C. *The Moral Economy of the Peasant.* New Haven, Conn.: Yale University Press, 1976.

Taylor, Philip. *Fragments of the Present: Searching for Modernity in Vietnam's South.* Sydney: Allen & Unwin, 2001.

Thrift, Nigel, and Dean Forbes. *The Price of War: Urbanization in Vietnam, 1954–1985.* London: Allen & Unwin, 1986.

Thanh-Cam Vecchi, Nicole. *Viet Nam: HIV, the New Epidemic.* New Haven, Conn.: Yale School of Medicine, 1992.

Winston, Jane Bradley, and Leakthina Chau-Pech Ollier (eds.). *Of Vietnam: Identities in Dialogue.* New York: Palgrave, 2001.

F. Tourism/Contemporary Accounts

Bekaert, Jacques. *Vietnam: A Portrait.* Hong Kong: Elsworth, 1994.

Brownmiller, Susan. *Seeing Vietnam: Encounters of the Road and Heart.* New York: HarperCollins, 1994.

Coffey, Maria. *Three Moons in Vietnam: A Haphazard Journey by Boat and Bicycle.* London: Little, Brown, 1996.

Cohen, Barbara. *The Vietnam Guidebook.* 3rd ed. New York: Houghton Mifflin, 1993.

Gift, Virginia. *Hanoi Today.* Columbia, Md.: Ebory, 1993.

Kamm, Henry. *Dragon Ascending: Vietnam and the Vietnamese.* New York: Arcade, 1996.

Lamb, David. *Vietnam, Now: A Reporter Returns.* New York: Public Affairs, 2002.

Leonard, Peter. *Saigon: A Guidebook.* 3rd ed. Denver, Colo.: Vietnam Trading Co., 1995.

Rodgers, Mary M. (ed.). *Vietnam: In Pictures.* Minneapolis, Minn.: Lerner, 1994.

Sachs, Dana. *A House on Dream Street: Memoir of an American Woman in Vietnam.* Chapel Hill, N.C.: Algonquin Books, 2000.
Schramm-Evans, Zoe. *A Phoenix Rising: Impressions of Vietnam.* London: Pandora, 1996.
Shillue, Edith. *Earth and Water: Encounters in Viet Nam.* Amherst, Mass.: University of Massachusetts Press, 1997.
Templer, Robert. *Shadows and Wind: A View of Modern Vietnam.* New York: Penguin, 1999.

G. Geography

Langlet, Philippe, and Quach Thanh Tam. *Atlas historique des six provinces du Sud (Nam Ky) du Viet Nam.* Paris: Les Indes Savantes, 2001.
Nguyễn Trọng Diệu. *Geography of Vietnam.* Hanoi: Thế Giới, 1992.
Papin, Philippe, and Philippe LeFailler. *Đồng Khánh địa dư chí. Géographie de l'Empereur Đồng Khánh.* Hanoi: Thống Nhất, 2001.
Robequain, Charles. *Le Thanh Hoá. Étude géographique d'une province annamite.* 2 vols. Paris: Éditions G. Van Oest, 1929.
Ulack, Richard, and Gyula Pauer. *Atlas of Southeast Asia.* New York: Macmillan, 1989.
Vietnam: The Land and the People. Hanoi: Thế Giới, 2001.

IV. The Economy
A. Agriculture

Anderson, Kym. *Vietnam's Transforming Economy and WTO Accession: Implications for Agricultural and Rural Development.* Singapore: Institute of Southeast Asian Studies, 1999.
Bredo, William et al. "Vietnam: Politics, Land Reform, and Development in the Countryside. A Symposium." In *Asian Survey* 10 (August 1970).
————. *Land Reform in Vietnam.* Menlo Park, Calif.: Stanford Research Institute, 1968.
Brocheux, Pierre. *The Mekong Delta: Ecology, Economics and Revolution, 1860–1960.* Madison, Wis.: University of Wisconsin Center for Southeast Asian Studies, 1994.
Chaliand, Gérard. *The Peasants of North Vietnam.* Baltimore: Penguin, 1969.
Dahm, Bernhard, and Vincent Houben (eds.). *Vietnamese Villages in Transition. Background and Consequences of Reform Policies in Rural Vietnam.* Passau, Germany: Passau Contributions to Southeast Asian Studies, 1998.
Dumont, René. *La culture du riz dans le delta du Tonkin.* Pattani, Thailand: Prince of Songkla University, 1995. (reprint)
Fforde, Adam. *The Agrarian Question in North Vietnam, 1974–1979.* Armonk, N.Y.: Sharpe, 1989.
————. *The Historical Background to Agricultural Collectivization in North Viet-*

nam: *The Changing Role of Corporate Economic Power.* Discussion Paper 148 (November 1981). Birkbeck College, London.

———. "Problems of Agricultural Development in North Vietnam." Ph.D. dissertation, Cambridge University, 1982.

———. *Specific Aspects of the Collectivization of Wet-Rice Cultivation: Reflections on Vietnamese Experience.* Discussion Paper 159 (July 1984). Birkbeck College, London.

Gittinger, J. Price. "Communist Land Policy in North Vietnam." *Far Eastern Survey* 28 (8) (August 1959).

———. "Agrarian Reform." In *Vietnam: The First Five Years,* ed. Richard W. Lindholm. East Lansing, Mich.: Michigan State University, 1959.

Gourou, Pierre. *L'utilisation du sol en Indochine Française.* Paris: Hartmann, 1940.

Hargrove, Thomas R. *A Dragon Lives Forever: War and Rice in Vietnam's Mekong Delta, 1969–1991.* New York: Ballantine, 1994.

Henry, Yves. *Économie agricole de l'Indochine.* Hanoi: Imprimerie d'Extrême-Orient, 1932.

Hy Van Luong. *Revolution in the Village: Tradition and Transformation in North Vietnam, 1925–1988.* Honolulu: University of Hawaii Press, 1992.

Kerkvliet, Benedict. *The Power of Everyday Politics: How Peasants Transformed National Policy.* Ithaca, N.Y.: Cornell University Press, 2005.

Ladejinsky, Wolf. "Agrarian Reform in Vietnam." In *Problems of Freedom: South Vietnam since Independence,* ed. Wesley Fishel. New York: Free Press of Glencoe, 1961.

Liljeström, Rita et al. *Profit and Poverty in Rural Vietnam: Winners and Losers of a Dismantled Revolution.* Richmond, UK: Curzon, 1998.

The Mekong Delta: Social and Economic Conditions. Vietnamese Studies 75 (New Series 5). Hanoi: Foreign Languages Press, 1984.

Moise, Edwin. *Land Reform in China and Vietnam.* Chapel Hill, N.C.: University of North Carolina Press, 1983.

Nguyen Tien Hung. "The Red River, Its Dikes, and North Viet-Nam's Economy." *Vietnam Bulletin* 7 (September 1972).

Quang Truong. *Agricultural Collectivization and Rural Development in Vietnam: A North/South Study (1955–1985).* Amsterdam: Vrije Universiteit te Amsterdam, 1987.

Sanson, Robert L. *The Economics of Insurgency in the Mekong Delta of Vietnam.* Cambridge, Mass.: MIT Press, 1970.

Tạ Thị Thùy. *Les concessions agricoles françaises au Tonkin de 1884 à 1918.* Hanoi: Thế Giới, 2001.

U.S. Department of Agriculture. *Agricultural Economy of North Vietnam.* Washington, D.C.: Government Printing Office, 1965.

Vickerman, Andrew. *The Fate of the Peasantry: Premature "Transition to Socialism" in the Democratic Republic of Vietnam.* New Haven, Conn.: Yale University Southeast Asian Series, 1980.

Wurfel, David. "Agrarian Reform in the Republic of Vietnam." *Far Eastern Survey* 26 (6) (June 1957).

Zasloff, Joseph J. "Rural Resettlement in South Vietnam." *Pacific Affairs* 35 (Winter 1962).

B. Economic Development

Bassino, Jean-Pascal et al. (eds.). *Quantitative Economic History of Vietnam, 1900–1990.* Tokyo: Hitotsubashi University Institute of Economic Research, 2000.

Beresford, Melanie. *National Unification and Economic Development in Vietnam.* London: Macmillan, 1989.

Bernard, Paul. *Le problème économique indochinois.* Paris: Nouvelles Éditions Latines, 1934.

Boarman, Patrick M. (ed.). *The Economy of South Vietnam: A Beginning.* Los Angeles: Center for International Business, 1973.

———. "Viet-Nam's Postwar Development: A Symposium." *Asian Survey* 11 (April 1971).

Boothroyd, Peter, and Pham Xuan Nam. *Socioeconomic Renovation in Vietnam: The Origin, Evolution, and Impact of Doi Moi.* Ottawa: International Development Research Centre, 2000.

Chan, Anita, Benedict Kerkvliet, and Jonathan Unger. *Transforming Asian Socialism: China and Vietnam Compared.* Lanham, Md.: Rowman & Littlefield, 1999.

Chin, Anthony, and Ng Hock Guan (eds.). *Economic Management and Transition towards a Market Economy: An Asian Perspective.* Singapore: World Scientific, 1996.

Dacy, Douglas C. *Foreign Aid, War, and Economic Development: South Vietnam, 1955–1975.* London: Cambridge University Press, 1986.

Đặng Đức Đàm. *Vietnam's Economy, 1986–1995.* Hanoi: Thế Giới, 1995.

———. *Vietnam's Macro-Economy and Types of Enterprises.* Hanoi: Thế Giới, 1997.

Descours-Gatin, Chantal. *Quand l'opium finançait la colonisation en Indochine.* Paris: L'Harmattan, 1992.

DiGregorio, Michael. *Urban Harvest: Recycling as a Peasant Industry in Northern Vietnam.* Honolulu: East-West Center, 1994.

Diollet, Dominique. *L'épopée des douaniers en Indochine, 1874–1954.* Paris: Kailash, 1998.

Dollar, David, Paul Glewwe, and Jennie Litvack (eds.). *Household Welfare and Vietnam's Transition.* Washington, D.C.: World Bank, 1998.

Fforde, Adam. *Vietnam: Economic Commentary and Analysis: A Bi-annual Appraisal of the Vietnamese Economy.* No. 6. Canberra: Aduki, 1995.

——— (ed.). *Doi Moi: Ten Years after the 1986 Party Congress.* Canberra: Australia National University Research School for Pacific and Asian Studies, 1997.

Fforde, Adam, and Anthony Goldstone. *Vietnam to 2005: Advancing on All Fronts.* London: Economist Intelligence Unit, 1995.

Fforde, Adam, and Stefan de Vylder. *From Plan to Market: The Economic Transition in Vietnam.* Boulder, Colo.: Westview, 1996.

Glewwe, Paul, Nisha Agrawal, and David Dollar (eds.). *Economic Growth, Poverty, and Household Welfare in Vietnam.* Washington, D.C.: World Bank, 2004.

Griffin, Keith (ed.). *Economic Reform in Vietnam.* New York: St. Martin's, 1998.

Harvie, Charles. *Vietnam's Reforms and Economic Growth.* New York: St. Martin's, 1997.

Hiebert, Murray. *Chasing the Tigers: A Portrait of the New Vietnam.* Tokyo: Kodansha International, 1996.

Hy Van Luong (ed.). *Postwar Vietnam: Dynamics of a Transforming Society.* Lanham, Md.: Rowman & Littlefield, 2003.

Kaye, William. "A Bowl of Rice Divided: The Economy of North Vietnam." *China Quarterly* 9 (January–March 1962).

Kerkvliet, Benedict (ed.). *Dilemmas of Development: Vietnam Update 1994.* Canberra: Australian National University Department of Political and Social Change, 1995.

Kimura, Tetsusabura. "Vietnam: Ten Years of Economic Struggle." *Asian Survey* 26 (October 1986).

———. *Vietnam: International Relations and Economic Development.* Tokyo: Institute of Developing Economies, 1986.

Le Manh Hung. *The Impact of World War II on the Economy of Vietnam 1939–45.* Singapore: Eastern Universities Press, 2004.

Le Thanh Khoi. *Socialisme et développement au Vietnam.* Paris: Presses Universitaires de France, 1978.

Lê Văn Toàn. *Vietnam Socio-Economy, 1991–1992.* Hanoi: Statistical Publications, 1993.

LeFailler, Philippe. *Monopole et prohibition de l'opium en Indochine. Le pilori des chimères.* Paris: L'Harmattan, 2001.

Lilienthal, David. "Postwar Development in Vietnam." *Foreign Affairs* 67 (January 1968).

Lindhold, Richard W. *Economic Development Policy: With Emphasis on Vietnam.* Eugene, Ore.: University of Oregon Press, 1964.

Litvack, Jennie, and Dennis Rondinelli. *Market Reform in Vietnam: Building Institutions for Development.* Westport, Conn.: Quorum, 1999.

Meuleau, Marc. *Des pionniers en Extrême-Orient. Histoire de la Banque de l'Indochine.* Paris: Fayard, 1990.

Murray, Martin. *The Development of Capitalism in Colonial Indochina (1870–1940).* Berkeley, Calif.: University of California Press, 1980.

Nguyen Anh Tuan. *South Vietnamese Trial and Experience: A Challenge for Development.* Athens, Ohio: Ohio University Southeast Asian Monograph Series, 1980.

Nguyen Tien Hung. *Economic Development of Socialist Vietnam, 1955–1980*. New York: Praeger, 1977.

Nørlund, Irene, Carolyn Gates, and Vu Cao Đam (eds.). *Vietnam in a Changing World*. Richmond, UK: Curzon, 1995.

Pham Hoang Mai. *FDI and Development in Vietnam: Policy Implications*. Singapore: Institute of Southeast Asian Studies, 1994.

Phạm Xuân Nam (ed.). *Rural Development in Vietnam: The Search for Sustainable Development*. Hanoi: Social Sciences Publishing House, 1999.

Robequain, Charles. *The Economic Development of French Indochina*. London: Oxford University Press, 1944.

Ronas, Per, and Orjan Sjoberg. *Socio-Economic Development in Vietnam: The Agenda for the 1990s*. Stockholm: Swedish International Development Authority, 1992.

Scigliano, Robert, and Guy H. Fox. *Technical Assistance to Vietnam: The Michigan State University Experience*. New York: Praeger, 1965.

Shabad, Theodore. "Economic Development in North Vietnam." *Pacific Affairs* 31 (March 1958): 36–53.

Taylor, Milton C. "South Vietnam: Lavish Aid, Limited Progress." *Pacific Affairs* 34 (Fall 1961): 242–256.

Trương Quang (ed.). *Vietnam: Gearing up for Integration*. Pathum Thani, Thailand: Asian Institute of Technology, 2001.

Turley, William S., and Mark Selden. *Reinventing Vietnamese Socialism: Doi Moi in Comparative Perspective*. Boulder, Colo.: Westview, 1993.

Việt Nam, 20 Years of Reunification and Development/Việt Nam, 20 Năm Thống Nhất và Phát Triển. Hồ Chí Minh City: Trung Tâm Hội Chợ Triển Lãm Việt Nam, 1995.

Võ Đại Lược et al. *Vietnam's Economic Renovation and Foreign Economic Policies*. Hanoi: Social Sciences Publishing House, 1995.

Võ Nhân Tri. *Croissance économique de la République Démocratique du Vietnam, 1945–1965*. Hanoi: Éditions en Langues Étrangères, 1967.

———. *Socialist Vietnam's Economy, 1975–1985*. Tokyo: Institute of Developing Economies, 1987.

Vu Van Thai. "Vietnam's Concept of Development." In *Problems of Freedom: South Vietnam since Independence*, ed. Wesley Fishel. New York: Free Press of Glencoe, 1961.

White, Christine P., and David G. Marr (eds). *Postwar Vietnam: Dilemmas in Socialist Development*. Ithaca, N.Y.: Cornell Southeast Asia Program, 1988.

C. Business and Finance

Aumiphin, Jean-Pierre. *La présence financière et économique française en Indochine (1859–1939)*. Hanoi: Éditions des Statistiques du Vietnam, 1997.

Borton, Lady. *Learning to Work in Vietnam*. New York: USIRP, 1994.

Dacy, Douglas C. *The Fiscal System of Wartime Vietnam.* Arlington, Va.: Institute for Defense Analysis, 1969.

Daniel, Howard. *Republic of Viet Nam Coins and Currency.* Dun Loring, Va.: BNR Press, 1992.

Dollar, David (ed.). *Viet Nam: Transition to the Market: An Economic Report.* Washington, D.C.: U.S. Vietnam Trade Council, 1993.

Elliott, Vance L. *The Agricultural Marketing/Finance System of Vietnam.* Arlington, Va.: Institute of Defense Analysis, nd.

Emery, Robert F. *The Financial Institutions of Southeast Asia.* New York: Praeger, 1970.

Engholm, Christopher. *Doing Business in the New Vietnam.* Englewood Cliffs, N.J.: Prentice Hall, 1995.

Leung, Suiwah (ed.). *Vietnam Assessment: Creating a Sound Investment Climate.* Richmond, UK: Curzon, 1996.

Macpherson, Neill. *The Business Guide to Indochina.* Hong Kong: International Securities Institute, 1994.

Murray, Geoffrey. *Vietnam Dawn of a New Market.* Richmond, UK: China Library, 1997.

Nguyen Tan Hai, and William Magennis (eds.). *Foreign Investment Laws of Vietnam: Official English Version.* Melbourne: Vietnam Laws, 1992.

Nguyen Tien Hung. "An Analysis of Money and Credit in Vietnam, 1884–1962." Ph.D. dissertation, University of Virginia, Charlottesville, 1965.

Nguyễn Xuân Oanh. *Vietnam: The New Investment Frontier in Southeast Asia.* Hồ Chí Minh City: Hồ Chí Minh City Publishers, 1992.

The 1994 U.S.–Vietnam Business Guide. Washington, D.C.: Vietnam Trade Council.

Price Waterhouse. *Vietnam: A Guide for the Foreign Investor.* 3rd ed. Hong Kong: Price Waterhouse, 1998.

Quinlan, Joseph P. *Vietnam: Business Opportunities and Risks.* Berkeley, Calif.: Pacific View Press, 1995.

Regulations of Export and Import Operations. Hồ Chí Minh City: Hồ Chí Minh City Publishers, 1994.

Robinson, James W. *Doing Business in Vietnam.* Rocklin, Calif.: Prima, 1995.

Romn, Lisa. *Institutions in Transition: Vietnamese State Bank Reform.* Boston: Kluwer, 1999.

Tan Cheng Leong et al. *Vietnam Business and Investment Opportunities.* Singapore: Institute of Southeast Asian Studies, 1992.

Tan Teck Meng (ed.). *Business Opportunities in Vietnam.* Upper Saddle River, N.J.: Prentice Hall, 1997.

Taylor, Milton C. *The Taxation of Income in Viet-Nam.* Saigon: Michigan State Advisory Group, 1959.

Tran Van Ho (ed.). *Prospects in Trade, Investment and Business in Vietnam and East Asia.* New York: St. Martin's, 2000.

D. Industry

Labour Code of the Socialist Republic of Vietnam. Hồ Chí Minh City: Chính Trị Quốc Gia, 1994.

Moody, Dale L. "The Manufacturing Sector in the Republic of Viet-Nam." Ph.D. dissertation, University of Florida, Gainesville, 1975.

Morrison, Lawrence. "Industrial Development Efforts." In *Viet-Nam: The First Five Years*, ed. Richard Lindolm. East Lansing, Mich.: Michigan State University Press, 1959.

Trued, M. N. "South Vietnam's Industrial Development Center." *Pacific Affairs* 33 (September 1960): 250–267.

E. Foreign Aid

Dacy, Douglas. *Foreign Aid, War, and Economic Development: South Vietnam, 1955–1975.* London: Cambridge University Press, 1986.

Dahm, Henrich. *French and Japanese Economic Relations with Vietnam since 1975.* Richmond, UK: Curzon Press, 1999.

Fforde, Adam. *Economic Aspects of the Soviet–Vietnamese Relationship: Their Role and Importance.* Discussion Paper 156 (April 1984). Birkbeck College, London.

F. Science and Technology

Annerstedt, Jan, and Tim Sturgeon. *Electronics and Information Technology in Vietnam.* Roskilde, Denmark: Roskilde Universite-Center, 1994.

Bezanson, Keith. *Viet Nam at the Crossroads: The Role of Science and Technology.* Ottawa: International Development Research Centre, 1999.

V. Culture
A. General

Crawford, Ann. *Customs and Culture of Vietnam.* Rutland, Vt.: Tuttle, 1966.

Ellis, Claire. *Culture Shock! Vietnam.* Singapore: Times Books International, 1995.

Huard, Pierre A., and Maurice Durand. *Connaissance du Vietnam.* Paris: École Française d'Extrême Orient, 1954.

Huard, Pierre A., and Maurice Durand. *Vietnam, Civilization and Culture.* Hanoi: École Française d'Extrême-Orient, 1994.

Hữu Ngọc, *Sketches for a Portrait of Vietnamese Culture.* Hanoi: Thế Giới, 1995.

Huynh Dinh Te. "Vietnamese Cultural Patterns as Expressed in Proverbs." Ph.D. dissertation, Columbia University, 1962.

Indochina: Social and Cultural Change. Claremont, Calif.: Regina, 1994.

McLeod, Mark, and Nguyễn Thị Diệu. *Culture and Customs of Vietnam.* Westport, Conn.: Greenwood Press, 2001.

Nguyễn Đình Hoà (ed.). *Some Aspects of Vietnamese Culture.* Carbondale, Ill.: Southern Illinois University, 1972.

Nguyễn Khắc Kham. *Celebrations of Rice Culture in Viet-Nam*. Saigon: Vietnamese Council on Foreign Relations, nd.

———. *Introduction to Vietnamese Culture*. Saigon: Vietnamese Culture Series, nd.

Nguyen Van Huy, and Laurel Kendall (eds.). *Vietnam: Journeys of Body, Mind, and Spirit*. Berkeley, Calif.: University of California Press, 2003.

Nguyễn Văn Huyền. *The Ancient Civilization of Vietnam*. Hanoi: Thế Giới, 1995.

Nhất Hạnh, Thích. *A Taste of Earth: And Other Legends of Vietnam*. Berkeley, Calif.: Parallax Press, 1993.

Phan Kế Bình. *Việt Nam Phong Tục (Moeurs et coutumes du Vietnam)* (trans. and ed. Nicole Louis-Henard). 2 vols. Paris: Maisonneuve, 1975.

Quang Van Nguyen, and Marjorie Pivar. *Fourth Uncle in the Mountain: A Memoir of a Barefoot Doctor in Vietnam*. New York: St. Martin's Press, 2004.

B. Architecture

Mai Ứng-Đạo Hùng. *Hue: Monuments of an Ancient Capital*. Hanoi: Foreign Languages Press, 1993.

Nguyễn Năng Đắc, and Nguyễn Quang Đức. *Vietnamese Architecture*. Vietnamese Information Service, Number 34. Washington, D.C.: Embassy of the Republic of Vietnam, 1970.

Võ Văn Tường. *Việt Nam Danh Lãm Cổ Tự/Famous Ancient Pagodas of Vietnam*. Hanoi: Social Science Publishing House, 1992.

C. Art

André-Pallois, Nadine. *L'Indochine, un lieu d'échange culturel? Les peintres français et indochinois (fin XIXe–XXe siècles)*. Paris: École Française d'Extrême-Orient, 1997.

Bezacier, Louis. *L'art vietnamien*. Paris: Éditions de l'Union Française, 1955.

Groslier, Bernard P. *The Art of Indochina*, trans. George Lawrence. New York: Crown, 1962.

Hejzlar, Josef. *The Art of Vietnam*. New York: Hamlyn, 1973.

Rawson, Philip. *The Art of Southeast Asia*. New York: Praeger, 1967.

Taylor, Nora. *Painters in Hanoi: An Ethnography of Vietnamese Art*. Honolulu: University of Hawaii Press, 2004.

Trần Văn Cẩn, Hữu Ngọc, and Vũ Huyên. *Contemporary Vietnamese Painters*. Hanoi: Foreign Languages Press, 1987.

Young, Carol M. et al. *Vietnamese Ceramics*. New York: Paragon House, 1982.

D. Language and Literature

Balaban, John. *Spring Essence: The Poetry of Hồ Xuân Hương*. Port Townsend, Wash.: Copper Canyon Press, 2000.

Bao Ninh. *The Sorrow of War*, trans. Phan Thanh Hao. New York: Pantheon, 1994.

Boudarel, Georges. *Cents fleurs écloses dans la nuit du Vietnam.* Paris: Bertoin, 1992.

De Francis, John. *Colonialism and Language Policy in Vietnam.* The Hague: Mouton, 1977.

Duong Thu Huong. *Memories of a Pure Spring,* trans. Phan Huy Duong and Nina McPherson. New York: Hyperion East, 2000.

———. *Paradise of the Blind,* trans. Phan Huy Dương and Nina McPherson. New York: Penguin, 1994.

Durand, Maurice, and Nguyễn Trần Huấn. *Introduction à la littérature viêtnamienne.* Paris: Maisonneuve et Larose, 1969.

Glimpses of Vietnamese Classical Literature. Vietnamese Studies. Hanoi: Foreign Languages Press, 1972.

Hoang Ngoc Thanh. *Vietnam's Social and Political Development as Seen through the Modern Novel.* New York: Lang, 1991.

Hue, Bernard et al. (eds.). *Littératures de la Péninsule Indochinoise.* Paris: Karthala-AUF, 1999.

Huỳnh Sanh Thông. *An Anthology of Vietnamese Poems: From the Eleventh through the Twentieth Centuries.* New Haven, Conn.: Yale University Press, 1996.

"Fishes and Fisherman: Females and Males in Vietnamese Folklore." *Vietnam Forum* 8 (Spring–Fall 1986).

——— (ed.). *The Heritage of Vietnamese Poetry.* New Haven, Conn.: Yale University Press, 1979.

The Light of the Capital: Three Modern Vietnamese Classics, trans. Greg Lockhart, and Monique Lockhart. New York: Oxford University Press, 1996.

Nguyễn Đình Hoà. *Language in Vietnamese Society: Some Articles.* Carbondale, IL: Asia Books, 1980.

Nguyễn Huy Thiệp. *The General Retires and Other Stories,* trans. Greg Lockhart. Singapore: Oxford University Press, 1992.

Nguyễn Khắc Viện et al. *Anthologie de la littérature viêtnamienne.* 3 vols. Hanoi: Foreign Languages Press, 1972–1975.

Nguyễn Ngọc Bích. *A Thousand Years of Vietnamese Poetry.* New York: Knopf, 1975.

Vo Phien. *Literature in South Vietnam, 1954–1975,* trans. Vo Dinh Mai. Victoria, Australia: Vietnamese Language and Culture Publications, 1992.

———. "Writers in South Vietnam, 1954–1975." *Vietnam Forum* 7 (Winter–Spring 1986).

Vũ Trọng Phụng. *Dumb Luck: A Novel,* trans. Peter Zinoman and Nguyễn Nguyệt Cầm. Ann Arbor, Mich.: University of Michigan Press, 2002.

Vương Lộc. *Glimpses of the Evolution of the Vietnamese Language.* Vietnamese Studies 40. Hanoi: Foreign Languages Press, 1975.

Wolters, O. W. "A Stranger in His Own Land: Nguyễn Trãi's Sino–Vietnamese

Poems, Written during the Ming Occupation." *Vietnam Forum* 8 (Spring–Fall 1986).

E. Music

Addiss, Stephen. "Theater Music of Vietnam." *Southeast Asia: An International Quarterly* 1 (Winter–Spring 1971).
Arana, Miranda. *Neotraditional Music in Vietnam*. Kent, Ohio: Nhạc Việt, the Journal of Vietnamese Music, 1999.
———. "Hat A Dao, the Sung Poetry of North Vietnam." *Journal of the American Oriental Society* 93 (January–March 1973).
Balaban, John. *Ca Dao Vietnam*. Greensboro, N.C.: Unicorn, 1980.
Đào Trọng Tu et al. *Essays on Vietnamese Music*. Hanoi: Red River Publishing House, 1984.
Le Tuan Hung. *The Dynamics of Change in Hue and Tu Tai Music of Vietnam between c. 1890 and c. 1920*. Melbourne: Monash University, 1991.
Nguyen Phong (ed.). *New Perspectives on Vietnamese Music: Six Essays*. New Haven, Conn.: Yale Council on Southeast Asia Studies, 1991.
———. *Textes et chants liturgiques bouddhiques viêtnamiens en France*. Kent, Ohio: ARVM, 1990.
Norton, Barley. "Music and Possession in Vietnam." Ph.D. dissertation, University of London, 1999.
Pham Duy. *The Musics of Vietnam*. Carbondale, Ill.: Southern Illinois University Press, 1975.
Thai Van Kiem. "Panorama de la musique classique viêtnamienne des origines à nos jours." *Bulletin de l'École Française d'Extreme-Orient* 39 (First Trimester, 1964).
Tran Van Khe. *La musique vietnamienne traditionnelle*. Paris: Presses Universitaires de France, 1962.
Vĩnh Long, and Đào Trọng Tu (eds.). *Folksongs of Vietnam*. Hanoi: Thế Giới, 1994.
Whiteside, Dale R. *Traditions and Direction in the Music of Vietnam*. Museum of Anthropology 28. Greeley, Colo.: University of Northern Colorado Anthropology Museum, 1971.

F. Films

Anderegg, Michael (ed.). *Inventing Vietnam: The War in Film and Television*. Philadelphia: Temple University Press, 1991.
Lanning, Michael L. *Vietnam at the Movies*. New York: Fawcett Columbine, 1994.

VI. Official Documents
A. Colonial Period

Bodinier, Gilbert (ed.). *1945–1946. Le retour de la France en Indochine. Textes et documents*. Vincennes, France: Service Historique de l'Armée de Terre, 1987.

———. *Indochine 1947. Règlement politique ou solution militaire. Textes et documents.* Vincennes, France: Service Historique de l'Armée de Terre, 1989.
Doumer, Paul. *Situation de l'Indochine, 1897–1901.* Hanoi: Schneider, 1902.
Gouvernement-Général de l'Indochine. *Contribution à l'histoire des mouvements politiques de l'Indochine Française.* 5 vols. Hanoi: Gouvernement-Général de l'Indochine, 1933–1934.

B. Vietnam Wars

Doumer, Paul. *Declassified Documents Reference Service.* Washington, D.C.: Carrollton, 1976.
Pentagon Papers. Senator Gravel edition. 4 vols. Boston: Beacon, 1971.
South Vietnamese National Liberation Front: Documents. South Vietnam: Liberation Publishing House, 1968.
U.S. Department of Defense. *United States–Vietnam Relations, 1945–1967.* 12 vols. Washington, D.C.: Government Printing Office, 1971.
U.S. Department of State. *Aggression from the North: The Record of North Vietnam's Campaign to Conquer South Vietnam.* Washington, D.C.: Government Printing Office, 1961.
———. *Foreign Relations of the United States.* Washington, D.C.: Government Printing Office.
———. *A Threat to the Peace: North Viet-Nam's Effort to Conquer South Viet-Nam.* Washington, D.C.: Government Printing Office, 1965.
United States Information Service. *Viet-Nam Documents and Research Notes.* 117 volumes. Saigon: U.S. Information Service, 1967–1972.
Vietnam: The Anti-U.S. Resistance War for National Salvation, 1945–1975. War Experiences Recapitulation Committee of the High Level Military Institute, 1980.

C. Postwar Period

Democratic Kampuchea. *Black Paper: Facts and Evidences of the Acts of Aggression and Annexation of Vietnam against Kampuchea.* Phnom Penh: Ministry of Foreign Affairs, 1978.
People's Republic of Kampuchea. *Undeclared War against the People's Republic of Kampuchea.* Phnom Penh: Ministry of Foreign Affairs, 1985.
Socialist Republic of Vietnam. *The Truth about Vietnamo–Chinese Relations over the Past Thirty Years.* Hanoi: Ministry of Foreign Affairs, 1979.

VII. Bibliographies

Boudet, Paul. *Bibliographie de l'Indochine française.* 4 vols. Hanoi: Imprimerie d'Extrême-Orient, 1913–1935.
Brune, Lester H. *America and the Indochina Wars, 1945–1990: A Bibliographical Guide.* Claremont, Calif.: Regina, 1991.

Burns, Richard D. *The Wars in Vietnam, Cambodia, and Laos, 1945–1982: A Bibliographic Guide*. Santa Barbara, Calif.: ABC-Clio, 1984.

Chen, John H. M. *Vietnam: A Comprehensive Bibliography*. Metuchen, N.J.: Scarecrow, 1973.

Cordier, Henri. *Bibliotheca Indosinica, dictionnaire bibliographique des ouvrages relatifs à la Péninsule Indochinoise*. 4 vols. Paris: Leroux, 1912–1915.

Cotter, Michael. *Vietnam: A Guide to Reference Sources*. Boston: Hall, 1977.

Dunn, Joe P. *Teaching the Vietnam War: Resources and Assessments*. Occasional Papers Series 18. Los Angeles: California State University, 1990.

Embree, John F., and B. O. Dotson. *Bibliography of the Peoples and Cultures of Mainland South-East Asia*. New Haven, Conn.: Yale University Press, 1950.

Hastie, Diane. *Viet-Nam: Une bibliographie des publications récentes*. Québec: Université Laval, 1992.

Hobbs, Cecil C. et al. *Indochina: A Bibliography of the Land and People*. Washington, D.C.: Library of Congress, 1950.

Jumper, Roy, and Nguyen Thi Hue. *Bibliography of the Political and Administrative History of Viet-Nam, 1802–1962*. East Lansing, Mich.: Michigan State University Advisory Group, 1962.

Kutler, Stanley I. (ed.). *Encyclopedia of the Vietnam War*. New York: Scribner's, 1996.

Leitenberg, Milton, and Richard Burns. *The Vietnam Conflict: Its Geographical Dimensions, Political Traumas, and Military Developments*. Santa Barbara, Calif.: ABC-Clio. 1973.

Marr, David G. *World Bibliographic Series. Vol. 147. Vietnam*. Santa Barbara, Calif.: ABC-Clio, 1993.

Nguyen Dinh Tham. *Studies on Vietnamese Language and Literature: A Preliminary Bibliography*. Ithaca, N.Y.: Cornell Southeast Asia Program, 1992.

Nguyễn Thế Anh. *Bibliographie critique sur les relations entre le Viêt-Nam et l'Occident (Ouvrages et articles en langues occidentales)*. Paris: Maisonneuve & Larose, 1967.

Nha Trang, Cong Huyen Ton Nu. *Vietnamese Folklore: An Introduction and Annotated Bibliography*. Berkeley, Calif.: University of California Press, 1970.

Phan Thien Chau. *Vietnamese Communism: A Research Bibliography*. Westport, Conn.: Greenwood, 1975.

Ruscio, Alain et al. *La guerre française d'Indochine, 1945–1954. Les sources de la connaissance. Bibliographie et filmographie*. Paris: Les Indes Savantes, 2001.

Schafer, John C. *Vietnamese Perspectives on the War in Vietnam: An Annotated Bibliography of Works in English*. New Haven, Conn.: Yale Council on Southeast Asia Studies, 1997.

Sugnet, Christopher L., and John T. Hickey. *Vietnam War Bibliography*. Lexington, Mass.: Heath, 1983.

Whitfield, Danny J. *Historical and Cultural Dictionary of Vietnam*. Metuchen, N.J.: Scarecrow, 1976.

Wittman, Sandra M. *Writing about Vietnam: A Bibliography of the Literature of the Vietnam Conflict*. Boston: G.K. Hall, 1989.

Internet Websites

Virtual Vietnam Archive, Texas Tech University: http://archive.vietnam.ttu.edu/ virtualarchive

Foreign Relations of the United States online: www.state.gov/www/about_state/ history/frus.html.

International Cold War History Project: cwihp.si.edu.

Vietnam Studies Internet Resource Center: www.vstudies.org.

Vietnamese Communist Party: www.cpv.org.vn. This site (with some English pages) provides information on current political developments in Vietnam. Readers of Vietnamese who are interested in Party history can also download many of the published documents from the various Party Congresses.

United Nations Development Program: www.undp.org.vn/ehome.htm. The UNDP website provides contemporary socioeconomic data and information on development programs.

United States Vietnam Trade Council: www.usvtc.org website provides useful information on current developments in Vietnam's trade relations.

Vietnam News Agency: ww.vnanet.vn/default.asp (includes English pages)

Voice of Vietnam: www.vov.org.vn (includes English pages)

About the Authors

William J. Duiker is liberal arts professor emeritus of East Asian Studies at the Pennsylvania State University in University Park, Pennsylvania. A former Foreign Service officer with the Department of State, he served in Taiwan and at the U.S. Embassy in Saigon before resigning from the government in 1965. In 1968, he received his doctorate in Far Eastern History at Georgetown University in Washington, D.C.

At Penn State, Professor Duiker specialized in the modern history of China and Vietnam, with a special interest in nationalism and revolution. He has written several books on Vietnam, including *The Communist Road to Power in Vietnam* (Westview, 1981), which received a Choice Outstanding Book Award in 1982; a second edition appeared in 1996. His more recent publications include *U.S. Containment Policy and the Conflict in Indochina* (Stanford University Press, 1994), *Sacred War: Nationalism and Revolution in a Divided Vietnam* (McGraw-Hill, 1995), and *Ho Chi Minh: A Life* (Hyperion, 2000). In 1994 he received an endowed professorship from the university, and in 1996 was awarded a Faculty Scholars Medal for Outstanding Achievement. He has served as a consultant for a number of documentary films on Vietnam and is a regular lecturer at the Foreign Service Institute in Washington, D.C.

In recent years, Professor Duiker has also developed a growing interest in the field of global history and is coauthor with Jackson Spielvogel of a textbook entitled *World History* (West Educational Publishers, 1994). A revised edition of the book appeared in 1997.

Bruce M. Lockhart is assistant professor of history at the National University of Singapore. He first became interested in Vietnam while still in high school after the arrival of refugees from South Vietnam in the summer of 1975. After his undergraduate studies at Cornell, he did a master's in East Asian Studies at Yale and then returned to Cornell

513

for his Ph.D. in Southeast Asian history, which he completed in 1990. He then left the academic world to spend several years teaching in Laos and Vietnam. He has been in Singapore since 1998. His main areas of interest in terms of teaching and research are Vietnam, Laos, and Thailand. Part of his dissertation was published as *The End of the Vietnamese Monarchy* (Yale Council on Southeast Asian Studies, 1993) and he is currently completing a manuscript on the Thai monarchy. He has published a journal article and several book chapters on Vietnamese and Lao historiography. He has served as associate editor and editor of the *Journal of Southeast Asian Studies.*